T4-BBL-690

CHURCH MUSIC

AN INTERNATIONAL BIBLIOGRAPHY

Richard Chaffey von Ende

The Scarecrow Press, Inc.
Metuchen, N.J., & London
1980

Library of Congress Cataloging in Publication Data

Von Ende, Richard C
Church music.

Includes index.
1. Church music--Bibliography. I. Title.
ML128. C54V66 016. 783 79-23697
ISBN 0-8108-1271-1

Manufactured in the United States of America

This book is dedicated to

The Glory of God

and with deep gratitude to those
to whose lives and to whose influence
I owe an unrepayable obligation:

- In Memoriam -

Florence von Ende; Herrmann von Ende; John W. Brady;
Veretta Brady; Jean D. Seaman; Will Earhart;
Lee M. Thurston; Amy Graves Ryan; Basil E. Ryan,

and to those living

Genevra von Ende
and my family

Matthew N. Frey

Willis P. Gerhart

Lena Ryan

CONTENTS

ACKNOWLEDGMENTS

It is a pleasant obligation to express my gratitude to the persons and organizations that have helped in the gathering of the information and in the compilation of the materials that have made this bibliography possible.

Our sincere appreciation is due to the numerous libraries and to their personnel (often anonymous) that have assisted us during our research visits to Ireland, England and the major cities of Europe. Thanks are given to my son, Dr. Frederick von Ende, and to Dr. John W. Johnson, for their additional aid in research in the holdings of the British Museum. We also thank our anonymous helpers in the Vatican Library.

Joe W. Specht and his library staff at McMurry College have been of great assistance in making available the valuable Library of Congress Reference Series, Authors and Subject listings.

The staff of the Reference Section of the Music Division of the Library of Congress has been quite helpful in this research. Special mention is due William Lichtenwanger, Irving Lowens and Mary Rogers. MLA's *Notes* merits many thanks for their contribution.

The staffs of the British Consulate and of the Irish and Greek Embassies have graciously assisted in the translations and transliterations from the Welsh, the Gaelic and the Greek.

Dr. Michael Winesanker has aided in furnishing information about the literature on Jewish music. Joseph Blanton, author of *The Organ in Church Design*, has generously assisted in providing bibliographical data for the categories of Organs and Organists.

My daughter, Eleanor Theresa, has been very helpful in transcribing, filing and proofreading; and her assistance has been truly appreciated. We thank Catharyn von Ende for her assistance in the preparation of the manuscript.

Our clerical assistants--transcribers and typists--deserve credit for the interest and the care they have demonstrated in handling the sometimes difficult work in languages foreign to them. Also, acknowledgment is made to Agnes Schroeder and to the late Frederick Block for proofreading some of the Teutonic entries.

To my son, Richard Lance, and to his wife, Kathryn, special thanks are given for their special contribution to the progress of this work.

A debt of gratitude is due to Dr. Carl von Ende and to Dr. Davis Scarborough, whose professional counsel and assistance have been a large factor in the completion of this book.

It would be difficult to name and thank each person who has made some contribution to the collecting and compiling of the materials that have gone into this project. Many have helped, and to each I would say thanks.

Finally, I wish to acknowledge my indebtedness to my wife, Genevra, for her assistance in research, and for her constant support and encouragement during the years of work that have gone into this bibliography.

Richard C. von Ende

INTRODUCTION

Raison d'être

This bibliography had its source in one prepared some years ago for my students in classes in church music. This earlier list contained about nine hundred titles, and was duplicated and distributed to the students for their use and reference. Very shortly thereafter, requests were received from libraries, college music departments and seminaries for copies of this study. Since this earlier bibliography was considerably less than complete, the interest expressed in it was a motivation to expand the study. The succeeding six or seven years were employed in collecting the bibliographical information and in necessary translations for purposes of categorizing the books for the readers' most efficient use.

The following several years were used in organizing and typing the materials. Since some twenty-five languages were involved, the typing, proofreading, and correcting of the typescript represented a time-consuming task.

Delimitations

The books included are principally those of the western world, and, to a considerable extent, of the Christian Church. The area of Hebrew music has been well covered in Alfred Sendrey's excellent book, Bibliography of Jewish Music (Columbia University Press, 1951). A limited number of references to books on the music of the Jewish faith and of the religions of the Orient are included here.

The Categories

It was felt that the most helpful presentation of the bibliographical information would be by categorization into specific areas of church music. Each book has been assigned to a principal category and has been given an identifying number, with additional listings (by prime number reference) under other appropriate categories. There are 284 of these categories. A few titles carry only one categorical assignment, most have three or four listings, and some, where the content coverage is broad, are listed under seven or eight categories.

Inclusions

In addition to books, some articles, catalogs, and music lists have been included, where it was felt they would be helpful.

Originally it was planned to incorporate a complete list of master's and doctoral theses that dealt with church music. However, another author has completed a volume on research in this area. I have included such titles as I had collected prior to the release of this other study, but have not done major research to extend this category further.

In the categories of organs and organists, some books that might be considered secular have been included, since the organ and the organist are so thoroughly identified with the church.

Similarly, materials about Johann Sebastian Bach that are in part secular have been included since Bach represents church music to such a high degree.

Books about and of national anthems have also been included since these generally are both patriotic and devotional, if not specifically religious in nature.

History of Church Music

One of the larger categories in this bibliography is that of "History." It should be noted also that quite a considerable number of the listed books, not categorized as "History," nor considered as such by the author of the book, may be helpful as historic references. I would consider most books with a publication date earlier than the twentieth century useful as resource books in the study of the history of church music.

Language

In deciding to list titles and other bibliographic information in the original language of the books, it was felt that such listing would facilitate locating the books; and that the person interested in a particular book would have some competence in the language in which it was written, or could obtain assistance in its reading; it was also felt that the categorizations of the listings would identify the areas of application of the books. Russian books are presented in transliteration rather than in the Cyrillic orthography. Similarly, Greek and Gaelic books are presented in transliteration.

Errata

This book is the product of the work of a number of clerical helpers. It also represents transcriptions, transcriptions of transcriptions, transcriptions of translations, and of transliterations. Our typists have had limited abilities in foreign languages. The manuscript and the typescript have been proofread, checked, and rechecked for error. Numerous mistakes have been corrected, but it is quite possible that others have been overlooked. Our regrets are extended for any that have been undetected. The reader's advice regarding any discovered will be appreciated.

Completeness

It would be presumptuous to claim that the present list is an all-inclusive, exhaustive listing of the books about church music. It would take several lifetimes and unlimited funds to approach such an accomplishment. I do feel that the research represented here does make available a useful and quite extensive bibliographical tool which should be of service to the church, the clergy, the church organist and choir director, colleges and universities, libraries, and writers of theses and dissertations, and to the interested layman.

In the case of some of the entries, complete bibliographical data were not available. These were included, in the belief that the information could be helpful, even though incomplete. Where it was known, the Library of Congress or British Museum identification number has been supplied for titles which are short on bibliographical data. Also, in a very few cases, the name of a bookhandler has been furnished in lieu of an unfound publisher.

Extension

The usefulness of a bibliography is limited in part by the degree to which it is current. The present volume may be used in conjunction with the periodical, *Notes*, published by the Music Library Association. *Notes* is a quarterly listing of the new books about music published in the Americas, Europe, Australia, Africa and the Orient. Inquiries may be addressed to: Business Mgr. for *Notes*, Music Library Association, 2017 Walnut St., Philadelphia, Pa. 19103.

A second useful source for extending the information contained in this bibliography is to be found in the quarterly, *Music Article Guide*, P. O. Box 12216, Philadelphia, Pennsylvania.

Numbering of Titles

The bibliographic entries are numbered in sequence through the categories.

Alphabetizing of Titles

Within each category, except PERSONALITIES, the entries

are alphabetized in standard bibliographic manner.

In the category PERSONALITIES, entries are arranged alphabetically by the last name of the person featured. Where there are a number of books about one person, these are entered with a subcategory heading, as:

Sub-cat. - BACH, JOHANN SEBASTIAN

The sub-categories are ended with asterisks.

Throughout the category of Personalities, to facilitate locating any given person, the full name of that person will be printed in capitals and underlined.

Aspiration and Commitment

Johann Sebastian Bach inscribed on many of his manuscripts, "Soli Dei Gloria." The author humbly echoes this dedication. I have been granted a professional career of forty years as a musician. This experience, coupled with a modest ability in languages, has given me the somewhat special qualifications for the development of this bibliography. This task has been conducted in a spirit of gratitude and with the hope that it will be useful.

SOME COMMON ABBREVIATIONS

Anh.	Appendix
Aufl.	Edition
Auft.	Commission
Ausg.	Edition, issue or publication
Bearb.	Compiler (d) Author (ed) Reviser (ed)
BM	British Museum
C.	Approximately
Coll.	Collated
Comp.	Compiler
Corr.	Correspondent or Corresponding
D.	The or of the
Del.	" " " "
Diss.	Dissertation
Distr.	Distributed
E.	A, one, or of one
Ed.	Edited, Edited by, Editor, Edition
Einf.	Introduction
Enl.	Enlarged
Erw.	Enlarged or expanded
Facs.	Facsimile
Förf	Forthcoming
Fwd.	Foreword
Gen.	General
Hrsg.	Edited
I.	In, in the
Illus.	Illustrated
Intro.	Introduction
ISBN	International Standard Book Number

LC.	Library of Congress
Lib. bdg.	Library binding
Microf.	Microfilm
Mitarb.	Collaborator
Nar.	Published
Nat.	National
N. d.	No date given
N. G.	Not given
Neuaufl.	Reprint
Neudr.	Reprint
Nouv.	New
N. p.	No pages given or not published
op.	Opus
Otv.	Abstract
P., or pp.	Page(s)
Pbk.	Paperback
Photos.	Photostatic (copy)
Popul.	Popular
Pref.	Preface
Pub. /Publ.	Publisher
R. C.	Roman Catholic
Rep. or Repr.	Reprint
Rev.	Revised
Slov.	Slovak
S. P. C. K.	Society for Promoting Christian Knowledge
Trans.	Translate or translation
Transc.	Transcribed
U.	And
Ubers.	Translated
Univ.	University

V. or v.	Volume
Ver. or Verl.	Publishing or Publisher
Vollst.	Complete
wd	withdrawn
Z.	To or to the

THE BIBLIOGRAPHY

ABBEYS

1. BURNEY, Charles. Account of musical performances in the Westminster-Abbey and the Pantheon. Amsterdam: F. A. M. Knuf, 1964.

2. HAMMER, Hubert-Gabriel. Die Alleluiagesange in der Choralüberlieferung der Abtei Altenberg. Köln: Volk, 1968.

3. OTTOBEUREN. Beiträge zur Geschichte der Abtei. Augsburg, Germany: Winfried-Werk in Kommission, 1964.

4. SCHMID, Mannfred Hermann, ed. Salzburg: Erzabtei St. Peter, Katalog (der Musikaliensammlung), Erster Teil: Leopold und Wolfgang Amadeus Mozart, Joseph und Michael Haydn. Salzburg: Publikationen des Institut für Musikwissenschaft der Universität Salzburg, 1970.

5. VOIX de St. Gall. Fribourg, Switzerland: Suisse, Impr. Canisienne, 1907.

See also: 3014

ACCOMPANIMENTS

6. ADLER, Kurt. The art of accompanying and coaching. Minneapolis: Minnesota University Press, 1965.

7. ________. The art of accompanying and coaching. (Reprint of entry no. 6.) New York: Da Capo Press, 1976.

8. ANGERSTEIN, Johann Carl. Theoretisch-practische Anweisung Choralgesänge nicht nur richtig, sondern auch schön spielen zu lernen. Stendal: Bei Franzen V. Grosse, 1800.

9. ARNOLD, F. T. The art of accompaniment from a thorough-bass. New York: A. Broude Inc., 1965.

10. ARNOLD, J. H. Accompaniments for the Ordinary of the mass (Anglican). London: The Faith Press, 1949.

11. _______. Plainsong accompaniment. London: Oxford University Press, 1927.

12. BAIRSTOW, E. C. Organ accompaniments to the unison verses of twenty-four hymn-tunes from the English hymnal. London: Oxford University Press, ng.

13. BECKER, Alfred. Der Mehrstimmige instrumental begleitete Kirchengesang in der Erzdiözese Köln zur Zeit der vier letzten Kurfursten. Würzburg-Aumühle: K. Triltsch, 1938.

14. BENNETT, J. Lionel (ed.). English hymnal organ and choir book of varied accompaniments and descants. New York: Carl Fischer, 1926.

15. _______. Varied harmonies for organ accompaniment. London: William Clowes & Sons, 1912.

16. BRAGERS, Achille P. Accompaniment to the Vatican Kyriale. New York: Pius X School of Liturgical Music, n.d.

17. _______. Accompaniments to gregorian chants. Boston: McLaughlin & Reilly Co., 1941.

18. _______. Chant motet book; accompaniment to the most frequently used gregorian hymns and motets. Boston: McLaughlin & Reilly Co., 1939.

19. _______. Plainsong accompaniment. New York: Carl Fischer, 1934.

20. BRIDGE, J. Frederick. Organ accompaniment of the choral service. London: Novello & Co., 1885.

21. BUELOW, George J. Thorough-bass accompaniment. New York: A. Broude, Inc., 1965.

22. BURGESS, Francis. The teaching and accompaniment of Plainsong. London: Novello & Co., 1914.

23. CATALOGUE of liturgical books & organ accompaniments to gregorian chants & of approved Catholic church music. New York: F. Pustet & Co., n.d.

24. COLEMAN, H. Varied hymn accompaniments. London: Oxford University Press, n.d.

25. CONWAY, Marmaduke Percy. Church organ accompaniment, etc. London: Canterbury Press, 1952.

26. EMMANUEL, M. Traité de l'accompagnement modal des psaumes. Lyon, France: Janin frères, 1913.

27. EVANS, E. The modal accompaniment of plain chant. London: W. Reeves, 1911.

28. FLEMMING, Michael P. M. The accompaniment of plainsong. Croydon, England: Royal School of Church Music, 1963.

29. GROOM, Lester W. Accompanying harmonies for the Plainsong Psalter. London: Novello & Co., 1914.

30. HARKNESS, R. Gospel song accompaniment. South Pasadena: R. Harkness, 1938. Rev. & enl. ed., 1942.

31. HERBEK, Raymond. Organ accompaniments for congregational singing. Nashville: Broadman Press, n. d.

32. JEANNIN, J. C. Sur l'importance de la tierce dans l'accompagnement grégorien. Paris: H. Herelle et cie. 1926.

33. KRAPF, Gerhard. Organ improvisation: A practical approach to chorale elaboration for the service. Minneapolis: Augsburg Publishing House, 1967.

34. KUNZELMANN, Adalbero. Die Begleitung des deutschen Kirchenliedes. Tübingen, Germany: C. L. Schultheiss, 1950.

35. LAPIERRE, Eugene. Gregorian chant accompaniment. Toledo: Gregorian Institute of America. 1949.

36. LATROBE, John Antes. The instructions of Chenaniah. London: L. B. Seeley & Sons, 1832.

Plain directions for accompanying the chant or the psalm-tune to which are annexed the canticles of the morning and evening church services, so arranged as to enable all persons to unite in the chant.

37. LI͡UBLINSKIĬ, Aleksandr Aleksandrovich. Teorii͡a i pratika akkompanementa. Leningrad: Muzyk Leningr. otd-nie, 1972.

38. LLOYD, Charles Harford. Free accompaniment of unison hymn singing. London: The Year Book Press, n. d.

39. MATHIAS, Dr. Fr. X. Die Choralbegleitung. Regensburg and New York: F. Pustet, 1905.

40. MOLITOR, P. Gregor. Die Diatonisch-rhytmische Harmonisation der gregorianischen choral melodien. Leipzig: Breitkopf und Härtel, 1913.

41. NIEDERMEYER, L. & J. d'Ortigue. Gregorian accompaniment. New York, Chicago: Novello, Ewer & Co., 1905.

42. NOBLE, T. Tertius. Fifty free organ accompaniments to well-known hymn tunes. New York: J. Fischer & Brothers, 1948.

43. _______. Free organ accompaniments to one hundred well-known hymn tunes. New York: J. Fischer & Brothers, 1946.

44. OLDROYD, George and Charles W. Pearce. The accompaniment of plain chant. London: J. Curwen & Sons, 1924.

45. PEARCE, Charles William. Organ accompaniment to the Psalms. London: Winthrop Rogers, n.d.

46. PEETERS, Flor. Méthode pratique pour l'accompagnement du chant grégorien. Malines: H. Dessain, 1949.

47. POTIRON, Henri. Treatise on the accompaniment of gregorian chant. Tournai, Belgium: Desclée and Co., 1933.

48. RENOUX, Marcel. Harmonie moderne et harmonie grégorienne, trait complete d'harmonie, application à l'accompagnement du grégorien. Besançan: Impr. Jacques et Demondtrond, 1948.

49. RICHARDS, H. W. The organ accompaniment of the church service. Boston: The Boston Music Co., 1911.

50. RIDDLE, Blanche Lee. Gospel song and hymn playing. Nashville: Broadman Press, 1950.

51. ROWLEY, A. Extemporisation. London: Joseph Williams Ltd., 1955.

52. SHAW, G. Thirty-six descants with accompaniment for use with the English hymnal. London: Oxford University Press, n.d.

53. SOEHNER, L. Die Orgelbegleitung zum gregorianischen gesang. Regensburg: F. Pustet, 1936.

54. SPRINGER, Max. The art of accompanying plain chant. New York: J. Fischer and Brothers, 1908.

55. THIMAN, Eric H. Varied accompaniments to 34 well-known tunes for unison singing. London: Oxford University Press, n.d.

56. _______. Varied harmonies to hymn tunes. New York: Carl Fischer, Inc., 1934. London: Oxford Univ. Press, 1934.

57. VARIED harmonizations of favorite hymns for organ. New York: H. W. Gray, n.d.

58. WAGENER, Heinz. Die Begleitung des gregorianischen Chorals im neunzehnten Jahrhundert. Regensburg, Germany: Bosse, 1964.

59. WEAKLAND, Rembert. Modal accompaniment. Latrobe, Pa.: Archabbey Press, 1959.

See also: 260, 261, 286, 459, 471, 517, 595, 641, 656, 2780, 3762, 3854, 4069, 5266, 5282.

ADDRESSES

60. ABERT, Hermann Joseph. Gesammelte Schriften und Vorträge von Hermann Abert herausgegeben von Friedrich Blume. Halle (Saale), Germany: M. Niemeyer, 1929.

61. CONVERSE, Charles Crozat. Symposium on church music. New York: The Homiletic Review, 1899.

62. GAY, Julius. An historical address delivered at the annual meeting of the Village Library Company of Farmington, Connecticut. Hartford, Ct.: Lockwood and Brainard Co., 1891.

63. GRESLEY, William. A sermon on church music, preached in St. Paul's Church, Brighton. London: J. Masters, 1852.

64. HYMN SOCIETY OF AMERICA. Addresses at the 20th anniversary of the Hymn Society of America. New York: The Society, 1943.

65. KNAUFF, Christopher Wilkinson. A sermon by the Reverend Christopher W. Knauff. New York: Theo. C. Knauff Co., 1890.

66. KRÜGER, Eduard. Beiträge für Leben und Wissenschaft der Tonkunst. Leipzig, Germany: Breitkopf und Härtel, 1847.

67. LUCAS, George Washington. An address on music. Northhampton, England: J. H. Butler, 1833.

68. METTENLEITER, Dominicus. Philomele. Brixen, Germany: A. Weger's Buchhandlung, 1867.
Noten und Klänge aus dem Reiche der Töne zur Belehrung und Unterhaltung. 2. Folge.

69. MITCHELL, Ammi R. An address on sacred music. Portland: Hyde, Lord & Co., 1812.

70. NAISH, Thomas. A sermon preached at the Cathedral Church of Sarum, November 30, 1726. London: J. Lacy, 1726.

71. NATIONAL Catholic Education Association, Proceedings and Addresses, 45th Annual Meeting. N.G.: N.G., 1948.

72. PRACTICAL discourses of singing in the worship of God. London: J. Darby for N. Cliff, 1708.

73. ROCHLITZ, Friedrich. Für Freunde der Tonkunst. Leipzig, Germany: C. Cnobloch, 1824-32.

74. ROLLE, Christian Carl. Neue Wahrnehmungen zur Aufnahme und weitern Ausbreitung der Musik. Berlin: A. Wever, 1784.

75. ROSSI, Lauro. Sulla Musica religiosa. Napoli: The Academy, 1871.
Parole di Lauro Rossi, lette all'Accademia di archeologia, lettere e belle arti nella tornata del di 8 Luglio 1876.

76. STANFORD, Charles Villiers. Studies and memories. London: A. Constable and Co., Ltd., 1908. Illustrated.

77. STEARNS, Charles. A sermon preached at an exhibition of sacred musick. Boston: Isaiah Thomas and Ebenezer T. Andrews, 1792.

78. TRUMMER, Carl. Die Musik von vormals und jetzt, vom Diesseits und Jenseits. Frankfurt, Germany: H. L. Bronner, 1856.

79. WORCESTER, Samuel. An address on sacred musick. Boston: Manning & Loring, 1811.

See also: 1022, 1091, 1092, 2446, 3410, 3411, 5057.

ADVENT

80. PATTEN, Simon N. Advent songs. New York: B. W. Huebsch, 1916.

81. WERTHEMANN, Helene. Studien zu den Adventsliedern des 16. und 17. Jahrhunderts. Zurich: EVZ-Verlag, 1963.
Basler-Studien zur historischen und systematischen Theologie, 4.

ANTHEMS

82. ANTHEMS for soprano, alto, baritone (Bks. 1 & 2). Anaheim, Cal.: National Music Service, n. d.

83. ANTHEMS for the adult choir. Anaheim, Cal.: National Music Service, n. d.

84. ANTHEMS for the junior choir. (Bks. 1, 2, 3, 4, 5) Anaheim, Cal.: National Music Service, n. d.

85. ANTHEMS for the mixed choir. Anaheim, Cal.: National Music Service, n. d.

86. ANTHEMS for the youth choir. Anaheim, Cal.: National Music Service, n.d.

87. BOWER, John Dykes and Allan Wicks. A repertory of English cathedral anthems. Fair Lawn, N.J.: Oxford University Press, 1965.

88. BURNETT, Coyne G. The selection and analysis of one hundred sacred anthems for mixed voices. Missoula, Mont.: Montana State University. M.M.E., 1954.

89. CHUA, Gloria. The development of the English anthem. Houston: University of Houston. M.M., 1959.

90. COLLINS, W. S., II. The anthems of Thomas Weelkes. Ph.D., Music. Michigan: University of Michigan, 1960.

91. CURRY, W. Lawrence (ed.). Anthems for the adult choir. Westminster Press, 1961.

92. ________. Anthems for the junior choir. Westminster Press, n.d.

93. ________. Anthems for the mixed choir. Westminster Press, 1948.

94. ________. Anthems for the youth choir. Westminster Press, 1952.

95. ________. Junior choir anthems for Advent and Christmas. Westminster Press, 1961.

96. DANIEL, Ralph Thomas. The anthem in New England before 1800. (Unpublished Ph.D. dissertation) Cambridge, Mass.: Harvard University, 1955.

97. ________. The anthem in New England before 1800. Evanston, Ill.: Northwestern University Press, 1966.

98. DANKERT, Mary Ruth. A study of the Lutheran hymnal as a source of anthem material for the church year. Austin, Tx.: The University of Texas, 1963.

99. DAVIES, H. W. and Henry G. Ley. The church anthem book. London: Oxford University Press, 1933.

100. DAVISON, A. T. and H. W. Foote. The Concord anthem book. Boston: E. C. Schirmer, n.d.

101. ________. ________. The second Concord anthem book. Boston: E. C. Schirmer, n.d.

102. DUNLAVY, Katharine. The basis of the early American anthem. Greencastle, Ind.: Master's Thesis, De Pauw University, 1935.

103. FOSTER, Myles Birket. Anthems and anthem composers. London: Novello & Co., Ltd., 1901.
An essay on the development of the anthem from the time of the reformation to the end of the nineteenth century.

104. GEORGIADY, Nicholas P. and Louis Romano. Our national anthem. Chicago, Ill.: Follett, 1963.

105. HIEBERT, Arlis John. Anthems and services of Samuel S. Wesley (1810-1876). Ann Arbor: Univ. Microfilms, 1965.

106. KING, William Joseph. The English anthem from the early Tudor period through the Restoration era. Ann Arbor, Mich.: Boston University Graduate School dissertation, 1962.

107. PRICE, Shelby Milburn, Jr. The restoration verse anthem. Ann Arbor: Univ. Microfilms, 1967.

108. RIMBAULT, Edward F. A collection of anthems for voices and instruments. London: Printed for the members of the Musical Antiquarian Society by Chappel, 1945.

109. ROMERO, Jesus C. Verdadera historia del himno nacional Mexicano. Mexico: Universidad Nacional Autónoma de México, 1961.

110. SHAW, Martin and Henry Coleman. National anthems of the world. New York, London, and Toronto: Pitman Publishing Corporation, 1960.

111. ________, ________ and T. M. Cartledge, eds. National anthems of the world. 3rd rev. ed. (2nd. ed., 1963; orig. ed., 1960). New York, London, Toronto, Tel Aviv: Pitman Publishing Corp., 1969.

112. WIENANDT, Elwyn Arthur and Robert H. Young. The anthem in England and America. New York: Free Press, 1970.

113. WORDS of anthems. London: Novello & Co., 1946.

See also: 151, 155, 156, 164, 166, 173, 178, 184, 360, 377, 380, 390, 443, 877, 1207, 1640, 2637, 4649, 4666, 5025, 5028.

ARCHITECTURE AND ACOUSTICS

114. ADDLESHAW, G. W. D. and Frederick Etchells. The architectural setting of Anglican worship. London: Faber & Faber, 1948.

115. ATKINSON, C. Harry. Protestant church buildings and equipment. (Periodical.) New York: Ford Stewart, November 1965.

116. BAGENAL, Hope and Alexander Wood. Planning for good acoustics. New York: Methuen & Co., Ltd., 1931.

117. BERANEK, Leo L. Music, acoustics and architecture. London and New York: John Wiley & Sons, Inc., 1962.

118. BERRY, Ray. "The importance of acoustics." Organ Institute Quarterly, Spring 1952.

119. BIEHLE, Johannes. Theorie des Kirchenbaues vom Standpunkte des Kirchenmusikes und des Redners, mit einer Glockenkunde in irher Beziehung zum Kirchenbaues mit vierzehn Abbildungen und zwei Tabellen. Wittenberg, Germany: A. Ziemsen, 1913.

120. BOND, Francis. An introduction to English church architecture. London and New York: H. Milford, 1913.

121. DE LASTEYRIE, R. L'architecture religieuse en France à l'époque Gothique. Paris: A. Picard, 1927.

122. ________. L'architecture religieuse en France à l'époque romane. rev. & aug. ed. Paris: A. Picard, 1929. (orig. Paris: A. Picard, 1912.)

123. DONISELLI, C. Udito e sensi generali: L'ordine geometrico musicale dei rapporti fra senso, moto, intelletto spazio, tempo, numero, forze. Milano: Istituto Editoriale Scientifico, s.a., 1927, 1933.

124. GLENDENNING, Frank John. The church and the arts. London: SCM Press, 1960.

125. HAMBERG, Per Gustav. Tempelbygge för protestanter; arkitekturhistorika studier i äldre reformert och evangelisk-luthersk miljö. Stockhölm: Svenska Kyrkans diakonisstyrelses bokförlag, 1955.

126. HOLTZ, John C. "Planning and equipping choir rooms." Protestant church buildings and equipment, Nov. 1965.

127. KIRCHER, Athanasius. Phonurgia nova. (Facsimile in original format.) New York: Broude Brothers Ltd., 1673-reprint.

128. KORNERUP, T. Die akustische Atomtheorie angewandt auf das pythagordische Tonsystem. Kopenhagen: Levin & Munksgaards sortiment, 1931.

129. KOSTOF, Spiro K. The Orthodox baptistry of Ravenna. New Haven, Ct.: Yale University Press, 1965.

130. LOWERY, H. A guide to musical acoustics. New York: Dover Publications, Inc., June 1966.

131. LUTHERAN Church--The Commission on Church Architecture. Architecture and the church. St. Louis: Concordia, 1961.

132. MARKS, Percy L. Acoustics. London: The Technical Press, Ltd., 1940.

133. SABINE, Wallace C. Architectural acoustics. Boston: Proceedings of American Academy of Arts and Sciences. Vol. XLII, No. 2, June 1906.

134. ________. Collected papers on acoustics. New York: Dover Publications, Inc., 1964. (Repr. of Amer. Acad. Arts & Science Proc., 1906.)

135. TIBY, O. Acustica musicale e organologia degli strumenti musicali. Palermo: Industrie riunite editoriali siciliane, 1933.

136. WALTON, A. C. W. Architecture and music. Cambridge: W. Heffer & Sons, Ltd., 1934.
A study in reciprocal values.

See also: 446, 448, 1591, 1605, 1784, 1856, 1945, 2955, 3232, 3781, 4704.

ARTICLES

137. CHURCH Music Society. Occasional papers. London: H. Frowde, 1912.

138. HUGHES, H. V. Church music monographs. London: Faith Press, 1920.

BELLS AND GLOCKEN

139. ADAMS, Saxe, and Susan Logan York. I heard the bells. New York: Carl Fischer, Inc., 1961.
Seventeen arrangements for handbells.

140. BARTLETT, Alice T. Bells around the world. New York: Harold Flammer, Inc., 1962.
A collection of bell choir music.

141. BEDFORD, Philip. An introduction to English handbell ringing. Chelmsford: Handbell Ringers of Great Britain, 1974.

142. BIGELOW, Arthur Lynds. The acoustically balanced carillon, graphics and the design of carillons and carillon bells. Princeton, N.J.: School of Engineering, Princeton Univ., 1961.

143. CAMP, John M. F. Bell ringing; chimes, carillons, handbells, the world of the bell and the bell-ringer. Newton Abbot: David and Charles, 1974.

144. CROCKETT, Marg. Bells in our lives. Newton Abbot: David and Charles, 1973.

145. DAVIES. Easter bell carol (SA). New York: Harold Flammer, n.d.

146. DAVIS, K. K. Ding-dong! Merrily on high (SATB, SA). New York: G. Schirmer, n.d.

147. ELPHICK, George Philip. Sussex bells and belfries. Chichester: Phillimore, 1970.

148. HANDEL, G. F. Sonata for a musical clock. Oxford Press, n.d. Adaptable for thirteen bells--C to A.

149. HART, Leen't. Campanology: A handbook for the carilloneur. Ann Arbor: Univ. of Mich. Press, 1972.

150. HOLST. Christmas song (Personent Hodie-Unison). New York: Oxford Press, n.d.

151. ______. A festival chime (St. Denio). (SATB or U) London: Stainer & Bell, n.d.

152. JENNINGS, Trevor S. A short history of surrey bells and ringing customs. Kingston-upon-Thames: Marchants, 1974.

153. JOHE, Edward. Carols and songs for ringing. New York: Harold Flammer, Inc., n.d.

154. KOUNTZ. Carol of the Christmas Chimes (all arr.). N.G.: Galaxy, n.d.

155. ______. Carol of the sheep bells (all arr.). New York: Galaxy, n.d.

156. LOCKWOOD. Lightly, lightly, bells are pealing. New York: H. W. Gray, n.d.

157. MACFARLANE. Evening bells and cradle song. Boston/Chicago: Summy-Birchard, n.d.

158. MARRYOTT, Carols for the Christ Child. New York: G. Schirmer, n.d.

159. MORRIS, Ernest. Legends of the bells, being a collection of legends, traditions, folk-tales, myths, etc., centered around the bells of all lands. Folcroft, Pa.: Folcroft Library Editions, 1974.

160. MOUNTS, Slater C. Collection for handbells and voices. New York: Harold Flammer, Inc., 1965.

161. OHK, Vera. Das Glockenmuseum in Laucha a. Unstrut, Germany: Rat des Kerises, 1962.

162. PARRY, Scott. Handbell ringing. New York: C. Fischer, n.d.

163. PURCELL. Bell symphony. London: Novello, n.d.

164. RAWLS. Bells of spring (SA or U). New York: J. Fischer, n.d.

165. ROBERTS. Carillon.

166. ROBSON. An awakening (U). London: Novello, n.d.

167. ROTKIN, Shirley Berger. "The wonderful sounds of bells in Shakespeare's plays: bell references, by the author for the American Bell Association." Skokie, Ill.: The Bell Tower, Vol. 31, No. 4, 1973.

168. RUNKLE, Helen M. A handbell concert. New York: J. Fischer, n.d.

A collection of 23 hymns, carols, folk songs, and others, arranged for a small ring of bells from middle C up.

169. RUSSELL. Bells of St. Anne de Beaupré. New York: J. Fischer, n.d.

170. SCHILLING, Franz Peter. Erfurter glocken. Berlin: Union Verlag, 1968.

171. SHARPE, Frederick. The church bells of Herefordshire. Launton-Oxon, England: F. Sharpe, 1972.

172. STEPHENS, Norris L. (arr.). Christmas music for handbell choirs. New York: G. Schirmer, Inc., n.d.

A collection of 51 carols.

173. THIMAN, E. A song of praise. London: J. Curwen; New York: G. Schirmer, n.d.

174. TUFTS, Nancy P. The art of hand-bell ringing. London: Jenkins, 1962.

175. ______. The bell ringers' handbook. New York: Harold Flammer, Inc., 1965.

176. ______. Original compositions for handbells. New York: Harold Flammer, Inc., n.d.

177. VAN HEUVEN, E. W. Acoustical measurements on church bells and carillons. Amsterdam: van Cleef, 1949.

178. WALTERS, Henry Beauchamp. The church bells of Wiltshire. Bath: Kingsmead Reprints, 1969.

179. WARNER. Alleluia! To the Triune majesty (SA). Summy-Birchard, n.d.

180. WEAVER. Bell Benedictus. New York: Galaxy, n.d.

181. WHEELDON. The Munster bells. New York: H. W. Gray, n.d.

182. WHITTLESEY, Federal Lee. (comp. & arr.). Familiar melodies for handbells. New York: Harold Flammer, Inc., 1959.

183. ______. Ringing and singing. New York: Harold Flammer, Inc., 1960.
A collection of twenty-three hymns and carols.

184. WIANT. A Chinese Christmas Carol (SATB or U). New York: H. W. Gray, n.d.

185. WILSON, Wilfred G. The art and science of change ringing on church and hand bells. New York: October House, Inc., 1966.

186. YOLEN, Jane. Ring out! A book of bells. Drawings by R. Cuffari. New York: Seabury Press, 1974.

See also: 2077, 3474, 3985.

BIBLICAL MUSIC

187. AVINGER, Thomas Dalton. The song of songs, which is Solomon's. Waco, Tex.: Baylor Univ. M.M., 1957.

188. BURGARD, Charles. La Bible dans la liturgie. London: Challoner Publications, 1960.

189. DEISS, Father Lucien. Biblical hymns and psalms. Cincinnati, Ohio: WLSM, 1965.

190. FINESINGER, Sol Baruch. Musical instruments in the Old Testament. (Research typescript) Baltimore, Md.: John Hopkins University, Ph.D., 1925-26.

191. GORALI, Moshe, ed. The Bible in English Music: W. Byrd-H. Purcell. Haifa, Israel: The Haifa Music Museum & AMLI, 1970.

192. GREEN, Joseph Franklin. Biblical foundations for church music. Nashville, Tenn.: Convention Press, 1967.

193. HA-MUZE'ON ve-sifriyat Amli le-musicah Hefah. The Old Testament in world music: exhibition. Haifa: Haifa Music Museum and AMLI Library, 1976.

194. HARTMAN, Elizabeth Rose. A project for making the musical instruments used in Solomon's Temple, with suggested programs of lectures and music. (Research typescript) New York: Union Theological Seminary. M.A. Music., 1943.

195. HOFMAN, Schlomo. Migra'ey musica: A collection of biblical references to music in Hebrew, English, French and Spanish. Tel-Aviv: Israel Music Institute, 1974.

196. HUNTER, Stanley Armstrong. (ed.). The music of the Gospel. New York: Abingdon Press, 1932.

197. HUTCHINSON, Enoch. Music of the Bible. Boston: Gould & Lincoln, 1864.
Explanatory notes upon those passages in the sacred scriptures which relate to music, including a brief view of Hebrew poetry.

198. McCOMMON, Paul. Music in the Bible. Nashville: Convention Press, 1956.

199. McELRATH, William N. Music in Bible times. Nashville, Tenn.: Convention Press, c1966.

200. SENDREY, Alfred and Mildred Norton. David's harp: The story of music in biblical times. New York: New American Library, 1964.

201. SILLAMY, Jean Claude. Essai de reconstitution de la musique de la Bible. Paris: Ajaccio, Si la Mi, 1966.

202. SMITH, William Sheppard. Musical aspects of the New Testament. Amsterdam: W. Ten Have, 1962.

203. STAINER, John. The music of the Bible. London: Cassell, 1882.

204. WARREN, Betsy. Make a joyful noise: Music of the Bible in instrument and song. Minneapolis, Minn.: Augsburg Publishing House, 1962.

205. WELTY, Frederick Arthur. Changing emphasis of music in the Bible. (Research typescript). Pittsburgh: Pittsburg, Pa., M.A., 1936.

See also: 1202, 1404, 2303, 2481, 2670, 2690, 2754, 2766, 2867, 2905, 4292, 4727, 4782, 4820, 5390.

BIBLIOGRAPHIES

206. L'ARCHIVIO musicale della Cappella Lauretana. Loreto, Italy: A cura dell'amministrazione di s. casa, 1921.
Catalogo storico-critico, con dieci illustrazioni e due tavole fuori testo.

207. BARTLETT, Hazel. Library of Congress catalogue (Catalogue of early books on music before 1800). Washington: Broude Brothers, 1944.

208. BESTERMAN, Theodore. "Music; musical instruments." A World Bibliography of Bibliographies. London: T. Besterman, 1947-49.

209. BIBLIOGRAPHIA musicologia, a bibliography of musical literature, Vol. 3: 1970. Utrecht: Joachimsthal, 1975.

210. BLUM, Fred. Music monographs in series. New York: Scarecrow Press, 1964.

211. BOBILLIER, Marie. "Bibliographie des bibliographies musicales." L'année musicale, 1913.

212. BÖHM, Carl. Das deutsche evangelische Kirchenlied, ein Führer durch die Literatur des lebenden, praktisch-verwertbaren Gutes unseres evangelischen Kirchenliedes. Hildburghausen, Germany: F. W. Gadow & Sohn, 1927.

213. BRITTON, Allen P. (ed.). Journal of research in music education. Washington, D.C.: Music Educators National Conference, 1959.
Music education materials.

214. BROOK, Barry S. A bibliography for music of the classic period. In progress and unpublished.

215. ________. Rilm (Inaugural Report: January 1967). Ithaca, N.Y.: Rêpertoire International de la Littêrature Musicale, 1967.

216. BUELOW, George J. "Music, rhetoric, and the concept of the affections: A selective bibliography." Notes, Vol. 30, Sept. 1973, p. 250.

217. COOVER, James B. Bibliography of music dictionaries. Denver, Colo.: Second Bibliographical Center for Research, 1958.

218. DEAKIN, Andrew. Outlines of musical bibliography: A catalog of early music and musical works. Hildesheim & New York: G. Olms, 1976.

219. DEUTSCH, Otto E. "Music bibliography and catalogues." The Library, March 1943.

220. DOUGLAS, Alan. Electronic musical instruments: A bibliography. London: Tottenham Public Library, 1962.

221. DUCKLES, Vincent. Music reference and research materials. London: The Free Press of Glencoe, Collier-Macmillan Ltd., 1964.

222. EITNER, Robert. Bibliographie der Musik-Sammelwerke des 16. und 17. Jahrhunderts. Hildesheim: Olms, 1963.

223. FISCHER, Wilhelm. "Verzeichnis von bibliographischen Hilfswerken für musikhistorische Arbeiten." Guido Adler. Methode der Musikgeschichte. Leipzig: Breitkopf & Hartel, 1919.

224. FREYSTATTER, Wilhelm. Die musikalischen Zeitschriften seit ihrer Entstehung bis zur Gegenwart. Amsterdam: Frits Knuf, 1964.

225. GREGORY, Julia. Catalogue of early books on music (before 1800). New York: Broude Brothers, n.d.

226. GROEBINGER, Eduard. Repertoire-untersuchungen zum mehrstimmigen Notre Dame-Conductus. Regensburg: G. Bosse, 1939.

227. HALL, G. K. Bibliographic guide to music: 1975. Boston: G. K. Hall, 1976.

228. LARSON, William S. Bibliography of research studies in music education, 1932-1948. Chicago, Ill.: Music Educators National Conference, 1949.

229. ________. Bibliography of research studies in music education 1949-1956. Washington, D.C.: Music Educators National Conference, 1958.
Journal of Research in Music Education.

230. LESURE, François, ed. Ecrits imprimé concernant la musique. 2 vols. München-Duisburg: G. Henle Verlag, c. 1971.

231. MATTEI-GENTILI, Guido. "Membra disiecta." Archivio musicale di Santo Spirito in Saxia con due facsimili ed una trascrizione. Roma: "Nova et vetera," 1937.

232. MÜNSTER, Universität. Die musikalischen Schätze der Santinischen Sammlung. Münster: Westfälische Vereinsdruckerei, 1929.

233. Die MUSIC-BUCH, ein nach Gruppen und Gattungen geodnete Zusammenstellung von Büchern über Musiker, die Musik und Instrument, mit Einführungen ... aus dem Verlage von Breitkopf und Härtel. Leipzig: Breitkopf & Härtel, 1913.

234. MLA index series # 3. Ann Arbor, Mich.: Univ. of Michigan, 1974.

235. PLESSKE, Hans-Martin. Zur geschichte der deutschen Musikbibliographie; die periodische Verzeichnung der praktischen Musik. Berlin: Verlag Neue Musik, 1963.

236. POLLARD, Arthur. English hymns. London: Longmans, Green & Co., 1960.

237. PROTESTANT Episcopal Church in the U.S.A. A bibliography of church music and allied subjects. Philadelphia: The Commission on Music of the Diocese of Pennsylvania, 1949.

238. REUTER, Rudolf. Bibliographie der Orgel; Literatur zur Geschichte der Orgel bis 1968. Kassel: Bärenreiter, 1973.

239. ROVELSTAD, Betsey. Notes. Ann Arbor: Music Library Association, June 1963.

240. SARTORI, Claudio. La cappella musicale del Duomo di Milano. Milano: Ven. Fabbrica del Duomo, 1957.
Catalogo delle musiche dell'archivio.

241. SCHREIBER, Max. Kirchenmusik von 1500-1600. Regensburg: St. Georgsheim Birkeneck, 1932.
Orginaldrucke und Manuskripte chronologische zusammengestellt.

242. SCHWANN, L. (Bookseller). Sale catalogues. Düsseldorf: Schwann, 1910? 1914?

243. SINGENBERGER, John Baptist. Supplement to guide to Catholic church music. St. Francis: N.G., 1911.

244. SOLOW, Linda. A checklist of music bibliographies and indexes in progress and unpublished. (3rd edition) Ann Arbor, Mich.: Music Library Assn., 1974.

245. WACKERNAGEL, K. E. Philipp. Bibliographie zur Geschichte des deutschen Kirchenliedes. Frankfurt, Germany: Jahrhundert, 1855.

246. WALTHER, Johann Gottfried. Musicalisches Lexicon, oder musicalische Bibliothek. New York: Scientific Library Service, 1732.

247. WEICHLEIN, William J. An introduction to the bibliography of music. Ann Arbor, Mich.: Univ. of Michigan, 1963.

See also: 341, 349, 350, 364, 383, 399, 425, 441, 494, 941, 1143, 1168, 1203, 1213, 1214, 1352, 1406, 1407, 1408, 1409, 1416, 1445, 1492, 1493, 1610, 1892, 1897, 1951, 1962, 1988, 2139, 2246, 2288, 2471, 2604, 2760, 2903, 2937, 3003, 3008, 3009, 3019, 3258, 3314, 3380, 3401, 3440, 3462, 3596, 3624, 3936, 4102, 4182, 4195, 4279, 4421, 4434, 4448, 4493, 4509, 4749, 4750, 4751, 4806, 4814, 4922, 4928, 4929, 4931, 4932, 4937, 4938, 4960, 4984, 4997, 5182, 5264, 5302, 5362.

CAMBIATA

248. COX, Rolla Kenneth. Contemporary plans for training the boy's changing voice. Denton, Tex.: North Texas State Univ., 1964.

249. LUCK, J. T. Study relating to the boy's changing voice in intermediate church choirs of the Southern Baptist convention. Tallahassee, Fla.: Florida State Univ., 1957.

250. MELLALIEU, W. N. The boy's changing voice. Fair Lawn, N.J.: Oxford Univ. Press, 1935.

See also: 850, 5336.

CANON

See: 532, 1040, 3684, 4249, 4787.

CANTATAS

251. BACH, J. S. Cantata texts, sacred and secular. London: Constable and Co., 1926.

252. ________. Geistliche und weltliche Kantatentext. Hrsg. von Rudolph Wustmann. Wiesbaden: Breitkopf u. Härtel, 1967.

253. BURROWS, David L. Antonio Cesti. Wellesley, Mass.: Wellesley College, 1964.
The Wellesley Edition Cantata Index Series, 1.

254. The CANTATA number two of Anton Webern. Vol. 2 (Dissertation). Ann Arbor: Univ. of Mich.-Zerox University Microfilms, 1972.

255. DAY, James. The literary background to Bach's Cantatas. New York: Dover Publications, Inc., June 1966.

256. HANNAM, William S. Notes on the church cantatas of John (sic.) Sebastian Bach. New York: Oxford University Press, 1928.

257. HANSELL, Sven Hostrup. The solo cantatas, motets, and antiphons of Johann Adolf Hasse. Ann Arbor: Univ. Microfilms, 1966.

258. HINDERMANN, Walter F. Die nachösterlichen Kantaten des Bachschen Choral-kantaten-Jahrgangs: Versuch e. Genesis-deutung mit synopt. Tab. u. ver-gleichenden Notenbeisp. Hofheim am Taunus: Hofmeister, 1975.

259. HOBSON, Stephen Gilbert. A performance edition and study of five sacred choral cantatas by selected German composers (ca. 1650-1720). Ames, Iowa: State University of Iowa, 1958.

260. HODGES, Daniel Houston. The day of the Lord. A Cantata for Soli and Mixed Chorus with Piano or Organ Accompaniment. Ft. Worth: Southwestern Baptist Theological Seminary, M.C.M., 1962.

261. JONES, Joyce Gilstrap. Psalm XVIII, cantata for solo and mixed chorus with organ accompaniment. Fort Worth: Southwestern Baptist Theological Seminary, M.S.M., 1957.

262. Die KANTATE. Hanssler-Verlag, 1964.

263. KRUMMACHER, Friedhelm. Die Überlieferung der Choralbearbeitungen in der frühen evangelischen Kantate. Berlin: Verlag Merseburger, 1965.

264. LANGE, M. F. W. Die Anfänge der Kantate. Dresden, Germany: M. Dittert & Co., 1938.

265. McKINNEY, James Carroll. The solo bass voice in the cantatas of J. S. Bach. Ann Arbor: Univ. Microfilms, 1969.

266. NEUMANN, Werner. Handbuch der Kantaten Joh. Seb. Bachs. Wiesbaden: Breitkopf und Härtel, 1966.

267. RIMBACH, Evangeline Lois. The church cantatas of Johann Kuhnau. Vols. I & II. Ann Arbor: Univ. Microfilms, 1966.

268. SAMUEL, Harold E. The cantata in Nuremberg during the seventeenth century. Ann Arbor, Michigan: Cornell Univ. dissertation, 1963.

269. SCHMITZ, Eugen. Geschichte der Kantate und des geistlichen Konzerts. Leipzig: Breitkopf & Härtel, 1914.

270. SCHWANBECK, G. F. H. Die dramatische Chorkantate der Romantik in Deutschland. Dusseldorf: Dissertations-Verlag-G. H. Nolte, 1938.

271. SCOTT, Robert C. The cantatas of Buxtehude. Kingsville, Tex.: Texas College of Arts and Industries, 1963.

272. SIRP, Hermann. Die Thematik der Kirchenkantaten J. S. Bachs in ihren Beziehungen zum protestantischen Kirchenlied. ML410/B1AC, 1931.

273. SMEND, Friedrich. Bach-Kirchen-Kantaten. Berlin: Christlicher Zeitschriftenverlag, 1966.

274. TUNLEY, David. The eighteenth century French cantata. London: Dennis Dobson, 1974.

275. WESTRUP, Sir Jack A. Bach cantatas. London: British Broadcasting Corp., 1966.

276. WHITTAKER, W. Gillies. Cantatas of Johann Sebastian Bach. 2 vols. London: Oxford Univ. Press, 1959.

277. WHITTEN, Royce Lynn. The German Baroque church cantata and its use in the 20th cent. corporate worship. Ann Arbor: Univ. Microfilms, 1966.

278. WOLF, Leonhard. J. Sebastian Bachs Kirchenkantaten. Walluf bei Wiesbaden: M. Sändig, 1972.

279. WOODMANSEE, Stanley Dennison. The three-part church cantatas of Dietrich Buxtehude. Austin: Univ. of Texas, M.M., 1958.

See also: 1294, 1649, 3227, 3459, 3715, 3739, 4097, 4230, 4235, 4280, 4299, 4304, 4306, 4314, 4316a, 4466, 4542, 4941.

CANTOR

280. CANTORINUS romanum. Rome: Editio Typica Vaticana, 1911.

281. FRASER, D. The passing of the precentor. Gall & Inglis, 1916.

282. NATIONAL Jewish Music Council. The cantorial art. New York: NJMC, 1966.

283. RIEDEL, Johannes, ed. Cantors at the crossroads; essays on church music in honor of Walter E. Buszin. St. Louis: Concordia Pub. House, 1967.

284. SCUFFERT, Josef. Kantorendienst. Trier: Paulinus-Verlag, 1970.

See also: 914, 2736, 3423, 3622, 4596.

CANTUS FIRMUS

285. DANNER, Peter Kolb. The miserere mihi and the English Reformation; a study of the evolution of a cantus firmus genre in Tudor music. Ann Arbor: Univ. Microfilms, 1967.

286. MARTINI, Giovanni Battista. Regola agli organisti per accompagnare il canto fermo. Bologna: Forni Editore, 1969.

287. MATTFELD, Jacquelyn. The cantus-firmus motet in the works of Joachim. New Haven, Conn.: Yale Univ., 1958.

288. NITSCHKE, Wolfgang. Studien zu den Cantus-Firmus-Messen Guillaume Dufays. Berlin: Verlag Merseburger, 1968.

289. PARTON, James Kenton. Cantus firmus techniques and the rhythmic elements of style in the organ music of the early Tudor era. Denton, Tex.: North Texas State Univ., 1964.

290. PORTA, Ferrari and Carlo Antonio. Il canto fermo ecclesiastico, spiegato a'seminaristi de Ferrara. New York: Scientific Library Service, 1732.

291. SHAFFER, Jeanne Ellison. The cantus firmus in Alessandro Scarlatti's motets. Ann Arbor: Univ. Microfilms, 1970.

292. SPARKS, Edgar H. Cantus firmus in mass and motet, 1420-1520. Berkeley, Calif.: Univ. of California Press, 1963.

293. ________. Cantus firmus in mass and motet--1420-1520. New York: Da Capo Press, 1975.

294. TETTAMANZI, Fabrizio. Breve metodo per apprendere fondamente e con facilita il canto fermo. New York: Scientific Library Service, 1756.

CAROLS

295. BANCROFT, Charles W. O little town of Bethlehem. Philadelphia: Church of the Holy Trinity, 1968.

296. BAYR, Rudolf. Still Nacht, heilige Nacht. Salzburg: Residenz-Verlag, 1965.

297. BOSSI-FEDRIGOTTI, Anton. Tirol und das Lied von der Stillen heiligen Nacht. Fügen: Argus-Rainer, 1967.

298. CAROLS of today. New Jersey: Oxford Univ. Press, 1965.

299. CHRISTMAS Songs and Verse. Pictures by T. Izawa and K. Kawamoto. New York: Grosset & Dunlap, 1971.

300. DEARMER, Percy, R. Vaughan-Williams, and Martin Shaw. The Oxford book of carols. Fair Lawn, N.J.: Oxford University Press, 1928.

301. DUNCAN, Edmonstoune. The story of the carol. New York: Charles Scribner's Sons, 1911.

302. The ENGLISH carol. New York: Oxford Univ. Press, 1959.

303. FISSINGER, Edwin. Here we come a-caroling. Cincinnati, Ohio: WLSM, 1965.

304. FRIEDEMANN, Lilli. Improvisieren zu Weihnactsliedern. Kassel: Bärenreiter, 1968.

305. GALLICO, Paul. The story of "Silent Night." New York: Crown Publishers, 1967.

306. GASSNER, Josef. Franz Xavier Grubers Autographen von Stille Nacht, heilige Nacht. Salzburg: Pfad Verlag, 1968.

307. GEHMACHER, Max. Stille Nacht, heilige Nacht. Salzburg: Pfad Verlag, 1968.

308. GREENE, Richard Leighton. A selection of English carols. Fair Lawn, N.J.: Oxford Univ. Press, 1962.

309. ________, ed. The early English carols. St. Clair Shores, Mich.: Scholarly Press, 1971.

310. INTERNATIONAL book of Christmas carols. Englewood Cliffs, N.J.: Prentice Hall, Inc., 1963.

311. JACQUES, Reginald and David Willcocks (ed. and arr.). Carols for choirs. Fair Lawn, N.J.: Oxford Univ. Press, 1961.

312. KEEFE, Mildred Jones. Carols. Boston, Mass.: Boston Univ., M.A. (Research typescript), 1936.
Their origin in and connection with dramatic ritual and folkways.

313. KORONA, Armin. Ein Unsterblich Lied. Die Geschichte des Weihnachtsliedes Stille Nacht, heilige Nacht in Wort und Bild. Salzburg, Rottau 20: Selbstverl, 1968.

314. MAYLE, Bessie H. History and interpretation of the pre-Reformation carol and the Negro spiritual. (Research typescript). Boston, Mass.: Boston Univ., 1932.

315. NOBLE, Tertius. A round of carols. New York: Oxford University Press, 1935.

316. OBERNDORFER, Marx and Anne. Noëls. Chicago: H. T. Fitz-Simons Co., 1932.

317. OLIVER, Robert E. A Canadian Christmas carol. Ontario: Huronia Historical Development Council, 1967.

318. OZLEY, Clara Elizabeth. Christmas customs and carols from Latin America. (Research typescript) Evanston, Ill.: Northwestern Univ., 1945.

319. PARKER, Mabel. "An historical study of the carol." In Dulci Jubilo. Denton, Tex.: North Texas State Univ., M.A., 1945.

320. PHILLIPS, William J. Carols: Their origin, music, and connection with the mystery-plays. New York: E. P. Dutton & Co., 1921.

321. ________. Carols: Their origin, music, and connection with the mystery plays. (Repr.) Westport, Conn.: Greenwood Press, 1970.

322. POSTON, Elizabeth (ed.). The Penguin book of Christmas carols. Baltimore, Md.: Penguin Books Inc., n.d.

323. REYNOLDS, William. Christ and the carols. Nashville: Broadman Press, 1967.

324. ROBBINS, Russell Hope (ed.). Early English Christmas carols. New York: Columbia University Press, 1961.

325. ROSEL, Paul. Silent Night, Holy Night. Minneapolis: Augsburg Pub. House, 1969.

326. ROUTLEY, Eric. The English carol. New York: Oxford Univ. Press, 1958.

327. ________. The English carol. Westport, Conn.: Greenwood Press, 1973. (reprint of entry 326)

328. SCHMAUS, A. & L. Kriss-Rettenbeck. Stille Nacht, Geschichte und Ausbreitung eines Liedes. München: Universitätsverlage, 1967.

329. SHAW, Martin and Percy Dearmer. The English carol book. London: A. R. Mowbray & Co., 1928-29.

330. STRICKLING, George F. Christmas carols for male voices. Minneapolis: Hall and McCreary, n.d.

331. TERRY, Sir Richard R. Two hundred folk carols. London: Burns, Oates, & Washbourne, 1934.

332. WOOD, Charles and George Ratcliffe Woodward. The Cambridge carol book. London: S.P.C.K., 1924.

333. WOODWARD, George Ratcliffe. The Cowley carol book. Boston: E. C. Schirmer Music Co., 1925.

See also: 153, 158, 172, 183, 820, 843, 1044, 1471, 1556, 1634, 1652, 2330, 2526, 2632, 2642, 3053.

CATALOGUES and LISTS

334. ASSISI. Basilica patriarcale di San Francesco. Milano, Italy: 1962.
Catalogo del fondo musicale nella Biblioteca Comunale di Assisi. A cura di Claudio Sartori, etc.

335. BAER, Kathi Meyer. Liturgical music incunabula. London: Bibliographical Society, 1962.

336. BECKER, C. F. Systematisch-chronologische Darstellung der musikalischen Literatur von der frühesten bis auf die neueste Zeit. New York: Broude Brothers Ltd. (Facsimile-original in Leipzig, 1836-39), 1964.

337. BRITISH Broadcasting Corporation. Central Music Library. London: British Broadcasting Corps., 1965.
Piano and organ catalogue.

338. BRITISH Union catalogue of early music. Washington, D.C.: Butterworths, 1800.

339. BUSSI, Francesco. Piacenza, archivio del Duomo. Milano: Istituto editoriale italiano, 1967.

340. A CATALOGUE of Catholic church music. New York: Schirmer, 1915.

341. CATALOGS of sacred music. New York: Novello, Eiver & Co., 1903.

342. CATALOGUES collectionis operum ortis musicae quae in bibliotheca Capituli metropolitani pragensis asseruantur. Prague: Typis Typographicae archiepiscopalis, 1926.

343. CATALOGUES of Catholic church music. Boston: Oliver Ditson Co., 1918.

344. CATALOGUES of Protestant church music. Boston: Oliver Ditson Co., 1918.

345. CATHOLIC church music. New York: Breitkopf & Härtel, 1904.

346. CHEVALIER, C. U. J. Repertorium hymnologicum. Louvain, Belgium, V. 1 Louvain, Imprimerie Lefêver 1892. V. 2, 3: Louvain, Imprimerie Polleunis & Ceuterick 1897-1904. V. 4: Louvain, Imprimerie Ceuterick, 1912. V. 5, 6: Bruxelles, Société des Bollandistes 1921, 1920.
Catalogue des chants, hymnes, en usage dans l'Eglise latine.

347. CHIESA di Santa Maria della Consolazione, Venice: catalago del fondo musicale a cura di Paolo Pancino. Milano: Istituto editoriale italiano, 1969.

348. CINCINNATI Diocesan Commission on Church Music. First official catalogue of church music. Cincinnati, Ohio: Press of Cincinnati-Litho Co., 1899.

349. CINCINNATI Diocesan Commission on Church Music. Second official catalogue of church music. Cincinnati, Ohio: Press of Keating and Co., 1900.

350. COATES, E. J. (comp.). British catalogue of music classification. London: Council of the British National Bibliography, Ltd., 1960.

351. COFFIN, Berton. Singer's repertoire. New Brunswick, N.J.: The Scarecrow Press, 1956.

352. COLEMAN, Henry. Hymn-tune voluntaries for the organ. New York: Carl Fischer, 1930.

353. COMPLETE Pepper guide to the sacred music of all publishers. Philadelphia: J. W. Pepper, n.d.

354. CUENCA, Spain. Cathedral Archivo. Catálogo musical del Archivo de la Santa Iglesia Catedral Basilica de Cuenca. Cuenca: Ediciones del Instituto de Música Religiosa, 1965.

355. DALMONTE, Rossana. Catalogo musicale del Duomo di Monza. Bologna: Forni, 1969.

356. DE ZULUETA, Francis M. List of church music, comprising evening services, vespers, short masses, motets, etc. London: R. T. Washbourne, n.d.

357. EIDGENÖSSISCHER, Sängerverein. Führer durch die gesamte a-cappella-Männerchor-literatur der Schweiz. Zurich: Hug, 1966.

358. ESCORIAL. Archivo de Musica. Catálogo del archivo de música del monasterio de San Lorenzo el Real de el Escorial. Cuenca: Instituto de Música Religiosa, 1976.

359. ESPINA, Nona. Vocal solos for protestant services; a descriptive reference of solo music for the church year, including a bibliographical supplement of choral works: sacred repertoire for concert and teaching. (2nd ed. rev. and enl.). New York: Vita d'Arte, 1974.

360. FELLOWES, Edmund Horace. A repertoire of English cathedral music. New York: H. Milford, Oxford Univ. Press, 1930.

361. FENLON, Iain. Catalogue of the printed music and music manuscripts before 1801 in the music library of Birmingham Barber Institute of Fine Arts. London: Mansell, 1976.

362. FENTUM, J. Catalogue of vocal and instrumental music. New York: Scientific Library Service, 1780.

363. FINELL, Judith Greenberg. American Music Center catalog of choral and vocal works. New York: American Music Center, 1975.

364. FINNEY, Theodore M. Union catalogue of music and books on music printed before 1801 in Pittsburgh libraries. Pittsburgh, Pa.: Univ. of Pittsburgh, 1963.

365. FLAMMER, H. The Harold Flammer choral catalogue. New York: H. Flammer, Inc., 1939.

366. FORTY years of cathedral music, 1898-1938. London: S.P.C.K., 1940.

367. GÖLLER, Gotfried. Die Liebliche Sammlung. Köln, Germany: Volk, 1964.

Katalog der Musikalien der Kölner Domcapelle. (Beiträge zur rheinischen Musikgeschichte, 57).

368. GRASBERGER, Franz. Code international de catalogage de la musique. Frankfurt, Germany and London: C. F.

Peters, 1957.
Der Autoren-Katalog der Musikdrucke.

369. INSTRUMENTAL church service selections. Winona Lake: Rodeheaver Hall-Mack Co., 1965.

370. INTERNATIONAL Catholic Association for Radio and Television. Catalogue du disque de musique religieuse. Fribourg, Switzerland: 1956.

371. KATALOG des Musik archives der St. Peterskirche in Wien. Wien: Kommissions-Verlag von A. Bohm & Sohn, 1908.

372. LLOYD'S church musicians' directory. New York: AMS Press, 1974.

373. MATTOS, Cleofe Person De. Catálogo temático das obras do Padre José Maurício Nunes Garcia. Rio de Janeiro: Ministério da Educacão, 1970.

374. MOORE, Edgar J. A guide to music in worship. A comprehensive, current index of sacred solos in print. Nassau, New York: Channel Press, 1959.

375. MUSIC recommended. London: S.P.C.K., 1935.
Musical Advisory Committee of the School of English Church Music.

376. OXFORD, Diocese of. Suggestions of the choice of music, with a first list of services and anthems. London: S.P.K.C., 1927.

377. PENNSYLVANIA Diocese, Commission on Music. List of service music and anthems. Philadelphia, Pa.: The Commission, 1946.

378. PLAINSONG and Mediaeval Music Society. Catalogue of the society's library. Burnham, Bucks: Nashdom Abbey, 1928.

379. PROTESTANT Episcopal Church in the U.S.A. Joint Commission on Church Music. A selected list of works relating to church music for the use of reverend clergy and choirmasters of the Protestant Episcopal church in the United States of America. New York: The H. W. Gray Co., 1927.

380. PROTESTANT Episcopal Church in the U.S. A. Joint Commission on Church Music. Service music and anthems, for the non-professional choir. Greenwich, Conn.: Seabury Press, 1955.

381. REICH, Wolfgang. Threnodiae sacrae. Dresden: Sachsische Landesbibliothek, 1966.

382. RKLITKAYA, comp., and G. P. Koltypina, ed. Muzikalnye biblioteki i muzykalnye fondy v bibliotekakh SSSR. (Russia's libraries of music in universities, conservatories, research institutes, publishers, etc.) Moskva: Tsentri, 1972.

383. ROEDIGER, Karl Erich. Die geistlichen musik handschriften der Universitätsbibliothek Jena. Jena: Frommann (W. Biedermann), 1955.

384. ROSSUM, Wed. J. R. and Utrecht Van. Kerkmuzie kuitgaven. Frankfurt, Germany: J. Baer & Co., 1905.

385. ROYAL School of Church Music. A selected list of church music recordings. Croydon: Royal School of Church Music, 1967.

386. SCHIRMER, G. (Pub.). Catalogue of sacred songs and duets. New York: G. Schirmer, Inc., 1920.

387. SCHLAGER, Karl-Heinz. Thematischer Katalog der ältesten Alleluia-Melodien aus Handschriften des 10. und 11. Jahrhunderts. München: W. Ricke, 1965.

388. SCHNURL, Karl. Das alte Musikarchiv der Pfarrkirche St. Stephan in Tulln. Wien: In Kommission bei Hermann Böhlaus Nachf.

389. SCOTLAND. List of music approved for use in the Catholic churches and chapels of Scotland. Edinburgh: Otto Schulze & Co., 1906.

390. SELECTED list of anthems, chorales & motets, psalters & hymnbooks. Chicago, Ill.: British American Music Co., n. d.

391. SLENK, Howard J. A well-appointed church music. Grand Rapids: Eerdmans Publishing Co., 1961.

392. STEVENS, R. J. S. (ed.). Sacred music for one, two, three and four voices. 3 vols. London: Charterhouse, 1798-1802.

393. STOUGHTON Musical Society. The Stoughton Musical Society's Centennial collection of sacred music. Consists of selections from the earliest American authors, as originally written, together with a few selections from European and modern composers. Boston: Ditson & Company, 1878.

394. STURE, D. Music for the protestant church choir. Richmond, Va.: John Knox Press, 1955.

395. SUBIRANA, E. Música sagrada. Barcelona: E. Subirana, 1912.

396. SUGGESTIONS of the choice of music. London: S. P. C. K., n. d.

397. TERRY, Richard Runciman. Catholic church music. London: Greening & Co., Ltd., 1907.

398. VERLAGS-katalog. Kirchen-musikalische Werke. New York: F. Pustet Co., 1901.

399. WALLON, Übersetzung von Simone. Code international de catalogage de la musique. London: C. F. Peters, 1961. Code restreint. Redigé par Yvetta Federoff. Kurzgefasste Anleitung. Limited Code.

400/1. WEEKES and Co. Music, sacred, and secular for church choirs, singing classes, choral societies and schools. London: Weekes, 1909.

See also: 4, 206, 207, 218, 219, 225, 231, 233, 242, 253, 425, 443, 488, 720, 779, 877, 918, 933, 934, 1096, 1101, 1207, 1299, 1389, 1642, 1647, 1937, 1938, 1940, 2069, 2285, 2466, 2615, 2679, 2829, 2939, 3006, 3012, 3015, 3020, 3068, 3069, 3245, 3273, 3284, 3307, 3316, 3365, 3513, 3646, 3723, 3815, 3836, 3837, 3941, 3962, 4012, 4022, 4068, 4253, 4300, 4385, 4390, 4492, 4552, 4754, 4924, 5279, 5429.

CATHEDRALS and BASILICAS

402. ADCOCK, E. E. "St. Paul's Cathedral." The American Organist, September 1921, 295.

403. ANTUNEZ, Francisco. La capilla de musica de la Catedral de Durango, Mexico, siglos XVII & XVIII. Aguascalientes: Author, 1970.

404. BAILEY, Terence William. The ceremonies and chants of the processions of the Western church. Ann Arbor: University Microfilms, 1968.

405. BALAGUER, Pablo Hernández. Catalogo de música de los archivos de la Catedral de Santiago de Cuba y el del Museo Bacardi. Havana: Biblioteca Nacional José Martí, 1961.

406. BARACHETTI, Gianni. La domus magna e il Collegio della Misericordia. Bergamo: Industrie grafiche Cattaneo, 1968.

407. BENDINER, M. Das Strassburger Münster. Stuttgart: W. Seifert, 1906.

408. BERETHS, Gustav. Beiträge zur Geschichte der Trierer Dommusik. Mainz: Schott, 1974.

409. BONY, Jean. French cathedrals. London: 1951.

410. BOSTON, Joseph Noel T. The musical history of Norwich Cathedral. Norwich, England: 63 The Close, Norwich Cathedral, 1963.

411. BOWERS, Roger and Anthony Crossland. The organs and organists of Wells Cathedral. Wells: Friends of Wells Cathedral, 1974.

412. BUMPUS, John Skelton. A history of English cathedral music, 1549-1889. London: T. W. Laurie, 1908.

413. _______. A history of English cathedral music, 1549-1889. (Reprint) Farnborough, England: Gregg, 1927.

414. BUMPUS, T. Francis. The cathedrals and churches of Norway, Sweden and Denmark. London: 1908.

415. BURNEY, Charles. An account of the musical performances in Westminster Abbey and the Pantheon, May 26, 27, 29 and June 3, 5, 1784 in commemoration of Händel. New York: Broude Brothers Ltd., 1964. (Reprint--orig. 1785)

416. CHARTIER, Francois Leon. L'ancien chapitre de Notre-Dame de Paris et sa maîtrise, d'après les documents capitulaires avec un appendice musical comprenant plusiers fragments d'oeuvres des anciens maîtres de chapelle. Paris: Perrin, 1897.

417. CHRIST, Yvan. Cathédrales de France. Paris: N.G., 1950.

418. CHURCH Music Society. Cathedral music today and tomorrow. London: Oxford Univ. Press, 1941.

419. CHURCH of England. Cathedral music today and tomorrow. London: S.P.C.K., 1941.

420. COOK, G. H. English cathedral through the centuries. London: Phoenix House, Ltd., 1957.

421. CRAM, Ralph Adams. The cathedral of Palma de Mallorca. Cambridge, Mass.: 1932.

422. DAY, J. Godfrey F. and Henry C. Patton. The cathedrals of the Church of Ireland. London: Society for Promoting Christian Knowledge, 1932.

423. DELHOMMEAU, L. Orgues et organistes de la cathédrale de Luçon. Luçon: S. Pacteau, 1967.

424. DELZENNE, Abel. Le chanoine Nicolas Joachim, 1872-1945: un maître de chappelle de la cathédrale de Tournai; con-

tributión à l'histoire de la Cathédrale de Tournai. Louvain: Bibliotèque centrale de l'Université catholique de Louvain, 1973.

425. DURHAM Cathedral. Library. *A catalog of the printed music and books on music in the Durham Cathedral library.* Compiled by R. Alec Harman. London: Oxford Univ. Press, 1968.

426. FELLOWES, Edmund H. *English cathedral music.* Revised by J. A. Westrup. New York: Barnes & Noble, 1969.

427. ________. *English cathedral music.* New 5th edition. London: Methuen; New York: Barnes & Noble, 1973.

428. FRIIS, Niels. *Domkirken vor frue kirkes orgel.* København: through th. Frobenius & Co., Orgelbyggeri, 1965.

429. FROST, William Alfred. *Early recollections of St. Paul's Cathedral.* London: Simpkin, Marshall, Hamilton, Kent & Co., Ltd., 1926.

430. GEE, Henry. *Gloucester Cathedral, its organs and organists.* London: Chiswick Press, 1921.

431. KIRWAN, A. Lindsey. *The music of Lincoln Cathedral.* London: Stainer and Bell, 1973.

432. LEFLON, Jean. *Henri Hardouin et la musique de chapitre de Reims au XVIII siècle.* Ouvrage orné de six gravures. Reims, France: Matot, 1934.

433. LOOTENS, Willem. *Beschrijving van het oude en nieuwe orgel in de Groote--of St. Lievens Monster-kerk der stad Zierikzee.* Baarn: De Praestantpers, 1966.

434. LOPEZ-CALO, José. *La música en el la catedral de Granada en el siglo XVI.* Granada: Fundación Rodriguez-Acosta, n. d.

435. MALE, Emile. *La cathédrale d'Albi.* Paris: P. Hartmann, 1950.

436. ________. *Notre-Dame de Chartres.* Paris: P. Hartmann, 1948.

437. MILMAN, H. H. *Handbook to the cathedrals of England-St. Paul's.* London: J. Murray, 1879.

438. MUONI, Damiano. *Gli antignati organari insigni e serie dei maestri di cappella del Duomo di Milano.* Bologna: Forni, 1969.

439. SARTHOU CARRERES, Carlos. Catedrales de España. Madrid, Spain: Espaso, 1907; Calpe, 1946.

440. SCOTT, David. The music of St. Paul's Cathedral. London: Stainer & Bell (also Galaxy Music Corp.), 1972.

441. SHAW, Harold Watkins. Eighteenth-century cathedral music. London: Oxford Univ. Press, 1952.

442. SIXTY years of cathedral music. Fair Lawn, N.J.: Oxford Univ. Press, 1963.

443. SOCIETY for Promoting Christian Knowledge. Forty years of cathedral music, 1898-1938. London: H. Milford, 1940.

444. STEVENSON, Robert Murrell. Spanish cathedral music in the Golden Age. Berkeley, Calif.: Univ. of California Press, 1961.

445. ________. Spanish cathedral music in the Golden Age. (A reprint of the 1961 edition) Greenwood Press, 1976.

446. STODDARD, Whitney S. Monastery and cathedral in France. Middletown, Conn.: Wesleyan Univ. Press, 1966.

447. TAGMANN, Pierre M. Archivalische Studien zur Musikpflege am Dom von Mantua (1500-1627). Bern: Haupt, 1967.

448. WERNER, Rudolf. Einflüsse raumakustischer Faktoren auf das Musikhören in Kirchen. Berlin: Merseburger, 1970.

449. WESLEY, S. S. A few words on cathedral music. New York: A. Broude Inc., 1965.

450. WEST, John E. Cathedral organist past and present. London: Novello & Co., 1899.

451. WILKES, Roger. English cathedrals and collegiate churches and chapels. London: Friends of Cathedral Music, 1968.

See also: 1, 87, 226, 240, 245, 339, 354, 355, 366, 367, 741, 1205, 1213, 1214, 1224, 1298, 1683, 1699, 1854, 2031, 2219, 3332, 3342, 3347, 3396, 3414, 3419, 3445, 3465, 3485, 3526, 3575, 3587, 3742, 3743, 3768, 3822, 3869, 3874, 3924, 3948, 3954, 3997, 4006, 4010, 4016, 4041, 4064, 4065, 4071, 4079, 4083, 4093, 4099, 4112, 4175, 4603, 4606, 4716, 4899, 5025, 5243.

CHANT

General

452. ANTONOWYEZ, Myroslaw. The chants from Ukrainian heirmologia. Bilthoven: A. B. Creygton, 1974.

453. AUBRY, Pierre. Le role du chant liturgique et sa place dans la civilisation générale du moyen age. Paris: Aux bureaux de la Schola Cantorum, 1897.

454. BAILEY, Terence. The intonation formulas of western chant. Toronto: Pontifical Institute of Mediaeval Studies, 1974.

455. BANNISTER, H. M. Anglo-French sequelae. London: Plainsong & Mediaeval Music Society, 1934.

456. BENZ, Ernst. Das Buch der heiligen Gesänge der Ostkirche. Hamburg: Furche-Verlag, 1962.

457. BOGAERTS, Jacques. S. Alphonse de Liguori, musicien, et la reforme de chant sacré. Paris: P. Lethielleux, 1899.

458. BOURDEAU, Celestin Charles Marie. Le chant réligieux de l'église orthodoxe russe. Paris: 1913.
In Encyclopédia de la musique et dictionnaire du conservatoire.

459. BRAGERS, Achille P. Bragers chant service book. Accompaniments to various masses, motets, litanies, hymns, canticles; principal propers of the mass; vespers of the B. V. M. and compline service. Boston, Mass.: McLaughlin & Reilly Co., 1954.

460. BUNJES, Paul. The formulary tones annotated. St. Louis, Mo.: Concordia Publishing House, 1965.

461. CALDWELL, John. Medieval music. New York: Barnes Noble & Harper Row, 1976.

462. CANDOTTI, Giovanni Battista. Sul canto ecclesiastico e sulla musica da chiesa. Venezía: Dalla tip. di G. B. Menlo, 1847.

463. CASIMIRI, Raffaele Casimiro. Cantantibus organis! Raccolta di seriti per la cultura delle Scholae Cantorum. Roma: Edizione del "Psalterium," 1924.

464. CLOET, N. De la restauration du chant liturgique, ou ce qui est à faire pour arriver a posséder le meilleur chant romain possible. Plancy: Societé de St.-Victor, 1852.

465. ________. Recueil de melódies liturgiques restituées d'après un très-grand nombre de monuments, tant manuscrits

qu'imprimes, pour servir a la restauration du chant romain, avec des préliminaires sur la méthode qu'on a suivie. Paris: J. Lecoffre etc., 1863-64.

466. CONGRES parisien et regional de chant liturgique et de musique d'église. Paris: 1911.

467. CROOK, Hubert. Chanting for beginners. Croydon, England: Royal School of Church Music, 196-.

468. DANJOU, Jean Louis Felix. De l'état et de l'avenir du chant ecclésiastique en France. Paris: Parent Desbarres, 1844.

469. DAUX, Camille. Deux livres choraux monastiques des Xe et XIe siècles étude historique, analytique et musicale par M. l'abbé Camille Daux. Paris: A. Picard et fils, 1899.

470. DENIS, P. Etudes sur la question du chant liturgique. Paris: R. Haton, 1891.

471. DESROCQUETTES, Dom Jean Hebert, O. S. B. Chant accompaniments for Solemn Matins invitatories of major feasts. Boston, Mass.: McLaughlin & Reilly Company, 1953.

472. DIVINI Cultus Sanctitatem. The chant of the church. Collegeville, Minn.: The Liturgical Press, 1930.

473. GAISSER, Ugo Atanasio. Les "Heirmoi" de Paques dans l'office grec. Rome: Impr. de la Propagando, 1905.
Etude rythmique et musicale.

474. GASTOUE, Amédée. Histoire du chant liturgique à Paris. Paris: C. Poussielgue, 1904.

475. GELINEAU, Joseph. Chant et musique dans le culture chretien. Paris: Editions Fleurus, 1962.
Principles lois et applications.

476. GEVAERT. La mélopée antique dans le chant de l'église Latine. Gand, Belgium: Hoste, 1895.

477. _______. Les origines du chant liturgique de l'église latine. Gand, Belgium: A. Hoste, 1890.
Etude d'histoire musicale.

478. GRADUALE Sarisburiensis. London: The Plainsong and Mediaeval Music Society, 1895.

479. H 159 MONTPELLIER. Tonary of St. Bénigne of Dijon. (transcribed and annotated by Finn Egeland Hansen.) Copenhagen: Dan Fog Musikforlag, 1974.

480. HEYWOOD, John. The art of chanting. London: William Clowes and Son, 1893.

481. HIRT, Charles C. Graeco-Slavonic chant traditions evident in the part-writing of the Russian Orthodox Church. (Research typescript). Los Angeles: So. California Univ., 1946.

482. KARPOV, Gennod Fedorovich. Krug tserkovnag drevniago znamennago pienia. St. Petersburg, Russia: Tip. U. S. Balasheva, 1884.

483. L., V. G. The chant. St. Louis: Herder Book Co., 1938.
A simple and complete method for teachers and students.

484. LACASSAGNE, Joseph. Traité général des éléments du chant. New York: Broude Brothers (Facsimile, orig. Paris: Chez l'auteur, 1766).

485. ________. Traité général des éléments du chant, dédie à monseigneur le Dauphin. (Réimpr.). Genève: Minkoff Reprints, 1972.

486. LARSEN, Jens Peter. Messetoner efter gammel kirkelig tradition. København: Samfundet Dansk Kirkesang, 1965.

487. LEUPOLD, Ulrich. A manual on intoning, for the Commission on Worship, Lutheran Church in America. Philadelphia: Lutheran Church in America Board of Publication, 1967.

488. LIST of Members. London: Plainsong and Mediaeval Music Society, 1934.

489. MACWILLIAM, I. M. Steps towards good chanting. London: S. P. C. K., 1938.

490. METALLOV, Vasiliĭ Mikhaĭkovich. Bogosluzhebnoe pienie russkoi tserkvi. (Transliteration). Divine service hymns of the Russian church (Translation). Moscow: N. G., 1912.

491. MOLITOR, Raphael. Eine werte Geschichte. Graz, Austria: Verlags Buchhandlung "Styria," 1903.
Erinnerungsvolle Gedanken über "Geschichte und Wert der offiziellen Choralbücher."

492. MUSICA sacra. Gand: C. Poelman, Impr., 1881-85.

493. MUSICA sacra. (unrev'd). Toulouse: Impr. L. Hebrail, Durand et Delpuech, 1875.
Revue du chant liturgique et de la musique réligieuses.

494. NUTTING, Sister Bertrand Marie. A thesis on trends in teaching liturgical singing. Lansing, Mich.: Univ. of Michigan, 1949.

495. PEARSALL, R. L. Pearsall on chanting. Leipsig: W. B. Squire, 1907.

496. PETER, Saint and apostle, benedictine monastery of Solesmes. Solesmes: The Monastery, 1963.
La notation musicale des chants liturgiques latins. Présentée par les moines de Solesmes (with plates and a map).

497. POTT, F. An introduction to the principles and practice of chanting. London: N. G., 1896.

498. PREOBRAZHENSKII, Antonin. Po cerkovnomoo peniyoo ookaztel knig, broshyoor, zhoornalnich stageii rukoiiseii (Transliteration). Moscow: 1900.

499. _______. Vopros o edinogtasnom pienii u russkoi tserkvi xvii go vilka. Tipografiia I. N. Skorokhòdov, 1904.
Istoricheskiia sviedieniia: pis'mennye pamiatniki.

500. RAZUMOVSKII, Dimitrii Vasilevich. Tserkovnoe pienie u rossii. Moscow: Tipograf T. Ris, 1867-69.
Iz urokov, chitannykh.

501. REBOURS, J. B. Traité de psaltique. Paris: A. Picard et fils, 1906.
Théorie et pratique du chant dans l'Eglise Grecque.

502. RUELLE, C. E. Le congrès européen d'Arezzo pour l'étude du chant liturgique. BM. Paris: N. G., 1884.

503. SAMSON, Joseph. Musique et chant sacrés. Paris: Gallimard, 1957.

504. SCHAFHAUTL, Karl Franz. Ein spraziergang durch die liturgische Musik-geschichte der katholischen Kirche. München, Germany: J. Lindauersche Buchhandlung, 1887.
Mit 4 notentafeln und 1 Titelbilde.

505. SEMAINE d'Etudes Internationales, Fribourg, 1965. Le chant liturgique après Vatican II. Paris: Editions Fleurus, 1966.

506. SISTERS of St. Benedict, St. Joseph, Minnesota (comp. and arr.). Chant melodies. Boston, Mass.: McLaughlin & Reilly Co., 1953.

507. SWAN, Alfred J. The nature of the ancient Russian liturgical chant. Rome: American Musicological Society, 1938. LC 4.1M6342.

508. _______. Russian music and its source in chant and folk song. New York: W. W. Norton, 1973.

509. TOVAR, Librado. La musica sagrada (su arreglo y fomento). Guadalajara: Albondiga y J. Manuel, 1907.
Breve comentario al Motu proprio respectivo de S. S. Pio X, de 22 de noviembre de 1903, y suscinto compendio de las doctrinas de autores de nota, en relacion a esta importante materia.

510. TYPIS Society S. Joannis Evang. Liber usualis--Missae et officii. Paris, Tornai, Rome: Desclée et Soc., 1954.

511. VALADEZ SANTOS, Jose. Los cabildos y el servicio coral. Morelia, Méxicó: Escuela Superior de Musica sagrada, 1945.

512. VELIMIROVIC, Milòs, ed. Studies in Eastern chant. London: Oxford Univ. Press, 1973.

513. VOZNESENSKII, Ivan Ivanovich. O sovremennikh nam'nuzhakh' i zadachakh russkavo tserkovnavo pieniia. Moscow and Leipzig: Cobctvennost-izdatelia-P. Yourgensona, 1899.

514. ________. Obshchedostupniia chteniia o tserkovnomi pienii-izdanie 2 . . . Protoiereia I. Voznesenskago. Kostroma: Fv Gubernskoi tipografii, 1897.

515. ________. Otserkovnom pienii provoslavnoi greko-rossiisko fserkvi. Riga: E. Plates, 1890.
Several volumes, bound in blue velvet, with gold letter inscriptions on front cover.

516. WACHSMANN, Klaus. Untersuchungen zum vorgregorianan-ischen Gesang. Regensburg: F. Pustet, 1935.
Veroffentlichungen der Gregorianischen Akademie zu Freiburg, Schweiz.

517. WAGENER, Heinz. Die begleitung des gregorianischen Chorals im neunzehnten Jahrhundert. Regensburg: Bosse, 1964.

518. WAGNER, Peter. Origine et Development du chant Liturgique jusqu'à la Fin du Moyen Age. Tournai: N. G., 1904.

519. ________. A handbook of plainsong. 2nd ed., rev. and enl. Part. 1. Origin and development of the forms of the liturgical chant up to the end of the middle ages. Translated by Agnes Orme and E. G. P. Wyatt. London: The Plainsong and Mediaeval Music Society, 1901.

520. WEISSENBRUCH, Publ. Essai sur la theorie du chant. New York: Scientific Library Service, 1820.

521. WOODWARD, D. R. Piae Cantiones. London: The Plainsong and Mediaeval Music Society, 1910.

See also: 5, 8, 346, 404, 813, 971, 1083, 1084, 1085, 1091, 1093, 1109, 1121, 1124, 1126, 1129, 1136, 1142, 1144, 1145,

1153, 1154, 1166, 1167, 1168, 1180, 1181, 1249, 1253, 1261, 1265, 1282, 1306, 1382, 1396, 1413, 1526, 1629, 1630, 1671, 1867, 1868, 1873, 1919, 1931, 1949, 1950, 1968, 2007, 2050, 2091, 2306, 2309, 2662, 2811, 2817, 2820, 2821, 2844, 2904, 2945, 3033, 3103, 3137, 3192, 3196, 3300, 3356, 3394, 3434, 3491, 3545, 3577, 3608, 3658, 4119, 4673, 4682, 4808, 4825, 4826, 4933, 4946, 5007, 5010, 5284, 5285.

Ambrosian

522. CATTANEO, Enrico. Note storiche sul canto ambrosiano. Milan: S. Benedello, 1950.

523. JESSON, Roy Hart. Ambrosian chant: The music of the mass. Bloomington: Indiana Univ., 1955.

524. MANUALE di canto Ambrosiano. Turin: Sten, 1929.

525. SESINI, Ugo. La notazione comasco nel cod. Ambrosiano E. 68. sup. Milano: Casa edetrice d'arte e liturgia B. Angelico, 1932.

See also: 2426, 3695, 3703, 4801.

Anglican

526. BRIDGES, Robert. Collected essays, papers, etc. Vol. III. New York: Oxford Univ. Press, 1935.

527. BRIGGS, Henry Brembridge (ed.) rev. and enl. by J. H. Arnold. A manual of plainsong for Divine Service. London: Novello, 1951.

528. PROTESTANT Episcopal Church in the U. S. A. Liturgy and ritual diurnal, benedictine. Kenosha, Wisconsin: St. Mary's Convent, 1952.

See also: 2807, 3332, 4847, 4853, 4855, 5014.

Byzantine (Includes Eastern Orthodox)

529. ALEKSANDR Mezenets. Azbuka znamennago pieniia. Kazan, Soviet Union: Tip. N. Danilov, 1888.

530. ALLEMANOV, Dimitri. Kurs istorii russkago tserkovnage pieniia. Moscow: P. Iurgensona, 1914.

531. ATHANASOPOULOS, Giorgios D. Theoria tes Büzantines musikes. Meta praktikon áskeseon kai perileptikes Istorias, etc. Patria: N. G., 1950. BM-7900. f. 28.

532. BIEZEN, Jan Van. The middle byzantine kanon-notation of manuscript. Bilthoven: A. B. Creyghton, 1969.

533. BURKHALTOR, A. Louis. Byzantine and medieval music by Romain Goldron. np: H. S. Stuttman Co., Distr. Doubleday, 1968.

534. CHOURMOUZIOS, S. Methodos pros eükolon didasklion tes büzantines. 'En Leükosia: N. G., 1936. (BM)

535. ________. 'O Damaskenos ètoi theoretikon pleres tes büzantines mousikes. 'En Leükosia: N. G., 1934.

536. CIOBANU, Gheorghe. Studii de etnomuzicologie şi bizantinologie. Bucharest: Editura muzicală, 1974.

537. FELLERER, Karl Gustav (gen. ed.). "The music of the Byzantine church." Anthology of Music. Vol. 13. New York: A. Broude, Inc., n. d.

538. HATHERLY, Stephen G. A treatise on byzantine music. Paisley and London: A. Gardner, 1892.

539. HISTOIRE de la musique ... Moyen âge. Paris: N. G., 1913.

540. HOEG, Carsten. The oldest slavonic tradition of byzantine music. Fair Lawn, N. J.: Oxford Univ. Press, 1953.

541. MARZI, Giovanni. Melodia e nomos nella musica bizantina. Studi pubblicati dall' Istituto di Filologia Classica. (with illustrations). Bologna: N. G., 1960.

542. RAASTED, Jørgen. Intonation formulas and modal signatures in byzantine musical manuscripts. Copenhagen: E. Munksgaard, 1966.

543. STRUNK, William Oliver. Essays on music in the byzantine world. Foreword by K. Levy. New York: W. W. Norton, 1975.

544. TARDO, Lorenzo. L'antica melurgia bizantina nell' interpretazione della scuola monastica di Grottaferrata. Grottaferrata: "S. Nilo." 1938.

545. TIBY, Ottavio. La musica bizantina. Milano: Fratelli Bocca, 1838.
Teoria e storia.

546. TILLYARD, Henry Julius Wetenhall. Byzantine music and hymnography. (Reprint London Faith Press, 1923.) New York: AMS Press, 1976.

547. VELIMIROVIC, Miloš M. Byzantine elements in early Slavic chant: The Hirmologion. Copenhagen: Ejnar Munksgaard, 1960.
Studies on the Fragmenta Chiliandarica palaeoslavica. no. 1, with musical illustrations.

548. WELLESZ, Egon. Aufgaben und Probleme auf dem Gebiete der byzantinischen und orientalishchen Kirchenmusik. Münster, Germany: Aschendorff, 1923.

549. ________. A history of Byzantine music and hymnography. Oxford, England: Clarendon Press, 1949.

550. ________. A history of Byzantine music and hymnography. Oxford, England: Clarendon Press, 1961.
Second edition, revised and enlarged, with musical illustrations. (Good bibliography.)

551. ________ and Miloš Velimirović (ed.). Studies in Eastern chant. New York: Oxford Univ. Press, 1966.

552. WILSON, N. G. and D. I. Stefanovic. Manuscripts of Byzantine chant in Oxford. Oxford: Bodleian Library, 1963.

See also: 512, 1254, 1255, 1262, 1275, 1279, 1280, 2932, 2041, 2285, 3162, 3304, 3574, 3684, 3692.

Gregorian

553. AGUSTONI, Luigi. Gregorianischer choral. Freiburg: Herder, 1973.
Elemente und Vortragslehre mit besonderer Berücksichtigung der Neumenkunde (with musical illustrations).

554. ________. Le chant grégorien. Rome: Herder, 1969.

555. ALTISENT, Miguel. El canto gregoriana, un modelo de música religiosa. Version castellana del P. Vicente Pérez-Jorge O. F. M. Tarrega, (Lérida): F. Camps Calmet, 1973.

556. APEL, Willi. Gregorian chant. Bloomington, Ind.: Indiana Univ. Press, 1958.

557. BANNWART, P. Roman. Gregorianischer Choral. Zurich: Panton Verlag, 1968.

558. BARON, Ludovic. L'expression du chant grégorien. Commentaire liturgique et musical des messes des dimanches et des principales fêtes de l'année. Plouharnel-Morbihan: Abbaye Sainte-Anne de Kergonan, 1947-1950.

559. BAS, G. *Rythme grégorien.* Rome: Desclée, Le Febvre et cie., 1906.
Les théorias de Solesmes et Dom T. A. Burge.

560. BECKER, L. *Kurzer Leitfaden für den Unterricht im gregorianischen Choral.* Regensburg and New York: F. Pustet, 1911.

561. BOER, Nicholas. *Confessio et pulchritudo, belijdenis en schoonheid; commentaar op de gregoriaanse misenofficiegezongen.* Rotterdam: De Forel, 1952.

562. BONUZZI, A. *Metodo di canto gregoriano.* Solesmes: N.G., 1894.

563. BOURDON, A. *Essai pratique de rhythmique grégorienne rationnelle.* Tours: A. Mame et fils., 1920.

564. BOYER D'AGEN, A. J. *Introduction aux mélodies grégoriennes.* Paris: H. Ovdin, 1894.

565. BOYER, Louis. *Musique et musiciens d'église.* L'art grégorien, le chant populaire et la chanson; études et leçons, silhouettes et portraits. Lyon: E. Gloppe, 1925.

566. BRAGERS, Achille P. *Standard gregorian chants.* Boston, Mass.: McLaughlin & Reilly Co., 1952.

567. BRAMBACH, Wilheim. *Gregorianisch. Bibliographische Lösung der Streitfrage über den Ursprung des gregorianischen Gesanges.* Leipzig: M. Spirgatis, 1895. Sammlung bibliothekswissenschaftlicher Arbeiten, 1895.

568. BROTHERS of the Christian Schools. *Solfége- manuel de chant grégorien.* Montreal: The School, 1914.

569. BRYDEN, John R. and David G. Hughes. *An index of gregorian chant.* Cambridge, Mass.: Harvard Univ. Press, 1969.

570. BURGESS, Francis. *The rudiments of gregorian music.* London: Wm. Reeves, 1908.

571. CARDINE, Eugene. *Semiologia gregoriana.* Roma: Pontifico Istituto di musica sacra, 1968.

572. CATHOLIC Church Liturgy and Ritual, Gradual. *Forty hours' adoration, gregorian chant and simple settings by A. Edmonds Tozer.* New York: J. Fischer, 1949.

573. CHARLIER, Henri et André. *Le chant grégorien.* Limoges: Drouget et Ardant, 1967.

574. COMBE, Don Pierre. Histoire de la restauration du chant grégorien d'après des documents inédits. Solesmes, Fr.: Abbaye de Solesmes, 1969.

575. COMES Y DE PUIG, Bernardo. Fragmentos musicos. New York: Scientific Library Service, 1739.
Caudalosa fuente gregoria, en el Arte de canto llano. Cuyos fundamentos, teorica, reglas, pratica, y exemplos, copiosamente se explican sobre los ocho tonos. . . .

576. DAVID, L. Analyses grégoriennes pratiques. Grenoble: Bureau de la Revue du chant grégorien, 1920.

577. _______. La prononciation romaine du latin et la chant grégorien. Grenoble: Libraire Saint Grégoire, 1937.

578. DECHEVRENS, Antoine. Les varies mélodies grégoriennes. Wiesbaden: M. Sändig, 1971. (repr. of Paris: G. Beauchesne et cie, 1902).

579. DESROCQUETTES, Dom J. Hébert. Flash cards-guide book, an extract from "A simple introduction to plainsong." Boston, Mass.: McLaughlin & Reilly Co., n. d.

580. _______. Gregorian musical values: Chappell. Cincinnati, Ohio: R. Jusko Publisher, 1963.

581. DOBBELSTEEN, Lambert Adrion. Kyriale, selective, containing gregorian chant and organ accompaniment. Milwaukee: M. L. Nemmers, 1949.

582. ECCHER, Celestino. Chironomia gregoriana, dinamica, movimento, trasporto; ossia, come leggere ed eseguire il canto gregoriano. Rome: Desclée, 1952.

583. EKVALL, Bo. Fran Gregoriansk sang till Bach. Stockholm: Verbum, 1967.

584. ERNETTI, Pellegrino Maria. Canto gregoriano. Trattato generale ad uso dei seminari ed istituti religiosi. Venezia, Roma: Istituto per la collaborazione culturale, 1960.

585. FELLERER, Karl Gustav. Anthology of Music, Vol. 18. Gregorian chant. New York: Broude Inc., n. d.

586. _______. Deutsche Gregorianik im Frankenreich. Regensburg: G. Bosse, 1941.

587. FERRETTI, P. M. Estetica gregoriana, ossia trattato delle forme musicali del canto gregariano. Roma: Pontificio istituto di musico sacra, 1934.

588. _______. Il cursus metrico e il ritmo delle melodie gregoriane. Roma: Tip. del Senato, 1913.

589. FREISTEDT, H. Die liqueszierenden Noten des gregorianischen Chorals. Freiburg: Publication of The Gregorian Akademy, 1929.

590. GAJARD, Joseph. Grondslagen van het gregoriaanse rythme. Roermond: Arsis, 1950.

591. GASTOUE, Amédée. L'art grégorien. 3. éd. (orig. Paris: F. Alcan, 1920.) New York: AMS Press, 1975.

592. ________. Cours théorique et pratique de chantegrégorien d'après les travaux les plus récents. Paris: Au bureau d'édition de la Scola Cantorum, 1904.

593. ________. Les origines du chant romain: l'antiphonaire grégorien. (Repr. Paris: A. Picard et fils, 1907.) New York: AMS Press, 1975.

594. ________. Les principaux chants liturgiques du choeur et des fidèles. Paris: C. Poussielgue, 1903.

Plain chant grégorien traditionnel d'après les manuscrits. Notation musicale, avec indication du rythme et de la tonalité.

595. ________. Traite d'harmonisation du chant grégorien sur un plan nouveau. Lyon: Janin frères, 1910.

596. GOEDE, N. de. Aanvags-cursus gregoriaans. Hilversum: Gooi & Sticht, 1963.

Uitg. in opdracht van de Nederlaandse St. Gregoriusvereniging.

597. GREGORIAN Institute Staff. Gregorian Institute of America Quarterly, Vol. 6, No. 2. Toledo, Ohio: Gregorian Institute of America, 1967.

598. HECKENLIVELY, Lura F. Fundamentals of gregorian chant. Tournai: Desclée & Co., Printers, 19__ (LC-MT860. H4)

599. HIGGINSON, J. Vincent. Revival of gregorian chant. New York: Papers of the Hymn Society, 1949.

Papers on the Hymn Society on its influence on English hymnody.

600. HOCKNEY, J. C. comp. Final antiphons of the Blessed Virgin Mary; the exact Solesmes melodies. Hammond: N.G., 1947. (LC-M2154. 8. H3FS)

601. HODES, Karlheinrich. Der Gregorianische Choral: eine Einfang. Darmstadt: Wissenschaftliche Buchgesellschaft, 1974.

602. HOUDARD, G. L'art dit grégorien d'après la notation neumatique. Paris: Fischbacher, 1897.

603. _______. Le rythme du chant dit Grégorien d'après la notation neumatique. Paris: Fischbacher, 1898.

604. HÜGLE, G. Catechism of gregorian chant. New York: G. Fischer, 1928.

605. HURLEY, E. G. Gregorian chant. New York: G. Schirmer, 1907.

606. JANSSEN, Nocolaas Adrianus. Wahre Grundregeln des Gregorianischen oder Choralgesanges hersg. von J. C. B. Smeddinck. Wallufbei Wiesbaden: M. Sändig, 1972.

607. JANSSENS, L. Le chant grégorien. Tournay, France: N. G., 1890. (BM)

608. JEANNIN, J. C. Accent bref ou accent long en chant grégorien? Paris: H. Hérelle et cie., 1929.

609. _______. Etudes sur le rythme grégorien. Lyon: E. Gloppe, 1926.

610. JOHNER, Rev., Dom Dominic. Der Gregorianische Choral. Stuttgart: J. Engelhorns Nachl., 1924.

611. _______. A new school of gregorian chant. New York: F. Pustet, 1906.

612. _______. Wort und Ton im choral. Leipzig: Breitkopf u. Härtel, 1940.
Ein Beitrag zur Aesthetik des gregorianischen Gesanges.

613. JUDITH, O. P., Sister M. Square notes: A notebook in gregorian chant. Boston, Mass.: McLaughlin & Reilly Co., 1962.

614. KELLER. Fundamentals of Gregorian chant. 5th ed. Collegeville, Minn.: Liturgical Press, 1959.

615. KESSLER, E. Über die leiterfremden Tonstufen im gregorianischen Gesang. Dornbirn: Voralberger Verlaganstalt, 1922.
Veröffentlichungen der gregorianischen Akademie zu Freiburg. Hft. 10.

616. KLIMISCH, Mary Jane. A cumulative index of gregorian chant sources. Yankton, S. D.: Sacred Music Resource Center, Mount Marty College, 1973.

617. KUPPER, Hubert. Statistische Untersuchungen zur Modusstruktur der Gregorianik. Regensburg: Bosse, 1970.

618. LABAT, Paule Elisabeth. Louange à Dieu et chant grégorien. Paris: P. Téqui, 1975.

619. LESPONNE, J. General principles and directions for the direction of the gregorian melodies. Trichinopoly, India: N. G., 1914. (BM)

620. LHOUMEAU, A. Rhythme exécution et accompagnement du chant grégorien. Lille: N. G., 1892.

621. LOOTENS, L. (Bishop of Castabola). La théorie musicale du chant grégorien. Paris: Thorin et fils, 1895.

622. LORY, Jacques. Guide des disques, l'aventure de la musique occidentale, du chant grégorien à la musique électronique racontée en 2,500 microsillons. Paris: Buchet, Chastel, 1967.

623. MATHE, A. Over Gregoriaansche muziek, oude handschriften en rhytmische opvattingen. Antwerpen: Drukkerij K. Dirix-van Riet, 1937.

624. MOCQUEREAU, Dom Andre. The art of gregorian chant. Washington: The Catholic Education Press, 1923.

625. ________. Le nombre musical grégorien, Part 1. English translation, Original French--Parts 1 and 2. Rome, Tournai: Desclée, 1908.

626. MOLITOR, Raphael. Der Gregorianische Choral als Liturgie und Kunst. Hamm: Breer & Thiemann, 1904.

627. MORIN, Germain. Der ursprung des gregorianischen Gesanges. Paderborn: F. Schöningh, 1892.
Eine Antwort auf Gevaerts Abhandlung über "den Ursprung des römischen Kirchengesanges."

628. ________. Les véritables origines du chant grégorien. Saint-Gerard: N. G., 1890. (BM)

629. MURRAY, Anthony Gregory. Gregorian chant according to the manuscripts. London: L. T. Cary & Co., 1963.
With a detachable musical supplement; with musical examples.

630. NACHBAR, K. J. Der Gregorianisch Kirchengesang. Schwiebus, Poland: C. Wagner, 1852.
Oder die Kirchentonarten, deren Ursprung, Entwickelung, Notenschrift und Harmonie, mit Berücksichtigung der polnischen Kirchenlieder und musikalischen Kunstausdruckes.

631. NEISS, Benoit. Le chant grégorien en France. Paris: Ministère des affaires culturelles, 1975.

632. NOLTHENIUS, Hélène. Oud als de weg naar Rome? Vragen round de herkomst van het gregorians (with phonodisc). Amsterdam: Noord-Hollandsche Uitgevers Mij, 1974.

633. NORMAND TORFS, T. E. X. [T. Nisard, pseud.]. L'archéologie musicale et le vrai chant grégorien. Paris: P. Lethielleux, 1890.

634. OLSEN, Bent. Gregoriansk sang. Egtved: Musikhøjskolens Forlag, 1968.

635. PIERIK, Marie. Dramatic and symbolic elements in gregorian chant. New York: Desclée Co., 1963.

636. ________. Gregorian chant analyzed and studied. St. Meinrad, Ind.: Grail Publications, 1951.

637. ________. The song of the church. New York: Longmans, Green, 1947.

638. ________. The spirit of gregorian chant. Boston: McLaughlin and Reilly, 1939.

639. POTHIER, J. Der Gregorianische Choral. Tournay: N. G., 1881.

640. ________. Les melodies grégoriennes. Ger. transl., Kienle.

641. POTIRON. Treatise on gregorian chant accompaniment. N. G.: N. G., n. d.

642. PRADO, German. El canto gregoriano. Barcelona: N. G., 1945.

643. RAYBURN, John. Gregorian chant rhythms: A history of the controversy concerning its interpretation. New York: Teachers College, Columbia Univ., 1961.

644. ROUSSEAU, N. L'école grégorienne de Solesmes, 1833-1910. Rome, etc.: Deslée et cie, 1910.

645. RUAULT, Jean and Roger Blin. Commentaires d'oeuvres musicales. Paris: A. Colin, 1964.
Evolution de la musique du chant grégorien au jazz.

646. SANDVIK, Ole Mork. Gregoriansk sang. Oslo: Aschehoug, 1945.
Norsk messe, koral og folketone. Med ooteeksempler og illustrasjoner.

647. SCHMITT, Jean Pierre. Geschichte des gregorianischen Choralgesanges. Trier: Paulinus Verlag, 1952.

648. SCHNAUS, E. U. The communicative role of Christian liturgy and gregorian chant. New York: Ed. D. Education, Columbia Univ., 1960.

649. SCHOLA Cantorum--Bureau d'Edition. Chant grégorien. Paris: Editions musicales de la Schola Cantorum, 1928.

650. SCHREMBS, Joseph, Sister Alice Marie, and Gregory Huegle. The gregorian chant manual of the Catholic music hour. New York: Silver, Burdett and Co., 1935.

651. SCHREMS, Theobald. Die geschichte des gregorianischen Gesanges in den protestantischen Gottesdiensten. Freiburg: St. Paulusdruckerei, 1930.

652. SERRANO, Luciano. ¿Qué es canto gregoriano? Barcelona: G. Gill, 1905.

653. SESINI, Ugo. La "Romana catilena." Roma: Cremonese, 1942.

Corso completo, storico, didattico, critico di canto gregoriano.

654. SHEBBEARE, A. Choral recitation of the divine office. Toledo: Gregorian Institute of America, 1954.

655. SODERLUND, G. F. Examples of gregorian chants and works by Orlandus Lassus, Palestrina, and Ingegneri. New York: F. S. Crofts, 1946.

656. SOEHNER, Leo. Die Geschichte der Begleitung des gregorianischen chorals in Deutschland, vornehmlich im 18. Jahrhundert. Inaugural-Dissertation, etc. Augsburg: B. Filserg. m. b. h., 1934.

657. SOLESMES Abbey. Manual of gregorian chant. Rome: The City, 1903.

658. SUÑOL, G. Méthode compléte de chant grégorien. Paris: Desclée & Co., 1918.

659. SUÑOL, Dom Gregory. Text book of gregorian chant. New York: J. Fischer and Brothers, 1930. Also Tournai: Desclée and Co., 1930.

660. SUSCA, Anselmo. Il canto gregoriano. Arte e preghieri. La scala: n. p., 1969. ML3082. S84.

661. TACK, Franz. Gregorian chant (Translation by Everett Helm). New York: Oxford, 1960.

662. THIERY. Etude sur le chant grégorien. Bruges: Desclée, de Brouwer cie, 1883.

663. URIARTE, E. De. Tratado de canto gregoriano segun la verdadera tradición. Madrid: N. G., 1896.

664. VALOIS, Jean de. Le chant grégorien. Que sais-je? 1041. Paris: Presses universitaires de France, 1963.

665. VAN POPPEL, P. Balduinus, O. C. R. Cours élémentaire et pratique de plain-chant grégorien. Boston, Mass.: McLaughlin & Reilly Co., and Westmalle: Imprimerie Cistercienne, 1963.

666. ________. Plain-chant gregorian. Boston, Mass.: McLaughlin & Reilly Co., 1963.

667. VENHODA, Miroslav. Uvod do studia gregoriánského chorálu. V. Praze: Vyšehrad, 1946.

668. WAESBERGHE, Jos. Smits Van. Gregorian chant and its place in the Catholic liturgy. Stockholm: Continental Book Co., 1949.

669. WAGNER, Peter. Einführung in die gregorianischen Melodien. Ein Handbuch der Choralwissenschaft. Leipzig: Breitkopf & Härtel, 1911-21. (Neudr. Freiburg, 1895)

670. ________. Einführung in die gregorianischen Melodien. Hildesheim: G. Olms, 1962. Reprint, 1970.
Ein Handbuch der Choralwissenschaft. Band 1: Ursprung und Entwicklung der liturgischen Gesangsformen bis zum Ausgange des Mittelalters. c. Auflage. Band 2: Neumenkunde, Paläographie Gregorianische Formenlehre; eine choralische Stilkunde. 2. Auflage.

671. ________. Elemente des gregorianischen Gesanges. Regensburg, Rome, New York, & Cincinnati: F. Pustet, 1909.

672. ________. Introduction to the gregorian melodies. 1957-1958. Part 1 reprinted in Caecilia, Vols. 84-85.

673. WARD, Justin. Gregorian chant. Washington: The Catholic Education Press, 1923.

674. WELLESZ, Egon. Eastern elements in western chants. Gregorian chant. Oxford, England: Byzantine Institute of America, 1947.

675. WYATT, E. G. P. St. Gregory and the gregorian music. London: Plainsong and Mediaeval Music Society, 1904.

See also: 17, 19, 35, 40, 41, 46, 47, 48, 53, 58, 517, 718, 804, 1869, 2535, 2841, 3009, 3322, 3619, 3683, 3689, 3703, 3709, 3973, 4232, 4918, 4948, 4953, 4954, 4955, 4992, 5201, 5221.

Hebrew (Jewish)

676. RAVETCH, Isadore Shalom. Shalom layeled sefer haftorah. Long Beach, Cal.: Shalom layeled, haftora primer. 1946.

Mozarabe

677. ALLINGER, Helen. The mozarabic hymnal and chant. With special emphasis upon the hymns of Prudentius. Research typescript. New York: Union Theological Seminary, D. S. M., 1953.

678. BROCKETT, Clyde Waring. Antiphons, responsories and other chants of the mozarabic rite. Brooklyn: Institute of Mediaeval Music, 1968.

679. RANDEL, Don Michael. An index to the chant of the mozarabic rite. Princeton, N. J.: Princeton Univ. Press, 1973.

680. ________. The responsorial psalm tones for the mozarabic office. Princeton: Princeton Univ. Press, 1969.

681. ROJO, Casiano. El canto mozarabe. Estudio historico-critico de su antiquedad y estado actual. Barcelona: Diputació provincial, 1929.

Plain

682. ANTIPHONALE sarisburiense. London: The Plainsong and Mediaeval Music Society, 1901-24.

683. ARNOLD, J. H. The approach to plainsong. London: Oxford Univ. Press, 1937.

684. BENEDICTINE of Stanbrook, A. A grammar of plainsong. Worcester: N. G., 1926. (BM)

685. ________. A grammar of plainsong. Liverpool: N. G., 1934. (BM)

686. ________. A grammar of plainsong. New York: J. Fischer and Brothers, 1936.

687. BISCHOFF, J. B. La pratique du plain-chant. Paris: N. G., 1890. (BM)

688. BRIGGS, H. B. The elements of plainsong. London: Quaritch, 1895.

689. ________. Recent research in plainsong. London: Charles Vincent, 1898.

690. ________ and W. H. Frere. A manual for plainsong. London: Novello & Co., 1902.

691. BURGESS, Francis. The rudiments of plainchant. London: Office of Musical Opin., 1923.

692. ________. Textbook of plainsong and gregorian music. N. G.: Vicent Music Co., 1906. (BM)

693. BURKARD, S. Manual of plain chant. New York: Fischer & Brothers, 1906.

694. CLARKE, Arthur W. What is plainsong? Croydon, England: Royal School of Church Music, 1963.

695. COOK, Edgar T. The use of plainsong. London: Plainsong & Mediaeval Music Society, 1928.

696. COORNAERT, V. J. Traité de plain-chant sacré. Burges: N. G., 1890. (BM)

697. CROFT, John Bonham. Practical plainsong. London: Society of SS. Peter & Paul, 1921.

698. DAVIS, Vernon Perdue. The church's one music. "The tones of plainsong." Boston, Mass.: E. C. Schirmer Music Co., 1963.

An excerpt from The Church's One Music. Part of "The Virginia Music Series."

699. DESROCQUETTES. Plain song for musicians. Liverpool: Rushworth & Dreaper, 1956.

700. FISH, James Leonard. On the application of plain song to services of church. Oxford, England: T. Vincent, 1850.

701. FRERE, Rt. Rev. W. H. Plainsong in Oxford history of music. New York: Oxford University Press, n. d.

702. GAJARD, Joseph. The rhythm of plainsong according to the Solesmes school.... Liverpool: Rushworth & Dreaper, 1943.

703. GATARD, Dom Augustine. Plainchant. London: The Faith Press, 1921.

704. GEERING, Arnold. Die Organo und mehrstimmigen Conductus in den Handschriften des deutschen Sprachgebietes vom. 13. bis 16. Jahrhundert. Bern: P. Haupt, 1952.

705. HUGHES, Dom Anselm. Anglo-French sequelae. London: The Plainsong & Mediaeval Music Society, 1934.

706. ________. Plainsong for English choirs. London: Faith Press, 1966 (i. e. 1967).

707. JUMILHAC, P. B. De. La science et la pratique du plain-chant, ou tout ce qui appartient à la pratique est etably par les principes de la science, et confirme par le témoignage des anciens philosophes, des père de l'église et des plus illustres musiciens ... par un religieux benedictin de S. Maur. Paris: Chez L. Bilaine, 1673, also same--Paris, Chez A. LeClerq, 1847, also same--thru' New York: Scientific Library Service, no date given.

708. LA FAGE, Juste Adnen Lenar de. De la reproduction des livres de plain-chant romain. Paris: Blanchet, 1853.

709. LA FEILLEI, François. De méthod nouvelle pour apprendre parfaitement les règles du plain-chant et de la psalmodie. A. Poitiérs, & se venda Paris, chez: J. T. Herissant, 1748.

710. LEGARE, E. Methode de plain-chant. Québec: N. G., 1898.

711. LEMMENS, J. N. Du chant grégorien, sa melodie, son rhythme. Gand: N. G., 1886.

712. LIBER antiphonarius pro Dirnis Haris. Rome: Vatican Press, 1912.

713. LITTLE, Vilma Gertrude. The chant, a simple and complete method for teachers and students. Tournai: Society of St. John, Evang. Desclée, 1949.

714. MARSHALL, Perry D. Plainsong in English: An historical and analytical survey. Ann Arbor, Mich.: Univ. Microfilms, Union Theological Seminary in the City of New York, Diss., 1964.

715. MOCQUEREAU, R. P. Dom André. Monographies gregoriennes. Paris: R. P. Dom André Mocquereau, 1924-31.

716. NICHOLSON, Sydney H. A plainsong hymnbook. London: William Clowes & Sons, 1932.

717. PERDUE-DAVIS, Vernon. A plainsong primer. Boston: E. C. Schirmer Music Co., 1966.

718. ________. The tones of plainsong. Boston: E. C. Schirmer, 1963.

719. PLAINSONG and Mediaeval Music Society. Hymn--melodies and sequences. London: The Plainsong and Mediaeval Music Society, 1920.

720. ________. List of gramophone records of plainsong in English and Latin and of mediaeval music. London: Burnhan, Bucks & London, 1932.

721. PUGIN, Augustus W. N. An earnest appeal for the revival of the ancient plain song. New York: Benziger Brothers, 1905.

722. ROBERTSON, Alec. The interpretation of plainsong. New York: Oxford Univ. Press, 1937.

723. SEYMAT, A. M. Raison du nouveau systéme de notation sur la vraie portée pour le plain-chant. Tournai: N. G., 1892. (BM)

724. SHELDERS, Philip. A beginner's plain-song. Tenbury Hills, Worcester, England: Fowler Wright Bks., 1964.

725. SINGENBERGER, John B. Short instructions on the art of singing plain chant. New York: F. Pustet, 1880.

726. SNOW, Francis W. Plain-song settings of the morning and evening canticles, together with Easter day, Thanksgiving and burial psalms. Boston, Mass.: Parish Choir, Trinity Church, 1925.

727. SOLFEGE. A primer of plainsong according to the Solesmes method. Rome: The City, 1906.

728. TARDIF, J. Méthode élémentaire et pratique de plain-chant. Angers: E. Barassé, 1860.

729. ________. Méthode théorique et pratique de plain-chant. Angers: E. Barassé, 1860 and 1883.

730. TURIN. Biblioteca Nazionale. Cypriot plainchant of the manuscript torino, biblioteca Nazionale J. II 9. Facsimile ed. Rome: American Institute of Musicology, 1968.

731. VALE, Walter S. Plainsong. London: The Faith Press, 1937.

See also: 10, 11, 18, 22, 27, 28, 29, 39, 44, 54, 378, 527, 528, 1525, 3055, 3133, 3344, 4859, 4956.

Thibetan Buddhist

732. KAUFMANN, Walter. Thibetan Buddhist chant: musical notations and interpretations of a song book by the Bkah Brgyud Pa and Sa Skya Pa sects. Translations from the Thibetan by Thubten Jigme Norbu. Bloomington, Ind.: Indiana Univ. Press, 1975.

CHAPELS-MUSIC

733. CAFFI, Francesco. Storia della musica sacra nell' già Cappella ducale di San Marco, Venezia. (2 vols.) Bologna: Forni, 1972.

734. COOK, George Henry. Medieval chantries and chapels. London: Phoenix House, 1947.

735. DEWER, Catherine Anne. Eighteenth-century Sistine chapel. Ann Arbor: Univ. Microfilms, 1968.

736. DIETSCH, Joseph. Souvenirs musicaux de la Sainte-Chapelle. Dijon: Impr. de l'Union typographique, 1884.

737. DUCROT, Ariane. Histoire de la Cappella Giulia au XVI siècle. Rome: Ecole Française, 1963.
With plates. Mélanges d'archélogie et d'histoire.

738. FEDERHOFER, Hellmut. Musikpflege und Musiker am Grazer Habsburgerhof der Erzherzöge Karl und Ferdinand von Innerosterreich. Mainz: Schott's Söhne, 1968.

739. FELLOWES, E. H. The music of Saint George's Chapel. Dent: N.G., 1927. (BM)

740. ________. Organists and masters of the choristers of St. George's Chapel in Windsor Castle. London: Society for the Promotion of Christian Knowledge for the Dean and Canons of St. George's Chapel in Windsor Castle. (orig. publ. in 1939.), 1974.

741. La CAPPELLA sistina de germania, ossia la settimana santa nella cattedrale di Ratisbona, per un prete milanese. Milano: Presso la direzione del periodico musica sacr., 1880.
Considerazioni e voti per la restaurazione della musica sacra in Italia.

742. LAUX, Karl. La staatskapelle de Dresde. Leipzig: Edition Leipzig, 1964.

743. LORETO, Italy. Santa Casa. L'archivio musicale della cappella lauretana. Loreto: S. Casa, 1921.
Catalogo storico-critico, con dieci illustrazioni e due tavole fuori testo.

744. The OLD cheque book or book of remembrance of the Chapel Royal. New York: Da Capo Press, 1966. Reprint, (original date, n.d.).

745. RAST, Benedict. Kappelen im Wallis. Zürich: R. Mühlemann, 1949.

746. SANDBERGER, Adolf. Beiträge zur Geschichte der bayerischen Hofkapelle unter Orlando di Lasso. (Neudr., 2 v. in 1) Walluf bei Wiesbaden: M. Sändig, 1973.

747. SCHELLE, Eduard. Die papstliche Sängerschule in Rom genannt die Sistinische Capelle. Wien: J. P. Gotthard, 1872. Ein musikhistorisches Bild.

748. _______. Die sixtinische Kapelle. Wien: Gotthard, 1872.

749. WISOKO-MEYTSKY, Karl. Die hofmusikkapelle und die Hofburgkapelle in Wien. Wien: Selbstverlag der Hofmusikkapelle, 1965.

750. _______. The hofmusikkapelle; the musical establishment of the Vienna Court and the Hofburg Chapel. (Translated from the German by Richard Rickett.) Wien: Hofmusikkapelle, 1965.

See also: 206, 240, 334, 389, 451, 2463, 2860, 2962, 3001, 3024, 3054, 3342, 3368, 3371, 3389, 3400, 3415, 3509, 3513, 3514, 3519, 3834, 3855, 4008, 4748.

CHILDREN'S MUSIC

751. BROCK. Children's hymn-book. London: N.G., 1881.

752. CATHOLIC child's hymn-book. London: N.G., 1882.

753. DEARMER, Percy. Prayers and hymns for little children. Fair Lawn, N.J.: Oxford University Press, 1932.

754. _______. Songs of praise for boys and girls. New York: Oxford University Press, 1929.

755. _______. Songs of praise for little children. London: Oxford Univ. Press, 1932.

756. FARRINGTON, Charlotte. Hymns for children. With opening and closing services and songs and hymns for bands of mercy and of hope. London: Sunday School Association, 1894.

757. HYMNS for children. London: N.G., 1881.

758. JACOBS, Ruth Krehbies. The children's choir. Rockland, Ill.: Augustana Press, 1958.

759. JONES, N. Hymn book for young people's mission services. London: N.G., 1890. (BM)

760. PARKER, Caroline Bird and Carlington G. Richards. Hymnal for boys and girls. New York: D. Appleton-Century Co., 1935.

761. POOLER, Marie. Children's choir book. Minneapolis: Augsburg Publishing House, n.d.

762. SONGS of praise for little children. New York: Oxford Univ. Press, 1933.

763. TUFTS, Nancy Poore. The children's choir, Vol. 2. Philadelphia: Fortress Press, series 1958-65.

764. WHITTEMORE, W. M. Our children's hymnal. London: N.G., 1894.

765. WINTERS, W. Sunday school hymnal. London: N.G., 1892. (BM)

766. WISEMAN, Herbert and W. H. Hamilton. Children praising. Fair Lawn, N.J.: Oxford Univ. Press, 1937.

See also: 250, 886, 1361, 1747, 2248, 2573, 2751, 3072, 4964, 4970, 5259, 5330.

CHOIR: ORGANIZATION AND DEVELOPMENT

767. ALLEMANOV, D. and Zvyerev. 'N semerine parasemantike tes êllnikes ekklesias. St. Petersburg: N.G., 1907.

768. ANISIMOV, Aleksandr Ivanovich. Dirizher-khormeĭster: tvorcheskometodicheskie zapiski. Leningrad: Muzyka, 1976.

769. ARMITAGE, M. Therese (ed.). Concert songs for girls. New York: Summy-Birchard, 1932.

770. ATKINSON, Thelma and Esther Mary Fuller. Handbook for choir directions. Westbury, N.Y.: Pro-Art Publications, n.d.

771. BAIRSTOW, Sir Edward. Practical choir-training. Croydon Royal School of Church Music, 1969.

772. BARDOS, György. 99 szabâly minderfajta ênekkarok tagjai számára, etc. Karenekes kiskâte. Budapest: N.G., 1944. (BM)

773. BENTALL, Elg. Suggestions for training choirboys. London: N.G., 1894.

774. BERNIER, A. Saint Robert Bellarium de la Compagnie de Jêsus et la musique liturgique. Montreal: N.G., 1939. (BM)

775. BOBBITT, Paul. The youth choir leadership manual. Nashville: Convention Press, 1967.

776. BOSTOCK, Donald. Choirmastery: A practical handbook. London: Epworth, 1966.

777. BOYD, Jack. Rehearsal guide for the choral director. West Nyack, N.Y.: Parker Publ. Co., 1970.

778. BRAUER, Friedrich Ernst. An evaluation of selected sixteenth-century choral music from representative composers with application for use by junior high school and by junior church choirs. Austin, Tex.: Univ. of Texas, 1964.

779. BRECK, Flora Elizabeth. Choir ideas for choir members, directors, preachers, and congregations. Boston: W. A. Wilde, 1952.

780. BREWER, A. Herbert. Memories of choirs and cloisters. London: John Lane, 1931.

781. BUTLER, A. M. The choristers' own book. N.G.: F. H. Morland, 1908.

782. CLEALL, Charles. The selection and training of mixed choirs in churches. Based on three lectures delivered at the Royal School of Church Music, etc. London: Independent Press, 1960.

783. CLOUGH-LEIGHTER (ed.). A cappella singer. Boston: E. C. Schirmer, n.d.

784. COLEMAN, Henry. The amateur choir trainer. London: Oxford Univ. Press, 1932.

785. ________. Youth club choirs. London: Oxford Univ. Press, 1950.

786. ________ and Hilda West. Girl's choirs. London: Oxford Univ. Press, (1st ed. 1932, 1936, etc.) 1962.

787. COWARD, H. "C.T.I." The secret. London: Novello & Co., 1938.

788. ________. Choral techniques and interpretation. London: Novello & Co., 1914.

789. CROOK, Hubert. How to form a choir. Croydon, England: Royal School of Church Music, 1963.

790. CURWEN, J. S. The boy's voice: information on training of boys for church choirs. London: N.G., 1891.

791. DARROW, Gerald F. Four decades of choral training. Metuchen, N.J.: Scarecrow Press, 1975.

792. DAVIES, H. Walford. Church choirs. Glasgow: Paterson Sons & Co., ltd., 1924; also New York: Carl Fischer, Inc.

793. DAVIES, R. C. Choir regulations and rules. Liverpool: Davies & Company, 1907.

794. DAVISON, A. T. Choral conducting. Cambridge: Harvard Univ. Press, 1940.

795. DAWSON, John J. The voice of the boy. Chicago, Ill.: Laidlaw Brothers, 1919.

796. DEMETRIA, Sister Mary. Basic gregorian chant and sight reading. Movable Do edition (with musical examples). Toledo, Ohio: Gregorian Institute of America, 1960.

797. DICKINSON, H. A. and C., and P. A. Wolfe. The Choir loft and the pulpit. New York: H. W. Gray and Co., 1943.

798. DUBROWSKI, Jerzy. Z mazdwszem w krajach azji. Warsaw: Ludowa Spóldzielnia Wydawnicza, 1961.

799. EARHART, Will. Choral technics. New York: M. Witmark & Sons, 1937.

800. ________. The eloquent baton. New York: M. Witmark & Sons, 1931.

801. ________. Teacher's manual for choral technics. New York: M. Witmark & Sons, 1938.

802. EHMANN, Wilhelm. Das chorwesen in der Kulturkrise. Eine hochaktuelle kulturpolitische Schrift. Ehmann entwickelt die geschichtlichen Grundlagen und Wesenszüge des modernen Chorwesens und zeigt, wie es aus der Kulturkrise des 18. Jahrh. Als ein Versuch zu seiner Überwindung herangewachsen ist und damit den Boden für die Musikkultur des bürgerlichen Zeitalters legen half. Dann weist er vor allem die Möglichkeiten, die dem Chorwesen in der Bewältigung unserer heutigen Kulturkrise, bei der das bürgerliche Zeitalter versinken will, gegeben sind. 40 Seiten, Kartoniert. Regensburg: G. Bosse, 1953.

803. EHRET, Walter. The choral conductor's handbook. With musical illustrations. London: Augener, 1961.

804. EVANS, J. J. Llawlyfr y Cynganeddion. Caerdydd, Gwasg: Prifyszol Cymru., 1960.

805. FEDERL, Ekkehard. Spätmittelalterliche Choralpflege in Würzburg und in mainfränkischen Klöstern. Oberbayern: Missionsdruckerei St. Ottilien, 1937.

806. FINN, Father. An epitome of some principles of choral technique. Boston: Francis James, 1935.

807. FINN, W. J. The art of the choral conductor. Boston: C. C. Birchard & Co., 1939.

808. FINNEY, Theodore M. We have made music. Pittsburgh, Pa.: Univ. of Pittsburgh Press, 1955.

809. FOJICK, Jan. Materialy do dziejów ruchu śpiewaczego na Slasku. Material for the history of the choral movement in Silesia. With illustrations and maps. Katowice: N. G., 1961.

810. FOTSCH, Willy. Der Kirchenchorleiter. Adliswil-Zürich: E. Ruh, 1966.

811. FUCHS, Carl Dorius J. Der taktgerechte Choral, Nachweisung seiner sechs Typen an 431 Beispielen mit einer. Berlin: C. E. Vieweg, 1923.

812. GASTOUE, A. L'église et la musique. Paris: B. Grasset, 1936.

813. GEARHART, Livingston. Gentlemen songsters. New York: Shawnee Press, n. d.

814. GLENN, Mabelle, and V. French, ed. Glenn Glee Club Book for girls. N. G.: Oliver Ditson Publisher, n. d.

815. GRACE, H. The training and conducting of choral societies. London: Novello's Music Primers and Educational Series (# 113), 1938, New York: The H. W. Gray Co., 1938.

816. GWYNN, Denis Rolleston. Edward Martyn and the Irish revival. London: J. Cape, 1930.

817. HALL, J. J. On the choice, the duty, and education of choristers. Slough, England: N. G., 1888.

818. HALTER, C. The Christian choir member. St. Louis, Mo.: Concordia Publishing House, 1959.

819. HAMMAR, Russell Alfred. The principles and practices in developing a volunteer church choir program. ED. D., Vocal Music. New York: Columbia Univ., 1961.

820. HARDY, T. M. How to train children's voices. London: J. Curwen & Sons, 1937.

821. HARRIS, Ernest Charles. Johann Mattheson's der vollkommene Chapellmeister: A translation and commentary. Ann Arbor: Univ. Microfilms, 1969.

822. HEATON, C. H. How to build a church choir. St. Louis, Mo.: The Bethany Press, 1959.

823. INGRAM, Madeline D. A guide for youth choirs. Nashville, Tenn.: Abingdon Press, 1967.

824. ______. Organizing and directing children's choirs. New York: Abingdon Press, 1959.

825. INSKIP, O. D. Church choirs. London: N.G., 1892. (BM)

826. JACOBS, Ruth Krehbiel. The children's choir. Rock Island, Ill.: Augustana Press, 1958.

827. ______. The successful children's choir. Chicago: H. T. Fitz-Simons Co., 1959.

828. JONES, Robert L. The junior choir leadership manual. Nashville, Tenn.: Convention Press, 1967.

829. KAELIN, Pierre. L'art choral. Avant propos d'Ernest Ansermet. Paris: Berger-Levraultet PRECIS. Propositions S.I.L.P. Montréal: Ministère de l'éducation du Québec, 1974.

830. KEITH, Gwendolyn Edwards. The status of negro church youth choirs in the State of Ohio. Columbus, Ohio: Ohio State Univ., 1950.

831. KETTRING, Donald. Steps toward a singing church. Philadelphia: Westminister Press, 1948.

832. KORTKAMP, I. One hundred things a choir member should know. Decorah, Iowa: Kortkamp, 1954.

833. LJUBLJANA. Delavsko prosveino društvo "svoboda" ljubljana-center. Spominski bornik Pevskega društva Ljubljanski Zvon. Ob 50-letnici ustanovitve društva. 1905-1955. (Zbral J. Brencic--uredil T. Seliskar) With illustrations. Ljubljana: N.G., 1955.

834. LONG, Kenneth R. Church choir management. London: The Faith Press, 1946.

835. LOVELACE, Austin C. The youth choir. Nashville, Tenn.: Abingdon Press, 1964.

836. LYALL, Jack. The adult volunteer choir in churches having primarily non-liturgical services: A handbook. New York: Columbia Univ. Teachers College, 1952.

837. MACNAUGHT, W. G. Hints on choir training for competitions. London: N.G., 1896. (BM)

838. MARTIN, Florence M. (ed.). Christmas carols for treble choirs. Chicago: Hall and McCreary, 1941.

839. MARTIN, G. C. Art of training choir-boys. New York: Novello's Music Primers, 1892.

840. MCKENZIE, Duncan. Training the boy's changing voice. New Brunswick, N.J.: Rutgers Univ. Press, 1956.

841. MEES, Arthur. Choirs and choral music. New York: Charles Scribner's Sons, 1924.

842. MILLARD, James Elwin. Historical notices of the office of choristers. London: J. Masters, 1848.

843. MILLER, P. J. Youth choirs. New York: Harold Flammer, Inc., 1953.

844. MOFFATT, Nona Stein. How to organize a music department for a church. New York: Exposition Press, 1963.

845. MOODY, C. H. The choirboy in the making. London: Oxford Univ. Press, 1923.

846. MUSIK im Gottesdienst: ein Handbuch zur Grundausbildung in der katholischer Kirchenmusik. Im Auftrag der Konferenz der Leiter katholischer kirchenmusikalischer Ausbildungsstätten Deutschlands, hrsg. von H. Musch. Regensburg: G. Bosse, 1975.

847. NICHOLSON, Peter. The adventures of a chorister, 1137-1937. London: S.P.C.K., 1944.

848. NICHOLSON, Sydney Hugo. Boy's choirs. Glasgow; New York: Paterson's Publications, Ltd., 1922.

849. _______. Practical methods in choir training. London: S.P.C.K., 1947.

850. _______. Quires and places where they sing. London: G. Bell & Sons, Ltd., 1932.

851. NOBLE, T. T. Training the boy chorister. New York: G. Schirmer, Inc., 1943.

852. NORDIN, Dayton W. How to organize and direct the church choir. W. Nyack, N.Y.: Parker Publ. Co., 1973.

853. OREL, D. Hudebni prvky Svatovaclavské-La musique dans le culte de Saint Wenceslas. V. Prage: N.G., 1937.

854. PHILLIPS, Evelyn Marney. A suggested course of study for the graded choir program of the Southern Baptist Churches

--first grade level. Fort Worth, Tex.: Texas Christian Univ., 1963.

855. PRITCHARD, Arthur J. How to train a choir of men and women. Croydon, England: Royal School of Church Music, 1963.

856. RICHARDS, H. W. Church choir training. N.G.: Joseph Williams Series on Handbooks, 1921.

857. ______. Course of lectures on choir training. N.G.: Royal College of Organists, 1903.

858. RICHARDSON, A. M. Choir training based on voice production. London: Vincent Music Co., 1899.

859. RING, Frands Johan. Oluf Ring. Et liv i dansk folkesangs tjeneste. With plates, including portraits. Odense, Denmark: N.G., 1961.

860. ROBERTS, J. V. Treatise on a practical method of training choristers. London: H. Frowde, 1910.

861. ROBERTSON, H. S. Mixed voice choirs. Glasgow: N.G., 1923.

862. ROBINSON, Ray and Allen Winold. The choral experience. New York: Harpers College Press, 1976.

863. ROUTLEY, Erik. Music leadership in the church. Nashville, Tenn.: Abingdon Press, 1967.

864. SATEREN, Leland B. The good choir. Minneapolis, Minn.: Augsburg Publishing House, 1963.

865. SAUNDERS, Percy G. Choir-training. Croydon, England: Royal School of Church Music, 1963.

866. SCHNEIDER, M. Geschichte der Mehrstimmigkeit. Historische und phanomerologische Studien. Berlin: J. Bard, 1934.

867. SEWELL, W. H. Choir instructions: Friendly hints for church singers. London: N.G., 1884. (BM)

868. SIMS, M. A. Sight reading for choir-boys. London: Novello & Co., 1939.

869. SIMS, Walter Hines. Church music administration. Nashville, Tenn.: Convention Press, 1969.

870. SOEHNER, L. Die Geschichte der Begleitung des gregorianischen Chorals in Deutschland, vornehmlich in 18. Jahr-

hundert. Veröffentlichungen der gregorianischen Akademie zu Freiburg i. d. Schweiz. Augsburg: B. Filser, g. m. b. h., 1931.

871. STEERE, D. Music for the protestant church choir. Richmond, Va.: John Knox Press, 1955.

872. STESHKO, F. Cesti hudebnici v ukrajinske cirkevni hudbe. N. G.: Rozpravy Ceske Akadamie Veda Umeni-Trid. I cis. 83, 1935. (BM)

873. STUBBS, G. E. Practical hints on the training of choir boys. London, New York, & Chicago: Novello, Ewer & Co., 1897.

874. SUNDERMAN, Lloyd F. Choral organization and administration. Rockville Center, N. Y.: Belwin, Inc., 1954.

875. ________. Organization of the church choir. Rockville Center, N. Y.: Belwin, Inc., 1957.

876. ________. Some techniques for choral success. Toledo: Univ. of Toledo, 1952.

877. SWENEY, J. R. and Wm. J. Kirkpatrick. Anthems and voluntaries for the church choir. Philadelphia: John J. Hood, 1881.

878. SYDNOR, James Rawlings. The training of church choirs. New York and Nashville: Abingdon Press, 1963.

879. TATE, John Paul. The carry-over of school music to church youth choirs at the jr. and sr. high level. Dallas: Southern Methodist Univ., 1958.

880. THORNDIKE, A. R. Children of the garter; memoirs of a Windsor Castle choir-boy, during the last years of Queen Victoria. London: Rich and Cowan, 1937.

881. TRUSLER, I. H., Jr. A plan for developing a closer relationship between the high school choral organization and church choirs. New York: Columbia Univ., 1955.

882. VALE, Walter S. The training of boys' voices. London: The Faith Press, 1932.

883. VANDEVERE, J. Lilian and Stuart B. Noppin, (ed.). Birchard choral collections. (No. 1) N. G.: Summy-Birchard, n. d.

884. VENERABLES, Edward M. Sweet tones remembered. Magdalen choir in the days of Varley Roberts. Oxford: Basil Blackwell, 1947.

885. VIVO, Gabriel. Formación de coros. Madrid: Ediciónes Santillana (Distribución: Delsa), 1963.
Colección Aficiones, 15.

886. VOSSELLER, Elizabeth Van Fleet. Junior choirs-more helps and suggestions. Flemington: Democrat Printing Office, 1939.

887. ______. The use of a children's choir in the church. New York: H. W. Gray Co., 1907.

888. WATERMAN, C. R. Planning for music rooms and buildings. Laramie, Wyo.: Univ. of Wyoming, 1955.

889. WATTS, H. E. Choir training in church and school. New York: Boosey, 1935.

890. WEST, Hilda. Girls' choirs. Fair Lawn, N.J.: Oxford Univ. Press, 1962.

891. WHITTAKER, W. G. Class singing. New York: Oxford Univ. Press, 1925.

892. WHITTLESEY, Federal Lee. A comprehensive program of church music. Philadelphia: Westminster Press, 1957.

893. WILLIAMS, C. L. and H. G. Chance. Annals of the three choirs of Gloucester, Hereford, and Worcester. Gloucester: Minchins & Gibbs, 1931.

894. WILSON, Harry Robert and Jack L. Lyall. Building a church choir. Minneapolis: Hall & McCreary, Co., 1957.

895. WRIGHT, E. Basic choirtraining. Croydon, England: Royal School of Church Music, 1955.

See also: 30, 91, 92, 93, 94, 95, 126, 140, 172, 248, 250, 260, 261, 311, 330, 365, 394, 399, 400, 419, 488, 489, 576, 587, 589, 609, 658, 761, 896, 905, 908, 914, 915, 916, 927, 938, 943, 946, 949, 950, 951, 981, 1013, 1014, 1016, 1017, 1020, 1073, 1077, 1167, 1209, 1222, 1324, 1325, 1453, 1473, 1640, 1655, 1679, 1744, 1820, 1881, 1893, 1896, 1904, 1907, 1908, 1911, 1914, 1926, 1927, 1930, 1932, 2318, 2498, 2553, 2572, 2646, 2712, 2713, 2723, 2727, 2732, 2737, 2743, 2747, 2750, 2992, 2994, 3001, 3124, 3178, 3226, 3250, 3321, 3360, 3385, 3393, 3396, 3419, 3420, 3444, 3456, 3565, 3589, 3658, 3737, 3846, 3937, 3955, 4084, 4139, 4140, 4143, 4184, 4307, 4317, 4338, 4712, 4717, 4724, 4729, 4781, 4787, 4870, 4963, 5010, 5028, 5029, 5061, 5069, 5071, 5072, 5077, 5080, 5085, 5238, 5245, 5275, 5314, 5330, 5331, 5341, 5349, 5366, 5376.

CHOIRMASTERS

896. BACHELIN, Henri. Les maitrises et la musique de choeur. Paris: Heugel, 1930.

897. BUCKLEY, Kevin. A handbook for Catholic choirmasters and organists. London: Cary & Co., 1948.

898. The CHOIR and musical record. London: T. Wright, 1863.
A journal chiefly devoted to the interests and advancement of church music.

899. The CHOIR magazine. Boston: The Choir Magazine Company, 1907.
Devoted to the advancement of church music.

900. CHURCH music: magazine for clergy, choirmasters, and organists. Philadelphia: American ecclesiastical review, 1905.

901. CLAIE, H. N. The choirmaster's manual. New York: G. Schirmer, 1908.

902. COLEMAN, Henry. The church choir trainer. Fair Lawn, N.J.: Oxford University Press, 1964.

903. CURTISS, M. J. The youth choir director. Boston: B. F. Wood, 1963.

904. HASTINGS, Thomas. The history of forty choirs. (repr. of New York: Mason Bros., 1854) New York: AMS Press, 1976.

905. HJORTSVANG, C. The amateur choir director. Nashville, Tenn.: Abingdon Press, 1941.

906. HOFFMEISTER, Joachim. Der Kantor zu St. Nikolai. Berlin: Evangelische Verlagsanstalt, 1964.
Beschreibung des Lebens von Johann Crügern, Direct.

907. MONTANI, N. A. (ed.). The Catholic choirmaster. Baltimore: Society of St. Gregory of America, 1915.
A magazine for those interested in liturgical music.

908. PHILLIPS, C. Henry. Psychology and the choir trainer. London: J. M. Dent & Sons, 1936.

909. PLANCHEF, Dominique Charles. L'art du maître de chapelle. Paris: N.G., 1913-31.

910. RICHARDSON, A. M. The choir-trainer's art. New York: G. Schirmer, 1914.

911. STAPLES, H. J. The choirmaster and the organist. London: Epworth Press, 1939.

912. VOLBACH, F. Der chormeister. Neue erweiterte Ausg. Mainz, Germany: B. Schotts Söhne, 1936.

913. WEINGARTNER, F. Erhebnisse eines "Königlichen Kapellmeisters" in Berlin. Berlin: P. Cassirer, 1912.

914. WERNER, A. Geschichte der Kantorei-Gesellschaften im Gebiete des ehemaligen Kurfürstentums Sachsen. Leipzig: Publikationen der Internationalen Musikgesellschaft, 1902.

915. WOODGATE, H. L. The chorus master. London: Archerberg, Hopwood & Crew, 1944.

916. ZECCHI, Adone. Il direttore di coro. Milano, Italy: Ricordi, 1965.
Teoria e pratica.

See also: 416, 424, 467, 427, 740, 780, 788, 797, 799, 808, 817, 827, 833, 859, 863, 864, 866, 874, 876, 882, 959, 1016, 1019, 1066, 1712, 1862, 1876, 1887, 1896, 1904, 1915, 1925, 1927, 1928, 1929, 1931, 1932, 1935, 2172, 2830, 2996, 3477, 3846, 3855, 4080, 4082, 4087, 4097, 4338, 4357, 4904, 5045, 5366.

CHORAL MUSIC

917. AIZPURUA, Pedro. Conjunto coral: nociones elementales de cultura coral. Valladolid: Imp. Aldecoa, 1975.

918. AMERICAN choral review. New York: N. G., 1959.
Articles, reviews, lists of new music and books.

919. BISGROVE, Mildred E. Sacred choral music in the Calvinistic tradition of the Protestant Reformation in Switzerland and France from 1541 to 1600. Ann Arbor: Univ. Microfilms, 1969.

920. CAIN, Noble. Choral music and its practice. New York: M. Witmark & Sons, 1932.

921. CHORAL responses. Anaheim, Calif.: National Music Service, n.d.

922. CRAWFORD, David. Sixteenth century choirbooks in the Archivo capitolare et Casale Monferrato. (n.p.) American Institute of Musicology; Renaissance manuscript studies, 2. Neuhausen-Stuttgart: distr. by Hänssler-Verlag, 1975.

923. CRUEGER, Johann. Sacred choral music. New York: C. F. Peters Corp., 1967.

924. DMITREVSKAIA, Kleopatra Nikolaevna. Russkaia sovetskaia khorovaîa muzyka. (Vol. 1) Moskva: Sov. Kompozitor, 1974.

925. FORSYTH, Cecil. Choral orchestration. New York: H. W. Gray Co., 1920.

926. GROTE, Gottfried (ed.). Geistliches Chorlied. Vol. 1 & 2. New York: C. F. Peters Corporation, 1967.

927. JACOBS, Arthur. Choral music. A symposium. Harmondsworth: Penguin Books, 1963.
With musical examples.

928. KLEIN, Johann Baptist. Der Choralgesang der Kartauser in Theorie und Praxis unter besonderer Berücksichtigung der deutschen Kartauser. Berlin: Druck der Germania, 1910.

929. LINDSLEY, Charles Edward. Early 19th century American collections of sacred choral music 1800-1810: Part 1. Ann Arbor: Univ. Microfilm, 1968.

930. MANNING, Rosemary. From Holst to Britten: A study of modern choral music. London: Worker's Music Association, 1949.

931. MATHIS, William S. Thirty six choral works of the 16th century: Adapted and annotated for performance by non-professional church groups. Tallahassee: Florida State Univ., 1952.

932. MOLITOR, Raphael. Die Nach-tridentinische Choral-Reform zu Rom. Ein Beitrage zur Musikgeschichte des XVI und XVII. Jahrhunderts. Leipzig: F. E. C. Leuckart, 1901-02. Also (repr.) Hildesheim: Georg Olms, 1966.

933. NARDONE, Thomas R. (ed.). Choral music in print, 1976 Supplement. Philadelphia: Musicdata, 1976.

934. ______, James H. Nye, and Mark Resnick, (eds.). Sacred choral music. (1st ed.) Vol. I of Choral Music in Print. Philadelphia: Musicdata, 1974.

935. OCHS, Michael (comp.). An index to "Das Chorwerk" Vols. 1-110. Ann Arbor, Mich.: Music Library Association, 1970.

936. SACRED choral music. Bryn Mawr: Theodore Presser Co., 1964.

937. SATEREN, L. B. The new song. Minneapolis: Augsburg Publishing House, 1958.

938. SCHUENEMANN, G. Führen durch die deutschen Choralliteratur. Wolfenbuttel: Verlag für musikalis Kultur und Wissenschaft, 1935.

939. SPARK, William. Lecture on church music. London: G. Bell, 1851.

940. STEERE, Dwight. Music for the protestant church choir. Richmond, Va.: John Knox Press, 1955 & 1957.

941. TUCHER, Von Simmelsdorf. Über den Gemeindegesang der evangelischen Kirche; ein Nachtrag zu des Verfassers "Schatz des evangelischen Kirchengesangs im ersten Jahrundert der Reformation." Leipzig: Breitkopf und Härtel, 1867.

942. ULRICH, Homer. A survey of choral music. New York: Harcourt Brace Jovanovich, 1973.

943. VAN NICE, John Robert. The larger sacred choral works of William Boyce: A study and edition of selected compositions for choir and orchestra. Iowa City: State University of Iowa, 1956.

944. VOZNESENSKII, I. O tserkovnom pienii pravoslavnoi greko-russkoii tserkvi. Riga: E. Plates, 1889.

945. WEAVER, Paul John. A study outline; sacred choral music. Ithaca, N.Y.: Music Clubs Magazine, 1938.

946. WEBB, Charles Haizlip, Jr. The development of choirs and choral music during the Renaissance. Dallas, Tex.: Southern Methodist Univ., 1955.

947. WIENANDT, Elwyn A. Choral music of the church. New York: The Free Press, 1965.

948. WIGNALL, Janice L. Sacred choral music in the secondary school: Its place and importance in the curriculum. Los Angeles: Univ. of Southern California, 1954.

949. WILSON, Harry R. Choral program series (Books 1 & 2). Morristown, N.J.: Silver Burdett, n.d.

950. _______. Choral program series (Book 3). Morristown, N.J.: Silver Burdett, n.d.

951. _______. Choral program series (Books 4, 5, & 6). Morristown, N.J.: Silver Burdett, n.d.

952. _______. Five master choruses. Minneapolis: Schmitt, Hall, & McCreary, n.d.

953. YARBROUGH, Sarah Aulona. The performance of sacred choral music of the fifteenth and sixteenth centuries. Dallas, Tex.: Southern Methodist Univ., 1959.

954. YOUNG, Percy Marshall. The choral tradition. An historical, analytical survey from the sixteenth century to the present day. With musical examples. London: Hutchinson, 1962.

955. ZIVKOVIC, Milenko. Umetnost xorskog pevatia. Hoeu Cad: N. G., 1946. (BM)

See also: 14, 82, 83, 84, 85, 86, 100, 101, 239, 311, 330, 357, 363, 779, 787, 820, 843, 846, 890, 969, 991, 1013, 1021, 1067, 1147, 1170, 1308, 1326, 1342, 1352, 1815, 1856, 1881, 1937, 1938, 1944, 2120, 2701, 2705, 2712, 2892, 2989, 3096, 3244, 3418, 3604, 3592, 3846, 4101, 4216, 4265, 4321, 4336, 4343, 4429, 4457, 4465, 4512, 4526, 4543, 4608, 4714, 4722, 4815, 4853, 4897, 4905, 4906, 4987, 5010, 5012, 5019, 5039, 5119, 5187, 5188, 5197, 5247, 5302, 5308.

CHROMATICISM

956. JACOBSTHAL, Gustav. Die chromatische Alteration im liturgischen Gesang der abendländischen Kirche. Berlin: J. Springer, 1897.

See also: 956, 3195, 4227.

CHURCH YEAR

957. ALEXANDER, Charles. The church's year. London: Oxford Univ. Press, 1950.

958. CHURCH of Scotland--Liturgy and Ritual. Prayers for the church year. 2nd ed., rev. and enl. London & New York: Oxford Univ. Press, 1952.

959. GILBERT, Harold W. Introits and graduals for the church year, set to music and pointed for speech rhythm singing, Vol. 1: Advent to Pentecost. Philadelphia: Fortress Press, 1964.

960. GUERANGER, Prosper. L'année liturgique. Ed. nouv., rev. et mise à jour par les moines de Solesmes. Tournai: Desclée, 1948-52.

961. GUIDE to music for the church year, A. Minneapolis: Augsburg Publishing House, 1962.

962. HELLMANN, D. Gesaenge zum Kirchenjahr (30). New York: C. F. Peters Corporation, 1967.

963. HOPHAN, Otto. Das Anlitz der Tage. Luzerne: Räber, 1947.

964. KIRCHENMUSIKALISCHES Jahrbuch. Köln: Luthe-Druck, 1962-63.

965. McARTHUR, A. The evolution of the church year. London: SCM Press, 1953.

966. MONTESSORI, Maria. La vita in Cristo. Anno liturgico. Milano: Garzanti, 1949.

967. STALEY, Vernon. The liturgical year. Milwaukee: Morehouse Publishing Co., 1907.

968. STRASSER, Bernard. With Christ through the year. Tenbury, Wells: Shalloner Publications, 1963.

969. STRASSLER, Paul Gene. Diego Ortiz: Hymns for the church year and other sacred choral works. Chapel Hill, N.C.: Univ. of North Carolina, 1961.

970. WALLIS, Charles L. Worship resources for the Christian year. New York: Harper, 1954.

See also: 80, 98, 1894, 2570, 2900, 2977, 4149, 4150, 4526, 4734, 5024, 5056, 5388.

CLERGY
(Books on Church Music for the Clergy)

971. ARNOLD, J. H. Priest's music. London: Oxford Univ. Press, 1936.

972. BAIRSTOW, E. C. The music of the minister. London: S.P.K.C., 1927.

973. BELTZ, Oliver Seth. The minister and the hymnal. Chicago: Northwestern Univ., 1933.

974. CAPUA, Seminario. La festa letteraria musicale per l'inaugurazione del nuovo anno scolastico 1904-1905 e la premiazione degli alunni d'il Seminario di Capua, etc. An offprint from "Campania Sacra." Capua: The Seminary, 1904.

975. CONGREGATIO Sacrorum Rituum (ed.). New instruction for American pastors. On sacred music and liturgy. Boston, Mass.: McLaughlin & Reilly Company, 1959.

976. GROVERR, G. F. Fifty musical hints to clergymen. London: N.G., 1893. (BM)

977. HATZFELD, Johannes Heinrich. Priester und musiker. Dusseldorf, Germany: Musikverlag Schwann, 1954.

978. HOWSE, W. L. The church staff and its work. Nashville: Broadman Press, 1959.

979. JOWETT, J. H. The preacher: His life and work. New York: Oxford Univ. Press, 1936.

980. KRIESSMANN, Alfons. Kleine Kirchenmusikgeschichte für Studierende, Kirchenmusiker und Geistliche. Tubingen: C. L. Schultheiss, 1948.

981. KUNSTLER, William M. The minister and the choir singer. The Hall-Mills Murder Case. New York: Morrow, 1964.

982. LEONARD, William J. (ed. and introd.). The new instruction for American Pastors. On sacred music and the Liturgy. Boston, Mass.: McLaughlin and Reilly, 1959.

983. LORENZ, Edmund Simon. Church music. What a minister should know about it. With foreword. New York: Fleming H. Revell, 1923.

984. QUADERNI di Rivista Liturgica, N6. Musica sacra e azione pastorale. Torino Leumann/collegno: Elle di Ci, 1967.

985. RHEA, Claude H., Jr. An investigation of the musical offerings for theological students in Southern Baptist colleges, universities, and seminaries. Tallahassee: Florida State University, M.M.E., 1954.

986. ROUTLEY, Erik. The church and music; an enquiry into the history, nature, and scope of christian judgement on music. Revised ed. London: Duckworth, 1967.

987. STEELE, James Nevell. The importance of musical knowledge to the priesthood of the church. New York: J. Pott & Co., 1894.

988. WILLIS, Richard Storrs. Our church music. A book for pastors and people. New York: Dana & Company, 1856.

989. ________. Our church music; a book for pastors and people. New York: AMS Press, 1973.

See also: 788, 805, 869, 900, 1793, 1855, 1862, 1892, 1896, 1921, 1927, 1928, 1948, 2468, 2543, 2719, 2908, 2947, 2989, 3131, 4037, 4169, 4904, 5045, 5046, 5371, 5372, 5401.

COLLECTIONS

990. DIEWALD, Josef, Adolf Lohmann, and Georg Turmair. Kirchenlied. Freiburg: Christophorus-Verlag, 1963.
Eine Auslese geistl. Lieder. Textausgabe T. 1.

991. HARRISON, Frank L. (ed. and transcriber). The Eton choirbook, II, III. London: Stainer & Bell, 1958, e.g. (also New York: Galaxy Music Corp., 1961.)

992. RAMBACH, August Jakob. Anthologie christlicher Gesänge aus allen Jahrhunderten der Kirche. reprt. of Altona & Leipzig 1917-33 ed. vol. 6. Hildesheim: G. Olms, n.d.

See also: 160, 222, 1646, 1647, 2262, 2465, 2475, 2560, 2565, 3022, 3023, 3297, 3532, 3539, 3586, 5138, 5417.

COMPOSERS

993. ANDERSON, Ruth. Contemporary American composers: A biographical dictionary. Boston: G. K. Hall, 1976.

994. ANGOFF, Charles. Palestrina, savior of church music. New York: Bernard Ackerman, 1944.

995. BARRETT, William Alexander. English church composers. Freeport, N.Y.: Books for Libraries Press, 1969.

996. BRIDGE, Sir Frederick. Twelve good musicians. New York: Dutton & Co., 1920.

997. BROWN, Maurice J. E. Essays on Schubert. New York: St. Martin's Press, 1966.

998. DOUGLAS, John R. Musician and composer societies: A world directory. Ann Arbor: Music Library Ass'n. in "Notes," Vol. 34, No. 1--Sept., 1977.

999 HUGHES. Contemporary American composers. Boston, Mass.: Page, 1900.

1000. SCHEIBE, J. A. Cristischer Musikers. Leipzig: B. C. Breitkopf, 1745.

1001. SMITH, Laura B. Sixteenth and seventeenth century composers of music forms which influenced the organ works of J. S. Bach. Denton, Tex.: North Texas State Univ., 1941.

1002. WRIGHT, Mary E. The musical contribution of five French organ composers from Widor to the present time. Denton, Tex.: North Texas State Univ., 1941.

See also: 103, 789, 2508, 2639, 2663, 2780, 3032, 3050, 3148, 3253, 3297, 3350, 3366, 3578, 3726, 4090, 4211, 4224, 4265, 4301, 4323, 4361, 4369, 4380, 4385, 4409, 4410, 4411, 4415, 4432, 4456, 4468, 4471, 4516, 4525, 4529, 4555, 4618, 4647, 4945, 5003, 5136, 5151, 5311, 5423.

COMPOSITION

1003. APFEL, Ernst. Grundlagen einer Geschichte der Satztechnik von 13. bis zum 16. Jahrhundert. Saarbrücken: Selbstverlag; also Kassel: Bärenreiter, 1974.

1004. DAVISON, A. T. The technique of choral composition. Cambridge: Harvard University, 1945.

1005. ILLING, C. H. Zur Technik der Magnificat-Komposition des 16. Jahrhunderts. Wolfenbuttel: N. G., 1936. (BM)

1006. POTIRON, Henri. La musique d'église; esquisse d'un traite de composition. Cinquante exemples musicaux. Paris: H. Laurens, 1945.

1007. SHAW, Martin. The principles of English church music composition. London: Office of "Musical Opinion," 1921.

1008. WALTER, Samuel. Music composition and arranging. New York: Abingdon Press, 1965.

See also: 176, 956, 1663, 1960, 2375, 3030, 3064, 3081, 3124, 3126, 3780, 4035, 4113, 4156, 4490, 4711, 4726, 4727, 4794, 5241, 5244, 5246, 5248, 5268, 5274.

CONCERTS

1009. ADRIO, A. Die anfänge des geistlichen Konzerts. Berlin: Junker und Dünnhaupt, 1935.

1010. PIERRE, Constant. Histoire du concert spirituel, 1725-1790. (Publications de la Société Française de musicologie. 3. sér., 3. Paris: Huegel, 1975.

See also: 2072, 4442.

CONDUCTING

1011. EISENBURG, H. & L. How to lead group singing. New York: Association Press, 1955.

1012. FINN, William J. Conductor raises his baton, The. New York: Harper & Brothers, 1944.

1013. GARRETSON, Robert L. Conducting choral music. Boston: Allyn & Bacon, 1961.

1014. GEHRKENS, Karl Wilson. Essentials in conducting. Philadelphia: Oliver Ditson Co., 1919.

1015. HOFFELT, Robert O. How to lead informal singing. New York: Abingdon Press, 1963.

1016. JONES, Archie N. Techniques in choral conducting. New York: Carl Fischer, Inc., 1948.

1017. LINDEMAN, Trygve Henrik. Laerebok i taktering for kordirigenter. 5 utg. Oslo: Aschehoug, 1974.

1018. SMIT, Jan. De diregent en zijn koor; een boek over koordirectie. Utrecht, Antwerpen: Het spectrum, 1961.

1019. THOMAS, C. Lehrbuch der chorleitung. Leipzig: N. G., 1937. (BM)

1020. WEISSMANN, A. Der Dirigent im 20. Jahrhundert. Berlin: Propyläen-verlag, 1925.

1021. WOODGATE, Hubert Leslie. The choral conductor. London: Archerberg, Hopwood and Crew, 1949.

See also: 802, 808, 811, 815, 821, 822, 857, 905, 1926, 3440.

CONFIRMATION

See 594.

CONGRESS (KONGRESS)

1022. CATHOLIC Church. National Catholic Education Association, proceedings and addresses, 45th annual meeting. 1948.

1023. CONGRES gregorien compte rende. Nantes: Imprimerie A. Dugas et cie., 1909.

1024. CONGRES international de musique sacrée, chant et orgue. Paris: Desclée, de Brouwer, 1937.

1025. CONGRESO nacional de música sagrada. Cronica y actas officiales del tercer Congreso nacional de musica sagrada. Barcelona: Tolleres tipográficos la Hormiga de oro, 1913.

1026. CONGRESO Nacional de Musica Sagrada. Quinto congreso nacional de musica sagrada celebrado en Madrid del 18 al

22 de noviembre de 1954; cronica. Madrid: Graficas dos de Mayo, 1956.

1027. CONGRESSO de musica sacra. Torino: M. Capra, 1905.

1028. DEUTSCHER Kongress für Kirchenmusik. Bericht über den deutschen Kongress für Kirchenmusik vom 19-22, April, 1927. Kassel: Bärenreiter-Verlag, 1928.
Im Auftrage des Preuss. Ministeriums für Wissenschaft, Kunst und Volksbildung hrsg. von der Staatlichen Akademie für Kirchen und Schulmusik in Charlottenburg.

1029. HAAG, Herbert. Evangelisches kirchenmusikalisches Institut, Heidelberg; eine Festgabe zum 25 jährigen Bestehen. Heidelberg: 1956. (LC-A 57-4692) avail.--Univ. of Oregon Lib.

1030. HAYDN-Zentenarfeier III Kongress der Internationalen Musikgesellschaft. Wien: Artaria & Co., 1909.

1031. INTERNATIONAL Church Music Congress. Musica sacra und Liturgiereform nach dem 2. vatikanischer Konzil. Regensburg: Fr. Pustet, 1968.

1032. INTERNATIONAL Church Music Congress--5th--(1966) Chicago and Milwaukee. Sacred music and liturgy reform after Vatican II, proceedings of the fifth International Church Music Congress--ed. by Johannes Overrath. Rome: Consociatio Internationalis Musicae Sacrae, 1969.

1033. INTERNATIONALER Kongress für katholische Kirchenmusik. Wien: N.G., 1955. (LC. A56-8942)

1034. LUEGER, Wilhelm, ed. Internationaler Kongress für Kirchenmusik (Köln -22-30. Juni 1961). Wilhelm Lueger: Kongressburo, 1961.
Hrsg. vom Präsidium des Kongresses. [Köln (Stadtisches Verkersamt): Kongressburo, 1961.]

1035. ________. Lobt den Herrn. Bonn: Allgemeiner Cäcilien-Verband, Sekretariat, 1965.

1036. REPORT of the fourth congress of the International Musical Society. London: Novello & Co., 1912.

1037. REVUE Musicale (LA). La musique sacrée au 3me Congres International. Paris: Editions de la Nouvelle revue française, 1957.

1038. ROME Pontificio Istituto di Musica Sacra. Atti del congresso internazionale di musica sacra organizzato dal istituto. Tournai: Descleé, 1952.

1039. WEINMANN, Karl. Das Konzil von Trient und die Kirchenmusik; eine historisch-kritische Untersuchung. Leipzig: Breitkopf & Hartel, 1919.

See also: 71, 466, 502, 1287, 1326, 1327, 1420, 1569, 2446, 2923, 2958, 3405, 3507, 3561, 3591, 3634, 4075, 4449.

COUNTERPOINT

1040. GOETSCHIUS, Percy. Counterpoint applied in the invention, fugue, canon, and other polyphonic forms: an exhaustive treatise on the structural and formal details of the polyphonic or contrapuntal forms of music, for the use of general and special students of music. (reprint, New York: G. Schirmer.) Westport, Conn.: Greenwood Press, 1975.

See also: 4725.

CRITICISM

See History and Criticism

DANCE-SACRED

1041. BARKSDALE, Rubie Jeanni. Social, religious and economic influences on the origin of dance. Nashville: George Peabody Univ., 1930.

1042. BONNET, Jacques. Histoire gênerale de la danse sacrée et profane. Genève: Slatkine Reprints, 1969.

1043. CARRUTH, Wincie Ann. The significance of religion in the dance. Baton Rouge, La.: Louisiana State Univ., 1937.

1044. CHAPMAN, A. D. English folk-carols and the dance. Québec, Canada: McGill Univ., 1937.

1045. COLE, Arthur C. The Puritan and Fair Terpsichore. Brooklyn: Dance Horizons, 1966.

1046. COVINGTON, Louise Donaldson. The religious dance of ancient civilizations and its modern revival. Nashville: George Peabody Univ., 1936.

1047. CUMMING, Janet. An annotated bibliography relating to the study of dance. Madison, Wis.: Wisconsin Univ., 1939.

1048. DEISS, Lucien. Dancing for God. Cincinnati: World Library of Sacred Music, 1969.

1049. DONALDSON, Martha. Primitive motivations of the dance. Nashville: George Peabody Univ., 1936.

1050. LAWLER, Lillian. The dance in ancient Greece. Middletown, Conn.: Wesleyan Univ. Press, 1966.

1051. OESTERLEY, W. O. E. The sacred dance. New York: Dance Horizons, 1968.

1052. TAYLOR, Margaret Fisk. A time to dance; symbolic movement in worship. Philadelphia: United Church Press, 1967.

1053. WALDROP, Rebecca. Sacred, classic, court and ritual dances of the Far East. Nashville: George Peabody Univ., 1935.

1053A. ZDENEK, Marilee and Marge Champion. Catch the new wind. Waco, Tex.: Word Books, Publ., 1972.

DENOMINATIONS, FAITHS and ORDERS--(DFO)

General

1054. BLUME, Friedrich, in collaboration with L. Finscher and others. Foreword by P. H. Lang. 1st ed. Protestant church music. New York: N. G., n. d.

1055. GÜLKE, Peter. Mönche, Bürger, Minnesänger: Musik in d. Gesellschaft des europ. Mittelalters. Wien: Böhlau, 1975.

1056. MEAD, Frank S., ed. Handbook of denominations in the United States, 4th Edition. Nashville: Abingdon Press, 1965.

1057. MELTON, John Gordon. A directory of religious bodies in the United States. New York: Garland Publ., 1977.

1058. STUBER, Stanley I. How we got our denominations. New York: Associated Press, 1927.

See also: 739, 5031.

African Methodist Episcopal

1059. DIVERS, Jessyca Pauline. The African Methodist Episcopal Church and its hymnal. Evanston, Ill.: Northwestern Univ., 1944.

Amish

1060. HOHMANN, Rupert Karl. The church music of the old order Amish of the United States. Evanston, Ill.: Northwestern Univ., 1959.

Anabaptist

1061. DUERKSEN, Rosella Reimer. Anabaptist hymnody of the 16th century: A study of its marked individuality coupled with a dependence upon contemporary secular and sacred musical style and form. New York: Union Theological Seminary, 1956.

See also: 3443.

Anglican

1062. AUTON, John G. Music at the parish church. New York: Oxford University Press, 1952.

1063. CHAPPELL, Paul. Music and worship in the Anglican Church 597-1967. London: Faith Press, 1968.

1064. RAINBOW, Bernarr. The choral revival in the Anglican church (1839-1872). New York & London: Oxford Univ. Press, 1970.

1065. TITCOMB, H. Everett. Anglican ways; a manual for Episcopal choirmasters. New York: H. W. Gray Co., 1954.

1066. ________. A choirmaster's notebook on Anglican services and liturgical music. Boston: Schola Cantorum Publications, 1950.

See also: 114, 1207, 1212, 1269, 1294, 1935, 1936, 2012, 2839, 3161, 3343, 4136, 4604, 4649, 5316.

Baptist

1067. ANGELL, Warren M. A plan for the improvement of choral music in the Southern Baptist Church. New York: Columbia University, 1944.

1068. BAKER, John Wesley. A study of the factors and influences involved in the administration of music in the rural church. Ft. Worth, Tex.: Southwestern Baptist Theological Seminary, 1960.

1069. The BAPTIST church hymnal. London: N.G., 1900.

1070. BENSON, David Paul. Church music in theory and practice in selected Baptist churches; an exploratory study. Ft. Worth, Tex.: Southwestern Baptist Theological Seminary, 1961.

1071. COLLIER, Shelby L. The status of music in one hundred Baptist churches of Texas. Austin, Tex.: Univ. of Texas, 1949.

1072. DILLARD, James Albert. Developing music activities in the negro church with emphasis especially on the Concord Baptist Church of Christ, Brooklyn, New York. New York: Columbia Univ., Teachers College, 1950.

1073. GAYLE, Mrs. Joe. Youth choirs and their place in Southern Baptist Churches. Ft. Worth, Tex.: Southwestern Baptist Theological Seminary, 1947.

1074. PATTERSON, Floyd H., Jr. Pioneering in church music; the organization and development of the state-wide church music program among Baptists in Texas. Waco: Baylor Univ. Press, 1949.

1075. REYNOLDS, Isham. Church music. Nashville: The Sunday School Board of the Southern Baptist Convention, 1935.

1076. THOMPSON, George S. Music programs of Baptist supported colleges in the southwest. Austin, Tex.: Univ. of Texas, 1935.

1077. WEBSTER, Imogene. A study of youth choirs in the Baptist churches of Texas. Austin, Tex.: Univ. of Texas, 1951.

See also: 198, 858, 985, 1562, 1567, 1568, 1898, 1899, 1900, 1920, 2173, 2177, 2178, 2226, 2247, 2328, 2384, 2404, 2407, 2592, 2704, 2794, 4556, 4785, 4969, 5424.

Benedictine, St.

See: 506, 652, 2742, 2844, 3014, 3571, 3683, 4808.

Bömischer Brüder

1078. SKARKA, Antonin, (k vyd pripravil.) Duchoví písně. Praha, Vysehrad, 1952.

1079. WOLKAN, Rudolf. Das Deutsche Kirchenlied der Böhmischen Bruder im XVI Jahrhundert. Hildesheim: Georg Olms Verlag, 1968.

Brethren in Christ

1080. SALTZMAN, Herbert R. A historical study of the function of music among the Brethren in Christ. Los Angeles, Calif.: Univ. of Southern California, 1964.

See also: 2377.

Carmelite Order

1081. ORLANDO, Danila. Elia Vanninida Medecina; musico carmelitano. Roma: Istitutum Carmelitanum, 1973.

1082. ZIMMERMAN, B. La cultura musicale nell' Ordine dei Carmelitani. Firenze, Italy: N.G., 1930.

Catholic Church, Roman

1083. AGRESTI, Michele. Il requiescat in pace della civiltà cattolica. Andria: Stab. tip. B. Terlizzi, 1888.

1084. ______. Risposta ad una severa critica della civiltà cattolica sul metodo teorico-pratico di canto ecclesiastico. Andria: Stab. tip. B. Terlizzi, 1887.

1085. ALFIERI, Pietro. Ristabilimento del conto e della musica ecclesiastica; considerazioni scritte in occasione de' moltiplici reclami contro gli abresi insorti invarie chiese d' Italia e di Francia. Roma: Tip. delle belle arti, 1843.

1086. AMADEI, Amadeo. Intorno allo stile della moderna musica da chiesa. Bologna: Tip. della Volpa, 1841.

1087. ASSOCIAZIONE Degli Amici Del Pontificio Istituto di Musica Sacra. Bollettino anno 1. Roma: the authors, 1949.

1088. BARATTA, Carlo Maria. Musica liturgica e musica religiosa. Parma: Scuola tipografica salesiaña, 1903.

1089. BÄUMKER. Das Katholische--deutsche Kirchenlied. Freiburg: Herder, 1886.

1090. BECK, Karl August. Geschichte des katholischen Kirchenliedes von seinen ersten Anfängen bis auf die Gegenwart. Köln: M. DuMont--Schauberg, 1878.

1091. BELLAIGUE, Camille. Etudes musicales. Paris: C. Delagrave, 1907.

1092. ______. Notes brèves. Paris: C. Delagrave, 1914.

1093. BERTOLA, Arnaldo. La musica sacra nelle leggi della chiesa. Torino: Societa tipografico--editrice nazionale, 1930.

1094. BÖCKELER, Heinrich. Wesen und Eigenschaften der katholischen Kirkenmusik im Anschlusse an d. Verordnungen d. Kölner Provinzial-concils vom Jahre 1860. (Pars. II, Tit. II, Cap XX, p. 121) nebst e Anh. "Zur Geschichte der Singschulen": Festgabe z. 1300 jahrigen Jubiläum d. Thronbesteigung d. h. Gregor d. Grossen, 3. Sept. 1890. (Unveränd Neudr. d. Ausg. von 1890.) Walluf (Aachen): Sändig (reprint by A. Jacobi), 1974.

1095. BONTINCK, François. La lutte autour de la liturgie chinoise aux XVII et XVIII siècles. Paris: Louvain, 1962.

1096. BOSTON (Archdiocese). Church music regulations and catalogue for the Archdiocese of Boston. Boston: Archdiocese, 1908.

1097. BUOMMATTEI, Benedetto. Modo di consecrar le vergini, secondo l'uso del pontifical romano. Venezia: A. Pinelli, 1622.

Con la Dichiarazion de' misteri delle cerimonie, che in quell' azion si fanno. Aggiuntori in fine l'ordine, çhe in alcuni monasteri si tiene nel dar l'abito a esse vergini. E nel ricever da loro i voti, e velarle.

1098. CALA, Antonin. Duchovni hudba. Olomouc: N. G., 1946.

1099. CANDOTTI, Giovanni Battista. Sul carattere della musica di chiesa. Milano: G. Ricordi, 1851.

1100. CECILIE; časopis pro katolickou hudbu pasvatnou v cechach, na morave a ve slezsku. V. Praze: Knĕhtiskárna Mikuláše e Knappa, 1874.

1101. CHURCH music regulations and catalogue for the Archdiocese of Boston. Boston: Archdiocese, 1908.

1102. La CIVILTA Cattolica: notizie critiche e biografiche sulle musica. Roma, N. G., 1887-1892. (LC. MO3033 ML 3830 ML410)

1103. CONGREGATIO Sacrorum Rituum, ed. Die Entscheidungen der Heiligen Riten-Kongregation in Bezug auf Kirchenmusik. New York: F. Pustet, 1901.

1104. ________. Istruzione. Milano: Societá editrine Vita e pensiero, 1958.

1105. COUTURIER, of Lengres, The Elder. Dêcadence et restauration de la musique religieuse. Paris: E. Repos, 1862.

1106. DOLD, Alban and Klaus Gamber. Das Sakramentar von Salzburg, seinem Typus nach auf Grund der erhaltenen Fragmente rekonstruiert, in seinem Verhältnis zum Paduanum untersucht. Hohenzollern: Beuron, 1960.

1107. DOREZ, Léon. La cour du Pope Paul III d'après les registres de la trésorerie secrête. Paris: Librairie Ernest Leroup, 1932.

1108. DRINKINELDER, Otto. Gesetz und Praxis in der Kirchenmusik; praktische Erklärung aller kirchenmusikalischen Gesetze. New York: F. Pustet & Co., 1914.

1109. DUCLOS, Adolphe Julien. Sa Saintetê Piex et la musique religieuse commentaire sur les motu proprio et les piêces. connexes, par Ad. Duclos. Rome: Journal, Societê de St. Jean L' Evangêliste & c., 1905.

1110. ECHO muzyczne; miesiecznik poswiecony muzyce koscielnej i swiekiej oraz zespolom muzycznym ï teatralnym. Chicago: B. J. Zalewski, 1924.

1111. EDITTO sopra la musica. Roma: Stamperia della reverenda Camera apostolica, 1698.

1112. L'ENCICLICA "Musicae sacrae discipline" di Sua Santitá Pio XII. Roma: Associazione italiana S Cecilia, 1957.

1113. ENGELHARDT, Zephyrin. Mission San Juan Bautista, a school of church music. Santa Barbara: Mission Santa Barbara, 1931.

1114. ________. Santa Barbara Mission. San Francisco: James H. Barry Co., 1923.

1115. ERLEMANN, Gustav. Die Einheit im katholischen deutschen Kirchenliede. Eine kritische Würdigung der Lieder der heutigen Diozesan--Gesangbücher ... Zugleich eine Auswahl und Festlegung der Lieder, die für ein einheitliches Gesangbuch in Betracht kommen konnten. Trier: Bantus--Verlag, 1911.

1116. FALCONARA, Pietro Battista da. Una crítica musicale della Civiltá cattolica. Roma: Tip. editrice-industriale M. Lovesio, 1890.

1117. FELLERER, Karl Gustav. Geschichte der Katholischen Kirchenmusik. Vol. 1. Kassel: Bärenreiter, 1972.

1118. ________. Geschichte der Katholischen Kirchenmusik. Vol. 2. Kassel: Bärenreiter Verlag, 1976.

1119. ________. The history of Catholic church music. Baltimore: Helicon Press, 1961.

1120. GABLER, Joseph. Die Tonkunst in der Kirche; kirchenmusikalische Excurse in sechs Büchern. Linz: Buchdruckerei des kath. Pressvereines, 1883.

1121. GALLI, Amintore. Corso di musica sacra; l' omofonia della chiesa latina e sua armonizzazione; nozioni teorico--pratiche. Milano: A. Bertarelli & Co., 1908.

1122. GASTOUE, Amédée. La musique d'église; études historiques, esthetiques et pratiques. Lyon: Janin frères, 1911.

1123. ______. Variations sur la musique d'église. Paris: Bureau d'édition de la "Schola," 1912.

1124. GEERING, Arnold. Die Organa und mehrstimmigen Conductus in den Handschriften des deutschen Sprachgebietes vom 13. bis 16. Jahrhundert. Bern: P. Haupt, 1952.

1125. GIGOUT, Eugène. Musique liturgique et rêligieuse catholique. Paris: In Encyclopédie de la musique et dictionnaire du Conservatoire, 1913-31.

1126. GIRAUD, Ludovic. La musique d'église telle que l'église la vent. Marseille: Editions Publiroc, 1934.

1127. GLORIA Deo pax hominibus: Festschrift zum 100-jährigen. Bestehen der Kirchenmusikschule Regensburg affiliiert der päpstlichen Hochschule für Kirchenmusik in Rom. Fachakademie für katholische Kirchenmusik und Musikerziehung am 22 November 1974. Hrsg. von F. Fleckenstein. Bonn: Allgemeiner Cäcilienverband, Sekretariat, 1974.

1128. GOOVAERTS, Alphonse Jean. De kerkmuziek; bedenkingen over haren huidigen toestand en beknopte geschiedenis aller scholen Europa's. Antwerpen: L. Dela Montagne, drukker, 1876.

1129. GOTTRON, Amad. Kirchemusik und Liturgie, die kirchlichen Vorschriften für Gesang und Musik beim Gottesdienst. Regensburg: F. Pustet, 1937.

1130. GRANDJEAN, Wolfgang. Das Katholische Kirchenlied in den trierischen Gesangbüchern von seinen Anfängen bis heute. Mainz: Selbstverlag der Gesellschaft für Mittelreinische Kirchengeschichte, 1975.

1131. GREGORIUS Blatt, Organ für katholische Kirchenmusik. Aachen: A. Jacobi & Co., 1877-87.

1132. GREGORY St.--Association of. Dublin, The Association, 1934.

1133. GRIESBACHER, Peter. Reaktion und Reform; historische Entwicklung und systematische Bewertung ihrer Formfaktoren mit besonderer Rücksicht auf moderne Komposition und Praxis dargestellt. Rogensburg: A. Coppenrath, 1916.

1134. GRISAR, Hartmann. History of Rome and the popes of the Middle Ages. London: K. Paul, Trench, Trübner & Co., 1911-12.

1135. HAMMERICH, Angul. Mediaeval musical relics of Denmark. Leipzig: Breitkopf & Härtel, 1912.

1136. HANIN, Aloys. La législation ecclésiastique en matière de musique réligieuse. Tournai: Desclée & cie, 1933.

1137. HENRY, Hugh Thomas. Music reform in the Catholic church. New York: G. Schirmer, 1915.

1138. HUEGLE, Gregory. The spotlight on Catholic church music; answers to common inquiries during 1933-34. London: Cary & Co., 1935.

1139. HUME, Paul. Catholic church music. New York: Dodd, Mead & Co., 1956.

1140. KALLENBERG, Paschalis. Fontes liturgiae Carmelitanae. Romae: impressum Bracarae Augustae, 1962.
Investigatio in decreta, codices et proprium sanctorum.

1141. KIENLE, Ambrosius. Mass und Milde in kirchenmusikalischen Dingen. Gedanken über unsere liturgische Musikreform. Freiburg: Herder, 1901.

1142. KIRCHENMUSIKALISCHE Gesetzgebung. Regensburg: F. Pustet, 1949.

1143. KOTHE, Bernhard. Die Musik in der katholischen Kirche. Wegweiser durch das gesammte Gebiet der katholischen Kirchemusik, nebst Abhandlungen über Regeneration derselben und den kirchlichen Verordnungen. Ein Handbuch für Chordirigenten und Kirchenvorstände. Breslau: F. E. C. Leuckart, 1862.

1144. KRIEG, Franz. Katholische Kirchenmusik, Geist und Praxis. Mit geschichtlichen Beiträgen. Teuffen: Niggli & Verkauf, 1954.

1145. KRIEGER, Ferdinand. Musica ecclesiastica catholica. Die katholische Kirchenmusik. Eine leichtfassliche Darstellung der allgemeinen Musik-Harmonic-und Compositionslehre nach den grundsätzen der Meister wahrer kirchlicher Tonkunst. Freiburg in Breisgau: Herder, 1872.

1146. LALOY, Louis. The musiclover's Calendar, illustrated and published annually. Boston: The Musiclovers Co., 1905.

1147. LÖBMANN, Hugo. Pflegt das deutsche Kirchenlied. Mit eine Anhang vom schönen Singen. Wien: Verlagsanstalt Tyrnlia, 1937.

1148. McNASPY, Clement James. The motu proprio of church music of Pope Pius X: a new translation and commentary. Toledo: Gregorian Institute of America, 1950.

1149. MANGANELLI, P. Sulla restaurazione della musica sacra. Roma: Tip. de la Pace, 1880.

1150. MAYNARD, Theodore. The story of American catholicism. New York: Macmillan Co., 1941.

1151. MOEHLER, A. Compendium der katholicshen Kirchenmusik. Ravensburg: F. Alber, 1909.

1152. MORONI, Gaetano. Le cappelle pontificie cardinalizie e prelatizie; opera storico-liturgica. Vol. 1. Venezia: Dalla tipografia Emilians, 1841.

1153. MOTU proprio of Pope Pius the Tenth on Christian democracy and sacred music. London: Catholic Truth Society, 1911.

1154. The MOTU proprio on church music. St. Meinrad's Abbey, Inc., 1951.

1155. MURPHY, Rose Marie. An historical survey of the National Catholic Music Educators Association. Washington, D.C.: D.C.: National Catholic Educators Assoc., 1963.

1156. MUSICAE Sacrae Disciplina. La voz del papa Pio XII enciclica "Musicae sacrae disciplina" sobre la musica sagrada. Barcelona: Editorial Balmes, 1957.

1157. MUSICA religiosa Catolica. New York: Schirmer, G. Inc., 19--. (BM.S3c34)

1158. Della MUSICA sacra; norme e regolamento per la citta ed archidiocesi di Urbino. Torino: Tip. G. Marietti, 1866.

1159. MUSICA sacra, "Sancta Sancte"; revue trimestrielle de chant d'église et de musique sacrée. Bruges: Desclée, 1881-19--.

1160. The MUSIC of the Roman rite. London: Burns, Oates & Washbouren, 1931.

1161. MUSIK und Altar. Freiburg: Christophorusverlag Herder, 1948.

1162. OLMEDA, Federico. Memoria de un viaje á Santiago de Galicia. Burgos: Impr. y estereotipia de Polo, 1895.

1163. ONGANIA, Ferdinando. A glance at the Grimani Breviary preserved in S. Mark's Library, Venice. Venezia: Ferd. Ongania, 1903.

1164. O'SHEA, William J. The worship of the church. A companion to liturgical studies. Revised Edition. London: Darton, Longman & Todd, 1960.

1165. PONS, André. Droit ecclêsiastique et musique sacrêe. St. Maurice, Suisse: Editions de l'oeuvre St. Augustin, 1958.

1166. PRADO, German. Mozarabic melodies. The mozarabic Liber ordinum. Cambridge: The Mediaeval Academy of America, 1928.

1167. PREDMORE, George Vincent. Sacred music and the Catholic church. Boston: McLaughlin & Reilly Co., 1936.

1168. PROKSCH, Joseph. Aphorismen über katholische Kirchenmusik nebst einem geschichtlichen Ueberblicke des gregorianischen Choralgesanges. Prag: C. Bellmann, 1858.

1169. PROVINCIAL Council. Catholic church in the United States. Milwaukee: H. H. Zahn & Co., 1891.

Guide in Catholic Church music, published by order of the first Provincial councils of Milwaukee and St. Paul, with a preface by Rt. Rev. Bishop M. Marty, D.D.

1170. RENNER, Josef. Moderne Kirchenmusik und Choral. Eine Abwehr. Leipzig: F. E. C. Leuckart, 1902.

1171. ROBERTSON, Alec. Music of the Catholic church. London: Burns & Oates, 1961.

1172. ROME, Church of. Motu Proprio of H. H. Pius X on sacred music. N.G.: Burns & Oates, 1923. (BM)

1173. ________ - Congregatio Rituum. Instructio de musica sacra et sacra liturgia ad mentem litterarum encyclicarum Pii Papae XII "Musicae sacrae disciplina" et "Mediator Dei." In: Acta Apostolicae Sedis. Vol. 50. No. 12/13. pp. 630-663. - 1958.

1174. SABEL, Hans. Die liturgischen Gesänge der katholischen Kirche. Wolfenbüttel und Zurich: Möseler, 1965.

1175. SAYAS, Juan Francisco de. Musica Canonica, motetica y sagrada, su origen, y pureza con que la erigio Dios para sus alabanzas divina. Pamplona: M. J. de Rada, 1761.

1176. SCHNEIDERWIRTH, Matthaeus. Das Katholische deutsche Kirchenlied unter dem einflusse Gellerts und Kopstocks. Münster: Aschendorff, 1908.

1177. SCHOLA cantorum, revista mensual de cultura sacro musical. N.G.: Morelia, 1939.

1178. SHEPPARD, Lancelot Capel. The liturgical books. London: Burns & Oates, 1962.

1179. STEIN, Albert Gereon. Die Katholische Kirchenmusik nach ihrer Bestimmung und ihrer dermaligen Beschaffenheit dargestellt. Koln: J. P. Bachem, 1864.

1180. A SZENTZENE töruenyei. Budapest: Magyar Kôrus, 1940.

1181. Die TONKUNST im Heiligtum: von der heiligen Ritenkongregation approbierte deutsche Übersetzung durch Mönche. Regensburg: F. Pustet, 1929.

1182. UDINA, Antonio. Participación en la Misa y música sagrada. Barcelona: Centro de Pastoral Litúrgica, 1959.

1183. URBINA, (Archbishop). Della musica sacra; norme e regolamente per la sitta. Torino: Tip. G. Marietti, 1866.

1184. URSPRUNG, Otto. Die Katholische Kirchenmusik. Potsdam: Akademische Verlagsgesellschaft Athenaion, 1931.

1185. ______. Die Katholisches Kirchenmusik. (Reprint) New York: Johnson Reprint Corp., 1973.

1186. ______. Restauration und Palestrina--Rennaissance in der katholischen Kirchenmusik der letzten zwei Jahrhundert Vergangenheitsfragen und Gegenwartsaufgaben, mit sieben Bildtafeln. Augsburg: B. Filser, 1924.

1187. VATICAN Council. Schema constitutionis de Sacra Liturgia. Modi a patribus conciliaribus propositi a Commissione Conciliari de Sacra Liturgia examinati. Vatican City: Vatican Council, 1963. See also "The Liturgy Constitution"--Glen Rock, N.J.: Paulist Press, 1964.

1188. WACHTEL. Die liturgische Musikpflege im Klosten Adelhausen seit Grundung des Klosters 1234 bis um 1500. Freiburg: N.G., 1939.

1189. WAGNER, Peter Josef. Einführung in die katholische Kirchenmusik; Vorträge, gehalten an der Universität Freiburg in der Schweiz für Theologen und andere Freunde kirchlicher Musik. Düsseldorf: L. Schwann, 1919.

1190. WEINMANN, Karl. History of church music. New York: F. Pustet, 1910.

1191. WERDER, Richard H., ed. Developing teaching skills in music. Washington: Catholic Univ. of America Press, 1960.

1192. WERNER, Alajos. A z Ëneklo egyház. Szombathely: Martineum Könyvnyomda, 1937.

1193. WESTGATE-on-Sea. Hallowed by thy Name. London: St. Paul Publications, 1959.

Written and illustrated by the Canonesses Regular of St. Augustine, English Vicarate, Westgate-on-Sea.

1194. ZEITSCHRIFT für Katholische Kirchenmusik. Gmünden: J. F. Habert, n.d.

See also: 5, 13, 16, 23, 34, 71, 78, 188, 189, 206, 226, 231, 232, 240, 241, 243, 292, 341, 342, 343, 345, 346, 349, 356, 383, 384, 389, 395, 397, 398, 416, 444, 453, 457, 462, 463, 464, 465, 466, 468, 472, 473, 476, 477, 491, 496, 503, 504, 506, 509, 510, 511, 558, 565, 577, 586, 594, 597, 598, 626, 627, 630, 637, 644, 649, 650, 668, 681, 682, 699, 708, 712, 735, 736, 741, 747, 752, 813, 822, 851, 896, 897, 907, 909, 926, 930, 956, 968, 975, 977, 980, 1006, 1022, 1023, 1024, 1025, 1026, 1027, 1030, 1031, 1032, 1033, 1036, 1038, 1039, 1262, 1268, 1270, 1370, 1511, 1518, 1520, 1543, 1561, 1598, 1599, 1600, 1636, 1641, 1642, 1644, 1649, 1657, 1723, 1736, 1740, 1806, 1871, 1873, 1880, 1897, 1901, 1905, 1925, 1927, 1931, 1933, 1948, 1949, 1950, 1977, 1978, 1989, 2006, 2007, 2013, 2031, 2032, 2041, 2045, 2054, 2069, 2077, 2086, 2087, 2091, 2095, 2116, 2149, 2150, 2152, 2169, 2196, 2233, 2244, 2281, 2282, 2356, 2385, 2412, 2424, 2448, 2494, 2506, 2515, 2568, 2598, 2617, 2662, 2693, 2715, 2720, 2729, 2742, 2809, 2810, 2812, 2814, 2816, 2817, 2818, 2819, 2820, 2821, 2842, 2852, 2856, 2863, 2868, 2871, 2876, 2877, 2880, 2881, 2883, 2885, 2892, 2897, 2900, 2901, 2904, 2911, 2912, 2913, 2914, 2916, 2918, 2920, 2923, 2926, 2936, 2937, 2938, 2939, 2941, 2945, 2946, 2948, 2951, 2958, 2960, 2961, 2963, 2964, 2968, 2979, 2985, 2988, 2991, 3003, 3004, 3005, 3010, 3016, 3017, 3019, 3020, 3025, 3029, 3033, 3034, 3038, 3039, 3041, 3044, 3045, 3046, 3047, 3048, 3054, 3057, 3059, 3060, 3062, 3065, 3074, 3083, 3087, 3099, 3103, 3104, 3112, 3114, 3117, 3121, 3128, 3131, 3136, 3137, 3139, 3149, 3153, 3155, 3164, 3192, 3228, 3243, 3244, 3255, 3279, 3281, 3285, 3286, 3287, 3289, 3293, 3295, 3300, 3301, 3325, 3356, 3387, 3389, 3390, 3405, 3419, 3429, 3434, 3435, 3440, 3453, 3460, 3465, 3469, 3471, 3474, 3491, 3500, 3507, 3509, 3511, 3512, 3513, 3515, 3516, 3518, 3519, 3525, 3541, 3545, 3548, 3550, 3551, 3552, 3553, 3554, 3570, 3571, 3591, 3598, 3601, 3602, 3607, 3619, 3624, 3627, 3647, 3682, 3711, 3913, 4022, 4108, 4149, 4169, 4174, 4177, 4187, 4195, 4207, 4264, 4328, 4355, 4401, 4530, 4551, 4604, 4673, 4682, 4725, 4734, 4772, 4787, 4791, 4808, 4826, 4891, 4904, 4911, 4916, 4917, 4921, 4933, 4979, 4981, 4982, 4994, 5011, 5019, 5035, 5043, 5074, 5093, 5094, 5196, 5198,

5199, 5200, 5230, 5281, 5312, 5316, 5317, 5321, 5326, 5381, 5398, 5426, 5442.

Christian Reformed Church

See: 2207.

Church of Christ

1195. BALES, James D. Instrumental music and New Testament worship. Searcy, Ark.: N.G., 1973.

1196. COLEMAN, Mina P. An examination of the technical aspects of music relevant to an understanding of music in the church. N.P.--avail. Abilene Christian Univ., 1966.

1197. FERGUSON, William E. A cappella music in the public worship of the church. Abilene, Tex.: Biblical Research Press, 1972.

1198. KURFEE, Marshall Clement. Instrumental music in the worship, or Greek verb "psallo" philologically examined, together with a full discussion of kindred matters relating to music in christian worship. Nashville: Gospel Advocate Publ., 1911.

1199. LEWIS, John Thomas. The voice of the pioneers on instrumental music and societies. Nashville: Gospel Advocate Publ. Co., 1932.

1200. LUTTRELL, William Leon. Instrumental music in New Testament worship. (Master's thesis, d.n.g.) n.p.--avail. Abilene, Tex.: Library, Abilene Christian Univ.

1201. McKINNON, James Wm. The church fathers and musical instruments. Ann Arbor: Univ. Microfilms, 1965.

1202. VAN DYKE, Frank. Is instrumental music scriptural? Murfeesboro, Tenn.: Dehoff Publ., 1949.

See also: 202, 4757, 4758, 4759, 4761, 4762, 4765, 4766.

Church of England

1203. AMERICAN Choral Foundation, Inc., The. The English Service. New York: American Choral Foundation, n.d.

1204. BOX, Charles. Church music in the metropolis: Its past and present condition. London: W. Reeves, 1884.

1205. BRIDGE, Sir Frederick. A Westminster pilgrim, being a record of service to church, cathedral, and abbey, college, university, and concert-room. New York: H. W. Gray Co., 1919.

1206. BURGE, William. On the choral service of the Anglo-Catholic church. London: G. Bell, 1844.

1207. BYRD, William. English church music. New York: Oxford Univ. Press, 1922.

1208. CHALFONT St. Giles Church ... history of the church ... account of mural paintings ... lives and work of the earlier English church musicians. High Wycombe: The Bucks Free Press, 1934.

1209. DANIEL, Richard Blackburne. Chapters on church music. London: E. Stock, 1894.

1210. DIXON, R. W. History of the Church of England. London: Oxford Univ. Press, n.d.

1211. DRYDEN, Sir Henry Edward Leigh. On church music and the fitting of churches for music. London: Savill & Edwards, 1853.

1212. ENGLISH church music Vol. 1. Canterbury: Royal School of Church Music, 1931.

1213. FELLOWES, Edmund Horace. English cathedral music from Edward VI to Edward VII. London: Methuen & Co., Ltd., 1941.

1214. ________. English cathedral music from Edward VI to Edward VII, 2nd ed. London: Methuen & Co., Ltd., 1945/1948.

1215. GAIRDNER, James. The English church in the 16th century. London, New York: The Macmillan Co., 1902.

1216. GARDNER, George Lawrence Harter, and S. H. Nicholson, (ed.). A manual of English church music, with an appendix bringing it up to date. New York: Macmillan Co., 1936.

1217. GRAY, Jonathan. An inquiry into historical facts, relative to parochial psalmody. York: T. Wolstenholme, 1821.

1218. GREGORY, John Herbert. A letter to the Right Rev. the Lord Bishop of Melbourne, on church music. Melbourne: Lucas Brothers, Printers, 1857.

1219. JEBB, John. The choral responses and litanies of the United Church of England and Ireland. London: George Bell, 1847.

1220. ________. The choral service of the United Church of England and Ireland. London: J. W. Parker, 1843.

1221. KING, J. Anglican hymnology. London: Hatchards, 1885.

1222. LA TROBE, John Antes. The music of the church considered in its various branches, congregational and choral; an historical and practical treatise for the general reader. London: R. B. Seeley and W. Burnside, 1831.

1223. LONG, Kenneth R. The music of the English church. New York: St. Martin's Press, 1971.

1224. MASON, William. Essays, historical and critical, on English church music. York: W. Blanchard, 1795.

1225. THORNE, E. H. A course of lectures on the music of the English church, from the Reformation to S. S. Wesley. London: Royal College of Organists, 1905. (BM)

1226. VINCENT, William. Considerations on parochial music. London: T. Cadell, 1790.

1227. WORDSWORTH, Christopher. The old service-books of the English church. London: Methuen & Co., 1904.

See also: 10, 103, 114, 412, 415, 418, 700, 716, 847, 855, 880, 939, 1374, 1629, 1690, 1708, 1820, 1825, 1956, 2012, 2124, 2141, 2190, 2210, 2393, 2493, 2654, 2660, 2857, 2902, 2932, 2933, 2997, 3105, 3107, 3247, 3343, 3347, 3361, 3368, 3376, 3377, 3809, 4045, 4071, 4651, 4730, 4737, 4740, 4743, 4747, 4748, 4774, 4807, 4850, 4885, 4898, 4899, 4909, 4930, 4947, 5014, 5016, 5342.

Church of Ireland

See: 1220, 3499.

Church of the Latter Day Saints (Mormon)

1228. DURHAM, Lovell M. The role and history of music in the Mormon church. Iowa City: Iowa Univ. Press, 1942.

1229. HATCH, Verena Ursenbach. Worship and music in the Church of Jesus Christ of Latter-Day Saints. Provo, Utah: M. E. Hatch, 1968.

1230. LAYCOCK, Harold R. A history of music in the academics of the Latter-Day Saints Church. Los Angeles: Univ. of Southern California, 1961.

1231. MACARE, H. H. The singing saints: A study of the Mormon hymnal 1835-1950. Los Angeles: Univ. of California, 1961.

1232. MAXWELL, William Le Grand. Revision of music study programs of the Church of Jesus Christ of Latter-Day Saints. New York: Columbia Univ. Teachers College Press, 1952.

1233. PURDY, William Earl. Music in Mormon culture, 1830-1876. Evanston, Ill.: Northwestern Univ., 1960.

1234. SLAUGHTER, Jay Leon. The role of music in the Mormon Church, school and life. Bloomington, Ind.: Indiana Univ., 1964.

1235. WEIGHT, Newell Bryan. An historical study of the origin and character of indigenous hymn tunes of the Latter-Day Saints. Los Angeles: Univ. of Southern California, 1961.

1236. WILKES, William. Borrowed music in Mormon hymnals. Los Angeles: Univ. of Southern California, 1957.

See also: 1940, 2516, 3673.

Church of the Nazarene

1237. BENNER, Hugh C. Singing disciples; toward better music. Kansas City, Mo.: Nazarene Publishing House, 1959.

1238. MOORE, Muriel Payne. History and practice of music in the Church of the Nazarene. Austin, Tex.: Univ. of Texas, 1966.

Church of Scotland

1239. HURLBUT, Stephen Augustus, ed. The liturgy of the Church of Scotland since the Reformation. Washington and (Part IV) Charleston, S.C.: St. Albans Press, 1944-52.

See also: 5327.

Congregational Church

See: 2184, 2185.

Coptic

1240. BENNETT, John Paul. Music in the Coptic Church of Egypt and Ethiopia. Seattle: Univ. of Washington, 1945.

1241. CRAMER, Maria. Koptische Hymnologie in deutscher Übersetzung. Wiesbaden: Harrassowitz, 1969.

1242. KEBEDE, Ashenafi. Äthiopien; Musik der Koptischen Kirche. Berlin: E. Blaschker, 1969.

1243. NEWLANDSMITH, E. The ancient music of the Coptic Church. N.G.: New Life Movement, 1931.

Disciples of Christ (Christian Church)

1244. HEATON, Charles. The disciples of Christ and sacred music. New York: Union Theological Seminary, School of Sacred Music, n.d.

See also: 2179, 4757, 4761.

Eastern Churches

1245. ADAIR, Gregory, ed. Orthodox Eastern Church; liturgy and ritual. Maitland, Fla.: Three Hierarchs Seminary, 1966.

1246. ALLEMANOV, Dimitri. Tserkovnye lady i garmonizatsiia ikh po teorii drevnikh didaskalov vostochnago osmoglasiia. V'soglasovanil s'novie ishimi akusticheskimi i dosche--muzykal'nymi zokonami. Moskva: P. Lurgensona, 1900.

1247. ARAKISHVILI, Dmitrii. Kratkii ocherk razvitia gruzinskoi, kartolinokakhetinskoi narodnoi piesni. Moskva: Mehlmosa, 1905.

1248. ARNOL'D, Iurii Karlovich. Garmonizatsiia drevne--russkago tserkovnago pieniia po ellen--skoi i vizantiiskoi teorii i akusticheskomii analizu sostavil. Moskva: Izdanie psalomtsika mikh Dmitr Razumovskago, 1886.

1249. ARRO, Elmar in verbindung mit Hans Heinrich Eggebrecht. Music Slavica. Wiesbaden: Franz Steiner Verlag, 1976.

1250. BELIAEV, Viktor M. Prevnerusskaya moozlkar'naya pisennost'. Moscow: Sovetskii Kompozitor, 1962.

1251. BOURGAULT-DUCOUCRAY, Louis Albert. Etudes sur la musique ecclèsiastique grècque; mission musicale en grèce et en orient janvier - mai 1875. Paris: Hachette et cie., 1877.

1252. BRAZHNIKOV, M. Pootii razvetiya i zapachi raspifrovkii znamennova rospeva XII-XVII vekov. Leningrad: Moozyookalinaya yezo-vo, 1949.

1253. CASTRO, Juan de. Methodus cantus ecclesiastici Graeco-Slavici auctore loanne de Castro. Roma: Typographia polyglotta. Accedit Enchiridion canticorum eiusdem ecclesiae ab eodem auctore concinnatum. 1881.

1254. CATHOLIC Church. Liturgy and Ritual. Ein Syro-Melkitisches Tropologion mit altbyzantischer Notation Sinai Syr. 261. Hrsg. von H. Husmann. Wiesbaden: Harrassowitz, 1975.

1255. CAVARNOS, Constantine. Byzantine sacred music; the traditional music of the Orthodox Church, its nature, purpose, and execution. Belmont: Institute for Modern Greek and Byzantine Studies, 1956.

1256. DALMAIS, Irênée Henri. Les liturgies d'orient. Paris: N.G., 1959.

1257. ________. (Les liturgies d'orient) The Eastern Liturgies. London: Burns & Oates, 1960.

1258. DORESSE, Jacques et Dom E. Lanne. Un têmoin archaïque de la liturgie copte de S. Basile. Louvain: Publications Universitaires, et, Institut orientaliste, 1960.
With the Coptic text in facsimile, a transcription and Greek and Latin translations.

1259. EDITING Committee. Recordings and music of the Greek Orthodox Church. Los Angeles: Greek Sacred and Secular Music Society, Inc., n.d.

1260. FOLLIERI, Henrica. Initia hymnorum ecclesiae Graecae. Vatican City: Vatican, 1960.

1261. GAISSER, Huguls. Les "Heirmoi" de Pâques dans l'office grec; êtude rythmique et musicale. Roma: Impr. de la Propagande, 1905.

1262. GAISSER, Ugo Atanasio. I canti ecclesiastici italo--greci. Roma: Desclêe, Lefèbvre & Co., 1965.

1263. HAMMERSCHMIDT, Ernst. Studies in the Ethiopic Anaphoras. Berlin: Akademie--Verlag, 1961.

1264. HANSSENS, J. M. Institutiones liturgicae de ritibus orientalibus. Roma: Pont. Institutum Orientalium Stud., 1930.

1265. KOSCHMIEDER, Erwin. Przyczynki do zagadnienia chomonji w hirmosach rosyjskick. Wilno: Instytutu Naukowo Badawezego Wschedniej, 1932.

1266. LIESEL, Nicholas. (Die Liturgien der Ostkirche) The Eastern Catholic Liturgies. London: Sands & Co., 1961.

1267. ______. Die Liturgien der Ostkirche. Freiburg: Herder, 1960.

1268. ______. (Die Liturgien der Ostkirche.) Les Liturgies catholiques orientales par l'image. Paris: Letovzey, 1959.

1269. MAYFIELD, Guy. An Anglican guide to the Orthodox Liturgy. London: Fellowship of St. Alban & St. Sergius, 1949.

1270. MOEHLER, A. Die griechische, griechischrömische und altchristlichlateinische Musik. 2. aufl. Leipzig: G. J. Göschen, 1907.
(1. aufl. Römische Quartalschrift für Christliche Alterthumskunde. Supplementheft. 9. 1898). (BM)

1271. NICHOLAS, Cabasilas. (Die divino altaris sacrificio.) A commentary on the divine liturgy. London: S. P. C. K., 1960.

1272. PAPADOPOULOS, Georgios I. Sümbolai eis ten istorian tes par' èmîn ékklesiastikes moüsikes, kai oi ton emeron èmon ákmásantes epiphanésteroi melodi, moüsikoi kai monsikochoi. En Athenais: Tüpogratheion kai Bibliopolēion Konsoülinoü and Athanasiádou, 1890. (LC-10-24596)

1273. RAES, Alphonsus. Introduction in liturgiam orientalem. Rome: The City: Pontificio Istituto per gli Studi Orientale, 1947.

1274. SALAVILLE, Sévérien and G. Nowack. Le rôle du diacre dans la liturgie orientale. Etude d'histoire et de liturgie. Paris: Institut Français d'Etudes Byzantines, 1962.

1275. SCHOLLMEYER, Pater Chrysologus. Die Ostkirche betet. Hymnen aus den Tagzeiten der byzantinischen Kirche. Münster: Verlag Regensberg, 1960.
Übertragen aus dem Originaltext des Triodion und herausgegeben von Pater Kilian Kirchhoff. In zweiter Auflage überarbeitet von Pater Chrysologus Schollmeyer.

1276. SMOLENSKII, Stepan Vasilevich. O sobranii russikh drevnepi͡evcheskikh rukopisei. St. Petersburg: Tipografiia-M. D. Rudometova, 1, 1899.

1277. SWAINSON, C. A. The Greek liturgies chiefly from original authorities. Hildesheim, Germany: Georg Olms-Reprint, 1967.

1278. THEREIANOS, Eustathios. Peri moüsikes ton 'Ellénon kai idiüs tēs ekklesiastikes üpo Eustathiou Thereianoū. 'En Tergéste: Tüpois tou Aùstroggmikou Aöüd, 1875.

1279. TILLYARD, H. J. W., transcriber. The hymns of the Octoechus. Copenhagen: E. Munksgaard, 1940-49.

1280. TZETZES, Johannes. Über die altgriechische Musik in der griechischen Kirche. München: vondr. C. Wolf and Sohn, 1874.

1281. VAJS, Josef. Recensio croatico-glagolitici fragmenti verbenicensis. Veglae: Glagolitica. Publicationes Palaeoslavicae Academiae Veglensis, 1903.
With the text in glagolitic and in cyrillic characters.

1282. VOZNESENSKII, Ioanniu Isannovich. Obraztsy grecheskago tserkovnag asmoglasiia s primi͡echani͡iami prilozhenie k' sochineniiu pienii v provoslavnykh tserkrakh grecheskago vostoka. Moskva: Sinodal nais Tipografia, 1897.

1283. WELLESZ, Egon Joseph. Die hymnen der Ostkirche. Basel: Basilienses de musica orationes, 1962.
With musical illustrations.

See also: 456, 458, 481, 490, 499, 513, 514, 515, 529, 530, 531, 534, 535, 539, 540, 541, 544, 548, 549, 550, 551, 552, 777, 944, 1526, 2033, 2284, 2285, 2506, 2570, 2628, 2630, 2634, 2686, 2858, 2888, 2931, 2937, 3028, 3484, 3559, 3562, 3566, 3570, 3576, 3577, 3692, 3707, 3710, 3711, 4150, 5213, 5229.

Episcopal

1284. PROTESTANT Episcopal Church in the U.S.A.--Editorial Committee. Report to General Convention. New York: H. W. Gray Co., 1961.

1285. PROTESTANT Episcopal Church--Joint Commission. The Hymnal: What it is. New York: Protestant Episcopal, 1951.

1286. ________. Report of the Joint Commissions on Church Music. New York: Protestant Episcopal Church, Joint Comm., 1919, 1922, 1930, 1961.

1287. PROTESTANT Episcopal Church--Joint Commission. Report of the Joint Commission on Church Music. Providence: St. Dunstan's College of Sacred Music, 1930.

1288. SHEPHERD, Massey Hamilton. The Oxford American prayer book commentary. New York: Oxford Univ. Press, 1958.

1289. SOULE, William E. Music in the town and country church. New York: National Council of the Protestant Episcopal Church, 1958.

See also: 237, 379, 1509, 1676, 1887, 1935, 1936, 2267, 2433, 2434, 2435, 2436, 2876, 2989, 3055, 3104, 3310, 4740, 4742, 4745, 4854, 4853, 5000, 5028, 5357.

Evangelical and Lutheran Churches
(In Germany: Evangelical, Protestant, or Lutheran)

1290. ALTHAUS, Paul. Forschungen zur evangelischen Gebetslitteratur. reprt.--of Gütersloh 1927 ed. Hildesheim: G. Olms, 1966.

1291. BACHMANN, F. Grundlagen und Grundfragen zur evangelischen Kirchenmusik. N.G.: Gütersloh, 1899. (BM)

1292. BEITRÄGE zur Geschichte der evangelischen Kirchenmusik und Hymnologie in Kurhessen und Waldeck. Kassel: Bärenreiter, 1968.

1293. BLUME, Friedrich. Die evangelische Kirchenmusik. Vol. 10 of Handbuch des Musikwissenschaft. Potsdam: Akademische Verlagsgesellschaft, 1931.

1294. ______. Geschichte der evangelischen Kirchenmusik. Kassel, New York: Bärenreiter--Verlag, 1965.

1295. BORLISCH, Hans. Kleine Geschichte der evangelischen Kirchenmusik. Berlin: Merseburger, 1961.

1296. BUNNERS, Christian. Kirchenmusik und Seelenmusik. Göttingen: Vandenhoeck und Ruprecht, 1966.

1297. BURKHARD, Willy and Walter Tappolet. Evangelische Kirchenmusik; die Briefe von Willy Burkhard and Walter Tappolet. Zürich u. Stuttgart: Zwingli Verlag, 1964.

1298. COMMISSION on Hymnal. The Lutheran hymnal. St. Louis: Concordia Publishing House, 1941.

1299. DAVISON, A. J. Protestant church music in America. Boston: E. C. Schirmer Music Co., 1933.

1300. DICKINSON, Clarence. The influence of the Reformation on music, 1517-1917. New York: H. W. Gray Co., 1917.

1301. DIETZ, Philipp. Die Restauration des evangelischen Kirchenliedes. Eine Zusammenstellung der hauptsachlichsten literarischen Erstscheinungen auf hymnologischem Gebiete, namentlich dem Gebiete der Gesangbuchslitteratur seit dem Wiedererwachen des evangelischen Glaubenslebens in Deutschland. Marburg: N. G. Elwert, 1903.

1302. EGGE, Mandus A. Liturgy, theology, music in the Lutheran church; a series of lectures. Minneapolis: N.G., 1959.

1303. ETHERINGTON, Charles L. Protestant worship music. New York: Holt, Rinehart, and Winston, Inc., 1962.

1304. FEST der deutschen Kirchenmusik; Werke unserer Zeit. Berlin: Eckart-Verlag, 1937.

1305. FRANKE, Doris Elaine. Performance practices of the liturgy in the service book and hymnal of the Lutheran church. Abilene, Tex.: Hardin-Simmons Univ., 1961.

1306. GLABN, Henrik. Melodistudier till den lutherske salmesangs historie, fra 1524 til ca. 1600. København: Rosenkilde og Bagger, 1954.

1307. GRAUER, Albert W. The vocal style of Sixt Dietrich and Johann Eccard and their contributions to Lutheran church music. New York: Univ. of Rochester, 1959.

1308. HOELTY-NICKEL, Theodore. The musical heritage of the church. Valparaiso: Valparaiso Univ. Pamphlet Series, No. 2, 1946.

1309. ________. The musical heritage of the Lutheran church. St. Louis: Concordia Publishing House, 1959.

1310. HOOPER, William L. Church music in transition. Nashville, Tenn.: Broadman Press, 1963.

1311. HORN, Henry E. O sing unto the Lord; music in the Lutheran church. Philadelphia: Muhlenberg Press, 1956.

1312. HULTBERG, Mary Louise Hendricks. The chorale concertata per omnes versus. Ann Arbor: Univ. Microfilms, 1964.

1313. JENNY, Markus. Die Zukunft des evangelischen Kirchengesanges. Zurich: Theologischer Verlag, 1970.

1314. KEMPFF, G. Der Kirchengesang in lutherischen Gottesdienst und seine Erinnerung. Leipzig: M. Heinsius nachtfolger, 1937.
Schriften des Vereins für Reformationsgeschichte.

1315. KIDD, B. J. Documents illustrative of the continental reformation. Oxford: The Clarendon Press, 1911.

1316. KNAUTZ, Phillip Frederick. The status of music in the Texas District of the American Lutheran Church Synod. Austin: Univ. of Texas, 1954.

1317. KOCH, Eduard Emil. Geschichte des Kirchenlieds und Kirchengesangs der christlichen, insbesondere der deutschen evangelischen Kirche. reprt.--of Stuttgart 1866-77 ed. vol. 8. Hildesheim: G. Olms, 1972.

1318. KÜMMERLE, Salomon. Encykopädie der evangelischen Kirchenmusik. (Nachdr. d. Ausg. Gütersloh--1888-1895, Hildesheim.) New York: Olms, 1974.

1319. LANG, P. H. Church music--what's left of it. From Saturday Review of Literature, June 29, 1946.

1320. LEHMAN, Arnold Otto. The liturgical music of the Lutheran church in the first century of the Lutheran church: its sources and development and its influence upon church and sacred music. Cleveland, Ohio: Western Reserve Univ., 1964.

1321. ______. Music of the Lutheran church. Ann Arbor: Univ. Microfilms, 1967.

1322. LEUPOLD, Ulrich. Die liturgischen Gesänge der evangelischen Kirche im Zeitalter der Aufklärung und der Romantik. Kassel: Bärenreiter-Verlag, 1933.

1323. ______. A manual on intoning. Philadelphia: Board of Publication of the Lutheran Church in America, 1967.

1324. LEWIS, George Daniel. Factors common to protestant church choirs in Helena, Montana, and their relationship to public school music. Missoula, Mont.: Montana State Univ., 1952.

1325. LIEMOHN, Edwin. The organ and choir in protestant worship. Philadelphia: Fortress Press, 1968.

1326. LILIENCRON, Rochus. Die Aufgaben des Chorgesänges im heutigen evangelischen Gottesdienste. Oppeln: G. Maske, 1895.

1327. LUTHERAN Church--First and Second Convocation Addresses. Essays on church music. Pittsburgh, 1899 and Philadelphia: N.G., 1898. (LC-42-11497)

1328. ______--Curriculum Committee of the Board of Christian Education of the Evangelical Missouri and Ohio Synods, Ed. Missouri Synod curriculum in music for Lutheran schools. St. Louis: Concordia Publishing House, 1936.

1329. MATTFELD, Victor. Rhau's publications in the liturgy of the Lutheran church. New Haven, Conn.: Yale Univ., 1959.

1330. MOSER, Hans Joachim. Die evangelische Kirchenmusik en volkstümlichem Überblick. Stuttgart: J. Engelhorns nachf, 1926.

1331. NELLE, Wilhelm. Geschichte des deutschen evangelischen Kirchenliedes ... mit einem Titelbilde und 40 Abbildungen im Text. Vierte, unveränderte Auflage. Hildesheim: G. Olms, 1962.

1332. NORTH, Louise. The psalms and hymns of Protestantism. Madison, N.J.: Fairleigh Dickenson, 1936.

1333. PICARD, Isaac. La musique dans le culte protestant. In Encyclopédie de la musique et dictionnaire du Conservatoire ... Paris: 1913-31. 2 ptie (v. 4, 1929 p. 2399-2444).

1334. PROTESTANT church music in America. Boston: Schirmer Music Co., 1933.

1335. PROTESTANTISME et musique. Paris: Editions "Jesers," 1950.

1336. RABICH, Ernst. Der evangelische Kirchenmusikstil. Langensalza: H. Beyer & Söhne, 1909.

1337. RASELIUS, Andreas. Deutsche sonntaegliche Evangelienspruech. New York: C. F. Peters Corporation, 1967.

1338. REED, Luther D. Lutheran liturgy, The. Philadelphia: Muhlenberg Press, 1960.

1339. RESPONSE. St. Paul, Minn.: Lutheran Society for Worship, n.d.

1340. SANDER, Hans Adolf. Beiträge zur Geschichte des lutherischen Gottesdienstes und der Kirchenmusik in Breslau; die lateinischen Haupt--und Nebengottes--dienste im 16. and 17. Jahrhundert. Breslau: Priebatsch, 1937.

1341. SCHULZ, W. A. H. Studien über das deutsche protestanische monodische Berücksichtigung der Länder. Breslau: "Quader," Druckerei und Verlagsanstalt, g.m.b.h., 1934.

1342. SEELEY, Gilbert Stewart. German protestant choral music since 1925. Ann Arbor: Univ. Microfilms, 1969.

1343. SMITH, Carlton York. Early Lutheran hymnody in America, from the Colonial period to the year 1850. Los Angeles: Univ. of Southern California, 1956.

1344. SMITH, Florence. Protestant church music: With an account of its history and development. Butler, Ind.: Higley Press, 1949.

1345. SPEAKER, Lucy Lee. The status of the music education program in the churches of the Texas-Louisiana Synod of the United Lutheran Church in America. Austin: Univ. of Texas, 1958.

1346. STERN, Hermann. Leitfaden zur Grundausbildung in der evangelischen Kirchenmusik. Stuttgart-Hohenheim: Hänssler, 1969.

1347. STEVENSON, Robert M. Patterns of Protestant church music. Durham, N.C.: Duke Univ. Press, 1953.

1348. ________. Protestant church music in America: A short survey of men and movements from 1564 to the present. New York: Norton, 1966.

1349. STIER, Alfred. Kirchliches Singen. Gütersloh: Rufer-Verlag, 1952.

1350. THOMPSON, Doris B. Practical approach to Protestant Church Music. Denton, Tex.: North Texas State Univ., 1947.

1351. THULIN, Gabriel. Utredning angaende klockar, organist--och kantors--befattningarna, efter nadigt uppdrag utgiven. Stockholm: Tryckt hos P. Palmquists, 1919.

1352. TOLLE, Wilhelm. Grundformen des reformatorischen Schulliederbuches vorwiegend um 1600. Berlin: G. Kallmeyer, 1936.

1353. TRAMPE, Ronald Charles. Music administration in Texas District Missouri Synod Lutheran churches. Austin, Tex.: Univ. of Texas, 1958.

1354. TUCHER, Gottlieb. Schatz des evangelischen Kirchengesangs im ersten Jahrhundert der Reformation. Hildesheim, Ger.: Georg Olms--Reprint, 1967.

1355. VALPARAISO Seminars--Essay. The musical heritage of the church. St. Louis: Concordia Publishing House, 1944.

1356. WALDERSEE, Paul H. O. Sammlung musikalischer Vorträge. Leipzig: Breitkopf u. Härtel, 1878-79.

1357. WEBER, Heinrich. Über den evangelischen Kirchengesang; mit Notenbeispielen. Zurich: Druck von Orell Fussli & Co., 1889.

1358. WISLPHAL, Johannes. Das evangelische Kirchlied. Berlin: Auflage, Union--deutsche, 1925.

1359. WOLF, Edward Christopher. Lutheran church music in America during the eighteenth and early nineteenth centuries. Urbana, Ill.: Univ. of Illinois, 1960.

1360. WOLFRUM, Phillip. Die Enstehung und erste Entwicklung des deutschen evangelischen Kircheliedes Beziehung.

(neudr. Leipzig: Breitkopf u. Härtel, 1890.) Walluf bei Wiesbaden: M. Sandig, 1972.
The beginning and development of German protestant church songs (hymns) in musical in reference.

1361. ZEDDIES, L. R. Music education principles and practices in the elementary schools of the Lutheran church--Missouri Synod. Evanston: Northwestern Univ. Diss., 1958.

1362. ZIELKE, Dorothy Helen Meyer. A study of the liturgical settings for the communion service of the Lutheran church --Missouri Synod. Austin, Tex.: Univ. of Texas, 1966.

See also: 98, 115, 212, 263, 272, 344, 380, 391, 394, 487, 651, 818, 871, 892, 941, 988, 1029, 1287, 1363, 1452, 1497, 1519, 1564, 1624, 1644, 1681, 1696, 1698, 1713, 1785, 1790, 1794, 1797, 1839, 1835, 1892, 1894, 1898, 1909, 1918, 1939, 1989, 2028, 2030, 2043, 2064, 2065, 2080, 2081, 2128, 2129, 2151, 2156, 2157, 2240, 2241, 2253, 2260, 2272, 2274, 2279, 2305, 2345, 2378, 2471, 2478, 2508, 2533, 2546, 2565, 2575, 2589, 2591, 2594, 2596, 2659, 2678, 2705, 2719, 2728, 2729, 2736, 2759, 2767, 2775, 2780, 2788, 2800, 2835, 2890, 2918, 2966, 2893, 3090, 3126, 3130, 3138, 3179, 3183, 3186, 3188, 3289, 3294, 3302, 3323, 3385, 3406, 3408, 3416, 3421, 3424, 3425, 3426, 3431, 3441, 3442, 3454, 3455, 3459, 3461, 3466, 3472, 3474, 3477, 3583, 3608, 3615, 3628, 3672, 3738, 3826, 3827, 3839, 3919, 3922, 3944, 3963, 4199, 4208, 4258, 4393, 4398, 4477, 4478, 4481, 4484, 4488, 4567, 4588, 4709, 4746, 4815, 4835, 4838, 4839, 4857, 4878, 4907, 4968, 4976, 5021, 5100, 5101, 5107, 5124, 5129, 5131, 5132, 5214, 5320, 5324, 5420, 5443.

Evangelical and Reformed Church

See: 271, 1320, 1895, 2403, 2533, 4900.

Franciscans

See: 2485, 2539.

Holy Land Christians

See: 1636.

Huguenots

1363. DOUEN, Orentin. Clément Marot et le Psautier huguenot, étude historique, litteraire, musicale et bibliographique, contenant les mélodies primitives des psaumes et des specimens d'harmonie. Paris: Imprimerie nationale, 1879.

1364. VER, J. La cantilène huguenote de XVI siècle. Le psaume huguenot: structure, physionomie; renseignements; interpretation par le chant et l'harmonie. Realville: Chez l'auteur, 1918.

See also: 4488, 4832, 4858, 4868, 4878.

Islam

1365. BESMER, Fremont E. Kídan clárán sállà: music for the eve of Muslim festivals of Id al-fitr and Id al-Kabir in Kano, Nigeria (Indiana Univ. Diss.). Bloomington, Ind.: African Studies Program of Indiana Univ., 1973.

1366. EL KHOLY, S. A. The function of music in Islamic culture (in the period up to A.D. 1100). Edinburgh, Scotland: Edinburgh Univ., 1953-1954.

1367. FRIEDLANDER, Ira. The whirling dervishes, being an account of the Sufi order known as the Mevlevis and its founder, the poet and mystic Mevlana Jalau'ddin Rumi. Music section by Nezih Uzel. New York: Collier Books, 1975.

1368. JENKINS, Jean and Paul Rovsing Olsen. Music and musical instruments in the world of Islam. Line drawings by J. Pringle. London: World of Islam Festival Publ. Co., 1976.

Jesuit (R.C.)

1369. CULLEY, Thomas D. Jesuits and Music, Volume 1. St. Louis and Rome: Jesuit Historical Institute, 1970.

1370. WITTWER, Max. Die Musikpflege im Jesuitenorden unter besonderer Berücksichtigung der Länder deutscher Zunge. Greifswald: Inaug. diss.--Greifswald, 1934. (LC-ML3002. W83MS)

Jewish

1371. ADLER, Israël. Hebrew writings concerning music in manuscripts and printed books from Geonic times up to 1800. München: G. Henle Verlag, 1975.

1372. _______. La pratique musicale savante dans quelques communautes juives en Europe aux XVIIe et XVIIIe siècles. Gravenhage: Mouton & Co., 1966.

1373. BACH, Carl Philipp Emanuel. Die Israeliten in der Wüste. Berlin: Bote & Bock, 1955.

1374. BEDFORD, Arthur. The temple musick; an essay concerning the method of singing the Psalms of David in the temple, before the Babylonish captivity. London: H. Morthlock, 1706.

1375. BINDER, Abraham Wolf. The Jewish movement in America: an informal lecture. New ed. with additional information. New York: Jewish Music Council of the National Jewish Welfare Board, 1975.

1376. BOX, Rev. G. H. Judaism in the Greek period. London: Oxford Univ. Press, 1932.

1377. BROD, Max. Die musik Israels. (rev. ed.) Kassel: Bärenreiter, 1951.

1378. DRUBECK, Ida M. Ritual music of the Jewish synagogue. Madison, Wis.: Univ. of Wisconsin, 1937.

1379. EISENSTEIN, Judith (Kaplan). The scope of Jewish music. New York: National Jewish Music Council, 1948.

1380. FELLERER, Karl Gustav, Gen. Ed. Anthology of music, Vol. 20. Hebrew music. (Werner) New York: A. Broude, Inc., n.d.

1381. FRIEDLANDER, Arthur M. Facts and theories relating to Hebrew music. London: Reeves, 1924.

1382. GRAVER, Victor. Hebrew chant in the daily liturgy of the synagogue. Middletown, Conn.: Wesleyan Univ., 1961.

1383. HESKES, J. (prepared by). Jewish music programs: concerts, liturgical services, and special events; a sampling from the Jewish music festivals, 1970-1973. New York: Jewish Music Council of the National Jewish Welfare Board, 1974.

1384. IDELSOHN, Abraham Zebi. Hebräisch--Orientalischer Melodienschatz. Leipzig: N.G., 1914.

1385. _______. Jewish liturgy and its development. New York: Henry Holt & Co., 1932.

1386. _______. Jewish liturgy and its development. (Reprint) New York: Schocken Books, 1967.

1387. _______. Jewish music in its historical development. New York: Henry Holt & Co., 1929.

1388. ________. Jewish music in its historical development. (Reprint) New York: Schocken Books, 1960.

1389. KAISER and SPARGER. A collection of the principal melodies of synagogue. Chicago: Rubovits, 1893.

1390. LENTSCHNER, Sofie. The four hymns appended to the Passover Haggadah of the German Jews. New York: New York Univ., 1939.

1391. MANN, Isak. Zur Geschichte der synagogalen Musik. Vienna: Vienna Univ., 1931.

1392. MILHAUD, Darius. Sacred service for the Sabbath morning. Westminster: Trans. fr. "Service-sacré" pour le samedi matin. Paris: Salabert, 1950.

1393. MOORE, George Foot. Judaism. Cambridge: Harvard Univ. Press, 1927.

1394. NETTL, Paul. Some early Jewish musicians. From Musical Quarterly, January, 1931.

1395. NULMAN, Macy. Concise encyclopedia of Jewish music. New York: McGraw-Hill, 1975.

1396. ________. Ma'ariv chants. New York: Cantorial Training Institute of Yeshive University, n.d.

1397. OESTERLY, W. O. E. The Jewish background of the Christian Liturgy (pre-Gregorian Period). London: Oxford, 1925.

1398. ________. Music of the Hebrews in Oxford history of Music. London: Oxford Univ. Press, 1925.

1399. PALM, Richard C. Hebrew origins and vocal practice of music in the early Christian church to 500 A.D. Denton, Tex.: North Texas State Univ., 1954.

1400. PORTNOY, Joseph L. Music curriculum for Jewish religious schools. New York: Union of American Hebrew Congregations, 1967.

1401. ROTHMÜLLER, Aron Marko. Du Musik der Juden. Zürick: Pan Verlag, 1951.

1402. ________. The music of the Jews: An historical appreciation. (New and rev. ed.) Cranbury, N.J.: A. S. Barnes, 1975.

1403. SALESKI, Gdal. Famous musicians of Jewish origin. New York: Bloch Pub. Co., 1949.

1404. SAMINSKY, Lazare. The music of the Ghetto and the Bible. New York: Bloch Publishing Co., 1934.

1405. SCHAUSS, Hayyim. The Jewish festivals. Cincinnati: Union of American Hebrew Congregations, 1938.

1406. SCHÖNBERG, Jakob. Die traditionellen Gesänge des israelitischen Gottesdienstes in Deutschland. Musikwissenschaftliche Untersuchung der in A. Baers "Baal T'fillah" gesammelten Synagogengesänge. Erlangen, Germany: Erlangen Univ., 1925.

1407. ________. Die traditionellen Gesänge des israelitischen Gottesdienstes in Deutschland. Nürnberg: Buch-und Kunstdruckerei E. Spandel, 1926.

1408. ________. Die traditionellen Gesänge des israelitischen Gottesdienstes in Deutschland; musikwissenschaftliche Untersuchung der in A. Baers Baal T'fillah gesammelten Synagogengesänge. (repr.--Spandel, 1926) Hildesheim and New York: G. Olms, 1971.

1409. SENDREY, Alfred. Bibliography of Jewish music. New York: Columbia Univ. Press, 1951.

1410. SHERMAN, Shirley Biller. The history of Hebrew and Jewish music in the temple and synagogue. Evanston, Ill.: Northwestern Univ., 1949.

1411. SINGER, Benedikt. Beiträge zur Geschichte der Musik Synagogale Gesänge. Prag: J. W. Pascheles, 1887.

1412. SINGER, Josef. Die Tonarten des traditionellen Synagogengesänges (steiger); ihr Verhältnis zu den Kirchentonarten und den Tonarten der vorchristlichen Musikperiode. Erläutert und durch Notenbeispiele erklärt. Wien: E. Wetzler, 1886.

1413. SPECTOR, Johanna L. A comparative study of scriptural cantillation and accentuation: Pentatuch. Cincinnati: Hebrew Union College, 1950.

1414. WAGNER, Richard. Die Kunst und die Revolution. Das Judentum in der Musik. Was ist deutsch? Hrsg. u. kommentiert von T. Kneif. München: Rogner und Bernhard, 1975.

1415. WALBE, Joel. Der Gesang Israels und seine Quellen: ein Beitrag zur hebräischen Musikologie. Hamburg: H. Christians, 1975.

1416. WEISSER, Albert. Bibliography of publications and other resources on Jewish music. New York: Nat. Jewish Council, 1969.

1417. WERNER, Eric. Contributions to a historical study of Jewish music. New York: KTAV Publishing House, 1976.

1418. ______. Contributions to a systematic study of Jewish music. New York: KTAV Publishing House, 1975.

1419. ______. A voice still heard: The sacred songs of the Ashkenazic Jews. University Park, Pa.: Penn. State Univ. Press, 1976.

See also: 282, 283, 676, 1644, 2152, 2251, 2729, 2877, 4762, 5352.

Knights of Jesus Christ

See: 3552.

Maronite Church

1420. PHARES, Emmanuel. La semaine des liturgies catholiques. La liturgie de l'église maronite. Paris: Eglise maronite de Nôtre Dame du Liban, 1926.

See also: 4119.

Mennonites

1421. HOSTETLER, Lester. Handbook to the Mennonite hymnary. Newton, Kan.: Mennonite Church Board of Publications, 1949.

1421a. ______ and Walter Hohmann. The Mennonite Hymnary. Newton, Kan.: Mennonite Publication Office, 1940.

1422. JOST, Walter James. Hymn tune tradition of the General Conference--Mennonite Church. Ann Arbor: Univ. Microfilms, 1966.

1423. Ein UNPARTHEYISCHES Gesang-buch enthaltend gristreiche Lieder und Psalmen, zum allgemeinen Gebrauch des wahren Gottesdienstes. Auf Begehren der Bruderschaft der Menonisten Gemeinen aus vielen Liederbüchern gesammelt. Mit einem dreyfachen Register. Lancaster, Pa.: Gedruckt bey Georg und Peter Albrecht, 1808.

1424. YODER, P. M. Nineteenth century sacred music of the Mennonite Church in the United States. Tallahassee: Florida State Univ., Diss., 1961.

Methodist

1425. CHRISTOPHERS, S. W. The Epworth singers and other poets of Methodism. New York: Randolph & Co., 1874.

1426. CREAMER, David. Methodist hymnology: comprehending notices of the poetical works of John and Charles Wesley. New York: David Creamer, 1848.

1427. HOOKS, Sylvia Marquita. The status of music in the Methodist churches of Texas. Austin, Tex.: Univ. of Texas, 1954.

1428. LIGHTWOOD, J. T. Music of the Methodist hymn book, The. London: The Epworth Press, 1935.

1429. ________. Stories of Methodist music. London: The Epworth Press, 1928.

1430. MANTRIPP. J. C. The devotional use of the Methodist hymn book. London: The Epworth Press, 1934.

1431. OUR hymnody: A manual of the Methodist hymnal. Nashville: Abingdon Press, 1937.

1432. PRICE, Carl F. The music and hymnody of the Methodist Hymnal. New York: Eaton and Maixs, 1911.

1433. STEVENS, Abel. The history of the religious movement called Methodism. 3 Vols. New York: Carlton and Porter, 1858-1861.

1434. TELFORD, John. The new Methodist hymn book illustrated in history and experience. London: The Epworth Press, 1934.

1435. VOIGT, Edwin E. Methodist worship in the church universal. New York: Abingdon Press, n.d.

1436. WALKER, Albert H. How to receive and use the new Methodist hymn book. London: The Epworth Press, 1933.

1437. WILLIAMS, Huw. Tonau a'u hawduron. Caernarfon: Llyfrfa'r Methodistiaid, 1967.

See also: 1911, 2206, 2300, 2348, 2353, 2384, 2390, 2467, 2610, 2691, 2993, 3056, 3273, 3499, 4650, 4652, 4654, 4656, 4661, 4662, 4665, 4667, 4669, 5087.

Methodist Episcopal

1438. HILL, Double E. A study of tastes in American church music as reflected in the music of the Methodist Episcopal church to 1900. Urbana, Ill.: Illinois Univ., 1962.

1439. WALKER, John Mann, et al. Better music in our churches. New York: Methodist Book Concern, 1923.

Moravian

1440. BIRD, Ruth Holmes. Music among the Moravians. Rochester: Univ. of Rochester Press, 1956.

1441. DAVID, Hans T. Music of the Moravians in America from the archives of the Moravian church at Bethlehem, Pennsylvania. N.G.: N.G., n.d.

1442. KEEN, James A. Some musical aspects of the Moravian church including Easter service at Winston-Salem. Iowa City: Iowa Univ., 1935.

1443. McCORKLE, Donald Macomber. An introduction to the musical culture of the North Carolina Moravians in the eighteenth century. Bloomington, Ind.: Indiana Univ., 1953.

1444. ________. Moravian music in Salem; a German-American heritage. Bloomington, Ind.: Indiana Univ., 1958.

1445. RAU, Albert George. A catalogue of music by American Moravians. Bethlehem, Pa.: Moravian Seminary and College for Women, 1938.

See also: 1100, 3301, 3638, 5317.

Mozarabe

See: 1151, 2474, 3703.

Orthodox Greek Catholic

1446. CAVARNOS, Constantine. Byzantine sacred music: The traditional music of the Orthodox church, its nature, purpose and execution. Belmont, Mass.: Institute for Byzantine and Modern Greek Studies, 1974.

1447. RUELLE, Charles Emile. Etudes sur l'ancienne musique grecque. Paris: Imprimerie nationale, 1875.

Pilgrim and Pentecostal

1448. ALFORD, Delton L. Music in the Pentecostal church. Cleveland, Tenn.: Pathway Press, 1967.

1449. RONANDER, Albert G. and Ethel K. Porter. Guide to the Pilgrim hymnal. Philadelphia: United Church Press, 1966.

Presbyterian

1450. The CHURCH harmony. (British Presbyterian) New York: Oxford Univ. Press, 1927.

1451. MARTIN, Raymond Jones. The transition from psalmody to hymnody in Southern Presbyterianism, 1753-1901. New York: Union Theological Seminary, 1963.

1452. MILO, D. W. L. Zangers en speellieden, bijdrage tot de ontwikkeling van een calvinistische kerkmuziek. Goes: Oosterbaan & Le Cointre, 1946.

1453. OHLSSON, Gordon Lewis. A proposed program for improving choral music in the Presbyterian churches of a three-state area (Nebraska-Colorado-Wyoming) through the facilities of Hastings College, Hastings, Nebraska. New York: Columbia Univ., 1961.

1454. SHORT, Naomi Carrington. The status of music in the Presbyterian churches of Texas. Austin, Tex.: Univ. of Texas, 1957.

1455. TAYLOR, H. V. and J. M. Kelly. Our singing church. Philadelphia: Board of Christian Education, Presbyterian Church in the U.S.A., 1951.

See also: 1884, 2228, 3499.

Protestant Episcopal in the U.S.A.

1456. DOUGLAS, Charles Winfred, ed. The Saint Dunstan edition Kyrie rex splendens elevson. New York: H. W. Gray Co., n.d.

1457. FENTON, William Conner. The role of music in the Protestant Episcopal Church of the Diocese of Southern Ohio. Ann Arbor: Univ. Microfilms, 1967.

1458. LOWRIE, Walter. St. Paul's Within-the-Walls. from Historical Magazine of the Protestant Episcopal Church. March, 1750.

1459. REPORT to General Convention 1961. New York: H. W. Gray Co., Inc., 1961. (Protestant Episcopal Church)

1460. SOWERBY, Leo. Ideals in church music. Greenwich, Conn.: Seabury Press, 1956.

See also: 2167, 4853, 4855, 5028, 5357.

Puritans

1461. EARLE. The Sabbath in Puritan New England. New York: Scribner, 1891.

1462. SCHOLES, Percy. The Puritans in music in England and New England. New York: Russell & Russell, Inc., 1962.

See also: 1045.

Reformed Church of Switzerland

1463. SCHNEIDER, Charles. L'évolution musicale de l'Eglise réformée de 1900 à nos jours. Avec cinq oeuvres musicales de Luther et Calvin. Neuchâtel: Delachaux & Niestlé, 1952.

Salvation Army

1464. SLATER. The Salvation Army dictionary of music. London, New York: Salvation Army Book Department, 1908.

See also: 2164.

Santiago

See: 3554.

Shaker

1465. COOK, Harold. Shaker music: A manifestation of American folk culture. Cleveland, Ohio: Western Reserve Univ., 1947. Also avail. as repr. Lewisburg, Pa.: Bucknell Univ. Press, 1973.

1466. PEARSON, E. J. Neal and W. Whitehall. The Shaker image. New York: Graphic Publ., 1974.

1467. THOMASON, Jean Healan. Shaker manuscript hymnals from South Union, Kentucky (Shakers--The Millenial Church). Bowling Green: Kentucky Folklore Soc., 1967.

Society of Friends

1468. FRIENDS, Society of. A gateway to good will, by Peace Education Committee of Philadelphia Yearly Meeting of Friends. Philadelphia: Society of Friends, 1924.

See also: 3182.

Society of St. Gregory

See: 1125, 4207.

Syrian

See: 2862.

Unitarian

See: 2328.

United Church of Canada

See: 2613.

United Presbyterian

1469. DOUGHTY, Gavin Lloyd. The history and development of music in the United Presbyterian Church in the U.S.A. Ann Arbor: Univ. Microfilms, 1966.

DESCANT

1470. BUKOFZER, Manfred. Geschichte des englischen Diskants und des Fauxbourdons nach den theoretischen Quellen. Sammlung musikwissenschaftlicher Abhandlungen. Strassburg: Heitz and Co., 1936.

1471. The DESCANT carol book. London: Novello & Co., n.d.

1472. FRY, Henry S. Eighteen descants on well-known hymn tunes. Philadelphia: Theodore Presser Co., 1931.

1473. GEORGIADES, T. Englische diskanttraktate aus der ersten Hälfte des 15. Jahrhunderts. Munich: N.G., 1937. Schriftenreihe des Musikwissenschaftliches Seminars der Universität München, 1937.

1474. GRAY, Alan. A book of descants. London: Oxford Univ. Press, 1926.

1475. SHAW, Geoffrey. The descant hymn-tune book. London: Novello & Co., 1956.

1476. _______. The descant hymn-tune book. New York: H. W. Gray, n.d.

1477. The TENOR tune book. London: The Faith Press, 1921.

1478. THIRTY-six descants with accompaniments for use with the English hymnal. London: Oxford Univ. Press, n.d.

1479. WILLIAMS, David McK. Thirty-four hymn descants. New York: H. W. Gray Co., 1948.

1480. WINN, Cyril. Forty-one descants to familiar hymn tunes. Fair Lawn, N.J.: Oxford Univ. Press, 1961.

See also: 14, 52, 689, 1629, 1632, 1652, 2534.

DICTIONARIES, LEXICONS and GLOSSARIES

1481. APEL, Willi. The Harvard dictionary of music. Cambridge, Mass.: Harvard Univ. Press, 1944, 1956.

1482. BAKER, Theodore. Baker's biographical dictionary of musicians. N.G.: Paul Pisk, 1938. (New York: G. Schirmer, 1940, 4th ed. rev.)

1483. BELL, Holly. A Christmas dictionary. Boston: Whittemore Associates, Inc., 1953.

1484. BONACCORSI, Alfredo. Nuovo dizionario musicale curci, con zilografie di Diego Pettinelli. Milano: Curci, 1954.

1485. BOUMAN, Leon C. Vreemden woorden in de musiek. Gronigen: E. P. Noordhoof, 1950.

1486. BRINKHOFF, Lucas. Liturgisch woordenboek. Roermond: J. J. Romen, 1958-1962.

1487. BROSSARD, Sebastien de. Dictionnaire de musique, contenant une explication des termes Grecs, Latins, Italiens et Français, les plus usitês dans la musique. New York: Broude Brothers Limited (Facsimile), 1964. (Orig. -- Paris: C. Ballard, 1703)

1488. BULL, Sverre Hagerup. Musikkens verden. Oslo: Musikkens verden forlag, 1951.

1489. CLAYTON, D. A dictionary of music terms. Croydon: N.G., 1932. (BM)

1490. COCKING, F. H. The composer's vade-mecum: English-Italian dictionary of musical terms. London: Augener, 1913.

1491. COOK, E. F. Dictionary of musical terms. N.G.: H. J. Drane, 1911. (BM)

1492. COOVER, James B. *A bibliography of music dictionaries.* Denver: Denver Public Library, 1952.

1493. _______. *Music lexicography--(third edition).* Carlisle, Pa.: Carlisle Books, 1971.

1494. CORTE, Andrea della. *Diccionario de la musica.* Buenos Aires: Ricordi Americana, 1950.

1495. _______. *Dizionario di musica.* Torino: G. B. Paravia, 1952.

1496. CUMMINGS, W. H. *Dictionary of musicians.* London: Novello & Co., 1934.

1497. DAVIDSON, James Robert. *A dictionary of protestant church music.* Metuchen, N.J.: Scarecrow Press, 1975.

1498. DOLZHANSKII, A. *Kratiĭ muzuikalniĭ slovar.* Leningrad: Gos. muzuikalnoyu izd-vo, 1952.

1499. ECKEL, Frederick L. *A concise dictionary of ecclesiastical terms.* Boston: Whittemore Associates, Inc., 1963.

1500. *ENCYCLOPEDIE des musiques sacrées.* Publiée sous la direction de Jacques Porte. Paris: Editions Lagergerie, 1968.

1501. ENGEL, Yu D. *Kratkii muzikalnii slovar,* (translit.). Mockva: N.G., 1907.

1502. FISCHER, Albert Friedrich Wilheim. *Kirchenlieder-Lexikon.* reprt.--of Gotha 1878-79 ed. vol. 1. Hildesheim: G. Olms, 1967.

1503. GILBERT, Will G. *Musikall zaklexicon; een vraagbaak vor de muziek beoefenaar en concertbezoeker.* Den Haag: J. P. Kruseman, 1951.

1504. GORDON, H. A. *Gordon's pocket dictionary of musical terms.* New York: Estate of Hamilton S. Gordon, 1923.

1505. GRASSINEAU, James. *A musical dictionary, being a collection of terms and characters, as well ancient as modern, including the historical, theoretical and practical parts of music.* London & New York: Broude Bros., 1965. (Facs. Repr. of 1st ed. 1740.)

1506. _______. *A musical dictionary, containing a full explanation of all the terms made use of ... new edition, with an appendix selected from the dictionnaire de musique of M. Rousseau.* New York: Scientific Library Service, 1966.

1507. GROVE, Sir George. Dictionary of music and musicians. London, New York: Macmillan and Co., 1879-89, 1890. New editions issued periodically.

1508. GROVE'S dictionary of music and musicians. (Vol. 1-6.) Philadelphia, Pa.: Theodore Presser Co., 1927, 1958.

1509. GRUM, Rolfe P., comp. A dictionary of the Episcopal church. Baltimore, Md.: Trefoil Publishing Society, 1950.

1510. HOPKINSON, Cecil. Dictionary of Parisian music publishers, A. London: The author, 1954.

1511. HUGHES, Anselm. Liturgical terms for music students: A dictionary. Boston: McLaughlin & Reilly Co., 1940.

1512. HULL, A. E. Dictionary of modern music and musicians. London & Toronto: J. M. Dent & Sons, Ltd., 1924.

1513. ILLING, Robert. A dictionary of music. Harmondsworth, Middlesex: Penguin Books, 1950.

1514. JULIAN, John. A dictionary of hymnology. New York: Alexander Broude, Inc., n.d.

1515. _______. A dictionary of hymnology. Vol. II. New York: Dover Publications, Inc., 1957.

1516. _______. Dictionary of hymnology. London: J. Murray, 1891. also--rev. eds. London: J. Murray, 1907, 1915, 1925.

1517. KORNMÜLLER, Utto. Lexikon der kirchlichen Tonkunst. Nachdr. d. Ausg. 1891 u. 1895. 2 vols. Hildesheim and New York: Olms, 1975.

1518. KOTHE, Bernhard. Musikalisch-liturgisches Wörterbuch. Für alle Freunde der Kirchenmusik, insbesondere zum Handgebrauche für Chordirigenten. Breslau: F. Goerlich, 1890.

1519. KÜMMERLE, Salomon. Encyklopädie der evangelischen Kirchenmusik bearbeitet und herausgegeben. Gütersloh: C. Bertelsmann, 1895.

1520. LESAGE, Robert. Dictionnaire pratique de liturgie romain. Paris: Bonne Press, 1952.

1521. LICHTENTHAL P. Dizionario di musica. New York: Scientific Library Service, 1826.

1522. MUSIKIN, Tietokirja. Toimitsukunta: Toivo Haapanen (et al.). Helsingissä: Kustannusosakeyhtiö Otava, 1948.

1523. NIECKS, F. Consise dictionary of musical terms. London: Augener & Co. also New York: G. Schirmer, 1884.

1524. OLLARD, S. L. A dictionary of English church history. London: A. R. Mowbray & Co., also Milwaukee: The Young Churchman Co., 1912.

1525. ORITGUE, Joseph Louis D'. Dictionnaire liturgique, historique et théorique de plain-chant et de musique d'église au Moyen Age et dans les temps modernes. Paris: J. P. Migne, 1860. Also, reprint--New York: Da Capo Press, 1971.

1526. PREOBRAZHENSKII, Antonin Viktorovich. Slovar' russkavo tserkovnago pieniia A. Preobrazhenskii. Moscow: A. A. Levenson, 1896.

1527. PULVER, Jeffrey. Biographical dictionary of old English music. New York: Kegan Paul, French, Frubner, 1927.

1528. RIEMANN, C. W. J. H. Dictionary of music. 4th ed. Trans.-J. S. Shadlock. London: Augener, 1908.

1529. _______. Dictionnaire de musique. Trans. G. Humbert. Lausanne: Payot et cie, 1913.

1530. _______. Hugo Riemanns Musik-Lexikon. Leipzig: Verlag des Bibliographischen Instituts, 1882.

1531. _______. Hugo Riemanns Musik-Lexikon. Leipzig: Hesse, 1900; 1905; 1916; 1919; 1912; 1929 and Mainz: B. Schott, 1939.

1532. _______. Moozikalnuii slovar. Moskva: P. I͡urgenson, 1904.

1533. ROUSSEAU, Jean Jacques. Dictionnaire de musique. Amsterdam: M. M. Rey, 1768.

1534. SACHS, Curt. Real-Lexikon der Musikinstrumente. New York: Dover Publications, Inc., 1964.

1535. SAINSBURY, John S. A dictionary of musicians from the earliest times. New York: Alexander Broude, Inc., 1966.

1536. SARDA, A. Lexico tecnologica musical en varios idiomas. Madrid: Unión Musicala Española, 1929.

1537. SCHOLES, Percy A. The Oxford companion to music. New York: Oxford Univ. Press, 1947.

1538. SLONIMSKY, ed. Baker's biographical dictionary of musicians. New York: G. Schirmer, 1958.

1539. SOHLMANS Musiklexikon: nordiskt och allmänt uppslags-verk för tonkonst, musikliv och dans. Redaktion: Carl Allan Moberg, och, Einar Sundström. Stockholm: Sohlman, 1948; 2nd ed. 1975.

1540. STAINER and Barrett. Dictionary of musical terms. Boston: O. Ditson & Co.; New York: C. H. Ditson & Co., 1876.

1541. STUBBINGS, G. W. Dictionary of church music, A. New York: Philosophical Library, Inc., 1950.

1542. VOWLES, W. Tenebrae Tonale. London: Burns & Oates, 1914.

1543. WEISSENBACK, Andreas. Sacra musica: lexikon der katholischen Kirchemusik. Klosterneuburg: Verlag der Augustinus-druckerei, 1937.

1544. WILLIAMS, Nyal and Peggy Daub. Coover's music lexicography-two supplements (I) dictionaries in RISM and not in Coover and (II) [A] corrections and additions to entries, and [B] additional dictionaries. Ann Arbor: Music Library Association, --in "NOTES" Vol. 30, March, 1974.

1545. WOTTON, T. S. Dictionary of foreign musical terms. New York: Breitkopf & Härtel, 1907.

See also: 217, 246, 1172, 1464, 1695, 2086, 2738, 2783, 2952, 3253, 3439, 3715, 3903, 3938, 5210, 5222, 5224, 5226, 5230, 5231, 5319.

DRAMA--RELIGIOUS

1546. BAXTER, Kay. The church and contemporary theater. England: SCM Press, 1964.

1547. BENNETT, Gordon. The reader's theater comes to church. Richmond, Va.: John Knox Press, 1971.

1548. COLLINS, Fletcher. The production of medieval church music-drama. Charlottesville: Univ. Press of Virginia, 1972.

1549. COUSSEMAKER, Edmond de, ed. Drames liturgiques du Moyen-Age: texte et musique. (Text in Latin, critical matter in French. reprint, 1860 Rennes ed.) Genève: Statkine Reprints, 1975.

1550. _______. Drames liturgiques de Moyen Age. New York: Broude Brothers, 1965.

1551. DOMINGOS DO ROSARIO, Padre. Theatro ecclesiastico, em que se acham muitos Documentos de Cantochao para qualquer pessoa dedicada ao Culto Divino nos officios do coro e altar offerecido a Virgem Santissima Ordem, correcto e accrescentado ... pelo Padra Angelo da conceicao. Quinto Impressao. New York: Scientific Library Service, 1774.

1552. EHRENSPERGER, Harold. Religious drama: Ends and means. Nashville, Tenn.: Abingdon Press, 1966.

1553. GREENBERG, Noah. The play of Daniel. Fair Lawn, N.J.: Oxford Univ. Press, 1959.

1554. _______. The play of Herod. Fair Lawn, N.J.: Oxford Univ. Press, 1965.

1555. HOLLMAN, Wilbur W., adapted by. The Maastricht Easter play (a twelfth century liturgical music drama). A modern adaptation. New York: G. Schirmer, Inc., n.d.

1556. HOWELL, Cyril Edwin. Twenty questions on pageants in church. London: A. R. Mowbray & Co., 1950.

1557. LE FLEMING, Christopher. The use of music in religious drama. London: S.P.C.K., 1950.

1558. LEWIS, A. and N. Fortune, eds. Opera and church music. London and New York: Oxford Univ. Press, 1975.

See also: 1650, 1856.

ECUMENICAL

1559. ROBBINS, Howard Chandler. Ecumenical trends in hymnody. New York: Commission on Worship, 1941.

See also: 2380.

ENCYCLOPEDIAS

1560. BARDY, Gustave. Le Crist: encyclopêdie populaire des connaissances christologiques, publicée sous la direction de m. l'abbê G. Bardy et de m. l'abbê A. Tricot ... avec le concours de m. l'abbê R. Aigrain. Preface de s. ex. m Pic ... collaborateurs; abbê Aigrain, abbê Amann, abbê Bardy. Paris: Bloud et Gay, 1932.

1561. The CATHOLIC encyclopedia. New York: The Encyclopedia Press, 1913.

1562. COX, Norman W. Encyclopedia of Southern Baptists. Vol. I & II. Nashville, Tenn.: Broadman Press, 1958.

1563. ELSON, Louis C., Ed. University musical encyclopedia. New York: The University Society, 1912-14.

1564. KUEMMERLE, S. Encyklopädie der evangelischen Kirchenmusik. Gütersloh: C. Bertelsmann, 1888-95.

1565. McCLINTOCK and Strong. Cyclopaedia of biblical, theological, and ecclesiastical literature. New York: Harper, 1867-85.

1566. THOMPSON, Oscar, ed. The international cyclopedia of music and musicians. New York: Dodd, Mead & Co., 1964. 10th ed. Bruce Bohle, ed., 1975.

See also: 1318, 1395, 1519, 1542, 3251.

EPHRATA

1567. SACHSE, Julius Friedrich. The music of the Cloister: A critical and legendary history of the Ephrata Cloister and the Dunkers. N.G.: N.G., n.d. (LC; Bx7817 P453 v.2)

1568. ______. The music of the Ephrata Cloister. Lancaster: The Society, 1903.

ESSAYS

1569. ESSAYS on church music. Pittsburgh: N.G., 1899. (LC-4211497)

1570. HODGES, Edward. An apology for church music and music festivals, in answer to the Animad versions of the standard and the record. London: Rivingtons, 1834.

1571. LAW, Andrew. Essays on music. Philadelphia: printed for the author, 1814. (LC 5-20197 res.)

1572. OLTE, Rudolf. The idea of the holy; religious essays. London: Oxford Univ. Press, 1931.

1573. PARKHURST, Howard Elmore. Rambles in music-land. New York: C. Fischer, 1914.

1574. PRATT, Waldo Selden. The church music problem. New York: The Century Co., 1887.

1575. SECCOMB, Joseph. An essay to excite a further inquiry into the ancient matter and manner of sacred singing. Boston: S. Kneeland & T. Green, 1741.

See also: 76, 526, 997, 1754, 3269, 4645, 4665, 4688, 4811.

ESTHETICS

1576. ANGELOV, Krum. *Osnovi na muzikalnata estetika.* Sofia: Nauka i izkystvo (IAmbol, pech. G. Dimitrov), 1973.

1577. BEARDSLEY, Monroe. *Aesthetics from classical Greece to the present.* New York: Macmillan Company, 1966.

1578. BENESTAD, Finn. *Musikk og tanke: Hovedretninger i musikkestetikkens fra antikken til vår egen tid.* Oslo: H. Aschehoug & Co., 1976.

1579. BERNSTEIN, Leonard. *The joy of music.* New York: Simon and Schuster, Inc., 1959.

1580. BUSONI, Ferruccio. *The essence of music and other papers.* New York: Dover Publications, Inc., n.d.

1581. DEBUSSY, Claude, Ferrucio Busoni, and Charles Ives. *Three classics in the aesthetic of music.* New York: Dover Publications, 1962.

1582. DUDLEY, Louise and Austin Faricy. *The humanities: Applied aesthetics, fourth edition.* New York: McGraw-Hill Book Co., 1967.

1583. EGGLI, Eva. *Probleme der musikalischen Wertästhetik im 19. Jahrhundert. Ein Versuch zur schlechten Musik.* Winterthur: Keller, 1965.

1584. FUBINI, Enrico. *L'estetica musicale dall' antichità al settecento.* 1. ed. Torino: G. Einaudi, 1976.

1585. GOLDSCHMIDT, Hugo. *Die Musikästhetik des 18. Jahrhunderts.* Hildesheim, Germany: Georg Olms-Reprint, 1967. (orig. Zurich: 1915.)

1586. HAND, F. *Aesthetics of musical art.* London: W. Reeves, 1911.

1587. HANNUM, Harold Byron. *Christian search for beauty: a review of the relationship of the arts, particularly music, to the principles of Christianity.* Nashville: Southern Pub. Association, 1975.

1588. HANSLICK, Edward. *The beautiful in music.* London: Novello and Co., 1891.

1589. HARMAN, A. and A. Milner. *Man and his music.* London: Barrie and Rockliff, 1959.

1590. HASTINGS, Thomas. *Dissertation on musical taste; general principles of taste applied to the art of music.* New York: Mason Brothers, 1853, (earlier edition, 1822).

1591. HELMHOLTZ, Hermann. Die Lehre von dem Tonempfindungen als physiologische Grundlage für die Theorie der Musik. Braunschwieg, F. Vieweg, 1865. On the sensations of tone as a physiological basis for the theory of music. Translated, thoroughly rev. and corrected by Alex. J. Ellis. 4th ed. London, New York: Longmans, Green, 1912.

1592. HILBRICH, Paul Day. The aesthetic of the counter-reformation and religious painting and music in Bologna. Ann Arbor: Univ. Microfilms, 1969.

1593. JAKOB. Die Kunst im Dienste der Kirche. Laudshut: Thomann, 1885.

1594. LEE, H. N. Perception and aesthetic value. New York: Prentice-Hall, inc., 1938 also Johnson Reprint.

1595. McCLINTON, K. M. Christian church art through the ages. New York: Macmillan Co., 1962.

1596. MEYER. Emotion and meaning in music. Chicago: Univ. of Chicago Press, 1966.

1597. MILA, Massimo. L'esperienza musical e l'estetica. Torino: Einaudi, 1965.

1598. MÖHLER, Anton. Ästhetik der katholischen Kirchenmusik. Ravensburg: F. Alber, 1910 (First edition).

1599. ________. Ästhetik der katholischen Kirchenmusik. Rottenburg: W. Bader, 1915 (Second edition).

1600. SCHELL, Johanna. Ästhetische Probleme der Kirchenmusik in Lichte der Enzyklika Pius' XII, "Musicae sacrae disciplina." Berlin: N.G., 1961. available--IU, KyU, NNC, MH.

1601. SCHERCHEN, Hermann. The nature of music. New York: Dover Publications, Inc., and Chicago: H. Regnery Co., 1950.

1602. SCHLOEZER, Boris de. Entwurf einer Musikästhetik; zum Verständnis von Johann Sebastian Bach. Hamburg & München: Ellermann, 1964.

1603. SCHOLES, Percy. The mirror of music. London: Novello and Oxford Univ. Press, 1947.

1604. SEASHORE, Carl E. In search of beauty in music. New York: Ronald Press, 1947.

1605. SUREMAIN-MISSERY, A. Theorie acoustico--musicale, ou de la doctrine des sons, rapportée aux principes de leur combinaison. New York: Scientific Library, 1793.

1606. THIBAUT, Anton Friedrich Justus. On purity in musical art. London: J. Murray, 1877.

1607. WEILER, W. J. An investigation of qualities of music essential to the Roman Catholic liturgy. Evanston, Ill.: Northwestern Univ., Ph.D. Music, 1960.

1608. WELLEK, Albert. Musikpsychologie und Musikästhetik: Grundriss der systematischen Musikwissenschaft. 2., durchgesehene underw. Aufl. Bonn: Bouvier, 1975.

1609. WOLFF, E. G. Grundlagen einer autonomen Musikasthetik. Strassburg: Heitz & Co., 1934.
Sammlung musikwissenschaft-licher Abhandlungen.

See also: 587, 612, 660, 1122, 1981, 2077, 2090, 2098, 2104, 2928, 4447, 4672, 4679, 4688, 4693, 4696, 4699, 4704, 4705, 4706, 4895, 5190, 5193, 5201, 5218, 5395.

ETHNOMUSICOLOGY and FOLK MUSIC

1610. GILLIS, Frank and Alan P. Merriam. Ethnomusicology and folk music. Middletown, Conn.: Wesleyan Univ. Press, 1966.
An international bibliography of dissertations and theses.

1611. JACKSON, George Pullen. The story of the Sacred Harp. Nashville: Vanderbilt Univ. Press, 1944.

1612. NETTL, Bruno. Theory and method in ethnomusicology. Riverside, N.J.: The Free Press (division of Macmillan Co.), 1964.

See also: 508, 646, 2971, 3063, 5137, 5139, 5142, 5153, 5168, 5181, 5183.

EVANGELISTIC, GOSPEL and REVIVAL MUSIC

1613. CORNELL, Jean Gay. Mahalia Jackson, queen of gospel song. (Illustrated by V. Mays) Champaign, Ill.: Garrard Publ. Co., 1974.

1614. DOWNEY, James Cecil. The music of American revivalism. (Tulane Univ. Diss.) Ann Arbor: Univ. Microfilms, 1968.

1615. FIFE, Austin and Alta. Heaven on horseback. Revivalist songs and verse in the cowboy idiom. Logan, Utah: Utah State Univ. Press, 1970.

1616. GOLD, Charles E. A study of the gospel song. Los Angeles, Calif.: Univ. of Southern California, 1953.

1617. GOSPEL Music Association, ed. Gospel music directory and yearbook. Nashville: Gospel Music Assoc., 1972-73.

1618. HALL, T. H. Biography of gospel song and hymn writers. New York: Fleming H. Revell, 1914.

1619. HEILBUT, Tony. The gospel sound: Good news and bad times. Garden City, N.Y.: Anchor Press, 1975.

1620. JACKSON, Jesse. Make a joyful noise unto the Lord! The life of Mahalia Jackson, queen of gospel singers. New York: Dell also publ.--New York: Crowell, 1975. (c. 1974).

1621. KERR, Phillip Stanley. Music in evangelism and stories of famous Christian songs. Glendale, Calif.: Gospel Music Publishers, 1964.
A handbook of information for evangelists, gospel singers, church musicians, choir members, song directors, and all others who are interested in Christian music.

1622. McDEARMON, Kay. Mahalia: gospel singer. Ill. by N. and P. Washington. New York: Dodd Mead, 1976.

1623. McKINLEY, Frank Arnold. The American gospel song. Westminister Choir College Library. Princeton, N.J.: Westminister Choir College, M.A., 1946.

1624. McNEELY, Edwin. Evangelistic music. Fort Worth: Seminary Hill Press, 1959.

1625. NEW gospel treasure select-a-song. First edition. Nashville: New Gospel Treasure Pub. Co., 1976.

1626. PEACH, Everett. The gospel song; its influences on Christian hymnody. (pp. 113) Wayne State Univ. Detroit, Mich.: Wayne State Univ., M.A., 1960.

1627. SMALL, Katharine Lucille. The influence of the gospel song on the Negro church. Columbus, Ohio: Ohio State Univ. Library, M.A., 1945.

1628. TERRY, Lindsay. How to build an evangelistic church music program. Nashville: T. Nelson, 1974.

See also: 30, 50, 1922, 2188, 2256, 2332, 2401, 3653, 4396, 4507, 4508, 4562, 5050, 5152, 5185, 5325.

FAUXBOURDON

1629. RILEY, Athelstan. A collection of faux-bourdons and descants for the French ecclesiastical melodies and other tunes in the English hymnal. London: A. R. Mowbray & Co., Ltd., 1916.

1630. SCEATS, Godfrey. The Fa-Burden chant book. London: The Faith Press, n.d.

1631. THIMAN, Eric H. Twenty faux bourdons. London: Bayley & Ferguson, Ltd., n.d.

1632. WHITEHEAD, Alfred. Eighteen faux-bourdons and descants. New York: Carl Fischer, 1930.

1633. WILLAN, Healey. Ten faux-bourdons on well known hymns. New York: Oxford Univ. Press, 1927.

See also: 690, 1470, 1472, 1479.

FESTIVALS--CHRISTMAS, EASTER, ETC.

1634. A CHILD Is born in Bethlehem. Cincinnati: World Library of Sacred Music, Inc., 1965.

1635. DOLAN, Diane. Le drame liturgique de Pâques en Normandie et en Angleterre au Moyen-Âge. Paris: Presses universitaires de France, 1975.

1636. FOLEY, Rolla. The religious ceremonies, shrines, and folk music of the Holy Land Christians. Southern California University Library. Los Angeles, Calif.: Univ. of Southern California, 1951.

1637. GEISTLICHE Chormusik für Advent und Weihnachten. 7 Stuttgart-Hohenheim, Postfach 70: Hänssler-Verlag, 1965.

1638. HYMNI ofte loff-sangen op den christelycke feest-dagen ende andersins. Forthcoming reprints, 1966. New York: Broude Brothers Limited, (Orig. 1615), n.d.

1639. HYMNI ofte loff-sangen op den christelycke feest-dagen ende andersins. Hilversum, Netherlands: Frits Knuf-Reprint, 1966 (orig. 1615).

1640. JUNIOR choir anthems for Palm Sunday and Easter. Anaheim, Calif.: National Music Service, n.d.

1641. LECLERCQ, Louis. La semaine sainte au Vatican, étude musicale et pittoresque. Texte et musique. Paris: L. Hachette et. c., 1867.

1642. LE SUEUR, Jean François. Exposé d'une musique une, imitative, et particulière à chaque solemnité; ou l'on donne les principes généraux sur lesquels on l'établit & le plan d'une musique propre à le fête de Noël. Paris: Veuve Herissant, 1787.

1643. LE SUEUR, Jean François. Suite de l'essai sur la musique sacrée et imitative, ou l'on donne le plan d'une musique propre à la fête de Paque. Paris: Chez la veuve Herissant, 1787.

1644. LEVY, Ezekiel. Sacred music and the festivals of the Catholic, Jewish and Protestant faiths. New York: New York Univ., School of Education, Ed.D., 1955.
A source book, including suggestions for its use in the furtherance of mutual respect and understanding among persons who differ in religious backgrounds.

1645. LIPPHARDT, Walther. Die Wiesen der lateinischen Osterspiele des 12. und 13. Jahrhunderts. Kassel: Musikwissenschaftliche Arbeiten, 1948.
With musical illustrations, p. 39.

1646. REED, Dr. Will (ed.). The treasury of Christmas music. London: Blandford Press Ltd., n.d.

1647. ________. The treasury of Easter music. London: Blandford Press Ltd., n.d.

1648. SCHEEL, Ernst Erich. Musik zur Weihnachtszeit. Ruhr, Leineweberstrasse/Mülheim: Stadtbücherei, Musikbücherei, 1964.

1649. SCHOLA Cantorum, Bureau d'édition de la. Cantiques et Noëls cantates and concerts spirituels. Paris: Editions musicales de la Schola Cantorum, 1927.

1650. SCHULER, Ernst August. Die Musik der Osterfeiern, Osterspiele und Passionen des Mittelalters. Kassel: Bärenreiter Verlag, 1951.

1651. TUCK, John Erskine. Singing salvation: The James McRobert's story of the Festivals of Male Voice Praise. London, Eastbouren: Victory Press, 1966.

1652. TWENTY Christmas carols with descants. Cincinnati, Ohio: World Library of Sacred Music, Inc., 1965.

1653. WERNECKE, Herbert H. Christmas songs and their stories. Philadelphia: Westminster Press, 1957.

See also: 145, 146, 150, 154, 155, 156, 184, 300, 302, 303, 310, 322, 324, 330, 473, 726, 1261, 1442, 1555, 1880, 2285, 2570, 2607, 2642, 2695, 2904, 2986, 3720, 4494, 4995, 5027, 5358.

FIGURED MUSIC

See: 5080.

FINANCE

See: 839, 3617.

FORM

1654. BERRY, Wallace. Form in music; an examination of traditional historical and contemporary styles. Englewood Cliffs, N.J.: Prentice-Hall, Inc., 1966.

1655. BOER, C. L. W. Chansonvormen op het einde van de xude eeuw. Een studie naar aanlieding. Leipzig: Petrucci's "Harmonice musices odhecation," 1935.

1656. HODIER, André and Nöel Barch (trans. from French). The Forms of Music. New York: Walker, 1966. (from: Presses Universitaires de France, 1951.)

1657. MARIE CECILE, Sister. Art forms in sacred music. Milwaukee: The Bruce Publishing Company, 1931.

See also: 587, 1133, 1659, 1661, 3213, 3233, 4287, 4653, 4719, 4723, 4999, 5196, 5201, 5412.

FUGUE

1658. BULLIVANT, Roger. Fugue. New York: Hillary House Publ., Ltd. (Univ. of Sheffield), to be published.

1659. DICKINSON, A. E. F. Bach's fugal works. Chester Springs, Pa.: Dufour Editions, 1955.

1660. FELLERER, Karl Gustav (ed.). Anthology of music. Vol. 19. The Fugue, I (Adrio). New York: A. Broude Inc., n.d.

1661. GEDALGE, André. Treatise on the fugue. Norman, Okla.: Univ. of Oklahoma Press, 1965.

1662. GIZLANZONI, Alberto. Storia della fuga. Trattato didattico. Roma: Edizioni dell' Ateneo, 1953.

1663. GOULD, Glenn. So you want to write a fugue. New York: G. Schirmer, n.d.

1664. HANSEN, Edward A. Anomaly in the organ fugue subject of J. S. Bach. Ann Arbor, Mich.: Univ. Microfilms, 1965.

1665. HORSLEY, Imogene. Fugue, history and practice. New York: Free Press, 1966.

1666. LOVELOCK, William. The examination fugue. London: A. Hammond, n.d. (LC-MT 59. L7)

1667. MANN, Alfred. The study of fugue. N. G.: N. G., 1960.

1668. PORTER, Quincy. A study of fugue writing; based on Bach's Well-tempered clavichord. Boston: Loomis, 1951.

1669. THORKILDSEN, John. Kontrapunkt; kanon og fuge. Oslo: Aschehoug, 1949.

1670. VACHON, Monique. La fugue dans la musique religieuse de W. A. Mozart. Québec: Les Presses de L'Université, 1970.

See also: 1040, 4037, 4249, 4287, 4629.

FUNERAL MUSIC

1671. BORGA, Horatiu D. Les chants funèbres chez les peuples du Bas-Danube. Etude descriptive de folklore albanais, bulgare, roumain et serbe (p. 370). Strasbourg Library. Strasbourg, France: Strasbourg, thé lettres, 1954.

1672. IRION, Paul E. The funeral: Vestige or value? Nashville, Tenn.: Abingdon Press, 1965.

1673. JUNG, Michael von. Die erhebendsten Grablieder des Michael von Jung, weiland Pfarrer zu Kirchdorf bei Menningen. Kempten (Allgau): Verlag für Heimatpflege, 1963.

1674. LANTZ, Russell A. Music for funerals. Newton, Kans.: Faith and Life Press, 1965.

1675. MUSIC for funerals. Greenwich: The Seabury Press, 1952. This is also by Protestant Episcopal in the U. S. A.

1676. PROTESTANT Episcopal Church in the U. S. A. --The Joint Commission on Church Music. Music for funerals. New York: The H. W. Gray Company, Inc., 1963.

See also: 381, 594.

GALLERY MINSTRELS--CHURCH

1677. MACDERMOTT, Kenneth Holland. The old church gallery minstrels. London: S. P. C. K., 1948.
An account of the church bands and singers in England from about 1660 to 1860.

See also: 2067.

GENERAL

1678. ALLEN, M. F. Church music. Mowbray: Oxford, 1921. (BM)

1679. ALLGEMEINE CAECILIEN--Verein für Deutschland Oester-Reich und die Schweiz. Die Kirchenmusik. Dusseldorf: The Society, 1938.

1680. ANDEL, Cornelius P. van. Tussen de regels. De samenhang van kerkgeschiedenis en kerklied. 's-Gravenhage: Boekencentrum, 1968.

1681. ANTHES, Friedrich Conrad. Die Tonkunst im evangelischen Cultus, nebst einer gedragten Geschichte der kirchlichen Musik. Ein Handbuch für Geistliche, Organisten, Vorsanger und Lehrer. Wiesbaden: Friedrichsche Buchhandlung, 1846.

1682. ARMSTRONG, Thomas. Church music today. London: Oxford Univ. Press, 1946.

1683. ARNOLD, Samuel. Cathedral music (4 vols.). London: N. G., 1790.

1684. BACH, Johann Sebastian. Kurtzer, jedoch höchstnöthiger Entwurff einer wohlbestallten Kirchen music; nebst einigen unvorgreiflichen Bedencken von dem Verfall derselben. Leipzig: VEB Deutscher Verlag für Musik, 1965.

1685. BACON, A. The true function of church music. Stockton: The Printwell Press, 1953.

1686. BAILEY, A. E. (ed.). The arts and religion. New York: The Macmillan Company, 1944.

1687. BAINTON, Roland. The church of our fathers. New York: Charles Scribner's, 1941.

1688. BATTELL, Ralph. The lawfulness and expediency of church-musick asserted. London: J. Heptinstall, 1694.

1689. BEECHER, Henry Ward. The religious uses of music. Abilene, Tex.: Community Service of Abilene (3rd floor, Reporter building), Music Week, May 7-13, n.d.

1690. BELL, Maurice Frederick. Church music. Milwaukee: Morehouse Publishing Company, 1922.

1691. BERG, David Eric. The music of the church. New York: Caxton Institute Incorporated, 1927.

1692. BERNSTEIN, Martin. An introduction to music. New York: Prentice-Hall, Inc., 1951.

1693. BERTRAM, Hans George and Karl Dienst. Kirchenmusik in der Petrusgemeinde Giessen. Giessen: Evang. Petrusgemeinde, 1968.

1694. BIAGGI, G. A. Della musica religiosa e delle questioni inerenti discurso. Milano: F. Lucca, 1856.

1695. BISCHOFES Institut für Kirkenmusik. Deutsches Sing-Lektionar. Freiburg i. Br.: Christophorus-Verlag, 1965.

1696. BLANKENBURG, Walter. Kirchenlied und Volksliedweise. Gütersloh: Rufer-Verlag, 1953.

1697. ________, Friedrich Hofmann, and Erich Hübner, eds. Kirchenmusik im Spannungsfeld der Gegenwart. Kassel: Bärenreiter, 1968.

1698. BÖHM, Hans (ed.). Kirchenmusik heute; Gedanken über Aufgaben und Probleme der musica sacra. Berlin: Union Verlag, 1959.

1699. BOYCE, William. Cathedral music. (3 vols.) London: By editor, 1760-1778.

1700. BOYDEN, David O. An introduction to music. New York: Alfred Knopf, Inc., 1956.

1701. BRINKMANN, Clemens. Albert Gereon Stein. (1809-1881); Kirchenmusik und Musikerziehung. Köln: Volk, 1974.

1702. BRUNNER, Adolf. Musik im Gottesdienst. Zurich: Zwingli Verlag, 1968.

1703. BUSZIN, Walter E., ed. by Johannes Riedel. Cantors at the Crossroads. St. Louis: Concordia Publ. House, 1967.

1704. CANNON, Beckman Cox; Alvin H. Johnson, and William Waite. The art of music. New York: Thomas Crowell Company, 1960.

1705. CANTATE domino. Liverpool: Rushworth and Dreaper, 1932.

1706. CARLSSON, Sten L. Kyrkomusiker och kyrkokörer. Lund: H. Ohlsson, 1969.

1707. CHARLES, Elizabeth R. The voice of Christian life in song. New York: Robert Carter & Brothers, 1859.

1708. CHURCH of England, Archbishop's Committee on Music in the Worship of the Church. Music in worship. London:

Press & Publications Board of the Church Assembly; Society for Promoting Christian Knowledge, 1947.

1709. CLOKEY, Joseph W. In every corner sing, an outline of church music for the layman. New York: Morehouse-Gorham, 1945-1948.

1710. CONFERENZE Pronunciate Alla Radio Vaticana. Presente e futuro della musica sacra. Roma: Desclée, 1967.

1711. CONSOLO, F. Cenni sull' origine e sul progresso della musica liturgica. Firenze: Successori le Monnier, 1897.

1712. COPLAND, A. Music for a great city. New York: Alexander Broude, Inc., 1966.

1713. CORBIN, Solange. L'église à la conquête de sa musique. Part of the series "Pour la Musique." Paris: Gallimard, 1960.

1714. CRAFTS, Wilbur Fisk. Trophies of song. Articles and incidents on the power of sacred music. Boston: D. Lothrop & Co., 1875.

1715. DAKERS, Lionel. Church music at the crossroads: A forward looking guide for today. London: Marshall Morgan & Scott, 1970.

1716. DAVISON, Archibald Thompson. Church music. Illusion and reality. With musical illustrations. Cambridge, Mass.: Harvard Univ. Press, 1952.

1717. DEUTSCHER Kirchenmusikertag. Musica sacra in unserer Zeit; die Vorträge des ersten Deutschen Kirchenmusikertages. Berlin: Merseburger, 1960.

1718. DEVORE, U. Faith in music. New York: Book Dealer (J. B. Muns, 842 Hyperlon Ave., Los Angeles, California 90029), 1958.

1719. DIAZ GUERRA, Carlos José. La música del Cristianismo apuntes para contribuir a su estudio. Rosario: R. A. Ruiz, 1956.

1720. DICKINSON, Edward. Music in the history of the western church. New York: Greenwood Press, 1969.

1721. ________. Music in the history of the western church. St. Clair Shores, Mich.: Scholarly Press, 1970.

1722. DOUGLAS, Charles Winfred. Church music in history and practice: Studies in the praises of God. New York: Charles Scribner's Sons, 1937. (rev., 1962).

1723. DUNCAN-JONES, Arthur S. Church music (Catholic). Milwaukee: The Morehouse Publishing Company, 1920.

1724. EASTERLING, R. B., Jr. Church music for youth. Nashville: Convention Press, 1969.

1725. EDEN, John. Church music. Bristol: J. M. Gutch, 1822. A sermon preached at the opening of the new organ in the parish church of St. Nicholas, in the city of Bristol. Designed particularly to encourage parochial psalmody, and to suggest effectual means of forming a congregation to this edifying part of divine service.

1726. EHMANN, Wilhelm (ed.). Kirchenmusik. Vermächtnis, und Aufgabe. 1948-1958. Festschrift zum zehnjährigen Bestehen der Westfälishen Landeskirchenmusikschule in Herford. Darmstadt-Eberstadt: Tonkunst-Verlag, 1958.

1727. EMERSON, Samuel. An oration on music. Portland: E. A. Jenks, 1800.

1728. ENGEL, Carl. Reflections on church music. London: Gustav Scheurmann and Co., 1856.

1729. EVERSOLE, Finley (ed.). Christian faith and the contemporary arts. New York and Nashville: Abingdon Press, 1962.

1730. FERRARI, Giulio. Il legno nell' arte Italiana. Milano: U. Hoepli, 1911.

1731. FESTSCHRIFT, Theodore Hoelty-Nickel. A collection of essays on church music. Valparaiso, Ind.: Valparaiso Univ., 1967.

1732. FORD, W. Morris. Music in worship. Nashville: Convention Press, 1960.

1733. FORTUNE, Nigel and Anthony Lewis. The new Oxford history of Music--Vol. V--Opera and church music--1630 to 1750. New York and London: Oxford Univ. Press, n.d.

1734. FRANTZ, Klamer Wilhelm. Vorschläge zur Verbesserung des musikalischen Theils des Cultus. Quedlinburg: G. Basse, 1816.

1735. FRICK, Christoph. Musik Büchlein, oder nützlicher Bericht von dem Ursprunge Gebräuche und Erhaltung christlicher Musik und also von dem Lobe Gottes/welches die Christe ... verrichten sollen ... mit vorher gesetztem summarischem Tinhalt/und zu Ende hinzu-gethanem Register. Lüneburg: J. und H. Sternen, 1631.

1736. FRIEBERGER, Rupert Gottfried. Entwicklung der Kirchenmusik und des Orgelbaues im Praemonstratenserstift Schlägl von der Grundung 1218 bis 1665, dem Todesjahr des Abtes Martin Greysing. Beitrage zu einer Musikgeschichte des Praemonstratenserstiftes Schlägl im Oberen Mühl Viertel. (Als Ms. vervielf.) Wien: Kirchenhist. Inst., 1973.

1737. GABRIEL, Charles H. Church music of yesterday, to-day and for to-morrow. Chicago: The Rodeheaver Company, 1921.

1738. GARDNER, George. Worship and music. New York: The Macmillan Co., 1918.

1739. GARVIE, Peter. Music and western man. New York: Philosophical Library, 1958.

1740. GASTOUE, Amédée. L'église et la musique. Paris: B. Grasset, 1936.

1741. GEORGIADES, Thrasuboulos. Sakral und Profan in der Musik. München: Münchener Universitätsreden, 1960.

1742. GERBERT, Martin and Freiherr von Hornau. De cantu et musica sacra a prima ecclesiae aetate usque ad praesens tempus. (Hrsg. von Othmar Wessely) Graz: Akademische Druck und Verlagsanstalt, 1968.

1743. GRIWING, Rudolf. Kirikumusika. Tartus, Syria: "Odamehe" kirjastus, 1921.

1744. HADOW, William Henry. Church music. London, New York: Longmans, Green & Company, Ltd., 1926. also Liverpool Diocesan Board of Divinity Publications.

1745. ________. Music. London: Williams & Norgate, 1924.

1746. HALTER, Carl. The practice of sacred music. St. Louis: Concordia Publishing House, 1955 (1956).

1747. HAM, Richard. Church music for children. Nashville: Convention Press, 1969.

1748. HAMBOURG, Mark. From piano to forte: A thousand and one notes. London: Cassell & Co., 1931.

1749. HANNUM, Harold Byron. Music and worship. Nashville: Southern Pub. Assn., 1969.

1750. HARMS, Gottlieb. Bemerkungen zur kultischen Musik. Kleine Veröffentlichungen der Glaubensgemeinde Ugrino. Klecken: Glaubensgemeinde Ugrino, 1922.

1751. HARPER, Earl Enyeart. Progress in church music. Chicago: Univ. of Chicago, 1930.

1752. HEDLEY, J. C. Church music. A pastoral letter. London: N.G., 1897.

1753. HINKLE, Donald. Music in Christian education. Philadelphia: Lutheran Church Press, 1969.

1754. HODGES, Edward. An essay on the cultivation of church music. New York: J. A. Sparks, 1841.

1755. HOELTY-NICKEL, Theodore, ed. The musical heritage of the church. St. Louis: Concordia Publishing, 1970.

1756. HOFFMANN, Hans. Vom Wesen der zeitgenössischen Kirchenmusik. Kassel: Bärenreiter--Verlag, 1949.

1757. HOOKER, Edward William. A plea for sacred music. New York: American Tract Society, 1850 (?).

1758. HOOPER, William Loyd. Church music in transition. Nashville: Broadman Press, 1963.

1759. HORTON, Isabelle. High adventure. New York: The Methodist Book Concern, 1928.

1760. HOWES, Charles. Free church musicians. London: Novello & Company, 1909.

1761. HUGHES, Edwin Holt, Robert G. McCutchan, Peter Christian Lutkin, and others. Worship in music. New York: The Abingdon Press, 1929.

1762. HUGHES, William. Remarks upon church Musick. To which are added several observations upon some of Mr. Handel's oratorios, and other parts of his work. Worcester: R. Lewis, 1763. (LC-9-7853)

1763. HUNT, Joseph Marion. Music in the church. A series of practical talks upon all the departments of music in public services. Kansas City, Mo.: The J. M. Hunt Music Company, 1900.

1764. HUNTER, Stanley Armstrong (ed.). Music and religion. New York: Abingdon Press, 1930.

1765. IN Caritate et veritate: Kirchenmusik u. Liturgie 10 Jahre nach Beginn. d. II. Vatikan Konzils, 70 Jahre nach Erlass d. Motu proprio Pius X; Dokumentationen u. Beitrag; Festschrift f. Johannes Overath; Z. Vollendung d. 60 Lebensjahres von Johannes Overath. Saarbrucken: Minerva-Verlag Thinnes U. Nolte, 1973.

1766. INTERNATIONALE Studienwoche. Kirchenmusik nach dem Konzil. Freiburg: Christophorus-Verlag, 1967.

1767. JUNKER, Karl Ludwig. Portefeuille für Musikliebhaber. Charakteristik von 20 Komponisten; und Abhandlung uber die Tonkunst. Bern: Leipziger Ostermesse, 1792.

1768. Von KIRCHENMUSIKEN. Leipzig: N.G., 1780.

1769. Der KIRCHENMUSIKER. Berlin: Verlag Merseburger, 1950.

1770. KIRK, Kenneth E. The vision of God. London: Longmans, Green & Company, 1931.

1771. KNIGHT, Gerald Hocken. Twenty questions on church music. Answered by G. H. Knight. London & Oxford: A. R. Mowbray & Company, 1950.

1772. KRESSMANN, Edouard. De la musique rêligieuse. Paris: Editions "Jesers," 1944.

1773. KRONSTEINER, Hermann. Kirchenmusik heute. Wien: Veritas, 1967.

1774. KRUTSCHEK, P. Die Kirchenmusik nach dem Willen der Kirche. Regensburg: New York: E. Pustet, 1901.

1775. LILLIE, Amy Morris. I will build my church. Philadelphia: Westminster Press, 1950.

1776. LONGFORD, William Wingfield. Music and religion. A survey. London: K. Paul, Trench, Trubner & Company, Ltd., 1916.

1777. LOPEZ CALO, José. Presente e futuro della musica sacra. Roma: Desclée, 1967.

1778. LORENZ, Edmund Simon. Music in work and worship. A discussion of church music as an applied art. New York: Fleming H. Revell Company, 1925.

1779. ______. Practical church music. New York: Fleming H. Revell Company, 1909.

1780. LUTKIN, Peter C. Music in the church. Milwaukee: Young Churchman Company, 1910.

1781. MANSFIELD, Orlando A. "What is sacred music?". The Musical Quarterly. Vol. XIII/3, July, 1927. See pp. 451-75.

1782. MANZARRAGA, Tomas de. La música sagrada a la luz de los documentos pontificios. Madrid: Editorial Coculsa, 1968.

1783. MATTHESON, Johann. Matthesonii Plvs vitra, ein Stückwerk von neuer und mancherlei Art. Hamburg: J. A. Martini, 1754.

1784. MAUS, Cynthia Pearl. The church and the fine arts. An anthology of pictures, poetry, music and stories.... By C. P. Maus in collaboration with John P. Cayarnos, Jean Louise Smith, Ronald E. Osborn, Alfred T. Degroot. New York: Harper & Brothers, 1960.

1785. MEHRTENS, Frits. Kerk & muziek. Gravenhage: Boekencentrum, 1961.

1786. MENDL, Robert W. S. The divine quest in music. New York: Philosophical Library, 1957.

1787. MEYER, Joachim. Unvorgreiffliche Gedanken über die neulich eingerissene theatralische Kirchenmusik und denen darinnen bisher üblich geworden Cantaten mit Vergleichung der Musik voriger Zeiten, zur Verbesserung der unserigen vorgestellt von J. M. D. Lemgo: J. M. D., 1726.

1788. MORAN, Owen W. Church music for the whole church. Lakeland: The Church Press, 1938.

1789. MORLEY, Thomas. A plain and easy introduction to practical music ed. by A. Harman. New York: Norton, 1973.

1790. MOSER, Hans Joachim. Die Gottesdienstmusik der Protestanten. Wolfenbüttel: Möseler Verlag, 1961.

1791. MUSICA divian: Monatsschrift für Kirchenmusik (periodical). Wien: Universal-Edition, 1913.

1792. MUSIK der Götter, Geister und Menschen: die Musik in d. myth., fabulierenden u. histor. Uberlieferung d. Völker Afrikas, Nordasiens, Amerikas u. Ozeaniens; eine Quellensammlung. Hrsg. von W. Laade. 1. Auflag. Baden-Baden: Koerner, 1975.

1793. MUSIK und Altar. Freiburg: Christophorus-Verlag Herder, 1948.

1794. MUSIK und Kirche (editorial in "Organ of the Neue Schütz" --Gesellschaft.) Kassel: Im Bärenreiter-Verlag, 1929 (Jan. -Feb.).

1795. NININGER, R. Church music comes of age. New York: Carl Fischer, Inc., 1957.

1796. O'CONNELL, J. B. (trans.). Sacred music and liturgy. Westminister, Md.: The Newman Press, 1959.

1797. OESTERLEY, Hermann. Handbuch der musikalischen Liturgik in deutschen Evangelischen Kirche. Göttingen: Vandenhoeck und Ruprecht, 1863.

1798. OSBORNE, Stanley R. The strain upraise. Toronto: The Ryerson Press, 1957.

1799. OVERATH, Johannes. Musicae sacrae ministerium. Bonn: Cäcilien-Verband, 1962.

1800. PALMER, Albert W. Art of conducting public worship. New York: The Macmillan Company, 1939.

1801. PARIS. Memoires de musicologie sacrée. Paris: Schola Cantorum, 1900.

1802. PINSK, Johannes. Towards the centre of Christian living. (Schritte zur Mitte.) A liturgical approach. Translated by H. E. Winstone. Edinburgh, London: Herder, Freiburg, Nelson, 1961.

1803. PRATT, Waldo Selden. The problem of music in the church. Chicago: Northwestern Univ., 1930.

1804. PUSHEE, Ruth. Music in the religious service. New York: Fleming H. Revell Company, 1938.

1805. RHYS, Stephen and King Palmer. ABC of church music. London: Hodder & Stoughton, 1967.

1806. ROBERTSON, Alec. Christian music. New York: Hawthorn Books, 1961.

1807. _______. Sacred music. New York: Chanticleer Press, 1950.

1808. ROBERTSON, Festus G., Jr. Church music for adults. Nashville: Convention Press, 1969.

1809. ROSSI, Isidoro. Intorno alla musica ecclesiastica. N.G.: Finale, 1854. (LC-ML3869. R82)

1810. ROUTLEY, Erik. The church and music. Chester Springs, Pa.: Dufour Editions, 1952.

1811. _______. The church and music. (revised ed.) London: Gerald Duckworth, 1967.

1812. _______. Music leadership in the church. The historical, theological, and biblical background of church music discussed practically and informally, putting the problems of the church musician in proper perspective. Nashville, Tenn.: Abingdon Press, 1967.

1813. ________. Twentieth century church music. Vol. I. of Studies in Church Music. New York: Oxford Univ. Press, 1964.

1814. ________. Words, music and the church. Nashville: Abingdon Press, 1968.

1815. ROYAL School of Church Music. Church music recommended by the Musical Advisory Board. Croydon (SY.): Royal School of Church Music., 1967.

1816. RUETZ, Caspar. Widerlegte Vorurtheile von der Wirkung der Kirchenmusik, und von den darzu erfoderten Unkosten, nebst einer Vorrede von der musikalischen Liebhaberei, ans Licht gestellt. Rostock: J. A. Berger & J. Boedner, 1753.

1817. SALAZAR, Adolfo. Music in our time. New York: W. W. Norton, 1946.

1818. SAMINSKY, L. Music of our day. Essentials and prophecies. New York: Thomas Y. Crowell Co., 1932.

1819. SCHEIBEL, Gottfried Ephraim. Zufällige Gedanken von der Kirchen-musik wie sie heutigen tages beschaffen ist, allen rechtschaffnen Liebhabern der Musik zur Nachlese und zum ergötzen wohlmeinende ans Licht gestellet. Frankfurt: zu finden beym authore, 1721. (LC-9-6442.)

1820. SCHOOL of English Church Music--London. Principles and recommendations. Tenbury Wells: N.G., 1943. See p. 60. (BM7891a. 32)

1821. SCHUBERT, Guilherme. A música sacra na histôria da musica. Rio de Janeiro: Electra Editoria e Distribuidora, 1970.

1822. SCUDO, Paul. Critique et litterature musicales. Paris: V. Lecou, 1852.

1823. SERPAGLI, Francesco. La music religiosa negli ultimi due secolo. Parma: S.T.B., 1972.

1824. SHAW, Martin. Up to now. New York: Carl Fischer, 1929.

1825. SHUTLLEWORTH, Henry Cary. The place of music in public worship. London: E. Stock, 1892.

1826. SIGL, M. Die Kirchenmusik in ihren Grundfragen. Regensburg: F. Pustet, 1922.

1827. SMITH, Henry Augustine. "The expression of religion in music." The Arts & Religion. New York: Macmillan Company, 1944.

1828. _______. Lyric religion. Westwood, N.J.: Fleming H. Revell Company, 1931.

1829. SÖDERSTEN, Gunno. Fran Munksäng til gospel. Stockholm: Evangelska fosterlands-stiftelsens studieförband, 1966.

1830. SÖHNGEN, Oskar. Die wiedergeburt der Kirchenmusik; Wandlungen und Entscheidungen. Kassel: Bärenreiter, 1953.

1831. _______. Wiedergewonnene Mitte? Die Rolle der Kirchenmusik in der modernen Musik. Berlin: C. Merseburger, 1956.

1832. SOLITARIO. L'apostolato della musica sacra nel secolo XX. Visione nel XIII centenario di San Gregorio Magno dai 12 marzo al 12 aprile 1904. Per un Solitario. pp. 14. Montecassino: N.G., 1904. (BM 7903. c. 21.)

1833. SQUIRE, Russel N. Church music: musical and hymnological developments in western Christianity. St. Louis: The Bethany Press, 1962.

1834. STÄHLIN, Wilhelm. Kirchenmusik und Gemeinde. Kassel: Bärenreiter, 1955.

1835. STEERE, Dwight. Music in Protestant worship. Richmond: John Knox Press, 1960, 1964.

1836. STEWART, George W. Music in church worship. London: Hodder & Stoughton, 1926.

1837. SWISHER, W. S. Music in worship. Bryn Mawr, Pa.: The Oliver Ditson Company, 1929.

1838. SYDNOR, James R. Planning for church music. Nashville: Abingdon Press, 1961, 1964.

1839. _______. Music in the life of the church, a manual. Richmond: CLC Press, 1968.

1840. THOMAS, Owen James. The divine mission of music. A study in music and the Christian church ... Annual public lecture, etc. pp. 16. London: London Bible College, 1961.

1841. THOMPSON, F. Fagan. Music and worship. Nashville: Whitmore & Smith, 1935.

1842. THURLINGS, Adolf. Wir entstehen Kirchengesänge Rektorrede, gehalten am 73. Stiftungsfeste der Universität Bern. Leipzig: Breitkopf & Härtel, 1907.

1843. TOPP, Dale. Music in the Christian community. Grand Rapids: W. B. Eerdmans Publ. Co., 1976.

1844. TOWLSON, Clifford W. A mightier music. London: The Epworth Press, 1934.

1845. TRAMBUSTI, Giuseppe. Della musica ecclesiastica, passato, il presente, il futuro. Roma: Tip. di G. Gentili, 1862.

1846. TURNER, Walter James. Music and life. London: Methuen & Co., Ltd., 1921.

1847. URANG, Gunnar. Church music, for the glory of God. Moline: Christian Service Foundation, 1956.

1848. VAUGHAN WILLIAMS, Ralph. The making of music. Ithaca: Cornell Univ. Press, 1955.

1849. WALLAGH, Constant. Spiritual en Gospel. Amsterdam: Koninginneweg 62, Stichting IVIO, 1967.

1850. WALTERS, William R. Modern trends in church music. Cleveland: Western Reserve Univ., 1961.

1851. WARING, Peter. Above the noise; a handbook on worship, Christian education and music. Cazenovia, N.Y.: N.G., 1973. (LC. ML-3166.W37)

1852. WERNER, Eric. The sacred bridge; the interdependence of liturgy and music and music in synagogue and church during the first millennium. New York: Columbia Univ. Press, 1959.

1853. WERNSDORF, Gottlieb. De prudentia in cantionibus ecclesiasticis adhibenda. Wittenbergae: Literis vidvae Gerdisiae, 1723.

1854. WESLEY, Samuel Sebastian. A few words on cathedral music and the musical system of the church, with a plan of reform. London: F. & J. Rivington, et al., 1849.

1855. WESTENDORF, Omar. Music lessons for the man in the pew. Cincinnati, Ohio: World Library of Sacred Music, Inc., 1965.

1856. WHITTLE, Donald Carey G. Christianity and the arts. Philadelphia: Fortress Press, 1967 (c. 1966).

1857. WHITTLESEY, Federal Lee. A comprehensive program of church music. Philadelphia: Westminster Press, 1957.

1858. ________ (ed.). Music and worship. Philadelphia: Board of Christian Education, Presbyterian Church in the U.S.A., 1951.

1859. WIBBERLEY, Brian. Music and religion; a historical and philosophical survey. London: The Epworth Press, 1934.

1860. WIENANDT, Elwyn Arthur (comp.). Opinions on church music; comments and reports from four-and-a-half centuries. Waco, Tex.: Markham Press Fund of Baylor Univ. Press, 1974.

1861. WILLIAMS, Charles L. Church music. Gloucester: Minehin & Gibbs, 1918.

1862. WILLIAMSON, Francis Hildt. The Lord's song and the ministry of the church. Ann Arbor: Univ. Microfilms, 1967.

1863. WINTERFELD, Carl von. Zur geshichte heiliger Tonkunst. Hildesheim: Georg Olms Verlag, 1966.

1864. WOOD, J. Nonconformist church music. London: Lindsey Press, 1921.

1865. WOODS, E. R. Music and meaning. Cambridge, Mass.: Harvard Univ. Press, 1932.

1866. WOODS, Leonard. A discourse on sacred music. Salem: Joshua Cushing, 1804.

See also: 63, 67, 68, 69, 72, 74, 192, 606, 819, 864, 869, 892, 941, 984, 986, 988, 1029, 1075, 1088, 1099, 1108, 1130, 1139, 1151, 1164, 1171, 1172, 1173, 1211, 1243, 1284, 1286, 1289, 1291, 1296, 1299, 1303, 1308, 1310, 1319, 1331, 1333, 1334, 1336, 1347, 1350, 1439, 1460, 1500, 1572, 1573, 1587, 1588, 1593, 1606, 1879, 1883, 1888, 1898, 1916, 1943, 1945, 1965, 2005, 2018, 2084, 2112, 2113, 2119, 2133, 2136, 2142, 2153, 2549, 2550, 2576, 2580, 2581, 2619, 2665, 2695, 2748, 2759, 2850, 2892, 2895, 2909, 2921, 2940, 2967, 2982, 2984, 3254, 3266, 3271, 3272, 3326, 3346, 3361, 3372, 3406, 3417, 3422, 3466, 3473, 3475, 3476, 3531, 3543, 3641, 3650, 3655, 3661, 4132, 4199, 4214, 4306, 4447, 4470, 4545, 4567, 4671, 4677, 4682, 4683, 4685, 4689, 4691, 4694, 4695, 4696, 4697, 4700, 4701, 4705, 4706, 4707, 4763, 4771, 4777, 4778, 4781, 4786, 4907, 4931, 4967, 4971, 5026, 5059, 5192, 5208, 5215, 5234, 5287, 5288, 5299, 5329, 5369, 5376, 5379, 5386, 5390, 5391, 5392, 5396, 5399, 5400, 5405, 5406, 5407, 5409, 5414, 5419, 5420.

GRADUAL

1867. BURGESS, Francis. The English Gradual. London: Plainchant Publications Committee, 1933.

1868. BURGUN Plainchant Publications (ed.). The English Gradual. London: Burgun-Oxford, n. d.

1869. DELALANDE, Dominique. Vers la version authentique du Graduel grégorien. Le Graduel des Prêcheurs. Recherches sur les sources et la valeur de son texte musical. Paris: Bibliothèque d'histoire dominicaine, 1949.

1870. FRERE, Walter Howard. Graduale Sarisburiense. Ridgewood, N.J.: Gregg Press-Reprint, March 31, 1967 (orig. 1894).

1871. GASTOUE, Amédée. Musique et liturgie. Le Graduel et l'Antiphonaire Romains: Histoire et description. Lyon: Janin Frères, 1913.

1872. HERZO, Marie Sister. Five aquitanian Graduals: Their mass propers and Alleluia cycles. Ann Arbor: Univ. Microfilms, 1967.

1873. JOHNER, Dominicus. The chants of the Vatican Gradual. Collegeville: St. John's Abbey Press, 1940.

1874. KINGO, Thomas. Gradual. København: Dan Fog Musikforlag, 1967.

1875. WAGNER, Peter. Das Graduale der St. Thomaskirche zu Leipzig. Hildesheim: Georg Olms Verlag, 1967.

See also: 959, 2904, 3403, 4985.

GUIDEBOOKS and HANDBOOKS

1876. BADEN POWELL, James. Choralia (a handy book for parochial precentors and choirmasters). London: Longmans Green & Co., 1901.

1877. BAILEY, M. B. Guide to church hymnals. London: N.G., 1890. (BM)

1878. BUCHHANDELS-adress für die Bundesrepublik Deutschland und West-Berlin; Adressbuch des Oesterreichischen Buch-, Kunst-, Musikalien-und Zeitschriftenhandels; Schweizer Buchhandel Adressbuch; Verzeichnis des Buchhandels anderer Länder. Frankfurt am Main: Buchhändler-Vereinigung, 1963.

1879. CAMPBELL, Sidney Scholfield. Music in the church. A handbook of church music. London: Dennis Dobson (Student's Music Library), 1951, e.g. (also Springs, Pa.: Chester Dufour, 1965).

1880. CARROLL, Joseph Robert. A choirmaster's guide to Holy Week. Toledo: Gregorian Institute of America, 1957.

1881. CHRISTY, Van A. Glee club and chorus. New York: G. Schirmer, Inc., 1940.

1882. COLWYN, A. W. Music student's handy-book. N.G.: Hutchings & Romer, 1907.

1883. COMMUNITY music. A practical guide. Boston: Playground and Recreation Association of America, 1926.

1884. COVERT, William Chalmers (ed.). Handbook to the hymnal. Philadelphia: Presbyterian Board of Christian Education, 1935.

1885. DARRELL, R. D. Guide to books on music and musicians. New York: G. Schirmer, 1951.

1886. DEARMER, P. Short handbook of public worship. London: Oxford Univ. Press, 1931.

1887. DIOCESE of Minnesota Education Committee. The Episcopal Choirmaster's handbook 1965-1966. Sauk Centre, Minn.: Department of Music Diocese of Minnesota, 1965.

1888. DOMMER. Handbuch der Musikgeschichte. Leipzig: Grunow, 1878.

1889. EDWARDS, Frederick George. United praise. A practical handbook of nonconformist church music. London: J. Curwen & Sons, 190-.

1890. ELLERHORST, W. Handbuch der Orgelkunde. Einsiedeln, Switzerland: Benziger, 1936, e.g. (also New York: Broude Brothers).

1891. GELINEAU, Joseph. Voices and instruments in Christian worship; principles, laws, application. Translated from French by Clifford Howell, London: Burns & Oates. Collegeville, Minn.: Liturgical Press, 1964.

1892. GILBERT, Harry. Gilbert's manual for choir-loft and pulpit. New York: G. Scribner's Sons, 1939.

1893. GRACE, H. A handbook for choralists. (Novello's Music Primers and Educational Series, no. 104). London and New York: Novello, 1928.

1894. A GUIDE to music for the church year. Minneapolis: Augsburg Publishing House, 1962.

1895. HAEUSSLER, Armin. The story of our hymns: The handbook to the hymnal of the Evangelical and Reformed Church. St. Louis: Eden Publishing House, 1952.

1896. HATCHETT, Marion J. Music for the church year; a handbook for clergymen, organists, & choir directors. New York: Seabury Press, 1964.

1897. HAYBURN, Robert F. Digest of regulations and rubrics of Catholic church music. Boston, Mass.: McLaughlin and Reilly Company, 1961.

1898. HEATON, Charles Huddleston. A guidebook to worship services of sacred music. St. Louis: Bethany Press, 1962.

1899. HOLCOMB, Clifford A. The associational church music guidebook. Nashville: Convention Press, 1957.

1900. ________. Guidebook to church music promotion. Nashville: Convention Press, 1959.

1901. JONES, Arthur S. D. Church music. N.G.: Handbooks of Catholic Faith and Practice, 1920. (BM)

1902. JONES, F. O. A handbook of American music and musicians. Buffalo: C. W. Moulton & Co., 1887.

1903. KAGEN, Sergius. On studying singing--on vocal science-techniques-repertoire. New York: Rinehart & Co., Inc., 1950.

1904. KORTKAMP, Ivan. One hundred things a choir member should know. Tower, Minn.: Mohawk Pub. Co., 1969.

1905. LEMACHER, Heinrich. Handbuch der katholischen Kirchenmusik. Essen: Fredebeul & Koenen, 1949.

1906. LONDON--Warham Guide. The Warham guide handbook, etc. London: Mowbray & Co., 1963. (second edition).

1907. LOVELACE, Austin C. The youth choir. New York & Nashville: Abingdon Press, 1964.

1908. LUNDSTROM, Linden J. The choir school; a leadership manual. Minneapolis, Minn.: Augsburg, 1963.

1909. MAHRENHOLZ, Christhard (ed.). Handbuch zum evangelischen Kirchengesangbuch. Göttingen: Vandenhoeck u. Ruprecht, 1970.

1910. MANUAL of church praise. Edinburgh: The Church Committee on Publications, 1932.

1911. MINISTER. A guide for Methodist choirs. London: Epworth Press, 1935. (BM)

1912. MOFFATT, J. and Millar Patrick (ed.). Handbook of the church hymnary. London: Oxford Univ. Press, 1933.

1913. _______. Handbook to the church hymnary. London: Oxford Univ. Press, H. Milford, 1927. Reiss, with supplement, - 1935.

1914. MOFFATT, Nona S. How to organize a music department for a church; a handbook by a successful choir director. New York: Exposition Press, 1963.

1915. NEWTON, J. The organist and choirmaster (plain guides to lay work). London: S. P. C. K., 1927.

1916. NICHOLSON, Sydney H. Church music: a practical handbook. London: The Faith Press, 1927.

1917. NORMAN, James Roy. Handbook to the Christian liturgy. New York: The Macmillan Company, 1944.

1918. POLACK, W. G. The handbook to the Lutheran hymnal. St. Louis: Concordia Publishing House, 1942.

1919. PREOBRAZHENSKII, Antonin Viktorovich. Po Tserkovnomu pieniiu ukazatelh kniga, broshiurh, zhurnalhnuichh statei i rukopisei. Izd. 2. Moscow: Tip. Vilde, Malaia Kislovka Sob. Domh, 1900.

1920. REYNOLDS, William J. Hymns of our faith; a handbook for the Baptist hymnal. Nashville, Tenn.: Broadman Press, 1964.

1921. RICHARDSON, A. M. Church music. A handbook for the clergy. New York and Bombay: Longmans, Green & Co., 1904.

1922. RODEHEAVER, Homer. Hymnal handbook for standard hymns and gospel songs. Chicago: The Rodeheaver Co., 1931.

1923. ROSS, William. Secrets of singing. On the science of singing--has unique section on the comparative methods of singing. Bloomington, Ind.: Author, through Indiana Univ. Bookstore, 1948.

1924. ROUTLEY, Erik. The organist's guide to congregational praise. London: Independent Press, Ltd., 1957.

1925. ROWLANDS, Leo F. Guide book for Catholic Church choirmasters. Boston, Mass.: McLaughlin & Reilly Co., 1962.

1926. SCHERCHEN, H. Handbook of conducting. London: Oxford Univ. Press, 1956.

1927. SCHMID, Eugen. Die neuen kirchenmusikalischen Vorschriften; ein Handbuch für Geistliche und Chorregenten. Regensburg: F. Pustet, 1919.

1928. SELLERS, Ernest Orlando. How to improve church music; a practical handbook for pastors and choir leaders. New York: Fleming H. Revell, 1928.

1929. SHEHAN, Lawrence J. A manual for choir musicians. Washington, D.C.: The Liturgical Conference, 1964.

1930. SMALLMAN, John and E. H. Wilcox. The art of a cappella singing. Boston: Oliver Ditson Company, 1933.

1931. TERRY, Sir Richard Runciman. The music of the Roman Rite. A manual for choirmasters in English-speaking countries. London: Burns, Oates, & Washbourne, Ltd., 1931.

1932. THAYER, Lynn W. The church music handbook; a handbook of practical procedures and suggestions. Grand Rapids: Zandervan Pub. House, 1971.

1933. THEOPHANE, Sister M., O.S.E. Handbook for Catholic church organist. Boston: McLaughlin & Reilly Company, 1961.

1934. THEUERKAUF, W. (ed.). Mit Herzen, Mund und Händen; Kunst-und-Handwerk im Dienst kirchlicher Verkündigung. Berlin: Evangelische Verlagsanstalt, 1963.

1935. TITCOMB, H. Everett. Anglican ways. A manual on liturgical music for Episcopal choirmasters. New York: H. W. Gray Company, 1954.

1936. ______. A choirmaster's notebook on Anglican services and liturgical music. Boston: Schola Cantorum Publications, 1950.

1937. VALENTIN, Erich. Handbuch der Chormusic, Band I. Regensburg: G. Bosse Verlag, 1953.

1938. ______. Handbuch der Chormusik, Band II. Regensburg: G. Bosse Verlag, 1953.

1939. ______ and Friedrich Hoffmann. Die evangelische Kirchenmusik. Regensburg: G. Bosse, 1967.

1940. WEDDLE, Franklyn S. O worship the king. A manual of helps and materials for priesthood, ministers of music, and others who assist in worship. Independence: Herald House, 1952.

1941. WHISTLING, Carl Friedrich and Friedrich Hofmeister. Handbuch der musikalischen Literatur. (A facsimile of the 1817 edition and ten subsequent supplements. (Introduction by Neil Ratliff.) New York: Garland Publ. Inc., 1977.

1942. Whitlock, J. A. (A) Handbook of Bible and Church. London: N. G., 1898.

1943. WIPF, Gerhard. Das Kirchenlied; ein Handbuch für den Religionsunterricht. Hrsg. vom Kirchenrat des Kantons Zürich. Zürich: Schulthess & Co. in Kommission, 1964.

1944. YOUNG, Percy M. A handbook of choral technique. London: Dobson, 1953, 1964.

See also: 126, 130, 175, 243, 266, 336, 353, 374, 467, 579, 657, 669, 670, 693, 717, 724, 780, 784, 785, 788, 797, 801, 811, 829, 841, 859, 866, 874, 876, 885, 897, 901, 961, 1056, 1065, 1066, 1160, 1269, 1346, 1421, 1431, 1449, 1621, 1838, 1851, 2169, 2177, 2253, 2468, 2551, 2596, 2631, 2654, 2797a, 2815, 2948, 2997, 2999, 3167, 3244, 3259, 3446, 3840, 3925, 3926, 3949, 4028, 4084, 4086, 4087, 4176, 4191, 4287, 4291, 4742, 4870, 4904, 5044, 5055, 5169, 5191, 5213, 5223, 5228, 5238, 5247, 5255, 5274, 5332.

HISTORY and CRITICISM

1945. ABRAHAM, Gerald (ed.). The history of music in sound. (10 vol.). New York: Oxford Univ. Press, 1953-1959.

1946. ________. A hundred years of music. London: Duckworth, 1938, and 4th ed. 1974.

1947. AGRAM. Crkveno glazbeno drůstvo Cirilo metodov kor. Cirilometod ski vjesnik. Smotra za crkvenoslovensku glazbu i unjetnost. Zagreb: N. G., 1938. (BM)

1948. AGRESTI, Michele. Il clero e la riforma della musica sacra; alcuni articoli estratti dal periodico musica sacra di Milano. Andria: Stab. tip. B. Terlizzi, 1891.

1949. AIGRAIN, René. La musique religieuse. Paris: Bloud & Gray, 1929.

1950. ________. Religious music. A further section on English and Irish religious music is added. London: Sands & Co., 1931.

1951. ALLEN, Warren Dwight. Philosophies of music history--Bibliography of 317 works. New York, London: American Book Company, 1939.

1952. ________. Philosophies of music history: A study of general histories of music, 1600-1960. New York: Dover, 1962.

1953. AMBROS. Geschichte der Musik. 5 volumes and index. Leipzig: Leuckart, 1880-1887.

1954. ANDERTON, H. Orsmond. Early English music. With preface by R. R. Terry. London: "Musical Opinion," 1920.

1955. AUBRY, Pierre. La musique et les musiciens d'église en Normandie au 13. siècle. (Réimpr.) Genève: Minkoff Reprints, 1972.

1956. BAILLE, Hugh. "A London church in early Tudor Times." Music and Letters. Vol. XXVI/I. N. G.: N. G., January, 1955 (55-64).

1957. BAINTON, Roland H. The reformation of the 16th century. Boston: The Beacon Press, 1952.

1958. BALAN, George. O istorie a muzicii europene. Epoci si curente. Personalitati şi capodopere. Bucureşti: Albatros, 1975.

1959. BAUER, Marion and Ethel Peyser. How music grew, from prehistoric times to the present day. New York: G. P. Putnam's Sons, 1939.

1960. BECKER, Carl Ferdinand. Die Tonwerke des XVI und XVII Jahrhunderts, oder systematisch--chronologische Zusammenstellung der in diesen zwei Jahrhunderten gedruckten Musikalien. Leipzig: E. Fleischer, 1855.

1961. BEKKER, Paul. Story of music. New York: W. W. Norton & Company, 1927.

1962. BERNOULLI, Eduard. Aus Liederbüchern der Humanistenzeit. Eine bibliographische und notentypographische Studie (Pp. 116). Zürich Library. Zürich: Leipzig, Breitkopf & Härtel (res. type script), 1910.

1963. BIRD, Joseph. Gleanings from the history of music. Boston: Benjamin B. Mussey & Company, 1850.

1964. BLUME, C. and Guido Maria Dreves. Analecta hymnica medie aevi. Leipzig: Reesland, 1886-1922.

1965. BLUME, Friedrich (ed.). Die Musik in Geschichte und Gegenwart. Kassel: Bärenreiter-Verlag, 1949-1964.

1966. _______. Renaissance and Baroque music. New York: Norton, February, 1967.

1967. BOETTICHER, Wolfgang. Orlando di Lasso und seine Zeit, 1532-1594. Repertoire-Untersuchung zur Musik der Spätrenaissance. Band 1. Monographie. Kassel & Basel: Bärenreiter-Verlag, 1958.

1968. BOTTEE DE TOULMON, Augusto. Lettre adressée à M. le president de la Scua-commission musicale des chantes religieux et historiques. Paris: Imprimerie d'E. Daverger, 1845.

1969. BRONARSKI, Ludwig. Die Lieder der heiligen Hildegard: ein Beitrag z. Geschichte d. geist. Musik d. Mittelalters. (Neudr.) Walluf bei Wiesbaden: M. Sändig, 1973.

1970. BROWN, Howard Mayer. Music in the Renaissance. Englewood Cliffs, N. J.: Prentice-Hall, 1976.

1971. BROWNLOW, J. M. E. Church music in the Middle Ages. York: N. G., 1911. (BM)

1972. BUKOFZER, Manfred F. Music in the Baroque era. New York: W. W. Norton and Company, 1947.

1973. ________. Studies in Medieval and Renaissance music. New York: W. W. Norton, 1950.

1974. CHAILLEY, Jacques. Forty thousand years of music. (Translated by Rollo Meyers [229 pp.]). New York: Farrar, Straus, and Giroux, 1964.

1975. CHAPPELL, William. History of music from the earliest records to the fall of the Roman empire. London: Chappell & Co., 1824.

1976. CHAUNCEY, Nathanial. Regular singing defended, and proved to be the only true way of singing the songs of the Lord. "Mr. Chauncey's arguments for regular singing." London: T. Green, 1728.

1977. CLEMENT, Felix. Histoire générale de la musique religieuse. Paris: A. Le Clere et c., 1860.

1978. CODEX Ult-Raiectensis. Liber sequentiarum ecclesiae capitularis Sanctae Mariae Ultraiectensis saeculi XIII. Amsterdam: Vereninging voor Nederlandse Musiek, 1965 (66).

1979. COLLES, Henry Cope. English church music; lantern lecture by H. C. Colles. London: Press & Publication Board of the Church Assembly, 1933.

1980. CORNWALL, Nathanael Ellsworth. Music: As it was, and as it is. New York: Appleton & Company, 1851.

1981. CROXALL, Samuel. The antiquity, dignity, and advantages of music. London: J. Watts & B. Dod, 1741.

1982. DANNREUTHER, Edward. Musical ornamentation (complete in one volume: Part 1--from Diruta to J. S. Bach, Part

II--From C. P. E. Bach to the present.) New York: Edwin F. Kalmus, n. d.

1983. _______. The Oxford history of music. Vol. VI. London: Oxford, 1905.

1984. DAVIS, Louis S. Studies in musical history. New York: G. P. Putnam's Sons, 1887.

1985. DAVISON, Archibald T. Bach and Handel: The consummation of the Baroque in music. Cambridge: Harvard Univ. Press, 1951.

1986. _______ and Willi Apel (ed.). Historical anthology of music. 2 volumes. Cambridge, Mass.: Harvard Univ. Press, 1959.

1987. DEICHGRABER, Reinhard. Gotteshymnus und Christushymnus in der frühen Christenheit. Göttingen: Vandenhoeck u. Ruprecht, 1967.

1988. DICKINSON, Edward. The history of church music. Syllabus, with bibliographical references for a course of 25 lectures given at Oberlin theological seminary. Oberlin: Pearce & Randolph, 1896.

1989. _______. Music in the history of the western church. New York: C. Scribner's Sons, 1902, 1937, 1953.

1990. _______. Music in the history of the western church. New York: Haskell House of Publishers, 1969. (Repr.)

1991. DICKINSON, Helen A. and Clarence. Excursions in musical history. New York: H. W. Gray Co., 1919.

1992. DORIAN, Frederick. The history of music in performance. New York: W. W. Norton & Co., 1942.

1993. DOUGLASS, Robert. Church music through the ages. Nashville, Tenn.: Convention Press, 1967.

1994. EASTCOTT, Richard. Sketches of the origin, progress, and effects of music, with an account of the ancient bards, and minstrels. Illustrated w/various historical facts, interesting anecdotes, and poetical quotations. Bath: S. Hazard, 1793.

1995. EINSTEIN, Alfred. Music in the Romantic era. New York: W. W. Norton, 1950.

1996. _______. A short history of music. New York: A. A. Knopf, 1947.

1997. ELLINWOOD, Leonard. The history of American church music. New York: Morehouse-Gorham Co., 1953.

1998. ELLIS, Alexander J. The history of musical pitch. New York: Broude Brothers, 1965.

1999. ENGEL. The music of the most ancient nations. London: Murray, 1864.

2000. ENGEL, Lehman (ed.). Renaissance to Baroque. Vol. I., French-Netherland Music. (Three centuries of choral music.) New York: H. Flammer, Inc., 1939.

2001. EWEN, David. Music comes to America. New York: Allen, Town, & Heath, 1947.

2002. FASSETT, Agatha. The naked face of genius. (under the heading: mid-century man and his music--a Christian view). Boston: Houghton Mifflin Co., 1958.

2003. FEIFEL, Erich. Grundzüge einer Theologie des Gottesdienstes. Motive und Konzeption der Glaubensverkündigung Michael Heldings, 1506-1561, als Ausdruck einer katholischen "Reformation." Freiburg: Untersuchungen zur Theologie der Seelsorge, 1960.

2004. FELITZ, Friedrich. Über einige Interessen der älteren Kirchenmusik. München: C. Kaiser, 1853.

2005. FELLERER, Karl Gustav. "Church music and the Council of Trent." The Musical Quarterly. Vol. XXXIX/4. Oct., 1943. (pp. 576-94).

2006. ______. Geschichte der katholischen Kirchenmusik. Düsseldorf: L. Schwann, 1939 and 1949.

2007. ______. Gründzüge der Geschichte der katholischen Kirchenmusik. Paderborn: F. Schöningh, 1929.

2008. ______. Der Palestrinastil und seine Bedeutung in der vokalen Kirchenmusik des achtzehnten Jahrhunderts; ein Beitrag zur Geschichte der Kirchenmusik in Italien und Deutschland. Augsburg: Dr. B. Filser Verlag G. m. b. H., 1929.

2009. FINN, William. Sharps and flats decades. New York, London: Harper & Brothers, 1947.

2010. FINNEY, Theodore M. A history of music. New York: Harcourt, Brace, & World, Inc., 1947. (also repr. Westport, Conn.: Greenwood Press, 1965-66).

2011. FLOOD, William H. G. Early Tudor composers--(period 1485-1555). Reprint of London: Oxford Univ. Press,

1925.) Freeport, New York: Books for Libraries Press, 1968.

2012. FORD, D. W. English church music, a brief historical survey. Christchurch: Caxton Press, 1949.

2013. GASTOUE, Amédée. La vie musicale de l'église. Paris: Bloud & Gray, 1929.

2014. GEROLD, Theodore. Les pères de l'église et la musique. Paris: F. Alcan, 1931.

2015. GIESLER, Walter. Studien zur klavischen Musik-und Liturgiegeschichte. Köln: Volk, 1968.

2016. GOLDRON, Romain. Histoire de la musique. Lausanne: Editions Rencontre, 1965.

2017. GOULD, Nathaniel. History of sacred music in America. Boston: A. N. Johnson, 1853.

2018. GRAY, Cecil. The history of music. London: K. Paul, Trench, Trubner & Co., 1928; also New York: A. Knopf, 1928; and rev. ed. Knopf, 1935.

2019. GREENBERG, N. (ed.). An English songbook: Part songs and sacred music of the Middle Ages and the Renaissance for 1-6 voices. New York: Anchor Books, 1961.

2020. GROUT, Donald J. A history of western music. New York: W. W. Norton & Co., 1960.

2021. HAAPANEN, Toive. Dominikanische Vorbilder im mittelalterlichen nordischen Kirchengesang. N. G.: N. G., n. d. (LCML55. G39).

2022. HADOW, W. H. The Viennese period. The Oxford History of Music. Vol. V. London: Oxford Univ. Press, 1931.

2023. HALBIG, H. Musikgeschichte--leicht gemacht. Berlin: N. G., 1943.

2024. HAMEL and Hurlimann (ed.). Das Atlantis Buch der Musik. Zürich: Atlantis-Verlag, 1946.

2025. HANUSZ, Jan. O ksiażce do nabożeństwa "Króla Zygmunta I." Wrekopisie monachijskim ... Odbitka z XI tomu Rozpraw Wydz. filolog. Akad. Umiej. Kraków: N. G., 1884. (BM 3071. a. 3.)

2026. HARMAN, Alec. Mediaeval and early Renaissance music. New York: Oxford Univ. Press, 1958.

2027. _______ and Anthony Milner. Late Renaissance and Baroque music. New York: Oxford Univ. Press, 1959.

2028. HAUSER, Johann Ernst. Geschichte des Christlichen, insbesondere des evangelischen Kirchengesänges und der Kirchenmusik ... nebst Andeutungen und Vorschlägen zur Verbesserung des musikalischen Theiles des evangelischen Cultus. Ein historisch--ästhetischer Versuch. Leipzig: G. Basse, 1834.

2029. HAWKINS. General history of the science and practice of music. 3 Vols. London and New York: Dover Publications, 1853.

2030. HEYDT, Johann von der. Geschichte der Evangelischen Kirchenmusik, 1926. Second Edition. Berlin: Trowizset & Sohn, 1932.

2031. HIRNER, Rose Gertrude. The Catholic church in music. Techny: Mission Press, S. V. D., 1932.

2032. HISTOIRE de la musique ... Moyen age (in "Encyclopédie de la musique et dictionnaire du conservatorie.) Paris: N. G., 1913. (LC-A44-2416)

2033. HÖEG, C. Monumenta musicae byzantinae. N. G.: N. G., 1935. (BM)

2034. HOPE. Mediaeval music. London: Stock, 1894.

2035. HUGHES, Dom Anselm. The new Oxford history of music. Vol. I (Ancient and Oriental Music). London: Oxford Univ. Press, 1957.

2036. _______. The new Oxford history of music. Vol. II (Early Medieval music--up to 1300). London: Oxford Univ. Press, 1954.

2037. _______ and Gerald Abraham (eds.). The new Oxford history of music. Vol. III (Ars Nova and the Renaissance). London: Oxford Univ. Press, 1960.

2038. HUMPHREYS, Francis Landon. The evolution of church music. With preface by Rt. Rev. H. C. Potter. New York: C. Scribner's Sons, 1896.

2039. HUOT-PLEUROUX, Paul. Histoire de la musique réligieuse des origines à nos jours. Paris: Presses universitaires de France, 1957.

2040. HUTCHINGS, Arthur. Church music in the nineteenth century. London and New York: Herbert Jenkins, Oxford Univ. Press, 1967.

2041. JAMMERS, Ewald. Musik in Byzanz, im päpstlichen Rom und im Frankenreich. Der Choral als Musik der Textaussprache, Akademie der Wissenschaften, philosophisch-historische Klasse, Jahrgang 1962, 1. Abhandlung.

2042. JUNG, Hans Rudolf. Geschichte des Musiklebens der Stadt Greiz. T. I: Von den Anfängen bis zum Stadtbrand 1802. (Schriften des Heimatmuseums Greiz, 4). Greiz: Heimatmuseum, 1963.

2043. KAHNIS, C. F. A. Internal history of German Protestantism. Edinburgh: N. G., 1856.

2044. KEHREIN, Joseph. Kirchen - und religiöse Lieder aus dem 12.-15. Jahrhundert. Repr. Hildesheim, Germany: Georg Olms, 1967. (orig. Paderborn, 1853.)

2045. KILLING, Joseph. Kirchenmusikalische Schätze der Bibliothek des Abbate Fortunato Santini; ein Beitrag zur Geschichte der katholischen Kirchenmusik in Italien. Düsseldorf: L. Schwann, 1910. (Neudr.--Münster: Aschendorffsche Buchdr., 1908).

2046. KIRBY, F. E. A short history of keyboard music. New York: Free Press, 1966.

2047. KIRCHENMUSIKALISCHE Vierteljahrs-Schrift. Salzburg: M. Mittermüller, 1887.

2048. KIRSCH, Winfried. Die Quellen der mehrstimmigen Magnificat-und Te Deum-Vertonungen bis zur Mitte des 16. Jahrhunderts. Tutzing: Schneider, 1966.

2049. KOCH. Geschichte des Kirchenliedes und Kirchengesänges. Stuttgart: Belser, 1866. Reprint, Hildesheim: Georg Olms, 1967.

2050. KONEVSKII, Mikhail Ferapontovich. Kratkaya istoriia tserkovnavo pieniia v tserkvi vselenskoi i melodicheskavo pieniia v tserkvi russkoi. sostabilh ... diakonh M. F. Konevskii. Moscow: Piurgersona, 1896.

2051. KÖSTLIN. Geschichte des christlichen Gottesdienstes. Freiburg: Mohr, 1887.

2052. KRAUSE, G. Geschichte des musikalischen Lebens in der evangelischen Kirche Westfalens von der Reformation bis zur Gegenwart. Kassel: N. G., 1932. (BM)

2053. KREMP, Werner. Quellen und Studien zum Responsorium prolixum in der Überlieferung der euskirchener Offiziumsantiphonare. Köln: Beiträge zur rheinischen Musikgeschichte, 1958. (BM-WP c. 455/30)

2054. KRIESSMANN, Alfons. Kleine Kirchenmusikgeschichte für studierende, Kirchenmusiker und Geistliche. Stuttgart: C. L. Schultheiss, 1938.

2055. LA BORDE, J. B. de. Essai sur la musique ancienne et moderne. New York: Scientific Library Service, 1780.

2056. LANG, Paul Henry. Music in western civilization. New York: W. W. Norton & Co., 1887.

2057. LANGHANS. Geschichte der Musik des 17., 18. und 19. Jahrhunderts. Leipzig: Leuckart, 1887.

2058. LA RUE, Jan (ed.). Aspects of Medieval and Renaissance music. New York: W. W. Norton & Co., 1966.

2059. LAURENCIN D'ARMOND, F. P. Zur Geschichte der Kirchenmusik bei den Italienern und Deutschen. Leipzig: H. Matthes, 1856.

2060. LAURENTIUS VON SCHNUFFIS. Mirantische Maultrummel. reprt. -of Konstanz 1698. ed. Hildesheim: G. Olms, n. d. (LC-35985)

2061. LAW, Andres. Select harmony, containing in a plain and concise manner, the rules of singing, together with a collection of psalm tunes, hymns, and anthems. New York: Scientific Library Service, 1792.

2062. LEICHTENTRITT, Hugo. Music, history, and ideas. Cambridge: Harvard Univ. Press, 1947.

2063. LILIENCRON, R. Deutsches Leben im Volkslied um 1530. Stuttgart: Spemann, 1884.

2064. ________. Liturgisch-musikalische Geschichte der evangelischen Gottesdienste von 1523 bis 1700. Schleswig: J. Bergas, 1893.

2065. LINDSAY, T. M. History of the Reformation. New York: C. Scribner's Sons, 1906-07.

2066. LOVELOCK, William. A concise history of music. London: G. Bell, 1953, also New York: Crowell, 1954.

2067. MACDERMOTT, Kenneth Holland. Sussex church music in the past. Chichester: Moore & Wingham, 1922.

2068. MACE, Thomas. Musick's monument. London: T. Radcliffe & N. Thompson, 1676.

2069. MANITIUS, M. Geschichte der christlich-lateinischen Poesie bis zur Mitte des 8. Jahrhunderts. Stuttgart: J. G. Cotta, 1891.

2070. MATTFELD, Victor H. Georg Rhaw's publication for vespers. Brooklyn: Institute of Mediaeval Music, 1966.

2071. MCKINNEY, Howard D. and William R. Anderson. Music in history. New York: American Book Co., 1940.

2072. MEYER, Kathi. Das Konzert; ein Führer durch die Geschichte des Musizierens in Bildern und Melodien. Stuttgart: J. Engelhorns nachf., 1925.

2073. MILLER, Hugh Milton. History of music, 2nd edition. New York: Barnes and Noble, Inc., 1947.

2074. MINSHALL, E. Fifty year's reminiscences of a free church musician. Lancaster, Mass.: J. Clarke & Co., 1910.

2075. MITTERER, Sigisbert. Zwölfhundert Jähre Kloster Schaftlarn, 762-1962; Blätter zum Gedächtnis. (Beiträge zur altbayerischen Kirchengeschichte, Band 22, Heft 3.) München: Seitz, 1962.

2076. MIZLER, Lorenz Christoph. Neu eröffnete musikalische Bibliothek. Hildesheim, Germany: Georg Olms, June 30, 1967. (orig. Leipzig, 1739-52).

2077. MÖHLER, Anton. Compendium der katholichen Kirchenmusik. Ravensburg: F. Alber, 1909.

2078. MÖNEKEBERG, Adolf. Die Stellung der Spielleute im Mittelalter. Berlin: Rothschild, 1910.

2079. MOSHEIM, Johann L. von. Institutes of ecclesiastical history. New Haven: A. H. Maltby, 1832, also--New York: Harper Bros., 1839 and 1941; New York: Stanford and Swords, 1854; New York: R. Carter Bros., 1867.

2080. MÜTZELL, Julius. Geistliche Lieder der evangelischen Kirche aus dem sechzehnten Jahrhundert. Reprt. -of Berlin 1855 ed. vol. 3. Hildesheim: G. Olms, n. d.

2081. ________. Geistliche Lieder der evangelischen Kirche aus dem siebzehnten und der ersten Hälfte des achtzehnten Jahrhunderts. reprt. of Braunschweig 1858 ed., Hildesheim: G. Olms, n. d.

2082. MUSIC in the Renaissance. New York: W. W. Norton & Co., 1959.

2083. MUSIC through the ages. New York: G. P. Putnam's Sons, 1946.

2084. The MUSICAL heritage of the church. St. Louis: Concordia Publishing House, 1944.

2085. NEIVERGELT, Edwin. Die Tonsätze der deutsch-schweizerischen reformierten Kirchengesangbücher im XVII. Jahrhundert. Zürich: Zwingli, 1944.

2086. NEMMERS, Erwin Esser. Twenty centuries of Catholic church music. Milwaukee: Bruce Publishing Co., 1949.

2087. NIKEL, Emil. Geschichte der katholischen Kirchenmusik. Breslau: F. Goerlich, 1908.

2088. NINDE, E. S. Nineteen centuries of christian song. Westwood, N. J.: Fleming H. Revell Co., 1938.

2089. NORMAND, Théodula. Musique réligieuse au moyen âge. N. G.: N. G., n. d. (LC ML 60:068)

2090. OLLARD, S. L. Short history of the Oxford movement. London: A. Mowbry & Co., 1915; also Milwaukee: The Young Churchman Co., 1915.

2091. ORTIGUE, Joseph Louis D'. La musique à l'église. Paris: Didier etc., 1861.

2092. OXFORD history of music. 6 vols. Oxford: Clarendon Press, Hadow, ed., 1901-05, 2nd ed., London: Oxford Univ. Press, 1929, 1954.

2093. PARRISH, Carl (compd. & ed.). A treasury of early music. An anthology of masterworks of the middle ages, the Renaissance, and the Baroque Era. New York: W. W. Norton & Co., Inc., 1958.

2094. ________ and John E. Ohl (compd. & ed.). Masterpieces of music before 1750. An anthology of musical examples from Gregorian chant to J. S. Bach. New York: W. W. Norton & Co., Inc., 1951.

2095. PETROSINI, Francesco. La musica sacra attraverso i secoli. Renevento: G. de Martini, 1928.

2096. PRATT, Waldo Selden. The history of music. New York: G. Schirmer, 1907.

2097. QUASTEN, Johannes. Musik und Gesang in den heidnischen Kulten der Antike und im Christentum der ersten Jahrhunderte. (pp. xii, 274). Münster Univ. Library. Münster, Germany: Aschendorff, 1928.

2098. ________. Musik und Gesang in den Kulten der heidnischen Antike und christlichen Frühzeit. Münster: Aschendorff, 1930; also Nachdr. 1973.

2099. RANTA, Sulho. Sävelten mestareita Palestrinasta nykypäiviin. Toimit, tanut S. Ranta. Porvoossa: N. G., 1945. (BM-7892. S. 3.)

2100. REESE, Gustave. Music in the Middle Ages. New York: W. W. Norton & Co., 1940-48.

2101. _______. Music in the Renaissance. New York: W. W. Norton & Co., 1959.

2102. RICE, William C. A concise history of church music. New York: Abingdon, 1964.

2103. RIEMANN. Catechism of musical history. 2 vols. London: Augener & Co., 1892. (also New York: G. Schirmer, 1902.)

2104. RINALDI, M. Musica e verismo. Critica ed estetica d'una tendenza musicale. Roma: Fratelli de Santis, 1932.

2105. ROBERTSON, A. and D. Stevens (ed.). The Pelican history of music. Vol. I., "Ancient forms to Polyphony"; Vol. II., "Renaissance and Baroque." Baltimore, Md.: Penguin Books, 1960, 1963.

2106. ROBERTSON, Dora H. Sarum close. London: Jonathan Cape, 1938.

2107. ROCKSTRO, W. S. A general history of music. New York: Scribner and Welford, 1886.

2108. ROOS, S. P. de. Beginselen van kerkmuziek. Amsterdam: H. J. Paris, 1946.

2109. ROUSSIER, Pierre Joseph. Mémoire sur la musique des anciens, ou l'on expose le principe des proportions authentiques, dites de Pythagor, et de divers systèmes de musique chez les Grecs, les Chinois et les Egyptiens. Monuments of Music & Music Literature. Rochester, N.Y.: Univ. Rochester Press, 1959. (orig. Paris, Chez Lacombe, 1770.)

2110. ROWBOTHAM, John. A history of music. London: Richard Bentley and Son, 1893.

2111. RUDOLF, Benedictine. Die Quaestiones in musica. Ein Choraltraktat des zentralen Mittelalters und ihr mutmasslicher Verfasser Rudolf von St. Trond, 1070-1138. Beihefte: International Musicale Society, 1911.

2112. SACHS, Curt. Our musical heritage. New York: Prentice-Hall, Inc., 1948 (1955).

2113. _______. The rise of music in the ancient world. New York: W. W. Norton & Co., 1943.

2114. SCHAUER, Johann Karl. Geschichte der biblisch-kirchlichen Dicht-und Tonkunst und ihrer Werke. Jena: T. Mauke, 1850.

2115. SCHERING, Arnold. Zur Frage der Orgelmitwirkung in der Kirchenmusik des 15. Jahrhunderts. Freiburg: Deutsche Orgelkunst, 1927.

2116. SCHLECHT, Raymund. Geschichte der Kirchenmusik. Zugleich Grundlage zur vorurtheilslosen Beantwortung der Frage: "Was ist echte Kirchenmusik." Regensburg: A. Coppenrath, 1871, 1879.

2117. SCHLETTERER. Studien zur Geschichte der Französischen Musik. Berlin: Dumköhler, 1884-1885.

2118. SCHOLES, Percy A. The Columbia history of music through ear and eye. London: Oxford Univ. Press, 1930-38.

2119. SCHRADE, Leo. Zum sechzigsten Geburtstag. Musik und Geschichte. Köln: Arno Volk Verlag, 1963.

2120. SCHUBERTH, Johannes. Das Wechselverhältnis von Choral und Orgelchoral im sechzehnten und siebzehnten Jahrhundert. Kassel: Bärenreiter-Verlag, 1931.

2121. SCOTT, Cyril. Music: Its secret influence throughout the ages. London: Rider & Co., 1933.

2122. SEAY, Albert. Music in the medieval world. Englewood Cliffs, N.J.: Prentice-Hall, Inc., 1965.

2123. SHAW, Harold Watkins. From Tallis to Tomkins; a survey of church music with foreword by A. S. Duncan-Jones. London: Oxford Univ. Press, 1954.

2124. SHORE, S. R. English church musical history of the Reformation period. Birmingham: N.G., 1911. (BM)

2125. SMITH, Leo. Music of the seventeenth and eighteenth centuries. London: J. M. Dent & Sons, 1931.

2126. SOEHNER, Leo. Die Geschichte der Begleitung des gregorianischen Chorals in Deutschland, vornehmlich im 18. Jahrhundert. Inaugural Dissertation, etc., pp. vvi-129. Augsburgh: N.G., 1931. (BM7900.g.16)

2127. SOLITT, Edna Nicholson. Dufay to Sweelinck. New York: Ives Washburn, 1933.

2128. SPELMAN, Leslie P. Art and the Reformation: A critical study of the effects of the Protestant Reformation on the continental arts of the 16th and 17th centuries, and in particular on the organ music of France and Germany up to the time of J. S. Bach. Claremont, Calif.: Claremont Graduate School, 1946.

2129. SPITTA, Philipp. Die wiederbelebung protestantischer Kirchen-musik auf geschichtlicher Grundlage. Berlin: N. G., 1892. (LC-ML 60. 377.)

2130. ________. Musik geschichtliche Ausfätze. Berlin: Paetel, 1894.

2131. STÄBLEIN, Bruno. Schriftbild der einstimmigen Musik. (Musikgeschichte in Bildern, III/4). Leipzig: VEB Deutscher Verlag für Musik, 1975.

2132. STANFORD and Forsyth. A history of music. London: Oxford Univ. Press, 1916.

2133. STARR, Blanche Ellis. The story of sacred and ecclesiastical music from the earliest times. Rockford, Ill.: Horton Printing Co., 1938.

2134. STATHAM, Heathcote. Restoration church music. New York: Oxford Univ. Press, 1949.

2135. STEVENS, Denis (ed.). A history of song. New York: Norton, 1961.

2136. ________. Tudor church music. New York: Norton, 1961.

2137. STEVENSON, R. Music before the classic era. London: Macmillan & Co., Ltd., 1958.

2138. STRUNK, William Oliver. Source readings in music history. New York: W. W. Norton, 1950.

2139. SYMMES, Thomas. Utile dulci. A joco-serious dialogue, concerning regular singing. Boston: B. Green, 1723.

2140. TAUNTON, E. L. History of church music. London: Lippincott, 1887.

2141. TAYLOR, Edward. The English cathedral service, its glory, its decline, and its designed extinction. London: Simptin, Marshall, & Co., 1845.

2142. TOVEY, Donald Francis. The main stream of music. New York: Oxford Univ. Press, 1949.

2143. TUDOR church music. London: Oxford Univ. Press, 1923.

2144. ULRICH, Homer and Paul A. Pisk. A history of music and musical style. New York, Burlingame: Harcourt, Brace, & World, Inc., 1963.

2145. WACKERBARTH, Francis Diederich. Music and the Anglo Saxons: Being some account of the Anglo-Saxon orchestra. With remarks on the church music of the 19th century. London: W. Pickering, 1837.

2146. WACKERNAGEL, Philipp. Das deutsche Kirchenlied von der ältesten Zeit bis zu Anfang des xvii. Jahrhunderts. Mit Berücksichtigung der deutschen kirchlichen Liederdichtung im weiteren Sinne und der lateinischen. Revised. Leipzig: B. G. Teubner, 1864-77.

2147. WAND, J. C. History of the modern church. London: Methuen, 1930.

2148. WEBER, Heinrich. Kirchenlied und Voekslied im 16. Jahrhundert. Züruch: Druck von Orell, Füssli & Co., 1872.

2149. WEINMANN, Karl. La musique d'église. Translated from German by Paul Landormy. Paris: P. Delaplane, 1912.

2150. WEITZEL, Wilhelm. Führer durch die katholische Kirchenmusik der Gegenwart. Freiburg: Herder & Co., 1930.

2151. WERNER, Arno. Vier Jahrhunderte im Dienste der Kirchenmusik; Geschichte des Amtes und Standes der evangelischen Kantoren, Organisten und Stadtpfeifer seit der Reformation. Leipzig: C. Merseburger, 1933.

2152. WERNER, Eric. The conflict between Hellenism and Judaism in music of early Christian church. Cincinnati: Offprint from Hebrew Union College Annual, Vol. 20., 1947.

2153. WESTERVELT, Caroline Castle. Early church Music. Honolulu: N. G., 1914. (LC-ML3400.W4)

2154. WESTRUP, Jack. An introduction to musical history. London: Hutchinson's Univ. Library, 1955.

2155. WILLIAMS, John. Gwaith Glanmor. yn cynnwys: hanes cerddoriaeth gyssegredig, yn cael ei egluro a thonau a darluniau; yn nghyda chaniadau amrywiaethol Cymreig. Gwrecsam: R. Hughes a'i pah, 1865.

2156. WINTERFELD, Carl von. Der evangelische Kirchengesang und sein Verhältniss zur Kunst des Tonsätzes. Leipzig: Breitkopf und Härtel, 1843-47.

2157. _______. Zur geschichte heiliger Tonkunst. Eine Reihe einzelner Abhandlungen. Leipzig: Breitkopf und Härtel, 1852.

2158. WIORA, Walter. The four ages of music. May. ref. Translated by M. D. Herter Norton. New York: W. W. Norton, 1965.

2159. WOOLDRIDGE, H. E. and G. E. P. Arkwright. Musica antiquata. New York: Carl Fischer, Inc., n. d.

2160. WOOLDRIGE. Oxford history of music, c. 1400-1600. London: Oxford, 1932.

2161. WRIGHT, Thomas. Anglo-Latin satirical poets of XII century. Vol. II. London: Longman & Co., 1872.

2162. YOUNG, Karl. The drama of the mediaeval church. 2 vols. New York: Oxford Univ. Press, 1933.

2163. ZENCK, Hermann. Sixtus Dietrich; ein Beitrag zur Musik und Musikanschauung im Zeitalter der reformation. Mit einem Notenanhang. Leipzig: Breitkopf & Härtel, 1928.

See also: 3, 5, 13, 62, 78, 81, 96, 97, 100, 101, 102, 103, 106, 107, 120, 121, 122, 199, 200, 201, 207, 216, 218, 225, 230, 235, 240, 245, 264, 268, 269, 277, 285, 289, 292, 314, 319, 324, 336, 338, 361, 364, 392, 410, 412, 413, 415, 416, 419, 420, 428, 432, 436, 439, 441, 444, 445, 453, 455, 456, 473, 476, 477, 478, 481, 486, 488, 491, 504, 511, 516, 518, 521, 530, 533, 539, 540, 545, 546, 549, 550, 567, 574, 583, 586, 605, 629, 636, 643, 644, 647, 651, 652, 653, 656, 663, 669, 670, 675, 681, 689, 692, 697, 698, 705, 707, 714, 719, 734, 735, 737, 743, 787, 789, 813, 847, 855, 884, 914, 919, 922, 928, 929, 931, 941, 945, 946, 953, 954, 980, 1001, 1002, 1005, 1039, 1042, 1046, 1050, 1055, 1060, 1063, 1079, 1080, 1085, 1090, 1091, 1095, 1117, 1118, 1119, 1122, 1128, 1133, 1134, 1135, 1142, 1150, 1155, 1168, 1174, 1175, 1184, 1186, 1189, 1192, 1204, 1205, 1208, 1210, 1213, 1214, 1215, 1227, 1228, 1230, 1235, 1238, 1240, 1243, 1244, 1248, 1252, 1255, 1260, 1265, 1267, 1277, 1280, 1293, 1294, 1295, 1299, 1301, 1303, 1306, 1308, 1309, 1315, 1317, 1320, 1322, 1331, 1343, 1344, 1349, 1352, 1354, 1355, 1363, 1364, 1366, 1372, 1374, 1376, 1387, 1391, 1393, 1397, 1398, 1399, 1402, 1410, 1411, 1413, 1429, 1443, 1462, 1467, 1469, 1473, 1481, 1504, 1507, 1524, 1527, 1535, 1548, 1550, 1561, 1575, 1578, 1583, 1584, 1586, 1592, 1595, 1601, 1616, 1645, 1654, 1657, 1662, 1665, 1677, 1681, 1692, 1711, 1713, 1720, 1721, 1722, 1733, 1735, 1736, 1737, 1742, 1751, 1755, 1760, 1766, 1784, 1787, 1804, 1806, 1812, 1821, 1845, 1847, 1852, 1850, 1861, 1865, 1871, 1885, 1888, 1941, 1946, 1947, 2048, 2183, 2194, 2249, 2259, 2274, 2284, 2289, 2326, 2345, 2359, 2362, 2372, 2374, 2376, 2380, 2382, 2385, 2388, 2392, 2393, 2394, 2399, 2400, 2402, 2416, 2417, 2422, 2429, 2438, 2442, 2443, 2448, 2456, 2458, 2469, 2470, 2475, 2478, 2485, 2487, 2494, 2501, 2503, 2519, 2541, 2542, 2544, 2546, 2562, 2568, 2593, 2594, 2603, 2620, 2621, 2626, 2627, 2636, 2638, 2641, 2643, 2652, 2662, 2663, 2666, 2667, 2671, 2672, 2675, 2676, 2689, 2691, 2695, 2700, 2701, 2706, 2723, 2742, 2755, 2757, 2760, 2761, 2776, 2779, 2780, 2784, 2785, 2786, 2787, 2789, 2791, 2795, 2807, 2812, 2814, 2818, 2838, 2859, 2860, 2871, 2873, 2877, 2881, 2884, 2892,

2898, 2900, 2907, 2914, 2915, 2920, 2922, 2929, 2932, 2933, 2934, 2937, 2939, 2945, 2952, 2953, 2954, 2958, 2961, 2968, 2969, 2970, 2975, 2978, 3001, 3004, 3008, 3010a, 3016, 3017, 3020, 3026, 3027, 3030, 3033, 3043, 3050, 3057, 3059, 3060, 3066, 3068, 3069, 3070, 3076, 3083, 3085, 3087, 3090, 3091, 3096, 3106, 3125, 3126, 3129, 3135, 3137, 3142, 3153, 3154, 3155, 3162, 3165, 3166, 3169, 3174, 3175, 3192, 3193, 3198, 3201, 3202, 3203, 3205, 3214, 3218, 3221, 3225, 3226, 3227, 3229, 3230, 3234, 3235, 3239, 3241, 3247, 3248, 3249, 3252, 3253, 3254, 3255, 3256, 3263, 3264, 3272, 3275, 3279, 3290, 3291, 3292, 3295, 3296, 3297, 3299, 3300, 3302, 3303, 3305, 3308, 3312, 3315, 3317, 3322, 3325, 3328, 3331, 3332, 3333, 3335, 3336, 3339, 3340, 3341, 3342, 3343, 3344, 3345, 3347, 3348, 3349, 3350, 3351, 3352, 3353, 3356, 3358, 3359, 3360, 3361, 3362, 3364, 3365, 3366, 3367, 3369, 3373, 3374, 3375, 3376, 3378, 3379, 3384, 3387, 3388, 3389, 3395, 3396, 3397, 3399, 3400, 3401, 3404, 3407, 3409, 3410, 3412, 3415, 3416, 3418, 3420, 3421, 3426, 3427, 3430, 3432, 3433, 3436, 3437, 3439, 3441, 3444, 3447, 3450, 3452, 3457, 3458, 3460, 3461, 3464, 3465, 3468, 3471, 3475, 3483, 3485, 3488, 3489, 3490, 3491, 3497, 3501, 3506, 3509, 3510, 3512, 3515, 3517, 3518, 3520, 3522, 3523, 3524, 3525, 3527, 3535, 3537, 3538, 3542, 3545, 3551, 3556, 3557, 3562, 3566, 3577, 3582, 3587, 3588, 3589, 3593, 3594, 3597, 3598, 3599, 3603, 3604, 3607, 3608, 3612, 3613, 3614, 3615, 3617, 3619, 3621, 3622, 3624, 3626, 3627, 3628, 3629, 3632, 3633, 3634, 3636, 3637, 3639, 3640, 3641, 3642, 3643, 3645, 3646, 3649, 3651, 3653, 3654, 3655, 3656, 3657, 3660, 3661, 3663, 3666, 3670, 3672, 3675, 3676, 3678, 3680, 3681, 3682, 3689, 3693, 3696, 3704, 3705, 3706, 3710, 3712, 3714, 3716, 3723, 3728, 3733, 3724, 3736, 3749, 3754, 3755, 3767, 3771, 3790, 3797, 3807, 3826, 3827, 3834, 3844, 3845, 3854, 3866, 3868, 3869, 3880, 3884, 3885, 3893, 3895, 3896, 3916, 3919, 3920, 3921, 3927, 3932, 3951, 3964, 3970, 3984, 3986, 3997, 3999, 4004, 4018, 4028, 4030, 4031, 4038, 4041, 4057, 4058, 4059, 4063, 4065, 4071, 4074, 4077, 4093, 4102, 4104, 4107, 4108, 4111, 4112, 4113, 4116, 4119, 4123, 4127, 4128, 4129, 4131, 4143, 4145, 4152, 4156, 4160, 4164, 4213, 4214, 4215, 4217, 4218, 4226, 4227, 4232, 4233, 4235, 4242, 4250, 4251, 4252, 4253, 4254, 4255, 4256, 4257, 4258, 4259, 4260, 4261, 4262, 4268, 4272, 4278, 4281, 4284, 4286, 4288, 4296, 4297, 4303, 4304, 4305, 4306, 4308, 4309, 4310, 4311, 4318, 4329, 4340, 4342, 4344, 4350, 4364, 4367, 4369, 4374, 4389, 4392, 4393, 4400, 4401, 4412, 4419, 4420, 4421, 4422, 4426, 4428, 4429, 4432, 4435, 4436, 4437, 4441, 4443, 4447, 4451, 4453, 4467, 4470, 4475, 4477, 4478, 4479, 4499, 4506, 4520, 4527, 4547, 4556, 4566, 4569, 4581, 4611, 4612, 4613, 4640, 4651, 4681, 4697, 4698, 4699, 4713, 4716, 4719, 4720, 4721, 4723, 4728, 4730, 4732,

4733, 4749, 4750, 4751, 4754, 4755, 4756, 4760, 4774, 4776, 4785, 4790, 4791, 4801, 4803, 4804, 4809, 4820, 4825, 4827, 4828, 4838, 4841, 4852, 4857, 4874, 4875, 4876, 4878, 4887, 4888, 4895, 4914, 4916, 4917, 4940, 4946, 4948, 4950, 4955, 4959, 4961, 4979, 4981, 4982, 4984, 4988, 5004, 5006, 5013, 5014, 5015, 5017, 5018, 5019, 5020, 5033, 5034, 5042, 5068, 5069, 5070, 5072, 5076, 5078, 5081, 5086, 5087, 5091, 5093, 5094, 5096, 5098, 5101, 5102, 5103, 5105, 5106, 5108, 5109, 5110, 5114, 5117, 5122, 5124, 5125, 5126, 5127, 5128, 5149, 5156, 5185, 5189, 5190, 5193, 5194, 5195, 5196, 5197, 5198, 5199, 5200, 5219, 5220, 5237, 5239, 5240, 5241, 5250, 5267, 5275, 5281, 5284, 5285, 5288, 5313, 5316, 5320, 5321, 5323, 5340, 5358, 5379, 5380, 5387, 5391, 5405, 5427, 5428, 5432.

HYMNAL COMPANIONS

2164. AVERY, Gordon. Companion to the song book of the Salvation Army. Compiled by G. Avery. London: Salvationist Publishing & Supplies, 1961.

2165. BICKERSTETH, E. H. (ed.). The hymnal companion to the Book of Common Prayer. Third edition, revised and enlarged. London: Sampson Low, Marston & Co., 1896 (?)

2166. CONCORDANCE to Christian Science hymnal and hymnal notes. Boston: Christian Science Publishing Society, 1961.

2167. EPISCOPAL Church--Joint Commission on Church Music. The hymnal 1940 companion. Third edition, revised. New York: The Church Pension Fund, 1956.

2168. GEALY, Fred Daniel, Austin Lovelace and Carlton R. Young. Companion to the Hymnal; a handbook to the 1964 Methodist Hymnal. Nashville, Tenn.: Abingdon Press, 1970.

2169. HIGGINSON, J. Vincent. Handbook for American Catholic hymnals. New York: Hymn Society of America, 1976.

2170. HILL, F. C. Tables to aid the selection of hymns for use in connection with hymns ancient and modern. London: N. G., 1891. (BM)

2171. HUTCHINS, Charles L. Annotations of the hymnal. Hartford, Conn.: M. H. Mallory & Co., 1872.

2172. JEAYES, I. H. Choirmaster's companion to hymns ancient and modern. London: N. G., 1889. (BM)

2173. LORENZ, Ellen Jane. Two-hundred hymn stories. Dayton, Ohio: Lorenz Publishing Co., 1941.

2174. MARTIN, Hugh (ed.). The Baptist hymn book companion. London: Psalms & Hymns Trust, 1962.

2175. MOORSOM, R. M. Historical companion to hymns ancient and modern. London: C. J. Clay, 1889 and 2nd ed., 1903.

2176. PARRY, K. L. and Erik Routley. Companion to congregational praise. London: Independent Press Ltd., 1953.

2177. REYNOLDS, William J. Hymns of our faith; a handbook for the Baptist hymnal. Nashville: Broadman Press, 1964.

2178. ______. Companion to Baptist hymnal. Nashville: Broadman Press, 1976.

2179. SMITH, Oswald J. Hymn stories. Winona Lake, Ind.: Rodeheaver Co., 1969.

2180. WAKE, Arthur N. Companion to hymnbook for Christian worship. St. Louis: Bethany Press, 1970.

See also: 2613.

HYMNALS and SONGBOOKS

Recent Hymnals (England and America)

2181. ALTENBURGISCHES Gesangbuch nebst gebeten. Altenburg: Hofbuchdruckerei, 1846.

2182. AMACULO enkonzo. Kransfontein: N.G., 1947. (BM-3438, g. 55.)

2183. BAEUMKER, W. Ein deutsches geistliches Liederbuch mit Melodien aus dem XV. Jahrhundert II. Leipzig: N.G., 1895. (BM) also-Neudr., Hildesheim: G. Olms, 1967.

2184. BARRETT, George Slatyer. Congregational church hymnal. Edited for the Congregational Union of England and Wales by G. S. Barrett. London: Congregational Union of England and Wales, 1905.

2185. ______. Congregational church hymnal; or, hymns of worship, praise, and prayer, for Congregational Churches. Edited for the Congregational Union of England and Wales by G. S. Barrett. The pointing arranged and the music selected by Josiah Booth. London: N.G., 1914. (BM)

2186. ______. Congregational mission hymnal. London: N.G., 1890. (BM)

2187. BAYLY, Albert Frederick. Rejoice O people. With tunes by various composers. N. G.: N. G., 1951. (BM-3437. fro)

2188. BECKER, Paula. Let the song go on; fifty years of gospel singing with the Speer family. Nashville, Tenn.: Impact Books, 1971.

2189. The BELIEVERS hymn book. With supplement. For use at assemblings of the Lord's people. London: Pickering & Inglis, 1963.

2190. BELL, C. D. and H. E. Fox. The church of England hymnal. London: Church of England, 1894.

2191. BENNETT, Clifford A. and Paul Hume. Hymnal of Christian unity. Toledo, Ohio: Gregorian Institute of America, 1964.

2192. The BERWICK hymnal. London: N. G., 1886. (BM)

2193. BLATCHFORD, Ambrose Nichols. Ministry in song. London: Reid Brothers, 1916.

2194. BODE, W. Quellennachweis über die Lieder des hannoverischen und lüneburgischen Gesangbuches. Hannover: N. G., 1881. (BM)

2195. BRADFORD Band of Hope Union. The band of hope melodist. Compiled under the direction of the committee. Bradford: M. Field, 1900.

2196. BRAGERS, Achille P. The monastery hymnal. Boston: McLaughlin & Reilly Co., n. d.

2197. BRIDGES, Robert and H. E. Wooldridge. The Yattendon hymnal. London: Oxford Univ. Press, 1920.

2198. BRITISH and Foreign Unitarian Association. The Essex hall hymnal. London: British and Foreign Unitarian Association, 1890.

2199. BUCHANON, E. S. The early Latin song book. New York: Charles A. Swift, Inc., 1930.

2200. CALL to praise. Winona Lake: Rodeheaver Hall-Mack Co., 1965.

2201. CALVARY'S blessing in song. Winona Lake: Rodeheaver Hall-Mack Co., 1965.

2202. CANADA--Church of England In. The book of Common Praise, being the hymn book of the Church of England in

Canada. Compiled by a committee of the General Synod. London: Oxford Univ. Press, e. g. (also Toronto: Henry Frowde.), 1910.

2203. CARMICHAEL, Amy B. W. (ed.). Wings. A book of Dohnavur songs. London: N. G., 1960. (BM-3054. f. 6.)

2204. CARTER, F. E. Truro mission hymn-book. London: N. G., 1892. (BM)

2205. CENTENARY missionary hymnal. London: N. G., 1895. (BM)

2206. CHRISTIAN asor ndwom. Na anapa asor mu nyebea. Fantse, etc. England: Methodist Book Depot, 1962.

2207. CHRISTIAN Reformed Church--Liturgy and Ritual. Psalter hymnal. Supplement with liturgical studies and forms. Grand Rapids, Mich.: Board of Publications of the Christian Reformed Church, 1974.

2208. CHRISTIAN service songs. Winona Lake: Rodeheaver Hall-Mack Co., 1965.

2209. The CHURCH hymnary. London: Oxford Univ. Press, 1927.

2210. CHURCH of England. The book of common praise. Compiled by a committee of the General Synod. Toronto: Oxford Univ. Press, 1938.

2211. CHURCH service hymns. Winona Lake: Rodeheaver Hall-Mack Co., 1965.

2212. CLARK, W. Thorburn. Hymns that endure. Nashville: Broadman Press, 1961.

2213. COBB, William Frederick. Hymns for men and women. Compiled by W. F. Cobb (afterwards Geikie-Cobb). London: Church of Saint Ethelburga the Virgin, 1907.

2214. COIT, S. and G. Spiller (ed.). Ethical hymn book. London: Swan Sonnenschein & Co., 1905.

2215. The COKESBURY worship hymnal. Nashville, Tenn.: Abingdon-Cokesbury Press, n. d.

2216. CORONATION hymns. Chicago: E. O. Excell, 1910.

2217. COUSINS, G. Missionary hymn book. London: N. G., 1888. (BM)

2218. CRUSADE songs. Winona Lake: Rodeheaver Hall-Mack Co., 1965.

2219. CUTTS, John P. Roger Smith, his book. Bishop Smith's part-song books in Carlisle Univ. Cathedral library. N. G.: American Inst. of Musicology, 1972.

2220. A DAILY hymn book. London: Burns, Oates, and Washbourne, 1931.

2221. The DAILY hymns throughout the year at Mattins and Evensong, to which are added the principal sequences, with appendix and supplement. London: W. Walker, 1903.

2222. DANIELS, Louis E. Songs of praise for America. New York: Oxford Univ. Press, 1938.

2223. DAVISON, A. T. The Harvard University hymn book. Cambridge, Mass.: Harvard Univ., 1926.

2224. DEARMER, Percy. The English hymnal. New York: Oxford Univ. Press, 1933.

2225. DEMAREST, A. (ed.). The canyon hymnal for boys and girls. East Orange: Canyon Press, 1958.

2226. DENSON, T. J., Music Committee. Original Sacred Harp. Has section on rudiments of music with particular reference to the use of 'shaped notes' and their solmization. Haleyville, Ala.: Sacred Harp Publishing Co., Inc., 1936.

2227. DEW, E. N. Guild hymn book. London: N. G., 1889. (BM)

2228. DICKINSON, Clarence and Calvin Weiss Laufer. The hymnal (American Presbyterian). Philadelphia: Presbyterian Board of Christian Education, 1933.

2229. DIEHL, Katherine S. Hymns and tunes. An index. New York: Scarecrow, 1966.

2230. EARLEYWOOD school hymnal. N. G.: N. G., 1910. (BM3440. tt87.)

2231. The ENGLISH hymnal service book. London: Oxford Univ. Press, 1962.

2232. The ENGLISH hymnal with tunes. Oxford Library. Fair Lawn, N. J.: Oxford Univ. Press, 1933.

2233. ERLEMANN, Gustav. Das neue Einliefungsgesangbuch. Trier: Bantus-Verlag, 1913.

2234. EVANGELICAL Union Conference. The evangelical union hymnal. Compiled by a committee. Glasgow: Thomas D. Morison, 1890.

2235. FAVORITE hymns and choruses. Winona Lake: Rodeheaver Hall-Mack Co., 1965.

2236. FROST, Maurice (ed.). Hymns ancient and modern. With accompanying tunes. Historical edition. London: William Clowes & Sons, 1962. Reiss., Frere ed., 1909.

2237. FULL redemption songs. Winona Lake: Rodeheaver Hall-Mack Co., 1965.

2238. GABRIEL, Charles (ed.). Hymnal--sacred songs for men. New York: Fleming H. Revell Co., 1904.

2239. _______. Sixty years of gospel song. Chicago: Hope Publishing Co., n.d.

2240. GASTLER, Bernard. A study of the music of the Lutheran hymnal as a tool for musical growth in the Lutheran elementary school. U.T. Library, M.M. Austin, Tex.: Univ. of Texas, 1963.

2241. GESANGBUCH der evangelischen Brüdergemeine. Gnadua: N.G., 1893. (BM)

2242. GLAD gospel songs series. Winona Lake: Rodeheaver Hall-Mack Co., 1965.

2243. GLAD tidings in song. Winona Lake: Rodeheaver Hall-Mack Co., 1965.

2244. GODSDIENSTIG gezangboek voor Oud-Katholieken. Rotterdam: N.G., 1890. (BM)

2245. GOOD news in song. Winona Lake: Rodeheaver Hall-Mack Co., 1965.

2246. GOUCHER, Valmore X. American hymnbooks through 1875. Index cards. In progress and unpublished, to be published by the American Antiquarian Society.

2247. GRACE and glory hymn book. London: Grace Advent Testimony, 1963.

2248. GRAMMAR school hymn book. For normal and grammar schools, and families. New York, Chicago: Woolworth, Ainsworth & Co., 1871.

2249. GRAY, Charles Eugene. A survey of early American hymnals from 1762 to c. 1962; from James Lyon's Urania to the publications of the "Lowells Mason School" Noting changing trends and styles in texts and tunes. Baylor Univ. Library, M.M. Waco, Tex.: Baylor Univ., 1965.

2250. GREER, E. Harold (ed.). Hymnal for colleges and schools. New Haven: Yale, 1964.

2251. GROSSMAN, Robert L. A hymnal for the American synagogue. New York: Columbia Univ. Teachers College--Ed. D., 1955.

2252. HALL, Charles Cuthbert and Sigismond Lasar. The evangelical hymnal and tunes. New York, Chicago: A. S. Barnes and Co., 1880.

2253. HANDBUCH zum Evangelischen Kirchengesangbuch. Göttingen: Vandenhoeck & Ruprecht, 1965.

2254. The HARVARD University hymn book. Cambridge: Harvard Univ. Press, 1926 and 1964.

2255. HAVEN of rest favorites. Winona Lake: Rodeheaver Hall-Mack, 1965.

2256. HEILBUT, Tony. The gospel sound; good news and bad times. New York: Simon and Schuster, 1971.

2257. HIGGINS, James. The new Baptist hymnal. SBS, M. C. M. Fort Worth, Tex.: Southwestern Baptist Theological Seminary, 1965.

2258. HINOS em portuguȇs e congo. Nkunga mia yimbidila nzambi. London: Baptist Missionary Society, 1924.

2259. HOFFMANN, Heinz. Tradition und Aktualität im Kirchenlied. Göttingen: Bandenhoeck & Ruprecht, 1967.

2260. HOLLWEG, Walter. Geschichte der evangelischen Gesangbücher vom Niederrhein. Hildesheim, Germany: Georg Olms--reprint, 1967, (orig. Gütersloh, 1923).

2261. HOPPS, John Page. Hymns for special services. Leicester: Hopps, 1885.

2262. HORDER, William Garrett. The treasury of hymns. New York, London: H. Frowde, 1896.

2263. ________. Worship-song. One leaf is mutilated. London: Elliot Stock, 1900.

2264. HUTCHINSON, W. O. Apostolic faith church hymnal. A subsequent edition is entered under "Hutchinson." Bournemouth: W. O. Hutchinson, 1921.

2265. HYMN book. Concordia: W. C. A., 1964.

2266. HYMNAL. Concordia: Pew ed., 1964.

2267. The HYMNAL of the Protestant Episcopal Church. New York: The Church Pension Fund, 1930.

2268. HYMNAL and prayerbook. N. G. : Herder, 1964.

2269. HYMNARY for mission and special services. London: N. G. , 1889.

2270. HYMNS for Churches of Christ. Second, revised, edition. Birmingham: Publishing Committee of Churches of Christ, 1910.

2271. HYMNS Committee of Church of St. Martin-in-the-Fields, London. The people's hymn book. London and Oxford: A. R. Mowbray & Co. , 1924.

2272. HYMNS in harmony. Winona Lake: Rodeheaver Hall-Mack Co. , 1965.

2273. HYMNS we love. Winona Lake: Rodeheaver Hall-Mack Co. , 1965.

2274. IN hoc signo ... 106th thousand, etc. London: S. P. C. K. , 1915.

2275. INNARIO cristiano. Sestaristampa ... Con l'aggiunta di 40 nuovi inni. Torre Pellice: N. G. , 1960.

2276. JACKSON, A. G. Missioner's hymnal. London: N. G. , 1885. (BM)

2277. JÄGER, Ernst. Unser neues Kirchen-gesangbuch; eine Handreichung an die Gemeinde. Bischofszell: A. Salzmann Schildknecht, 1942.

2278. JAMES, Lionel. Songs of Zion. London: John Murray, 1936.

2279. JENNY, Markus. Geschichte des deutschschweizerischen evangelischen Gesangbuches im 16. Jahrhundert. With illustrations and musical examples. Kassel: Basel, 1962.

2280. JUBILATE. Winona Lake: Rodeheaver Hall-Mack Co. , 1965.

2281. KATHOLISCHES Gesang- und Gebetbuch. Mannheim: N. G. , 1885.

2282. KEATINGE, C. The Army Catholic hymn book. London: N. G. , 1893. (BM)

2283. KEYMER, N. Durham mission hymn-book. London: N. G. , 1885. (BM)

2284. KIRCHHOFF, Pater Kilian. Hymnen der Ostkirche. Dreifaltigkeits-, Marien-und totenhymnen. Revised by Schollmeyer. Münster: Verlag Regensberg, 1960.

2285. ______. Osterjubel der Ostkirche. Hymnen aus der fünfzigtägigen Osterfeier der byzantinischen Kirche. Revised by Schollmeyer. Münster: Verlag Regensberg, 1961.

2286. The LEWIN'S Mead hymnal. Compiled for the use of the ancient society of Protestant dissenters worshipping in Lewin's Mead, Bristol. Bristol: John Wright & Sons, 1911.

2287. LEWIS, John Daniel Vernon. Mawl i'r goruchaf. Emynau a chyfieithiadau. Llandyssul: Gwasg Gomer, 1962.

2288. LIBRARY of Congress, Music Division. Eddy hymn book index. In progress and unpublished. Washington, D. C.: Library of Congress, n. d.

2289. LIPPHARDT, Walther. Johann Leisentrits Gesangbuch von 1596 (Studien zur katholischen Bistums-und Klostergeschichte, 5). Leipzig: St.-Benno-Verlag, 1963.

2290. LORETTO hymn book. Manch: N. G., 1895.

2291. LOWENS, Irving (ed.). Wyeth's repository of sacred music, part second. New York: Da Capo Press, 1963.

2292. McCUTCHAN, Robert G. The deluge of new hymnals. N. G.: A reprint from the MTNA proceedings, 1933.

2293. McELRATH, Hugh T. How to use a hymnal. Nashville: Baptist School Board of the Southern Baptist Convention, 1968.

2294. MAXWELL, Richard. BMI hymnal. New York: Broadcast Music, Inc., 1940.

2295. MEARNS, James. Early Latin hymnaries. Cambridge: Cambridge Univ. Press, 1913.

2296. MELODIES of life. Winona Lake: Rodeheaver Hall-Mack Co., 1965.

2297. MELODIES of praise. Winona Lake: Rodeheaver Hall-Mack Co., 1965.

2298. MEN'S songs. Winona Lake: Rodeheaver Hall-Mack Co., 1965.

2299. METHODIST Church--Hymnal Revision Committee. The Methodist hymnal. Nashville, Tenn.: The Methodist Publishing House, 1932.

2300. METHODIST Conference Office--British Methodist. Methodist hymn book. London: Methodist Publ. House, 1933.

2301. MEYER, Frederick Brotherton and Walter John Mayers. Hymns for heart and life, for use at missions and conventions. London: Marshall Brothers, 1900.

2302. MISSION hymns for private use in the parish of St. John the Divine, Kennington. London: H. J. Wright, 1885.

2303. MORGAN, George Campbell. The song companion to the scriptures. London: Morgan & Scott, 1911.

2304. NATIONAL spiritualists' propaganda hymn book. Manchester: "The Two Worlds" Publishing Co., 1916.

2305. NELLE, W. Das neue evangelische Gesangbuch für Rheinland und Westfalen. Dortmund: N. G., 1890. (BM)

2306. The NEW office hymn book. London: Novello & Co., 1908.

2307. NEW songs for service. Winona Lake: Rodeheaver Hall-Mack Co., 1965.

2308. The OFFICE hymn book, 2 pt. London: Pickering & Chatto, 1889.

2309. The OFFICE hymn book. London: Pickering & Chatto, 1891.

2310. O'HALLORAN, Leo (ed.). Redemptorist hymn book and prayers. Dublin: Cahill & Co., 1963.

2311. OLD fashioned revival hour songs. Winona Lake: Rodeheaver Hall-Mack Co., 1965.

2312. ONE hundred and twelve familiar hymns and gospel songs. Winona Lake: Rodeheaver Hall-Mack Co., 1965.

2313. OULD, Dom S. G. (ed.). The book of hymns. Edinburgh: Sands & Co., 1910.

2314. PARKER, Alice Stuart. Creative hymn-singing: A collection of hymn-tunes and texts with notes on their origin, idiom, and performance, and suggestions for their use in the service. Chapel Hill, N. C.: Hinshaw Music, 1976.

2315. PARRY, William John. The English hymnal. Bethesda: J. E. Williams, 1907.

2316. PAULSEN. Das neue Gesangbuch. Altona: N. G., 1882. (BM)

2317. PFATTEICHER, Carl F. The Oxford American hymnal. New York: Oxford Univ. Press, 1930.

2318. POPPEN, H. Das erste Kurpfälzen Gesangbuch und seine Singweisen. Karlsruhe: N. G., 1938. (BM)

2319. POWELL, Francis Edward. Bromyard parish church. The National Mission of Repentance and Hope. Supplementary hymns, with a litany of penitence and hope, and a short dissertation on love as the supreme aim and object of the Christian Church. Leominster: Orphans' Printing Press, 1916.

2320. PRAISES in song. Winona Lake: Rodeheaver Hall-Mack Co., 1965.

2321. PRICE, Carl F. Curiosities of the hymnal. New York: Methodist Book Concern, 1926.

2322. RAEL, Juan Bautista. The New Mexican alabado. With transcription of music by Eleanor Hague. Stanford: Stanford Univ. Press, 1951.

2323. REEKS, J. St. George's hymn book. London: N. G., 1895.

2324. ROBERTS, Enid Pierce. Emynau hen a newydd. Bangor, Wales: N. G., 1962.

2325. RODEHEAVER and Sanville. Hymns for praise and service. Winona Lake: Rodeheaver Hall-Mack Co., 1965.

2326. RUCKER, E. and W. Schadendorf. Bibel und Gesangbuch im Zeitalter der Reformation, 1517-1967. Nurnberg: Germanisches Nationalmuseum, 1967.

2327. SAMPSON, Gerard. Hymns of devotion for every day of the year. Bradford: Blakey & Co., 1921.

2328. SANDERS, Robert L. and Edward P. Daniels. Hymns of the spirit (Unitarian and Universalist). Boston: The Beacon Press, 1937.

2329. SCRIPTURE verse chorus melodies. Winona Lake: Rodeheaver Hall-Mack Co., 1965.

2330. SHORTT, John Purser (compl.). Tables relating to the hymns and carols contained in the last two forms of church hymnal. Dublin: A. P. C. K., 1960.

2331. SIEVERS, Eduard. Die Murbacher Hymnen. Hildesheim, Germany: Georg Olms, June 30, 1967, (Orig. Halle, 1874).

2332. SINGING evangelism. Winona Lake: Rodeheaver Hall-Mack Co., 1965.

2333. SMITH, Augustine. The new church hymnal (Liberal Protestant). New York: D. Appleton-Century Co., 1937.

2334. The SOLDIER'S hymn book. Aldershot: N. G., 1890.

2335. SONGS. Winona Lake: Rodeheaver Hall-Mack Co., 1965.

2336. SONGS for the new day. Winona Lake: Rodeheaver Hall-Mack Co., 1965.

2337. SONGS of faith and triumph combined. Winona Lake: Rodeheaver Hall-Mack Co., 1965.

2338. STANTON, W. K. (ed.). The BBC hymn book. London: Oxford Univ. Press, 1951.

2339. STEVENSON, W. R. School hymnal. London: N. G., 1881. (BM)

2340. STICKNEY, Marion Faye. Twenty-five hymns with art picture illustrations. New York: Century-Appleton Co. (now Fleming H. Revell), n. d.

2341. STONE, Thompson and Sidney A. Weston. The Pilgrim hymnal. Boston: The Pilgrim Press, 1935.

2342. SUPPLEMENT to hymns for christian worship. Glasgow: Dunlop & Foote, 1899.

2343. SWAHILI hymn book in Arabic characters. London: N. G., 1898.

2344. TALEK and Gunwyn. Lyver hymnys ha salmow. Bardic names of compilers--E. G. Retallack Hooper and G. Pawley White. Camborne: An Lef Kernewek, 1963.

2345. TELEMANN, Georg Philipp. Fast allgemeines Evangelisch-Musicalisches Lieder-Buch. reprt. --of Hamburg 1730. Hildesheim: G. Olms, n. d.

2346. THANK you, Jesus. Winona Lake: Rodeheaver Hall-Mack Co., 1965.

2347. THIRTY gospel choruses. Winona Lake: Rodeheaver Hall-Mack, 1965.

2348. THOMPSON, Van Denman and Robert G. McCutchan. The Methodist hymnal (American Methodist). New York: The Methodist Book Concern, 1935.

2349. TREASURY of gospel hymns and poems. Winona Lake: Rodeheaver Hall-Mack, 1965.

2350. TRIUMPHANT service songs. Winona Lake: Rodeheaver Hall-Mack Co., 1965.

2351. TWEEDY, Henry Hallam. Christian worship and praise. New York: A. S. Barnes & Co., 1939.

2352. UNION mission hymnal. London: N. G., 1894.

2353. The UNITED Methodist church hymnal. London: United Methodist Church Publishing House, 1904.

2354. UPJOHN, Edward. A selection of favourite hymns for home use. Leeds: Alfred W. Inman, 1892.

2355. VERE, L. G. The abridged Catholic hymn book. London: N. G., 1882.

2356. VERRET, Sister Mary Camila, R. S. M. A preliminary survey of Roman Catholic hymnals published in the U. S. A. Washington, D. C.: The Catholic Univ. of America Press, 1964.

2357. VOIGHT, Louis. Hymnbooks at Wittenberg: a classified catalog of the collections of Hamma School of Theology, Wittenberg School of Music and Thomas Library. (1084 titles.) Springfield, Ohio: Chantry Music Press, 1975.

2358. WALES--Undeb Bedyddwyr Cymru a Mynwy. Emynau llawlyfr moliant at wasanaeth cynulleidfaoedd y Bedyddwyr. Argraffiad diwvgiedig ... Golygyddion: yr emynau. Abertawe: E. Cefni Jones, 1952.

2359. WALKER, William. The southern harmony. An unabridged reproduction of the 1854 edition, edited by Glenn C. Wilcox. Los Angeles: Pro Musicamericana, 1966.

2360. WARD, J. Round and through the Wesleyan hymn book. Leeds: B. W. Sharp, 1868.

2361. WARKENTIN, Larry Ray. "The 'Geistliches Gesangbuechlein' of Johann Walter and its historical environment." Ann Arbor: Univ. Microfilms, 1967.

2362. WEDDERBURN, James and A. F. Mitchell (ed.). The Gude and Godlie ballatis (A compendious book of Godley and spiritual songs ... 1567). New York: Johnson Reprint Corp., 1966, (orig. Edinburgh & London, 1897).

2363. WELSH, R. E. and F. G. Edwards. Romance of psalter and hymnal. London: Holder and Stoughton, 1889.

2364. WENDE luo. Wende kanisa. London: S. P. C. K., 1952.

2365. WERNER, J. Die ältesten hymnensammlungen von Rheinau. Zürich: Gesellschaft für Erforschung vaterländischer Alterthümer, 1891.

2366. WHITEFIELD, George. A collection of hymns for social worship. London: W. Strahan, 1753.

2367. WILLIAMS, Ralph VAUGHAN and Martin Shaw. Songs of praise (Church of England). New York: Oxford Univ. Press, 1931.

2368. WILSON, E. C. Duncan house hymnal. Bristol: E. Austin & Son, 1914.

2369. WORD of life melodies. Winona Lake: Rodeheaver Hall-Mack Co., 1965.

2370. YOUTH hymnal. Winona Lake: Rodeheaver Hall-Mack Co., 1965.

2371. ZELLE, Friedrich. Das älteste lutherische Haus-Gesangbuch 1524. Mit Einleitung und textkritischem Kommentar hrsg. Göttingen: Vandenhoeck & Ruprecht, 1903.

See also: 12, 14, 52, 98, 390, 677, 716, 719, 751, 752, 754, 755, 756, 759, 760, 762, 764, 765, 964, 973, 1069, 1115, 1236, 1275, 1285, 1298, 1305, 1421a, 1423, 1428, 1430, 1434, 1436, 1449, 1450, 1475, 1476, 1616, 1629, 1638, 1877, 1884, 1895, 1909, 1913, 1918, 2019, 2172, 2181, 2425, 2433, 2434, 2435, 2436, 2493, 2512, 2523, 2578, 2666, 2696, 2919, 2993, 3386, 4370, 4886, 4976, 5135, 5239, 5329.

HYMNODY and HYMNOGRAPHY

2372. AMELN, K. Roots of German hymnody of the Reformation era. St. Louis: Concordia Publ. House, 1964.

2373. BENSON, Louis F. The hymnody of the Christian church. Richmond, Va.: John Knox Press, 1956.

2374. BURNETT, Madeline Land. The development of American hymnody, 1620-1900. Southern Calif. Library. Los Angeles, Calif.: Southern California, M.A., 1946.

2375. BUTTERWORTH, Hezekiah. The story of the tunes. New York: American Tract Society, 1890.

2376. CHEEK, Curtis Leo. The singing school and shaped-note tradition residuals in twentieth-century American hymnody. Ann Arbor: Univ. Microfilms, 1968.

2377. CHURCH of the Brethren, Editorial Committee. The ministry of music. Introducing the father of modern hymnody. Elgin, Ill.: Church of the Brethren, 1948.

2378. DEVELOPMENT of Lutheran hymnody in America, The. (A reprint of article from the Encyclopedia of the Lutheran Church). Minneapolis: Augsburg Publishing House, 1967.

2379. EVANS, Ifor Leslie and David de Lloyd. Mawl yr oes oedd. Casgliad o donau ac emynau. A wnaethpwyd gan Ifor L. Evans a David de Lloyd. Caerdydd: Gwasg Prifysgol Cymru, 1951.

2380. FEDERAL Council of the Churches. Ecumenical trends in hymnody of Christ in America. New York: Commission on Worship, 1941.

2381. FOOTE, Henry Wilder (The younger). Recent American hymnody. New York: Repr. Papers of American Hymn Soc., Vol. 27, 1952.

2382. ______. Three centuries of American hymnody. Hamden, Conn.: The Shoe String Press, 1961, e.g. (also Harvard Univ. Press, 1940.)

2383. GREEN, S. G. Hymnody in our churches. London: N.G., 1895. (BM)

2384. GREENLAW, Kenneth Hould, Jr. Traditions of Protestant hymnody and the use of music in the Methodist and Baptist churches of Mexico. Ann Arbor: Univ. Microfilms, 1967.

2385. HABAN, Sister M. The hymnody of the Roman Catholic church--historical survey with an analysis of musical styles. Princeton, N.J.: Princeton Univ. Pr., 1956.

2386. HEYWOOD, J. Our church hymnody. London: N.G., 1881. (BM)

2387. KEITH, Edmond D. Christian hymnody. Nashville: Convention Press, 1956.

2388. KROLL, Josef. Die Christliche Hymnodik bis zu Klemens von Alexandreia. Darmstadt: Wissenschaftliche Buchgesellschaft, 1968.

2389. LOVELACE, Austin C. The anatomy of hymnody. New York, Nashville: Abingdon Press, 1965.

2390. MORGAN, Wesley K. The development of the Wesleyan hymnody. Union Theological Seminary Library. New York: Union Theological Seminary, M.A., 1946.

2391. NEVE, Paul. Scandinavian hymnody. New York: Union Theological Seminary, School of Sacred Music, n. d.

2392. PERDUE-DAVIS, Vernon. A primer of ancient hymnody. Boston: E. C. Schirmer Music Co., 1968.

2393. PHILLIPS, Charles Stanley. Hymnody past and present. New York: Macmillan Co., 1937.

2394. REEVES, Francis. The evolution of our Christian hymnody. Philadelphia: The John C. Winston Co., 1912.

2395. REVITT, Paul J. The George Pullen Jackson collection of southern hymnody. A bibliography compiled, with an introduction by Paul J. Revitt. Los Angeles, Cal.: Univ. of California, 1964.

2396. REYNOLDS, William Jensen. A survey of Christian hymnody. With musical examples. New York: Holt, Rinehart & Winston, 1963.

2397. ROUTLEY, Erik. The music of Christian hymnody. Naperville, Ill.: Alec R. Allenson, Inc., 1957 also London: Independent Press, Ltd., n. d.

2398. ________. I'll praise my maker. A study of the hymns of certain authors who stand in or near the tradition of English Calvinism, 1700-1850. London: Independent Press, 1951.

2399. RYDEN, E. E. The story of Christian hymnody. Rock Island, Ill.: Augustana Press, 1959.

2400. SICCO, Anacleto. De ecclesiastica hymnodia, libri tres, in (quibus) de presentatia, effectibus, et modo rite in choro psallendi agitur copiose. New York: Scientific Library Service, 1634.

2401. SIMS, John Norman. The hymnody of the camp-meeting tradition. Union Theological Seminary. New York: Union Theological Seminary, D. S. M., 1960.

2402. SMITH, Charles Howard. The hymnody of the free churches of Scandinavia: Its background and development. Ann Arbor: Univ. Microfilms, 1968.

2403. STOUGHTON, Marion W. The influence of the Kirchenlied of the Reformation on Protestant hymnody in England and America. Evanston, Ill.: Northwestern Univ., 1934.

2404. WALL, Woodrow W. The development of Baptist hymnody with particular emphasis on the Southern Baptist Convention. Denton: North Texas State Univ., M. M., 1955.

2405. WASHBURN, Charles. Hymnic interpretations. Nashville: Cokesbury, 1938.

2406. WETZEL, Johann Caspar. Hymnopoeographia. Hildesheim, Germany: Georg Olms--Reprint, 1967. (orig. Herrnstadt, 1718-28).

2407. YOUNG, R. H. The history of Baptist hymnody in England from 1612 to 1800. New York: Columbia, Music Ed. D., 1959.

See also: 295, 296, 297, 546, 599, 1061, 1299, 1343, 1431, 1432, 1451, 1559, 1626, 1912, 2088, 2262, 2269, 2410, 2417, 2431, 2481, 2489, 2529, 2547, 2576, 2637, 2993, 3638, 3678, 4359, 4639, 4644, 4760, 4947, 4994, 5327.

HYMNOLOGY

2408. ADAMS, Juliette. Studies in hymnology. A textbook designed for study groups where attention is given to the subject of church music. Also for colleges, schools, the music teacher, and all inquiring students. Nashville: Cokesbury Press, 1938.

2409. ALBRECHT, Christoph. Einfürung in die Hymnologie. Göttigen: Vandehoeck und Ruprecht, 1973.

2410. ARVASTON, Allan Togo Gustav. Den Thomander-Wieselgenska psalmboken. With a summary in English. Stockholm: Samlingar och studier till svenska kyrkans historia, 1949.

2411. BACHMANN, Johann F. Zur Geschichte der Berliner Gesangbücher. reprt.--of Berlin 1856 ed. Hildesheim: G. Olms, 1970.

2412. BAUMKER, Wilhelm. Das katholische deutsche Kirchenlied in seinen Singweisen. reprt.--of Freiburg 1883-1891 ed. Hildesheim: G. Olms, 1962.

2413. BENSON, Louis F. Studies of familiar hymns. Philadelphia: The Westminster Press, 1921, 1933.

2414. BERNAID, J. H. and R. Atkinson. The Irish liber hymnorum. N. G., Henry Bradshaw Society Publication, 1898. (BM)

2415. BONSALL, Elizabeth Hubbard. Famous hymns. Philadelphia: Union Press, 1923.

2416. BRAWLEY, Benjamin. History of the English hymn. New York: The Abingdon Press, 1932.

2417. BREED, David Riddle. The history and use of hymns and hymn tunes. (Reprint) New York: AMS Press, 1975.

2418. BROOKE, S. A. Christian hymns. London: N. G., 1891.

2419. CAMPBELL, Duncan. Hymns and hymn makers. London: A & C. Black, 1899, also The Guild Library, 1898.

2420. The CHURCH and the hymn-writers. New York: Doubleday, Doran, and Co., Inc., n. d.

2421. CLARK, William. Sing with understanding. Notes on hymns. With a portrait. Exmouth: The author, 1952.

2422. CLARKE, William Kemp Lowther. A hundred years of hymns ancient and modern. London: William Clowes & Sons, 1960.

2423. DANIEL, H. A. Thesaurus hymnologicus. Hildesheim, Germany: Georg Olms--Reprint 1967, (orig. Leipzig, 1841-56).

2424. DECHEVRENS, A. Du rythme dans l'hymnographie latine. Paris: Delhomme et Briguet, 1895.

2425. DORRICOTT, I. and L. Collins. Lyric studies: A hymnal guide. Handbook to the primitive Methodist hymnal of England. London: J. Toulson, 1891.

2426. DREVES, Guido Maria. Aurelius Ambrosius, der Vater des Kirchengesänges. Amsterdam: B. R. Gruner, 1968.

2427. DUFFIELD, Samuel. English hymns: their authors and history. New York: Funk & Wagnalls, 1888.

2428. DUNCAN, Joseph. Popular hymns: their authors and teachings. London: Skeffington & Son, 1919.

2429. EIN Jahrtausend Lateinischer Hymnendichtung. "Eine Blutenlese aus den Analecta hymnica mit liter-historischen Erlauterungen von Guido Maria Dreves." Leipzig 1909 ed. Bologna: Forni, 1969.

2430. ELLERTON, J. J. Ellerton. Being a collection of his writings on hymnology. New York: E. B. J. Young & Co., 1896.

2431. ENGLAND, M. W. and J. Sparrow. Hymns unbidden: Donne, Herbert, Blake, Dickinson and the hymnographers. New York: N. Y. Public Library, 1966.

2432. ESKEW, Harry Lee. Shape-note hymnody in the Shenandoah Valley, 1816-1860. Ann Arbor: Univ. Microfilms, 1966.

2433. FARLANDER, A. W. The hymnal outsings the ages. A pamphlet. New York: Protestant Episcopal Church, 1951.

2434. ______. The hymnal: How it grew. Pamphlet. New York: Protestant Episcopal Church, 1951.

2435. ______. The hymnal: How to use it. Pamphlet. New York: Protestant Episcopal Church, 1951.

2436. ______. The hymnal: What it is. Pamphlet. New York: Protestant Episcopal Church, 1951.

2437. FISCHER, A. and J. Linke. Blaetter für hymnologie. Hildesheim, Germany: Georg Olms--Reprint, 1967, (orig. Gotha, 1883-94).

2438. GILLMAN, Frederick John. The evolution of the English hymn. New York: Macmillan Co., 1927.

2439. GRAY, George Francis Selby. Hymns and worship. London: S. P. C. K., 1961.

2440. H., W. O. Hymns we shall always cherish. Twenty-four little talks giving interesting information about twenty-four favourite hymns. Stirling: Stirling Tract Enterprise, 1951.

2441. HART, William J. Hymns in human experience. New York: Harper Bros., 1931.

2442. HUNICH, Fritz Adolf. Das fortleben des älteren Volksliedes im Kirchenliede des 17. Jahrhunderts. Leipzig: R. Voigtländer, 1911.

2443. HYMNOLOGISCHE Beiträge. Quellen und Forschungen zur Geschichte der Lateinischen Hymnendichtung. reprt.--of Leipzig 1897 ed. Hildesheim: G. Olms, 1971.

2444. HYMN Society of America. Addresses at the International Hymnological Conference (Second). New York City: Hymn Society of America, 1962.

2445. ______. Miscellaneous notices, programmes, etc. New York: Hymn Society of America, 1949.

2446. INTERNATIONAL Hymnological Conference, Ed. Committee. Addresses at the International Hymnological Conference. New York: Hymn Society of America, 1962.

2447. JONES, William and William Price Robinson. Hymns and their authors. How some of our best known hymns came to be written. Liverpool: A. Wood & Co., 1962.

2448. KAYSER, Johann. Beiträge zur Geschichte und Erklärung der ältesten Kirchenhymnen. Mit besonderer Rücksicht auf das römische Brevier.... Zweite, umgearbeitete und vermehrte Auflage. 2Bd. Paderborn: Paderborn & Münster, 1881.

2449. KENLOCH, T. F. An historical account of the church hymnary. Cambridge: W. Heffert & Sons, Ltd., 1926.

2450. KING, James. Anglican Hymnology. London: Hatchards, 1885.

2451. LAUFER, Calvin W. Hymn lore. Philadelphia: Westminister Press, 1932.

2452. LAUSBERG, Heinrich. Der hymnus Jesu dulcis memoria. München: Hueber, 1967.

2453. LEVY, E. Poésies religieuses provençales et françaises. Paris: N.G., 1887. (BM)

2454. LEWIS, Howell Elfet. Cyflwyno tysteb genedlaethol i'r Parchedig H. Elfed Lewis. Cardiff: Teml Heddwch, Caerdydd, 1948.

2455. LUNDGUIST, Matthew D. Hymnological studies. Chicago: Wartburg, 1926.

2456. MALMIM. English hymn tunes from the sixteenth century to the present. London: Reeves, n.d.

2457. MÜLLER, Heinrich. Hymnologia sacra ... zehn andächtige Betrachtungen von geistlichen Liedern, nebst einer besondern Vorrede von dem so-genannten Gregorius-Fest und Liedern, aufs Neue heraus-gegeben. Nurnberg: Bey Johann Daniel Taubers sel. erben, 1728.

2458. NEALE, John Mason. "English hymnology: Its history and prospects," Christian Remembrances. N.G.: N.G., Oct., 1849.

2459. NUTTER, Charles. Hymn studies. New York: Eaton & Mains, 1897.

2460. PARISOT, J. Hymnographie poitevine. Liège: N.G., 1898.

2461. POLLARD, Arthur. English hymns. London: Longmans, Green & Co., 1960.

2462. POTEAT, Hubert MacNeill. Practical hymnology. (Reprint. Boston: R. C. Badger, 1921). New York: AMS Press, 1975.

2463. REHMANN, Theodor Bernhard. "Klingende Kathedrale." Das hymnische Geheimnis der Aachener Pfalzkapelle. Brussel: Mededelingen van de Koninklijke Vlaamse Academie voor Wetenschappen, 1961.

2464. REYNOLDS, W. J. Sources for college teaching of Christian hymnology. Nashville, Tenn.: George Peabody College for Teachers, 1961.

2465. RHODES University Grahamstown, South Africa. James Rodger hymnological collection. Grahamstown: Univ. Library, 1966.

2466. RICHARDSON, Alice Marion. Index to stories of hymns: Analytical catalog of twelve much used books. New York: AMS Press, 1975.

2467. ROBERTS, Gomer Morgan. Morgan Rhys, Llanfynydd. Caernarfon: Lyfrfa'r Methodistiaid Calfinaidd, 1951.

2468. RODEHEAVER, Homer A. Hymnal handbook for standard hymns and gospel songs: a collection of stories and information about hymns, gospel songs, and their writers, designed to help ministers and music directors create greater appreciation and interest in congregational singing. New York: AMS Press, 1975.

2469. SCHLETTERER. Geschichte der kirchlichen Dichtung und geistlichen Musik. Dodlingen: Beck, 1866.

2470. SIMONETTI, Manlio. Studi sull'innologia popolare cristiana dei primi secoli. Roma: Atti dell' Accademia Nazionale dei Lincei, 1952.

2471. STEPKA, Karel Václav. Hymnologie; repetitonum dějin církevni hudlrf a zpevu Husovy ceskoslovenské bohoslovecké fakulty v Praze. Praha: Blahoslav, 1952.

2472. STEVENSON, Arthur Linwood. The story of Southern hymnology. Roanoke: Stone Printing and Manufacturing, 1931, also Repr. New York: AMS Press, 1975.

2473. THICKENS, John. Emynau a'u hawduriaid ... Argraffiad newydd, wedi ei ddiwygio, gydag ychwanegiadau, gan ... Gomer M. Roberts. Caernarfon: L'yfrf'r Methodistiaid Calfinaidd, 1961.

2474. THORSBERG, Birgitta. Etudes sur l'hymnologie mozarabe. (Acta Universitatis Stockholmiensis. Studia latina stockholmiensai, 8.) Stockholm: Almqvist & Wiksell, 1962.

2475. WETZEL, Johann Caspar. Analecta hymnica. reprt. of Gotha 1751-56 ed. vol. 2. Hildesheim: G. Olms, n.d.

2476. WOLFRUM, P. Die entstehung des deutschen evangelischen Kirchenliedes in musikalischer Beziehung. Leipzig: Brietkopf und Härtel, 1890.

2477. WOLKAN, R. Das Kirchenlied der Böhmischen Brüder im xvi. Jahrhunderte. Prag: N. G., 1891. (BM)

See also: 236, 305, 306, 307, 309, 313, 323, 325, 328, 549, 1219, 1241, 1275, 1283, 1285, 1292, 1422, 1426, 1514, 1515, 1516, 1833, 1987, 2169, 2179, 2187, 2223, 2229, 2231, 2314, 2321, 2322, 2324, 2344, 2358, 2373, 2377, 2381, 2482, 2495, 2496, 2501, 2502, 2505, 2521, 2530, 2532, 2536, 2543, 2545, 2565, 2566, 2579, 2620, 2629, 2637, 2639, 2641, 2647, 2648, 2649, 2650, 2656, 2657, 2661, 2672, 2682, 2689, 2837, 2901, 2975, 3328, 3630, 3679, 4188, 4232, 4366, 4383, 4469, 5143, 5425, 5426, 5437, 5438, 5441, 5443.

HYMNS and HYMN TUNES

2478. ALLARD, F. M. Från Luther till Bach. Liturgisk-musikaliska studier från den evangeliska kyrkosångens klassiska tid. Stockholm: N. G., 1932. (BM)

2479. BÄCK, A. Huru hafva våra förfäder sjungit sina psalmer. Stockholm: N. G., 1891. (BM)

2480. BACON and Allen (eds.). The hymns of Martin Luther set to their original melodies with an English version. New York: Scribner, 1883.

2481. BAILEY, Albert Edward. The gospel in hymns. Backgrounds and interpretations. New York: Scribner's Sons, 1950.

2482. BANKS, L. A. Immortal hymns and their story. Cleveland: N. G., 1898. (BM)

2483. BARLOW, J. H. The Bach chorale book. New York: H. W. Gray, 1922.

2484. BARNLEY, Joseph. Hymn tunes. London: Novello, Ewer & Co., 1897.

2485. BARR, Sister M. Cyrilla, FSPA. The Laude Francescane and the Disciplinati of thirteenth century Umbria and Tuscany. A critical study of the Cortona Codex 91. Ann Arbor, Mich.: Univ. Microfilms, 1965.

2486. BARTON, William Eleazar. Old plantation hymns. New York: AMS Press, 1972.

2487. BELCHER, Joseph. Historical sketches of hymns. Philadelphia: Lindsay & Blakiston, 1859.

2488. BELSHEIM, J. Oversigt over Kirkens Salmesang. Kristiania: N. G., 1889. (BM)

2489. BENSON, Louis F. The English hymn. New York: George H. Doran Co., 1915 (1962).

2490. ________. Hymns of John Bunyan. New York: Hymn Society, 1930.

2491. BERNOULLI, Eduard. Die Choralnotenschrift bei Hymnen und Sequenzen. Wiesbaden: Breitkopf & Härtel, 1966.

2492. BERRY, William. Stories about hymns. Elgin, Ill.: Brethren Publishing House, 1921.

2493. BLEW, William John. Hymns and hymn-books, with a few words on anthems. London: Rivingtons, 1858.

2494. BOBOWSKI, M. Polskie piésni katolicke do kónca xvi. wieku. Cracow: N. G., 1893. (BM)

2495. BODINE, William. Some hymns and hymn writers. Philadelphia: The John C. Winston Co., 1907.

2496. BONNER, Clint. Hymn is born. Nashville: Broadman, 1959.

2497. BOSE, A. C. Hymns from the Vedas. Taplinger: Asia Pub., 1965.

2498. BOSTON, J. N. F. Norwich note book of hymns and hymn tunes. Norwich: N. G., 1940. (BM)

2499. BOYD, Charles Arthur. Stories of hymns for creative living. Philadelphia: Judson Press, 1938.

2500. BOYD, Malcolm. Harmonizing "Bach" chorales. London: Barrie & Rockliff, 1967.

2501. BREED, David R. The history and use of hymns and hymn tunes. New York: Fleming H. Revell, 1903.

2502. BROCKLEHURST, William. Hymns and how they were inspired. London: Brown and Sons, 1944.

2503. BROWN, Donald Clayton. The role of the hymn in the doctrinal controversies of the fourth century. SBS Library, M. C. M. Fort Worth, Tex.: Southwestern Baptist Theological Seminary, 1964.

2504. BROWN, Theron and Hezekiah Butterworth. The story of the hymns and tunes. New York: George W. Doran Co., 1906.

2505. BROWNLIE, John. The hymns and hymn writers of the church hymnary. London: Henry Frowde, 1899 and 1911.

2506. ________. Hymns from east and west: Translation from the poetry of the Latin and Greek churches. London: N. G., 1898. (BM)

2507. BRUMBACK, Carl, comp. Holy Land hymns. Plainfield, N. J.: Logos International, 1974.

2508. BUSCH, Martin Paul. The Luther hymn--its sphere of influence on Protestant church music. Vermillion: Univ. of South Dakota M. M., 1954.

2509. CARLONI, L. L'arpa liturgica, ossia gl'inni della chiesa Cattolica. Forli: N. G., 1891. (BM)

2510. CLAGHORN, Charles Eugene. Battle hymn: The story behind the battle hymn of the Republic. New York: Hymn Society of New York, 1974.

2511. CLOKE, Rene. Favourite hymn painting books. Edited by Ernest H. Hayes. Wallington: Religious Education Press, 1950.

2512. COELENBIER, L. C. Hymns for congregations, convents, and missions. London: N. G., 1900. (BM)

2513. COLES, A. Latin hymns with translations. New York: N. G., 1892. (BM)

2514. COLSON, Elizabeth. Hymn stories. Boston: Pilgrim Press, 1925.

2515. CONNELLY, Joseph. Hymns of the Roman liturgy. Westminster: Newman, 1957.

2516. CORNWALL, J. Spencer. Stories of our Mormon hymns. Salt Lake City, Utah: Deseret Book Co., 1963.

2517. COVELL, Frank Jack. The national hymns of the Spanish-American Republics. Stanford Univ. Lib. Stanford, Calif.: Stanford Univ., M. A. (Romance Langs.), 1940.

2518. CRAINE, Anne Porter. Picture stories of favorite hymns. Cincinnati, Ohio: Standard Publ., 1964.

2519. CRAWFORD, Benjamin Franklin. Religious trends in a century of hymns. Carnegie, Pa.: Carnegie Church Press, 1938.

2520. CRONHAM, C. R. *How to play hymns.* New York: Harold Flammer, Inc., 1961.

2521. CRUCEFIX, R. H. *Hymns to well-known tunes.* London: N. G., 1886. (BM)

2522. DAHLE, John. *Library of Christian hymns.* English trans. by M. C. Johnshoy (Reprint). New York: AMS Press, 1975.

2523. DANIEL, Clifford Haworth. *Order of service for children, with a selection of hymns.* Compiled in the first instance for use in the Parish Church of St. Paul, Birmingham, by the Rev. C. H. Daniel. Birmingham: Midland Educational Co., 1899.

2524. DARIES, F. R. *Book of chorales and supplementary hymns.* St. Louis: Eden Publishing House, 1957.

2525. DEMPE, Rolf. *Die Syrischen Hymnen von Ephrem.* (pp. iv, 501.) (Res. tyscript.) Jena: Goethehalle 7, 1958.

2526. DOUGLAS, Winfred. *A brief commentary on selected hymns and carols.* Evanston, Ill.: Northwestern Univ., 1936.

2527. DRINKER, Henry S. *The Bach chorale texts in English translation.* New York: Association of American Colleges, 1941.

2528. DYSON, Verne. *A Hong Kong governor and his famous hymns.* N. G.: N. G., 1930.

2529. EGGE, Mandus A. and Janet Moede (ed.). *Hymns; how to sing them.* Minneapolis: Augsburg Publishing House, 1966.

2530. EMURIAN, Ernest K. *Famous stories of inspiring hymns.* Grand Rapids: Baker Book House, 1975.

2531. EPHRAEM, Syrus Saint. *Hymnen aus dem Zweiströme land.* Mainz: N. G., 1882. (BM)

2532. ESCOTT, Harry. *Isaac Watts, hymnographer; a study of the beginnings, development, and philosophy of the English hymn.* London: Independent Press, 1962.

2533. EUBANKS, Ruby Bloxom. *The influence of secular music on the Protestant chorale.* SMU, M. M. Library. Dallas, Tex.: Southern Methodist Univ., 1959.

2534. *FAMILIAR hymns with descants.* Anaheim, Calif.: National Music Service, n. d.

2535. FELLERER, C. G. Der Gregorianische Choral im Wandel der Jahrhunderte. Regensburg: N. G., 1936. (BM)

2536. FERENCZI, K. Halotti zsolozsmák könyve. Csik-Szeredában: N. G., 1885. (BM)

2537. FLEMING, J. R. The highway of praise. New York: Oxford Univ. Press, 1937.

2538. FLEW, R. N. The hymns of Charles Wesley. London: The Epworth Press, 1953.

2539. FORTINI, Arnaldo. La Lauda in Assisi e le origini del teatro italianó. Assisi: A cura della Società internationale di studi Francescani-Santa Maria degli Angeli, 1961.

2540. FOUR-part chorales of J. S. Bach. Fair Lawn, N. J.: Oxford Univ. Press, 1929. (Reprint, 1964.)

2541. FRERE, W. H. Introduction to hymns ancient and modern. Historical edition. London: Clowes, 1909.

2542. FROST, Maurice (ed.). Historical companion to hymns ancient and modern. London: Clowes, 1962.

2543. FRY, J. S. Selection of hymns. London: N. G., 1894. (BM)

2544. GARDNER, G. L. H. "Victorian hymn tunes." Musical Opinion. N. G.: N. G., 1917. (BM)

2545. GERLEY, M. Gyászénekek. Esztergom: N. G., 1890. (BM)

2546. GEROLD, Theódore. Les plus anciennes mélodies de l'église protestante de Strasbourg et leurs auteurs. Paris: F. Alcan, 1928.

2547. GOODENOUGH, Caroline L. L. Highlights on hymnists and their hymns. New York: AMS Press, 1974.

2548. GRASBERGER, Franz. Die Hymnen Österreichs. Tutzing: H. Schneider, 1968.

2549. GREGORY, A. S. Hymns and the faith. London: The Epworth Press, n. d.

2550. ________. Praises with understanding. London: The Epworth Press, 1936.

2551. A GUIDE to the use of hymns ancient and modern. London: William Clowes & Sons, 1925.

2552. HABERL. Magister chorales. New York: Prestel, 1892.

2553. HADOW, W. H. Hymn tunes. N. G.: Church Music Society, 1914. (BM)

2554. HARKNESS, Robert. Harkness piano method of evangelistic hymn playing. A home-study course. Kansas, Mo.: Lillenas Publishing Co., 1962.

2555. HARROW school hymns. Harrow: N. G., 1881.

2556. HART, William J. Unfamiliar stories of familiar hymns. Boston: W. A. Wilde Co., 1940.

2557. HARVEY, Robert. Best-Loved hymn stories. Grand Rapids, Mich.: Zondervan, 1963.

2558. HERZEL, Catherine and Frank Herzel. To thee we sing. Philadelphia: Muhlenberg Press, 1949.

2559. HIMNOS y Banderas de América. Ediciones San Cristobal (without music). N. P. (LC-M1680. H5)

2560. HORDER, W. G. Congregational hymns. London: E. Stock, 1884.

2561. _______. The hymn lover. London: Curwen, 1889, 1905.

2562. HOSTINSKY, O. 36 nápěvů světských písni českého lidu z XVI. století. Praze: N. G., 1892. (BM)

2563. HUGHES, H. V. Latin hymnody. London: Faith Press, 1922.

2564. HUNGARY, Lutheran Church in. Kéresztyén énekes-könyv. Budapest: Editorial Committee of the Lutheran Church in Hungary, 1895.

2565. HUNTER, J. Hymns of faith and life. Glasg.: N. G., 1896. (BM)

2566. HUNTON, William Lee. Favorite hymns; stories of the origin, authorship, and use of hymns we love. Philadelphia: The General Council Publication House, 1917.

2567. The HYMN. New York: Hymn Society of America, Oct., 1949.

2568. HYMNARIUM parisiense. Das Hymnar der Sisterzienser-Abtei Pairis im Elsass. Aus zwei Codices des 12. und 13. Jahrhunderts herausgegeben und kommentiert. Regensburg: Druck von F. Pustet, 1904.

2569. HYMN lovers magazine. Yucaipa, Cal.: N. G., Aug., 1947.

2570. HYMNS for Christmas day and Epiphany by early Greek authors. Cambridge: N. G., 1888.

2571. HYMNS for creative living. N. G.: Judson, 1964.

2572. HYMNS for junior worship. Westminster: N. G., 1964.

2573. HYMNS for mission churches and children's services. London: N. G., 1885. (BM)

2574. HYMNS for the celebration of life. N. G.: Beacon, 1963.

2575. HYMNS ... how to sing them. Minneapolis, Minn.: Augsburg Press, 1945.

2576. HYMNS in the lives of men. Nashville: Abingdon Press, 1945.

2577. HYMNS of praise. Chicago: Hope Publishing Co., n. d.

2578. INNI nuovi per l'innario cristiano. A cura della commissione Interdenominazionale per la revisione dell' innarion. Torre Pellice: N. G., 1960. (BM-3111 aa15).

2579. J. M. K. Bright talks on favourite hymns. Philadelphia: John C. Winston, n. d.

2580. JACKSON, R. C. His presence. Spiritual hymns of the Blessed Sacrament. London: N. G., 1886. (BM)

2581. ________. The risen life. London: N. G., 1883. (BM)

2582. JEFFERSON, H. A. L. Hymns in christian worship. London: Rockliff, 1950.

2583. JIROVEC, K. Zachovej nám hospodine. Praze: N. G., 1896. (BM)

2584. JONES, Francis Arthur. Famous hymns and their authors. (Second edition). London: Hodder and Stoughton, 1903.

2585. JONES, R. C. Hymns of duty and faith. London: N. G., 1886. (BM)

2586. JORDAHL, Robert A. A study of the use of the chorale in the works of Mendelssohn, Brahms and Reger. Ann Arbor: Univ. Microfilms, 1965.

2587. JUBILEE hymns. London: N. G., 1887. (BM)

2588. KELLER, Walter B. The Italian organ hymn, 1500-1700. Cambridge, Mass.: Harvard Univ., 1957.

2589. KELLEY, W. A. The relationship of the early Lutheran hymns to certain features of Martin Luther's theories of religious education. Ann Arbor: Univ. Microfilms, 1958.

2590. KELLY, J. Hymns of the present century from the German. N. G.: N. G., 1885. (BM)

2591. KERR, Marjorie A. The Protestant chorale. Nashville, Tenn.: George Peabody College for Teachers, 1953.

2592. KEY, Jimmy Richardson. The use of the Wesley hymns in Southern Baptist worship. Austin, Tex.: Univ. of Texas, M. M., 1962.

2593. KINLOCK, T. F. An historical account of the church hymnary. Cambridge: W. Heffer & Sons, 1926.

2594. KROHN, Ilmari. Der Lutherische Choral in Finnland. With musical examples. Helsinki: N. G., 1948. (BM)

2595. KRONKEL, Wilbur. Next hymn, please: A delightful quest for hymn stories. New York: Carlton, 1963.

2596. KULP, Johannes. Handbuch zum Ostgesangbuch. Dortmund: W. Crüwell, 1931.

2597. LAUB, T. Om kirkesangen. Kjbenh: N. G., 1887. (BM)

2598. LAWSON, J. A. Hymni usitato latine redditi. London: N. G., 1883. (BM)

2599. LAZARKI. Die Haydn Hymne, ihre melosophische Deutung. Wien: Rubato-Verlag, 1972.

2600. LE FORT, Gertrud. Hymnen an die Kirche. München: M. Beckstein, 1924, 1946.

2601. LIEMOHN, Edwin. The chorale. Philadelphia: Muhlenberg Press, 1953.

2602. LIGHTWOOD, James T. Hymn tunes and their story. London: Epworth Press, 1923.

2603. LIUZZI, Fernando. La lauda e i primordi della melodia italiana. Roma: La Libreria dello stato, 1935.

2604. LOOTS, P. J. Ons kerklied deur die eeue Hoofstukki 4(b) en 7 oor die musick van die Psalms en die Gesange is opgestel deur. Prof. Dr. G. G. Cillié. Stellenbosch: N. G., 1948. (BM)

2605. LOVELACE, Austin C. The organist and hymn playing. New York, Nashville: Abingdon Press, 1962, 1964.

2606. LUTKIN, P. C. Hymn singing and hymn playing. Evanston: Northwestern Univ., Dept. of Church Music, Bulletin III, 1930.

2607. McALL, Reginald Ley. The hymn festival movement in America. New York: Hymn Society of America, 1951.

2608. McCUTCHAN, Robert Guy. Hymn tune names. Nashville, Tenn.: Abingdon Press, 1957; also: St. Clair Shores, Mich.: Scholarly Press, 1974.

2609. ________. Hymns in the lives of men. Nashville: Abingdon Press, 1945.

2610. MacDONALD, F. W. Latin hymns in the Wesleyan hymn-book. Studies in hymnology. London: N. G., 1899. (BM)

2611. McDORMAND, Thomas B. and Frederic S. Crossman. Judson concordance to hymns. Valley Forge: Judson Press, 1965.

2612. MacGILTON, Alice King. A study of Latin hymns. Boston: Richard H. Badger, 1918.

2613. MacMILLAN, Alexander. Hymns of the church: A companion to the hymnary of the United Church of Canada (second edition). Toronto: The United Church Publishing House, 1945.

2614. MADSEN, W. Til belysning af den nye himesseliturgi. Bergen: N. G., 1887. (BM)

2615. MAIN, Walter J. The Stirling three hundred. Selected psalms and hymns. Stirling: Stirling Tract Enterprise, 1951.

2616. MANNING, Bernard Lord. The hymns of Wesley and Watts. London: Epworth Press, 1942.

2617. MARCH, F. A. Latin hymns, with English notes. New York: Harper & Bros., 1874, 1888, 1898. also American Book Co., 1874.

2618. MASON, G. M. Church militant hymns. Dover: N. G., 1883.

2619. MERRILL, William Pierson. The religious value of hymns. New York: The Hymn Society, 1931.

2620. MERRYWEATHER, Frank B. The evolution of the hymn: Outline of history or origin and development from first century to the present. London: Clowes, 1966.

2621. MESSENGER, Ruth Ellis. The medieval Latin hymn. Washington: Capital Press, 1953.

2622. _______, (ed.). The public hymn. New York: The Hymn Society of America, n. d.

2623. METCALF, Frank J. Stories of hymn tunes. New York: Abingdon Press, 1928.

2624. MILCHSACK, G. Hymni et sequentiae. Halis: N. G., 1886.

2625. MISSET, E. and Pierre Aubry. Les proses d'Adam de Saint Victor. Paris: H. Welter, 1900.

2626. MOBERG, Carl Allan. Die liturgischen Hymnen in Schweden, Beiträge zur Liturgie und Musikgeschichte des Mittelalters und der Reformationszeit. Kopenhagen: E. Munksqaard, 1947.

2627. MOORE, Robert Lee. A theoretical and historical analysis of selected hymn-tunes published since 1900. Rochester, N. Y.: Univ. of Rochester, Eastman School of Music, n. d.

2628. MOORSOM, Robert Maude. Renderings of church hymns from eastern and western office books. London: C. J. Clay and Sons, 1901.

2629. MORRISON, Duncan. Great hymns of the church. London: N. G., 1890. (BM)

2630. MORTON, Helen and Murry Brooks (eds.). Hymns for worship. N. G.: Associated Press, n. d.

2631. MOYER, J. Edward. The voice of his praise. A practical, functional guide to interpreting and singing hymns. Nashville: Cokesbury, 1964.

2632. NEALE, John Mason. Collected hymns, sequences, and carols. London: J. Masters, 1863.

2633. _______. Echoes from Easter: Selections from the hymns of the Eastern church. Trans. by Rev. J. M. Neale. New York: A. D. F. Randolph & Co., 1885.

2634. _______. Hymns of the Eastern church. London: N. G., 1866, 1882.

2635. NORTHCOTT, Cecil. Hymns we love. Philadelphia: Westminister Press, 1955.

2636. NOTT, Charles C. Seven great hymns of the Medieval church. Annotated Rev. Ed. New York: Edwin S. Gorham, 1902.

2637. NUNN, Henry Praston Vaughan. An introduction to Ecclesiastical Latin. Third edition, with an appendix of Latin hymns. Eton: Alden & Blackwell, 1951.

2638. ODINGA, T. Das deutsche Kirchenlied der Schweiz im Reformationszeitalter. Frauenfeld: N. G., 1889. (BM)

2639. OLDING, B. S. Hymns and their writers. London: N. G., 1899. (BM)

2640. OTIS, Philo Adams. The hymns you ought to know. Chicago: Clayton F. Summy, 1928.

2641. PALMER, R. Hymns, their history and development. London: Adam and Charles Black, 1892.

2642. PARKER, Alice and Robert Shaw. Hymns and carols. New York: Lawson-Gould Music Publishing, Inc., n. d.

2643. PARKS, Edna Dorintha. English hymns and their tunes in the sixteenth and seventeenth centuries. Boston Univ. Library. Boston, Mass.: Boston Univ., Ph. D., 1957.

2644. ________. The hymns and hymn tunes found in the English metrical psalters. New York: Coleman-Ross Co., Inc., 1966.

2645. PARRY, K. L. and Erik Routley. Christian hymns. London: Student Christian Movement Press, 1956.

2646. PHELPS and Park. Hymns and choirs. Andover: Warren F. Draper, 1860.

2647. PRATT, John B. Present day hymns and why they were written. New York: A. S. Barnes, 1940.

2648. PRESCOTT, J. E. Christian hymns and hymn writers. Cambridge: N. G., 1886.

2649. PRICE, Carl F. More hymn stories. New York and Nashville: Abingdon-Cokesbury Press, 1929.

2650. ________. One-hundred and one hymn stories. New York and Nashville: Abingdon-Cokesbury Press, 1923.

2651. PRUDENTIUS, Clemens. Preface and hymns for cock-crow, day-break, and before sleep. Cambridge: N. G., 1887.

2652. RABY, F. J. E. A history of Christian Latin poetry. Oxford: Oxford Univ. Press, 1927.

2653. RAND, S. T. Hymni recentes latini. Halifax: S. Selden, 1888.

2654. RANDALL, Mallinson. The choirmaster's guide to the selection of hymns and anthems for the services of the church. New York: H. W. Gray Co., 1911.

2655. RANKIN, J. Exposition of the Apostles' creed. Edinburgh: W. Blackwood and Sons, 1890.

2656. REEVES, Jeremiah Bascom. The hymn as literature. New York: The Century Co., 1924.

2657. REID, William Watkins. Sing with the spirit and understanding, The story of the Hymn Society of America. New York City: Hymn Society of America, 1962.

2658. RELLY, James and John Relly. Christian hymns, poems, and spiritual songs. Burlington: Isaac Collins, 1776.

2659. RIEDEL, Johannes. The Lutheran chorale: Its basic traditions. Minneapolis: Augsburg Pub. House, 1967.

2660. RILEY, Athelstan. Concerning hymn tunes and sequences. London: A. R. Mowbray & Co., Ltd., 1915.

2661. RIZK, Helen S. Stories of the Christian hymns. Boston: Whittemore, 1964.

2662. ROTH, R. W. E. Lateinische Hymnen des Mittelalters. Augsburg: N.G., 1887. (BM)

2663. ROUTLEY, Erik. Hymn tunes; an historical outline. Croydon, England: Royal School of Church Music, 1964.

2664. ________. Hymns and human life. New York: Philosophical Library, 1952.

2665. ________. Hymns and the faith. London: Murray, Ltd., 1955; also--Grand Rapids, Mich.: Eerdmans, 1968.

2666. ________. Hymns today and tomorrow. Nashville: Abingdon Press, 1964.

2667. ________. Words of hymns, a short history. Croydon, Eng.: Royal School of Church Music, 1963.

2668. RUDIN, Cecilia M. Stories of hymns we love. Chicago: John Rudin & Co., 1937.

2669. RYLE, J. C. Hymns for the church. London: N.G., 1882. (BM)

2670. SCHATTENMANN, Johannes. Studien zum neutestamentlichen Prosahymnus. München: C. H. Beck, 1965.

2671. SCHILLE, Gottfried. Frühchristliche Hymnen. Berlin: Evangelische Verlagsanstalt, 1965.

2672. SHEPPARD, William John Limmer. Great hymns and their stories. London: Lutterworth Press, 1950.

2673. SHIPLEY, O. Annus sanctus. Hymns translated from the Sacred offices. London: N. G., 1884.

2674. SILTMAN, Bobby. The three-voice folk hymns of William Walker found in Southern harmony. Abilene, Tex.: Hardin-Simmons Univ., 1957.

2675. SMEND, Julius. Das Evangelishe Lied von 1524. Leipzig: M. Heinsius nachfolger, Eger v. S. Ivers, 1924.

2676. SMITH, Nicholas. Hymns historically famous. Chicago: Advance Publishing Co., 1901.

2677. SMITH, Robert Elmer. Modern messages from great hymns. New York: Abingdon Press, 1916.

2678. STANTON, Royal Waltz. The quality of permanence in Protestant hymn tunes. UCLA, Lib., Los Angeles: Univ. of Calif. at L. A., M. A., 1946.

2679. STELLHORN, Martin H. (comp.). Index to hymn preludes. St. Louis: Concordia Publishing House, 1948.

2680. STEPHAN, Dom John. The adeste fideles. South Devon: Buckfast Abbey, 1947.

2681. STUBBINS, George C. Reminiscences and gospel hymn stories. New York: George H. Doran Co., 1924.

2682. SUTHERLAND, Allan. Famous hymns of the world. Their origin and their romance, etc. New York: Fredrick A. Stokes, Co., 1906 and 1923.

2683. SYDNOR, James Rawlings. The hymn and congregational singing. Richmond, Va.: John Knox Press, 1960.

2684. TERRY, Charles Sanford. Bach's chorales (3 vols.). New York: G. P. Putnam's Sons, 1915.

2685. TILESTON, Mary W. Hymns of comfort. Boston: Little, Brown & Co., 1877.

2686. TILLYARD, H. J. W. The hymns of the Pentecostarium. Trans. by H. J. W. Tillyard. Copenhagen: N. G., 1940. (BM)

2687. _______. The hymns of the Octoechus. Copenhagen: E. Munksgaard, 1940-49.

2688. TRENCH, Richard Chenevix. Sacred Latin poetry. London: MacMillan & Co., 1874.

2689. TUCKER, W. H. Hymns ancient and modern. London: N. G., 1891. (BM)

2690. VESELOVSKY, A. N. Raziskoniya f oblasti russkix cloohovnich stichoff. N. G., 1879-83. (BM)

2691. VICTORIAN hymns. London: N. G., 1887. (BM)

2692. The VOICE of praise. London: N. G., 1887. (BM)

2693. WALPOLE, A. S. Early Latin hymns. Cambridge, Eng.: Univ. Press, 1922.

2694. WASHBURN, Charles C. Hymn stories. Nashville: Whitmore E. Smith, 1935.

2694a. WATTS, Isaac. Hymns and spiritual songs. London: John Lawrence, 1707.

2695. WEIGELT, C. Aus dem Leben der Kirche in der Geschichte ihrer Lieder. Wrocław, Poland: Breslau, 1885.

2696. WELLS, Amos R. A treasure of hymns. Boston, Chicago: United Society of Christian Endeavor, 1914.

2697. WESLEY, John and Charles Wesley. Hymns and sacred poems. Bristol: F. Farley, 1745.

2698. WESTBROOK, Francis Brotherton. Reading hymn-tunes and singing psalms. London: Epworth, 1969.

2699. WHITLEY, W. T. Congregational hymn singing in England. London: Dent & Sons, Ltd., 1933.

2700. WILHELM, James J. (comp.). Medieval song, an anthology of hymns and lyrics. New York: Dutton, 1971.

2701. WILSON, Archibald Wayet. The chorales; their origin and influence. London: The Faith Press, Ltd., 1920.

2702. WINKWORTH, Catherine. Chorale book. London: Longman, Green, Roberts, 1863.

2703. WRANGHAM, Digby S. The liturgical poetry of Adam of Saint Victor. London: Kegan, Paul, Trench, & Co., 1881.

2704. WRAY, J. Campbell. A proposed plan of procedure in teaching the hymns of the Baptist church through the Sunday school. San Marcos: Southwest Texas State College, M.A., 1943.

2705. ZELLE, Friedrich. Die Singweisen der ältesten evangelischen Lieder. Berlin: R. Gaertner, 1899-1900.

2706. ________. Geschichte des Chorals: komm Heiliger Geist, Herre Gott. Berlin: R. Gaertner, 1898.

See also: 12, 14, 24, 38, 42, 43, 50, 56, 64, 183, 189, 212, 236, 346, 352, 390, 459, 554, 606, 612, 639, 677, 683, 705, 719, 753, 757, 883, 969, 973, 1235, 1260, 1283, 1330, 1390, 1421, 1432, 1472, 1475, 1480, 1559, 1639, 1714, 1833, 1895, 1920, 1922, 1964, 2041, 2085, 2111, 2146, 2155, 2170, 2171, 2172, 2196, 2209, 2232, 2241, 2244, 2250, 2256, 2259, 2275, 2281, 2284, 2285, 2293, 2295, 2314, 2326, 2330, 2345, 2359, 2361, 2365, 2371, 2373, 2375, 2413, 2415, 2419, 2422, 2427, 2428, 2438, 2439, 2441, 2447, 2449, 2453, 2456, 2477, 2781, 3025, 3029, 3097, 3146, 3159, 3270, 3283, 3357, 3403, 3413, 3421, 3424, 3461, 3499, 3574, 3584, 3586, 3657, 3663, 3665, 3922, 3962, 3963, 4049, 4054, 4126, 4150, 4232, 4263, 4309, 4310, 4358, 4365, 4399, 4454, 4460, 4469, 4471, 4474, 4475, 4475a, 4476, 4489, 4492, 4493, 4521, 4540, 4600, 4601, 4638, 4643, 4652, 4653, 4654, 4658, 4660, 4661, 4670, 4721, 4810, 4814, 4815, 4824, 4857, 4873, 4965, 4966, 4994, 5029, 5042, 5092, 5099, 5101, 5106, 5127, 5128, 5129, 5417, 5423, 5424, 5425, 5430, 5434, 5435, 5436, 5438, 5440, 5441.

IMPROVISATION

2707. DUPRE, Marcel. Organ improvisation. (Trans. by J. Fenstermaker). Vol. 2 of "Complete Course in organ improvisation." Paris: A. Leduc, ix, Vol. 2, n. d.

2708. GEHRING, Philip K. Improvisation in contemporary organ playing. Ann Arbor: Syracuse Univ. diss., 1963.

2709. GÖRING, Ernst-Otto. Improvisation-leicht gemacht. Anleitung zum gottesdienstlichen Orgelspiel. Berlin: Evangelische Verlagsanstalt, 1971.

2710. NICHOLSON, Sir Sydney. The elements of extemporisation. Croydon: Royal School of Church Music, 1969.

See also: 33, 304, 4024.

INSTRUCTION, STUDY and EDUCATION

2711. BAIRD, Forrest J. Music skills for recreation leaders. Dubuque, Iowa: W. C. Brown, 1963.

2712. BATES, James. Voice culture for children (2 vols.). New York: H. W. Gray Co., 1907.

2713. BRISTOL, Lee H. Westminster Choir College, "A college to sing about." New York: Newcomen Society in North America, 1965.

2714. BUSHNELL, W. C. A plan of curriculum for the proposed church music school of the American Baptist Convention. New York: Columbia Univ., Ed. D. Vocal Music, 1961.

2715. CATHOLIC Church--Congratio Sacrorum Rituum. Instruktion über die Musik in die Liturgie. Trier: Paulinus-Verlag, 1967.

2716. CONGREGATIO (Sacra) Rituum. Elementi di educazione musicale. Milano: Vita e pensiero, 1967.

2717. DOWD, Philip. Charles Bordes and the Schola Cantorum of Paris. Ann Arbor: Univ. Microfilms, 1969.

2718. EMPEY, Louella Jeanette. Spanish folk music as source material for religious education. Chicago Univ. Library. Chicago, Ill.: Chicago, M. A., 1931.

2719. FINK, Fred M. Graduate music curricula in Protestant theological seminaries of America. SMU Library, M. M. Dallas, Tex.: Southern Methodist Univ., 1952.

2720. GOOVAERTS, Alphonse Jean Marie. La musique d'église; considerations sur son état actuel et histoire abregée de toutes les écoles de l'Europe. Anvers: La Féderation artistique, 1876.

2721. HALLER, M. Kompositionslehrer für polyphonen Kirchengesang. Regensburg: A. Coppenrath (H. Pawelek), 1891.

2722. HARRINGTON, Karl Pomeroy. Education in church music. New York: The Century Co., 1931.

2723. HARRISON, Frederick. Life in a medieval college. The story of the Vicars-Choral of York. Printed in Holland. London: John Murray, 1952.

2724. HEUBERGER, Julius. Lied und Musik in Religions-unterricht und Jugendarbeit. München: Kösel, 1976.

2725. HISPANIAE schola musica sacra. New York: Johnson Reprint Corp., n. d. (orig. Barcelona, 1894-1898).

2726. HOOPER, William Loyd. Master's degree, Music (church) in Protestant theological seminaries of the U. S. Ann Arbor: Univ. Microfilms, 1966.

2727. JAGGARD, C. M. Suggestions to choirmen. London: J. Curwen, 1919.

2728. JANKE, Betty Jean Sellers. An in-service training program in music for student teachers in the Lutheran schools of Denver, Colorado. UT Library, M. M. Austin, Tex.: Univ. of Texas, 1966.

2729. JENKINS, Richard R. Selected Protestant, Catholic and Jewish music for use in the junior high school program. Los Angeles, Cal.: Univ. of Southern California, L. H., M. M., 1953.

2730. KNIGHT, Gerald Hocken. The first forty years: The school of English church music. Croydon: Royal School of Church Music, 1968.

2731. KOSKI, George William. A plan for a graduate program in church music for Howard College, Birmingham, Alabama. New York: Columbia Univ., 1962.

2732. MARTIN, George C. The art of training choir boys. New York: H. W. Gray Co., n. d.

2733. METCALF, Frank Johnson. The easy instructor; a biographical study. N. G.: N. G., 1937. (LC-41 M5259)

2734. MORSCH, Vivian Sharp. The use of music in Christian education. Philadelphia: Westminister Press, 1956.

2735. MURRAY, Joseph J. Children's story sermons for today. Richmond: John Knox Press, 1946.

2736. NUECHTERLEIN, Herbert E. The sixteenth century Schulkantorei and its participation in the Lutheran service. Ann Arbor: Univ. Microfilms, 1969.

2737. NICHOLLS, M. School choir-training. London and New York: Novello's Elementary Music Manual, 1914.

2738. PHILLIPS, W. R. Dictionary of the tonic sol-fa system. London and New York: Novello, 1909.

2739. RINNOVAMENTO Liturgico e Musica Sacra. Bibliotheca "Ephimerides liturgicae." Sectio pastoralis, 4. Rome: Edizioni liturgiche, 1967.

2740. SCHEIDLER, Bernhard. Elementare Musikerziehung Teil 1--Notenkunde-Melodielehre. Ein mit viel Liebe und grosser Gründlichkeit in zwingender Darstellung geschriebenes Buch, das in die Hand des Junglehrers gehört. Pädagogische Welt, 177 Seiten, mit über 300 Notenbeispielen. Regensburg: G. Bosse, 1950.

2741. ________. Elementare Musikerziehung Teil II--Harmonieleher Rhythmik-Formenlehre. Allen Musikerziehern, die zur Gewinnung klarer musiktheoretischer Kenntnisse den Weg der Selbsthilfe beschreiten, seien die beiden Bände angelegentlichst empfehlen. 162 Seiten, mit über 300 Notenbeispielen. Hamburg: Hamburger Lehrerzeitung, 1953.

2742. SCHUBIGER, Anselm. Die sängerschule St. Gallens vom achten bis zwölften Jahrhundert. Ein Beitrag zur Gesanggeschichte des Mittelalters. Mit vielen Facsimile und Beispielen. New York: K. und N. Benziger, 1858.

2743. SEAGRAVES, Lila Fagan. A study of the music theory teaching practices of junior church choirs as compared with those of the public school classes at the same age level. Austin: Univ. of Texas, M. M., 1957.

2744. SHIELDS, Elizabeth. Music in the religious growth of children. Nashville: Abingdon Press, 1943.

2745. SIMMONS, R. E. Points for choral singers. N. G.: Vicent Music Co., 1906. (BM)

2746. SIMON, Richard George. The propriety of the study of sacred music in the public schools of Greeley. Ann Arbor: Univ. Microfilms, 1968.

2747. ST. Mary-of-the-Angels Song School. A day in the life of the choir school. Addlestone: N. G., 1946. (BM)

2748. THOMAS, Edith Lovell. Music in Christian education. Nashville: Abingdon Press, 1953.

2749. TRENT. Scuola diocesana di musica sacra. Trento: Arti grafiche Saturnia, 1967.

2750. TUKEY, Ruth S. A year's course of study for junior church choirs. East Lansing: Michigan State, 1948.

2751. WOODS, M. A. Hymns for school worship. London: N. G., 1890. (BM)

See also: 6, 483, 489, 494, 511, 558, 560, 568, 584, 619, 644, 657, 658, 692, 709, 747, 781, 787, 798, 804, 844, 854, 860, 862, 873, 879, 896, 909, 910, 948, 974, 985, 1016, 1019, 1070, 1113, 1127, 1147, 1191, 1212, 1324, 1345, 1352, 1361, 1400, 1696, 1701, 1725, 1807, 1882, 2240, 2339, 2464, 2520, 2555, 2704, 2921, 3190, 3368, 3405, 3623, 3823, 3943, 3978, 4144, 4324, 4337, 4724, 4826, 4894, 5035, 5039, 5247, 5331, 5334, 5335, 5338, 5339, 5343, 5397.

INSTRUMENTAL MUSIC
(Other Than Organ and Piano)

2752. AGRICOLA, Martin. Musica instrumentalis Deutsch. Rochester, N. Y.: Univ. of Rochester Press, 1954. (orig., Wittenberg: Georgen Rhaw, 1528, 1545).

2753. BESSE, H. T. The Bible on instrumental music. Syracuse: Wesleyan Methodist Publishing House, 1896.

2754. BLAIKIE, Alexander. The organ and other musical instruments as noted in the holy scriptures. Boston: Lee & Shepard, 1865.

2755. BONANNI, Filippo. The showcase of musical instruments. New York: Dover Publishing, n. d.

2756. BONNER, D. F. Instrumental music in the worship of God divinely authorized. Rochester: F. A. Capwell, 1881.

2757. BOWLES, Edmund A. A checklist of musical instruments in fifteenth century illuminated manuscripts at the Bibliothèque Nationale. Ann Arbor: Music Lib. Assn., publ. in "Notes" for Vol. 30, Mar., 1974.

2758. BRAUN, Richard W. Possible carry-over of school instrumental music into the Protestant church. Los Angeles: Univ. of Southern California, M. M., 1953.

2759. BRITTEN, B. Concerto, violin, and orchestra. New York: Alexander Broude Inc., 1966.

2760. BROWN, H. M. Instrumental music printed before 1600; a bibliography. Cambridge: Alexander Broude, Inc., 1965.

2761. CERVELLI, Luisa. Contributi alla storia degli strumenti musicali in Italia nel Rinascimento. Bologna: Tamari, 1965.

2762. CLUBB, Merrel Dare. Discussion: Is instrumental music in christian worship scriptural? Nashville, Tenn.: Gospel Advocate Company, 1927.

2763. DODWELL, Henry. A treatise concerning the lawfulness of instrumental musick in holy offices (first ed.). London: W. Hawes, 1700.

2764. ________. A treatise concerning the lawfulness of instrumental musick in holy offices (second ed.). London: W. Hawes, 1700.

2765. ________. A treatise concerning the lawfulness of instrumental musick in holy offices. (repr.). Rochester: Rochester Univ., 1954.

2766. DYSON, Jo Ann. The musical instruments of the Bible. Waco: Baylor Univ., M. M., 1955.

2767. EHMANN, Wilhelm. Das Bläserspiel. Kassel: Sonderdruck aus Liturgie, Handbuch des evangelischen Gottesdienstes, herausgegeben von W. Blankenburg und K. F. Müller, 1961.

2768. EISENACH, Bachmuseum. Verzeichnis der Sammlung alter Musikinstrumente im Bachhaus zu Eisenach, hrsg. von der Neuen Bachgesellschaft. Leipzig: Breitkopf & Härtel, 1964.

2769. ERARD, Sébastien. La maison Erard. Ses origines, ses inventions, ses travaux. 1780-1903. With illustrations, including a portrait. Paris: N. G., 1903. (BM07902. dc. 9).

2770. FIELDS, Warren C. Venetian influences on German instrumental music. Baylor Univ. Library. Waco, Tex.: Baylor Univ., M. M., 1963.

2771. GALPIN, Francis William. Notes on the old church bands and village choirs of the last century ... from "Proceedings" Dorset Natural History and Antiquarian Field Club. Dorchester: "Dorset County Chronicle" Printing Works, 1905.

2772. GIRARDEAU, John Lafayette. Instrumental music in the public worship of the church. Richmond: Whittet & Shepperson, 1888.

2773. GREEN, S. A. Tractate against instrumental music in churches. N. G.: N. G., 1911. (BM)

2774. HANCOCK, Tyre. Church error; or instrumental music condemned. Dallas: The Author, 1902.

2775. HONEMEYER, Karl. Die posaunenchöre im Gottesdienst. Gütersloh: Rufer-Verlag, 1951.

2776. JAMES, Philip. Early keyboard instruments. Chester Springs, Pa.: Dufour Editions, 1960.

2777. KURFEES, M. C. Instrumental music in the worship. Nashville: J. B. Muns, 1922.

2778. A LETTER to a friend in the country, concerning the use of instrumental musick in the worship of God. London: A. Baldwin, 1698.

2779. LEWER, Stanley Karl. Electronic musical instruments. London: Electrical Engineering, 1948.

2780. LILLEHAUG, L. A. A study of instrumentally-accompanied sacred vocal works of selected seventeenth century German Lutheran composers. Rochester: Univ. of Rochester, Mus. Ed., 1961.

2781. McCOY, Floyd. Hymns for instrumental ensemble. Nashville: Broadman, 1961.

2782. McKINNON, James William. Church fathers and musical instruments. New York: Columbia Univ. (Thesis), 1965.

2783. MARCUSE, Sibyl. Musical instruments, a comprehensive dictionary; a corrected reprint of the 1964 Doubleday edition. N. G.: The Norton Library, 1965-66. (LC-74-30050)

2784. MEYER, Ernst H. English chamber music. London: Wishart, 1946.

2785. MONTAGU, Jeremy. The world of medieval and Renaissance musical instruments. Newton Abbott: David and Charles, 1976.

2786. MUNROW, David. Instruments of the Middle Ages and Renaissance. Foreword by A. Previn. London: Oxford Univ. Press, 1976.

2787. RIEDEL, Friedrich Wilhelm. Quellenkundliche Beiträge zur Geschichte der Musik für Tasteninstrumente in der zweiten Hälfte des 17. Jahrhunderts, vornehmlich in Deutschland. Kassel & Basel: Schriften des Landesinstituts für Musikforschung, Kiel, 1960.

2788. ROEHRICH, Edouard. Les origines du choral luthérien. Paris: Fischbacher, 1906.

2789. ROKSETH, Yvonne. Musical instruments in the fifteenth century church. Cambridge: Bois de Boulogne, 1968.

2790. SACHS, Curt. Geist und Werden der Musikinstrumente. List of publications of forthcoming reprints 1966. New York: Broude Brothers Limited (Facsimile), 1965. (repr. Berlin: D. Reimer, 1929.)

2791. ________. The history of musical instruments. New York: W. W. Norton, 1940.

2792. SCHUBERTH, Dietrich. Kaiserliche Liturgie. Göttingen: Vanderhoeck und Ruprecht, 1968.

2793. SHANNON, James W. The use of brass instruments in Händel's oratorios. Dallas, Tex.: Southern Methodist Univ. M. M., 1960.

2794. SIMS, W. Hines. Instrumental music in the church. Nashville: Sunday School Board of the Southern Baptist Conventions, 1947.

2795. SMITH, S. E. Boyd. The use of the orchestra in the church during the seventeenth and eighteenth centuries. Austin, Tex.: Univ. of Texas, M.M., 1947.

2796. TRETHOWAN, Anthony M. Instruments in early church music. Guilford, W.A.: Guilford Grammar School, 1973.

2797. TROBIAN, Helen Johnette Reed. The implementation of instrumental ensemble music in religious education. New York: Columbia Univ., Teachers College, Ed.D., 1950; also New York and Nashville: Abingdon Press, 1961, 62, 63, 64.

2797a. ________. The instrumental ensemble in the church. Nashville: Abingdon Press, 1964.

2798. ULRICH, Homer. Chamber music. New York: Columbia Univ. Press, 1948.

2799. VERTKOV, K. A., G. Blagodatov, and E. I͡azovitskai͡a. Atlas muzykalnykh instrumentov narodov SSSR. (Atlas of musical instruments of the people inhabiting the USSR. 2-3 izd., dop. i pererab. Moskva: Muzyka, 1975.

2800. WAGGONER, William L. An investigation into the use of instrumental music in the Lutheran church of North America. Huntsville, Tex.: Sam Houston State College, M.A., 1961.

See also: 13, 135, 190, 194, 204, 362, 369, 925, 1195, 1199, 1200, 1201, 1202, 1224, 1240, 1368, 1534, 1891, 2060, 2068, 2145, 3014, 3374, 3382, 3486, 3502, 3516, 3762, 4113, 4121, 4123, 4308, 4630, 4759, 4762, 4766, 4779, 4782, 4794.

INTROITS

2801. DANGEL-HOFMANN, Frohmut. Der mehrstimmige Introitus in Quellen des 15. Jahrhunderts. (Würzburger Musikhistorische Beitrage.) Tutzing: Hans Schneider, 1975.

See also: 959.

JAZZ and ROCK in CHURCH MUSIC

2802. HAGEN, Rochus Andreas Maria. Jazz in der Kirche? Stuttgart: Kohlhammer, 1967.

2803. LARSON, Bob. Rock and the church. Carol Stream, Ill.: Creation House, 1971.

2804. OSTRANSKY, Leroy. The anatomy of jazz. Seattle, Wash.: Univ. of Washington Press, 1960.

2805. STEARNS, Marshall W. "What is happening to jazz?" Musical Journal. Jan., 1961. p. 48.

2806. WIENANDT, Elwyn A. "Jazz at the altar?" The Christian Century. March 23, 1960.

KYRIE and KYRIAL

2807. BOE, John. The ordinary in English: Anglican plainsong kyrials and their sources. Ann Arbor: Univ. Microfilms, 1969.

2808. CURRY, Jerry Lee. A computer-aided analytical study of Kyries in selected masses by Johannes Ockeghem. Ann Arbor: Univ. Microfilms, 1969.

2809. HABERL, Ferdinand. Das Kyriale Romanum: liturg. u. musikal. Aspekte. Bonn: Sekretariat d. ACV, 1975.

2810. JOHNER, Dominicus. Erklärung des Kyriale, nach Text und Melodie. Regensburg: F. Pustet, 1933.

2811. The KYRIAL. New York: H. W. Gray Co., 1930.

2812. LANDWEHR-MELNICKI, Margaretha. Das einstimmige Kyrie des lateinischen Mittelalters. Regensburg: Bosse, 1968.

See also: 3055, 3084.

LECTURES

2813. BATES, William. College lectures on Christian antiquities and the ritual of the English church. London: John Parker, 1895.

See also: 76, 194, 1225, 1694, 1979, 2986, 3537, 3362, 4286.

LEGISLATION, ECCLESIASTICAL

2814. FERLAND, David J. Plenary, provincial, and synodal legislation concerning liturgical music in U. S. Washington, D. C.: N. G., 1955.

2815. MacMANUS, Frederick Richard. Handbook for the new rubrics. London: Geoffrey Chapman, 1961.

2816. MYTYCH, Joseph F. Digest of church law on sacred music. Toledo: Gregorian Institute of America, 1959.

2817. OTAÑO, N. La música religiosa y la legislación eclesiástica; principales documentos de la Santa Sede desde Leon IV hasta nuestros dias acerca de la musica sagrada, con las conclusiones de los Congresos españoles de musica sagrada. Barcelona: V. de J. M. Llobet, 1912.

2818. ROME, Church of. Catholic church music. The legislation of Pius X, Benedict XV, and Pius XI. London: Burns & Oates, 1933.

2819. ________. The rubrics of the Roman Breviary and Missal. The general decree Novum Rubricarum of S. C. R., 26 July, 1960. With an English translation by J. B. O'Connell. London: Burns & Oates, (Search Press), 1960.

2820. ROMITA, Fiorenzo. Il codice giuridico della musica sacra. Roma: Desclée, 1952.

2821. ________. Jus musicae liturgicae, dissertatio historico-inridica. Taurini: Officina Libraria Marietti, 1936.

2822. VATICAN. Ex codice Vaticano Lat. 5129 edidit Albertus Seay Corpus scriptorum de musica, 9. Rome: American Institute of Musicology, 1964.

See also: 1136, 1140, 1162, 1337, 1600, 1782, 1897, 1978, 2485, 2860, 2865, 2939, 3276, 4682, 5074.

LIBRARY

2823. GROPP, Arthur. Guide to libraries and archives in Central America and the West Indies, Panama, Bermuda and British Guiana. Supplemented with information on private libraries. New Orleans: American Research Institute of Tulane Univ., 1941.

2824. LONGYEAR, R. M. Article citations and "obsolescence" in musicological journals. Ann Arbor, Mich.: Quarterly Journal--"Notes" Vol. 33, No. 3--p. 563--Music Library Assoc., 1977.

2825. MUSIC Library Association: Guidelines for Music Library. Consultants and clients. Ann Arbor, Mich.: Quarterly Journal--"Notes," Vol. 33, No. 3, p. 581--Music Library Assn., 1977.

2826. MUSIC Library Association--Technical Reports. Exceptions to the Anglo-American cataloging rules. Ann Arbor, Mich.: Music Library Association, 1970.

2827. OCHS, Michael. A taxonomy of qualifications for music librarianship: The cognitive domain. Ann Arbor, Mich.: MLA's "Notes," Vol. 33, No. 1, p. 27-50, 1976.

2828. PHILLIPS, Don (ed.). Directory of music librarians in the United States and Canada: A preliminary edition compiled by the Membership Committee of the Music Library Association. Ann Arbor, Mich.: Music Library Association, 1976.

2829. PUBLIC Libraries Commission of the International Association of Music Libraries, compilers. International basic list of literature on music. The Hague: Nederlands Bibliotheek en Lectuur Centrum., 1975.

2830. SCHMIDT, Wolfgang. Eine Fachbibliotek für Chorleiter. Wuppertal: Singende Gemeinde, 1974.

2831. VEREIN Deutscher Bibliothekare. Kommission für. Alphabetische Katalogisierung. Unterkommission für Musikalien- und Tonträgerkatalogisierung. Regeln für die alphabetische Katalogisierung von Musikalien und Tonträgen, 501-507. Ansetzung von Sachtiteln und Sammlungs--vermerken sowie Bestimmung des Einheitssachtitels; Vorabdruck. (a preprint.) München: Die Kommission, 1975.

2832. YOUNG, Margaret Labash, Harold Chester Young and Anthony T. Kruzas, eds. Subject directory of special libraries and information centers. Vol. 4: Social sciences and humanities libraries: "Music Libraries-United States," and "Music Libraries-Canada." Detroit, Mich.: Gale Research Co., 1975.

See also: 350, 425, 2739, 3006, 3018, 3311, 4862.

LITANIES

2833. MUELLER, Carl F. A litany of psalms. New York: G. Schirmer, n.d.

2834. ROTH, Joachim. Die mehrstimmigen lateinischen Litaneikompositionen des 16. Jahrhunderts. Regensburg: Kölner Beiträge zur Musikforschung, 1959.

See also: 1219.

LITURGY and RITUAL

2835. ABRAHAMSEN, Erik. Liturgisk musik i den danske kirke efter reformationen. Trykt paa Carlsbergfondets bekostning. København: Levin & Munksgaard, 1919.

2836. ADAM, De Saint Victor. Liturgical poetry of Adam of St. Victor. London: N. G., 1881. (BM)

2837. AMELN, Hrsg. von K., C. Mahrenholz, and K. F. Müller. Jahrbuch für Liturgik und Hymnologie. Kassel: Stauda, 1963.

2838. ARBEITSGEMEINSCHAFT für Reinische Musikgeschichte. Studien zur Klevischen Musik-und-Liturgiegeschichte. Köln: Volk, 1968.

2839. ARNOLD, J. H. (ed.). Anglican liturgies. London: Oxford Univ. Press, 1939.

2840. BAILEY, Terence. The processions of Sarum and the Western Church. Toronto: Mediaeval Studies, 1971.

2841. BARTON, Jane Johannes. Formulation and consolidation of the Gregorian musical liturgy. Lubbock, Tex.: Texas Technological College, M. Ed., 1964.

2842. BASTIAENSEN, A. A. R. Observations sur le vocabulaire liturgique dans l'itinéraire d'Egérie. Nijmegen, Utrecht: Latinitas Christianorum primaeva, 1962.

2843. BELL, Bernard Iddings. The altar and the world. New York: Harper & Brothers, 1944.

2844. BENEDICTINES of Solesmes. Liber Usualis Missal et. Officii. New York: J. Fischer & Brother, 1934.

2845. BERENDES, Sister M. Benedicta. The versus and its use in the medieval Roman literature. (Univ. of Iowa diss.) Ann Arbor, Mich.: Xerox Univ. Microfilms, 1973.

2846. BERNSTEIN, Meluin. The liturgical music of Giaches Wert. Chapel Hill, N. C.: Univ. of North Carolina, n. d.

2847. BIEHLE, J. Beiträge zur musikalischen Liturgik. Leipzig: N. G., 1919. (BM)

2848. _______. Die Liturgische Gleichung und die Stellung der Musik im Gottesdienste. Vortrag ... mit 7 graphischen Darstellungen. Berlin: Trowitzsch und Sohn, 1931.

2849. BIULETYN liturgiczny. Aylesbury: N. G., 1947. (BMP. P. 177. paa)

2850. BOUYER, Louis. Rite and man. The sense of the sacral and Christian liturgy. Le Rite de l'homme. Trans. by M. Joseph Costelloe. London: Burns & Oates, 1963.

2851. ______. Le rite et l'homme. Sacralité naturelle et liturgie. Paris: Lex orandi, 1962.

2852. BUGNINI, Annibale. Liturgia viva. Commento all'Istruzione della S. C. dei Riti sulla musica sacra e la Liturgia del 3 settembre 1958. Milano: N. G., 1962. (BM)

2853. CABROL, Ferdinand. Liturgical prayer, its history and spirit. London: Burns, Oates & Washbourne, 1925.

2854. CALVOER, Caspare. Ritualis Ecclesiastici. 1--Origines ac Causas Rituum; II--Nobile de Locis, Temporibus, personis Sacris. Includes a 67p. section De Cantu Ecclesiastico, with chapters on psalms, hymns, the litany, music in general, instruments, the organ, directing music, etc. New York: Scientific Library Service, 1966.

2855. CATHOLIC Church, Liturgy and Ritual. The Winchester troper from mss. of the Xth and XIth centuries, with other documents illustrating the history of tropes in England and France. Edited by Walter Howard Frere. (reprint). New York: AMS Press, 1973.

2856. CATHOLIC Church, Liturgy and Ritual. German. Volk vor Gott. St. Pölten: Universum-Verlagsgesellschaft, 1968.

2857. CEREMONIAL pictured in photographs, etc. London: A. R. Mowbray & Co., 1924.

2858. CHEVALIER, C. U. J. Poésie liturgique de l'église Catholique en Occident. Tournai: Desclée, Lefebvre, 1894.

2859. ______. Poésie liturgique du moyen âge. Paris: N. G., 1893. (BM)

2860. CHIFFLET, Jules. Aula sacra principum belgii. Sive Commentarius Historicus de Capellae Regiae in Belgio Principiis, Ministris, Ritibus atque Universo Appartu, accedunt Capella Sacrae Constitutiones, edente J. Chifflet. New York: Scientific Library Service, n. d. (Orig. -- Antwerp: B. Moreti, 1650.)

2861. CLARKE, W. K. Lowther. Liturgy and worship. New York: Macmillan Co., 1932.

2862. CODRINGTON, Humphrey William. Studies of the Syrian liturgies. Reprinted from the Eastern Churches Quarterly. London: Geo. E. J. Coldwell, 1953.

2863. CONGREGATIO Sacrorum Rituum, ed. Sacred music and liturgy; the instruction of the Sacred Congregation of Rites. Westminister: Newman Press, 1959.

2864. DALMAIS, Irénée Henri. Introduction to the liturgy. Initiation à la liturgie. Translated by Roger Chapel. Preface by Frederick R. McManus. London: Geoffrey Chapman, 1961.

2865. DANIEL, H. A. (ed.). Codex liturgicus. (repr.) Hildesheim, Germany: Georg Olms, Dec. 31, 1966, (orig. Leipzig, 1847-53.

2866. DANIEL, Vattel Elbert. Ritual in Chicago's south side churches for Negroes. Chicago Univ. Library. Chicago, Ill.: Chicago, Ph. D. (sociol.), 1940.

2867. DANIELOU, Jean. The Bible and the liturgy. Edited by Michael A. Mathis. London: Darton, Longman, & Todd, 1960, e.g. (also Hemmond, Indiana).

2868. DAVIS, Charles. Liturgy and doctrine. The doctrinal basis of the liturgical movement. London & New York: Sheed & Ward, 1960.

2869. DEUTSCHE Liturgie? Sind wir auf dem Weg dahin? Maria Laach: Verlag Ars Liturgica, 1967.

2870. DIEKMANN, Godfrey Leo. Come, let us worship, etc. Essays on the Mass and other parts of the liturgy. London: Darton, Longman, & Todd, 1962.

2871. DIJK, S. J. P. van. The urban and Papal rites in seventh and eighth-century Rome. With a summary in Latin. In: Sacris erudiri, 1961.

2872. DIX, Dom Gregory. The shape of the liturgy. London: Dacre Press, 1960.

2873. DOUGLAS, Winfred (ed.). The Monastic Diurnal or Day Hours of the Monastic Breviary according to the Holy Rule of St. Benedict. With additional rubrics and devotions for its recitation in accordance with The Book of Common Prayer. London: Oxford Univ. Press, 1957.

2874. ________. The Monastic Diurnal Noted. Kenosha: St. Mary's Convent, 1952-60.

2875. DUNNE, William. The ritual explained ... sixth edition. London: B. Herder, 1950, e.g. (also Ambleside: A. Hickling).

2876. EISENHOFER, Ludwig and Josef Lechner. The liturgy of the Roman Rite. Liturgik des römischen Ritus. Trans.

by A. J. and E. F. Peeler. Edinburgh, London: Nelson, 1961; also New York, Freiburg: Herder and Herder, 1961.

2877. ENSEL, Gustavus S. Ancient liturgical music. A comparative and historical essay on the origin and development of sacred music from the earliest times, with illustrations of the music employed in the worship of the synagogue, church and mosque. N. P. 1881 Hectographed.

2878. FARMER, H. H. Servant of the word. New York: Charles Scribner's Sons, 1942.

2879. FERREIRA, José Augusto. Estudos historico-liturgicos. Os ritos particulares das Igrejas de Braga e Toledo, etc. With facsimiles. Coimbra: N. G., 1924. (BM 3043. b. 15)

2880. FORTESCUE, Adrian Knottesford and John Betram O'Connell. The ceremonies of the Roman Rite described ... With ... an appendix on "The Ceremonies of the Ritual in the U. S. A." by Frederick R. McManus. London: Burns & Oates, 1962.

2881. FRANK, Hieronymus. Der älteste erhaltene Ordo defunctorum der römischen Liturgie und sein Fortleben in Totenagenden des frühen Mittelalters. In: Archiv für Liturgiewissenschaft, 1962.

2882. FRERE, Walter Howard. Bibliotheca musico-liturgica. Hildesheim, Germany: Georg Olms, 1966 (orig. London & Oxford, 1894-1932).

2883. GAMBER, Klaus. Codices liturgici latini antiquiores. Freiburg, Schweiz: Spicilegii friburgensis subsidia, 1963.

2884. GAUTIER, L. Histoire de poésie liturgique au moyen âge. Paris: N. G., 1886. (BM)

2885. GEMEINDE in der Liturgie. Arbeitsunterlage zum Jahresthema 1965-66 Katholischen Jugend Oesterreichs. Wien: Fahrmann-Verlag, 1967.

2886. GERBERT, Martin. Monumenta veteris liturgiae alemannicae. Hildesheim, Germany: Georg Olms, 1966 (orig. St. Blasien, 1777-79).

2887. ________. Vetus liturgia alemannica. Hildesheim, Germany: Georg Olms, 1966 (orig. St. Blasien, 1776).

2888. GOGOL, Nikolai Vasil'evich. The divine Liturgy of the Eastern Orthodox Church. Trans. by Rosemary Edmonds. London: Darton, Longman, & Todd, 1960.

2889. GÖLLNER, Theodor. Die mehrstimmigen liturgischen Lesungen. Tutzing: H. Schneider, 1969.

2890. HAMM, Fritz. Die Liturgischen Einsetzungsberichte im Sinne vergleichender Liturgieforschung untersucht. The Liturgical settings report in the sense of comparative investigation research. Münster in Westf: Liturgiegeschichtlichtliche Quellen und Forsungen, 1928.

2891. HANUSZ, Jan. O ksiazce do nabozenstwa "Krolo Zygmuntai." W. rekopisie mon-chij-skim ... Obditka z XI toma Rozp-raw Wydz. filog. Akad. Umiej. Krakow: N. G., 1884. (BM. 3071a. 3)

2892. HARPER, Earl Enyeart. Church music and worship, a program for the church of to-day. New York: Abingdon Press, 1924, 1925.

2893. HEBERT, A. G. Liturgy and society. London: Faber & Faber, 1935, 1961.

2894. HEMSJÖMANUALET. En liturgi-historisk studie av Hilding Johansson. With a summary in German. Stockholm: Samlingar och studier till svenska kyrkans historia, 1950.

2895. HEWINS, James M. Hints concerning church music, the liturgy, and kindred subjects. Boston: Ide & Dutton, 1856.

2896. HICKES, George. Devotions in the ancient way of offices. London: Printed by W. B. for R. Sare, 1715.

2897. HILDEBRAND, Dietrich von. Liturgy and personality (R. C.). New York: Longmans, Green & Co., 1943.

2898. HIPPOLYTUS, Saint of Rome. La tradition apostolique de Saint Hippolyte. Essai de reconstitution par Dom Bernard Botte. Münster: Liturgiewissenschaftliche Quellen und Forschungen, 1963.

2899. HORN, Michael (ed.). Gregorianische Rundschau Monatschrift für Kirchenmusik und Liturgie. Graz: Verlagsbuchhandlung "Styria," 190-.

2900. JAHRBUCH für Liturgik und Hymnologie. Kassel: J. Stauda, 1955.

2901. JANINI, José. Los sacramentarios de Tortosa y el cambio de rito. In: Analecta sacra tarraconensia, 1963.

2902. JEBB, John. The choral service of the United Church of England and Ireland: Being an enquiry into the liturgical system of the cathedral and collegiate foundations of the Anglican communion. London: J. W. Parker, 1843.

2903. JENKINS, Graham. A short-title English liturgical bibliography. London: Duckett, 1951.

2904. JOHNER, Dominicus. Die sonn-und-Festtagslieder des vatikanischen Graduale, nach Text und Melodie erklärt. Regensburg: F. Pustet, 1928.

2905. JONES, Bayard Hale. The American lectionary. New York: Morehouse-Gorham, 1944.

2906. JONES, Perry. English in the liturgy: Some aesthetic and practical problems. London: G. Chapman, 1966.

2907. JUNGMANN, Josef Andreas. The early liturgy. To the time of Gregory the Great. Trans. by Francis A. Brunner. London: Darton, Longman & Todd, 1960.

2908. ________. Liturgisches Erbe und pastorale Gengenwart. (Pastoral liturgy.) Tenbury Wells: Challoner Publications, 1962.

2909. KASKAMPAS, Giorgios K. Moüsikou apauthisma Leitourgias. N. G.: N. G., 1957. (BM 07903)

2910. KENNEDY, Sister Rose. Paraliturgical music in Italy, 1600-1650; with selected examples from the works of Giovanni Battista Beria. Ann Arbor: Univ. Microfilms, 1969.

2911. KING, Archdale Arthur. Liturgy of the Roman church. With plates. London: Longmans, Green, & Co., 1957.

2912. KIRCHGAESSNER, Alfons. Unto the altar. The practice of Catholic worship. Unser Gottesdienst. Edinburgh, London: Nelson, 1963; also Frieburg: Herder.

2913. KIRCHMEYER, Helmut. Liturgie am Scheideweg; Betrachtungen zur Situation der katholischen Kirchenmusik aus Anlass des Kölner Kongresses. Liturgy at the Crossroads. Regensburg: Bosse, 1962.

2914. KLAUSER, Theodor. The Western liturgy and its history. Abendländische Liturgiegeschichte. Some reflections on recent studies. Translated by F. L. Cross. London: A. R. Mowbray & Co., 1963.

2915. ________. The Western liturgy to-day. Die abendländische Liturgie von Aeneas Silvius Piccolomini bis heute. Erbe und Aufgabe. Translated by F. L. Cross. London: A. R. Mowbray & Co., 1963.

2916. KNIEWALD, Károly. A "hahóti kódex." Zágrábi MR 126. kézirat--jelentősége a magyarországi liturgia szempontjából ... Fordította Dr. Kühár Flóris. Különlenyomat a Magyar Könyvszemle 1938. évi 11. füzetéből. With facsimiles and a summary in German. Budapest: N. G., 1938. (BM4385 dd. 3)

2917. LADD, William Palmer. Prayer book interleaves. New York: Oxford Univ. Press, 1942.

2918. LANE, John. Notes on some ceremonies of the Roman rite. Fourth edition. Dublin: Burns, Oates & Washbourne, 1952.

2919. LAVANOUX, Maurice. Liturgical Arts. New York: Periodical.

2920. LEFEVRE, Pl. F. Les ordinaires des collégiales Saint-Pierre à Louvain et Saints-Pierre--et-Paul à Anderlecht d'après des manuscrits du XIV siècle. Louvain: Bibliotèque de l'Université, Bureaux de la Revue, 1960.

2921. LEONARD, William J., ed. Sacred music and the liturgy. Boston, Mass.: McLaughlin & Reilly Co., 1959.

2922. LILIENCRON, Rochus von. Liturgisch-musikalische Geschichte der evangelischen Gottesdienste von 1523-1700. reprt.--of Schleswig 1893 ed. Hildesheim: G. Olms, 1970.

2923. LITURGICAL Conference, Board of Editors. The book of Catholic worship. Washington, D.C.: The Liturgical Conference, 1966.

2924. The LITURGICAL portions of the Genevan service book. Edinburgh: N.G., 1931.

2925. LOWRIE, Walter. The Lord's supper and the liturgy. New York: Longmans, Green & Co., 1943.

2926. MANZETTI, Leo P. Church music and Catholic liturgy. Baltimore: St. Mary's Seminary, 1925.

2927. MARBACH, Carl. Carmina scripturarum. Scilicet antiphonas et responsoria ex Sacro Scripturae fonte in libros liturgicos Sanctae Ecclesiae Romanae derivata. Hildesheim: Olms, 1963.

2928. MARITAIN, Jacques Aimé Henri, and Raïssa Maritain. Liturgy and contemplation. Translated by Joseph W. Evans. London: Geoffrey Chapman, 1961.

2929. MARTENE, Edmond. De antiquis ecclesiae ritibus libri. Hildesheim, Germany: Georg Olms, 1966. (orig. Antwerp, 1736-38.)

2930. MARTINDALE, C. C. The prayers of the Missal. Vol. I--The Sunday Collect, 1936, Vol. II--The Offertory Prayers and Post-Communions, 1938. London: Sheed and Ward, 1936 and 1938.

2931. ______. The words of the Missal (R. C.). London: Sheed and Ware, 1933.

2932. MASKELL, William. Ancient liturgy of the Church of England. Original in Latin. Oxford: N. G., 1880.

2933. ______. Monumenta Ritualia Ecclesiae Anglicanae. Second edition. Oxford: N. G., 1882. (LC-1-3049)

2934. MATTFELD, Victor Henry. George Rhaw's publications for Vespers: A study of liturgical practices of Early Reformation. Vol. I & II. Ann Arbor: Univ. Microfilms, 1960.

2935. MAYER, Anton L. Liturgie und Barock. In: Jahrbuch für Liturgiewissenschaft. Bd. 15., 1941. (BM-AC. 2630. c)

2936. MENSBRUGGHE, Alexis Van der. La liturgie orthodoxe de rit occidental. Essai de restauration. Mélanges de l'Institut Orthodoxe Français de Paris. No. 3. Paris: N. G., 1948.

2937. MEYER-BAER, Kathi. Liturgical music Incunabula: A descriptive catalogue. London: The Bibliographical Society, 1962.

2938. MICHEL, Dom Virgil. The liturgy of the church (Roman Catholic). New York: The Macmillan Co., 1937.

2939. MOHLBERG, Cunibert (Leonard). Note su alcuni sacramentarii. 1. Nuovi frammenti di un sacramentario Gelasiano dell'Italia settentrionale, Budapest Cod. Lat. Med. Aevi 44. 11. Paolo Diacono e l'archetipo del sacramentario di Drogone, con un'aggiunta sul "Messale antico" di Montecassino, Cod. Casinensis rescript. 271, alias 348. Appendice. 1. Il testo dei frammenti di Budapest. 2. Alcune messe del Sacramentario di Drogone in confronto col sacramentario ambrosiano di Bergamo. In: Atti della Pontificia Accademia Romana. di Archeologia. ser. 3. Rendiconti. vol. 16. fasc. 3/4. N. G.: N. G., 1940. (BMAc. 5236)

2940. MORTIMER, Alfred G. The development of worship in the rites and ceremonies of the church. Philadelphia: George W. Jacobs & Co., 1911.

2941. MURRAY, Placid (ed.). Studies in pastoral liturgy. Foreword by Thomas Morris, Archbishop of Cashel and Emly. Lectures delivered to the Irish Liturgical Congress, 1954-1959. Maynooth: Furrow Trust, 1961.

2942. MUSIC and liturgy. Hickley: Society of St. Gregory, 1929.

2943. La MUSIQUE dans la liturgie, documents officiels. Paris: Editions Musicales de la Schola Cantorum, 1967.

2944. NORDEN, Norris Lindsay. The music of the Russian liturgy. New York: Burr Printing House, 1916.

2945. OREL, Alfred. Kirchenmusikalische Liturgik, ein Leitfaden. Augsburg: A. Böhm & Sohn, 1936.

2946. OXFORD, University of; Bodleian Library. Latin liturgical manuscripts and printed books. Guide to an exhibition held during 1952. Oxford: Oxford Univ., 1952.

2947. PEARCE, Charles William. The priest's part of the Anglican liturgy. Choir offices and litany. London: The Faith Press, 1922.

2948. PEIL, Rudolf. Handbuch der Liturgik für Katecheten und Lehrer. A Handbook of the liturgy ... translated by H. E. Winstone. Edinburgh, London: Nelson, 1960, also Freiburg: Herder.

2949. PIUS XII, Pope. On the Sacred liturgy. New York: American Press, 1948.

2950. POCKNEE, Cyril Edward. Liturgical vesture: Its origins and development. London: A. R. Mowbray & Co., 1960.

2951. PODHRADSKY, Gerhard. Lexikon der Liturgie; ein Ueberblick für die Praxis. A survey of practices. Innsbruck, Wien, München: Tyrolia-Verlag, 1962.

2952. PRIMUS, John Henry. The vestments controversy. An historical study of the earliest tensions within the Church of England in the reigns of Edward VI and Elizabeth. Kampen: J. H. Kok, 1960.

2953. PROBST, Ferdinand. Liturgie der drei ersten christlichen Jahrhundert. Darmstadt: Wissenschaftliche Buchgesellschaft, 1968.

2954. QUACQUARELLI, Antonio. Retorica e liturgia antenicena. With plates. Roma: N. G., 1960. (BM3042. h. 24)

2955. RAMSEYER, Jean. La parole et l'image. Liturgie, architecture et art sacré. Faize: Neuchaiel, 1963.

2956. REINHOLD, Hans Ansgar. The dynamics of liturgy. New York: Macmillan Co., 1961.

2957. ROME, The City. Quaestiones rituales ... de quibus deliberabitur in Pontificia Academia Liturgica anno 1924-1925, etc. Romae: N. G., 1924. (BM5034. de. 4)

2958. ROMEO, Galindo. El breviario y el ceremonial cesaraugustanos, siglos XII-XIV. With the text of the 'Kalendarium cesaraugustanum saec. XIV-XV." Zaragoza, Tudela: Estudios ec lesiásticos de Aragón, 1930.

2959. RÖNNAU, Klaus. Die tropen zum Gloria in excelsis Deo. Wiesbaden: Breitkopf und Härtel, 1967.

2960. RUTLEDGE, Denys. Catechism through the liturgy. London: Douglas Organ, 1949.

2961. SALMON, Dom Pierre. Le lectionnaire de Luxeuil. Edition et étude comparative. Contribution à l'histoire de la Vulgate et de la liturgie en France au temps des Mérovingiens. Roma: Città del Vaticano, 1944.

2962. SAY, William. Liber Regie Capelle. A manuscript in the Biblioteca Publica, Evora. Edited by Walter Ullmann. With a note on the music by D. H. Turner. London: Henry Bradshaw Society, 1961.

2963. SCHMIDT, Eberhard Kantor. Der Gottesdienst am kurfürstlichen Hofe zu Dresden. Ein Beitrag zur liturgischen Traditionsgeschichte von Johann Walter bis zu Heinrich Schütz. Göttingen: Veröffentlichungen der evangelischen Gesellschaft für Liturgieforschung, 1961.

2964. SCHMIDT, Herman A. P. Introductio in liturgiam occidentalem. Romae: Friburgi Brisg.--Barcinone: Herder, 1960.

2965. SHEPHERD, Massey Hamilton, Jr. At all times and in all places. Hartford: Church Congress of the United States, 1947.

2966. ________. The living liturgy. New York: Oxford Univ. Press, 1946.

2967. SMEND, Julius. Vortrage und Aufsätze zur Liturgik, Hymnologie und Kirchenmusik. Gütensloh: N. G., 1925. (BM)

2968. SÖHNER, Leo. Drei Zeremonialien aus dem 17. Jahrhundert. N. G.: N. G., 1931. (LC-ML5. K58)

2969. SOOS, Marie Bernard de. Le mystère liturgique d'après Saint Léon le Grand. Münster: Liturgiewissenschaftliche Quellen und Forschungen, 1958.

2970. SØRENSEN, Søren. Kirkens liturgi. København: Wilhelm Hansen, 1969.

2971. SOUZA, José Geraldo de. Folcmúsica e liturgia; subsidios para o estudo do problema. Petrópolis: Editora Vozes, 1966.

2972. STEFANI, Gino. L'espressione vocale e musicale nella liturgia. Torino Leumann Collegno: Elle Di Ci, 1967.

2973. STÖFFEL, Alexander Franz. An analysis of liturgical response by confirmed members of the American Lutheran Church. Ann Arbor: Univ. Microfilms, 1969.

2974. STUDIA liturgica. An international ecumenical quarterly for liturgical research and renewal. Rotterdam: N. G., 1962. (BM P. P. 7618)

2975. TELL, Werner. Kleine Geschichte der deutschen evangelischen Kirchenmusik; Liturgik und Hymnologie, bearb. von Georg Eberhard Jahn. Berlin: Evangelische Verlagsanstalt, 1962.

2976. TRETHOWAN, Illtyd. Christ in the liturgy. London & New York: Sheed & Ward, 1952.

2977. TREVES. Liturgisches Jahrbuch. Im Auftrage des Liturgischen Institute in Trier herausgegeben von Joseph Pascher. Münster: N. G., 1951. (BMAc. 2027. e)

2978. UNTERKIRCHER, Franz and Klaus von Gamber (eds.). Das killektar-Pontifikale des Bischofs Baturich von Regensburg, 817-848. Freiburg, Schweiz: Spicilegium friburgense, 1962.

2979. VAN DIJK, Stephen Joseph Peter and Joan Hazelden Walker. The origins of the modern Roman liturgy. The liturgy of the papal court and the Franciscan order in the thirteenth century. With plates. London: Darton, Longman & Todd, 1960.

2980. VISMANS, T. A. and Lucas Brinkhoff. Critical bibliography of liturgical literature. Kritische Bibliographie der Liturgie. Translated from German edition by Raymond W. Fitzpatrick ... and Clifford Howell. Nijmgen: Bestelcentrale der V. S. K. B. Publ., 1961.

2981. WEALE, W. H. S. Analecta liturgica. Insulis et Brugis: The Author, 1889.

2982. WESSELING, Dom Theodore. Liturgy and life. London: Longmans, Green, and Co., 1938.

2983. WEST, R. C. Western liturgies. London: S. P. C. K., 1938.

2984. WICKER, Brian. Culture and liturgy. London & New York: Sheed & Ward, 1963.

2985. WINNINGER, Paul. Langues vivantes et liturgie, etc. Paris: Editions du Cerf, 1961.

2986. WISEMAN. Lectures on the Offices and Ceremonies of Holy Week. Baltimore: Kelly, 1850.

2987. WORLD Council of Churches--Commission on Faith and Order. Ways of worship. Report of a theological commission of Faith and Order. London: SCM Press, 1951.

2988. ZUNDEL, Maurice. The splendour of the liturgy. New York: Sheed & Ward, 1939.

See also: 13, 23, 188, 312, 335, 453, 461, 465, 473, 474, 494, 496, 507, 518, 594, 597, 626, 648, 651, 668, 677, 681, 682, 783, 956, 967, 968, 977, 1031, 1032, 1053, 1093, 1095, 1103, 1104, 1106, 1125, 1126, 1129, 1136, 1142, 1144, 1148, 1153, 1154, 1160, 1163, 1164, 1165, 1166, 1167, 1178, 1180, 1181, 1182, 1187, 1188, 1193, 1227, 1240, 1253, 1256, 1257, 1258, 1261, 1262, 1263, 1264, 1266, 1267, 1268, 1269, 1271, 1273, 1277, 1288, 1302, 1305, 1320, 1322, 1326, 1329, 1338, 1362, 1374, 1378, 1382, 1385, 1397, 1405, 1406, 1407, 1408, 1420, 1435, 1486, 1511, 1518, 1520, 1525, 1607, 1686, 1711, 1764, 1793, 1796, 1841, 1864, 1917, 1931, 1935, 1936, 1940, 2015, 2025, 2064, 2079, 2091, 2137, 2162, 2478, 2509, 2515, 2686, 2715, 2739, 2792, 2813, 2815, 2821, 2974, 2990, 3028, 3042, 3047, 3048, 3054, 3058, 3062, 3065, 3090, 3098, 3099, 3107, 3108, 3112, 3121, 3122, 3136, 3137, 3146, 3149, 3153, 3159, 3195, 3265, 3332, 3374, 3419, 3434, 3443, 3461, 3491, 3516, 3520, 3541, 3551, 3593, 3695, 3913, 4013, 4030, 4053, 4119, 4139, 4149, 4169, 4186, 4351, 4354, 4393, 4478, 4642, 4728, 4734, 4735, 4736, 4738, 4741, 4744, 4746, 4772, 4791, 4830, 4834, 4843, 4865, 4896, 4903, 4908, 4910, 4913, 4927, 4930, 4946, 4988, 4991, 4995, 5011, 5032, 5035, 5043, 5056, 5214, 5215, 5216, 5221, 5226, 5237, 5284, 5285, 5313, 5324, 5326, 5371, 5373, 5374, 5378, 5380, 5381, 5382, 5383, 5387, 5390, 5391, 5397, 5398, 5399, 5412, 5414, 5419, 5420, 5443.

MANUALS

2989. The CHORAL service. A manual for clergy and organist. The Liturgical music for morning and evening prayer. The Litany and The Holy Communion according to the use of the Protestant Episcopal Church in the U. S. A. New York: H. W. Gray Co., 1927.

2990. HELMORE, Thomas. A manual of plainsong for divine service. As edited by H. B. Briggs and W. H. Frere. Revised and enlarged by J. H. Arnold. London: Novello & Co., 1951.

2991. HINES, Robert S. Singer's manual of Latin diction and phonetics. New York: Schirmer Books, 1975.

2992. JEKYLL, C. S. The choir boy's manual. London: N. G., 1899. (BM)

2993. McCUTCHAN, Robert Guy. Our hymnody: A manual of the Methodist hymnal. New York: The Methodist Book Concern, 1937.

2994. MARSHALL, M. The singer's manual of English diction. New York: G. Schirmer, Inc., 1946.

2995. MORIARTY, John. Diction: Italian, Latin, French, German: The sounds and 81 exercises for singing them. Boston: E. C. Schirmer Music Co., 1975.

2996. NEWTON, J. Don'ts for choirmasters. Cambridge: N. G., 1924.

2997. NICHOLSON. A manual of English church music. N. G.: N. G., 1923.

2998. SCOTLAND, Church of--Ed. Commission. Manual of church praise. Edinburgh: The Church of Scotland Committee on Publications, 1932.

2999. SHEIL, Richard F. A manual of foreign language dictions for singers. Fredonia, N. Y.: B. G. Print Co., 1975.

3000. A WEDDING manual. Nashville: Abingdon Press, 1959.

See also: 175, 560, 568, 650, 690, 693, 784, 801, 809, 833, 901, 964, 1216, 1323, 1839, 1879, 1901, 1906, 1929, 1940, 3056, 4191, 4870, 5039, 5055, 5056, 5228.

MANUSCRIPT

3001. AMANN, J. Allegris miserere und die Auffuhrungspraxis in der Sistine nach Reiseberichten und Musikhandschriften. Regensburg: F. Pustet, 1935.

3002. BIBLIOTEQUE Royale Albert Ier. Trésors musicaux de la Bibliothèque royale Albert Ier, 1220-1800: exposition du 8 au 27 septembre 1975. Catalogue de l'exposition redigé par B. Huys. Bruxelles: B. Huys, 1975.

3003. B., M. Manuscrits à peintures et livres d'heures imprimes appartenant à M. B. Vente aux enchères publiques ... le 7 decembre 1960. Paris: N. G., 1960. (BM)

3004. BURGOS, Spain. Las Huelgas. El codex musical de Las Huelgas. Barcelona: Institut d'estudis catalans: Biblioteca de Catalunya, 1931.

3005. CABROL, Ferdinand. The year's liturgy. 2 volumes. London: Burns, Oates, & Washbourne, 1938 & 1940.

3006. CODE for cataloguing of manuscripts, Vol. IV. New York: C. F. Peters Corporation, 1967.

3007. DONATO, Anthony. Preparing music manuscript. Englewood Cliffs, N. J.: Prentice-Hall, Inc., 1963.

3008. FAGE, A. de la. Essais de diphtérographie musicale ou descriptions, notices, analyses, extraits et reproductions de manuscripts rélatifs à la pratique à la théorie et à l'histoire de la musique. New York: Broude Brothers Limited, 1964. (original Paris, 1864.)

3009. FERRETTI, Paolo M. I manoscritti musicali gregoriani dell'archivio di Montecassino. In Casinensia: miscellanea di studi Cassinesi ... v. 1. Montecassino: Archivo Musicale, 1929.

3010. FRANKFURT Am Main. Stadtbibliothek (ed.). Kirchliche Musikhandschriften des XVII und XVIII Jahrhunderts. Katalog von Carl Suss, im Auftrage der Gesellschaft der Freunde der Stadtbibliothek bearbeitet und herausgegeben. Frankfurt am Main: Gesellschaft der Freunde der Stadtbibliotek, 1926.

3010a. FRERE, W. H., ed. Biblioteca Musico-Liturgica. A descriptive handlist of the musical and Latin-liturgical manuscripts of the Middle Ages, preserved in the libraries of Great Britain and Ireland. Hildesheim: Georg Olms, 1967.

3011. HUGHES, Anselm, compiler. Catalogue of the musical manuscripts at Peterhouse, Cambridge. Cambridge: University Press, 1953.

3012. JANINI, José. Manuscritos liturgicos de la Biblioteca Nacional. Madrid: Direccion General Archivos, 1969.

3013. JUST, Martin. Der Mensuralkodex Mus. ms. 40021 der Stadtbibliothek preussischer Kulturbesitz Berlin. Untersuchung zum Repertoire einer deutschen Quelle des 15. Jahrhunderts. (Würzburger musikhistorische Beiträge, 1.) 2 vols. Tutzing: Hans Schneider, 1975.

3014. KLIMA, Josef. Die lautenhandschrift der Benediktinerabtei Göttweig, N. O. Text, Tablatur 1, Anfangs d. 18 Jh., Tablatur 2, 1735-39; themat. Verzeichnis. Maria Enzersdorf bei Wien: Verl. Wiener Lautenarchiv, J. Klima, 1975.

3015. LISBON. Palacio da Ajuda. Biblioteca. Catálogo de música manuscrita. Lisboa: Palacio da Ajuda, 1958-63.

3016. LUDWIG, Friedrich. Repertorium. Die Handschriften, welche das Repertoire der späteren Organa und der Motetten bis zum Ausgang der 13. Jahrh. in Mensuralnotation geschrieben überliefern; ferner verwandte Texthandschriften kleinere Sammlungen des jüngeren Motetten-repertoires in verschiedener Notation und deutche Motettenhandschriften. Halle a S.: M. Niemeyer, 1910.

3017. MASSERA, Giuseppe. La "mano musicale perfetta" di Francesco de Brugis dalle prefazionia ai corali di L. A. Giunta. Venezia, 1499-1504. Con 7 tavv. f. t. e trascrizione integrale degli scritti teorici. "Historiae musicae cultores." Biblioteca. vol. 18. Firenze: N. G., 1963.

3018. NICHOLSON, Edward W. Introduction to the study of some of the oldest Latin musical manuscripts in the Bodleian Library. Oxford & London: Gregg, 1967.

3019. RUBIO PIQUERAS, Felipe. Códices polifónicos toledanos Estudio critico de los mismos con motivo del VII centenario de la catedral primada. Toledo: N. G., 1925.

3020. SAMPAYO, Ribeiro Mario de. Os manuscritos musicais. Coimbra: Impresso nas oficinas de Atlantida, 1941.

3021. SCHREIBER, Max. Kirchenmusik von 1600-1700. Originaldrucke und Manuskripte chronologisch zusammengestellt. Regensburg: Druckerei St. Georgsheim Birkeneck, 1934.

3022. THEMATISCHER Katalog der Musikhandschriften der Bendiktinerinnenabtei Frauenwörth und der Pfarrkirchen Indersdorf, Wasserburg am Inn und Bad Tölz. Unter der Leitung von R. Münster. Bearb. von U. Bockholdt et al. München: G. Henle, 1975.

3023. THEMATISCHER Katalog der Musikhandschriften der ehemaligen Klosterkirchen Weyarn, Tegernsee und Benediktebeurn. By Robert Münster and Robert Machold. (Katologe Bayerische Musiksammlungen, [1].) München: G. Henle, 1971.

3024. WINDSOR Castle, St. George's Chapel. The musical manuscripts of St. George's Chapel, Windsor Castle; a descriptive catalog by Clifford Mould. Windsor: Oxley, 1973.

See also: 206, 226, 231, 241, 341, 361, 383, 387, 416, 446, 477, 478, 532, 542, 623, 629, 730, 1207, 1467, 1919, 2141, 2628, 2742, 2946, 2962, 3204, 3356, 3371, 3386, 3416, 3491, 3513, 3588, 3598, 3624, 3684, 3690, 3697, 3700, 3703, 3735, 4723, 4724, 4754, 4842, 5030, 5034.

MARY, VIRGIN

3025. ALPHONSO X, King of Castile and Leon. La música de las cantigas de Santa María. Barcelona: Diputación Provincíal de Barcelona Biblioteca Central-Publicaciones de la Sección de Musica--No. 15., 1943.

3026. HANS, Bruder. Marienlieder aus dem vierzehnten Jahrhundert. Amsterdam: Gruner, 1967.

3027. MAIER, J. Studien zur Geschichte der Marienantiphon "Salve regina." Regensburg: F. Pustet, 1939.

3028. NASRALLAH, Joseph. Marie dans la sainte et divine liturgie byzantine. Paris: Nouvelles Editions latines, 1955.

3029. SCHMITZ, Eugen. Das madonnen-ideal in der tonkunst. Mit 7 Vollbildern in Tonatzung und 5 Notenbeilagen. Leipzig: C. F. W. Siegel, 1920.

See also: 2284.

MASS, and REQUIEM MASS

3030. ADLER, G. Zur Geschichte der wiener Messkomposition in der zweiten Halfte des XVII Jahrhunderts. Wien: N. G., 1916.

3031. ALLAIRE, Gaston G. The French 'Chanson-Mass' 1525-1575. Boston: Boston Univ., n. d.

3032. ________. The masses of Claudin de Surmisy. Boston: Boston Univ., 1960.

3033. BANK, J. A. Geschiedenis van de meerstemmige mis. Bilthoven: de Gemeeschap, 1938.

3034. BELLINI, Vincenzo. Mass. New York: Mills Music, 1959.

3035. BENEVOLI, Orazio. Missa Pastoralis. (Monumental liturgiae polychoralis sanctae ecclesiae Romanae, ordinarium missae cum duobus choris, No. 1). Rome: Societas Universalis Sanctae Ceciliae, 1957.

3036. BIGGLE, Lloyd, Jr. The masses of Antoine Brumel. Ann Arbor: Univ. of Michigan, 1953.

3037. BLUM, Klaus. "Hundert Jahre 'Ein Deutsches Requiem' von Johannes Brahms." Tutzing: H. Schneider, 1971.

3038. BORREL, Eugène. La forme musicale de la messe. Paris: N. G., 1929. (LC - A44-2508)

3039. BRAGERS, Achille P. Masses. Boston, Mass.: McLaughlin & Reilly Co., n. d.

3040. _______. Propers of the mass. Boston, Mass.: McLaughlin & Reilly Co., n. d.

3041. BRAND, Carl Maria. Die Messen von Joseph Haydn. (Unverändert Neudruck.) Walluf bei Wiesbaden: M. Sändig, 1973.

3042. BRENNAN, Gerard S. (ed.). Propers of the mass made easy. Toledo, Ohio: Gregorian Institute of America, 1961.

3043. BURNE, Martin Joseph. Mass cycles in early Graduals: A study of the Ordinary of the mass cycles found in Mediaeval and Renaissance Graduals in libraries in the U. S. New York: N. Y. Univ. School of Ed., n. d.

3044. BYRD. Mass of three voices. London: Stainer & Bell, n. d.

3045. _______. Mass for four voices. London: Stainer & Bell, n. d.

3046. _______. Mass for five voices. London: Stainer & Bell, n. d.

3047. CABROL, Ferdinand. The mass of the western rites. London: Sands & Co., 1934.

3048. CATHOLIC Church. The laws of the Holy Mass, being the general rubrics and other preliminaries of the Roman missal. New York: Sheed and Ward, 1949.

3049. CHRISTIAN, Sister M. Contemporary trends in the musical settings of the liturgical mass. Rochester, N. Y.: Univ. of Rochester, 1957.

3050. CLENDENIN, William Ritchie. The use of the French chanson in some polyphonic masses by French and Netherlands composers, 1450-1550. Iowa City: State Univ. of Iowa, 1952.

3051. COHEN, Judith. The six anonymous L'Homme armé masses in Naples, Biblioteca Nazionale. Dallas: American Institute of Musicology, 1968.

3052. DABIN, L. Célebrons l'eucharistie. Bruxelles: Editions "Vie ouvrière," 1970.

3053. DENKER, Fred Herman. A study of the transition from the cantus firmus mass to the parody mass. Rochester: Univ. of Rochester, Eastman School of Music, n. d.

3054. DIJK, S. J. P. The authentic missal of the Papal chapel. In: Scriptorium, Vol. 14, pp. 257-314., 1960. (BM. PP4453. B)

3055. DOUGLAS, Winfred (ed.). The Kyrial or Ordinary of the mass with the plainsong melodies. New York: H. W. Gray Co., 1933.

3056. DUTTON, W. E. The eucharistic manuals of John and Charles Wesley. London: Pull, Simmons, and Co., 1794.

3057. EISENRING, Georg. Zur Geschichte des mehrstimmigen proprium missae bis zum 1560. Düsseldorf: Druck von L. Schwann, 1913.

3058. ELLARD, Gerald. The mass of the future. Milwaukee: Bruce Publishing Co., 1948.

3059. FERRERES, Juan B. Historia del Misal romano, etc. Barcelona: E. Subirana., 1929.

3060. FICKER, Rudolf von. Die frühen Messenkompositionen der Trienter Codices. N. G.: N. G., 1924. (LC-ML55. 59)

3061. ________. Die kolorierungstechnik der Trienter Messen (Studien zur Musikwissenschaft). Wien: N. G., 1920. (BM7890)

3062. FLEMING, Jo Lee. The Bach B-minor Mass and its deviation from Roman Catholic Liturgy. Dallas, Tex.: Southern Methodist Univ., M. M., 1958.

3063. FREDRICH, Eva. Der Ruf, eine Gattung des geistlichen Volksliedes. reprt.--of Berlin: Eberling, 1936 ed. Nendeln/Liechtenstein: Kraus Reprint, 1967.

3064. FRITSCHEL, J. E. The study and performance of three extended choral works: Mass in G, by Francis Poulenc; Missa Brevis, by Dietrich Buxtehude; Stabat Mater, by Antonio Caldara; and: Original Composition. Introits and graduals for Holy Week for chorus and wind instruments. Ames: State Univ. of Iowa, Mus., 1960.

3065. GAMBER, Klaus. Das kampanische Messbuch als Vorläufer des Gelasianum 1st der hl. Paulinus von Nola der Verfasser? In: Sacris erudiri, 1961. (BM PP2421. 00)

3066. GHESQUIERE, Remi. Geschiedenis van de zingende Meisjes van Halle, 1928-1941. with illustrations including a portrait. Halle: N. G., 1963. (BM7903. bb40)

3067. GIEBLER, Albert C. The masses of Johann Kaspar Kerll. Ann Arbor: Univ. of Michigan, 1956.

3068. GÖHLER, K. A. Die Messkataloge im Dienst der Musikalischen Geschichtsforschung. Eine Anregung zur zeitgenössischen Buchbeschreibung. Unchanged reprint of the original edition, 1901. New York: Broude Brothers Limited, 1965.

3069. ________. Verzeichnis der in den Frankfurter und Leipziger Messkatalogen der Jahre 1546 bis 1759 angezeigten Musikalien. Angefertigt und mit Vorschlägen zur Förderung der musikalischen Bücherbeschreibung begleitet. New York: Broude Brothers Limited (Facsimile), 1965, (orig. 1902).

3070. GOTTLIEB, Louis F. Cyclic masses from the Trent Codices. Berkeley: Univ. of California at Berkeley, 1957.

3071. GOULD, Ronald Lee. The Latin Lutheran mass at Wittenberg 1523-1545: A survey of the early Reformation mass, and the liturgical writings of Martin Luther, the relevant Kircheordnungs and the Georg Rhau Musikdrucke for the Hauptgottesdienst. Ann Arbor: Univ. Microfilms, 1970.

3072. GROSSE-JÄGER, Hermann. Eucharistiefeier für Kinder. Düsseldorf: Patmos-Verlag, 1969.

3073. GUTHERIE, Claude E. Communion service (shortened form) with text according to the Book of Common Prayer. Denton, Tex.: North Texas State Univ., M. M., 1948.

3074. HAKE. Kyrie. London: Stainer & Bell, n. d.

3075. HAYDN, Joseph. Mass in time of war. (Paukenmesse). New York: G. Schirmer, n. d.

3076. HOWELL, Almonte C., Jr. The French organ mass in the 16th and 17th centuries. Chapel Hill: Univ. of North Carolina, 1953.

3077. HURST, Ronald S. Requiem. Denton, Tex.: North Texas State Univ., M. M., 1957.

3078. JACKSON, Philip Taylor. The masses of Jachet of Mantua, with Vol. II a musical supplement. Ann Arbor: Univ. Microfilms, 1968.

3079. JOHNSON, Orland W., Jr. Masses of Archangelo Crivelli. Ann Arbor: Univ. Microfilms, 1965.

3080. KEAHEY, Thomas Herman. The masses of Johannes Prioris. Ann Arbor: Univ. Microfilms, 1968.

3081. KIENBERGER, Franz Josef. Studien zur Geschichte der Messenkomposition der Schweiz im 18. Jahrhundert. Freiburg and Schweiz: Universitätsverlag, 1968.

3082. KNISELEY, S. Philip. Masses of Francesco Soriano. Gainesville: Univ. of Florida Press, 1967.

3083. KURTHEN, Wilhelm. Zur Geschichte der deutschen Singmesse. N. G.: N. G., 1931. (LCML5. k58)

3084. KYRIALE Simplex. Cum Missis ornatioribus et pro defunctis. Romae-Neo Eboraci, Parisiis-Tornaci: Desclée & socii, 1966.

3085. LEFEBURE, Dom Gasper (ed.). St. Andrew daily Missal. St. Paul, Minn.: Lohmann, 1945.

3086. LERNER, Edward R. The masses and motets of Alexander Agricola. New Haven, Conn.: Yale, 1957.

3087. LIPPHARDT, Walther. Die Geschichte des mehrstimmigen Proprium missae. Heidelberg: F. H. Kerle, 1950.

3088. LOCKWOOD, Lewis. The counter-Reformation and the masses of Vincenzo Ruffo. Vienna: Universal Edition, 1967.

3089. LUCE, H. T. The Requiem mass for its plainsong beginnings to 1600, vol. I.: Selected Requiem Masses, vol. II. Tallahassee: Florida State Univ., 1958.

3090. LUTHER, Martin. Deutsche Messe und Ordnung Gottesdienst. Wittemberg: Michael Lotther, 1526.

3091. LÜTOLF, Max. Die Mehrstimmigen Ordinarium Missae-Sätze vom ausgehenden 11, bis zur Wende des 13. zum 14. Jahrhundert. Bern: Komm. Paul Haupt, 1970.

3092. MACK, Gerald Raymond. Performance and analysis of Messa III a quattro voci da cappella (Monteverdi). Ann Arbor: Univ. Microfilms, 1966.

3093. McRAE, Donald. The masses of Claudin de Sermisy. Los Angeles: Univ. of California at Los Angeles, n. d.

3094. MAHRT, William Peter. The Missae ad Organum of Heinrich Isaac. Ann Arbor: Univ. Microfilms, 1969.

3095. MARBECKE. Benedictus (per arma justicie). London: Stainer & Bell, n. d.

3096. MARQUARDT, H. Die stuttgarter Chorbücher unter besonderer Behandlung der Messen. Studien zum erhaltenen Teil des Notenbestandes der württembergischen Hofkapelle des 16. Jahrhunderts. Tübingen: N. G., 1936. (BM)

3097. MARSHALL, Robert L. "The paraphrase technique of Palestrina in his masses based on hymns." Journal of the

American Musicological Society. XVI/3 pp. 347-72., 1963 (Fall).

3098. MARTINDALE, C. C. The mind of the Missal. New York: Macmillan Co., 1929.

3099. The MASS in pictures. Droitwich: Word Press, 1950.

3100. MICHAEL, George. The masses of Philippe de Monte. New York: New York Univ., Graduate School of Arts and Science, 1958.

3101. MINOR, Andrew C. The masses of Jean Mouton. Ann Arbor: Univ. of Michigan, 1951.

3102. MORLEY. Agnus Dei. London: Stainer & Bell, n.d.

3103. MULKEARN, Clement. The music of the mass. Ft. Worth: N.G., 1938, also Thesis-American Conservatory of Music, Chicago. (LC40-34385)

3104. NATIONAL Commission for Catholic Church Music. Music in the mass. London: Catholic Truth Society, 1969.

3105. NEYLAND, Elizabeth H. B. Music for the Episcopal communion service. Austin: Univ. of Texas, M.M., 1960.

3106. O'BRIEN. History of the mass. New York: Catholic Publishing Society, 1893.

3107. The OFFICE of the Holy Communion as set by John Merbecke. London: Oxford Univ. Press, 1949.

3108. OFFICIAL liturgical texts and music for the Ordinary of the mass. Cincinnati, Ohio: World Library of Sacred Music, Inc., 1966.

3109. OKELAND. Kyrie. London: Stainer & Bell, n.d.

3110. PACKE. Kyrie, Rex summe. London: J. & W. Chester, n.d.

3111. PALESTRINA, Giovanni Pierluigi. Pope Marcellus Mass: an authoritative score, backgrounds and sources, history and analysis, views and comments edited by L. Lockwood. New York: Norton, 1975.

3112. PASCH, Pius. The liturgy of the mass (R.C.). St. Louis: B. Herder Book Co., 1936.

3113. PAULY, Reinhard G. "Michael Haydn's Latin Proprium Missae compositions." New Haven: Yale Univ., 1956.

3114. PEOPLES mass book. Cincinnati, Ohio: World Library of Sacred Music, Inc., 1965.

3115. PIBERNIK, Lilian. The masses of Costanzo Porta. Chapel Hill: Univ. of North Carolina, 1956.

3116. PRESTON, Robert E. A stylistic comparison of the Machaut and Tournai masses. Ann Arbor: Univ. of Michigan, n. d.

3117. The PROPER of the mass. Vol. 1, Sundays and principal feasts (No. 707A); Vol. 2, Feasts which supersede Sundays (No. 2241A). From National Headquarters for Catholic Church and School music. Boston, Mass.: McLaughlin & Reilly Co., n. d.

3118. RICKS, Robert Wayne. The published masses of Joseph Eybler, 1765-1846. Ann Arbor: Univ. Microfilms, 1967.

3119. ROBERTSON, Alec. Requiem: Music of mourning and consolation. London: Cassell, 1967, and New York: F. A. Praeger, 1968.

3120. ________. Requiem: Music of mourning and consolation. (Repr. of New York: Praeger, 1968.) Westport, Conn.: Greenwood Press, 1976.

3121. ROME, Church of--Congregatio Rituum. Urbis et orbis. Approbationis officii ac missae propriae Sancti Roberti Bellarmino, etc. Rome, Vatican, 1931. (BM5034. E. 13)

3122. ROSNER, Sister Mary. Contemporary trends in the musical settings of the liturgical mass. Rochester: Univ. of Rochester, Eastman School, 1956.

3123. SALOP, Arnold. The masses of Jacob Obrecht. Bloomington: Indiana Univ., 1959.

3124. SANDER, H. A. Italienische Messkompositionen des 17. Jahrhunderts aus der Breslauer Sammlung des Daniel Sartorius. Birkeneck: N. G., 1934. (BM)

3125. SCHERING, Arnold. Die Niederländische Orgelmesse in Zeitalter des Josquin. Amsterdam: Breitkopf und Härtel, 1971.

3126. SCHILD, Emilie. Geschichte der protestantischen Messenkomposition im 17. und 18. Jahrhundert. Wuppertal-Elberfeld: F. W. Khöler, 1934.

3127. SCHMITZ, Eberhard. Die messen Johann David Heinischens. Hamburg: Diss. (Univ. Lib.), 1967.

3128. SCHNERICH, Alfred. Messe und Requiem seit Haydn und Mozart. Mit einem thematischen Verzeichnis. Wien-Leipzig: C. W. Stern, 1909.

3129. SCHNOEBELEN, Sister Mary N. The concerted mass at San Petronio in Bologna: ca. 1660-1730. Ann Arbor: Univ. Microfilms, 1966.

3130. SCHULZE, Willi. Die mehrstimmige Messe im frühprotestantischen Gottesdienst. Berlin: Wolfenbüttel, 1940.

3131. SELBST, Joseph. Der Katholische Kirchengesang beim heiligen Messopfer. In popularen Vorträgen für Geistliche und Laien dargestellt. New York: F. Pustet, 1890.

3132. SHEPHERD. The French mass. London: J. & W. Chester, n. d.

3133. ________. Playnsong mass for a mene. London: J. & W. Chester, n. d.

3134. SHERMAN, Charles Henry. The masses of Johann Michael Haydn. Ann Arbor: Univ. Microfilms, 1967.

3135. SHORE, S. Royle. The Choral Eucharist since the Reformation. London: Faith Press, 1914.

3136. SIFFRIN, Petrus. Missale Gothicum. Vat. Reg. lat. 317. dargeboten vom Petrus Siffrin. Konkordanztabellen zu den lateinischen Sakramentarien. 111. Roma: Rerum ecclesiasticarum documenta. Series minor. Sub-sidia studiorum. vol. 6., 1961.

3137. SIGL, Maximilian. Zur Geschichte des Ordinarium missae in der deutschen Choralüberlieferung. Regensburg: F. Pustet, 1911.

3138. SMEND, Kulius. Die evangelischen deutschen Messen bis zu Luthers deutschen Messen. (Nachdr. Ausgabe Gottingen, 1896 ed.) Hildesheim: G. Olms, n. d., auch Nieuwkoop: B. de Graaf, 1967.

3139. ________. Die Römische Messe. Tübigen: Mohr, 1920.

3140. SOPEÑA, Federico. El requiem, en la música romántica. Madrid: Ediciones Rialp, 1965.

3141. SPRATT, John F. The masses of Antoine de Fevin. Tallahassee: Florida State Univ., 1960.

3142. STEIN, Edwin Eugene. The polyphonic mass in France and the Netherlands, c. 1525 to c. 1560. Rochester: Univ. of Rochester, Eastman School of Music, 1941.

3143. TAVERNER, John. Kyrie Leroy. London: Oxford Univ. Press, n. d.

3144. _______. Mass, Gloria tibi Trinitas. London: Stainer & Bell, n. d.

3145. _______. The Westron Wynde mass. London: J. & W. Chester, n. d.

3146. THOMAS, De Celano. Dies Irae. Latin text, with a prose translation. Chicago: N. G., 1892.

3147. TIRRO, Frank P. American jazz mass. Evanston, Ill.: Summy-Birchard Publishing Co., 1960.

3148. TORTOLANO, William. The mass and the 20th century composer. Ann Arbor: Univ. Microfilms, 1964.

3149. TREXLER, Georg. Die Musik der römischen Messe; werkheft für liturgie und kirchenmusik. Leipzig: St. Benno-Verlag, 1963.

3150. TYE. Euge bone mass. London: Joseph Williams, n. d.

3151. VAIL, J. H. The Choral Eucharist in the Anglican church from the English Reformation to the Oxford movement. Los Angeles: Univ. of Southern California, 1961.

3152. VIVALDI, Antonio. Chamber mass. New York: G. Schirmer, n. d.

3153. VOGT, Walter. Die Messe in der Schweiz im 17 Jahrhundert. Schwarzenburg: Buchdruckerei H. Gerber, 1940.

3154. WAGNER, Lavern John. The octo missae of George de la Hèle, 1547-1587. Madison: Univ. of Wisconsin, 1956.

3155. WAGNER, Peter. Geschichte der Messe. Leipzig: Breitkopf & Härtel, 1913.

3156. WALSH, Thomas F. The mass. Data-guide solid plastic religion charts. Flushing, N. Y.: Data-Guide, Inc., 1963.

3157. WALTON, William. Gloria, for contralto, tenor, and bass soloists, chorus, and orchestra. London & New York: Oxford, 1961.

3158. WANNINGER, Forrest I. Dies Irae: Its use in non-liturgical music from the beginning of the nineteenth century. Ann Arbor: Northwestern Univ., diss., 1962.

3159. WARREN, C. F. S. The Dies Irae. On this hymn and its English versions. London: N. G., 1897. (BM)

3160. WARREN, Edwin Brady. The masses of Robert Fayrfax. Ann Arbor: Univ. of Michigan, 1952.

3161. WILHITE, Charles Stanford. Eucharistic music for the Anglican church in England and the U. S. at mid-twentieth century (1950-1965). Ann Arbor: Univ. Microfilms, 1968.

3162. WILLIAMS, Edward Vinson. John Koukouzeles' reform of Byzantine chanting for Great Vespers in the 14th-century, with musical supplement. Ann Arbor: Univ. Microfilms, 1968.

3163. WOOLLEN, Charles R. The mass ordinaries of the manuscript J. 11. 9 in the Biblioteca Nazionale of Turin. Urbana: Univ. of Illinois, n. d.

3164. ZEHR, Sister Maria D. A study of selected masses approved for use in the church. Austin: Univ. of Texas, M. M., 1960.

See also: 10, 189, 288, 292, 293, 459, 523, 558, 646, 654, 1124, 1160, 1182, 1268, 1872, 1874, 1875, 2141, 2655, 2807, 2808, 2810, 2819, 2844, 2870, 2904, 2923, 2930, 2931, 3013, 3192, 3229, 3374, 3528, 3587, 3608, 4077, 4139, 4147, 4186, 4222, 4275, 4354, 4372, 4395, 4442, 4572, 4661, 4722, 4836, 4933, 5025, 5187, 5202, 5203, 5284, 5285.

MASTERWORKS

3165. CARRUTH, Carroll Dodson. The St. Matthew Passion by Johann Sebastian Bach. Waco: Baylor Univ., M. M., 1953.

3166. EDWARDS, J. Malcolm. A historical and musical study of the St. Matthew Passion by J. S. Bach. Waco, Tex.: Baylor Univ., M. M., 1954.

3167. GRAVES, Richard. Your performance of "Messiah"; a guide for the amateur conductor. With a foreward by Sir Adrian Boult. London: Novello, 1962.

3168. MYERS, R. M. Handel's Messiah. New York: Macmillan & Co., 1948.

3169. SHAW, Harold W. The story of Handel's Messiah, 1741-1784; a short popular history. London: Novello, 1963.

3170. WOODWARD, Ralph. The large sacred choral works of Franz Liszt. Ann Arbor: Univ. Microfilms, 1964.

See also: 3037, 3727, 3739, 4307, 4426, 4711, 5188.

MELODY

3171. BURGER, Erich. Deutsche Kirchenmelodien in Schweden. Ein Beitrag zur Geschichte der Schwedischen Reformation. (pp. 108-271). Münich Library, Phil. Munic, Ger.: Kyrkohistorick Ärsskritt, 1932.

3172. RUNGE, P. Die Lieder und Melodien der Geissler des Jahres. Leipzig: Breitkopf and Härtel, 1900.

See also: 578, 619, 1247, 1341, 3429, 3536, 4475a, 5009, 5132.

MENSURAL NOTATION

3173. BELOMONDI, Prosdocimo de, ed. and transl. by Jay A. Huff. A treatise on the practise of mensural music in the Italian manner. N. P. American Institute of Musicology, 1972.

3174. JACOBSTHAL, Gustav. Mensuralnotenschrift des 12. und 13. Jahrhunderts. Walluf bei Wiesbaden: M. Sändig, 1973.

3175. WOLF, Johannes. Geschichte der Mensural-Notation von 1250-1460. Wiesbaden: Breitkopf & Härtel, 1965.

See also: 3013, 3713, 4369.

MINISTRY OF MUSIC

3176. BAUMAN, William A. The ministry of music: A guide for the practicing musician. Washington: Liturgical Conference, 1975.

3177. EVANGELISCHE Kirche der altpreussischen Union. Berlin: Evangelische Verlagsanstalt, 1950.

3178. GUNDY, Palmer Van. Some ministers of music. Los Angeles: First Methodist Church, 1935.

3179. HOFFLAND, R. D. The ministry to youth through music. Minneapolis: Augsburg Publishing House, 1956.

3180. MUSIC ministry. "Notes" Dec., 1966. Nashville, Tenn.: The Graded Press, n. d. (Monthly.)

3181. OSBECK, Kenneth W. The ministry of music. Grand Rapids: Zondervan Publishing House, 1961.

3182. PRATT, W. S. Musical ministries in the church; studies in the history, theory, and administration of sacred music. New York: G. Schirmer, Inc., 1901, 1915, 1923.

3183. ______. Musical ministries in the church; studies in the history, theory and administration of sacred music. (Repr., New York: Schirmer, 1923.) New York: AMS Press, 1976.

3184. RINEY, Cecil J. The emergence and development of a ministry of music within the Society of Friends. Ann Arbor: Univ. of Southern California, Diss., 1950 and 1963.

3185. SÖHNGEN, Oskar. Das kirchenmusikalische Amt in der Evangelischen Kirche der altpreussischen Union: die wichtigsten geltenden Verordnungen und Erlasse auf dem Gebiete der Kirchenmusik. Berlin: Evangelische Verlagsanstalt, 1950.

3186. STÖBE, Paul. Recht und Brauch im kirchenmusikalischen Amte; auf Grund amtlichen Materials und anerkannter liturgischer Darlegungen für die Kantoren, Organisten und Kirchschullehrer der Evangel-luther. Landeskirche im Königreich Sachsen zusammengestellt. Zittau i. Sachs: Druck von R. Menzel nachf., 1908.

3187. SÜDDEUTSCHE Blätter für Kirchenmusik. Tübingen: C. L. Schultheiss, 1948.

3188. WHITTLESEY, F. L. The ministry of music. Philadelphia: Board of Christian Education, Presbyterian Church in the U. S. A., n. d.

See also: 788, 1068, 1799, 1862, 2151, 2377, 2722, 4193, 4101.

MISSION MUSIC

3189. CLARO, Samuel. La musica en las misiones Jesuitas de Moxos. Santiago, Chile: Instituto de Investigaciones Musicales, 1967.

3190. ROGERS, Sister Mary James. Elements of musical study in the Missionary school and some Missions afar. (pp. 99). Washington, D. C.: Catholic Univ., 1938.

See also: 3652.

MODES, CHURCH

3191. AARON, Pietro. Trattato della natura et cognitione di tutti gli tuoni di canto figurato. A reprint of the Venice, 1525, ed. New York: Broude Brothers Ltd., 1966.

3192. BOMM, Urbanus. Der Wechsel der Modalitäts bestimmung in der Tradition der Messgesänge im Ix. bis XIII. Jahrhundert und sein Einfluss auf die Tradition ihrer Melodien. Einsiedeln: Benziger & Co., 1929.

3193. BRENNAN, Mary Ellen. The material used in ancient modes: Greek and Ecclesiastical. Evanston, Ill.: Northwestern Univ., M. M., 1947.

3194. EVANS, Paul. The early Trope repertory of Saint Martial de Limoges (Princeton Studies in Music, 2). Princeton, N. J.: Univ. Press, 1970.

3195. JACOBSTHAL, Gustav. Die chromatische Alteration im liturgischen Gesang der abendländischen Kirche. Reprt. --of Ausgabe Berlin: 1897 ed. Hildesheim: G. Olms, 1970.

3196. RICHARDSON, A. Madely. The mediaeval modes. New York: The H. W. Gray Co., 1933.

3197. SPENCER. Concise explanation of the church modes. London: Novello, n. d.

See also: 59, 542, 1240.

MONODY

3198. BLUME, Friedrich. Das monodische Prinzip in der protestantischen Kirchenmusik. Mit einem Notenanhang. Leipzig: Breitkopf & Härtel, 1925.

3199. FELLERER, Karl Gustav. Monodie und Polyphonie in der Musik des 16. Jahrhunderts. Brüssel: Paleis der Acamadiën, 1972.

3200. LEAVITT, Donald. The rise of Monody in English church music. Bloomington: Indiana Univ., 1963.

3201. TREITLER, Leo. The Aquitanian repertoires of sacred monody in the eleventh and twelfth centuries. Ann Arbor: Univ. Microfilms, 1964.

See also: 5034.

MOTETS

3202. ARMSTRONG, Donald Jan. The motets of Johannes Brahms: An historical analytical interpretative survey. Austin, Tex.: Univ. of Texas, M. M., 1965.

3203. AUBRY, Pierre. Cent motets du XIII siècle. Paris: A. Rouart, Lerolle & Co., 1908, e. g. (also New York: Broude Bros. --Reprint).

3204. BRAITHWAITE, James Roland. The introduction of Franco-Netherlandish manuscripts to early Tudor England. The motet repertory (with) volumes III-V, transcriptions. Ann Arbor: Univ. Microfilms, 1967.

3205. BROWN, Samuel E., Jr. The motet, 1400-1475. Bloomington: Indiana Univ., n. d.

3206. BRUNGARDT, Gilbert Ambrose. Some selected motets of Francesco Durante. Ann Arbor: Univ. Microfilms, 1967.

3207. BRYDEN, John Rennie. The motets of Orazio Benevoli. Ann Arbor: Univ. of Michigan, 1951.

3208. CAIRD, Armida. A stylistic analysis of the motets of Jacob Obrecht. Bloomington: Indiana Univ., 1963.

3209. CASTLE, Conan Jennings. The grand motets of André Campra. Ann Arbor: Univ. of Michigan diss., 1962.

3210. COLE, William Powell. The motets of Jean Baptiste Lully (with vol. II). Ann Arbor: Univ. Microfilms, 1967.

3211. DUGGAN, Sister Mary and C. S. J. Laurent. Marc Antonio Ingegneri: motets for four and five voices (with) Vol. II: transcriptions of the motets. Ann Arbor: Univ. Microfilms, 1968.

3212. DUNN, James P. The grand motets of Marc-Antoine Charpentier. Ann Arbor: State Univ. of Iowa diss., 1962.

3213. GLASER, Victoria M. Form and expression in some motets of Josquin des Prez. Cambridge, Mass.: Radcliffe College, n. d.

3214. HOFMANN, Klaus. Untersuchung zur Kompositions Technik der Motet im 13. Jahrhundert durchgef. an den Motetten d. Tenor in seculum. Neuhausen-Stuttgart: Hänssler, 1972.

3215. HOPPIN, Richard H. The motets of the early 15th century manuscript J. 11. 9 in the Biblioteca Nazionale of Turin. Cambridge, Mass.: Harvard Univ., 1952.

3216. JOHNSON, Mildred Jane. The thirtyseven motets of the Codex Ivrea. Bloomington: Indiana Univ., 1955.

3217. LAWRY, Eleanor McChesney. The psalm motets of Claude Goudimel. New York: New York Univ., Graduate School of Arts and Science, 1954.

3218. LEICHTENTRITT, Hugo. Geschichte der Motette. Hildesheim, Germany, Georg Olms-Reprint, 1966, (orig. Leipzig, 1908).

3219. LENGEFELD, William Chris. The motets of Pierre Colin. Ann Arbor: Univ. Microfilms, 1969.

3220. LEUCHTMANN, Horst. Die musikalischen Wortausdeutung in den Motetten des Magnum Opus Musikum von Orlando di Lasso (Neudr.). Baden-Baden: Koerner, 1972.

3221. LEVY, Kenneth Jay. "New material on the early motet in England: a report on Princeton Ms. Garrett 119." Journal of the American Musicological Society, IV/3. Fall, 1951.

3222. McELRATH, Hugh. A study of the motets of Ignatio Donati. Ann Arbor: Univ. Microfilms, 1967.

3223. McKELVY, J. M., Jr. A study of the double-choir motets of Johann Sebastian Bach in relation to their performance. Los Angeles: Univ. of Southern California, D. Mus. A., 1957.

3224. MARSHALL, H. Lowen. The four-voice motets of Thomas Crecquillon. Ann Arbor: Univ. Microfilms, 1968.

3225. MATTHIASSEN, Finn. The style of the early motet. Copenhagen: Dan Fog Musikforlag, 1966.

3226. MORGAN, Wesley. The chorale-choir motet between 1650 and 1750. Los Angeles: Univ. of Southern California, 1958.

3227. MOSER, Hans Joachim. Die mehrstimmige Vertönung des Evangeliums 1. Hildesheim, Germany: Georg Olms Reprint, 1966. (orig. Leipzig: Breitkopf and Härtel, 1931.)

3228. MOTETS et psaumes. Paris: Editions musicales de la Schola Cantorum, 1927.

3229. NOBLITT, Thomas Lee. The Motetti missales of the late fifteenth century. Austin, Tex.: Univ. of Texas, Ph. D., 1963.

3230. OREL, Alfred. Einige Grundformen der Motettkomposition im XV. Jahrhundert. N. G.: N. G., 1920. (ML55.69)

3231. PARKER, Robert L. The motets of Adam Rener (c. 1485-c. 1520) with part II: transcriptions. Ann Arbor: Univ. Microfilms, Univ. of Texas diss., 1963.

3232. PHILLIPS, Rubyrae. An acoustical analysis of vertical sonorities in three Palestrina motets. Fort Worth: Texas Christian Univ., M. M. E., 1965.

3233. PISANO, R. C. A study of the Bach motets based upon an analysis of their structure. New York: Columbia Univ., Ed. D., 1956.

3234. RAYNAUD, Gaston. Recueil de motets de 12e et 13e siècle. Hildesheim, Germany: Georg Olms--Reprint, 1967. (orig. Paris: N. G., 1881-1883.)

3235. RICHARDS, James E. The 'grand motet' of the late Baroque in France as exemplified by Michel-Richard de Lalande and a selected group of his contemporaries. Los Angeles: Univ. of Southern California, 1950.

3236. SHINE, Josephine M. The motets of Jean Mouton. New York: New York Univ., Graduate School of Arts and Science, 1953.

3237. STEINHART, Milton. Jacobus Vaet and his motets. New York: New York Univ., Graduate School of Arts and Science, 1950.

3238. STEPHAN, Wolfgang. Die burgundisch-niederlandische Mottete zur Zeit Okeghems. Kassel: Bärenreiter, 1973.

3239. TISCHLER, Hans. The motet in thirteenth century France. Ann Arbor: Univ. Microfilms, 1967. (Yale Univ. diss., 1942, Vols. 1 and 2.)

3240. WEBHOFER, Peter. Giovanni F. Sances (ca. 1600-79); biographisch-bibliographische Untersuchung und Studie über sein Motettenwerk. Innsbruch: Pontificio Institute di musica sacra, 1965.

3241. WICKS, John Doane. The motets and chansons of Pierre de Manchicourt: some Salient characteristics in the Art of Franco-Netherlandish vocal polyphony of the mid-16th century. Cambridge: Harvard Univ., 1958.

3242. WING, Henry Joseph, Jr. The polychoral motets of Leone Leoni. Ann Arbor: Univ. Microfilms, 1966.

See also: 19, 257, 287, 291, 292, 293, 459, 1294, 1643, 3004, 3016, 3086, 3374, 3534, 4104, 4314, 4328, 4352, 4354, 4390, 4489, 4542, 4544, 4560, 4649, 4712, 5202.

MOTU PROPRIO, IN LIGHT OF

3243. PIUS X, Pope. "Motu proprio" sur la musique sacrée. Liege: N. G., 1928. (ML 3095. M65)

3244. PREDMORE, George Vincent. Church music in the light of Motu Proprio. A guide for the Catholic choirmaster and organist. Rochester: The Seminary Press, 1924.

See also: 384, 509, 1153, 1154, 1172, 1765, 5310.

MUSIC WRITING

3245. HORTSCHANSKY, von Klaus. Katalog der Kieler Musiksammlungen. Die Notendrücke, Handschriften, Libretti und Bücher über Musik aus der Zeit bis 1830. Kieler Schriften zur Musikwissenschaft, Band 14. Kassel, New York: Bärenreiter, 1963.

See also: 5093, 5094.

MUSICIANS

3246. The CHURCH musician. Nashville: Sunday School Board of the Southern Baptist Convention, Oct., 1950.

3247. DONE, Agnes E. A short account of our great church musicians specially written for choristers. New York: H. Frowde, 1903.

3248. FETIS. Biographie universelle des musiciens. 8 vols. with 2 supp. vols. by Pangin. Paris: Didot, n. d.

3249. HAENSGEN, A. Zeitgenossen. Eine Zusammenstellung von 3000 der wichtigsten Geburts-und Sterbedaten berühmten und bekannter Musiker. Potsdam: N. G., 1926. (BM)

3250. LONDON--Guild of Church Musicians. The church musician. London: Guild, 1929.

3251. The NEW Encyclopedia of music and musicians. New York: N. G., 1931.

3252. PARKER, John R. A musical biography: Sketches of the lives and writings of eminent musical characters. Interspersed with an epitome of interesting musical matter. Boston: Stone and Fovell, 1825.

3253. REFARDT, E. Historisch-biographisches Musikerlexikon. Leipzig: Zürich: Gebrüder Hug & Co., 1928.

3254. SLONIMSKY, Nicholas (ed.). Baker's biographical dictionary of musicians (5th ed. rev.). New York: W. W. Norton, 1958.

See also: 1403, 1496, 1512, 1535, 1566, 1745, 1885, 2074, 3397, 4890, 5296.

MUSICOLOGY

3255. AUBRY, Pierre. La musicologie médiévale, histoire et méthodes, cours professé à l'institut catholique de Paris

1898-1899. Paris: H. Welter, 1900. (Reprint ed. --New York: Broude Brothers.)

3256. ______. La musicologie médiaevale: histoire et méthodes, cours professé à l'institut catholique de Paris, 1898-1899. (Reprint, 1900 Paris ed.) Genève: Slatkine Reprints, 1975.

3257. BARBLAN, Guglielmo, and Direttore. Rivista italiana di musicologia. Organo della Societa Italiana di Musicologia. Firenze: Leo S. Olschki, 1966.

3258. BIBLIOTHEK der schoenen Wissenschaften und der Freyen Kuenste. New York: Scientific Library Service, 1764.

3259. BÜCKEN, E. von. Handbuch der Musikwissenschaft. New York: Johnson Reprint Corp., 1966, (orig. Pottsdam, 1927-34).

3260. CURRENT musicology. (semi-annually). New York: Columbia Univ., Music Department, n. d.

3261. CURRENT thought in musicology. Ed. by J. W. Grubbs, with the assistance of R. A. Balzer et al. Austin: Univ. of Texas Press, 1976.

3262. DOUTEIL, Herbert. Studien zu Durantis Rationale divinorum officiorum als kirchenmusikalische Quelle. Regensburg: Bosse, 1969.

3263. FORKEL, J. N. Allgemeine litteratur der Musik; oder, Anleitung zur Kenntniss musikalische Buecher, welche von den aeltesten bis auf die neusten Zeiten bey den Griechen, Roemern, und den meisten neuern enropaeischen Nationen sind geschriebenworden. New York: Scientific Library Service, 1792.

3264. KASSLER, Jamie Croy. The science of music in Britain, 1714-1830. (a catalogue of writings, lectures, and inventions.) New York: Garland Publishing, Inc., 1977.

3265. MAHRENHOLZ, Christhard. Musicologia et liturgicia. Gesammelte Aufsätze von Christhard Mahrenholz. Als Festgabe zu seinem 60 Geburtstag am 11. August 1960 herausgegeben von Karl Ferdinand Müller. Kassel: N. G., 1960. (BM7888. c. 62)

3266. MATZKE, Hermann Karl Anton. Aus Grenzgebieten der Musikwissenschaft, eine Reihe von Vorträgen und Aufsätzen. Breslau: "Quader" Druckerei und Verlagsanstalt g. m. b. h., 1928.

3267. PARIS; Schola Cantorum (ed.). Memoires de musicologie sacrée lus aux Assises de musique religieuse les 27, 28 et 29 septembre 1900 a la Schola Cantorum. Paris: Aux Bureaux d'édition de la Schola, 1900.

3268. REVUE de musicologie. (semi-annually). Vivienne, Paris: Librairie Heugel, n. d.

3269. SACHS, Curt. A collection of Sachs' musicological and music-ethnographical essays, collected and annotated by Prof. Hans H. Draeger, Univ. of Texas. Originally published in periodicals. New York: Broude Brothers, Limited (Facsimile), 1966.

See also: 66, 1293, 1609, 1792, 1801, 3173, 3230, 3600, 3690, 3975, 4138, 4982, 5030.

MYTHOLOGY

3270. MYLONAS, George E. Hymn to Demeter and her sanctuary at Eleusis. Seattle: Washington Univ., 1942.

See also: 1792, 2666.

NATIONAL and/or GEOGRAPHIC ENTITIES

General

3271. SOUSA, John Philip. National, patriotic and typical airs of all lands. Boston: Longwood Press, Inc., 1911.

3272. VAUGHAN WILLIAMS, Ralph. National music. London: Oxford Univ. Press, 1934. (also New York: Carl Fischer, n.d.)

See also: 111, 3278.

Africa

3273. AFRICA, South, Wesleyan Methodist Church of. Gezangen der Wesleyaansche Gemeente van Zuid Afrika. Cape Town: N. G., 1899.

3274. BRANDEL, Rose. The music of Central Africa. The Hague: Martinus Nijhoff, 1962.

3275. JONES, A. M. Studies in African music. Fair Lawn, N. J.: Oxford Univ. Press, 1959.

3276. MBUNGA, Stephen B. G. Church law and Bantu music. Ecclesiastical documents and law on sacred music as applied to Bantu music. Schöneck-Beckenried: Neue Zeitschrift für Missionswissenschaft. Supplementa, 1963.

3277. WEMAN, Henry. African music and the church in Africa. Translated by Eric J. Sharpe. Uppsala: Lundequistska bokhandeln, 1960.

See also: 1365, 2182, 2206, 2258, 2343, 2364, 2587, 3383.

Albania

See: 1671.

Argentine Republic

3278. GARCIA MUÑOZ, Carmen, and Waldemar Azel Boldán. Un archivo musical americano. Buenos Aires: Editorial Universitaria de Buenos Aires, 1972.

3279. LANGE, Francisco Curt. La música eclesiástica en el perioda de la dominación hispanica, una investigación. Mendoza, Arg.: Impr. de la Universidad, 1954.

3280. _______. La música eclesiástica en Córdoba durante la dominación hispanica. Córdoba: Impr. de la Universidad, 1956.

Armenia

3281. GREGORY, Stephen Mesrope. The land of Ararat. Twelve discourses on Armenia, her history and her church. London: Chiswick Press, 1920.

Australia

3282. ORCHARD, William Arundel. Music in Australia; more than 150 years of development. Melbourne: Georgian House, 1952.

See also: 4, 3989, 4862, 4863, 4864.

Austria

3283. GRASBERGER, Franz. Die Hymnen Österreichs. Tutzing: Hans Schneider, 1968.

3284. GRASBERGER, Franz. The music collection of the Austrian National library (transl. by Hans Suesserott). Vienna: Federal Chancellory, Federal Press, and Information Dept., 1972.

3285. GUINAN, Alastair. The Catholic choir. Philadelphia: The Dolphin Press, 1936.

3286. GURTNER, Joseph. Die Katholische Kirchenmusik Österreichs im Lichte der Zählen. Baden: R. M. Rohrer, 1937.

3287. HUDAL, Alois (ed.). Der Katholizismus in Österreich, sein Wirken, Kämpfen und Hoffen; unter Mitwirkung zahlreicher Fachleute und mit einem Geleitworte. München: Verlagsanstalt Tyrolia, 1931.

3288. KRAUSE, Emil. Zur Pflege der religiösen Vokalmusik in Steiermark. Langensalza: H. Beyer & Mann, 1913.

3289. LORENZ, Franz. Haydn, Mozart und Beethoven's Kirchenmusik und ihre katholischen und protestantischen Gegner. Breslau: F. E. C. Leukart, 1866.

3290. ROSENTHAL, Karl August. Zur Stilistik der Salzburger Kirchenmusik von 1600-1730. Österreich: In-Studien der Musikwissenschaft, 193-.

3291. SCHNÜRL, Karl. Die Kirchenmusik einer niederösterreichischen Landpfarre im 19. Jahrhundert. Wordern: N. G., 1958. (LC-ML290. 8. 5353)

3292. TITTEL, Ernst. Österreichische Kirchenmusik. Werden, wachsen, wirken. With musical examples. Wien: Schriftenreihe des allgemeinen Cäcilien-Verbandes für die Länder der deutschen Sprache, 1961.

3293. ZAGIBA, Frantšek. Die ältesten musikalischen Denkmäler zu Ehren des Heiligen Leopold, Herzog und Patron von Österreich. Ein Beitrag zur Choralpflege in Österreich am Ausgange der Mittelalters, etc. Zürich: Amalthea-Verlag, 1954.

3294. ZAHN, Johannes. Die melodium der deutschen evangelischen Kirchenlieder. Gütersloh: C. Bertelsmann, 1889-93.

See also: 241, 388, 749, 750, 1194, 2548, 2885, 3030, 3736, 3737, 3860, 3992, 4145.

Belgium

3295. AUDA, Antoine. L'école musicale liégeoise aux siècle. Etienne de Liége, par Antoine Auda. Contains music. "Memoire presenté à la Classe des beaux-arts, dans la séance du 1er juin 1922," "Principaux ouvrages à consulter." Bruxelles: M. Lamertin, 1923.

3296. BRUSSELS. Bibliothèque royale de Belgique. Catalogue des imprimés musicaux du XVIIIe siècle: fonds général. Catalogus van de muziekdrukken van de XVIIIde eeuw: algemene verzamelung. Par B. Huys. Bruxelles: Bibliothèque royale Albert I., 1974.

3297. MALDEGHEM, Robert Julian von (ed.). Trésor musical, collection authentique de musique sacrée et profane des anciens maîtres belges. New York: Kraus Reprint Corp., 1965.

3298. MUSIC in Belgium. Brussels: A. Broude, Inc., 1964.

3299. WANGERMEE, Robert. Die flämische Musik in der Gesellschaft des 15. und 16. Jahrhunderts. Brussels: Kunstverlag, 1965.

See also: 623, 1018, 2860, 3066, 3959, 4059, 4751.

Bohemia

3300. KONRAD, Karel. Dějiny posvátnebo zpěvu starŏceského. V. Praze: Nakl. Cyrillo-Methodejské knehtiskarny, 1881. (LC-60-55780)

3301. LEHNER, F. J. (ed.). Cecile časopis pro katolickon hudbu pasvatnou v cechách, na Moravě a ve Slezsku. V. Praze: Knehuskarna Mikulase A. Knappa, 1874.

See also: 341, 383, 1100, 2562, 2583, 3320, 3638, 3955, 5317.

Brazil

3302. BRAGA, Henriqueta Rosa Fernandes. Musica sacra evangélica no Brasil; contribuicao à sua história. Rio de Janeiro: Livraria Kosmos Editôra, 1961.

3303. KIEFER, Bruno. História da música brasileira dos primórdios ao início do século XX. (Coleção Lúis Cosme, 9). Porto Alegre: Editora Morimento, 1976.

See also: 373.

Bulgaria

3304. PALIKAROVA, Verdeil R. La musique byzantine chez les Bulgares et les Russes (du IXe au XIVe siècle.) Copenhague: E. Munksgaard, and Boston: Byzantine Inst., 1953.

See also: 3547.

Canada

3305. AMTMANN, Willy. Music in Canada--1600-1800. Cambridge, Ont.: Habitex Books; dist. by Collier-Macmillan Canada, 1975.

3306. CANADIAN Broadcasting Corp., --International Service, ed. Thirtyfour biographies of Canadian composers. Saint Clair Shores, Mich.: Scholarly Press, 1972.

3307. JARMAN, Lynne. Canadian music, a selected checklist--1950-73. Buffalo, N.Y.: Univ. of Toronto Press, 1976.

3308. KALLMANN, Helmut. A history of music in Canada. New York: C. F. Peters Corp., 1967.

3309. MacMILLAN, Keith and John Beckwith. Contemporary Canadian composers. London and New York: Oxford Univ. Press, 1975.

3310. REPORT on conditions of church music in Western Canada. Winnepeg: Winnepeg Centre of the Canadian College of Organists, 1926.

See also: 317, 2202, 2800, 4924.

Caribbean

3311. DOWER, Catherine A. Libraries with music collections in the Caribbean Islands. Ann Arbor: Music Library Assn. (in "Notes"--Vol. 34, No. 1, Sept.), 1977.

3312. STEVENSON, Robert. A guide to Caribbean music history. (second rev. ed.). Washington, D.C.: Pan-American Union., 1962.

Chile

3313. URIBE-ECHEVARRIA, Juan. Cantos a lo divino y a lo humano en Aculeo; folklore de la provincia de Santiago (Santiago de Chile). Santiago de Chile: Editorial Universitaria, 1962.

See also: 3189.

China

3314. LIEBERMAN, Fredric. Chinese music. (An annotated bibliography second edition.) New York: Garland Publ., 1977. (1st ed., New York: Garland, 1970.)

See also: 184, 4110, 4111, 4114, 4117, 4123, 4125.

Colombia

3315. STEVENSON, Robert. La música colonial en Colombia. Cali, Colombia: Publicaciones del Instituto Popular de Cultura de Cali, Departamento de Investigaciones Folcloricas, 1, 1964.

Cuba

3316. HERNANDEZ BALAGUER, Pablo. Catálogo de música de los archivos de la Cathedral de Santiago de Cuba y del Museo Bacardí. La Habana: Biblioteca Nacional José Martí, 1961.

3317. MACIA DE CASTELEIRO, María. La música religiosa en Cuba. Habana: N. G., 1956. (LC-5721653)

See also: 405.

Czechoslovakia

3318. BERKOVEC, Jiri. The praise of music: Five chapters on Czech music and musicians. 1st ed. Prague: Orgis, n. d.

3319. GARDAVSKY, Čeněk. Contemporary Czechoslovak composers. Prague and Bratislava: Panton, 1965.

3320. NEWMARCH, Rosa. The music of Czechoslovakia. London: Oxford Univ. Press, 1942, 1943.

3321. NOVACEK, Zdeněk. Robotnícke spevokoly na Slovensku, 1872-1942. Bratislava: Vydatel' stvo Slovenskej akadémie vied, 1960.

See also: 2471, 3547.

Denmark

3322. ABRAHAMSEN, Erik. Eléménts romans et allemands dans le chant grégorien et la chanson populaire en Denmark.... Avec un resumé en danois. Copenhague: P. Haase & fils, 1923.

3323. DANSK kirkesangs aarsskrift. København: N. G., n. d. (LC 5139332)

3324. FOSS, Julius Christian. Kirkemusik og organistuddannelse: Denmark. København: W. Hansens musikforlag, 1930.

3325. HABERL, Ferdinand. Der Kirchenchorleiter. Tübingen: C. L. Shultheiss, 1949.

3326. LAUB, Thomas Linneman. Musik og kirke, 1920, paany unidvet af: Samfundet Dansk kirkesang. København: Ascheboug dansk forlag, 1937.

3327. NUTZHORN, H. Den dansk Menigheds Salmesang i Reformationstiden, dens Ord og Toner. København: N. G., 1909. (BM)

3328. POULSEN, P. Andelig sang gennem 100 år. Historisk, folkelig fremstilling af danske sang og deres for fattere. København: N. G., 1961. (BM 3042. i. 6)

3329. YOELL, John H. The Nordic sound: Explorations into the music of Denmark, Norway and Sweden. (Foreword by Antal Dorati.) Boston: Crescendo Publ. Co., 1974.

See also: 414, 1135, 2402, 2835, 3606, 3866, 3869, 4866, 5123, 5198, 5199, 5200.

Ecuador

3330. MORENO ANDRADE, Segundo Luis. Historia de la música en el Ecuador. Quito: Editorial Casa de la Cultura Ecuatoriana, 1972.

England

3331. ALDERTON, H. Orsmond. Early English music. London: Offices of "Musical Opinion," 1920.

3332. ANTIPHONAIRE monastique XIII siècle. Tournay: Desclée and Co., 1922.

3333. BLOM, Eric. Music in England. Revised ed. Baltimore: Penguin Books, 1947. (Also: Middlesex, England: N. G., 1957.)

3334. BORREN, Charles van den. The sources of keyboard music in England. London: Novello, 1913.

3335. BOYD, Morrison Comegys. Elizabethan music and musical criticism. 2nd ed. (orig. --1940.) Philadelphia: Univ. of Pennsylvania Press, 1962.

3336. BROWN, J. D. and S. S. Stratton. British musical biography. Stratton: Birmingham, 1897.

3337. COX, J. Charles. Pulpits, lecterns and organs in English churches. London & New York: N. G., 1915. (BM640)

3338. CROYDON, - Addington Palace, ed. by. English church music: A collection of essays. Croydon-Addington Palace: Royal School of Church Music, 1973.

3339. DANIEL, Ralph T. and Peter Le Huray. The sources of English church music, 1549-1660, (supplemental vol., parts I and II--Early English Church Music). London: Stainer and Bell, for the British Academy, 1972.

3340. DAVEY, Henry. History of English music. 2nd, ed., rev. --(orig.-1895). London: J. Curwen & Sons., 1921.

3341. DAVIES, G. The early Stuarts (1603-1660). London: Oxford Univ. Press, 1959.

3342. DEARNLEY, Christopher. English church music, 1650-1750, in Royal Chapel Cathedral, and parish church. New York and London: Oxford Univ. Press, 1970.

3343. DICKSON, William Edward. Fifty years of church music. Ely: T. A. Hills & Son, 1894.

3344. DONAHUE, Benedict Sister. From Latin to English: Plainsong in Tudor England. Ann Arbor: Univ. Microfilms, 1967.

3345. EARLY English church music. New York: A Broude Inc., 1965.

3346. FELLOWES, Edmund H. English cathedral music. London: Methuen & Co., 1948.

3347. FULLER-MAITLAND, J. A. English music in the XIXth century. New York: E. P. Dutton & Co., 1902.

3348. ________. English music in the XIX century. Portland, Me.: Longwood Press, 1976.

3349. GARDINER, S. R. Student's history of England. N. G.: N. G., 1895.

3350. GRATTAN-FLOOD, W. H. Early Tudor composers. London: Oxford Press, 1925.

3351. HADOW, William H. English music. London: Longmans Green & Co., 1931.

3352. HALEVY, Elie. History of the English people. Vol. III. (Trans. from Paris: Hachette et cie, 1913) and London: T. F. Hunwin, ltd., 1924-34.

3353. HARRISON, Frank L. Music in medieval Britain. New York: Routledge, 1958.

3354. HARRISON, Frederick. Life in a medieval college. The story of the Vicars-Choral of York Minster, etc. Printed in Holland. London: John Murray, 1952.

3355. HOWES, Frank S. The English musical renaissance. London: Secker & Warburg, 1966.

3356. HUGHES, Anselm. Worcester mediaeval harmony of the 13th and 14th centuries. Transcribed with general introduction, 15 facsimiles, and notes. Nashdom Abbey: Burnham, Bucks, the Plainsong and Mediaeval Music Society., 1928.

3357. KNIGHT, Gerald H. and William L. Reed. The treasury of English church music. 5 vols. London: Blandford Press Ltd., 1965.

3358. LE HURAY, Peter G. Church music in England, 1549-1644. London: Herbert Jenkins, 1966.

3359. ________. Music and the Reformation in England, 1549-1660. New York: Oxford Univ. Press, 1967.

3360. LEWER, David. A spiritual song. The story of the Temple choir and a history of divine service in the Temple Church, London. With plates and musical illustrations. London: Templars' Union, 1961.

3361. LONDON--School of English Church Music. English church music. London: The School, 1928.

3362. LONDON Musicians' Company. English music (1604 to 1904) being the lectures given at the music loan exhibition of the worshipful company of musicians. New York: C. Scribner's Sons, 1906.

3363. LONG, Kenneth R. The music of the English church. New York: St. Martin's Press, 1972.

3364. MACKERNESS, E. D. A social history of English music. London: Routledge & Kegan Paul, 1964.

3365. PARRY, W. H. Thirteen centuries of English church music. London: Hinrichsen Edition, 1946.

3366. PFEILSCHIFTER, Oskar. Die Englische Kirchenmusik der Tudorepoche; eine stilkindliche Untersuchung. München: N. G., 1949. (LC-56-26445)

3367. REANEY, Gilbert. English Renaissance music 1400-1625. New York: Hillary House Pub. Ltd., n. d.

3368. RIMBAULT, E. F. The old Cheque book of the Chapel Royal. New series III. N. G.: Camden Society, 1872.

3369. RITTER, F. L. Music in England. New York: Scribner, 1890.

3370. ROYAL School of Church Music. The Nicholson memorial. Canterbury: The School, 1948.

3371. SAY, William. Liber Regie Capelle. A manuscript in the Biblioteca Publica Evora. Edited by Walter Ullmann. Notes on the music by D. H. Turner. London: Printed for the Society by the Univ. Press, Cambridge, 1961.

3372. SMITH, Joseph. A musical pilgrimage in Yorkshire. Leeds: N. G., 1928.

3373. SPARK, William. Musical reminiscences; past and present. London: Simpkin, Marshall, Hamilton, Kent & Co., ltd., 1892.

3374. STEVENS, Denis. Tudor church music. New York: W. W. Norton, 1961.

3375. ________. Tudor church music. New York: Da Capo Press, 1973.

3376. SYKES, N. The English religious tradition. Rev. ed. London: SCM Press, 1961.

3377. USHER, R. G. The reconstruction of the English church. London and New York: D. Appleton & Co., 1910.

3378. WALKER, Ernest. A history of music in England. 3rd ed., revised by Jack Westrup. London: Oxford Univ. Press, 1952.

3379. WESTRUP, Jacob. British music. No. 15 of series British Life and Thought. London: Longmans, Green & Co. (The British Council), 1943.

3380. YEATS-EDWARDS, Paul. English church music: A bibliography. London and New York: White Lion, 1975.

See also: 12, 14, 52, 87, 89, 106, 112, 120, 147, 152, 171, 179, 191, 308, 326, 327, 329, 338, 410, 413, 415, 420, 426, 427, 429, 431, 440, 441, 451, 455, 706, 880, 893, 930, 995, 1044, 1208, 1210, 1213, 1214, 1215, 1216, 1217, 1218, 1219, 1225, 1470, 1473, 1524, 1527, 1677, 1715, 1725, 1820, 1868, 1889, 1931, 1950, 1954, 1956, 1979, 2011, 2012, 2019, 2067, 2123, 2124, 2143, 2145, 2209, 2224, 2231, 2232, 2403, 2416, 2427, 2438, 2458, 2461, 2489, 2532, 2626, 2627, 2723, 2771, 2784, 2932, 2933, 2952, 3024, 3161, 3204, 3221, 3247, 3456, 3674, 3716, 3742, 3768, 3786, 3813, 3845, 3855, 3863, 3895, 3948, 3954, 3985, 4006, 4099, 4184, 4342, 4344, 4366,

4432, 4438, 4451, 4494, 4499, 4547, 4549, 4606, 4730, 4739, 4760, 4785, 4798, 4810, 4824, 4828, 4887, 4989, 5014, 5047, 5048, 5049, 5122, 5227, 5287, 5316, 5318, 5376.

Ethiopia

3381. HAILU, Abba Pietros. Il canto sacro etiopico. Addis Ababa: Istituto italiano di Cultura, il., 1968.

3382. POWNE, Michael. Ethiopian music; an introduction and survey of ecclesiastical and Ethiopian music instruments. London: Oxford Univ. Press, 1966.

3383. SHACK, William A. and Habte Hariam Marcos. Gods and heroes: Oral traditions of the Gurage of Ethiopia. Oxford: Clarendon Press, 1974.

Europe

3384. DUNWELL, Wilfrid. Music and the European mind. New York: Thomas Yoseloff, Publ., 1962.

See also: 1372.

Finland

3385. LAGERCRANTZ, Ingeborg. Lutherska kyrkovisor. Helsingfors: Förbundet, 1948-52.

3386. ________. Roslagskullahandskriften. Acta Acadamiae Aboensis. Humaniora. Vol. 17, no. 2. Åbo: tt åboensiskt koralboks förlag, 1948.

See also: 2594, 3606, 4589.

France

3387. AUBRY, Pierre. La musique et les musiciens d'église en Normandie au XIII siècle. d'après le "Journal des visites pastorales" d'Odon Rigaud. Paris: H. Champion, 1906.

3388. BELLAIGUE, Camille. Un siècle de musique française. Paris: C. Delagrave, 1887.

3389. BLAZE, Called Castil Blaze. Chapelle--musique des Rois de France. Paris: Chez Paulin, 1832.

3390. BOBILLIER, Marie. Les musiciens de la Sainte-Chapelle du Palais. Documents inédits; recueillis et annotés. Paris: A. Picard et fils, 1910.

3391. ________. La musique sacrée sous Louis XIV. Conférence pronouncée le 12 janvier 1899 dans le grand Amphithéatre de l'Institut catholique. Paris: Bureau d'Edition de la Schola Cantorum, 1899.

3392. BOTTEE DE TOULMON, Auguste. Observations sur les moyens de restaurer la musique religieuse dans les églises de Paris. Paris: Imprimerie de Paul Dupont et cie., 1841.

3393. CAEN. Memoires sur la musique sacrée en Normandie. Caen: Ligugé, 1896.

3394. CHORON, Alexandre Etienne. Considérations sur la nécessité de rétablir le chant de l'église de Rome dans toutes les églises de l'empire. Paris: Chez Courcier, 1811.

3395. CHURCH music: Paris. Paris: N. G., 1786. (LC-ML 3027. 6. P212)

3396. CLANCHE, Gustave. La musique, le choeur, le bas-choeur de la cathédrale de Toul. Documents historiques. Préface du maître J. Oury. Toul: Imprimerie moderne, 1934.

3397/8. EXPERT, Henry. Les maîtres musiciens de la Renaissance Française. Collected editions Historical sets 1965-66. New York: Broude Brothers, n. d.

3399. ________. Monuments de la musique Française au temps de la Renaissance. Collected Editions, Historical sets 1965-66. New York: Broude Brothers, 196-.

3400. ROQUET, Antoine Ernest. Les origines de la chapelle-musique des souverains de France. Paris: A. Claudin, 1844.

See also: 121, 122, 226, 274, 409, 416, 417, 423, 432, 436, 455, 468, 474, 503, 586, 631, 736, 896, 919, 1002, 1010, 1103, 1126, 1335, 1363, 1364, 1510, 1955, 1968, 2117, 2128, 2453, 2961, 3031, 3050, 3076, 3132, 3142, 3209, 3212, 3235, 3239, 3534, 3753, 3763, 3780, 3795, 3804, 3820, 3833, 3877, 3990, 3995, 3997, 3988, 4036, 4056, 4062, 4064, 4326, 4488, 4808, 4867, 4876, 4877, 4897, 4943, 5096.

Germany

3401. BERLIN Akademisches Institut für Kirchenmusik. Festschrift zur Feier des hundertjährigen Bestehens des staatlichen akademischen Instituts für Kirchenmusik in Berlin. Berlin-Charlottenburg: N. G., 1922. (LC-25-12214)

3402. BUCHNER, Arno. Das Kirchenlied in Schlesien und der Oberlaufitz. Dusseldorf: Verl. Unser Weg, 1971.

3403. COX, F. E. Hymns for the German. London: N. G., 1890. (BM)

3404. CUNZ, F. A. Geschichte des deutschen Kirchenliedes vom 16. Jahrhundert bis auf unsere Zeit. Leipzig: J. T. Löschke, 1855.

3405. DEUTSCHER Kongress für Kirchenmusik. Im Auftrage des Preuss, Ministeriums für Wissenschaft, Kunst and Volksbildung, hrsg. von der staatlichen Akademie für Kirchen-und-schulmusik. Kassel: Bärenreiter-Verlag, 1928.

3406. EHMANN, Wilhelm. Das Schicksal der deutschen Reformationsmusik in der Geschichte der musikalischen Praxis und Forschung. Göttingen: Vandenhoeck & Ruprecht, 1935.

3407. ENCYCLOPEDIE de la Musique. Histoire de la musique ... Allemagne. Paris: C. Delagrave, 1913.

3408. Die EVANGELISCHE Kirchenmusik in Baden, Hessen und der Pfalz. Heidelberg: Hochstein, 1924.

3409. FELLERER, Carl. Beiträge zur Geschichte der Musik am Niederrhein ... Herausgegeben von K. G. Fellerer. Köln: Beiträge zur rheinischen Musikgeschichte, 1956.

3410. FESTSCHRIFT Max Schneider zum 60. Geburtstag. Überreicht von Kollegen, Freunden und Schülern. In Verbindung mit Arnold Schering, Walther Vetter, Hans Hoffman, und Walter Serauky herausgegeban von Hans Joachim Zingel. Halle: E. Schneider, 1935.

3411. FESTSCHRIFT Peter Wagner zum 60. Geburtstag gewidmet von Kollegen, Schülern und Freunden. Leipzig: Breitkopf & Härtel, 1926.

3412. FRANKFURT Am Main, Lessing-Gymnasium. Die musikalischen Schätze der Gymnasialbibliothek und der Peterskirche zu Frankfurt am Main. Frankfurt: Druck von Mahlau & Waldschmidt, 1872.

3413. FRIESE, Hans. Gib mir die Gnadenhände (thüringer Liederdichter aus der Barockzeit). Berlin: Evangelische Verlaganstalt Gmblt, 1962.

3414. GALL, E. Cathedrals and abbey churches of the Rhine. New York: Abrams, 1963.

3415. GARTEN, Alter. Mecklenburgische Staatskapelle, 400 Jahre, 1563-1963. Festwoche vom 6.-15. Juni 1963. Schwerin: Mecklenburgisches Staatstheater, Dramaturgie, 1963.

3416. GERHARDT, Carl. Die torgauer Walter-Handschriften; eine Studie zur Quellenkunde der Musikgeschichte der deutschen Reformationszeit. Kassel: Bärenreiter-Verlag, 1949.

3417. GERMANY, Deutscher Kirchenmusikertag. Musica sacra in unserer Zeit. Die Vorträge des ersten deutschen Kirchenmusikertages, Berlin 1959. By Oskar Söhngen and others. Berlin: N. G., 1960. (BM-07903. f. 27)

3418. GOSSLAU, Werner. Die religiöse Haltung in der Reformationsmusik, nachgewiesen an den "Newen deutschen geistlichen gesengen" des Georg Rhaw, 1544; ein Beitrag zur Musikanschauung des 16. Jahrhunderts, von Werner Gosslau. Kassel: Bärenreiter-Verlag, 1933.

3419. GUCKEL, Hans Erdmann. Katholische Kirchenmusik in Schlesien. Leipzig: Breitkopf & Härtel, 1912. (Reprt. by Walluf-bei-Wiesbaden: M. Sandig, 1972.)

3420. HAASE, Rudolf. Geschichte des Solinger Chorwesens. Beiträge zur rheinischen Musikgeschichte, with illustrations. Köln: Arno Volk Verlag, 1956.

3421. HAMPEL, Norbert. Deutschsprachige protestantische Kirchenmusik Schlesiens bis zum Einbruch der Monodie. Breslau: diss., n. p., 1937. (LC42-26082)

3422. HASSE, Karl. Von deutscher Kirchenmusik; zur neugestaltung unseres Musiklebens im newen Deudschland; ausgewählte Reden und Aufsätze. Regensburg: G. Bosse, 1936.

3423. HELD, Karl. Das Kreuzkantorat zu Dresdan. (reprint.) Walluf. bei Wiesbaden: M. Sandig, 1972.

3424. HENCHE, Heinz. Die Gottesdienstliche Aufgabe der Kirchenmusik. Gütersloh: Rufer-Verlag, 1951.

3425. HERFORD, Germany. Schriftenreihe Heft. Gütersloh: Rufer-Verlag, 1951.

3426. HEYDT, Johann Daniel. Geschichte der evangelischen Kirchenmusik in Deutschland. Berlin: Trowitzsch & Sohn, 1926.

3427. HOFFMANN von FALLERSLEBEN, August Heinrich. Geschichte des deutschen Kircheliedes bis auf Luthers Zeit, nebst einem Anhange "In dulci jubilo nun singet und seid froh." Ein Beitrag zur Geschichte der deutschen Poesie. Hannover: C. Rumpler, 1861.

3428. HOLMES, Edward. A ramble among the musicians of Germany. Giving some account of the operas of Munich, Dresden, Berlin, and others. With remarks upon the church music, singers, performers, and composers; and a sample of the pleasures and inconveniences that await the lover of art on a similar excursion. London: Hunt and Clarke, 1828.

3429. HOUEL, Reinhold. Melodische und rhythmische Wandlungen im katholischen deutschen Kirchenlied. Liepzig: Druck von Frommhold & Wendler, 1932.

3430. KETTERING, Heinz. Quellen und Studien zur Essener Musikgeschichte des hohen Mittelalters. Essen: Beiträge zur rheinischen Musikgeschichte, 1960.

3431. Der KIRCHENMUSIKER. Berlin: Verlag-Merseburger, 1950.

3432. KLEIN, Theodor Heinrich. Die prozessionsgesänge der Mainzer Kirche aus dem 14. bis 18. Jahrhundert. (Quellen und Abhandlungen zur mittelrheinischen Kirchengeschichte, 7.) Speyer and Rhein: Jaeger, 1962.

3433. KNICK, Bernhard. S(ank)t Thomas zu Leipzig; Schule und Chor, Strätte des Wirkens von Johann Sebastian Bach, Bilder und Dokumente zur Geschichte der Thommaschule und des Thomännerchores mit ihren zeitgeschichtlichen Beziehungen. Hrsg., mit einer Einführung von M. Mezger. Wiesbaden: Breitkopf & Härtel, 1963.

3434. KÖLLNER, Georg Paul. Der accentus Moguntinus; ein Beitrag zur Frage des "Mainzer Chorals." Mainz: N. G., 1950.

3435. KRIESSMANN, Alfons. Geschichte der katholischen Kirchenmusik in Württemburg, von der ältesten Zeit bis zur Gegenwart. Stuttgart: G. L. Schultheiss, 1939.

3436. KRUGER, Liselotte. Die hamburgische Musikorganisation im XVII Jahrhundert. Strassburg: Heitz & Co., 1933.

3437. LACROIX, Yves. La vie musicale réligieuse à Tréves. Tréves: Imprimerie-lithographie J. Lintz, 1922.

3438. LANG, Berthold. Bischof Sailer und die Kirchenmusik. N. G.: N. G., 1932. (LC-ML3029. 8)

3439. LEDEBUR, C. von. Tonkünstler-Lexikon Berlins von den ältesten Zeiten bis auf die Gegenwart. Berlin: L. Rauh, 1861. also Tutzing, Berlin: H. Schneider, 1965.

3440. MATYSIAK, Waldemar. Breslauer Domkapellmeister von 1831-1925. Düsseldorf: G. H. Nolte, 1934.

3441. MOSER, Hans Joachim. Die evangelische Kirchenmusik in Deutschland. Berlin: C. Merseburger, 1953-54.

3442. _______. Schütz und das evangelische Kirchenlied. Berlin: N. G., 1930. (LCML-32c. 3b 35)

3443. MUNZER, Thomas. Thomas Munzer's deutsche Messen und Kirchenämter, mit Singnöten, und liturgischen Abhandlungen herausgegeben von Oskar John Mehl. Grimmen and Pommern: A. Waberg, 1937.

3444. NIEMOELLER, Klaus Wolfgang. Kirchenmusik und reichsstädtische Musikpflege im Köln des 18. Jahrhunderts. Köln: Beiträge zur rheinischen Musikgeschichte, 1960.

3445. OPITZ, Paul. Kurze Geschichte des Königlichen Domchors in Berlin zum 50. Jahr. Jubiläum Ostern 1893. Berlin: H. Blanke, 1893.

3446. OPP, Walter. Handbuch des kirchenmusikalischen Dienstes in Nebenamt. Berlin: Merseburger, 1967.

3447. PEMBAUR, Karl. Drei Jahrhunderte Kirchenmusik am sächsischen Hofe, ein Beitrag zur Kunsigeschichte Sachsens. Dresden: Druck Stengel & Co., g. m. b. h., 1920.

3448. [no entry]

3449. PFLEGER, M. C. Untersuchungen am deutschen geistlichen Lied des 13. Jahrhundert. Berlin: N. G., 1937. (BM)

3450. PIETZSCH, Gerhard Wilhelm. Quellen und Forschungen zur Geschichte der Musik am kurpfälzischen Hof zu Heidelberg bis 1622. Mainz: Akademie der Wissenschaften und der Literatur. Abhandlungen der geistes-und sozialwissenschaftlichen Klasse, 1963.

3451. PROHLE, Heinrich Christoph Ferdinand. Weltliche und geistliche Volkslieder und Volksschauspiele. Aschersleben: O. Fokke, 1855.

3452. RAUTENSTRAUCH, Johannes. Die Kalandbruderschaften, das kulturelle Vorbild der sachsischen Katoreien. Ein Beitrag zur Geschichte der kirchlichen Musikpflege in vor- und nachreformatorischer Zeit. Dresden: Rammingsche Buchdruckerei-und-verlag, 1903.

3453. _______. Luther und die Pflege der kirchlichen Musik in Sachsen bis zum 2. Jahrzehnt des 17. Jahrhunderts. Ein Beitrag zur Geschichte der sachsischen Kantoreien und ihrer kulturellen Vorläufer der katholischen Bruderschaften. Leipzig: Druck von Breitkopf & Härtel, 1906.

3454. REICHSVERBAND für Evangelische Kirchenmusik. Fest der deutschen Kirchenmusik; Werke unserer Zeit. Berlin-Steglitz: Eckart-verlag, 1937.

3455. RIEDEL, Otto. Vom alten Wort und neuen Lied der Kirche. Konstanz: Christliche Verlagsanstalt, 1941.

3456. ROBERTON, Sir Hugh S. A German odyssey ... being an account of a tour in the British occupied zone of Germany by the Glasgow Orpheus Choir, May-June 1946. Glasgow: William Hodge & Co., 1946.

3457. SACHS, Curt. Musik und Oper am Kurbrandenburgischen Hof, 1533-1713. Broude Brothers Limited (facsimile), 1966. (orig.--Berlin: J. Bard, 1910.)

3458. SALMEN, Walter. Geschichte der Musik in Westfalen; bis 1800. Kasse: Bärenreiter, 1963.

3459. SCHILLING, Hans. Tobias Eniccelius, Freidrich Meister, Nikolaus Hanff; ein Beitrag zur Geschichte der evangelische Frühkantate in Schleswig-Holstein. Kiel: N.G., 1934. (LC-ML3129. S86T6)

3460. SCHMID, Otto. Die Kirchenmusik in der katholischen Kirche zu Dresden. Ihre Geschichte und ihre kunst-und kultur geschichtliche Bedeutung. Dresden: Henkler, 1921.

3461. SCHOEBERLEIN, Ludwig and F. Riegel. Schatz des liturgischen Chor-und Gemeindegesangs nebst den Altarweisen in der deutschen evangelischen Kirche; aus den Quellen vornehmlich des 16. und 17. Jahrhunderts geschöpft mit den nöthigen geschichtlichen und praktischen Erläuterungen versehen und unter der musikalischen Redaktion. Göttingen: Vandenhoeck & Ruprecht, 1865-72. (Reprint--Hildesheim, Germany: Georg Olms, 1967.)

3462. SIEVERS, Heinrich. Die musik in Hannover. Hannover: Sponholtz, 1961.

3463. SIMON, Heinrich. Das deutsche geistliche Volkslied als Gut unserer Kultur. (pp. V, 89). (Res. tp. sc.) Münster, Germany: Münster (phil.), 1924.

3464. SOCHER, O. Siebenhundert Jahre Dresdner Kreuzchor. Ein Abriss seiner Geschichte. Dresden: Selbstverlag des Kreuzchor, 1937.

3465. SÖHNER, Leo. Die Musik im Münchener Dom unserer lieben Frau in Vergangenheit und Gegenwart. München: Lentnersche Buchgandlung, 1934.

3466. SÖHNGEN, Oskar. Die neue Kirchenmusik; Wandlungen und Entscheidungen. Berlin-Steglitz: Eckart-Verlag, 1937.

3467. SPITTA, Friedrich. Das deutsche Kirchenlied in seinen charakteristischen Erscheinungen ausgewählt. Leipzig. G. U. Göschen, 1912.

3468. STEIN, Fritz Wilhelm. Zur Geschichte der Musik in Heidelberg. Heidelberg: Universitäts-Buchdruckerei J. Hörning, 1912.

3469. STEINDORF, Eberhard und Dieter Uhrig, (ed.). Staatskapelle Dresden. Mit einem Essay von Ernst Krause. Berlin: Henschelverlag, 1973.

3470. TAEGLICHSBECK, Johann F. Die musikalischen Schätze der St. Katharinenkirche zu Brandenburg. Ein Beitrag zur musikal. Literatur d. 16. u. 17. Jahrh. Brandenburg: A. H. Gedruckt bei A. Müller, 1857.

3471. VLEUGELS, Johannes. Zur Pflege der katholischen Kirchenmusik in Württemburg von 1500-1650, mit besonderer Berücksichtigung der Institutionen. Aachen: Druck von W. Siemes, 1928.

3472. VOLL, Wolfgang. Die musikalische Neuordnung unseres Gottesdienstes. Gütersloh: Rufer-Verlag, 1954.

3473. WACKERNAGEL, K. E. Phillipp. Das deutsche Kirchenlied. 4 vols. Stuttgart: C. G. Liesching, 1841.

3474. WEITZEL, Wilhelm. Kirchenmusikalische Statistik der Erzdiözese Freiburg mit einem Überblich über die Glocken und Orgeln der Erzdiözese. Karlsruhe: Badenia, 1928.

3475. WILSS, Ludwig. Zur Geschichte der Musik an den oberschwäbischen Klöstern im 18. Jahrhundert. Mit Notenbeilagen. Stuttgart: C. L. Schultheiss, 1925.

3476. WITT, Franz Xaver. Ausgewählte Aufsätze zur Kirchenmusik. Köln: Verlag des Diözesan--Cäcilien--Köln--Aachen, 1934.

3477. ZIMMER, F. Der Verfall des Kantoren. Und Organistenamtes in der evangelischen Landeskirche Preussens. Quedlinburg: C. F. Vieweg, 1885.

See also: 13, 34, 170, 212, 233, 235, 241, 245, 270, 277, 367, 371, 383, 407, 586, 651, 656, 742, 813, 913, 914, 936, 1028, 1029, 1089, 1090, 1106, 1147, 1176, 1291, 1292, 1293, 1301, 1304, 1314, 1322, 1330, 1336, 1337, 1340, 1341, 1352, 1360, 1370, 1380, 1406, 1407, 1408, 1567, 1693, 1726, 1727, 1790, 1830, 1943, 2052, 2053, 2059, 2115, 2120, 2128, 2129, 2146, 2156, 2163, 2183, 2194, 2260, 2305, 2318, 2372, 2411, 2412, 2442, 2476, 2546, 2590, 2596, 2638, 2701, 2752, 2770, 2780, 2787, 2837, 2856, 2886, 2887, 2963, 2978, 3010, 3066, 3069, 3071, 3083, 3090, 3096, 3171, 3183, 3184, 3186, 3188, 3198, 3245, 3253, 3265, 3294, 3723, 3728, 3798, 3799, 3826, 3827, 3854, 3858, 3880, 3916, 3919, 3924, 3950,

3966, 3980, 3984, 4026, 4063, 4078, 4101, 4102, 4143, 4208, 4217, 4218, 4260, 4297, 4389, 4432, 4449, 4475, 4477, 4479, 4494, 4588, 4654, 4660, 4709, 4717, 4755, 4940, 5003, 5037, 5067, 5070, 5076, 5077, 5081, 5085, 5093, 5101, 5102, 5106, 5108, 5111, 5112, 5127, 5128, 5129, 5132, 5281, 5320, 5437.

Great Britain

3478. BRITISH music yearbook: 1975. (continues "The Music Yearbook"). London; New York: Bowker, 1975.

3479. CROWEST, Frederick James. The story of British music from the earliest times to the Tudor period. Portland, Me.: Longwood Press, 1976.

3480. JACOBS, Arthur, ed. British music yearbook: A survey and directory with statistics and reference articles for 1975. New York: Bowker, 1975.

3481. ________. British music yearbook: A survey and directory with statistics and reference articles for 1976. London, New York: Bowker, 1976.

See also: 3261, 3498, 4094, 4752, 5016.

Greece

3482. MACRAN, H. S. Greek Music in Grove's Dictionary. 5th ed., New York: St. Martin's, n. d.

3483. TORR, Cecil. Greek Music in Oxford History of Music. London: Oxford Univ. Press, 1929.

3484. TZETZES, Johannes. Über die altgriechische Musik in der griechischen Kirche. (Neudr.) Walluf bei Wiesbaden: M. Sändig, 1973.

See also: 530, 534, 535, 1050, 1272, 2152, 4674, 5250.

Guatemala

3485. CORTES Y LARRAZ, Pedro. Reglas, y estatutos del choro de la santa Metropolitana iglesia de Santiago de Guatemala. Dispuestos por su arzobispo. N. G.: Joachin de Arevalo, 1770.

Hungary

3486. BANYAY, I. K. The history of the Hungarian music. Los Angeles, Cal.: Southern California, M. N., 1942.

3487. GOMBOSI, Otto. Die ältesten Denkmäler der mehrstimmigen Vokalmusik aus Ungarn. Berlin und Leipzig: W. de Gruyter & Co., 1931.

3488. SZABOLCSI, Bence. A concise history of Hungarian music. Chapter on modern music by G. Kroó. Trans. from the Hungarian by S. Karig and F. MacNicol. (2nd enl. ed.) Budapest: Corvina Press, 1974.

3489. ______. A concise history of Hungarian music. Translated from Hungarian by Sara Karig. London: Barrie & Rockliff, 1964.

3490. ______. Geschichte des ungarischen Musik. Available also in English translation. Budapest: Corvina, 1964.

3491. SZALKAI, Laszlo. Szalkai érsek zenei jegyzetei monostoriskolai diák korából. Das Musiklehrbuch einer ungarischen Klosterschule in der Handschrift. Budapest: Orsz. Széchényi Könyutár, 1934.

See also: 782, 2536, 2545, 2564, 2916, 3547.

Iceland

3492. THORSTEINSSON, Bjarni. Islenzk bjodlög. Kaupmannahöfn: Prentud hja S. L. Møller, 1906-1909.

India

3493. DANIELOU, Alain. Northern Indian Music. New York: F. A. Praeger, Publ., 1969.

3494. KAUFMANN, Walter. The ragas of North India. Bloomington, Ind.: Indiana Univ. Press, 1968.

3495. RAO, T. V. Subba. Studies in Indian music. London: Asia Publ. House, 1962.

See also: 4113, 4115, 4117, 4120, 4121, 4122.

Ireland

3496. FLOOD, William H. G. A history of Irish music. Boston: Milford House, 1974.

3497. ______. A history of Irish music. (3rd ed.) New York: Praeger, 1970. (1st ed., 1904; 2nd ed., 1906.)

3498. HOGAN, Itam. Anglo-Irish music, 1780-1830. Cork, Ireland: Cork Univ. Press, 1966.

3499. IRELAND, Church of. The daily service. Prayers and hymns for schools. Authorized by the Boards of Education of the Church of Ireland, the Presbyterian in Ireland and the Methodist Church in Ireland. London: Oxford Univ. Press, 1951.

3500. MOLUS Organ of the Association of St. Gregory. Dublin: The Association, 1934.

3501. PETRIE, G. (ed.). The Petrie collection of the ancient music of Ireland. Ridgewood, N.J.: Gregg Press, reprint, n.d. (orig. Dublin, 1855.)

3502. WALKER, Joseph C. Historical memoirs of the Irish bards, interspersed with anecdotes of the music of Ireland; also an account of the musical instruments of the ancient Irish. New York: Scientific Library Service, 1786.

See also: 422, 1132, 1219, 1950, 2414.

Israel

3503. GRADENWITZ, Peter. The music of Israel. New York: W. W. Norton & Co., 1949.

3504. LEEB, Helmut. Die Gesänge im Gemeindegottesdienst von Jerusalem. Wien: Herder, 1970.

See also: 4837.

Italy

3505. ALESSI, Giovanni d'. La cappella musicale del Duomo di Treviso. Vedelago: Ars et Religio, 1954.

3506. CAFFI, Francesco. Storia della musica sacra nella già cappella ducale di San Marco in Venezia dal 1318 al 1797. Venezia: G. Antonelli, 1854-55.

3507. CONGRESSO Cattolico Italiano. Sulla ristaurazione della musica sacra in Italia. Bologna: Dalla tip. Jelsinea, 1874.

3508. DAMILANO, Pietro. G. Giovenale Ancina e la lauda cinquecentesca. Milano: Fratelli Bocca, 1953.

3509. FEDELI, Vito. Le cappelle musicali di Novara, dal secolo XVI a'primordi dell' ottocento. Milano: Ricordi, 1933.

3510. GIACOMO, Salvatore di. Maestri di cappella, musici y istrumenti al Tesoro di San Gennaro nei secoli XVII y XVIII. Napoli: A spese dell' autore, 1920.

3511. GIULIARI, Giovanni Battista Carlo. Della musico sacra in Verona. Firenze: Coi tipi di M. Cellini e c., 1879.

3512. KATSCHTHOLER, Jean Baptiste. Storia della musica sacra, nuovamente rifusa e migliorata con un' appendice sull storia della riforma Ceciliana in Italia per cura del sacerdote. Torino: Societá tipografico editrice nazionale, 1910.

3513. L'ARCHIVIO musicale della cappella Antoniana in Padova; illustrazione storico-critica, con cinque eliotipie. Padova: Tip. e. libreria Antoniana, 1895.

3514. LEVRI, Mario. La cappella musicale di Rovereto. Trento: Biblioteca P. francescani, 1972.

3515. McELRATH, Hugh T. Milanese church music in the early Baroque. Rochester: Univ. of Rochester, Eastman School of Music, n. d.

3516. MAGGI, Sebastiano. Dissertazione sopra il grave disordine ed abuso della moderna musica vocale ed istrumentale che si e introdotta e si usa a nostri di nelle chiese e nei divini uffizii. Venezia: Alvisopoli, 1821.

3517. MASUTTO, Giovanni. Della musica sacra in Italia. Venezia: Fratelli Visentini, 1889.

3518. METTENLEITER, Dominicus. Aus der musikalischen Vergangenheit bayrischer Städte. Musikgeschichte der Stadt Regensburg. Aus Archivalien und sonstigen Quellen. Regensburg: J. G. Bössenecker, 1866.

3519. MILANESE Priest, by an Unidentified. La cappella sistina di Germania, ossia. La settimana santa nella cattedrale di Ratisbona, per un prete milanese; considerazioni e voti per la retaurazione della musica sacra in Italia. Milano: Presso la direzioni del periodico Musica sacra, 1880.

3520. MULLER, Walther. Johann Adolf Hasse als Kirchenkomponist. Ein Beitrag zur Geschichte der neapolitanischen Kirchenmusik; mit thematischem Katalog der liturgischen Kirchenmusik. Leipzig: Breitkopf & Härtel, 1911.

3521. SCHOLES, Percy Alfred. Crotchets, a few short musical notes. London: John Lane, 1924.

3522. STEFANI, Gino. Musica e religione nell'Italia barocca. Palermo: Flaccovio, 1975.

3523. TEBALDINI, Giovanni. La musica sacra in Italia. Milano: G. Palma, 1893.

3524. TERENZIO, Vincenzo. La musica italiano dell'Ottocento. (Storia della musica italiano da sant- Ambrogio a noi.) Milano: Bramante, 1976.

3525. WEBER, Heinrich. Von dem kunstreichen Kirchengesang Italiens im 16. Jahrhundert. Mit Steindruck Benedetto Marcello. Zürich: Druck von Orell Füssli & Co., 1888.

See also: 206, 231, 240, 281, 334, 339, 347, 355, 438, 447, 463, 733, 737, 743, 1086, 1087, 1152, 1158, 1592, 2007, 2045, 2059, 2588, 2603, 2761, 2770, 2910, 3124, 3129, 3163, 3215, 3935, 3956, 3960, 4356, 4372, 4401, 4405, 4527, 4546.

Mexico

3526. BARWICK, Steven (ed.). The Franco Codex of the Cathedral of Mexico. New York: A. Broude Inc., 1965.

3527. ______. Sacred vocal polyphony in early colonial Mexico. Cambridge, Mass.: Harvard Univ., n. d.

3528. LECLERC, Jean-Marc. Misa Tepozteca. Cuernavaca, Mexico: Centro Intercultural de Documentacion, 1966.

3529. SPELL, Lota May. Music in the Cathedral of Mexico in the sixteenth century. N. p., 1946. (LC-ML210. 8. Mc37)

See also: 109, 403, 507, 2384, 2823, 5040.

Netherlands

3530. FELLERER, Karl Gustav. Anthology of music. Vol. 22. The art of the Netherlands (Lanaerts). New York: A. Broude Inc., n. d.

3531. KAT, A. I. M. De geschiedenis der kerkmuziek in de Nederlanden sedert de hervorming. Hilversum: N. G., 1939. (BM)

3532. LENAERTS, René Bernard. The art of the Netherlands. New York: Oxford Univ. Press, 1964.

3533. NEDERLANDSE Hervormde Kerk Commissie Voor de Kerkmuziek. Die gemeente zingt. 's-Gravenhage: Boekencentrum, 1968.

3534. STEPHAN, Wolfgang. Die burgundisch-niederländ-ische Motette zur Zeit Ockeghems. Kassel: Bärenreiter-Verlag, 1937.

3535. STRAETEN, Edmond Vander. La musique aux pays-bas avant le XIXe siècle. New York: Broude Brothers, 1965. (reprint).

3536. VAN DUYSE, Florimond. De melodie van het nederlandsche lied en hare rhythmische vormen. 's-Gravenhage: M. Nijhoff, 1902.

3537. ________. Het oude nederlandsche lied. Wereldlijke en geestelijke liederen uit vroegere tijd. Teksten en melodieën, verzameld en toegelicht. New York: Broude Brothers Limited (Facsimile), 1965.

3538. WIEDER, F. C. De schriftuurlijke liedekens. De liederen de Nederlandsche hervormden tot op het jaar 1566. Gravenhage: M. Nijhoff, 1900.

See also: 433, 1638, 1978, 2108, 2244, 3033, 3050, 3142, 3778, 3791, 3882, 3900, 3929, 3931, 3969, 3983, 4025, 4057, 4059, 4207, 4751, 4792, 4860, 5201.

Norway

3539. HOVEY, Rolf Eggericks. An anthology of Norwegian Religious music. Ann Arbor: Univ. Microfilms, 1967.

3540. LANGE, Kristian, and Arne Ostvedt. Norwegian music; a brief survey. London: D. Dobson, 1963.

3541. OSLO. Libri liturgici provinciae Nidrosiensis medii aevi. Osloiae: Norsk Historisk Kjeldeskriftinstitutt. Reitshistoriske Kommisjon, 1962.

3542. SANDVIK, Ole Mork. Norsk kirkemusik og dens kilder. Kristiania: Steen, 1918.

See also: 414, 2402, 3329, 3606, 3868.

Philippines

3543. ESPINA, A. Beaunoni. Music in the Philippines and the development of sacred music there. (pp. XXVI, 314). New York: Union Tehological Seminary, D. S. M., 1961.

Poland

3544. ETAT des recherches sur la musique religieuse dans la culture polonaise. Ouvrage collectif sous la rédaction de J. Pikulik. Varsovie: Academie de théologie catholique, 1973.

3545. GIEBUROWSKI, Waclaw. Die "musica magistri Szydlovite," ein polnischer Choraltraktat des XV. Jahrh. und seine Stellung in der Choraltheorie des Mittelalters, mit Berücksichtigung der Choraltheorie-und-praxis des XV. Jahrh. in Polen, sowie der nachtridentinischen Choralreform. Posen: Druck und Verlag der St. Adalbert-Druckerei, 1915.

3546. KIRCHENGESANG-Verein der. Festschrift zur Feier des 75 jährigen Jubiläums St. Trinitatis-Gemeinde zu Lodz. 1859-1934. Lodz: Neue Lodzer Zeitung, 1934.

3547. LARUE, Jan. The bydgoszcz festival celebrating Poland's thousand years. New York: Polish Book Importing Company, n. d.

3548. STAN badán nad muzyka religijna w kulturze polskeij. Praca zbiorowa pod. red. J. Pilulika. Warszawa: Akademia Teologii Katolickiej, 1973.

See also: 630, 1406, 2494, 2891, 3020.

Portugal

3549. ANDRADE, Mario de. Ensaio sôbre la música brazileira. São Paolo: Livraria Martins Editôra, 1972.

3550. BRAGA, Theophilo. Joaquim Silvestre Serrao e a musica religiosa em Portugal. Lisboa: Typ. do Annuario Commercial, 1906.

3551. CORBIN, Solange. Essai sur la musique religieuse portugaise au Moyen Age. Paris: Les Belles Lettres, 1952.

3552. SOUSA VITERBO, Francisco. A ordem de Christo e a musica religiosa nos nosses dominios ultramarinos. Coimbra: Imprensa da Universidade, 1910.

3553. _______. A ordem de Christo e a musica sagrada nas suas igrejas do continente Propriedade e edicão da familia do autor. Coimbra: Imprensa da Universidade, 1911.

3554. _______. A ordem de Santiago e a musica religiosa nas igrejas pertencentes á mesma ordem. Coimbra: Imprensa da Universidade, 1912.

See also: 1406, 2879, 3761, 4060.

Puerto Rico

3555. THOMPSON, Annie Figueroa. An annotated bibliography of writings about music in Puerto Rico (MLA Index and Bibliographical Series No. 12). Ann Arbor, Mich.: Music Library Assn., 1975.

Rumania

3556. BRANÇUSI, Petre. George Breazul şi istoria necrisă a muzicii româneşti. Bucureşti: Editura muzicala, 1976.

3557. COSMA, Octavian. Hronicul muzicii româneşti muzicală. Bucaresti: Editura muzicală, 1973.

See also: 1671, 3543.

Russia

3558. BELIAEV, Viktor Mikhaĭlovich. Central Assian music: essays on the history of the music of the peoples of the U. S. S. R. Ed. and annotated by M. Slobin. Trans. from the Russian by M. and G. Slobin. 1st ed. Middletown, Conn.: Wesleyan Univ. Press, 1975.

3559. BRAZHNIKOV, M. Puti razvitiia i zadachi rasshifrovki znamennnovo rospeva XII-XVLL vekov. Primenenie nekotouich statisticheckich metodov k issledovaniiu muzhuikalhnuich yablenii. Leningrad: Gos Muzuikalhnoe Izd'vo, 1949.

3560. CUI, César. La musique en Russie. (Fotomechan. Neudr. d. orig. Ausg. Paris: 1880.) Leipzig: Zentralantiquariat der DDR., 1974.

3561. INTERNATIONAL Musical Society. Report of the fourth congress of the International musical society. London: Novello and Co., ltd., 1912.

3562. IUSUPOV, Nikolai Borisovich. Histoire de la musique en Russie. Première partie, musique sacrée, suivie d'un choix de morceaux de chants d'église anciens et modernes. Paris: Saint-Jorre, 1862.

3563. LAVASHEVA, Olga Evgenevka. Istoriîa russkoĭ muzki. Moskva: Muzyka, 1972.

3564. LEONARD, Richard Anthony. A history of Russian music. New York: Macmillan Co., 1956.

3565. LUUR, August. Tartu ühöpilasmeeskoor, 1912-1962. Vastutav toimetaja. Tartu: N. G., 1962. (BM 07902-bbb. 10)

3566. L'VOV, Alekseiĭ Fedorovich. Über den freien Rhythmus des altrussischen Kirchengesangs. St. Petersburg: Gedruckt in dem Polytechnographischen établissement, 1859.

3567. MODEST, Archbishop of Volhynia. O tserkovnom oktoik. Kiev: Tip. Kievo-Pecherskoi Iavry, 1885.

3568. MOLDON, David. A bibliography of Russian composers. London: White Lion, 1976.

3569. MONTAGU-NATHAN, Montagu. A history of Russian music. New York: Biblo and Tannen, 1969.

3570. OPALINSKI, Christine. Music and song of Ukraine. Weston, Ont.: St. Demetrius Ukranian Catholic Church, 1976.

3571. ORLOV, S. P. La musique réligieuse en Russie. Amay, Belgique: Prieuré d'Amay-sur-Meuse, 1939.

3572. POSELL, Elsa Z. Russian composers. Boston: Houghton Mifflin Co., 1967.

3573. RIESEMANN, Oskar von. Monographien zur russischen Musik. Hildesheim; New York: G. Olms, 1975.

3574. TCHYERKOYOI pisni Vidannia V'yato. Prudeimonil: Budaenuumeo una Co. Baculia Belunozo, 1961.

3575. VOLKOV, S. S. Odrevnerusskikh tserkovnykh napievakh io znachenii ikh dlia budushchnosti russkago musykall nago iskusstva. N.G.: N.G., 1906. (LC-ML2937)

3576. VOZNESENSKII, I. Osmotlasnye rospievy 4-kh Posliednikh viekov pravoslavnoi Russkoi tserkvi. N.G.: N.G., 1888-93. (LC-MT 860-V708 case)

3577. YUSUPOFF, Nikolai Borisovich. (Second transliteration of the name of author of number 3562.)

See also: 382, 456, 458, 482, 498, 499, 500, 507, 508, 513, 514, 515, 529, 924, 944, 1249, 1265, 1526, 1919, 2690, 2799, 2945, 3304, 3547, 3699, 3700, 3961, 4402, 4404, 5213.

Scandinavia

See: 2391, 2479, 2488, 2597, 2614, 3650.

Scotland

3578. BAPTIE, David. Musical Scotland. Hildesheim, Germany: Georg Olms-Reprint, 1967. (orig. Paisley, 1894.)

3579. COLLINSON, Francis. The traditional and national music of Scotland. Vanderbilt Univ. Library. London: Routledge & K. Paul, n. d.

3580. DALWELL, John Graham. Musical memoirs of Scotland. Edinburgh: T. G. Stephenson, 1849.

3581. ________. Musical memories of Scotland with historical annotations. Folcraft, Pa.: Folcraft Library Editions, 1976.

3582. LOVE, James. Scottish church music--its composers and sources. London: W. Blackwood & Sons, 1891.

3583. McMILLAN, William. The worship of the Scottish Reformed Church, 1551-1638. London: J. Clarke & Co., 1931.

3584. MILLER, W. M. Church of Scotland psalm and hymn tune book. Edinburgh: N. G., 1881. (BM)

See also: 389, 958, 3674, 4809, 4810, 4824, 4881, 4945, 5073, 5327.

Serbia

3585. SRPSKA muzika korz vevoke. La musique serbe à travers les siècles. Glavni urednik S. Durié-Klajn (In Serbian and French). Beograd: Srpska akademija nauka i umetnosti, 1973.

See also: 1671, 5354.

South Africa

3586. VERZAMELING van geestelijke liederen. Kaapstad: N. G., 1893.

See also: 2604.

South America

3587. STEVENSON, Robert. The earliest polyphonic imprint in South America. (Single copy at Cuzco Cathedral.) Rome: Dorico Brothers, 1544. --See "Notes," March, 1967.

See also: 4603.

Spain

3588. ANGLES, Higini. La música a Catalunya fins al segle XIII. Barcelona: Institut d'estudio catalans; Biblioteca de Catalunya, 1935.

3589. ARAIZ MARTINEZ, A. Historia de la música religiosa en España. Barcelona: Editorial Labor, s. a., 1942.

3590. ARANA MARTIJA, José Antonio. Música vasca. San Sebastián: Sociedad Guipuzcoana de Ediciones y Publicaciones, 1976.

3591. CONGRESO Nacional de Musica. Crónica y actas oficiales del tercer Congreso nacional de sagrada. Barcelona: Talleres tipograficos La Hormiga de oro, 1913.

3592. CORAL. Revista musical ilustrada. Organo de las agrupaciones corales de España e Hispanoamérica. Madrid: N. G., 1953.

3593. ELUSTIZA, J. B. de and G. Castrillo Hernandez. Antología musical. Siglo de oro de la música litúrgica de España. Polifonía vocal, siglos XV y XVI. Barcelona: R. Casulleras., 1933.

3594. ESLAVA, Miguel Hilarion. Breva memoria historica de la music religiosa en España. N. G.: N. G., n. d. (LC-M2E76)

3595. FERNANDEZ-CID, Antonio. La musica española en el siglo XX. Madrid: Riocluera, 1973.

3596. FOSTER, David W. and Virginia Ramos Foster. Manual of Hispanic bibliography. (second edition). New York: Garland Publ., 1977.

3597. HAMILTON, Mary Neal. Music in eighteenth century Spain. New York: Johnson Reprint Corp., 1966. (orig. Urbana, Ill.: N. G., 1937.)

3598. HUELGAS, Las. El còdex musical de Las Huelgas (musica a veus deis segles) XIII-XIV. Barcelona: Institut d'estudis catalans, Biblioteca de Catalunya, 1931.

3599. LOZANO GONZALEZ, Antonio. La música popular, religiosa y dramática en Zaragoza desde el siglo XVI hasta nuestros dias. Zaragoza: Tip. de J. Sanz y Navarro, 1895.

3600. MARTINEZ, Roger. Checklist of Spanish musicologists, chronologically arranged.... For the N. Y. U. Journal Club. In progress and unpublished.

3601. MILLET, Luis. El canto popular religiós. Barcelona: Henrich y comp., 1913.

3602. OLMEDA, Federiko. Estudio de la música sagrada en las parroquias. Burgos: Impr. y libreria del Centro catolico, 1907.

3603. PEDRELL, Felipe. La festa d'Elche ou Le drame lyrique liturgique espagnol.... Le trépas el l'assomption de la Vierge. Paris: Au bureau d'édition de la "Schola," 1906.

3604. TREND, John Brande. The music of Spanish history to 1600. New York: Kraus Reprint Corp., 1965. (orig. London, Oxford Univ. Press, H. Milford, 1926.)

See also: 354, 421, 434, 439, 444, 445, 652, 681, 917, 1025, 1026, 1151, 2718, 2725, 2879, 3004, 3019, 3696, 3743, 3744, 4060, 4355.

Südslawen

3605. CVETKO, Dragotin. Musikgeschichte der Südslawen. Kassel: Bärenreiter, 1975.

See also: 547.

Sweden

3606. BETANKANDE med förslag till nyorgansation ar kyrkomusikerbefattningarna. Stockholm: I. Haeggströms boktryckeri a.b., 1945.

3607. BUCHT, Bergljot Krohn (ed.). Nomus Katalog 76. Stockholm: Nordiskt Musik Samarbete, 1976.

3608. FRAN tyska Kyrkans glansdagar. Bilder ur svenska musikens historia från vasaregenterna til Karolinska tidns slut ... Av Tobias Norlind. Stockholm: N.G., 1944.

3609. FRANSEN, Hatanael. Svensk maosa präntad pa porgament. N.G.: N.G., 1927. (LC-ML 5.896)

3610. JACOBSSON, Jacob. Mässans budskap; en studie i de fasta sangpartierna i svenska massan under reformationstiden. Mit einer deutschen Zusammenfassung. Lund: Gleerup, 1958.

3611. JACOBSSON, Stig. Musiken i Sverige: skivlyssnarens handbok i svensk musik från äldsta tid till 1970-talet, med utförlig skivforteckning. Västerås: Ica-förlaget, 1975.

3612. MOBERG, Carl Allan. Från kyrko-och hovmusik till offentlig konsert; studier i stormaktstidens svenska musikhistoria. Leipzig: O. Harrassowitz, 1942.

3613. ________. Kyrkomusikens historia. Stockholm: Svenska kyrkans diakonistyrelses bokförlag, 1932.

3614. _______. Zur Geschichte des schwedischen Kirchengesangs. Liége: N. G., 1930. (LC-ML26. 185)

3615. NORLIND, Tobias. Från tyska kyrkans glansdagar; bilder ur svenska musikens historia från vasaregenterna till karolinska tidens slut. Stockholm: Musikhistoriska, museet, 1944-45.

3616. OLSEN, Helge. Svenska kyrkomusici. Biografisk uppslagsbok. Stockholm: H. Olsen, 1928 and rev., 1936.

3617. OLSON, Lee O. G. A history of Swedish church music. New York: Union Theological Seminary, School of Sacred Music, 1945.

3618. WALIN, Stig Alfred Ferdinand. Svensk musikhistoria; en översikt. Stockholm: Bonnier, 1949.

See also: 414, 1351, 2402, 2410, 2626, 2894, 3171, 3329, 3664, 4883, 4984, 5020.

Switzerland

3619. BENZINGER, Augustin. Beiträge zum katholischen Kirchenlied in der deutschen Schweiz nach der Reformation. Sarnen: L. Ehrli, 1910.

3620. DREIFALTIGKEITSKIRCHE. Geschichte des Pfarr-Cäcilienvereins Bern. Bern: Pfarr-Cäcilienverein, 1936.

3621. DUFT, Johannes. Bruder Klaus in der Musik; Beitrag zur Geschichte des deutschen Volks und Kirchenliedes der Schweiz. Kaltbrunn: Buchdrückerei Aug. Kühne, 1937.

3622. FALLET, Edouard. L'office de chantre dans les églises neuchâteloises de la réforme au XVIIIe siècle. N. G.: N. G., 1928. (LC-ML-5-s. -338)

3623. HILBER, Johann Baptist. Fünf-und-Zwanzig Jähre Kirchenmusikschule Luzern. Luzern: Kommission Haag, 1967.

3624. MARXER, Otto. Zur spätmittlelalterlichen Choralgeschichte St. Gallens. Mit 10 photographischen Tafeln. St. Gallens: Buchdruckerei "Ostschweiz," 1908.

3625. REIMANN, Hannes. Die Einführung des Kirchengesangs in der Züricher Kirche nach der Reformation. Zürich: Zwingli-Verlag, 1959.

3626. SALADIN, Josef Anton. Die Musikpflege am Stift S. Leodegar in Luzern. Stans: Buchdr. P. von Matt, 1948.

3627. SCHUBIGER, Anselm. Die Pflege des Kirchengesanges und der Kirchenmusik in der deutschen Katholischen Schweiz. Eine musikalischhistorische Skizze. New York: N. Benziger, 1873.

3628. STIERLIN, Leonhard. Der züricherische Kirchengesang seit der Reformation. Zürich: Druck von Orell, Füssli & Co., 1855.

3629. ZULAUF, Max. Der Musikunterricht in der Geschichte des bernischen Schulwesens von 1528-1798. Bern: P. Haupt, 1934.

See also: 241, 357, 919, 1463, 2085, 2268, 2281, 2638, 2742, 3081, 3153, 3793, 3908, 3964, 3965, 4079, 4177, 4764, 4897, 4936, 4982, 5065, 5084, 5086.

Syria

3630. NARSAI. Syrische Wechsellieder von Narses. Ein Beitrag zur altchristlichen syrischen Hymnologie. Leipzig: N.G., 1896.

See also: 2525, 2862, 3288.

Ukraine

3631. KOSHYTS, Oleksander Antonoyych. Pro henetychyi zviazok ta hrupvvannia ukrainskykh obriadovykh bisen. Genetic relationship and classificat ion of Ukrainian ritual songs. Winnipeg: Ukrainian Cultural and Educational Center, 1945.

United States

3632. ALLWARDT, Anton Paul. Sacred music in New York, 1800-1850. New York: Union Theological Seminary, School of Sacred Music, 1950.

3633. AMERICAN music before 1865 in print and on records: A Bibliodiscography. Preface by H. Wiley Hitchcock. Brooklyn: Institute for Studies in American music, Dept. of Music, School of Performing Arts, Brooklyn College of the City Univ. of New York, 1976.

3634. AMERICAN Musical Convention. Proceedings of the American Musical Convention. New York: Saxton & Miles, 1845.

3635. CARROLL, Alf Lindsay. All day singing. Mount Vernon: Xavier Printing Co., 1937.

3636. CHASE, Gilbert. America's music: From the Pilgrims to the present. New York: McGraw-Hill Book Co., Inc., 1955, 1956 (revised, 1966).

3637. COLONIAL Dames of America, National Society of. (ed. by William Lichtenwanger.) Church music and musical life in Pennsylvania in the 18th century. Philadelphia: Printed for the Society of Colonial Dames of America, 1926, 1947.

3638. DAVID, Hans Theodore. Musical life in the Pennsylvania settlements of the Unitas Fratrum. Winston-Salem: Moravian Music Foundation, 1959.

3639. ELLINGTON, Charles Linwood. The sacred harp tradition of the South: Its origin and evolution. Ann Arbor: Univ. Microfilm, 1969.

3640. ELLINWOOD, Leonard Webster. English influences in American church music. Taunton: Eng., 1954. (LC55-32624)

3641. ________. The history of American church music. New York: Da Capo Press, 1970. (repr. Of Morehouse-Gorham, 1953).

3642. ELSON, Louis. History of American music. New York: Macmillan Co., 1904.

3643. FISHER, William A. One-hundred and fifty years of music publishing in the U.S. (1783-1933). Boston: Oliver Ditson Co., 1933.

3644. GAY, Julius. Church music in Farmington in the olden time. An historical address delivered at the annual meeting of the Village library company of Farmington, Conn. Hartford, Conn.: Lockwood & Brainard Co., 1891.

3645. GERSON, Robert. Music in Philadelphia. Philadelphia: Theo. Presser Co., 1940.

3646. GOULD, Nathaniel Duren. Church music in America. Comprising its history and its peculiarities at different periods with cursory remarks on its legitimate use and its abuse; with notices of the schools, composers, teachers, and societies. Boston: A. N. Johnson, 1853.

3647. GRUBBS, Baalis. Modern use of California mission music. Los Angeles: Univ. of Southern California, L.A., M.M., 1955.

3648. HEARD, Priscilla S. American music, 1698-1800: An annotated bibliography. Waco, Tex.: Baylor Univ. Press, 1975.

3649. HITCHCOCK, H. Wiley. Music in the United States: A historical introduction. (2nd ed.) Englewood Cliffs, N.J.: Prentice-Hall, 1969, 1974.

3650. HJORTSUANG, Carl T. Scandinavian contributions to American sacred music. (p. 255). New York: Union Theological Seminary, D.S.M., 1951.

3651. HOOD, George. A history of music in New England: With biographical sketches of reformers and psalmists. Boston: Wilkins, Carter & Co., 1846 and New York and London: Johnson Reprint, 1970.

3652. HOPPS, Gloria Lorraine. Mission music of California. Evanston, Ill.: Northwestern Univ., M.M., 1949.

3653. HORN, Dorothy D. Sing to me of heaven: A study of folk and early American materials in three harp books. Gainesville: Univ. of Florida, 1970.

3654. HOWARD, John T. Music of George Washington's time. Washington, D.C.: Washington Bicentennial Commission, 1950.

3655. ________. Our American music. 3rd edition. New York: The Thomas Y. Crowell Co., 1946 (revised 1955).

3656. HUBBARD, William Lines, ed. History of American music. With introductions by G. Chadwick and F. Damrosch. New York: AMS Press, 1976.

3657. JACKSON, George Pullin. The story of the Sacred Harp 1844-1944. A book of religious folk song as an American institution. Nashville: Vanderbilt Univ. Press, 1944.

3658. KLUCKHOHN, C. and L. C. Wyman. An introduction to Navaho chant practice. Menasha: American Anthropological Assoc., 1940.

3659. LOWENS, Irving, ed. American composers and American music. (A list of 648 American composers and a list of 115 books on American music and American composers.) Boston: W. Schwann, 1975.

3660. ________. Music and musicians of early America. New York: W. W. Norton, 1965 and 1967.

3661. McKISSICK, Marvin Leo. A study of the function of music in the major religious revivals in America since 1875. Los Angeles, Cal.: Southern California, M.M., 1957.

3662. METCALF, Frank Johnson. American writers and compilers of sacred music. New York: Abingdon Press, 1925.

3663. ________. History of sacred music in the District of Columbia. Washington, D.C.: Columbia Historical Society, 1926.

3664. NELSON, C. L. The sacred and secular music of the Swedish settlers of the midwest, 1841-1917. New York: New York Univ., 1950. (avail.--Ann Arbor: Univ. Microfilms, 1951.)

3665. NINDE, Edward S. The story of the American hymn. New York: Abingdon Press, 1921.

3666. PRATT, Waldo Selden. The music of the Pilgrims. Boston: Oliver Ditson Co., 1921.

3667. REED, Andrew and James Matheson. A narrative of the visit to the American church by the deputation from the Congregation Union of England and Wales. 2nd Vol. London: Jackson and Walford, 1835.

3668. ROBLOWSKY, John. Music in America. New York and London: Crowell-Collier Press, 1967.

3669. ROHRER, Gertrude Martin. Music and musicians of Pennsylvania. Port Washington, N.Y.: Kennikat Press, 1940, and 1970.

3670. ROSENBERRY, Moris Claude. The Pennsylvania German in music. Harrisburg: Pennsylvania German Society, 1930.

3671. SOUTAMIRE, Albert. Music of the old south: Colony to Confederacy. Madison, N.J.: Fairleigh Dickinson U., 1972.

3672. STEVENSON, Robert. Protestant church music in America: A short survey of men and movements from 1564 to the present. New York: W. W. Norton, 1966.

3673. SWAN, Howard. Music in the Southwest: 1825 to 1950. San Marino, Cal.: The Huntington Library, 1952.

3674. WESTERHOFF, Gerhard. Christlich--religiöse Züge in den englischschottischen Volksballaden und ihren nordamerikanischen Fassungen. Bonn, Germany: Bonn, 1942.

3675. WRAGG, Eleanor Newton. The American Civil War era as reflected in the religious song of the age. Boston: Boston Univ., M.A., 1935.

3676. ZANZIG, Augustus D. Music in American life. London: Oxford Univ. Press, 1932.

See also: 96, 97, 112, 237, 348, 379, 835, 892, 918, 929, 982, 993, 999, 1056, 1060, 1071, 1073, 1074, 1076, 1077,

1150, 1169, 1284, 1286, 1288, 1289, 1299, 1310, 1316, 1319, 1324, 1328, 1343, 1344, 1345, 1348, 1349, 1353, 1359, 1361, 1424, 1427, 1438, 1440, 1441, 1442, 1443, 1444, 1445, 1453, 1454, 1457, 1461, 1467, 1562, 1568, 1615, 1623, 1797, 1838, 1902, 1976, 1989, 1997, 2001, 2017, 2222, 2226, 2246, 2249, 2267, 2374, 2376, 2380, 2382, 2395, 2403, 2404, 2432, 2472, 2480, 2607, 2683, 2719, 2726, 2728, 2733, 2799, 2814, 2900, 3161, 3712, 3766, 3951, 4080, 4081, 4129, 4456, 4491, 4495, 4611, 4745, 4790, 4797, 4803, 4806, 4814, 4886, 5043, 5050, 5062, 5079, 5155, 5156, 5158, 5160, 5165, 5170, 5172, 5179, 5183, 5233, 5420.

Wales

3677. CROSSLEY-HOLLAND, P. Music in Wales. New York: C. F. Peters Corporation, 1967.

3678. GRIFFITH, R. D. Hanes Canu Cynulleidfaol Cymru. Caerdydd: Gwasg Prifysgol Cymru., 1948.

3679. ROBERTS, Gomer Morgan. Cyfres yr emynwyr. Caernarfon: Edited by G. M. Roberts, 1951.

See also: 812, 1437, 2155, 2287, 2324, 2344, 2358, 2454, 2467, 2473.

Yugoslavia

See: 838, 1947, 3547, 4851.

NOTATION and MUSICAL PALEOGRAPHY

3680. APEL, Willi (ed.). The notation of polyphonic music, 900-1600. Cambridge, Mass.: Medieval Academy, 1961, 1949.

3681. ________. Die Notation der polyphonen Musik 900-1600. Revised und verb. Neuausgabe. Leipzig: Breitkopf & Härtel, 1962.

3682. BANNISTER, H. M. Monumenti Vaticani di paleografia musicale. Latina. Leipzig: A. Harrassowitz, 1913.

3683. BENEDICTINES Of Stanbrook. Gregorian music. An outline of musical paleography. London & New York: Benziger Brothers, 1897.

3684. BIEZEN, J. Van. The middle Byzantine kanon-notation of manuscript H. Bilthoven: A. B. Creyghton, 1968.

3685. BORETZ, Benjamin and Edward T. Cone, eds. Perspectives on notation and performance. New York: W. W. Norton, 1976.

3686. BROUDE. Paleographie musicale. New York: Broude Brothers, 1966.

3687. COLE, Hugo. Sounds and signs: Aspects of musical notation. London: Oxford Univ. Press, 1974.

3688. DITTERICH, Margerete. Untersuchungen zum altrussichen Akzent; Anhang von Kirchengesangs Handschriften. München: O. Sagner, 1975.

3689. FLEISCHER, Oskar Reinhold. Die germanischen Neumen als Schlüssel zum altchristlichen und gregorianischen Gesang. Frankfurt: M. Frankfurter Verlags-anstalt, 1923.

3690. GARDNER, Johann von. Zur Frage der Verwendung des Sema Fita in den altrussischen liturgischen Gesangshandschriften mit linierter Notation. Mainz: Verlag der Akademie der Wissenschaften und der Literatur, 1970.

3691. GEISLER, Christian P. V. Vokalnotation. Kopenhagen: Munksgaard, 1948.

3692. HAAS, Max. Byzantinische und slavische Notationen. Köln: Volk-Verlag Gerig, 1973.

3693. HENDERSON, Robert V. A historical study of some symbols used for notating musical pitch. San Diego, Cal.: San Diego, S. C., M. A., 1962.

3694. HOLTHAUS, Mary Joachim. Beneventan notation in the Vatican manuscripts. Ann Arbor: Univ. Microfilms, Univ. of Southern California Diss., 1961.

3695. HUGLO, Michel. Fontie paleografia del canto ambrosiano. A cura della revísta "Ambrosius." Milano: Schola tip. San Benedetto, 1956.

3696. JACOBS, Charles. Tempo notation in Renaissance Spain. Brooklyn: Institute of Medieval Music, 1964.

3697. JAMMERS, Ewald. Tafeln zur Neumenschrift. Tutzing: H. Schneider, 1965.

3698. KARKOSCHKA, Erhard. Notation in new music; a critical guide to interpretation and realization. (transl. from German by Ruth Koenig.) Tonbridge: Universal Edition, 1972. (also: New York: Praeger, 1972.)

3699. METALLOV, Vasilii Mikhailovich. Osmoglasie Znamenaago raspieva. Opyt rukovodstva. Moskva: Synodal 'naia tipografiia, 1899.

3700. ________. Russkaya simiografiia. Moscow: Moskovskii Arkheologicheskii Institut, 1912.

3701. MOCQUEREAU, André, and others (ed.). Paliographi musicale, 1889--music in church. London: Report of the Archbishops' Committee, 1951.

3702. NEDERLANDSE Verniging ter Verbreiding van het. Musikschrift Klavarskribo. Slikkerveer: Klavarskribo, 1947.

3703. PALEOGRAPHIE Musicale. Les principaux manuscrits de chant grégorien, ambrosien, mozarabe, gallican. Berne: Herbert Lang Publisher, n.d.

3704. PARRISH, Carl. The notation of medieval music. New York: Norton, 1957.

3705. READ, Gardner. Music notation. Boston: Allyn & Bacon, Inc., 1964.

3706. RIEMANN, Hugo. Studien zur Geschichte der Notenschrift. Hildesheim, Germany: Georg Olms-Reprint, 1967 (orig. Leipzig, 1878).

3707. RIESEMANN, Oskar von. Die notationen des altrussischen Kirchengesanges. Leipzig: Breitkopf & Härtel, 1909.

3708. STENZEL, Jürg. Repertorium der liturgischen Musikhandschriften der Diözesen Sitten, Lausanne und Genf. Freiburg: Universitätverlag, 1972.

3709. SUÑOL, Dom Gregorio Maria. Introduction à la paléographie musicale grégorienne.... Ouvrage traduit du catalan, etc. With plates, including musical examples and a map. Paris: Tournai, 1935. (also Paleografia Musical Gregoriana Abadiá de Montserrat. Spain, 1925.)

3710. THIBAUT, Jean-Baptiste. Monuments de la notation ecphonetique et hagiopolite de l'église grecque. Hildesheim, Germany: Georg Olms-Reprint, 1967 (orig. St. Petersburg, 1913).

3711. ________. Origine byzantine de la notation neumatique de l'église latine. Hildesheim: New York: Georg Olms, Reprint, 1975 (orig. Paris 1907).

3712. TUCK, Mary Lynn Cagle. Tablatures as processes of instrumental notation in the sixteenth century. Abilene, Tex.: Hardin-Simmons Univ., 1966.

3713. WOLF, Johannes. Geschichte der mensura-notation von 1250-1460. Wiesbaden: Breitkopf & Härtel, 1965.

See also: 361, 469, 479, 496, 452, 544, 552, 571, 579, 603, 669, 670, 1151, 1240, 1250, 1265, 1357, 1412, 1505, 1525, 1962, 2122, 2131, 2141, 2376, 2432, 3021, 4113, 4117, 4756, 4961, 4977, 5104, 5158, 5300, 5305.

ORATORIO

3714. ALALEONA, Domenica. Storia dell'oratorio musicale in Italia. (Storia della musica: studi e documenti per una storia della musica, ser. 2, no. 1.) Milano: Fratelli Bocca, Editori, 1945. (orig. Turin: Fratelli Bocca, 1908.)

3715. ALBINATI, G. Piccolo dizionario di opere teatrali, oratori, cantate. Milano: N. G., 1913.

3716. ARANT, Carl P., Jr. The characteristics of the English oratorio in the 18th and 19th centuries. Waco, Tex.: Baylor Univ., M. M., 1959.

3717. BITTER, Karl Hermann. Beiträge zur Geschichte des Oratoriums. Walluf bei Wiesbaden: M. Sändig, 1974. (Unveränd., Neudr. d. Ausg. von 1872.)

3718. BÖHME, Franz Magnus. Die Geschichte des Oratoriums. (reprint). Walluf bei Wiesbaden: M. Sändig, 1973.

3719. DANIELS, David W. Alessandro Stradella's oratorio San Giovanni Battista--Vol. 1: Commentary, a modern edition and commentary. Vol. 2: Score. Ann Arbor: Univ. Microfilms, State Univ. of Iowa diss., 1963.

3720. DÜRR, Alfred. Johann Sebastian Bach, Weihnachts--Oratorium BVW 248. München: Fink, 1967.

3721. EBENSBERGER, Gary Lee. Heinrich Schuetz and the development of the oratorio. Huntsville, Tex.: Sam Houston State College, M. A., 1962.

3722. EDWARDS, Frederick George. The history of Mendelssohn's oratorio, Elijah. (with an introduction by Sir G. Grove.) New York: AMS Press, 1976.

3723. GECK, Martin. Deutsche Oratorien 1800 bis 1840. Verzeichnis der Quellen und Aufführungen. Wilhelmshaven: Heinrichshofen, 1971.

3724. HANDEL, G. F. The sacred oratorios, as set to music. Part I only. New York: Scientific Library Service, 1770.

3725. MARTIN, Clarence James. Performance practices in Händel's Messiah. Ann Arbor: Univ. Microfilms, 1968.

3726. MEIER, Heinz. Typus und Funktion der Chorsätze in Georg Friedrich Händels Oratorien. Wiesbaden: Breitkopf u. Härtel, 1971.

3727. MENDELSSOHN, Felix. Oratorio St. Paul. New York: G. Schirmer, Inc., n. d.

3728. MILLER, Kenneth E. A study of selected German baroque oratorios. Ann Arbor: Univ. Microfilms, Northwestern Univ. diss., 1963.

3729. PANNAIN, Guido. L'oratorio dei Filippini e la scuola musicale di Napoli. Milano: Edizioni Ricordi, 1934.

3730. PAULI, Hertha Ernestine. Händel and the Messiah story. New York: Meredith Press, 1968.

3731. PROBST, Gisela. Robert Schumanns Oratorien. Wiesbaden: Breitkopf und Härtel, 1975.

3732. SCARLATTI, A. The complete edition of oratorios. New York: A. Broude, Inc., 1965.

3733. SCHERING, Arnold. Geschichte des Oratoriums. Hildesheim: G. Olms, 1966. (orig. Ausgabe Leipzig, 1911 ed.)

3734. SHAW, Harold W. A textual and historical companion to Händel's Messiah. London: Novello, 1965, also New York: Mills Music.

3735. TOBIN, John. Händel's Messiah; a critical account of the manuscript sources and printed editions. New York: St. Martin's Press, 1969, and London: Cassell, 1969.

3736. VOGL, H. Zur Geschichte des Oratoriums in Wien von 1725 bis 1740. Wien: N. G., 1927.

3737. WELLESZ, E. Der Begin des musikalischen Barock und die Anfänge der Oper in Wien. Wien, Leipzig: Wiener Literarische Anstalt, Gesellschaft m. b. n., 1922.

3738. WELLMER, August. Die geistliche, insonderheit die geistliche Oratorienmusik unseres Jahrhunderts. Ein Beitrag zur Würdigung der geistlichen Musik in ihrer Bedeutung für das christliche Gemeinde-und-Volksleben. Hildburghausen: F. W. Gadow & Sohn, 1885.

3739. WÖRNER, Karl H. Schoenberg's "Moses and Aaron." Transl. by Paul Hamburger. With the complete libretto in German and English. New York: St. Martin's Press, 1963.

3740. YOUNG, Percy M. The oratorios of Handel. London: Dobson, 1949.

See also: 1761, 2793, 3168, 4230, 4304, 4350, 4419, 4429.

ORGAN and ORGAN PLAYING
Concerti Organ and Pipe Organ

3741. ABERG, Jan Häkan. En liten orgelbok. Stockholm: Verbum, 1972.

3742. ADCOCK, Ernest E. "Concerning the organ in Norwich Cathedral." The American Organist. Feb., 1956, pg. 55.

3743. _______. "The organ in Seville Cathedral." The Organ. July, 1921, pg. 20.

3744. _______. "Some Spanish organs and their cases." The Organ. April 1954, and July 1954. P. 161 et seq. and p. 28 et seq. respectively.

3745. ADELUNG, Wolfgang. Einführung in den Orgelbau. 2. erw. und. neubearb. Aufl. Leipzig: Breitkopf u. Härtel, 1972.

3746. _______. Das elektrium. Beitrag zu Klärung der Frage Orgel--Orgelimitation (Veröffentlichung der Gesellschaft der Orgelfreunde, 22). Berlin: Merseburger, 1964.

3747. _______. Orgeln der Gegenwart. Kassel: Bärenreiter, 1972.

3748. AEOLIAN Company, The. The Aeolian pipe-organ and its music. New York: Vreeland Advertising Press, 1919.

3749. ALEWINE, Murry L. A comparison of modern and historical pipe organs. Huntsville, Tex.: Sam Houston State College, M.A., 1963.

3750. The AMERICAN organist (monthly). Staten Island, N.Y.: Organ Interests, Inc., n.d.

3751. ANDERSON, Poul-Gerhard. Organ building and design. Transl. by Joanne Cornutt. New York: Oxford Univ. Press, 1969.

3752. _______. Orgelbogen. København: Munksgaard, 1956.

3753. ANDOUREL, Robert. L'orgue de l'église Notre-Dame de Millau. Millau: Dépositaire, Association des amis de l'orgue, 1975.

3754. APEL, Willi. Early history of the organ. Cambridge, Mass.: N.G., 1948.

3755. ________. Geschichte der Orgel-und. Klaviermusik bis 1700. Kassel: Bärenreiter Verlag, 1967.

3756. APPLEBAUM, Max H., and Donald A. John. Servicing electric organs. With a specially written chapter for the guidance of the English reader by W. Oliver. Slough: Foulsham-Tab., 1974.

3757. ARNOLD, Corliss Richard. Organ literature; a comprehensive survey. Metuchen, N. J.: Scarecrow Press, 1973.

3758. AUDSLEY, George Ashdown. The art of organ-building. Comprehensive historical, theoretical, and practical treatise on the tonal appointment and mechanical construction of concert-room, church, and chamber organs. New York: Dover Publications, Inc., 1905.

3759. ________. The organ of the twentieth century. New York: N. G., 1919.

3760. ________. Organ-Stops and their artistic registration. New York: H. W. Gray Co., 1921.

3761. AZEVEDO, Carlos de. Baroque organ cases of Portugal. Amsterdam: Uitgeverij Frits Kruf, 1972.

3762. BACH, Carl Philipp Emanuel. Versuch über die wahre Art das Klavier zu spielen. Leipzig, New York, etc.: Breitkopf und Härtel, 1753.

3763. BAFFERT, Jean Marc. Les orgues de Lyon du XVIIe au XVIIIe siècle. Paris: L'orgue, 1974.

3764. BAGGIANI, Franco. L'organo di Azzolino B. Della ciaia nella chiesa conventuale dei Cavalieri di S. Stefano in Pisa. Pisa: Pacini, 1974.

3765. BANCHIERI, Adriano. Conclusioni nel suono dell'organo. Bologna: Heredi di G. Rossi, n. d.

3766. BARNES, W. H. The contemporary American organ. Glen Rock, N. J.: J. Fischer & Brother, 1959 (7th ed.).

3767. ________, and Edward B. Gammons. Two centuries of American organ building. Glen Rock, N. J.: Fischer & Bro., 1970.

3768. BARRETT, Philip. The organs and organists of the Cathedral Church of St. Thomas of Canterbury at Portsmouth. Portsmouth (Hants): Portsmouth City Council, 1968.

3769. BAURIT, Maurice. Orgues et vitraux de Saint-Germain-l'Auxerrois. Paris: L'Auteur, 1964.

3770. BEARD, R. C. Textures in twentieth century organ compositions. A study of selected recital work. New York: Columbia Univ., 1957.

3771. BEDOS DE CELLES, Francois. L'art du facteur d'orgues. Faksimile-Nachdruck (in Zweidrittelgrösse) mit Begleitwort hrsg. von C. Mahrenholtz. Band 1. (Documenta musicologia, Reihe 1, Nr. 24.) Kassel: Bärenreiter, 1963.

3772. BEER, Gisela. Orgelbau Ibach, Barmen, (1794-1904). Köln: A. Volk, 1975.

3773. BEGG, James. The use of organs and other instruments of music in Christian worship indefensible. London: M'Phun & Son, 1866.

3774. BENDER, Antoine. Les orgues Silbermann de Marmoutier et Ebersmünster. Avec la collaboration de Marcel Thomann. With illustrations. Strasbourg: Orgues d'Alsace, 1960.

3775. ________. Les orgues Silbermann de Soultz, Haut-Rhin. (Orgues d'Alsace.) With illustrations. Strasbourg: Editions Europa, 1960.

3776. BENDER, Jan. Organ improvisation for beginners: A book of self-instructions for church musicians. St. Louis: Concordia Publ. House, 1975.

3777. BERNAT, Emile. L'orgue de Saint Guilhem le Désert. Montpellier: Bonniol, 2, rue du Pavillon, 1970.

3778. BESSELAAR, Jan Hermanus. Het orgel in de Groote Kerk te Rotterdam. With plates. Rotterdam: N. G., 1931. (BM-7900. K. 11)

3779. BIASI, Franz. Heldenorgel Kufstein; die 1. grosse Freiorgel der Welt, eine Schilderung ihres Werdens und ihrer Bedeutung. Zusammenstellung unter Benützung der alten Heldenorgelbroschüre. Kufstein: Lippott, 1962.

3780. BIE, Peg Carol. The cavaillé-coll organ at Ste. Clothilde in Paris and the organ compositions of Cesar Franck. Dallas, Tex.: Southern Methodist Univ., M. M., 1956.

3781. BIEHLE, Johannes. Raumakustische, orgeltechnische und bauliturgische Probleme. Leipzig: N. G., 1922. (B640)

3782. BISHOP, C. K. K. Notes on church organs. London: Oxford and Cambridge, 1873.

3783. BLANTON, Joseph. The organ in church design. Albany, Tex.: The Venture Press, 1957.

3784. BLANTON, Joseph. The revival of the organ case. Albany, Tex.: Venture Press, 1965.

3785. BONAVIA-HUNT, Noel A. The church organ. London: The Faith Press, 1920.

3786. ______. The modern British organ. London: Weekes, 1943.

3787. ______. Modern organ stops. London: Musical Opinion, 1923.

3788. ______, and H. W. Lomer. The organ reed. New York: J. Fischer, 1950.

3789. BONER, C. P. "Acoustic spectra of organ pipes." N. G.: F. Acoustic Society of America, July, 1938.

3790. BOSTON, Noel and L. G. Langwill. Church and chamber barrel-organs: their origin, makers, music and location; a chapter in English church music. Edinburgh: Lyndesay Langwill, 1967.

3791. BOUMAN, A. Orgels in Nederland. Amsterdam: Tweede, vermeerderde druk, 1949.

3792. BRAUDO, Isaĭ Aleksandrovich. Ob organnoĭ i klavirnoĭ muzyke. Vstupit. stat'ia i komment. L. Kovnatskoĭ. Leningrad: Muzyke, Leningr. otd-nie, 1976.

3793. BRINER, Andres. Das Musikbild und die Hausorgel im Landgut "Zur Schipf" in Herrliberg-Zürich. With plates. Zürich: Hundertfünfundvierzigstes Neujahrsblatt der Allgemeinen Musikgesellschaft Zürich auf das Jahr, 1961.

3794. BROADHOUSE, John. The organ viewed from within. Chester Springs, Pa.: Dufour Editions, 1925.

3795. BRUNOLD, Paul. Le grand orgue de St. Gervais à Paris. Paris: Editions de l'Oiseau lyre, 1934.

3796. BRUNZEMA, Daniel. Die Gestaltung des Orgelprospektes im friesischen und angrenzenden Nordseeküstengebiet bis 1670 und ihre Bedeutung für die Gegenwart. With plates, including a map. Aurich: Abhandlungen und Vorträge zur Geschichte Ostfrieslands, 1958.

3797. BUCK, D. The influence of the organ in history. (New ed.) London: W. Reeves, 19--.

3798. BURGEMEISTER, Ludwig. Der Orgelbau in Schlesien. Strassburg: Heitz, 1925.

3799. ______. Der Orgelbau in Schlesien. 2. erw. Aufl. bearb. von H. J. Busch, R. Walter, und D. Grossman mit einem Beitrag über den Orgelbau Zwischen den beiden Weltkriegen, von R. Walter. Frankfurt am Main: W. Weidlich, 1973.

3800. BURGESS, Francis. The organ of fifty years hence. London: W. Reeves, 1908.

3801. BUSCH, Hermann J. Die Orgeln des Kreises Siegen. Berlin: Pape, 1974.

3802. BUTLER, Douglas Lamar. The organ works of Felix Mendelssohn-Bartholdy. Ann Arbor: Univ. Microfilms, 1973.

3803. BUXTEHUDE, D. Organ Works. New York: A. Broude Inc., 1965.

3804. CANTAGREL, Gilles and Harry Halbreich. Le livre d'or de l'orgue français. Paris: Calliope-Marval, 1976.

3805. CARLSSOHN, Sten L. Sveriges kyrkorglar. Lund: H. Ohlsson, 1973.

3806. CELLIER, Alexandre. L'orgue modern. Paris: Delagrave, 1913.

3807. ______, et Henri Bachelin. L'orgue. (Ses Eléments, son histoire, son esthétique.) Paris: Delagrave, 1933.

3808. CHURCH Music Association, London, Introduced by James Long. The church organ: Notes on design, specification, and installation. London: St. Martin's Publications, 1964.

3809. CHURCH of England--Organs Advisory Committee. Church organs. London: Church Information Office, 1970.

3810. CLARKE, William H. An outline of the structure of the pipe organ. Indianapolis: W. H. Clarke & Co. and Boston: O. Ditson, 1877.

3811. CLUTTON, Cecil. "The new organ at Doetinchem, Holland." The Organ. Oct. 1954. (B-640)

3812. ______, and George Dixon. The organ. Its tonal structure and registration. London: Greenville Publishing Co., 1950.

3813. ______, and Austin Niland. The British organ. London: B. T. Batsford, 1963.

3814. COMPTON, John, Organ Company. Leaflets and pamphlets on organs built by the company. London: Compton Organ Co., 1951.

3815. CONWAY, M. P. Organ voluntaries. London: Oxford Univ. Press, 1948.

3816. COUPER, Alinda B. Organ loft and belfry. New York: Harold Flammer, Inc., n. d.

3817. CROWHURST, Norman H. Electronic organs. Indianapolis: H. W. Sams, 1975.

3818. DÄHNERT, Ulrich. Der Orgel-und Instrumentenbauer Zacharias Hildebrandt. Sein Verhältnis zu Gottfried Silbermann und Johann Sebastian Bach. Leipzig: Breitkopf und Härtel Musikverlag, 1962.

3819. DE BRISAY, A. C. Delacour. The organ and its music. New York: E. P. Dutton & Co., 1935.

3820. DE FARCY, M. L. Notices archéologiques sur les orgues de la Cathédral d'Angers. Angers: The Cathédral, 1873.

3821. DE PONTECOULANT, A. Organographie. New York: Broude Brothers Limited (facsimile), 1966. (orig. Paris, 1861.)

3822. DICKSON, W. E. "Early organs in Ely Cathedral." The Organ. July, 1921.

3823. ______. Practical organ-building. London: C. Lockwood & Co., 1882.

3824. DIEDERICH, Susanne. Originale Registrieranweisungen in der französischen Orgelmusik des 17. und 18. Jahrhunderts. Beziehungen zwischer Orgelbau und Orgelkomposition im Zeitalter Ludwigs XIV. Kassel, Basel, Tours, London: Bärenreiter, 1975.

3825. DIENEL, O. Die moderne Orgel. Berlin: Hanneman's Buchhandlung., 1903.

3826. DIETRICH, Fritz. Elf Orgelchoräle des siebzehnten Jahrhunderts. Kassel: Bärenreiter-Verlag, 1932.

3827. DONAT, Friedrich Wilhelm. Christian Heinrich Rinck und die Orgelmusik seiner Zeit; ein Beitrag zur Geschichte der deutschen protestantischen Kirchenmusik um 1800. Bad Oehnhausen: Theine & Peitsch, 1933.

3828. DONINGTON, Robert. Tempo and rhythm in Bach's organ music. (School of Bach Playing for the Organist, Vol. 3.) London and New York: Hinrichsen, 1961.

3829. DOUGLAS, Alan Lockhart Monteith. Frequency divider organs for the constructor. London: Sir Isaac Pitman & Sons, 1963.

3830. ______. The electronic musical instrument manual.... Fourth edition. London: Sir Isaac Pitman & Sons, 1962.

3831. ______. "Pipe organ construction." Musical Opinion. May, 1949 (Pp. 362-7); June, 1949 (412-20); July, 1949 (487-98); Aug., 1949 (526-32); Sept., 1949 (560-6); Oct., 1949 (602-10).

3832. DÜCKERING, Heiko and P. H. Gottwald. Die Treutmann-Orgel im Kloster Grauhof: eine Monographie. Tutzing: H. Schneider, 1974.

3833. DUFOURCQ, Norbert. La musique d'orgue française, de Jehan Titelonze à Jehan Alain. Les instruments; les artistes et les oeuvres; les formes et les styles.... 2nd édition (revue et augmentée). Paris: Floury., 1949.

3834. ______. Nicolas Lebègue, 1631-1702, organiste de la Chapelle Royale, organiste de Saint-Merry de Paris. Etude biographique, suivie de nouveaux documents inédits relatifs à l'orgue français au XVIIe siècle. Paris: La Vie musicale en France au siècle de Louis XIV, 1954.

3835. DUPRE, M. Method for the organ. New York: A. Broude Inc., 1965.

3836. EDSON, Jean Slater. Organ-preludes. Metuchen, N.J.: Scarecrow Press, 1970.

3837. ______. Organ-preludes; an index to compositions on hymntunes, chorales, plainsong melodies, Gregorian tunes and carols. (Supplement.) Metuchen, N.J.: Scarecrow Press, 1974.

3838. EDWARDS, C. A. Organs and organ building. London: "The Bazaar" office, 1881.

3839. EHMANN, Wilhelm. Erziehung zur Kirchenmusik. Gütersloh: Rufer-Verlag, 1951.

3840. EHRENHOFER, Walther Edmund. Taschenbuch der Orgelbau-Revisors. Graz und Wien: Verlags buchhandlung "Styria.", 1909.

3841. EINWEIHUNG der neuen Orgel im Dom St. Blasii, Braunschweig 1962. Braunschweig: Zu beziehen-Westermann: Wolfenbüttel: Landes Kirchamt, 1962.

3842. ELLISTON, Thomas. Organs and tuning. London: Weekes & Co., 1898.

3843. ELVIN, Laurence. Forster and Andrews: Their barrel, chamber and small church organs. Foreword by P. Marshall. Lincoln: The Author, 1976.

3844. ______. Organ blowing: Its history and development. Lincoln, England: The Author, 1971.

3845. EMMERSON, John Michael. Four organs; being the history of the organs in the Churches of Holy Trinity and St. Peter, Hersham. Walton-on-Thames: J. M. Emmerson, 1968.

3846. ETHERINGTON, Charles L. The organist and choirmaster. New York: Macmillan, 1952.

3847. FANSELAU, Rainer. Die Orgel in Werk Edward Elgars. Kassel: Bärenreiter-Antiquariat, 1973.

3848. FARLEY, Charles (ed.). The organ concerti of George Frideric Handel. Ann Arbor: Univ. Microfilms, Univ. of Denver, diss., 1962.

3849. FAULKNER, Thomas. Designs for organs. 3rd ed. London: Printed and published by the author, 1838.

3850. FAUST, Oliver C. A treatise on the construction, repairing, and tuning of the organ. Boston: 1949, printed for the author 1905, rev. 1935.

3851. FELIX, Jean Pierre. Histoire des orgues de l'Eglise du Grand béguinage à Bruxelles. Bruxelles: Félix, 1976.

3852. ______. Histoire des orgues de l'Eglise St. Pierre à Uccle (XVIe-XX[e]s). Bruxelles: J. P. Félix, 1975.

3853. ______. Inventaire descriptif des archives du facteur d'orgues Emile Kerkhoff au Musée royal instrumental de musique à Bruxelles par J. P. Félix. Bruxelles: Félix, 1975.

3854. FELLERER, Karl Gustav. Beiträge zur Choralbegleitung und Choralverarbeitung in der Orgelmusik des ausgehenden 18. und beginneden 19. Jahrhunderts. Mit einer Musiknotenbeilage. Strassburg: Heitz & Co., 1932.

3855. FELLOWES, Edmund H. Organists and masters of the choristers of St. George's Chapel in Windsor Castle. London: S.P.C.K., 1939.

3856. FESPERMAN, John. The organ as musical medium. New York: Coleman-Ross Co., 1962.

3857. ______. Two essays on organ design. Raleigh, N.C.: Sunbury Press, 1975.

3858. FISCHER, Hermann and Theodor Wohnhaas. Süddeutsche Orgeln aus der Zeit vor 1900. Frankfurt am Main: Verlag das Musikinstrument, 1973.

3859. FLADE, Ernest. Der orgelbauer Gottfried Silbermann. Leipzig: K. Kistner & C. F. W. Siegel, 1926.

3860. FORER, Alois. Orgeln in Österreich. Wien; München: Schroll, 1973.

3861. FREEMAN, Andrew. Church organs and organ cases. London: S. P. C. K., 1942.

3862. ______. "Father Smith: Organ maker and master craftsman." The Organ. Jan., 1926, p. 129.

3863. ______. "The Father Smith organs at Cambridge." The Organ. Apr., 1922, p. 163.

3864. ______. "The organs of all hallows barking." The Organ. July, 1928, p. 91.

3865. FRESCOBALDI, G. Collected organ and keyboard works. New York: A. Broude Inc., 1965.

3866. FRIIS, Niels. Buxtehude. Hans by og hans Orgel. Helsinger Sct. Morce Kirkes Orgelhistorie i tre Aarhundre. With German and English summaries. Helsinger: N. G., 1960. (BM10060. f. 31)

3867. ______. Orgelbygning i Danmark: Renaesance og rokoko. (2nd ed.). Copenhagen: Dan Fog, 1971.

3868. ______. Trefaldighetskyrkoms orgel, Kristianstad, 1619-1961. With illustrations. Kristianstad: N. G., 1961. (BM7903. f. 24)

3869. ______. Viborg Domkirkes orgel 1570-1966. Viborg: Centralbiblioteket, 1967.

3870. GAGNEBIN, Henri. Orgue; musett et bourdon: souvenirs d'un musicien. Neuchâtel: Editions de la Baconnière 1975.

3871. GEER, E. H. Organ registration. Glen Rock, N. J.: J. Fischer and Brother, 1957.

3872. GELLERMAN, Robert F. The American reed-organ; its history, how it works, how to rebuild it. Vestal, N. Y.: Vestal Press, 1973.

3873. GLAUBENSGEMEINDE, Ugrino. Kleine Veröffentlichungen der Glaubensgemeinde. Klecken: Ugrino Abteilung Verlag, 1922.

3874. GÖBEL, Werner and Konrad Krieschen. Die Orgeln von St. Marien zu Danzig. Danzig: A. W. Kafemann, 1939.

3875. GOODE, Jack. Pipe organ registration. New York City: Abingdon Press, 1964.

3876. GOODELL, J. D. and E. Swedien. "Design of a pipeless organ." Electronics. Aug., 1949, p. 92.

3877. GOODRICH, Wallace. The organ in France. Boston: Boston Music Co., 1917.

3878. GOTTRON, Adam. Arnold Rucker, Orgelmacher von Seligenstadt. Mainz: Arbeitsgemeinschaft für mittelrheinische Musikgeschichte, 1962.

3879. GRANDES orgues de la cathédrale de Sées, Les. Alençon: Imprime alençonnaise, 1972.

3880. HAACKE, Walter. Die Entwicklungsgeschichte des Orgelbaus im Lande Mecklenburg-Schwerin von den Anfängen bis ins ausgehende 18. Jahrhundert. Wolfenbüttel, Berlin: N. G., 1935. (BM 7890. cc45)

3881. ______. Organs of the world. London: Allen & Unwin, 1966.

3882. HAARLEM, Tentoonstelling Nederlandse Orgelpracht. Catalogus der tentoonstelling Nederlandse Orgelpracht, 3-30 juli 1961 te Haarlem. Samengesteld en ingericht door; H. P. Baard, etc. In: Obermayr (J. F.) Nederlandse orgelpracht, 1961.

3883. HARDOVIN, Piérre. Le grand orgue de Notre Dame de Paris. Tours: Bärenreiter, 1973.

3884. HAVINGHA, Gerhardus. Oorsprong en Voortgang der Orgelen. Hilversum, Netherlands: Frits Knuf--Reprint, n. d. (orig. Alkmaar: Jan van Beyeren, 1727.)

3885. ______. Oorsprong en Voortgang der Orgelen. New York: Broude Brothers Limited (Facsimile), 1966. (orig. Alkmaar: Jan van Beyeren, 1727.)

3886. HAYCRAFT, Frank W. The organs of Bath and district. Bath: The Ralph Allen Press, 1932.

3887. HERRENSCHWAND, Franz. "The Bossard family, organ builders of Baar, and the organ in the former Abbey Church at St. Urban." Organ Institute Quarterly. Spring 1954. P. 24.

3888. HESS, Joachim. Dispositien der merkwaardigste Kerk-Orgelen. Hilversum, Netherlands: Frits Knuf--Reprint, n. d. (orig. Gouda, J. vander Klos, 1774.)

3889. _______. Dispositien der merkwaardigste Kerk-Orgelen, welke in de zeven Vereënigde Provincien als mede in Duytsland en Elders aangetroffen worden. New York: Broude Brothers Limited (Facsimile), 1966. (orig. Gouda 1774.)

3890. _______. Luister van het orgel. Buren and Hilversum, Netherlands: Frits Knuf--Reprint, 1976. (orig. Gouda: J. vander Klos, 1772.)

3891. _______. Luister van het orgel. New York: Broude Brothers Limited (Facsimile), 1966. (orig. Gouda: J. vander Klos, 1772.)

3892. HEURN, Johan van. De orgelmaaker. 3 vols. (Repr. -- Bibliotheca organologica, 56. Dordrecht: A. Blussé, 1804.) Arnheim: Gijsbers & Van Loon, 1976.

3893. HILL, Arthur George. The organ-cases and organs of the Middle-ages and the Renaissance. Hilversum, Netherlands: Frits Knuf-Reprint, 1966. (Orig. London, 1883-91.)

3894. _______. Vierzig Orgelgehäuse--Zeichnungen. Berlin: Merseburger, 1964.

3895. HOPKINS, Edward J. The English medieval church organ. Exeter: N.G., 1888. (BM)

3896. _______, and Edward F. Rimbault. The organ, its history and construction. A comprehensive treatise on the structure and capabilities of the organ with specifications and suggestive details for instruments of all sizes. New York: Broude Brothers Limited (Facsimile), 1966. (orig. London 1877.)

3897. HORNER, B. W. Organ pedal technique. London: Novello's Music Primers, 1895.

3898. HULL, A. Eaglefield. Bach's organ works. London: Office of "Musical Opinion," 1922.

3899. HUNT, Noel Aubrey B. Church organ: an introduction to the study of modern organ-building. London: W. Reeves, 1967.

3900. HUYGENS, Constantin. Heer van Zuilichem. Gebruych of ongebruych van t'orgel in de kercken der Vereenighde Nederlanden. Amsterdam: Noord Hollandsche Uitg. Mij., 1974.

3901. I Cataloghi originali degli organi fabricati da: Serassi di Bergamo (1816). G. B. Castelli: catalogo degli organi da chiesa dei fratelli Serassi (1858). Ristampa anastatica con appendici, postilla e indici. A cura di O. Mischiati. Bologna: Pàtron, 1975.

3902. IRWIN, Stevens. Dictionary of Hammond-Organ stops. Completely revised edition, etc. New York: G. Schirmer, 1952. (also 1961, 3rd ed.)

3903. _______. Dictionary of pipe organ stops. Detailed descriptions of more than 600 stops, together with definitions of many other terms connected with the organ, etc. New York: G. Schirmer, 1962.

3904. JÄGER, Eberhard. Die orgeln des ehemaligen Kreises Springe: ein Beitrag zur Geschichte vom Wandel des Klangideals. Und e. Anhang-Die Glocken des ehemaligen Kreises Springe. Berlin: Pape, 1975.

3905. JAKOB, Friedrich. Die Orgel als Gift und Heilmittel. Männedorf: T. Kuhn, 1973.

3906. _______. Die Orgel und der Blinde. Männedorf: T. Kuhn, 1973.

3907. _______. Die Orgel und ihre Namen. Männedorf: Orgelbau Th. Kuhn, 1974.

3908. _______. Der Orgelbauer, der Zinnpfeifen-macher: ein Berufsbild. Zürich: Gesellschaft Schweizerischer Orgelbaufirmen, 1975.

3909. JAMISON, J. B. Organ design and appraisal. New York: H. W. Gray, 1959.

3910. JOHNS, David Otto. The organ-reform movement. Ann Arbor: Univ. Microfilms, 1969.

3911. JOHNSON, David N. Method: an instruction book for beginners in organ. St. Olaf, Minn.: The Author, College Organist, St. Olaf College, 1962.

3912. JOINT Commission of the Protestant Episcopal Church in the United States. A prelude to the purchase of a church organ. Philadelphia: Fortress Press, 1964.

3913. JONES, Agnes Louise. A pedagogical study of the function of the organ in the Catholic liturgy. Rochester, N.Y.: Eastman School of Music, Univ. of Rochester, M.A., 1951.

3914. JUSTER, F. Orgues électroniques ultramodernes. Paris: Editions techniques et Scientifiques françaises, 1975.

3915. KARG-ELERT, Sigfrid. Karg-Elert festival. A series of ten organ recitals at St. Lawrence Jewry (London) May 5th to 17th, 1930. Wimbledon: E. Trim & Co., 1930.

3916. KAUFMANN, Walter. Die Orgeln des alten Herzogtums Oldenburg. "Nordoldenburgische Orgeltopographie." Oldenburg, Oldb.: Oldenburg Forschungen. Hft. 15, 1962.

3917. KELLER, H. The organ works of Bach. New York: C. F. Peters, 1967.

3918. KEMMELMEIER, Karl-Jürgen. Die gedruckten Orgelwerke Olivier Messiaens bis zum "Verset pour la fête de la dédicase." (2 vols.) Regensburg: G. Bosse, 1974.

3919. KESSLER, Franz. Neue Bestrebungen auf dem Gebiete des Orgelchorals. N. P. David, J. N., H. Distler, E. Pepping. (195-). (LC-M1647. k4)

3920. KINKELDEY, Otto. The organ and clavier in the music of the 16th century. New York: Dover Publishing, Inc., n. d.

3921. ______. Orgel und Klavier in der Musik des 16. Jahrhunderts. Leipzig: Breitkopf und Härtel, 1910. (Reprint--New York: Dover Publ., 1910, also [Neudr.]--Hildesheim: Georg Olms, 1967.)

3922. KITTLER, G. Geschichte des protestantischen Orgelchorals von seinen Anfängen bis zu den Lüneburger Orgeltabulaturbüchern. Äckermünde: W. Heyer, 1931.

3923. KLAIS, Hans Gerd. Überlegungen zur Orgeldisposition: Theorie und Praxis aus d. Orgel-Werkstatt. Frankfurt am Main: Verlag Das Musikinstrument, 1973.

3924. ______. Die Würzburger Domorgel. Frankfurt: Das Musikinstrument, 1970.

3925. KLOTZ, Hans. Das Buch von der Orgel. 7th ed. Kassel-Wilhelmshöhe: Bärenreiter Verlag, Karl Vötterle K. G., 1965.

3926. ______. The organ handbuch. (Transl. by Gerhard Krapf.) St. Louis and London: Concordia Publ. House, 1969.

3927. ______. Über die Orgelkunst der Gotik, der Renaissance und des Barock. Kassel: Bärenreiter-verlag, 1934. (Neudr. 1975.)

3928. KNAPP, Willem Hendrik Christiaan. Het orgel. Amsterdam: G. J. A. Ruys, 1952. (BM-7901 c. 5)

3929. KNOCK, Nicolaas Arnoldi. Dispositien der merkwaardigste kerkorgelen, welken in de provincie Friesland. Sneek: Boeijanga, 1968.

3930. KOCH, C. Organ student's Gradus ad Parnassum, The. Glen Rock, N. J.: J. Fischer & Brother, 1945.

3931. KRUIJS, Marius Hendrik Van't. Verzameling van disposities der verschillende orgels in Nederland, benevens een korte beschrijving van het orgel in de Groote Kerk te Rotterdam. Geheel bijgewerkte tweede druk. Amsterdam: F. A. M. Knuf, 1962. (BM-07903. s. 11)

3932. KUHNEMUND, Hans und Hans Eule. Sechshundert Jahre Orgelgeschichte im Dom zu Halberstadt. Halberstadt: Domgemeindekirchenrat, 1965.

3933. LAHEE, Henry Charles. The organ and its masters. Portland, Me.: Longwood Press, 1976. (Reprint--Boston: L. C. Page, 1903 and 1927.)

3934. LEWIS, W. and T. Lewis. Modern organ building. London: W. Reeves, 1956.

3935. LIBERA, Sandro Dalla. L'arte degli organi a Venezia. With plates. Venezia: Istituto per la collaborazione cultural, 1962.

3936. LIEBENOW, Walther. A bibliography of the history and construction of organs. Minneapolis: Martin Press, 1973.

3937. LIEMOHN, Edwin. Organ and choir in protestant worship. Philadelphia: Fortress Press, 1968.

3938. LOCHER, Carl. Dictionary of the organ. London: K. Paul, Trench, Trubner & Co., ltd., also New York: E. P. Dutton & Co., 1914.

3939. ______. Die Orgel-Register und ihre Klangfarben. Hilversum, Netherlands: Frits Knuf--Reprint, n. d. (orig. Bern 1912, 5th ed.)

3940. ______. Die Orgel-Register und ihre Klangfarben. New York: Broude Brothers Limited (Facsimile), 1966. (orig. Bern: 1912, 5th ed.)

3941. LOHMANN, Heinz. Handbuch der Orgelliteratur. Wiesbaden: Breitkopf und Härtel, 1975.

3942. LONDON, Yearbook, 1963-1964. London: Royal College of Organists, 1964.

3943. LOVETT, Sydney Harry. The use of small church organs. Church Music Society Occasional Paper. no. 20. London: Oxford Univ. Press, 1952.

3944. LUTHERAN Church in America, Commission on Worship. A prelude to the purchase of a church organ. Philadelphia: Fortress Press, 1964.

3945. MAAG, Max. Ein Tor geht auf im Orgelbau; Orientierung über dem Maag-System. Zürich: Altstetten, Genossenschaft Hobel, 1958.

3946. MARENHOLZ, Christhard. The calculation of organ pipe scales from the Middle Ages to the mid-nineteenth century. Trans. by A. H. Williams. Original title--"Die Berechnung der Orgelpfeifen--Mensuren vom Mittlealter bis zur Mitte des 19. Jahrhunderts." Oxford: Positif Press, 1975.

3947. MARTINI, Ulrich. Die Orgeldispositionssammlungen bis zur Mitte des 19. Jahrhunderts. Kassel: Bärenreiter, 1975.

3948. MATTHEWS, Betty. The organs and organists of Winchester Cathedral. Hants, England: Friends of Winchester Cathedral, 1966.

3949. MATTHEWS, John. A handbook of the organ. London: Augener, Ltd., n. d.

3950. MAURER, Karl. Die Orgelwerke der Lauterbacher Stadtkirche und ihre Spieler. Lauterbach und Hessen: Hohausmuseum, 1969.

3951. MEREDITH, Maudell Dukeminier. Organ music in America since 1900. Waco, Tex.: Baylor Univ., M. M., 1956.

3952. MEYER-SIAT, Paul. Die Callinet-Orgel zu Masevaux. Mulhouse: Impr. L'Alsace, 1962.

3953. ________. Les Orgues Callinet de Masevaux. Masevaux: Les Amis de Houppach, 1962.

3954. MEYRICK-ROBERTS, R. The organ at Liverpool Cathedral. London: Office of "Musical Opinion"., 1926.

3955. MINSHALL, E. Organs, organists, and choirs. London: N. G., 1887. (BM)

3956. MISCHIATI, Oscar. L'organo della Chiesa del Carmine di Lugo di Romagna. Bologna: Casa Editrice Prof. Riccardo Patron, 1968.

3957. MOEHLMAN, Carl B., Jr. A comparative analysis of the Orgelbuchlein by J. S. Bach and Choral-vorspiele für Orgel by Max Reger. Denton, Tex.: North Texas State Univ., M. M., 1963.

3958. MOORE, W. T. A study of the organ chorale prelude, 1624-1750, through analysis of representative works. New York: Columbia Univ., 1959.

3959. MOORTGAT, Gabriël. Oude orgels in Flaanderen. Antwerpen: Belgische Radio en Televisie, 196-.

3960. MORETTI, Corrado. L'organo italiano, 2nd ed. Milano: Eco, 1973.

3961. MOSCOW. Organy bolshoi zalui Moskovskoi Konservatorii. Moscow: N. G., 1904. (BM)

3962. MUELLER, John H. and Margaret Mueller. A selected list of organ works based on chorales. Winston-Salem, N. C.: N. G., 1966.

3963. MUENGER, Fritz. Protestantische Choräle und choralgebundene Orgelmuskik. Alphbetisches Choral-Verzeichnis mit Literaturangabe von Orgelsätzen. Zürich: "Der Organist," 1938.

3964. ________. Schweizer Orgeln von der Gotik bis zur Gegenwart. Ein Bildband, etc. Bern: Krompholz, 1961.

3965. ________. Schweitzer Orgeln von der Gotik zur Gegenwart. (Ein Bildband. 2., erw. Aufl.) Bern: Krompholz, 1973.

3966. NADLER, H. Die Orgeln von St. Stephan in Lindau, 1506 bis 1975. Lindau: Museumsverein Lindau, 1975.

3967. NARDONE, Thomas R. Organ music in print. 1st ed. (Music-in-print series. 3.) Philadelphia: Musicdata, 1975.

3968. Die NEUE Orgel in der Stadtkirche Aarau (Hrsg. von der Orgelbaukommission). Aarau: Orgelbaukommission der Stadtkirche Aarau, 1962.

3969. OBERMAYR, J. F. Nederlandse orgelpracht. Articles by various authors, together with the catalogue of the exhibition "Nederlandse Orgelpracht" at Haarlem. Haarlem: Commissie van redactie J. F. Obermayr, 1961.

3970. OCHSE, Orpha Caroline. The history of the organ in the United States. Bloomington, Ind.: Ind. Univ. Press, 1975.

3971. ORGAN Builders Manual 5th edition. Altadena, Cal.: Electronic Organ Arts, Los Angeles, Cal.: Artisan Organs, 1963.

3972. ORGAN hymn-tunes. Winona Lake: Rodeheaver Hall-Mack Co., 1965.

3973. ORGAN music based on gregorian chant themes. Boston: Mass.: McLaughlin & Reilly Co., n. d.

3974. The ORGANIST and the congregation. Lectures and sermon delivered at the first Conference of Congregational Organists, held at Mansfield College, Oxford, June 22, 23, and 24, 1951. London: Independent Press, 1952.

3975. ORGEL im Gottesdienst heute. Bericht über d. 3. Colloquium d. Walcker-Stiftung für Orgelwiss. Forschung. 13-15 Januar 1974. in Sinzig/Rhein. Hrsg. von H. H. Eggebrecht. Stuttgart: Musikwissenschaftliche Verlags-Gesellschaft, 1975.

3976. ORGELN der Willibrordikirche von Heinz Kirch, Die. Wesel: Willibrordi-dombauverein, 1972.

3977. ORGELWEIHE in der Epiphaniaskirche zu mannheim-Freudenheim. Mannheim: Waldkirch, 1966.

3978. PAGE, A. On organ playing. Hints to young organist. London: N. G., 1899. (BM)

3979. PAPE, Uwe. Die Orgel der Klosterkirche in Riddagshausen. Braunschweig (Am Tafelacker 6): U. Pape, 1962.

3980. _______. Die Orgeln der Stadt Wolfenbüttel. Berlin: U. Pape, 1973.

3981. _______. Orgelatlas. Heft 1: Die Orgeln des Kreises Peine. Braunschweig (Am Tafelacker 6): U. Pape, 1962.

3982. PEETERS, Flor. Ars Organi. (in 3 vol.) New York: C. F. Peters Corporation, 1967.

3983. _______, and Maarten Albert Vente. The organ and its music in the Netherlands 1500-1800. Antwerp: Mercatorfonds, 1971.

3984. PEINE, Theodor. Der Orgelbau in Frankfurt am Main und Umgebung von den Aufängen bis zur Gegenwart. With plates and illustrations. Frankfurt a. M.: N. G., 1956. (BM-07903. dd. 13)

3985. PERKINS, J. The organs and bells of Westminister Abbey. London: Novello and Co., 1937.

3986. PERROT, Jean. The organ, from its invention in the Hellenistic period to the end of the thirteenth century. London, New York: Oxford Univ. Press, 1971.

3987. PHILLIPS, Charles Henry. Modern organ pedalling ... with ... an editorial note by Leonard Blake. With musical illustrations. London: Oxford Univ. Press, 1951.

3988. PHILLIPS, Gordon. Articulation in organ-playing. The music text consisting of 31 chorale preludes and chorales by Bach, forming a Little Organ Book for Manuals only. With a foreward by Robert Donington. New York: Edition Peters, 1962.

3989. POLLARD, Howard F. The tonal design of organs (2nd part). Sydney, Australia: Organ Institute of New South Wales, 1972.

3990. PONS, Christian. Orgue: un joyau à découvrir, avec comme sujet l'orgue Notre-Dame de la Platé, Castres. Castres, France: Edition des amis de l'orgue et de la musique, 1976.

3991. PRICK von WELY, Max Arthur. Het orgel en zijn meesters. 3. geheel herz. druk. Den Haag: Kruseman, 1976.

3992. QUOIKA, Rudolf. Altösterreichische Hornwerke. Ein Beitrage zur Frühgeschichte der Orgelbaukunst. With illustrations. Berlin: N. G., 1959. (BM)

3993. ______. Vom Blockwerk zur Registerorgel. Kassel & Basel: Barenreiter, 1966.

3994. RADEKER, Johannes. Korte beschryving van het beroemde en prachtige orgel in de Groote of St. Bavoos-kerk te Haerlem. Opnieuw uitg. door. Herman S. J. Zandt, (Includes reprint, 1775 ed.) Amsterdam: F. Knuf, 1974.

3995. RAUGEL, Félix. Les grandes orgues des églises de Paris et du Departement de la Seine. Paris: Fischbacher, 1927.

3996. ______. Les organistes ... deuxième édition revue et complétée. With plates. Part of the series "Les Musiciens célèbres." Paris: H. Laurens, 1962.

3997. ______. Les orgue et les organistes de la Cathédrale de Strasbourg. Colmar: Editions Alsatia, 1948.

3998. REHM, Gottfried. Die Orgeln des ehemaligen Kreises Schlüchtern, mit Ergänzungen zu den Bänden Kreis Hünfeld, Landkreis Fulda, Stadt Fulda. Berlin: U. Pape, 1975.

3999. REITSCHEL, Georg. Die Aufgabe der Orgel im Gottesdienste bis in das achtzehnte Jahrhundert. Leipzig: Program-Univ. Leipzig, 1892.

4000. RHOADS, Larry Lynn. Themes and variations in twentieth century organ literature. Ann Arbor: Univ. Microfilms, Ohio State Diss., 1973.

4001. RIELANDER, Michael. Die elektronische Orgel. Frankfurt am Main: Verlag das Musikinstrument, 1975.

4002. RIMBAULT, Edward Francis. The early English organ builders and their works from the 15th century to the great Rebellion. New York: AMS Press, 1976. (orig. London: R. Cocks, 1865.)

4003. RIPON. Programmes of the organ. Re-opening recitals on Thursday, June 15th, Thursday, June 29th, and Thursday, July 20th, 1950. etc. Ripon: Cathedral Church, 1950.

4004. RITTER, August Gottfried. Zur Geschichte des Orgelspiels. Hildesheim, Germany: Georg Olms-Reprint, 1969. (orig. Leipzig: M. Hesse, 1884.)

4005. ROUNTREE, John Pickering, and John F. Brennan. The classical organ in Britain, 1955-1974. Oxford: Positif Press, 1975.

4006. ROUTH, Francis. Early English organ music from the Middle Ages to 1837. New York: Barnes and Noble, 1973.

4007. ROWELL, Lois. American organ music on records. Braintree, Mass.: Organ Literature Foundation, 1976.

4008. RUNT, E. van and J. P. H. van der Knaap. Het oude orgel in de Nieuwe Kapel te Hoorne. Het Künkelorgel van 1784. Hoorn, Nederlands: Edecea, 1973.

4009. RUPP, Ursula. Die Orgel in der Stadtkirche zu Lauterbach (Lauterbacher Sammlungen, 37.) Lauterbach/Hessen: Hohhausmuseum, Bibliothek, 1963.

4010. SABATIER, François. Les aventures du grand orgue de Notre Dame de Paris au XIXe siècle. Paris: L'Orgue, 1974.

4011. SACHS, Klaus-Jurgen. Mensura fistularum: Die Mensurierung der Orgelpfeifen im Mittelalter, Teil 1: Edition der Texte. Stuttgart: Musikwissenschaftliche Verlags-Gesellschaft MBH, 1970.

4012. SACRED songs for organ. Winona Lake: Rodeheaver Hall-Mack Co., 1965.

4013. SCEATS, Godfrey. The liturgical use of the organ. London: Office of "Musical Opinion," 1922.

4014. SCHAEFER, Marc. Les orgues Stiehr-Mockers de Riquewihr. With illustrations. Orgues d'Alsace no. 3. Strasbourg: Editions Européa, 1961.

4015. SCHÄFER, Johannes. Osteroder Orgelchronik; Geschichte der Orgelwerke in Osterode am Harz. (Osteroder Kirchengeschichtliche Nachrichten, 2.) Osterode und Harz (Schlossplatz 5): Superintendentur, 1961.

4016. SCHLATTER, Viktor. Die Orgel im Grossmünster Zürich. Zürich (Oberdorfstrasse 27): Kirchengutsverwaltung Grossmünster, 1962.

4017. SCHLEPPHORST, Winfried. Die Orgelbau im westlichen Niedersachsen. (vol. 1) Kassel: Bärenreiter, 1975.

4018. SCHLICK, Arnol. Spiegel der Orgelmacher und Organisten allen Stiften und Kirchen (1511). Facsimile, Mainz: P. Smet, 1932.

4019. SCHLIMBACH, Georg Christian Friedrich. Über die Structur, Erhaltung, Stimmung, Prufung etc. der Orgel. Hilversum: Frits Knuf, 1966. (reprint of the orig. edition, Leipzig, 1801.)

4020. ______. Über die Structur, Erhaltung, Stimmung, Prufung u. der Orgel. Leipzig: Breitkopf u. Härtel, 1801.

4021. ______. Über die Structur, Erhaltung, Stimmung, Prufung etc. der Orgel. New York: Broude Brothers Limited (Facsimile), 1966. (orig. Leipzig, 1801.)

4022. SCHOLA Cantorum, Bureau de la. Pièces d'orgue et d'harmonium. Paris: Editions musicales de la Schola Cantorum, 1927.

4023. SCHOUTEN, Hennie. Improvisation on the organ. London: W. Paxton & Co., and New York: Mills Music Co., 1963.

4024. ______. Improviseren op het orgel (2e, herz. en uitgebreide durk). Amsterdam: A. J. G. Strengholt, 1962.

4025. ______. Techniek van het orgelspel. Naarden: Strengholt, 1972.

4026. SCHUMANN, Otto. Quellen und Forschungen zur Geschichte des Orgelbaues im Herzogtum Schleswig vor 1800. München: Musikverlag Katzbichler, 1973.

4027. SCHWARZ, Peter. Studien zur Orgelmusik Franz Liszts. München: Musikverlag Katzbichler, 1973.

4028. SEIDEL, J. J. Die Orgel und ihr Bau. Ein systematisches handbuch. New York: Broude Brothers Limited (Facsimile), 1962. (orig. 1843.)

4029. SEIJBEL, Maarten. Zes eeuwen Veluwse orgels. Zaltbommel, Nederlands: Europese Bibliotheek, 1975.

4030. SIEBERT, F. Mark. Liturgical organ music in the 15th century. New York: Columbia Univ., 1961.

4031. SKUPNIK, Reinhard. Der Hannoversche Orgelbauer Christian Vater, 1679-1756. Kassel: Barenreiter, 1976.

4032. SMITH, William Joseph Thomas. The organ and organists. Chemsford, England: The Author, 1975.

4033. SNOW, Francis W. First principles of organ playing; a concise-practical-graduated course of study for the modern organ: organ technique, style, co-ordination of the hands and feet. New York: R. D. Row Music Co., 1963.

4034. SOUTHERN, Eileen. The Buxheim organ book. Brooklyn, N.Y.: Institute of Mediaeval Music, 1963.

4035. STEGALL, Ruth Ellen. Organ composition on the motive B-A-C-H. Denton, Tex.: North Texas State Univ., M.M., 1965.

4036. STIVEN, Frederic B. In the organ lofts of Paris. Boston: The Stratford Co., 1923.

4037. STROUD, William Paul. A prelude to the purchase of a church organ. Nashville, Tenn.: Cokesbury, n.d.

4038. STÜVEN, Wilfried. Orgel und Orgelbauer im halleschen Land vor 1800. Wiesbaden: Breitkopf & Härtel, 1964.

4039. SULZMANN, Bernd. Die Orgelbauerfamilie Martin in Waldkirch im Breslau. Wiesbaden: Breitkopf und Härtel, 1975.

4040. SUMNER, William Leslie. Bach's organ-registration (School of Bach-playing for the organist, 2). London and New York: Hinrichsen Edition, 1961.

4041. ________. A history and account of the organs of St. Paul's Cathedral. London: Office of "Musical Opinion," 1931.

4042. ________. The organ. Its evolution, principles of construction and use. London: Macdonald, 1952; 2nd edition, 1958; 3rd ed., 1964; 4th ed., 1973.

4043. ________. The organ, its evolution, principles of construction and use. (Reprint.) St. Clair Shores, Mich.: Scholarly Press, 1976.

4044. ________. The parish church organ. Croydon, England: Royal School of Church Music, 1963.

4045. SWANSON, Jean Phyllis. The use of the organ in the church of England (1600-1800). Ann Arbor: Univ. Microfilms, 1969.

4046. TACHEZI, Herbert. Ludus organi contemporarii; eine Einführung in das Spiel zeitgenossicher Orgelmusik. Wien: Dohlinger, 1973.

4047. TAYLOR, Bernard. The priory organ. An appreciation of a masterpiece of Victorian craftsmanship with some account of the life and work of its maker. London: St. Dominic's Priory, 1962.

4048. THIEL, Jörn. Die Orgel; Königin der Instrumenten. Frankfurt am Main: Verlag Das Musikinstrument, 1973.

4049. THIMAN, Eric. Varied harmonizations of favorite hymn tunes for organ. New York: H. W. Gray, 1934, and London: Oxford Univ. Press, 1934.

4050. TREVOR, Caleb H. A concise school of fugal playing for organ. London: Oxford Univ. Press, 1964.

4051. TRUETTE, Everett E. Organ registration. St. Clair Shores, Mich.: Scholarly Press, 1972.

4052. TÜRK, Daniel Gottlob. Von den wichtigsten Pflichten eines Organisten. Hilversum, Netherlands: Frits Knuf-Reprint, 1966. (orig. Halle, 1787.)

4053. ________. Von den wichtigsten Pflichten eines Organisten. Ein Beytrag zur Verbesserung der musikalische Liturgie. New York: Broude Brothers Limited (Facsimile), 1966. (orig. 1787.)

4054. TUSLER, Robert L. The style of J. S. Bach's Choral Preludes. New York: Da Capo Press, 1968.

4055. UNGELENK, Manfred. Geschichte der Silbermannorgel von Schloss Burgk. With illustrations. Schleiz: N. G., 1958.

4056. VANMACKELBERG, Maurice. Les orgues de Tourneheim. Paris: L'orgue, 1973.

4057. VAN'T KRUYS, M. H. Verzemeling van dispositics der verschillende orgels in Nederland. New York: Broude Brothers Limited (Facsimile), 1962. (orig. 1885.)

4058. VENTE, Maarten Albert. Bouwstoffen tot de Geschiedenis van het Nederlandse Orgel in de 16de eeuw. Amsterdam: N. G., 1942.

4059. ________. Die brabanter Orgel, etc. With plates. Amsterdam: Zweite Auflage, 1963.

4060. ________. "Organs in Spain and Portugal." The Organ. Apr., 1955, p. 193; Oct., 1955, p. 57; Jan., 1956, p. 136 et seq.

4061. VIDAL, Pierre. Bach et machine-orgue. Fontenay-sous-Bois, France: Stil, 1973.

4062. VITASSE, Henri. Le grandes orgues de la Cathédrale d'Amiens. Amiens: N. G., 1890.

4063. VOSS, Otto. Die sachsische Orgelmusik in der zweiten Hälfte des 17. Jahrhunderts. Jena: Universitäts-Buchdruckerei G. Neuenhahn, 1936.

4064. WALTER, Joseph and Jean Roubier. La cathédrale de Strasbourg. Paris: N. G., 1939.

4065. WELLS, Cathedral Church. A short history of the organs of Wells Cathedral. By L. S. C. With plates. Wells: N. G., 1951. (BM7900. S. 8924)

4066. WERCKMEISTER, Andreas. Werckmeister's erweiterte und verbesserte Orgel-Probe in English. Trans. by G. Krapf. Raleigh, N. C.: Sunbury Press, 1976.

4067. WESTERBY, Herbert. The complete organ recitalist. New York: H. W. Gray Co., 1927.

4068. ______. International repertoire guide. New York: H. W. Gray Co., 1933.

4069. WHITMER, T. Carl. The art of improvisation. New York: M. Witmark and Sons, 1934.

4070. WHITWORTH, Reginald. The electric organ. London: Musical Opinion, 1930.

4071. ______. "Manchester Cathedral organs of yesterday." The American Organist. Jan. 1945, p. 9.

4072. ______. Organ stops and their use. London: Sir Isaac Pitman & Sons, 1951.

4073. WILLIAMS, Alfred. Favorite registrations for the Wurlitzer organ, model 4100 series. With Song-dex "Chordmaster" and "Organmaster Guide." New York: Song-Dex, 1960.

4074. WISMEYER, Heinrich. Geschichte um die Orgel. Illus. Paul E. Rattelmüller. Altötting: Coppenrath, 1972.

4075. WOLFRAM, J. C. Anleitung zur Kenntnis, Beurtheilung und Erhaltung der Orgeln. New York: Broude Brothers Limited (Facsimile), 1962. (orig. Amsterdam: Knuf, 1815.)

4076. WYATT, Geoffrey. At the mighty organ. Oxford & Vestal, N. Y.: Oxford Illustrated Press and Vestal Press, 1974.

4077. YOUNG, Clawson. Sixteenth and seventeenth century organ-mass, a study in musical style. Ann Arbor: Univ. Microfilms, 1968.

4078. ZITKE, Hans-Joachim. Vorschlag zur Einrichtung einer Kalkulation im Orgelbau. Frankfurt am Main: Verlag Das Musikinstrument, 1975.

4079. ZURICH. Die Orgel im Grossmünster Zürich. By various authors. With illustrations. Glattbrugg: N. G., 1962.

See also: 12, 14, 15, 20, 25, 26, 28, 31, 32, 33, 42, 43, 45, 49, 51, 53, 54, 57, 65, 118, 157, 220, 238, 260, 261, 289, 337, 352, 411, 423, 428, 430, 435, 436, 439, 581, 855, 1001, 1002, 1209, 1308, 1325, 1351, 1525, 1634, 1660, 1664, 1725, 1736, 1815, 1890, 2015, 2077, 2115, 2120, 2128, 2151, 2588, 2605, 2679, 2707, 2708, 2709, 2710, 2754, 2776, 2778, 2783, 2785, 2786, 2999, 3040, 3076, 3265, 3286, 3324, 3337, 3373, 3409, 3617, 4084, 4091, 4095, 4096, 4157, 4176, 4215, 4229, 4254, 4264, 4266, 4302, 4388, 4458, 4459, 4496, 4501, 4555, 4587, 4723, 4778, 4779, 4842, 4902, 4925, 4926, 5004, 5044, 5091, 5205, 5206, 5265, 5282, 5445.

ORGANISTS

4080. AMERICAN Guild of Organists Quarterly. Interesting to choirmasters and organists. New York: 1956.

4081. The AMERICAN Organist. Edited by Scott T. Buhrman. New York: Organ Interests Inc., 1918.

4082. BOYD, C. The organist and the choirmaster. Nashville: Abingdon Press, 1936.

4083. BUMPUS, J. S. Organists and composers of St. Paul's Cathedral. London: Bowden, Hudson & Co., 1891.

4084. CHORAL and Organ Guide. Directed to organists and choirmasters. Mount Vernon, N. Y.: N. G., 1948.

4085. COLEMAN, Henry. The amateur organist. Oxford Library. Fair Lawn, N. J.: Oxford Univ. Press, 1955.

4086. CONELY, James. A guide to improvisation: an introductory handbook for church organists. Nashville: Abingdon Press, 1975.

4087. EPHEM. Organist and choirmaster's diary. London: N. G., 1893. (BM)

4088. FERRIS, John R. "Cantate Domino Canticum Novum." American Guild of Organists Quarterly, VII, No. 2, 51 et seq. April 1962.

4089. FRARY, Reginald Frederick. Don't blame the organist. With illustrations by Rod. London: A. R. Mowbray, 1963.

4090. GAY, Harry W. Four French organist-composers, 1549-1720. (book and cassette.) Memphis: Memphis State Univ. Press, 1975.

4091. GRACE, H. The complete organist. Third edition. London: The Richards Press Ltd., 1947.

4092. GUILMANT, Felix Alexandre, comp. Archives des maîtres de l'orgue. 10 vols. Paris: Durand, 1893-1909.

4093. LENZINGER, Gustav. Domorganist Hans Buchner. Eine Studie zur Konstanzer Musikgeschichte. In: Schriften des Vereins für Geschichte des Bodensees und seiner Umgebung. Hft. 63. pp. 55-114., 1936. (BMAC6963)

4094. LUKAS, Viktor. Reclams Orgelmusikführer. 3., neubearb. u. erw. Aufl. Stuttgart: Reclam, 1975.

4095. MOORTGAT, Gabriël. XVIe, XVIIe, eeuwse Franse orgelmeesters. With plates. Brugge: Verbecke-Loys, 1963.

4096. L'ORGANISTA D'Oggi. (Today's Organist.) Cincinnati: WLSM, 1965 (monthly subscription).

4097. The ORGANIST and Choirmaster. A mid-monthly musical magazine. Absorbed by "The Sackbut" in May, 1920. London: Office of the Organist and Choirmaster, 1920.

4098. STEINMETZ, C. Martin. AGO survey report. New York: American Guild of Organists, 1974.

4099. STOCKS, H. C. L. British cathedral organists. New York: C. F. Peters Corporation, 1967.

4100. THIMAN, Eric H. The beginning organist. London: Ascherberg, Hopwood & Crew, Ltd., 1954.

4101. VOGE, Richard. Fritz Heitmann; das Leben eines deutschen Organisten. Berlin: Merseburger, 1963.

4102. VOLLHARDT, Reinhard. Geschichte der Cantoren und Organisten von den Städten im Konigreich Sachsen. Berlin: W. Issleib, 1899.

4103. WEMBRIDGE, Arthur Selwyn. The deputy church organist. With a foreword by Garth Benson. London: Pitman, 1961.

See also: 286, 411, 418, 423, 430, 450, 740, 864, 897, 900, 911, 1862, 1896, 1915, 1924, 1929, 1933, 2605, 3000,

3244, 3310, 3471, 3477, 3750, 3768, 3933, 3950, 3955, 3974, 3978, 4032, 4037, 4238, 4371, 4388, 4487, 4904, 5045, 5064.

ORGANUM

4104. LUDWIG, Friedrich. Repertorium organorum recentioris et motetorum vetustissimi stili. Halle: S. M. Niemeyer, 1910.

4105. PEROTINUS MOGISTER, A. Das Organum Alleluja Nativitas gloriose Virginis Marie und seine Sippe. Hrsg. von Friedrich Gennrich. Darmstadt: N. G., 1955.

4106. SCHMIDT, H. Die drei-und-vierstimmige Organa. Kassel: Bärenreiter-verlag, 1933.

4107. WAELTNER, Ernst Ludwig. Die Lehre vom Organum bis zur Mitte des 11. Jahrhunderts; Band I, Edition. (Münchner Veroffentlichungen zur Musikgeschichte, 13.) Tutzing: Hans Schneider, 1975.

4108. ZAMINER, Frieder. Der vatikanische Organum-Traktat, Ottob. lat. 3025. Organum-Praxisder frühen Notre Dame-Schule und ihrer Vorstufen. Tutzing: Münchner Veröffentlichungen zur Musikgeschichte. Bd. 2. With facsimiles. 1959.

See also: 477, 704, 3016.

ORIENTAL MUSIC

4109. ARNOLD, T. W. and Alfred Guillaume. The legacy of Islam. Fair Lawn, N. J.: Oxford Univ. Press, Inc., 1931.

4110. BECKER, Babette Mimmie. Music in the life of ancient China as reflected in the ceremonial books: The I li, the Chou li, the Li Chi. Chicago, Ill.: (Res. type script) Chicago, M. A., 1954.

4111. _______. Music in the life of ancient China: from 1400 B. C. to 300 B. C. Chicago, Ill.: (Res. type script) Chicago, Ph. D. (Oriental language and literature), 1957.

4112. BROWN, E. A. St. Andrew's Cathedral and its music. A short history of church music in Singapore. Singapore: N. G., 1929.

4113. EVANS, Ruth Harriet. Music of India. Madison, Wisc.: (Res. type script) Wisconsin Univ., M. Phil., 1937.

4114. FAUROT, Albert Louis. Music in the Chinese church. Oberlin, Ohio: (Res. type script) Oberlin, M. A. (theol.), 1940.

4115. FOXSTRANGWAYS, A. H. The music of Hindostan. Fair Lawn, N. J.: Oxford Univ. Press, 1914 (reissued 1965).

4116. GOLDRON, Romain. Ancient and Oriental music. Garden City, N. Y.: H. S. Stuttmann & Co., Inc., Distrib. by Doubleday & Co., 1968.

4117. KAUFMANN, Walter. Musical notations of the Orient: National systems of continental East, South, and Central Asia. Bloomington, Ind.: Indiana Univ. Press, 1967.

4118. MALM, William P. Music cultures of the Pacific, the Near East, and Asia. Englewood Cliffs: Prentice-Hall, 1967.

4119. PARISOT, Jean. Rapport sur une mission scientifique en Turquie d'Asie. Paris: F. Leroux, 1899.

4120. PRAJNANANANDA, Swami. A historical study of Indian music. Calcutta, India: Anandadhārā Prakāshan, 1965.

4121. SACHS, Curt. Musikinstrumente Indiens und Idonesiens. New York: Broude Brothers Limited (Facsimile), 1966. (orig. 1915.)

4122. SIKH Sacred music. New Delhi: Sikh Sacred Music Society, 1967.

4123. THOMPSON, Jean Graham. China and her music. Evanston, Ill.: (Res. type script) Northwestern Univ., M. M., 1947.

4124. WIANT, Bliss Mitchell. The character and function of music in Chinese culture. Nashville, Tenn.: (Res. type script) George Peabody Univ., Ph. D. (music), 1946.

4125. ________. The music of China. Ma Liu Shui, N. T., Hong Kong, B. C. C.: Chung Chi Publications, The Chinese Univ. of Hong Kong, 1965.

4126. WOODROFFE, John. Hymn to Kali. Sanskrit and English. Madras: Ganesh, 1965.

See also: 548, 806, 1053, 1095, 1384, 1636, 2032, 2035, 2109, 2877, 3543, 5009.

ORNAMENTATION

4127. BROWN, Howard Mayer. Embellishing sixteenth century music. London: Oxford Univ. Press, 1976.

4128. EMERY, Walter. Bach's ornaments. London: Novello & Co., Ltd., 1953.

4129. ENGELKE, Hans. A study of ornaments in American tune-books, 1760-1800. Los Angeles, California: (Res. type script), Southern California Univ., Ph. D. (music), 1960.

4130. HAMILTON, Clarence Grant. Ornaments in classical and modern music. New York: AMS Press, 1976.

4131. KUHN, Max. Die Verzierungs-kunst in der Gesangs-Musik des 16.-17. Jahrhunderts, 1535-1650. Leipzig: Publikationen der Internationalen, 1902.

See also: 1982.

PAMPHLET

4132. CASTLE, L. Church music booklets. Church Music Review, 1931.

4133. CHURCH Music Society. Church music Society papers. London: Oxford Univ. Press, variable release dates.

4134. SÜDDEUTSCHE Blätter für Kirchenmusik. South German papers on church music. Tübingen: C. L. Schultheiss, 1948.

4135. WURTTEMBERGISCHE Blätter für Kirchenmusik. Wurtenberg papers on church music. Waiblinger: N. G., 1949.

See also: 2433, 2434, 2435, 2436, 3188, 4137, 4645.

PARISH and/or VILLAGE CHURCH

4136. AUTON, John G. and Patrick Wild. Music at the parish church. London & New York: Oxford Univ. Press, 1952.

4137. CHURCH music in town and country. London: N. G., 1882.

4138. GRACE, Harvey. Music in parish churches. Music in larger country and in smaller town churches. Music in parish churches. A plea for the simple. London: Humphrey Milford, 1917.

4139. HERBERT, A. G. The parish communion. London: S. P. C. K., 1937.

4140. MORGAN, Stuart M. Choirs in little churches. London: The Faith Press, 1931.

4141. _______. Music in the village church. An attempt at something practical. London: S. P. C. K., 1939.

4142. NICHOLSON, S. H. The improvement of music in parish churches. London: Faith Press, 1920.

4143. SCHNÜRL, Karl. Das alte Musikarchiv der Pfarrkirche St. Stephan in Tulln. Wien, Graz, Köln: Böhlau in Kommission, 1964.

4144. SMITH, W. K. The training of village choirs. London: S. P. C. K., 1911.

4145. VIENNA-Pfarrkirche St. Karl Borromäus. Das Musikarchiv der Pfarrkirche St. Karl Borromaus in Wien (von) Theophil Antonicek. Wien: Böhlau in Kommission, 1968.

4146. VOGT, V. O. Modern worship for village churches. New York: Agriculture Mission Foundation, 1939.

See also: 388, 939, 1226, 1289, 2771, 2923, 3575, 3602, 4044, 4871.

PARODY

4147. WILDER, Robert Dinsmoor. The masses of Orlando di Lasso with emphasis on his parody technique. Cambridge, Mass.: Harvard Univ., 1952.

See also: 3053.

PASSION MUSIC

4148. BACH, Johann Sebastian. Matthaeus Passion. Oorspronkelijke Duitse text naar het Evangelie van Matthaeus met bijvoegingen van C. F. Henrici. Utrecht: Spectrum, 1973.

4149. BURRETT, Alban Sydney Edward. We celebrate our Redemption. The liturgy of Holy Week. London: Challoner Pub., 1960.

4150. DRAPER, W. H. and J. V. Roberts. Hymns for Holy Week: translations from hymns of the Greek church. London: N. G., 1898.

4151. DÜRR, Alfred. Mattäus--Passion u. Markus-Passion: kritischer Bericht. Kassel: Bärenreiter, 1974.

4152. FREDERICHS, Henning. Das verhältnis von Text und Musik in den Barockespassionen Keisers, Händels, Telemanns und Mattesons: mit einer Einführung in ihre Entstehungs-- und Rezeptionsgeschichte sowie den Bestand ihrer literarischen und musikalischen Quellen. München: E. Katzbichler, 1975.

4153. GERBER, Rudolf. Das Passionsrezitativ bei Heinrich Schütz und seine stilgeschichtlichen Grundlagen. Hildesheim: G. Olms Verlag, 1972-1973. (reprt. of Gutersloh, 1929 ed.)

4154. HEUSS, Alfred Valentin. Johann Sebastian Bachs Matthäuspassion. (Neudr.) Walluf bei Wiesbaden: Sändig, 1972.

4155. JAKOBI, Theodor. Zur Deutung von Bachs Matthäus-Passion. Stuttgart: Reclam, 1966.

4156. KADE, Otto. Die ältere Passions Komposition bis zum Jahre 1631. Hildesheim, Germany: Georg Olms-Reprint, 1967. (orig. Gütersloh, 1893.)

4157. MADDEN, Evalynn. The Passion Chorale and its treatment on the organ. Austin, Tex.: Univ. of Texas, M. M., 1949.

4158. MENDEL, Arthur. Johannes--Passion: kritischer Bericht. (J. S. Bach: Neue Ausgabe sämtlicher Werke, Serie II, Band 4. Kassel: Bärenreiter, 1974.

4159. MOE, Donald George. The St. Mark Passion of Reinhard Keiser (with) vol. II: score. vol. no. I and II. Ann Arbor: Univ. Microfilms, 1968.

4160. MOSER, Hans Joachim. Die Passion von Schütz bis Frank Martin. Wolfenbüttel: Möseler Verlag, 1967.

4161. MÜLLER, Karl-Josef. Informationen zu Pendereckis Lukas-Passion. Frankfort am Main: M. Diesterweg, 1973.

4162. PASTELLI, Giorgio. La passione secondo Giovanni di J. S. Bach. Torino: G. Giappichelli, 1972.

4163. SMALLMAN. The background of Passion music: J. S. Bach and his predecessors. Chester Springs, Pa.: Dufour Editions, 1957.

See also: 1294, 1650, 4275, 5209.

PATRONAGE

4164. DORIAN, Frederick. Commitment to culture. Art patronage in Europe, its significance for America. Pittsburgh, Pa.: Pittsburgh Press, 1964.

4165. KEEFER, Lubov Breit. Music angels: a thousand years of patronage. Baltimore, Md.: The author, 1976.

PERIODICALS

4166. ACCENT Church Music Library. (ed. J. W. Brewer). Minneapolis: N.G., n.d. (Lc-582772)

4167. ACTA musicologica (Quarterly). Basel, Switzerland: Bärenreiter Verlag, n.d.

4168. ALLGEMEINE Musikalische Zeitung. New York: Broude Brothers, 1965.

4169. AMBROSIUS. Rivista liturgico-pastorale. Nuova serie. Anno 36. No. 1. Milano: N.G., 1960.

4170. ARCHIV für Musikwissenschaft (Viertel jährlich). Wiesbaden, Germany: Franz Steiner Verlag, n.d.

4171. ARTICLE Citations and "Obsolescence" in musicological journals, by R. M. Longyear. Ann Arbor: Music Library Assoc. in "Notes" for March, 1977, Vol. 33, No. 3.

4172. ASSOCIAZIONE degli amici del Pontificio istituto di musica sacra. Roma: Bollettino anno 1-, Apr. 1949.

4173. BLÄTTER für Haus-und-Kirchenmusik, unter Mitwirkung namhafter Musikschriftsteller und Komponisten, herausgegeben, -Ernest Rabich. Langensalza: Beyer & Söhne, 1897-1914.

4174. CAECILIA, a Review of Catholic Church Music (Quarterly). Omaha, Neb.: Society of St. Caecilia, n.d.

4175. The CATHEDRAL Quarterly and Church Music Review. A record of work in connection w/th. cathedral churches and chapels royal and collegiate and parish churches in communion w/th. see of Canterbury. London: Faith Press, 1914.

4176. CHORAL and Organ Guide. 10 issues yearly. Mt. Vernon, N.Y.: N.G., n.d.

4177. Der CHORWÄCHTER; Zeitschrift fur Kirchenmusik. Einsiedeln: Kirchenmusikverlag M. Ochsner, monthly.

4178. CHURCH Choral Service. Chicago: Choral Services, Oct. 1956.

4179. CHURCH Music Bulletin. Minneapolis: Augsburg Publishing House, n.d.

4180. The CHURCH Music Review. London: N. G., 1931.

4181. CONTEMPORARY Keyboard. The magazine for all keyboard players. Ed. by Tom Darter. Saratoga, Cal.: Keyboard Players International, current.

4182. A CRITICAL Annotated Bibliography of Periodicals (memo no. 33). American Choral Foundation, Inc. New York: Alexander Broude, 1962, also New York: Stechert-Hafner, Inc.: Riverside, Cal.: Central Magazine Service, Inc.

4183. The DIAPASON. Chicago: N. G., n. d.

4184. DUZREKORD. The magazine of the choir of St. Aidan's Church. Vol. 1. No. 2. Cheltenham: St. Aidan's July/Sept., 1962.

4185. EARLY Music. Ed. by J. M. Thomson. A quarterly Journal. London: Oxford Univ. Press, current.

4186. FOLK Mass and Modern Liturgy Magazine. Ed. by William Burns. (Eight issues a year.) San Jose, Cal.: Resource Publications, n. d.

4187. GREGORIUSBLAD. (5 issues yearly). Utrecht, Netherlands: Nederlandse Sint-Gregoriusvoreniging, Plompetorengracht, n. d.

4188. The HYMN. Periodical and bulletin of the Hymn Society of America. New York, 1949.

4189. JOURNAL of the American Musicological Society. 3 issues yearly. Philadelphia, Pa.: Univ. of Pennsylvania, n. d.

4190. JOURNAL of Church Music. 11 issues yearly. Philadelphia, Pa.: N. G., n. d.

4191. MUSIC Article Guide. 4 issues yearly. Philadelphia, Pa.: N. G., n. d.

4192. MUSIC Educators Journal. Washington: Music Educators National Conference.

4193. MUSIC Ministry. Nashville: Graded Press, 1959.

4194. "MUSIC Periodicals." Charles Lindahl comp. and reviewer. Ann Arbor: Music Library Assn. in "Notes" Dec., 1976, Vol. 33, No. 2.; also June, 1977, Vol. 33, No. 4.

4195. MUSICA sacra, revista mensal. Petropolis: Editora Vozes, 1941.

4196. MUSICAL Opinion. London: Minerva House.

4197. The MUSICAL Quarterly. New York: G. Schirmer.

4198. The MUSICAL Times. London: Novello & Co.

4199. MUSIK und Gottesdienst. Zeitschrift für evangelische Kirchenmusik. Zürich: Zwingli-Verlag, 1947.

4200. MUSIK und Kirche. Bimonthly. Kassel-Wilhelmshöhe, Germant: Bärenreiter-Verlag, Heinrich-Schütz-Allee.

4201. MUSIKALISCHEN Zeitschriften seit ihrer Entstehung bis zur Gegenwart. New York: Broude Brothers, 1965.

4202. Die MUSIKFORSCHUNG. Kassel-Wilhelmshöhe, Germany: Bärenreiter-Verlag, Heinrich-Schütz-Allee.

4203. The NEW Music Review and Church Music Review. New York: Novello, Ewer & Co., 1901.

4204. PERIODICAL Index. Library of Congress, Music Division.

4205. REPRINTS in Music, 1964-65. New York: Frits A. M. Knuf, sold by Broude Brothers, 1965.

4206. The SACRED Musician. South Pasadena, Cal.: N. G., 1932.

4207. SINT Gregorius-blad ... tijdschrift tot bevordering van kerkelijke toonkunst. Haarlem, Netherlands: Snelpersdrukkerij Sint Jacobs-Godshuis, 1876.

4208. WURTTEMBERGISCHE Blätter für Kirchenmusik. Waiblingen: N. G., 1942-52.

4209. ZEITSCHRIFT für Katholische kirchenmusik. Gmunden: J. E. Habert, n. d.

See also: 115, 224, 239, 492, 493, 597, 741, 898, 899, 900, 907, 918, 1110, 1131, 1159, 1161, 1177, 1194, 1212, 1270, 1339, 1458, 1791, 1794, 2567, 2569, 2824, 2849, 2852, 2899, 2910, 2919, 2974, 3187, 3246, 3257, 3260, 3276, 3408, 3431, 3592, 3750, 4067, 4080, 4081, 4084, 4895, 4924, 5289, 5294.

PERSONALITIES

In order to make the names of the personalities easier to locate, their full names are capitalized, and the names of the author(s) or editor(s), presented in lower case, except for the first letter of the names. Where there are a number of books about one personality they are presented in a sub-category, and concluded with asterisks. In this category only, the authors and editors will not be in alphabetic order, except in the subcategories.

4210. Johnson, John Preston. An analysis and edition of selected sacred choral works of JOHANN RUDOLF AHLE. Ann Arbor: Univ. Microfilms, 1969.

4211. Weissenback, Andreas. JOHANN GEORG ALBRECHTSBERGER als Kirchenkomponist. Österreich: Beihefte der Denkmäler der Tonkunst, 1927.

4212. _______. Thematisches Verzeichnis der Kirchenkompositionen von JOHANN GEORG ALBRECHTSBERGER. Leipzig: W. Braumüller, 1914.

4213. Augustine. ST. AUGUSTINE's de Musica. London: Orthological Issue, 1949.

4214. Davenson, Henri. Traité de la musique selon l'esprit de SAINT AUGUSTIN. Neuchatel: N. G., 1942.

The Bachs

4215. Aldrich, Putnam. Ornamentation in J. S. BACH's organ works. New York: Coleman-Ross Co., 1950.

4215a. BACH, CARL PHILIP EMANUEL. Autobiography. New York: Broude Brothers Limited (facsimile), n. d. (orig. 1773.)

4216. Bach, Johann S. JOHANN SEBASTIAN BACHS vierstimmige Choralgesänge. Hildesheim: G. Olms, n. d. (reprt. Berlin; Leipzig, 1765-69.)

4217. _______. JOHANN SEBASTIAN BACH's Werke. Herausgegeben von der Bach-Gesellschaft. Leipzig: Breitkopf & Härtel, 1851-1926. (Also Ann Arbor: J. W. Edwards, 1947.) 61 vols., in 47. (Vol. 47 not reprinted.)

4218. _______. Neue BACH Ausgabe. Kassel und Basel: Bärenreiter-Verlag, 1954.

4219. _______. Twelve sacred songs for mixed chorus. (From Geistliche Lieder.) New York: G. Schirmer, n. d.

4220. Bishop, Claire. JOHANN SEBASTIAN BACH: Music Giant. Champaign, Ill.: Garrard Publishing Co., 1972.

4221. Bizony, Celia. The family of BACH: a brief history. Horsham: Artemis Press, 1975.

4222. Blankenburg, Walter. Einführung in BACHS H-moll-Messe. BWV 232. 3., völlig neu bearb. Aufl. mit vollst text. Kassel: Bärenreiter, 1974.

4223. Blume, Friedrich. JOHANN SEBASTIAN BACH. Two centuries of Bach. (Trans. by Stanley Godman from "Im Wandel der Geschichte"--Kassel: Bärenreiter Verlag, 1947.) London and New York: Oxford Univ. Press, 1950.

4224. Boughton, Rutland. BACH the Master. New York: Harper & Brothers, 1930.

4225. Broyles, Michael Everett. Textual interpretation in the choral harmonizations of J. S. BACH. Ann Arbor: Univ. Microfilms, 1967.

4226. Buchet, Edmond. JEAN-SEBASTIEN BACH; l'oeuvre et la vie. (Club des libraires de France, Destins de l'art. 15.) Paris: Le Libraires associé, 1963.

4227. Bullivant, Roger. "Word-painting and chromaticism in the music of J. S. BACH." The Music Review, 1949. XX/ 3-4 (Aug.-Nov.). p. 186-216.

4228. Carrell, Norman. BACH the borrower. London: George Allen & Unwin, Ltd., 1967.

4229. Chailley, Jacques. Les chorals pour orgue de J. S. BACH. Paris: A. Leduc, 1974.

4230. Chamblee, James Monroe. The cantatas and oratorios of CARL PHILIPP EMANUEL BACH. Ann Arbor: Univ. Microfilms, Univ. of North Carolina diss., 1973.

4231. Chiapusso, Jan. BACH'S world. Bloomington and London: Indiana Univ. Press, 1968.

4232. Connor, Sister M. Gregorian chant and mediaeval hymn-tunes in the works of JOHANN SEBASTIAN BACH. Washington, D.C.: Catholic Univ. of America, 1957.

4233. David, Hans T. J. S. BACH'S musical offering, history, interpretation, and analysis. Magnolia, Mass.: P. Smith, 1973. (reprint G. Schirmer-1945.)

4234. ________, and Arthur Mendel (eds.). The BACH reader. New York: Norton, 1945.

4235. Davis, Richard C. Self parody among the cantatas of JOHANN SEBASTIAN BACH. (2 parts.) Ann Arbor: Univ. Microfilms, Boston Univ. diss., 1962.

4236. Davison, Archibald T. BACH and Handel. Cambridge, Mass.: Harvard Univ. Press, 1951.

4237. Dickinson, A. E. F. The Art of J. S. BACH. London: C. F. Peters Corporation, 1950. (Hinrichsen edition.)

4238. Dufourcq, Norbert. JEAN-SEBASTIEN BACH, le maître de l'orgue. (2nd edition.) Paris: A. & J. Picard, 1973.

4239. Eickhoff, Henry John. Volume I: The Ritornello principle of the organ works of BACH. Volume II: Appendix. Evanston, Ill.: Northwestern Univ., 1960.

4240. Emery, Walter. Notes on BACH'S organ works ... a companion to the revised Novello edition. London: Novello & Co., 1952.

4241. Felix, Werner, Armin Schneiderheinze, and Winfried Hoffman. JOHANN SEBASTIAN BACH: lebendiges Erbe. Leipzig: Johann-Sebastian-Bach Komitee der Deutschen Demokratischen Republik, 1973.

4242. Findeisen, Kurt Arnold. Der Gross Kantor und seine Orgel; Roman um JOHANN SEBASTIAN BACH. Berlin: Evangelische Verlagsanstalt, 1961.

4243. Finke-Hecklinger, Doris. Tranzcharaktere in JOHANN SEBASTIAN BACHS Vokalmusik. (Tübinger Bach-Studien, 6.) Trossingen: Hohner-verlag, 1970.

4244. Foelber, P. F. BACH'S treatment of the subject of death in his choral music. Washington, D.C.: Catholic Univ. of America, 1961.

4245. Forkel, Johann Nikolaus. JOHANN SEBASTIAN BACH. New York: Johnson Reprint Corp., 1966; also Berlin: Henschel, 1966. (orig. Leipzig, 1802.)

4246. ________. Über JOHANN SEBASTIAN BACHS Leben, Kunst und Kunstwerke. Kassel: Bärenreiter-Verlag, 1968.

4247. Franck, Hans. Cantate; das Leben des JOHANN SEBASTIAN BACH. Stuttgart: Kreuz-Verlag, 1965.

4248. Friedemann, Gerhard. BACH zeichnet das Kreuz; die Bedeutung der 4 Duetten aus dem 3 Theil der Calvierübung. Pinneberg, Im Bans: G. Friedemann, 1963.

4249. Gardonyi, Zoltán. J. S. BACH kánon-es fugaszerkeszö muveszete. Budapest: Editio Musica, 1973.

4250. Geiringer, Karl. The BACH family: seven generations of creative genius. New York: Oxford Univ. Press, 1954.

4251. ________. JOHANN SEBASTIAN BACH: the culmination of an era. New York: Oxford Univ. Press, 1966.

4252. ________. Music of the BACH family. Cambridge: Harvard Univ. Press, 1955.

4253. Göhler, K. A. Die Messkataloge im Dienst der musikalischen Geschichtsforschung. Eine Anregung zur zeitgenössischen Buchbeschreibung. (BACH). New York: Broude Brothers Limited. (Facsimile), 1965. (orig. 1901.)

4254. Grace, H. The Organ works of BACH. London: Novello & Co., 1922.

4255. Gurlitt, Wilibald. JOHANN SEBASTIAN BACH. Basel: E. Reinhardt, 1947; also Kassel: Bärenreiter-Verlag, 1949.

4256. Hajek, Egon. Alles nur nach Seinem Willen; Lebenspfade des Thomaskantors JOHANN SEBASTIAN BACH. Stuttgart: Steinkopf, 1963.

4257. Hemel, Victor Van. Het Leven van BACH en Händel; aan jonge mensen verteld. (2e druk.) Antwerpen: Cupido, 1963.

4258. Herbst, Wolfgang. JOHANN SEBASTIAN BACH und die lutherische Mystik. Erlangen: N. G., 1958. (LC61-85620)

4259. Hilgenfeldt, C. L. JOHANN SEBASTIAN BACHS Leben, Wirken und Werke. Ein Beitrag zur Kunstgeschichte des achtzehnten Jahrhunderts. New York: Broude Brothers, 1965. (orig. Leipzig 1850.)

4260. Hindemith, Paul. JOHANN SEBASTIAN BACH; ein verpflichtendes Erbe. (Insel-Bücherei, 575.) Frankfurt am Main: Insel, 1962.

4261. ________. J. S. BACH: heritage and obligation. New Haven: Yale Univ. Press, 1952.

4262. JUAN SEBASTIAN BACH (Genios y realidades). Buenos Aires: Compañia general Fabril editora, 1964.

4263. J. S. BACH'S original hymn tunes. London: Oxford Univ. Press, 1932.

4264. Kehrer, Jodoc. JOH. SEB. BACH als Orgelkomponist und seine Bedeutung für den katholischen Organisten. Regensburg: F. Pustet, 1920.

4265. Kellar, Allan Dean. The Hamburg Bach--CARL PHILIPP EMANUEL BACH as choral composer. vol. I & II. Ann Arbor: Univ. Microfilms, 1970.

4266. Keller, Hermann. The Organ works of BACH. New York, London, Frankfurt: C. F. Peters Corporation, 1967.

4267. Khubov, Georgii Nikitch. SEBASTIAN BACH. 3. ied. perer. i dop. Moskva: Gos. moozikalnayah yezd-vo, 1953.

4268. Kleinhaus, Theodore J. Hans liv var musik; en bok am JOHANN SEBASTIAN BACH. Oevers., Sven Larsson. Stockholm: Efs-forl, 1962.

4269. ______. The Music master; the story of JOHANN SEBASTIAN BACH (Reprint). Westport, Conn.: Greenwood Press, 1973.

4270. Lang, György. A Tamás-templom karnagya JOHANN S. BACH életének regenye. Budapest: Móra Kiadó, 1966.

4271. Mc All, May de Forest. Melodic index to the works of J. S. BACH. rev. and enl. ed. London, New York, Frankfurt: C. F. Peters Corporation, 1962.

4272. Marcel, Luc-André. JOHANN SEBASTIAN BACH in Selbstzeugnissen und Bilddokumenten. Aus dem Französischen übertragen von C. Waege und H. Weiher-Waege. Den Anhang bearb. H. Riege. (Rowohlts monographien, 83.) Reinbek bei Hamburg: Rowohlt, 1963.

4273. Meynell, Esther. BACH. New York: A. A. Wyn, Inc., 1949.

4274. Miles, Russell H. JOHANN SEBASTIAN BACH: an introduction to his life and works. Englewood Cliffs, N.J.: Prentice-Hall, 1962.

4275. Moberg, Carl Allan. BACHS passioner och höga mässa; en stilöversikt jämte ettbidrag till Bachrenässänsens historia i Sverige. Stockholm: H. Geber, 1949.

4276. Morozov, Sergei Aleksandrovich. BAKH. Moskva: Mol. gvardiía, 1975.

4277. Nägeli, Hans Georg. JOHANN SEBASTIAN BACH. Zürich: Hug, 1974.

4278. Neumann, Werner. Auf den Lebenswegen JOHANN SEBASTIAN BACHS. 4., verbesserte Auflage. Berlin: Verlag der Nation, 1962.

4279. ______. BACH, Eine Bildbiographie. Berlin & Wien: Deutsche Buch-Gemeinschaft, 1965.

4280. ______. JOHANN S. BACH: Sämtliche Kantaten Texte. New York: A. Broude, Inc., 1965.

4281. ______, und Hans-Joachim Schulz, editors. Fremdgeschichte und gedruckte Dokumente zur Lebensgeschichte JOHANN SEBASTIAN BACH 1685-1750. Kassel: Bärenreiter, 1969.

4282. Parry, C. Hubert H. JOHANN SEBASTIAN BACH. New York: G. P. Putnam's Sons, 1922.

4283. Philippsborn, Magali. Die Frühdrucke der Werke JOHANN SEBASTIAN BACHS in der ersten Hälfte des 19. Jahrhunderts: ein kritisch vergleichende Untersuchung anhand des Wohltemperierten Klaviers I. (Thesis-Frankfurt am Main. unpubl.) 1975.

4284. Pirro, André. J. S. BACH. Translated by Mervyn Savill. New York: The Orion Press, 1957.

4285. Preuss, Hans. BACH'S Bibliothek. Leipzig: N. G., 1928.

4286. Raupach, Hans. JOHANN SEBASTIAN BACH und die Gesellschaft seiner Zeit. (Vortrags--veranstaltung d. Bayer Akad. d. Schönen Künste am 21 Marz, 1973). München: Callwey, 1973.

4287. Rothschild, Fritz. A Handbook to the performance of the forty-eight preludes and fugues of BACH. Chester Springs, Pa.: Dufour editions; also London: A. & C. Black, 1955.

4288. Rüber, Johannes. Die Heiligsprechung des JOHANN SEBASTIAN BACH; eine papst-legende. Schwiegerdingen: G. Ruber, 1973. (Reprint of Olten: Hegner, 1962.)

4289. Rubin, Augusta. J. S. BACH: The modern composer. Boston: Crescendo Publ. Co., 1976.

4290. Ruiz Tarazona, Andrés. J. SEBASTIAN BACH: un padre venerable. Madrid: Real Musical, 1975.

4291. Sachse, Wolfgang. Thema con variationi; Erzählungen um JOHANN SEBASTIAN BACH. Mit einem Nachwort von K. Wiesner. Berlin: Union-Verlag, 1963.

4292. Scheide, William H. JOHANN SEBASTIAN BACH as a biblical interpreter. Princeton: Princeton Theological Seminary, 1952.

4293. Schering, Arnold. JOHANN SEBASTIANS BACH'S Leipziger Kirchenmusik; Studien und Wege zu ihrer Erkenntnis. Leipzig: Breitkopf & Härtel, 1936; also Wiesbaden: Breitkopf & Härtel, 1968.

4294. Schrade, Leo. BACH: the conflict between the sacred and the secular. New York: Da Capo Press, 1973.

4295. Schultz, H. J. (ed.). JOHANN SEBASTIAN BACH: Leben und Werk in Dokumenten. Als Taschenbuch zusammengearbeitet von H. J. Schulze. Kassel: Bärenreiter, 1975.

4296. Schweitzer, Albert. JOHANN SEBASTIAN BACH. (Vorrede von C. M. Widor.) Vols. 1 & 2. Leipzig: Breitkopf & Härtel, 1963.

4297. Spitta, Philipp. J. S. BACH: his work and influence on the music of Germany. Vols. 1, 2, 3. London: Novello, 1899; also New York: Dover, 1951.

4298. Stiller, Günther. JOHANN SEBASTIAN BACH und das Leipziger gottesdienstliche Leben seiner Zeit. Kassel, Basel: Bärenreiter-Verlag, 1970.

4299. Streck, Harald. Die Verskunst in den poetischen Texten zu den Kantaten J. S. BACHS. Hamburg: Verlag der Musikalienhandlung, 1971.

4300. Tamme, Carl. Thematisches Verzeichnis der Vocalwerke von JOH. SEB. BACH. Auf Grund der Gessamtausgaben von C. F. Peters und der Bach-Gesellschaft verfasst. Leipzig: N. G., 1890. (BM)

4301. Taylor, S. The Life of J. S. BACH in relation to his work as a church musician and composer. Cambridge: MacMillan & Bowes, 1897.

4302. Taylor, S. D. B. The Chorale Preludes of J. S. BACH. London: Oxford Univ. Press, 1942.

4303. Terry, Charles Sanford. BACH. A Biography. London: Oxford Univ. Press, 1928; also 2nd ed. rev., Oxford Univ. Press, 1933.

4304. ______. BACH: The Cantatas and Oratorios. (Musical Pilgrim Series) 2 vols. London: Oxford Univ. Press, 1926.

4305. ______. BACH: The historical approach. New York: Oxford Univ. Press, 1930.

4306. ______. BACH'S Cantata Texts, sacred and secular. Chester Springs, P.: Dufour Editions, 1926.

4307. ______. BACH'S Mass in B Minor. London: Oxford Univ. Press, Milford, 1924; also Glasgow: J. Maclehose & Sons, 1915.

4308. ______. BACH'S Orchestra. London: Oxford Univ. Press, 1932.

4309. ______. J. S. BACH'S four part chorales. London: Oxford Univ. Press, 1929.

4310. ______. J. S. BACH'S original hymn-tunes. London: Oxford Univ. Press, 1922.

4311. _______. The music of BACH; an introduction. Gloucester, Mass.: P. Smith, 1964. (available through A. Broude, New York, N.Y.)

4312. Valabrega, Cesare. La musica sacra di JOHANN S. BACH. Parma: Guanda, 1965.

4313. Vos, Adriaan Cornelius. JOH. SEB. BACH: de Thomascantor van Leipzig zijn voorouders en nakomelingen. Franeker, Nederlands: Werer, 1976.

4314. Whittaker, William Gillies. Fugitive notes on certain Cantatas and the motets of J. S. BACH. London: Oxford Univ. Press (H. Milford), 1924.

4315. Wotquenne, A. Thematisches Verzeichnis der Werke von CARL PHILIPP EMANUEL BACH. New York: A. Broude Inc., 1965.

4315a. Young, Percy Marshall. The BACHS, 1500-1850. New York: T. Y. Crowell Co., 1970.

4316. Zander, Ferdinand. Die Dichter Kantatentexte JOHANN SEBASTIAN BACH; Untersuchungen zu ihrer Bestimmung. Köln: Inaug. dissertation-Cologne, 1967.

* * *

4317. Bertault, P. BALZAC et la musique religieuse. N.G.: N.G., 1929.

4318. Calamy, Edward. An Abridgement of Mr. BAXTER'S history of his life and times. N.G.: N.G., 1713.

4319. Forbes, Elliot. The Choral music of BEETHOVEN, American Choral Review, V. 11, no. 3. New York: American Choral Foundation, 1969.

4320. Sullivan, J. W. N. BEETHOVEN: his spiritual development. New York: W. W. Norton, 1964.

4321. Welleford, Paul Bailey. The Sacred Choral Works of JEAN BERGER 1941-1963. Fort Worth, Tex.: Southwestern Baptist Theological Seminary, M.C.M., 1965.

4322. Barzun, Jacques. BERLIOZ and the romantic century. Vols. 1 and 2. Boston: Little, Brown & Co., 1950.

4323. Barbour, J. Murray. The Church music of WILLIAM BILLINGS. East Lansing: Michigan State Univ. Press, 1960.

4324. McKay, David P. and Richard Crawford. WILLIAM BILLINGS of Boston: eighteenth century composer. Princeton: Princeton Univ. Press, 1975.

4325. Miley, Malcolm Wayne. A Study of the life and works of WILLIAM BILLINGS. Fort Worth, Tex.: Southwestern Baptist Theological Seminary, M. C. M., 1961.

4326. Boucher, Joan Anne. The Religious music of GILLIS BINCHOIS. Boston: Boston Univ. diss., 1963.

4327. Currie, John. BINCHOIS' religious music. New Haven, Conn.: Yale Univ., n. d.

4327a. Riemer, Otto. ERHARD BODENSCHATZ und sein Florilegium portense. Leipzig: F. Kistner & C. F. W. Siegel, 1928.

4328. Cook, B. and E. H. Firth. THOMAS BRAMELD of Parkgate. Rothesham: Garnett & Co., 1916.

Johannes Brahms

4329. Drinker, Sophie. BRAHMS and his women's choruses. Merion, Pa.: Sophie Drinker under auspices of Musurgia Publ., 1952.

4330. Evans, Edwin. Historical, descriptive and analytical account of the entire works of JOHANNES BRAHMS. Vol. I--The Vocal Works. London: Wm. Reeves, Publ., 1912.

4331. Fuller-Maitland, John A. BRAHMS. Port Washington, N. Y. and London: Kennikat Press, 1972. (repr. of Dallas, Tex.: Taylor Publ. Co., 1911.)

4332. Gal, Hans.--trans. by Joseph Stein. JOHANNES BRAHMS, his work and personality. New York: Alfred Knopf, 1963. (orig. Frankfurt am Main: Fischer Bücherei KG, 1961.)

4333. Geiringer, Karl. BRAHMS: his life and work. (Second ed.--1st ed. German-1934; 1st English ed.-1936.) New York and London: Oxford Univ. Press, 1947.

4334. Niemann, Walter. BRAHMS. Trans. by Catherine Phillips. New Ed. New York: Tudor Publ. Co., 1937. (orig. Alfred A. Knopf, 1929.)

4335. Stanford, Charles V., Sir. BRAHMS. (of the Mayfair biographies, ed. by Emile Lesage.) London: Murdoch, Murdoch & Co., n. d.

* * *

4336. Corse, Larry B. The A Cappella choral music of BEN-

JAMIN BRITTEN. Denton, Tex.: North Texas State Univ., M.M., 1963.

4337. Griesbacher, P. BRUCKNER'S Te Deum. Studie. Regensburg: N.G., 1919.

4338. Koenig, W. ANTON BRUCKNER als Chormeister. Linz: N.G., 1936.

4339. Gallo, William K. Life and church music of DUDLEY BUCK. Ann Arbor: Univ. Microfilms, 1968.

4340. Geck, Martin. Die Vokalmusik DIETRICH BUXTEHUDES und der frühe Pietismus. Kassel & New York: Bärenreiter, 1965.

William Byrd

4341. Andrews, H. K. The Techniques of BYRD'S vocal polyphony. New York: Oxford Univ. Press, 1966.

4342. Fellowes, Edmund H. WILLIAM BYRD. New York: E. P. Dutton & Co., 1928; 2nd ed. London & New York: Oxford Univ. Press, 1948.

4343. Gray, Walter B. A Comparison of the Latin and English sacred choral compositions of WILLIAM BYRD. Ann Arbor: Univ. Microfilms, Univ. of Wisconsin, diss., 1962.

4344. Howes, Frank. WILLIAM BYRD. New York: E. P. Dutton & Co., 1928.

4345. Smith, Ronnie Lew. The Psalm-settings of WILLIAM BYRD. Fort Worth, Tex.: Southwestern Baptist Theological Seminary, M.C.M., 1961.

* * *

4346. Cinti, Italo. L'Arte nel mondo spirituale e l'Ikuhunaton di LAMBERTO CAFFARELLI. Bologna: Tamari, 1965.

4347. CALVIN, JOHN. Sermons upon the Book of Job. N.G.: Golding, 1574.

4348. Garside, Charles. "CALVIN'S preface to the Psalter: A Reappraisal." Musical Quarterly. N.G.: Oct. 1951.

4349. Castle, Conan. The Sacred works of ANDRE CAMPRA. Ann Arbor: Univ. of Michigan, 1961.

4350. Ardry, Roger W. The Influence of the extended Latin sacred works of GIACOMO CARISSIMI on the Biblical oratorios of George Frederic Händel. Ann Arbor: Univ. Microfilms, The Catholic Univ. of America diss., 1964.

4351. Beveridge, Lowell Pierson. GIACOMO CARISSIMI: A study of his life and his music with Latin texts in the light of the institutions which he served and through the perspective of liturgical, literary, and musical theory and practice. Cambridge, Mass.: Harvard Univ., 1944.

4352. Warren, Jerry Lee. The Motetti a voce sola of MAURITIO CAZZATI. Vol. No. II. Ann Arbor: Univ. Microfilms, 1967.

4353. Solkema, Sherman Van, Jr. The Liturgical music of PIERRE CERTON. Ann Arbor: Univ. Microfilms, 1963.

4354. Barber, Clarence Howard. The Liturgical music of MARC-ANTOINE CHARPENTIER: the masses, motets, leçons de Ténébres. Cambridge, Mass.: Harvard Univ., 1955.

4355. Collet, Henri. Le Mysticisme musical espagnol au XVI siècle, par HENRI COLLET. Paris: F. Alcan, 1913.

4356. McKinley, Ann W. FRANCESCO CORTECCIA'S music to Latin texts. Ann Arbor: Univ. of Michigan diss., 1963.

4357. Rodgers, J. A. Dr. HENRY COWARD, the pioneer chorus-master. New York: J. Lane, 1911.

4358. Wright, T. (ed.). Correspondence of WILLIAM COWPER. New York: Dodd, 1902.

4359. Ruffin, Bernard. FANNY CROSBY. Philadelphia: United Church Press, 1976.

4360. Hoyem, Nell-Marie. JOHN DAHLE: a positive development of church music in the American Midwest, 1876-1931. Ann Arbor: Univ. Microfilms, 1967.

4361. Colles, H. C. WALFORD DAVIES (a biography). London: Oxford Univ. Press, 1942.

4362. Essays in honor of ARCHIBALD THOMPSON DAVISON. Cambridge: N.G., 1957.

4363. Palmer, Larry. HUGO DISTLER and his church music. St. Louis: Concordia Publishing House, 1967.

4364. Rauchhaupt, Ursula von. Die Vokale Kirchenmusik HUGO DISTLERS; eine Studie zum Thema "Musik und Gottesdienst." Gütersloh: Gütersloher Verlagshaus (Mohn), 1963.

4365. Garland, Henry James. The Life and hymns of Dr. PHILIP

DODDRIDGE. A bicentenary tribute. Stirling: Stirling Tract Enterprise, 1951.

4366. Nuttall, Geoffrey Fillingham. PHILIP DODDRIDGE, 1702-51. His contribution to English religion. By various authors. Edited by G. F. Nuttall. With a portrait. London: Independent Press, 1951.

4367. Walton, Isaac. Lives of DONNE, WOTTON, HOOKER, HERBERT. London and New York: H. Milford, Oxford Univ. Press, 1927. (orig. 1670.)

4368. Poulton, Diana. JOHN DOWLAND: his life and works. Berkeley: Univ. of California Press, 1972.

4369. Hamm, Charles E. A Chronology of the works of GUILLAUME DUFAY, based on a study of mensural practice. Princeton, N.J.: Princeton Univ. Press, 1964.

4370. Stainer, J. F. R. and C. Stainer. DUFAY and his contemporaries. New York: Broude Brothers Limited (Facsimile), 1963. (orig. London, 1898.)

4371. DUPRE, MARCEL. Recollections. Foreword by O. Messiaen. Trans. and ed. by R. Kneeream. Melville, N.Y.: Belwin-Mills Pub. Corp., 1975.

4372. Auerbach, Johanna Maria. Die Messen des FRANCESCO DURANTE. Ein Beitrag zur Geschichte der neapolitanischen Kirchenmusik. München: N.G., 1954. (LC5822464)

4373. Roey, Johan de. AIME DUVAL en het religieuse chanson, etc. With plates and with a list of gramophone records. Tielt, Den Haag: Humanitas-boekje, 1960.

4374. ________. Pater DUVAL und das religiöse Chanson. (Aus dem Flämischen übertragen von G. Hermanowski.) München: Manz, 1961.

4375. Fischl, Viktor (ed.). ANTONIN DVORAK: his achievement. Westport, Conn.: Greenwood Press, 1970. (repr. of London: L. Drummond, 1943.)

4376. Mariánková, Jana. ANTONIN DVORAK, 8. 9. 1841-1. 5. 1904 (Edice KKKladno. Bibliografie. Malá rada, 39.) Kladno: Kraj. knihovna, 1974.

4377. Stefan, Paul. (Transl. by Y. W. Vance.) ANTON DVORAK. New York: Da Capo Press, 1971. (orig. New York: The Greystone Press, 1941.)

4378. Mittring, G. and G. Rödding. Musik als Lobgesang; Festschrift für WILHELM EHMANN. Darmstadt: Tonkunst-Verlag, 1964.

4379. Reed, W. H. ELGAR. New York: E. P. Dutton & Co., 1939.

4380. Koechlin, Charles L. GABRIEL FAURE (1845-1924). London: Dobson, n.d. 2nd ed. Paris: F. Alcan, 1927.

4381. Main, Alexander. The Sacred music of COSTANZO FESTA. New York: New York Univ., Graduate School of Arts and Science, n.d.

4382. Clinkscale, Edward. The Complete works of ANTOINE de FEVIN. New York: New York Univ., Graduate School of Arts and Science, 1961.

4383. Foote, Arthur, 2nd. HENRY WILDER FOOTE, hymnologist. New York: The Hymn Society of America, 1968.

4384. Sabatier, Paul. Life of ST. FRANCIS of Assisi. N.G.: N.G., 1894.

4385. Demuth, Norman. CESAR FRANCK. New York: Alexander Broude, Inc., n.d.

4386. D'Indy, Vincent. CESAR FRANCK. London: John Lane, 1909.

4387. Landgraf, Armin. Musica sacra zwischen Symphonie und Improvisation: CESAR FRANCK und sein Musik für den Gottesdienst. Tutzing: Schneider, 1975.

4388. Cametti, Alberto. GIROLAMO FRESCOBALDI in Roma, 1604-1643. Con appendice sugli organi, organaii ed organisti della basilica vaticana nel secolo XVII. With illustrations. Torino: Estratto dalla Rivista Musicale Italiana, 1908.

4389. Köchel, Ludwig Ritter von. JOHANN JOSEF FUX, Hofcompositor und Hofkapellmeister der Kaiser Leopold I., Josef I. und Karl VI, von 1698 bis 1740. (Reprint.) Hildesheim and New York: G. Olms, 1974.

4390. Arnold, Denis. GIOVANNI GABRIELI (Oxford Studies of Composers, 12). London: Oxford Univ. Press, 1974.

4391. Kenton, Egon. Life and works of GIOVANNI GABRIELI. Rome: American Institute of Musicology, 1967.

4392. Winterfeld, Carl Georg August. JOHANNES GABRIELI und sein Zeitalter. Berlin: Schlisenger, 1834.

4393. Moorefield, Arthur A. The Music of JOHANNES GALLICULUS and its function in the early Lutheran liturgy. Ann Arbor, Mich.: Univ. Microfilms, 1965.

4394. Chiuminatto, Anthony. The Liturgical works of BALDASSARE GALUPPI. Evanston, Ill.: Northwestern Univ., 1958.

4395. Pogemiller, Raymond. Selected works of FRANCESCO GASPARINI: Messa a quattro voci a cappella and Messa concertata a più voci con istrumenti. Ann Arbor: Univ. Microfilms, 1967.

4396. Funk, Theophil. ERNST GEBHARDT, der Evangeliums-Sänger. Stuttgart: Christliches, 1969.

4397. Rigsby, Oscar Lee. The Sacred music of ELZEAR GENET. Ann Arbor: Univ. of Michigan, 1955.

4398. Motz, Georg. Die vertheidigte Kirchen-Musik, oder klar und deutlicher Beweis/welcher Gestalten Hr. M. CHRISTIAN GERBER ... in seinem Buch/welches er unerkandte Sünden der Welt nennet/zu Verwerfung der musicalischen Harmonie und Bestraffung der Kirchen-Musik zu weit gegangen. Tilsit: N. G., 1703. (LC-ML-3001. M7)

4399. Hewitt, T. B. PAUL GERHARDT as a hymn writer. New Haven: Yale Univ. Press, 1918.

4400. Fellowes, Edmund H. ORLANDO GIBBONS. New York: Carl Fischer, Oxford Univ. Press, 1925.

4401. Winter, Carl. RUGGIERO GIOVANNELLI; eine stilkritische Studie zur Geschichte der römischen Schule um die Wende des 16. Jahrhunderts. München: Musikwissenschaftliches Seminar der Universität München, 1935.

4402. Brown, David. MIKHAIL GLINKA; a biographical and critical study. London and New York: Oxford University Press, 1974.

4403. Montagu, Nathan. GLINKA. New York: AMS Press, 1976.

4404. Orlova, Aleksandra Anatolevno. GLINKA v Peterburge. Leningrad: Lenizdat, 1970.

4405. Winter, Paul. GOETHE erlebt Kirchenmusik in Italien; Darstellung nach Selbstzeugnissen. Hamburg: H. Dulk, 1949.

4406. Santi, Angelo de. S. GREGORIO Mango, Leone XIII, e il canto liturgico; discorso letto ... nel saggio solenne di musica sacra ossequiosamente offerto a Sua Santita dagli alunni del ven. Roma: Tip. A. Befani, 1891.

4407. Vivell, C. Vom Musik-Traktate GREGORS des GROSSEN. Leipzig: Breitkopf & Härtel, 1911.

4408. GRETCHANINOFF, ALEXANDRE. My life. (Introduction and translation by Nicolas Slonimsky.) New York: Coleman-Ross Co., 1952.

4409. Monrad-Johansen, D. EDVARD GRIEG. New York: N.G., 1945.

4410. Maisel, E. M. CHARLES T. GRIFFES: Life of an American composer. New York: N.G., 1943.

Georg Friedrich Händel

4411. Abraham, Gerald (ed.). HÄNDEL: a symposium. London: Oxford Univ. Press, 1954.

4412. Antonicek, Theophil. Zur Pflege HÄNDELSCHER Musik in der 2. Hälfte des 18. Jahrhunderts. Graz: Böhlau in Kommission, 1966.

4413. Bell, Arnold Craig. HÄNDEL before England. Darley: Grian-Aig Press, 1975.

4414. ________. HÄNDEL: chronological thematic catalog. Darley: Grian-Aig Press, 1973.

4415. Chrysander. GEORG FRIEDRICH HÄNDEL. 3 vols. Leipzig: Breitkopf & Härtel, 1856-1867.

4416. Chrysander, Friedrich. G. F. HÄNDEL. Hildesheim, Germany: George Olms-Reprint, 1966. (orig. Leipzig, 1858-67.)

4417. ________. GEORG FRIEDRICK HÄNDELS Werke. 96 vols. and 6 supple. Leipzig: Breitkopf & Härtel (1854-1894), 1902.

4418. Clausen, Hans Dieter. HÄNDELS Direktionspartituren. Hamburg: Verlag der Musikalienhandlung, 1972.

4419. Dean, Winton. HÄNDEL'S dramatic oratorios and masques. New York: Oxford Univ. Press, 1959.

4420. Dent, Edward J. HÄNDEL. London: Duckworth, 1947.

4421. Deutsch, Otto E. HÄNDEL: A documentary bibliography. New York: Norton, 1955.

4422. Flower, Newman. GEORGE FRIDERIC HÄNDEL, his personality and his times. London: Cassell, 1959; also London: Panther, 1972.

4423. Hadden, James Cuthbert. Life of HÄNDEL. New York: AMS Press, 1976.

4424. HÄNDEL, G. F. Complete works. New York: A. Broude, Inc., 1965.

4425. Lang, Paul Henry. GEORGE FRIDERIC HÄNDEL. New York: W. W. Norton, 1966.

4426. Larsen, Jens Peter. HÄNDEL'S Messiah: Origins, compositions, sources. New York: W. W. Norton & Co., 1957.

4427. Laubscher, Friedrich. Ich weiss dass mein Erlöser lebt: HÄNDELS Glaubenbekenntnis. Lahr-Dinglingen, (Baden): Verlag der Sankt-Johannis-Druckerei Schweickhardt, 1974.

4428. Mainwaring, John. Memoirs of the life of the late GEORGE FREDERIC HÄNDEL. New York: Broude Brothers Limited (Facsimile), 1964. (orig. London, 1760.)

4429. Myers, Robert Manson. Early moral criticism of HÄNDELIAN oratorio. Williamsburg, Va.: Manson Park Press, 1947.

4430. ________. HÄNDEL'S Messiah: A touchstone of taste. New York: The Macmillan Co., 1948.

4431. Petzold, Richard. GEORG FRIEDRICH HÄNDEL. Sein Leben in Bildern. Kommentierter Bildt.: Eduard Crass. Leipzig: Bibliographisches Institut, 1965.

4432. Rackwitz, Werner and Helmut Steffens. GEORGE FRIEDRICH HÄNDEL. Leipzig: VEB Editions, 1963.

4433. Ramsy, William H. An Analytical report of "O Come Let Us Sing Unto the Lord" by GEORGE FRIEDRICH HÄNDEL and "Jonah" by Richard Wayne Dirksen. Ann Arbor: Univ. Microfilms, Columbia Univ. diss., 1963.

4434. Sasse, Konrad. HÄNDEL-Bibliographie. Leipzig: Deutscher Verlag für Musik, 1963.

4435. Streatfeild, Richard A. HÄNDEL. New York: Da Capo Press, 1964.

4436. Taylor, Sedley. The Indebtedness of HÄNDEL to works of other composers. Cambridge: Univ. Press, 1906.

4437. Tobin, John. HÄNDEL at work. New York: St. Martin's Press, 1964 (1965).

4438. Völsing, Erwin. G. F. HÄNDELS englische Kirchenmusik. Leipzig: F. Kistner & C. F. W. Siegel, 1940.

4439. Weinstock, Herbert. HÄNDEL. (2nd ed., rev.). New York: Alfred A. Knopf, 1959.

4440. Young, Percy M. HÄNDEL. London: J. M. Dent; New York: E. P. Dutton, 1947; rev. ed. London: J. M. Dent, 1975.

* * *

4441. Hiller, Johann Adam. Beyträge zu wahrer Kirchenmusik. (um J. A. HASSE.) Leipzig: Bey A. F. Böhme, 1791.

4442. Barlow, Carl Leland. Four-part through seven-part Sacrae Symphoniae collected and published in 1600 by CASPAR HASSLER. Ann Arbor: Univ. Microfilms, 1966.

4443. Dooley, James E. THOMAS HASTINGS: American church musician. Ann Arbor: Univ. Microfilms, Florida State Univ. diss., 1963.

Josef Franz Haydn

4444. Geiringer, Karl. HAYDN: a creative life in music. Berkeley: Univ. of California Press, 1967.

4445. ________. "The Small sacred works by HAYDN in the Esterhazy Archives at Eisenstadt," The Musical Quarterly, XLV/4, 460-72. Oct. 1959.

4446. Gotwals, Vernon. JOSEPH HAYDN: Eighteenth-century gentleman and genius. Madison: The Univ. of Wisconsin Press, 1963.

4447. Hadow, William Henry. Collected essays. Contains famous essay on HAYDN as a Croatian composer. London: H. Milford, 1928.

4448. Hobeken, Anthony van, editor. JOSEPH HAYDN: thematisch-bibliographisches Werkverzeichnis. Band II. Mainz: B. Schott's Söhne, 1971.

4449. International Music Society. HAYDN--zentenarfeier. Wien: Artaria & Co., 1909.

4450. Jacob, H. E. JOSEPH HAYDN: his art, times and glory. Westport, Conn.: Greenwood Press, 1971. (Repr. New York: Rinehart, 1950.)

4451. Landon, Howard C. R. HAYDN: chronicle and works. Vol. 1-5. Bloomington: Indiana Univ. Press, 1976-19--.

* * *

4452. Bronarski, Ludwig. Die Lieder der hl. HILDEGARD. Ein Beitrag zur Geschichte der geistlichen Musik des Mittelalters. Zürich: Buchdr. gerb. Leeman & Co., 1922.

4453. Hoffman, Ernst Theodor Wilhelm. E. T. A. HOFFMAN musikalische Schriften. Stuttgart: Greiner und Pfeiffer, 1907.

4454. Boyer, Daniel Royce. GUSTAY HOLST'S: The hymn of Jesus. Ann Arbor: Univ. Microfilms, 1968.

4455. Holst, Imogen. The Music of GUSTAV HOLST. New York: Oxford Univ. Press, 1951.

4456. Sonneck, Oscar G. T. FRANCIS HOPKINSON, the first American poet-composer and our musical life in colonial times. Philadelphia: Historical Society of Philadelphia, 1919; also Repr. New York: A. Broude, 1966.

4457. Kumlien, Wendell Clarke. The Sacred choral music of CHARLES IVES: a study in style development. Ann Arbor: Univ. Microfilms, 1969.

4458. Sceats, G. KARG-ELERT. New York: C. F. Peters Corporation, 1967.

4459. _______. The Organ works of KARG-ELERT. New York: C. F. Peters Corporation, n. d.

4460. Lock, Walter. JOHN KEBLE: A biography. London: N. G., 1893. Repr. London: Methuen & Co., 1905.

4461. Labat, Jean Baptiste. Ouvres litteraires-musicales de J. B. LABAT. Paris: J. Baur, 1879-83.

4462. Paladi, Marta. ORLANDO di Lasso. Bucureşti, Romania: Editura muzicalǎ.

4463. Sharp, Geoffrey B. LASSUS and Palestrina. Sevenoaks, London: Novello, 1972.

4464. Crawford, Richard. ANDREW LAW, American psalmodist. Evanston: Northwestern Univ. Press, 1968.

4465. MacDonald, John Alexander. The Sacred vocal music of GIOVANNI LEGRENZI. Ann Arbor: Univ. Microfilms, 1964.

4466. Souluri, James Joseph. The Concerti Ecclesiastici of LODOVICO GROSSI da VIADANA. Ann Arbor: Univ. Microfilms, 1963.

* * *

Martin Luther

4467. Achelis, E. Die Entstehungszeit von LUTHERS geistlichen Liedern. Marburg: N. G., 1884. (BM)

4468. Anton, Karl. LUTHER und die Musik. Zwickau: N. G., 1928.

4469. Bacon, Leonard Woolsey. The Hymns of MARTIN LUTHER. New York: Charles Scribner's Sons, 1883.

4470. Buszin, Walter. "LUTHER on music." The Musical Quarterly, XXXII/1 (January), 80-97, 1946.

4471. Gerbert, C. Die Abfassung des LUTHERliedes: "Ein feste Burg ist unser Gott." Zürich: N. G., 1884. (BM)

4472. Grew, Eva Mary. "MARTIN LUTHER and music," Music & Letters, XIX/1, 67-78. January 1938.

4473. Grisar, H. LUTHER. London: K. Paul, Trench, Trübner & Co., ltd., 1913-1917.

4474. Lambert, James F. LUTHER'S hymns. Philadelphia: General Council Publication House, 1917.

4474a. Linke, J. Wann wurde das LUTHERlied "Ein feste Burg ist unser Gott" verfast? Leipzig: Buchhandlung des Verinshäuses, 1886.

4475. Moser, H. J. Die Melodien der LUTHERlieden. Leipzig: G. Schloessmann (G. Fick), 1935.

4476. Moser, Hans Joachim, and Otto Daube. Die Wittenbergische Nachtigall; MARTIN LUTHER und die Musik (Quellenhefte zur Musikkunde und Musikgeschichte im Schulunterricht, 4.). Dortmund: Cruwell, 1962.

4477. Nettl, Paul. LUTHER and music. Philadelphia: N. G., 1948. (New York: Russell and Russell, 1967; [Repr. from New York Public Library]).

4478. Rambach, August Jakob. Ueber D. MARTIN LUTHER'S Verdienst um den Kirchengesang, oder Darstellung desjenigen, was er als Liturg, als Liederdichter und Tonsetzer zur Verbesserung des öffentlichen Gottesdienstes geleistet hat. Nebst einem aus den Originalen genommenen Abdrucke sämmtlicher Lieder und Melodien Luthers, wie auch der Vorreden zu seinem Gesangbuche. Hamburg: Bohnische Buchhandlung, 1813. (Also available Reprint-Georg Olms. Hildesheim, Germany, 1967.)

4479. Rautenstrauch, Johannes. LUTHER und die Pflege der kirchlichen Musik in Sachsen (14.-19. Jahrh.) Reprt. - of Ausgabe Leipzig 1907 ed. Hildesheim: G. Olms Verlag, 1970.

4480. Reed, Luther D. LUTHER and congregational song. New York: Hymn Society of America, 1947.

4481. Rotermund, Donald O. LUTHER'S ideas in the development of music in the Lutheran church. Denton, Tex.: NTSU, M.A., 1958.

4482. Wackernagel, Karl Eduard Philipp. MARTIN LUTHERS geistliche Lieder. Hildesheim, Germany: Georg Olms-Reprint, 1967. (orig. Stuttgart, 1848.)

4483. Winterfeld, Carl Von, hrsg. MARTIN LUTHERS deutsche geistliche Lieder. Hildesheim: G. Olms, 1966. (orig. Ausgabe 1840 ed.)

4484. Zelle, Friedrich. Ein Feste Burg ist unser Gott. Zur Entwickelung des evangelischen Choralgesanges. (LUTHER). Berlin: G. Gaertner, 1895.

* * *

4485. Levarie, Siegmund. GUILLAUME de MACHAUT (of series-"Great Religious Composers.") New York: Sheed & Ward, 1954.

4486. Blankenburg, Walter and others, editors. Keryama und Melos. CHRISTHARD MAHRENHOLZ 70 Jahre. Kassel: Bärenreiter, 1970.

4487. MANN, ARTHUR HENRY. A Memoir. Cambridge: Cambridge Univ. Press, 1930.

4488. Douen, Orentin. CLEMENT MAROT et le Psautier Huguenot. Paris: Imprimerie nationale, 1878-79.

4489. Brawley, John Gray, Jr. The Magnificats, hymns, motets, and secular compositions of JOHANNES MARTINI. Ann Arbor: Univ. Microfilms, 1968.

4490. Wiechens, Bernaward. Die Kompositions-theorie und das kirchenmusikalische Schaffen PADRE MARTINIS. Regensburg: Bosse, 1968.

4491. Gray, Arlene. LOWELL MASON'S contribution to American church Music. Rochester, N.Y.: Univ. of Rochester, Eastman School of Music, 1941.

4492. Mason, Henry L. Hymn-tunes of LOWELL MASON. Cambridge: Harvard Univ. Press, 1944.

4493. ________. Hymn-tunes of LOWELL MASON: a bibliography. New York: AMS Press, 1976. (Reprint--orig. Cambridge, Mass.: Univ. Press, 1944.)

4494. ________. Musical letter from abroad: including detailed accounts of the Birmingham, Norwich, and Dusseldorf musical festivals of 1852. New York: Mason Brothers, 1854.

4495. Rich, Arthur Lowndes. LOWELL MASON. Chapel Hill: Univ. of North Carolina Press, 1946.

4496. Hathaway, J. W. G. An Analysis of MENDELSSOHN'S organ works. London: W. Reeves, 1898.

4497. Jacob, Heinrich Eduard. FELIX MENDELSSOHN and his times. (Trans. by Richard and Clara Winston.) Englewood Cliffs, N. J.: Prentice-Hall, 1963.

4498. Werner, Eric. MENDELSSOHN: A new image of the composer and his age. (Trans. by Dika Newlin.) London: The Free Press of Glencoe-Collier-Macmillan, 1963.

4499. MERBECKE, JOHN (also spelled Marbecke). A Booke of Notes and commonplaces. London: N. G., 1581.

4500. Bastian, James George, Jr. The Sacred music of CLAUDIO MERULO. Ann Arbor: Univ. Microfilms, 1967.

4501. Ahrens, Sieglinde, Hans Dieter Möller and Almut Rössler. Das Orgelwerk MESSIAENS. Duisburg: Gilles und Francke, 1976.

4502. Johnson, Robert Sherlaw. MESSIAEN. Berkeley & Los Angeles, Cal.: Univ. of California Press, 1975.

4503. Samuel, Claude. Conversations with OLIVIER MESSIAEN. (Trans. by Felix Aprahamian.) New York: Galaxy Music Corp., n. d.

4504. Kammerer, Heinrich. HALLAR MICHAEL, katholischer Kirchenkomponist in Regensburg. München: N. G., 1956.

4505. Oberg, Paul Matthews. The sacred music of PHILIPPE de MONTE. Rochester, N. Y.: Univ. of Rochester, Eastman School of Music, n. d.

4506. An Alphabetical index to CLAUDIO MONTEVERDI-Tutte le Opere. New York: Music Library Association, 1965.

4507. Moody, W. R. D. L. MOODY. New York: N. G., 1930.

4508. The Life of DWIGHT L. MOODY. New York: N. G., 1900.

Wolfgang Amadeus Mozart

4509. Angermüller, Rudolph and Otto Schneider. MOZART-Bibliographie (bis 1970). (Mozart-Jahrbuch, 1975.) Kassel:

Bärenreiter auch Salzburg: Internationale Stiftung Mozarteum, 1976.

4510. Biancolli, Louis, comp. and ed. The MOZART handbook: a guide to the man and his music. Cleveland & New York: The World Publ. Co., 1954.

4511. Blom, Eric. MOZART. (rev. ed.) (orig. 1935.) London: J. M. Dent & Sons, 1962.

4512. Briggs, Wilfred Arnold. The Choral church music of WOLFGANG AMADEUS MOZART (1756-1791). Ann Arbor: Univ. Microfilms, 1966.

4513. Deutsch, Otto Eric. MOZART: A documentary biography. (Transl. by Eric Blom, Peter Branscombe and Jeremy Noble--from supplement to Neue Mozart-Ausgabe, publ. by Internationale Mozarteum, in Salzburg--date n. d.) Stanford, Cal.: Stanford Univ. Press, 1965-66.

4514. Einstein, Alfred. MOZART: his character and his work. (Transl. by Arthur Mendel and Nathan Broder--orig. data n. d.) London, New York and Toronto: Oxford Univ. Press, 1945.

4515. Hutchings, Arthur. MOZART: the man, the musician. New York: Schirmer Books (Macmillan), 1976.

4516. Millerick, Velberta A. A Stylistic analysis of MOZART'S eight offertories. Austin, Tex.: Univ. of Texas, M. M., 1961.

4517. Paap, Wouter. MOZART: portret van een muziekgenie. 3e, herz. en uitgebreide dr. Utrecht: Het Spectrum, 1976.

4518. Schenk, Erich. MOZART and his times. (Ed. and transl. by Richard and Clara Winston, orig. publ. as "Wolfgang Amadeus Mozart, eine Biographie." Wien: Almathea-Verlag, 1955.) New York: Alfred A. Knopf, 1959.

4519. Turner, W. J. (ed. & rev. by Christopher Raeburn). MOZART, the man and his works. (orig. c. 1945.)

* * *

4520. Schuler, Richard J. The Life and liturgical works of GIOVANNI MARIA NANINO (1545-1607). Ann Arbor: Univ. Microfilms, Univ. of Minnesota diss., 1963.

4521. Letters of JOHN MASON NEALE, D. D. London: N. G., 1910.

4522. Hutton, Richard H. CARDINAL NEWMAN. London: Methuen & Co., 1891.

4523. Martin Barnard Davis. An Ancient mariner. A biography of JOHN NEWTON. A revised ed. of "John Newton." London: Epworth Press, 1960.

4524. Henze, Marianne. Studien zu den Messenkompositionen JOHANNES OCKEGHEMS. Berlin: Merseburger, 1968.

4525. Krenek, Ernest. OCKEGHEM, JOHANNES (1430-1495). New York: Great Religious Composers, 1953.

4526. Strassler, Paul Gene. Hymns for the church year, Magnificats, and other sacred choral works of DIEGO ORTIZ (with) musical supplement. Ann Arbor: Univ. Microfilms, 1966.

Giovanni Pierluigi da Palestrina

4527. Baini, Giuseppe. Memorie storico-critiche della vita e delle opere di GIOVANNI PIERLUIGI da PALESTRINA. Hildesheim, Germany: Georg Olms-Reprint, 1966. (orig. Rome, 1828.)

4528. Boyd, Malcolm. PALESTRINA'S style; a practical introduction. London: Oxford Univ. Press, 1973.

4529. Coates, Henry. PALESTRINA. New York: E. P. Dutton & Co., 1938.

4530. Felix, Gabrielle. PALESTRINA et la musique sacrée. Bruges: Société de St. Augustin, Desclée, 1895.

4531. Jeppesen, Knud. The style of PALESTRINA and the dissonance. New York: Dover Publications, 1970.

4532. King, Ethel M. PALESTRINA, the prince of music. Brooklyn, N.Y.: Theo. Gaus' Sons, 1965.

4533. PALESTRINA, G. P. Opere complete. New York: A. Broude, Inc., 1965.

4534. Pyne, Zoe Kindrick. GIOVANNI PIERLUIGI da PALESTRINA, his life and times. Freeport, N.Y.: Books for Libraries Press, 1970.

4535. Roche, Jerome. PALESTRINA. London: Oxford Univ. Press, 1971.

* * *

4536. Semler, Isabel Parker. HORATIO PARKER. New York: C. P. Putnam's Sons, 1942.

4537. Tovey, Donald and Geoffrey Parratt. WALTER PARRATT. London: Oxford Univ. Press, 1941.

4538. Fuller-Maitland, J. A. The Music of PARRY and STANFORD. Cambridge: W. Heffer & Sons, 1934.

4539. Bruni, Massimo. LORENZO PEROSI; il cantore evangelico. Torino: Teca, 1972.

4540. Lyder, Peguy. The Latin sacred music of PETER PHILIPS. New York: New York Univ., Graduate School of Arts and Science, 1955.

4541. Cambon, Elise. Sacred music by FRANCIS POULENC. Guild of Organists Quarterly, Oct., 1963.

4542. Landreth, Joe Alton. The Unaccompanied mass, motets and cantatas of FRANCIS POULENC. Dallas, Tex.: Southern Methodist Univ., M.M., 1953.

4543. Neely, James Kilford. The Sacred choral music of FRANCIS POULENC. Austin, Tex.: Univ. of Texas, M.M., 1952.

4544. Gable, Frederick Kent. Polychoral motets of HIERONYMUS PRAETORIUS (1560-1629). Ann Arbor: Univ. Microfilms, 1966.

4545. Weinmann, C. KARL PROSKE der Restaurator der klassischen Kirchenmusik. Sammlung "Kirchenmusik." Regensburg & New York: F. Pustet, 1909.

4546. Bonaccorsi, Alfredo. Le Musiche sacre dei PUCCINI. Lucca: Scuola tip. Artigianelli, 1934.

Henry Purcell

4547. Arundell, Dennis. HENRY PURCELL. London: Oxford Univ. Press, 1927.

4548. Editorial Committee-Music Library Association, New York Chapter. The Works of HENRY PURCELL. An index to the Purcell Society Edition. In progress and unpublished. New York: Music Library Assn., 1963.

4549. Holland, A. K. HENRY PURCELL: The English musical tradition. London: G. Bell & Sons, 1932.

4550. Holst, Imogen (ed.). HENRY PURCELL 1659-1695; essays on his music. London: Oxford Univ. Press, 1959.

4551. Westrup, J. A. PURCELL. London: J. M. Dent & Sons, 1937.

4552. Zimmerman, Franklin B. HENRY PURCELL, 1659-1695; an analytical catalogue of his music. New York: Macmillan, 1963.

4553. ______. HENRY PURCELL, 1659-1695: melodic and intervallic indexes to his complete works. Philadelphia: Smith-Edwards-Dunlap, 1975.

* * *

4554. Bertensson, Sergei and Jay Leyda. SERGEI RACHMANINOFF: A Lifetime in music. New York: New York Univ. Press, 1956.

4555. Kalkoff, Artur. Das Orgelschaffen MAX REGERS im Lichte der deutschen Orgelerneuerungsbewegung. Kassel: Bärenreiter-Verlag, 1950.

4556. Spigener, Tommy Ray. The Contributions of ISHAM E. REYNOLDS to church music in the Southern Baptist Convention between 1915-1945. Fort Worth, Tex.: Southwestern Baptist Theological Seminary, M. C. M., 1962.

4557. Johnson, Alvin. The Liturgical music of CIPRIANO da RORE. New Haven: Yale Univ., 1954.

4558. Lockwood, Lewis. The Sacred music of VINCENZO RUFFO. Princeton, N. J.: Princeton Univ., 1959.

4559. SAINT-SAËNS, CAMILLE. Ecole buissonnière: notes et souvenirs. Paris: P. Lafitte et c., 1913.

4560. Webhofer, Peter. GIOVANNI FELICE SANCES, ca. 1600-1679; biographisch-bibliographische Untersuchung und Studie über sein Motettenwerk. Innsbruck: Pontificio Istituto di musica sacra, 1965.

4561. The IRA P. SANKEY centenary. New Castle: N. G., 1941.

4562. SANKEY, IRA D. My life and the story of gospel hymns. Philadelphia, Penn.: P. W. Ziegler Co., 1907.

4563. Dent, Edward J. ALLESSANDRO SCARLATTI: his life and his works. Repr. with preface and additional notes by Frank Walker. (orig. -1905.) London: Edw. Arnold Publ., 1960.

4564. Pagano, Roberto and Lino Bianchi. ALESSANDRO SCARLATTI. Torino, Italy: Editzioni RAI, 1972.

4565. Kirkpatrick, Ralph. DOMENICO SCARLATTI. Princeton, N. J.: Princeton Univ. Press, 1953.

4566. Reckziegel, Walter. Das Cantional von JOHAN HERMAN SCHEIN. Seine geschichtliche Grundlagen. With illustrations, including musical illustrations. Berlin: Berliner Studien zur Musikwissenschaft, 1963.

4567. Cornelius, Heinrich. Gesammelte und ausgewählte Werke der SCHEUSINGER Dichterbrüder. Lütjenburg: P. C. Groth, 1915.

4568. Stuckenschmidt, H. H. ARNOLD SCHOENBERG. New York: Grove Press, 1960.

4569. FRANZ SCHUBERT complete works, volume 6 (series 13 & 14): Masses and smaller pieces of sacred music. New York: Alexander Broude, Inc., 1966.

4570. Flower, Newman, Sir. FRANZ SCHUBERT: The man and his circle. (new ed.) (orig. ed. 1923.) New York: Tudor Publ. Co., 1935.

4571. Reed, John. SCHUBERT, the final years. New York: St. Martins Press, 1972.

4572. Stringham, Ronald S. The Masses of FRANZ SCHUBERT. Ann Arbor: Univ. Microfilms, Cornell Univ., diss., 1964.

Heinrich Schütz

4573. Agey, Calvin Buell. A Study of the kleine geistliche Concerte and geistliche Chormusik of HEINRICH SCHÜTZ. Tallahassee: Florida State Univ., School of Music, 1955.

4574. Brodde, Otto. HEINRICH SCHÜTZ, Weg und Werk. Kassel: Bärenreiter, 1972.

4575. Eggebrecht, Hans Heinrich. SCHÜTZ and Gottesdienst. Stuttgart: Musikwissenschaftliche Verlags Gesellschaft, 1969.

4576. Eppstein, Hans. HEINRICH SCHÜTZ. Stockholm: Nordiska musicförlaget, 1972.

4577. ________. HEINRICH SCHÜTZ. Neuhausen-Stuttgarts: Hänssler, 1975.

4578. Moser, Hans Joachim. HEINRICH SCHÜTZ: A short account of his life and works. (Transl. and ed. by Derek McCulloch. from orig. --"Kleines Heinrich-Schütz-Buch.) New York: St. Martin's Press, 1967.

4579. Osthoff, Wolfgang. HEINRICH SCHÜTZ: l'incontro storico fra lingua tedesca e poetica nel seicento. Venezia: Centro tedesco di studi veneziani, 1974.

4580. Petzold, Richard. HEINRICH SCHÜTZ und seine Zeit in Bildern. Leipzig: Deutscher Verlag für Musik, 1972.

4581. Varnai, Peter. HEINRICH SCHÜTZ. (Kis zenei könyvtár, 8.) A verseket ford. Ormay Imre. Budapest: Gondolat, 1959.

4582. Wolfenbüttel. Herzog-August-Bibliothek. HEINRICH SCHÜTZ (1585-1672) in seinen Beziehung zum Wolfenbütteler Hof. Wolfenbüttel: Hans Haase, 1972.

* * *

4583. Grabs, Rudolf. ALBERT SCHWEITZER, Dienst am Menschen; ein Lebensbild. 3., unveränderte Auflage. Halle/Saale: Niemeyer, 1963.

4584. Jacobi, Erwin Reuben. ALBERT SCHWEITZER und die Musik. Jahresgabe d. Internat. Bachges. Wiesbaden: Breitkopf und Härtel, 1975.

4585. Joy, Charles R. Music in the life of ALBERT SCHWEITZER. New York: Harper & Bros. also Boston: Beacon Press, 1951.

4586. Payne, Robert. ALBERT SCHWEITZER und seine drei Welten; Biographie. Konstanz & Zürich: Diana-Verlag, 1964.

4587. Quoika, R. ALBERT SCHWEITZER'S Begegnung mit der Orgel. New York: C. F. Peters Corporation, 1967.

4588. Günther, Siegfried. Die geistliche Konzertmusik von THOMAS SELLE nebst einer biographie. Giessen: N. G., 1935. (LC36-25651)

4589. Hannekainen, Iimari. SIBELIUS and the development of Finnish music. New York: C. F. Peters Corporation, 1967.

4590. Söhngen, Oskar. Gestalt und Glaube. Festschrift für ... OSKAR SÖHNGEN zum 60. Geburtstag am 5. Dezember 1960. Herausgegeben von einem Freundeskreis. (Check also SONGEN.) With plates. Witten, Berlin: N. G., 1960. (BM-07903aa28)

4591. Parks, O. G. A Critical analysis of the works of LEO SOWERBY. Denton, Tex.: North Texas State Univ., M. M., 1941.

4592. Perrin, Phil D. Forsaken of Man by LEO SOWERBY; A stylistic analysis. Fort Worth, Tex.: Southwestern Baptist Theological Seminary, M. C. M., 1964.

4593. Greene, Harry Plunket. CHARLES VILLIERS STANFORD. London: Edward Arnold & Co., 1935.

4594. Porte, John F. Sir CHARLES V. STANFORD. London: Kegan Paul, Trench, Trubner, & Co., 1921.

4595. STOCK, ELLIOT. My Jubilee as a church musician, 1862-1912. N. G.: Elliot Stock (ed.), 1914. (BM)

4596. Müsel, Albrecht. Der mitteldeutsche Kantor und Hofkapellmeister JOHANN STOLLE (um 1566 bis 1614); Leben und Schaffen. Koln: Böhlau Verlag, 1970.

4597. Corle, Edwin (ed.). IGOR STRAVINSKY. New York: Merle Armitage, distr. by Duell, Sloane & Pearce, 1949.

4598. Craft, Robert. STRAVINSKY: Chronicle of a friendship. New York: Alfred A. Knopf, 1972.

4599. Libman, Lillian. And music at the close. (re: STRAVINSKY.) New York: W. W. Norton, 1972.

4600. Sullivan, Herbert and Newman Flower. Sir ARTHUR SULLIVAN: his life, letters, and diaries. New York: George H. Doran Co., 1927.

4601. Sego, Charles M. The Chorale variation technique of JAN PIETERSZOON SWEELINCK. Dallas, Tex.: Southern Methodist Univ., M. M., 1959.

4602. Doe, Paul. TALLIS. London and New York: Oxford Univ. Press, 1968.

4603. Eyzaguirre, Roberto. MELCHIOR TAPIA and music in the Lima cathedral. Ann Arbor: Xerox Univ. Microfilms, 1973.

4604. TAVERNER, JOHN. Works, vocal. New York: Oxford Univ. Press, 1923-24.

4605. Petzold, Richard. GEORG PHILIPP TELEMANN (Transl. by Horace Fitzpatrick from "Georg Philipp Telemann: Leben und Werk" Leipzig: VEB Deutscher Verlag für Musik, 1967). New York & London: Oxford Univ. Press, 1974.

4606. Andrews, Hilda. Westminster retrospect. (TERRY) London: Oxford Univ. Press, 1948.

4607. Mackey, Elizabeth Jocelyn. The Sacred music of JOHANN THEILE. Ann Arbor: Univ. Microfilms, 1968.

4608. O'Neal, Jerry Marcus. ERIC HARDING THIMAN: His sacred choral and sacred solo music. Fort Worth, Tex.: Southwestern Theological Seminary, M. C. M., 1962.

4609. Hoover, Kathleen and John Cage. VIRGIL THOMPSON: His life and music. New York & London: Thomas Yseloff, Publ., 1959.

4610. Thompson, Virgil. VIRGIL THOMPSON. New York: Alfred A. Knopf, 1966.

4611. Knauff, Christopher W. Doctor TUCKER, priest-musician. New York: A. D. F. Randolph Co., 1897.

4612. Franklin, Don Oscar. The Anthems of WILLIAM TURNER (1652-1740): an historical and stylistic study with musical supplement: transcription. Ann Arbor: Univ. Microfilms, 1967.

4613. Satterfield, John Roberts. The Latin church music of CHRISTOPHER TYE. With musical supplement. Ann Arbor: Univ. Microfilms, Univ. of North Carolina at Chapel Hill diss., 1962.

4614. Dickinson, A. E. F. VAUGHAN WILLIAMS. London: Faber and Faber, 1963.

4615. Foss, Hubert. RALPH VAUGHAN WILLIAMS (Repr. of London: G. G. Harrap & Co.-1950). Westport, Conn.: Greenwood Press, 1974.

4616. Howes, Frank. The Music of RALPH VAUGHAN WILLIAMS. (Repr. of London: Oxford Univ. Press, 1954.) Westport, Conn.: Greenwood Press, 1975.

4617. Hurd, Michael. VAUGHAN WILLIAMS. New York: Thomas Y. Crowell Co., 1970.

4618. Kennedy, Michael. The Works of RALPH VAUGHAN WILLIAMS. London, New York: Oxford Univ. Press, 1964.

4619. Vaughan Williams, Ursula. R. V. W.: A Biography of RALPH VAUGHAN WILLIAMS. London: Oxford Univ. Press, 1964.

4620. Young, Percy M. VAUGHAN WILLIAMS, RALPH. London: D. Dobson, 1953.

4621. Rüegge, Raimund. ORAZIO VECCHIS geistliche Werke. Bern: Haupt, 1967.

4622. Sheean, Vincent. Orpheus at eighty. (re: G. VERDI) New York: Random House, 1958.

4623. Toye, Francis. GIUSEPPE VERDI: his life and his works. (Repr. --"First publ. 'elsewhere'.") New York: Alfred A. Knopf, 1946.

4624. Verfel, Franz and Paul Stefan, eds. (transl. by Edward Downes.) VERDI, the man in his letters. New York: L. B. Fischer, Co., 1942.

4625. Walker, Frank. The Man VERDI. New York: Alfred A. Knopf Co., 1962 & 1972.

4626. Souluri, James Joseph. The Concerti Ecclesiastici of LODOVICO GROSSI da VIADANA. Ann Arbor: Univ. Microfilms, 1963.

4627. Cramer, Eugene Casjen. The Officium hebdomadae sacrae of TOMAS LUIS de VICTORIA. Ann Arbor: Univ. Microfilms, Boston Univ. Press-Diss., 1973.

4628. Pruett, James W. The Works of FILIPPO VITALI. The hymns of Filippo Vitali; musical supplement. Ann Arbor: Univ. Microfilms, Univ. of North Carolina diss., 1962.

4629. Suess, John Gunther. GIOVANNI BATTISTA VITALI and the sonata da chiesa. Ann Arbor: Univ. Microfilms, 1963.

4630. Coral, Lenore. Concordance of the thematic indexes to the instrumental works of ANTONIO VIVALDI. Ann Arbor, Mich.: Music Library Assoc., 1965.

4631. Kolneder, Walter. (transl. by Bill Hopkins.) ANTONIO VIVALDI: his life. (orig. Wiesbaden: Breitkopf u. Härtel, 1965.) Berkeley and Los Angeles, Cal.: Univ. of Cal. Press, 1970.

4632. Luciano, S. A., ed. ANTONIO VIVALDI, note e documenti sulla vita e sulle opere. Siena: N. G., 1939.

4633. Natkin, Marcel. ANTONIO VIVALDI, l'homme, son milieu et sa musique. Paris: Seghers, 1965.

4634. Pincherle, Marc. VIVALDI. Paris: Editions Le Bon Plaisir, 1955.

4635. ________. VIVALDI, genius of the Baroque. (transl. by Christopher Hatch.) New York: W. W. Norton, 1957.

4636. Bekker, Paul. (Transl. by M. M. Bozman.) RICHARD WAGNER: his life in his work. Freeport, N. Y.: Books for Libraries Press.

4637. Jones, Matt B. Bibliographical notes on THOMAS WALTER'S "Grounds and Rules of Musick Explained." Worcester, Mass.: American Antiquarian Society, 1933.

Isaac Watts

4638. Bishop, Selma. ISAAC WATTS--Hymns and Spiritual songs--1707-1748. A study in early eighteenth century language changes. (A collation of the earliest editions. With a bibliography.) London: Faith Press, 1962.

4639. Davis, A. P. ISAAC WATTS, his life and works. New York: The Dryden Press, 1943.

4640. Gibbons, Thomas. Memoirs of Reverend ISAAC WATTS. London: Printed for James Buckland, 1780.

4641. Hymn Society of America. Observing the ISAAC WATTS Bicentennial, 1948. New York: The Society, 1948.

4642. ________. A Service of divine worship commemorating the 200th anniversary of the death of ISAAC WATTS, etc. New York: The Society, 1948.

4643. Lyell, James P. R. Mrs. Piozzi and ISAAC WATTS. London: N. G., 1934.

4644. Presbyterian, Fort George. A Hymn festival commemorating the bicentenary of the death of ISAAC WATTS. Sunday, November 14, 1948, etc. A Programme. New York: N. G., 1948.

4645. WATTS, ISAAC. Discourses on the love of God. (4th ed.) London: J. Waugh, for J. Buckland, 1760.

4646. Watts, Thomas. Memories of Dr. ISAAC WATTS. N. G.: N. G., 1780.

* * *

4647. Richards, James H. SAMUEL WEBBE as a church composer. Waco, Tex.: Baylor Univ., M. M., 1965.

4648. Moldenhauer, Hans, comp. and Demar Irvine, ed. ANTON von WEBERN: perspectives. Seattle and London: Univ. of Washington, 1966.

The Wesleys

4649. Ambrose, Holmes. The Anglican anthems and Roman Catholic motets of SAMUEL WESLEY. Ann Arbor: Univ. Microfilms, 1969.

4650. Bashford, James Whitford. WESLEY and Goethe. Cincinnati: Jennings and Page; also New York: Eaton and Mains, 1903.

4651. Edwards, Maldwyn. JOHN WESLEY and the eighteenth century. London: G. Allen and Unwin, 1933.

4652. Findlay, George Hudson. Christ's Standard Bearer; a study of the hymns of CHARLES WESLEY as they are contained in the last edition (1876) of The People called Methodists, by the Rev. John Wesley. London: Epworth Press, 1956.

4653. Flew, Robert Newton. The Hymns of CHARLES WESLEY, A study of their structure. London: Epworth Press, 1953.

4654. Hatfield, James T. JOHN WESLEY'S translations of German hymns. New York: Publications-Modern Language Assoc. XI, 1896.

4655. Jones, D. M. CHARLES WESLEY, a study. London: Skeffington & Son, 1919.

4656. Lee, Humphrey. JOHN WESLEY and modern religion. Nashville: Cokesbury, 1936.

4657. Lightwood, James Thomas. SAMUEL WESLEY--musician; the story of his life. New York: B. Blohm, 1972.

4658. Manning, Bernard, Lord. The Hymns of WESLEY (CHARLES) and Watts (Isaac); five informal papers. London: Epworth Press, 1942.

4659. Monk, Robert. JOHN WESLEY: his Puritan heritage. Nashville: Abingdon Press, 1966.

4660. Neulsen, John Louis. JOHN WESLEY and the German hymn. (Trans. from the German by Theo Parry, Sydney H. Moore, and Arthur Holbrook.) Calverly: A. S. Holbrook, 1972.

4661. Rattenbury, John Ernest. The Eucharistic hymns of JOHN and CHARLES WESLEY, to which is appended Wesleys's preface extracted from Brevint's Christian Sacrament and Sacrifice, together with hymns on the Lord's Supper. London: Epworth Press, 1948.

4662. ________. WESLEY'S legacy to the world. Nashville: Cokesbury Press, 1928.

4663. Routley, Erik. The Musical WESLEYS. New York: Oxford Univ. Press, 1968.

4664. ________. The Musical WESLEYS. Westport, Conn.: Greenwood Press, 1976.

4665. Rowe, Kenneth E. (ed.). The Place of Wesley in the Christian tradition. "Essays delivered at Drew University in celebration of the publications of the Oxford edition of the works of JOHN WESLEY." A selected bibliography by Lawrence D. McIntosh. Metuchen, N.J.: Scarecrow Press, 1976.

4666. Scales, William Albert. Selected unpublished anthems of CHARLES WESLEY, Jr. Ann Arbor: Univ. Microfilms, 1969.

4667. Telford, John. The Treasure house of CHARLES WESLEY. London: Epworth Press, 1933.

4668. Wesley, Sam. SAMUEL WESLEY'S famous Bach letters to Benjamin Jacob. New York and London: C. F. Peters, n.d.

4669. Wisemann, F. Luke. CHARLES WESLEY. New York: Abingdon Press, 1932.

* * *

4670. Watson, Bula Trueblood. An Analysis of the hymns of JOHN GREENLEAF WHITTIER. Abilene, Tex.: Hardin-Simmons Univ., M.A., 1960.

4671. Hines, Dixie and H. P. Hanaford (eds.). WHO'S WHO in music and drama. See also British Music List. London and New York: Hanaford, 1914.

See also: 4, 60, 90, 103, 105, 251, 252, 254, 255, 256, 258, 265, 266, 267, 271, 272, 273, 275, 276, 278, 279, 287, 288, 291, 347, 373, 457, 495, 530, 655, 675, 738, 783, 906, 943, 952, 969, 994, 995, 997, 998, 1001, 1207, 1307, 1308, 1329, 1426, 1452, 1538, 1543, 1602, 1622, 1659, 1664, 1668, 1670, 1760, 1762, 1765, 1832, 1902, 1967, 1985, 1989, 2003, 2008, 2045, 2289, 2430, 2480, 2483, 2490, 2500, 2508, 2527, 2532, 2538, 2540, 2586, 2589, 2592, 2597, 2674, 2684, 2697, 2703, 2733, 2768, 2793, 2808, 2836, 2846, 3036, 3037, 3041, 3056, 3062, 3067, 3071, 3078, 3079, 3080, 3082, 3086, 3088, 3090, 3092, 3093, 3094, 3097, 3100, 3101, 3113, 3115, 3116, 3118, 3123, 3125, 3127, 3128, 3134, 3141, 3154, 3160, 3162, 3164, 3165, 3166, 3167, 3168, 3169, 3170, 3202, 3206, 3207, 3208, 3209, 3210, 3211, 3212, 3213, 3217, 3219, 3220, 3222, 3224, 3231, 3233, 3235, 3236, 3237, 3240, 3241, 3269, 3273, 3289, 3368, 3410, 3411, 3433, 3438, 3453, 3525, 3534, 3550, 3600, 3621, 3719, 3720, 3721, 3722, 3725, 3726, 3730, 3731, 3740, 3780, 3802, 3818, 3828, 3834, 3839, 3847, 3848, 3859, 3865, 3866, 3898, 3915, 3917, 3918, 3933, 3957, 4027, 4035, 4040, 4054, 4061, 4101, 4128, 4147, 4148, 4153, 4154, 4155,

4158, 4159, 4162, 4712, 4760, 4789, 4798, 4799, 4805, 4818, 4822, 4832, 4854, 4856, 4858, 4863, 4864, 4888, 4902, 4921, 4934, 4998, 5008, 5018, 5027, 5068, 5083, 5110, 5113, 5118, 5134, 5143, 5187, 5188, 5198, 5199, 5200, 5202, 5203, 5205, 5206, 5207, 5209, 5212, 5218, 5219, 5266, 5269, 5286, 5320.

PHILOSOPHY

4672. ADAMS, Zabdiel. The nature, pleasure and advantages of church-musick. Boston: Richard Draper, 1771.

4673. AGRESTI, Michele. Ragionamento sulla musica sacra. Roma: Tip. -della Pace di F. Cuggiani, 1884.

4674. ANDERSON, Warren D. Ethos and education in Greek music: the evidence of poetry and philosophy. Cambridge, Mass.: Harvard Univ. Press, 1967.

4675. AUGUSTINUS, Aurelius. Aurelii Augustini "De Musica." Firenze: Sansoni, 1969.

4676. BRADY, Nicholas. Church-musick vindicated. London: J. Wilde, 1697.

4677. COPPAGE, L. J. A treatise on principles which should govern use of music of God including suggestions as to its design, method and limitations with an appendix showing what should be our attitude towards those who differ from us. Crawfordsville, Ind.: N. G., 1893. (LC ML 3001. C78)

4678. DALTRY, Joseph S. Religious perspectives of college teaching in music. New Haven, Conn.: Edward W. Hazen Foundation, 195-.

4679. DUCASSE, Curt John. The philosophy of art. New York: Dover Publications, 1966.

4680. EARHART, Will. A steadfast philosophy. Washington, D. C.: Music Educators National Conference, 1962.

4681. FERGUSON, Donald. A history of musical thought. New York: Appleton-Century-Crofts, Inc., 1948.

4682. GELINEAU, Joseph. Chant et musique dans le culte chrétien. Principes, lois et applications. Paris: Kinnor, 1962.

4683. GRUNSKY, Karl. Das Christus-ideal in der Tonkunst. Leipzig: C. F. W. Siegel, 1920.

4684. HAMMER, Wolfgang. Musik als Sprache der Hoffnung. (Theologische Existenz heute, Neue Folge 99.) München: Kaiser, 1962.

4685. HASTINGS, Thomas. Sacred praise: an earnest appeal to Christian worshipers, in behalf of a neglected duty. New York: A. S. Barnes & Co., 1856.

4686. HAWEIS, H. R. Music and morals. New York: Harper & Brothers Publishers, 1877.

4687. HEIMSOETH, Heinz. Hegels Philosophie der Musik. Bonn: Bouvier, 1964.

4688. HUBBARD, John. An essay on music. Boston: Manning and Loring, 1808.

4689. KENNEDY, James. Christ in the song. Boston: Bradley & Woodruff, 1890.

4690. LABAT, Soeur Elizabeth-Paule, O. S. B. Essai sur le mystère de la musique. (Kinnor, 3.) Paris Editions Fleurus, 1963.

4691. LOWLSON, Clifford W. A mightier music. London: Epworth Press, 1934.

4692. MELLERS, Wilfrid. Music and society. New York: Dover Publications, Inc., 1965.

4693. MENDELSSOHN, Arnold. Gott, Welt und Kunst. Aufzeichnen. Wiesbaden: Insel-Verlag, 1949.

4694. NATIONAL Council of Churches of Christ, Ed. Committee. Christianity and the Arts. New York: Department of Worship and the Arts, National Council of the Churches of Christ in the U. S. A., 1955.

4695. PARKER, William. The pleasures of gratitude and benevolence improved by church-musick. London: J. Fletcher, 1753.

4696. PARRY. Evolution of the art of music. New York: Appleton, 1896.

4697. RAWLINS, John. The power of musick, and the particular influence of church musick. Oxford: Clarendon Press, 1773.

4698. RIEMER, Siegfried. Philosemitismus im deutschen evangelischen Kirchenlied des Barock. Stuttgart: Studia Delitzschiana, 1963.

4699. SACHS, Curt. The commonwealth of art. New York: W. W. Norton, 1946.

4700. SCHMID, Sebastian. Disputatio theologica de musica. Argentorati: Johannis Wilhelmi Tidemanni, 1673. (LC 21-2018)

4701. SCHMIDT, Johann Michael. Musico-theologici, oder erbauliche Anwendung musicalisher Wahrheiten. Bayreuth und Hof: J. G. Vierling, 1754.

4702. SCHREMS, Theobald. Music und Ethos; Kult und Kulture, Singen und Seelsorge; Denkschrift und Mahnruf. Regensburg: Habbel, 1962.

4703. SENSE against sound; A succedaneum for Abbey music. London: Printed for C. Stalker, 17--.

4704. SMITH, Robert. Harmonics, or the philosophy of musical sounds. New York: Scientific Library Service, 1749. Also as reprint: Da Capo Press, N. Y., 1966.

4705. SOWERBY, Leo. "Ideals in church music." Greenwich: Seabury Press, 1956.

4706. STIEVENARD, E. Philosophie de l'expression musicale. Bruxelles; Paris: Schott Frères, 1934.

4707. THIBAUT, Anton Friedrich Justus. Über Reinkeit der Tonkunst. Mit einem Vorwort von dr. K. Ch. W. F. Blair. Freiburg: J. C. B. Mohr, 1884.

See also: 66, 1302, 1335, 1460, 1552, 1579, 1580, 1581, 1588, 1590, 1594, 1596, 1598, 1599, 1601, 1604, 1605, 1606, 1681, 1688, 1718, 1781, 1793, 1831, 1846, 1853, 1856, 1859, 1865, 1866, 1952, 1981, 2002, 2116, 2122, 2441, 2664, 2762, 2763, 2764, 2848, 2923, 3266, 4110, 4123, 4155, 4258, 4447, 4767, 4768, 4777, 4786, 4788, 4950, 5089, 5204, 5233, 5234, 5395.

PHRASING, THE ART OF

4708. KELLER, Hermann. Phrasing and articulation, a contribution to a rhetoric of music, with 152 examples. Trans., Leigh Gerdine. New York: W. W. Norton, 1966, also London: Barrie & Rockcliff, 1966.

4709. WINTERFELD, Carl von. Über Herstellung des Gemeinde- und Chorgesänges in der Evangelischen Kirche. Geschichtliches und Vorschläge. Leipzig: Breitkopf und Härtel, 1848.

See also: 1003, 3726, 5130.

PIANO and PIANIST

4710. MATHIS, William S. The pianist and church music. Nashville: Abingdon Press, 1962, 1964.

See also: 2015, 4842.

POLYCHORAL WORKS

4711. DÜWELL, Klaus-Ulrich. Studien zur Kompositionstechnik der Mehrchörigkeit im 16. Jahrhundert. Dargestellt an Werken von Lasso, Palestrina, Victoria, 1963. Köln: Händel und Giovanni Gabrieli, 1963.

4712. FLETCHER, William Harold. Polychoral music and the double-choir motets of J. S. Bach. Abilene, Tex.: Hardin-Simmons University, M. M., 1950.

4713. WINTER, Paul. Der Mehrchörige Stil; historische Hinweise für die heutige Praxis. Frankfurt, London, N. Y.: Peters, 1964.

4714. ________. History of polychoral style and its application in contemporary performance practice. New York: C. F. Peters Corporation, 1967.

See also: 3035, 3223, 3242, 4390, 4544.

POLYPHONY

4715. BESSELER, Heinrich and Peter Gülke. Schriftbild der mehrstimmigen Musik. 1. Aufl. Leipzig: Deutscher Verlag für Musik, 1973.

4716. CRAWFORD, David Eugene. Vespers polyphony at Modena's Cathedral in the first half of the sixteenth century. Ann Arbor: Univ. Microfilms, 1967.

4717. EICHENAUER, R. Polyphonie-die ewige Sprache deutscher Seele. Wolfenbüttel und Berlin: G. Kallmeyer., 1938.

4718. EISIKOVITS, M. Polifonia barocului. Stilul bachian. Bucaresti: Editura muzicala, 1973.

4719. FEININGER, L. J. Die Frühgeschichte des Kanons bis Josquin des Prez, um 1500. Emsdetten: H. & J. Lechtie, 1937.

4720. FELLERER, Karl G. Altklassische Polyphonie. Köln: Volk, 1965.

4721. GERBER, Rudolf. Zur Geschichte des mehrstimmigen Hymnus; gesammelte Aufsätze. Kassel & New York: Bärenreiter, 1965.

4722. GERKEN, Robert Edward. The polyphonic cycles of the proper of the mass in the Trent Codex 88 and Jena choirbooks 30 and 35. Ann Arbor: Univ. Microfilms, 1969.

4723. GOELLNER, Theodor. Formen früher Mehrstimmigkeit in deutschen Handschriften des späten Mittelalters. Mit Veröffentlichung der Orgelspiellehre aus dem Cod. lat. 7755 der Bayer, Staatsbibliothek München. Tutzing: Münchner Veröffentlichungen zur Musikgeschichte, 1961.

4724. HUSMANN, H. Die dreistimmigen Organa der Notre Dame-Schule, mit besonderer Berucksichtigung der Handschriften Wolfenbüttel und Montpellier. Leipzig: Druck von Frommold & Wendler, 1935.

4725. KAT, A. I. M. Studie en uitvoering van de klassieke polyphonie. Bilthoven: De Gemeenschap, 1939.

4726. MERRITT, A. Tillman. Sixteenth century polyphony. Cambridge: Harvard Univ. Press, 1939.

4727. MOSER, Hans Joachim. Die mehrstimmige Vertonung des Evangeliums. Hildesheim: Georg Olms Verlag, 1968.

4728. PRESTON, Alan Herbert. Sacred polyphony in Renaissance Verona: a liturgical and stylistic study. Ann Arbor: Univ. Microfilms, 1969.

4729. SALZER, F. Sinn und Wesen der abendlandischen Mehrstimmigkeit. Wien: Saturn-Verlag, 1935.

4730. SHORE, S. R. The place of polyphony in English Reformation church music. Birmingham: N. G., 1912.

4731. STEPANOV, Aliksei Alekseevich and Aleksander Giorgievich Chugaev. Polyfoniîo. Moskva: Muzyka, 1972.

4732. WAITE, William G. The rhythm of twelfth century polyphony, its theory and practice. Westport, Conn.: Greenwood Press, 1973. (repr. of New Haven, Conn.: Yale Univ. Press, 1954.)

4733. YATES, Wilbur C. The history of the cadency in polyphonic vocal music through the fifteenth century. Ann Arbor: Univ. Microfilms, Indiana Univ. diss., 1962.

See also: 1040, 1473, 2721, 2801, 2889, 3013, 3033, 3044, 3045, 3046, 3091, 3130, 3142, 3199, 3227, 3527, 3587, 3680, 3681, 4106, 5015, 5017, 5042, 5197, 5275.

PRAYER

4734. BROU, Louis. Les oraisons dominicales. Deuxième série. De l'Avent à la Trinité. With the text of the prayers in various versions. Bruges: Paroisse et liturgie, 1960.

4735. JUNGMANN, Josef Andreas. Die Stellung Christi im liturgischen Gebet ... 2. Auflage. Photo-mechanischer Neudruck ... mit Nachträgen des Verfassers. Liturgiewissenschaftliche Quellen und Forschungen, Hft. 19/20. Münster: Aschendorf, 1962.

4736. ________. The place of Christ in liturgical prayer. 2nd rev. ed. trans. by A. Peeler. Staten Island, N. Y.: Alba House, 1965.

See also: 660, 753, 1275, 1290, 2310, 2866, 3499.

PRAYER BOOK

4737. The BOOK of Common Prayer. - 1549 - (BM)

4738. BURGESS, Francis G. The romance of the Book of Common Prayer. Milwaukee: Morehouse Publishing Co., 1930.

4739. CHURCH of England. The prayer book of King Edward the VII. N. G.: N. G., 1549. Facsimile reprint, 1844. (LC. 522422t)

4740. DEARMER, Percy. Everyman's history of the Prayer Book. N. G.: N. G., 1912. American ed., ref. by F. C. Morehouse. Milwaukee: Morehouse Publ. Co., 1931.

4741. ________. The story of the Prayer Book. New York: Oxford Univ. Press, 1933. (Revision of "Everyman's history of the Prayer Book.")

4742. EPISCOPAL Church of America. The Oxford American Prayer Book commentary. By Massey Hamilton Shepherd, Jr. The text of the revised Prayer Book of 1928, with a commentary. Wanting the psalter. The pagination of the commentary is irregular.

4743. MARBECKE, John. (also spelled MERBECKE). The Book of Common Prayer with musical notes. London: Rimboult; Douello, 1845.

4744. MAXWELL, William Delbert. The Book of Common Prayer and the Worship of the non-Anglican churches. Friends of Dr. William's Library. Lecture. London: Oxford Univ. Press, 1950.

4745. PARSONS, Edward Lambe, and Bayard Hall Jones. The American Prayer Book, its origins and principles. New York: Charles Scribner, 1937.

4746. PRAYER Book Studies. New York: Standing Liturgical Commission of the Protestant Church, 1950.

4747. PROCTER and Frere. A new history of the Book of Common Prayer. London: Macmillan, 1901.

4748. RIMBAULT, Edward F. John Merbecke's Book of Common Prayers as used in the Chapel Royal of Edward VI. London: N. G., 1845. (BM)

See also: 2165, 2268, 2281, 2853, 2917, 2978, 3073.

PRINTING-MUSIC

4749. BOHN, Emil. Bibliographie der Musik-Druckwerke bis 1700 ... in der Stadtbibliothek ... zu Breslau. Hildesheim, Germany: Georg Olms-Reprint, 1967. (orig. Berlin, 1883.)

4750. DAVIDSSON, Ake. Bibliographie zur Geschichte des Musikdrucks. Uppsala: Almquist und Wiksells, 1965.

4751. GOOVAERTS, Alphonse. Histoire et Bibliographie de la Typographie Musicale dans les Pays-Bas. New York: Broude Brothers, 1965. (Repr. of orig., Bruxelles, 1880.)

4752. KIDSON, Frank. British music publishers, printers, and engravers. Bronx, N. Y.: Benjamin Blom, Inc., 1967.

4753. KRUMMEL, Donald William. English music printing, 1553-1700. London and New York: Bibliographical Society, by Oxford Univ. Press, 1975-76.

4754. MAGGINI, Emilio (ed.). Lucca, Biblioteca del Seminario; catalogo delle musiche stampate e manoscritte del fondo antico. Milano: Istituto Editoriale Italiano, 1965.

4755. MOLITOR, Raphael. Deutsche Choral-Wiegendrucke. Reprt. -of Ausgabe Leipzig 1901-02 ed. Hildesheim: G. Olms Verlag, Regensburg and New York: F. Pustet, 1904.

4756. ZIRNBAUER, Heinz. Geistliche Musik des Mittelalters und der Renaissance. Handschriften und frühe Drucke in Nürnberger Bibliotheken. Ausstellung, etc. A catalogue. With plates. Nürnberg: Ausstellungskatalog der Stadtbibliothek Nürnberg, 1963.

See also: 2946, 3021, 3281, 3587, 3697, 4283.

PROCESSIONS

See: 404, 2840, 4930.

PRO ET CONTRA

4757. BOOK, Morris B. and James P. Miller. Book-Miller debate on instrumental music in worship. Gainesville, Fla.: Phillips Publications, 1955.

4758. BOSWELL, Ira Matthews. Boswell-Hardeman discussion on instrumental music in the worship. Nashville: Gospel Advocate Publ. Co., 1924.

4759. BRINEY, J. B. Instrumental music and Christian worship. Cincinnati: Standard Publ. Co., 1914.

4760. BROWN, Gerald Wayne. The historical significance of Miles Coverdale's Ghostly Songs and Spiritual Songs in the Sixteenth Century English Hymnody-Psalmody controversy. Fort Worth, Tex.: Southwestern Baptist Theological Seminary, M.C.M., 1964.

4761. BUNTING, Robert H. and J. D. Marion. Both sides of the music question discussed. Athens, Ala.: The C.E.I. Store, 1957.

4762. BURGESS, Tom. Documents on instrumental music. Portland, Ore.: Scripture Suppl. House, 1966.

4763. CANNON, Richard L. Defense of classic church music. Cincinnati: Press of the Methodist Book Concern, 1921.

4764. CHERBULIEZ, Antoine E. Zum problem der religiösen musik. N.G.: In "Zachweizerisches Jahrbuch für Musikwissenschaft," 1924.

4765. CLUBB, Merrel Dare. Discussion: Is instrumental music in Christian worship scriptural? Between M. D. Clubb, affirmant, and H. Leo Boles, negant. Nashville: Gospel Advocate Publ. Co., 1927.

4766. COLLEY, A. O. Instrumental music reviewed. Privately publ. Avail. Abilene Christian Univ., no date.

4767. A FEW plain and serious remarks upon singing the praises of God in public worship. Sherborne: J. Langdon, n.d. (LC-ML-8001. F3)

4768. HAMMETT, John. Promiscuous singing no divine institution; having neither precedent nor precept to support it, either from the musical institution of David, or from the gospel dispensation. n.p., 1739.

4769. HICKMAN, Charles. A sermon preached at the anniversary feast of the lovers of musick. London: W. Kettelby, 1696.

4770. JACOBS, Heinrich. Kirchenmusikalische Gegenwartsfragen. Aachen: J. Volk, 1939.

4771. LITURGICAL Conference, Inc. Harmony and discord: an open forum on church music. Washington: (Proceedings)--The Liturgical Conference and the Church Music Assoc. of America, 1966.

4772. McDONALD, Dean Earl. An analysis of the attitudes of worship of Roman Catholics toward the music of the renewed liturgy. Ann Arbor: Univ. Microfilms, 1969.

4773. MARLOW, Isaac. The controversie of singing brought to an end. A treatise in three parts. The first is a tract on singing. The second hath some remarks on Mr. Richard Allen's book, called An essay, with answers to them. And the third containeth several queries presented to divers elders, and ministers about London. London: Isaac Marlow, 1696.

4774. MATTHESON, Johann. Der neue göttingische aber viel schlechter/als die alten ladedämonischen, urtheilende Ephorus, wegen der Kirchenmusik eines andern belehret. Hamburg: J. C. Kissern, 1727.

4775. MOISSL, Franz. Von neuer Kirchen Musik; reaktionares und fortschriftliches. New York: Universal-Edition, 1926.

4776. NÄGELI, Hans Georg. Der Streit zwischen der alten und der neuen Musik. Enthaltend Nägeli's Beurtheilung der Schrift: Die Reinheit der Tonkunst in der Kirche: nebst der Erwiederung des Verfassers, so wie Gotts: Weber's Ansicht über denselben Gegenstand. Mit Anmerkungen hrsg. von einigen Freunden des guten Alten, wie des guten Neuen. Breslau: C. G. Förster, 1826.

4777. NEWES from Pauls. London: N. G., 1642. (LC)

4778. NEWTE, John. The lawfulness and use of organs in Christian church. London: F. Collins, 1701.

4779. NEWTON, John. The natural, moral, and divine influences of musick. London: E. Cave, 1748.

4780. NORDEN, Norris Lindsay. What is wrong with church music? n. p., 194-. (LC-49-44039)

4781. OF the use and abuse of music, particularly the music of the choir. N. G.: N. G., 1753.

4782. PAYNE, O. E. Instrumental music is scriptural. Cincinnati: Standard Publishing Co., 1920.

4783. PRICE, Uvedale Thomas Shudd. The conservatism of "The Standard" proved to be spurious and not sound; its objections to musical festivals and church music in general proved erroneous. London: J. Ridgway and Sons, 1834.

4784. SÖHNGEN, Oskar. Erneurte Kirkenmusik: eine Streitschrift. Göttingen: Vanderhoek und Ruprecht, 1975.

4785. SPANN, Carry Edward. The seventeenth century English Baptist controversy concerning singing. Fort Worth, Tex.: Southwestern Baptist Theological Seminary, M. C. M., 1965.

4786. TASWELL, William. The propriety and usefulness of sacred musick. Gloucester: C. Hitch, 1742.

4787. WAGNER, P. Der Kampf gegen die Editio Vaticana. Gray: N. G., 1907. (BM)

See also: 567, 643, 1105, 1198, 1201, 1202, 1570, 1574, 1688, 1703, 1706, 1803, 1860, 1976, 2503, 2733, 2756, 2762, 2763, 2764, 2772, 2773, 2778, 2782, 2952, 3773, 4294, 4672, 4676, 4677, 4685, 4695, 4700, 4793, 4918, 5243, 5301, 5344.

PROPRIETIES OF CHURCH MUSIC

4788. ELLIS, Ferdinand. An address on music. Boston: Russell & Cutler, 1806.

See also: 2746.

PSALMODY

4789. ANDERSON, Terrance Alfred. The metrical psalmody of Jan Pieterzoon Sweelinck. Ann Arbor: Univ. Microfilms, 1968.

4790. BARRINGTON, James Oris. The beginnings of psalmody in the English speaking colonies (1607-1700). Fort Worth, Tex.: Southwestern Baptist Theological Seminary, M. C. M., 1962.

4791. BONA, Giovanni. De divina psalmodia, eusque causis, mysteriis, et disciplinis, deque variis ritibus omnium ecclesiarum in psallendis divinis officiis, tractatus historicus, symbolicus, asceticus. Parisiss: Apud Lvdovicvm Billaine, 1663.

4792. BRUINSMA, Henry Allen. The Souterliedekens and its relation to psalmody in the Netherlands. East Lansing, Mich.: Michigan, Ph. D. (Research type-script), 1949.

4793. CLAYBAUGH, Joseph. The ordinance of praise. or An argument in favor of the exclusive use of the book of Psalms, in singing praises to God. With additional notes and appendix. Rossville: J. M. Christy, 1843.

4794. COLE, William. A view of modern psalmody. Being an attempt to reform the practice of singing in the worship of God. Colchester: J. Chaplin, 1819.

4795. EVANS, John. Practical observations on the due performance of psalmody. With short postscript, on the present state of vocal music in other departments. Bristol: The Bristol Observer, 1823.

4796. FINNEY, Theodore M. The third edition of Tufts' Introduction to the Art of Singing Psalm-Tunes. Baltimore, Md.: Music Educators National Conference, 1966.

4797. FISHER, William Arms. Ye old New England psalm tunes. (1620-1820). Boston: Oliver Ditson Co., 1930.

4798. FLETCHER, Donald R. English psalmody and Isaac Watts. Ann Arbor: Univ. Microfilms, 1951.

4799. HAMEL, Fred. Die Psalmenkompositien Johann Rosenmüllers, mit e. Anhang. (Neudr. 2 Aufl.) Baden-Baden: Koerner, 1973. (neu. Strassburg: Hertz & Co., 1933.)

4800. KENNEDY, Rann. Thoughts on the music and words of psalmody. London: Longman, Hurst, Rees, Orme, and Brown, 1821.

4801. LEEB, Helmut. Die Psalmodie bei Ambrosius. Wien: Herder, 1967.

4802. LEONARD, William A. Music in the western church. A lecture on the history of psalmody, illustrated with examples of the music of various periods. London: F. Pitman, 1812.

4803. MacDOUGALL, Hamilton C. Early New England psalmody. Brattleboro: Stephen Daye Press, 1940.

4804. ________. Early New England psalmody. An historical appreciation. New York: Da Capo Press, 1969. (Repr. - Brattleboro: S. Daye, 1940.)

4805. MacMILLAN, John Buchanan. The Calvinistic psalmody of Claude le Jeune--reference to the Dodecacorde of 1958. Ann Arbor: Univ. Microfilms, 1966.

4806. METCALF, Frank Johnson. American psalmody. Containing tunes printed in America from 1721-1820. New York: C. F. Heartman, 1917.

4807. MILLER, Edward. Thoughts on the present performance of psalmody in the established Church of England. London: Printed for W. Miller, 1791.

4808. MOCQUEREAU, Andre. Piccolo trattato di salmodia dei rr. pp. benedittini di Solesmes. Roma: Società di San Giovanni Evangelista, Desclée, Lefébvre et cie, tip., 1904.

4809. PATRICK, Millar. Four centuries of Scottish psalmody. London: Oxford Univ. Press, 1949.

4810. ROGERS, Kirby. An index to Maurice Frost's "English and Scottish psalm and hymn tunes." (MLA Index Series No. 8.) Ann Arbor: Music Library Association, 1967.

4811. ROMAINE, William. An essay on psalmody. New York: Scientific Library Service, 1775.

4812. SYMMES, William. The duty and advantages of singing praises unto God. Appointed to promote and encourage the religious art of psalmody. Boston: E. Russell, 1754.

4813. WALTER, Thomas. The Sweet Psalmist of Israel. Preached for reforming the depravations and debasements our psalmody labours under, in order to introduce the proper and true way of singing. Boston: J. Franklin, 1722.

4814. WARRINGTON, James. Short titles of books relating to, or illustrating the history and practice of psalmody in the United States 1620-1820. Philadelphia: Private print, 1898. (Printed, New York: Burt Franklin--Lennox-Hill Publ. Co., 1971.)

See also: 709, 1217, 1224, 1451, 1725, 2698, 3582, 3629, 4324, 4464, 4760, 4826, 4835, 4875, 4909, 4992, 5158.

PSALMS AS WORSHIP

4815. BEHRENS, Johan Diderik. Om den Lutherske salmesang og dens gjenindforelse: den norske kirke. Kristiania: Feilberg & Landmark, 1858.

4816. BERGER, Hugo. Untersuchungen zu den Psalmdifferenzen. Regensburg: Bosse, 1966.

4817. BRADY, Nicholas and Hahum Tate. A new version of the Psalms of David. London: The Company of Stationers, 1711.

4818. BRESHEARS, Donald Lee. The three-part psalms of Claude le Jeune, Premier Livre: a performance edition and commentary. Ann Arbor: Univ. Microfilms, 1966.

4819. CALVIN, Jean (John). Commentary on the Book of Psalms. Edinburgh: N. G., 1845-1849; also Grand Rapids: W. Eerdmans Publ. Co., 1949.

4820. COTTON, John. Singing of psalmes, a Gospel-ordinance. London: John Rothwell, 1647.

4821. COVERDALE, Miles. Ghostly psalmes and spirituall songs. Cambridge, England: Univ. of Cambridge Press, 1846.

4822. CRAWFORD, Richard A. Andrew Law, American psalmodist. (Pi Kappa Lambda studies in American music.) Evanston, Ill.: Northwestern Univ. Press, 1968.

4823. D'ISRAELI, Isaac. Curiosities of literature; article on psalm singing. Orig.--London: printed; Philadelphia: W. Gibbons; num. eds. incl. New York: D. Appleton, 193-.

4824. FROST, Maurice. English and Scottish psalm and hymn tunes. London: S. P. C. K. and Oxford Univ. Press, 1953.

4825. GREGORY, Arthur. Psalms and chanting. London: Epworth Press, 1946.

4826. GROVES, R. E. Some hints on the chanting of the Psalms. London: Novello, 1915.

4827. HARASZTI, Zoltan. The Bay Psalm Book. Facsimile of the first edition of 1640 with a companion volume The Enigma of the Bay Psalm Book. Chicago: Univ. of Chicago Press, 1956.

4828. JENNINGS, Kenneth L. English festal psalms of the 16th and 17th centuries. Ann Arbor: Univ. Microfilms, 1966.

4829. KNECHT, Justin Heinrich. Neue Kirchenmusik, bestehend in dem drey-und-zwanigsten Psalm, mit vier Singestimmen, Orgel und einer willkührlichen Begleitung von verschiedenen Instrumenten. Leipzig: Schwickert, 1783.

4830. LAMB, John Alexander. The psalms in Christian worship. London: Faith Press, 1962.

4831. LE ROY, Adrian. Psaumes. Tiers livre de tabulature de luth (1552); Instruction (1574). Edition et transcription par Richard de Morcourt. (Les Luthistes.) Settings in French with lute accompaniments. Paris: Centre National de la Recherche Scientifique, 1962.

4832. LENSELINK, Samuel Jan. Les psaumes de Clément Marót. Kassel: Bärenreiter, 1969.

4833. LOBWASSER, Ambrose. Psalmorum Davidis, Prophetae regil, Paraphrasis metrorhythmica. New York: Scientific Library Service, 1596.

4834. McNAUGHER, John. The psalms in worship. Pittsburgh: The United Presbyterian Board, 1907.

4835. MEHL, Johannes G. Einführung in den Psalmengesang der Evangelisch-Lutherischen Kirche. Volkach: Evangelischen Kirchenchore, 1950.

4836. MISCHKE, Bernard, and Eugene Lindusky. Psalms in song. WLSM, 1965.

4837. MOWINCKEL, Sigmund. The psalms in Israel's worship. Nashville, Tenn.: Abingdon, 1963.

4838. NAUMANN, Emil. Nachklänge. Eine Sammlung von Vorträgen und Gedenkblättern aus dem Musik-, Kunst-und Geistesleben unserer Tage. Berlin: P. Oppenheim, 1872.

4839. ________. Über Einführung des Psalmengesanges in die evangelische Kirche. Berlin: G. Reimer, 1856.

4840. OESTERLEY, W. O. E. A fresh approach to the psalms. London: Ivor Nicholson & Watson, 1937.

4841. PAULSEN, Hans Hejselbjerg. Sonderjydsk psalmesang. 1717-1740, fra AEgidius til Pontoppidan. En kirkehistorisk undersogelse. Mit einer Zusammenfassung in deutscher Sprache. (a thesis.) Christiansfeld: Skrifter, udgivne af Historisk Samfund for Sonderjylland, 1962.

4842. PERKINS, Franklin Elwood. Keyboard and instrumental settings of Genevan psalm melodies in the Lubbenau manuscripts. Vol. I and II. Ann Arbor: Univ. Microfilms, 1968.

4843. PETERS, John P. The psalms as liturgies. New York: Macmillan, 1922.

4844. PLAYFORD, John. The whole book of psalms. London: J. Heptinstall, 1701.

4845. PROTHERO, Rowland E. The psalms in human life. London: Thomas Nelson & Sons, 1903.

4846. The PSALMS of David imitated in the language of (Author). London: N.G., 1719.

4847. RICHARDSON, A. Madeley. The psalms: their structure and musical rendering. London: The Vincent Music Co., 1903.

4848. SCAMMON, John H. Living with the psalms. Valley Forge, Pa.: Cankarjeva zalozba, 1967.

4849. STERNHOLD, Thomas and John Hopkens. The whole book of Psalms. London: The Company of Stationers, 1636.

4850. TODD, Henry John. Observations upon the metrical version of the psalms. London: F. C. & J. Rivington, 1822.

4851. TRUBER, Primus. Eni psalmi, ta celi Catehismus. Ljubljana: Cankarjeva zalozba, 1967.

4852. WILLIAMSON, Virginia Sue. A historical survey of psalm settings from the Reformation through Stravinsky's Symphonie des Psaumes. Denton, Tex.: North Texas State Univ., M. M., 1947.

See also: 26, 45, 187, 189, 501, 1207, 1306, 1332, 1363, 1364, 1616, 2068, 2604, 2615, 3217, 3228, 3327, 3561, 3584, 3651, 3657, 4345, 4857, 4868, 4869, 4874, 4875, 4882, 5029, 5185.

PSALTER

4853. The AMERICAN psalter. The Psalms and canticles according to the use of the Protestant Episcopal Church; pointed and set to Anglican chants together with the choral service. New York: H. W. Gray Co., 1930.

4854. BILLINGS, William. The New England psalm singer. Boston: Edes and Gill, 1770.

4855. BROWN, R. F. The Oxford American psalter. Fair Lawn, N.J.: Oxford Univ. Press, 1949.

4856. COBB, James V. The fifteen hundred-eighty-three psalter of Paschal de l'Estocart. Ann Arbor: Univ. Microfilms, 1966.

4857. CROSS, Earle Bennett. Modern worship and the psalter. New York: The Macmillan Co., 1932.

4858. DOUEN, Orentin. Clement Marót et le Psautier huguenot. Nieuwkoop: B. de Graaf, 1967.

4859. DOUGLAS, Winfred (ed.). The plainsong psalter. New York: H. W. Gray, 1932.

4860. ENGELBRECHT, J. H. A. and Tillman Seebass. Kunst-en muziekhistorische bijdragen tot de bestudering van het Utrechts Psalterium. Utrecht: Haentjens Dekker & Gumbert, 1973.

4861. GLASS, H. A. The story of the psalter. London: Paul, 1888.

4862. ILLING, Robert. Est-Barley-Ravenscroft and the English metrical psalter. Adelaide, South Australia: Libraries Board of South Australia, 1969.

4863. _______. Est's psalter; volume 1, commentary and transcriptions. Adelaides, South Australia: Libraries Board of South Australia, 1969.

4864. _______. Thomas Tallis and Ralph Vaughan Williams with Thomas Tallis's psalm tunes; a text for organists. Adelaide, South Australia: Libraries Board of South Australia, 1968.

4865. KEET, C. C. A liturgical study of the psalter. New York: The MacMillan Co., 1928.

4866. KIRKESALMER i Skolestus. Gennemgang af salmer i Den Danske Salmebok. København: Loshe, 1967.

4867. LANGHE, Rovert de (ed.). Le psautier; ses origines, ses problémes litteraires, son influence. Etudes présentées aux XIIe Journées Bibliques (29-31 août 1960). (Université de Louvain, Institut Orientaliste; Orientalia et biblioca Lovaniensia, 4.) Louvain: Publications Universitaires, 1962.

4868. MAROT, Clément. Le psautier Huguenot. New York: Broude Brothers Limited, n. d.

4869. MARSHALL, Walter and Seymour Pile. The barless psalter. London: Novello & Co., n. d.

4870. NEWTON, E. A. The choirboy's guide to the Cathedral psalter. New York: Novello, Ewer & Company's Music Primeres, 1907.

4871. NICHOLSON, Sydney H. The parish psalter. London: The Faith Press, 1932.

4872. PALMER, G. H. The sarum psalter. Wantage: St. Mary's Convent, 1916.

4873. PARKS, Edna. The hymns and hymn tunes found in the English metrical psalters. New York: Coleman-Ross Co., 1966.

4874. PIDOUX, Pierre. Le psautier huguenot du 16e siècle. Vol. 1: Les Mélodies. Vol. 2: Documents et bibliographie. Bâle (Basel): Bärenreiter, 1962.

4875. PIERIK, Marie. The psalter in the temple and the church. The Catholic Univ. of America Library, Washington, D. C.: The Catholic Univ. of America, n. d.

4876. PRATT, Waldo Seldon. The music of the French psalter of 1562. New York: Columbia Univ. Press, 1939.

4877. ________. The significance of the old French psalter begun by Clément Marót in 1532. New York: The Hymn Society, 1933.

4878. Le PSEAUTIER Huguenot du XVI siècle. Paris: Fischbacher, 1902.

4879. RAVENSHAW, Thomas F. and W. S. Rockstro. The ferial psalter. London: J. Master & Co., 1890.

4880. ROPER, Cecil Mizelle. The Strasbourg French psalters, 1539-1553. Ann Arbor: Univ. Microfilm, Univ. of Southern California diss., 1972.

4881. The SCOTTISH psalter 1929. Fair Lawn, N. J.: Oxford Univ. Press, 1929.

4882. STROUD, William Paul. The Ravenscroft psalter. (Repr. London: 2nd ed. (1st ed. 1633). Ann Arbor: Univ. Microfilms, 1959.

4883. SWEDEN. Psalmkommitté, 1969 års. Psalmer och visor: tillagg till Den svenska Psalmboken; förslag. Argivet av 1969 års Psalmkommitté. Stockholm: Liber Forlag/Allmänna forlaget, 1975-, v. 1, pt. 1-3, 1975.

4884. TERRY, Richard Runicman. A forgotten psalter and other essays. London & New York: Oxford Univ. Press and Carl Fisher, 1929.

4885. TRIMENHURE, G. H. The English psalter with the canticles. London: Faith Press, 1915.

4886. WESLEY, John. Collection of psalms and hymns for the Lord's Day. London: J. Mason, 1843.

4887. WORMALD, Francis. The Winchester psalter. Williamstown, Mass.: New York Graphic Society thru Nicholas Books, Williamstown, Mass., 1973.

4888. WRIGHT, Robert Foster. A history and analysis of the Sternhold and Hopkins psalter. Fort Worth, Tex.:

Southwestern Baptist Theological Seminary, D. C. M., 1965.

See also: 29, 390, 1124, 1867, 2061, 2207, 2363, 2410, 2644, 2844, 2923, 4348, 4940, 4947, 4996.

PSYCHOLOGY

4889. ALBERSHEIM, Gerhard. Zur Musikpsychology. Wilhelmshaven: Heinrichshofen, 1974.

4890. BUCK, P. C. Psychology for musicians. Fair Lawn, N. J.: Oxford Univ. Press, 1944.

4891. DREISOERNER, Charles. The psychology of liturgical music. Kirkwood: Maryhurst Press, 1945.

4892. REICH, O. Das qualitätsproblem der Psychologie und seine Lösung. Eine musikpsychologisch-psychologische Abhandlung. Prag: N. G., 1933. (BM)

4893. ROE, A. A study of the accuracy of perception of visual musical stimuli. New York: Archives of Psychology #158, 1933.

4894. SEASHORE, C. E. Studies in the psychology of music. Iowa City: Iowa Univ. Press, 1938.

4895. STUMPF, Karl. Tonpsychologie. New York: Broude Brothers Limited (Facsimile), 1965. (orig. Leipzig, 1883-1890.)

See also: 123, 908, 1581, 1596, 1608, 1865, 2956, 4951, 5167, 5204, 5322, 5420.

PUBLICATIONS

See: 3643, 5247.

REFORM

4896. BEILLIARD, Jean et Francois Picard. La musique sacrée après la réforme liturgique. Paris: Editions du Centurion, 1967.

4897. BISGROVE, Mildred E. Sacred choral music in the Calvinistic tradition of the Protestant Reformation in Switzerland and France 1541-1600. Ann Arbor: Univ. Microfilms, 1969.

4898. BISHOP, John. Remarks on causes of present generally degraded state of music in our churches. Cheltenham: John Bishop, 1860.

4899. BOWLES, William Lisle. A last and summary question "Of what use have been, and are, the English cathedral establishments?" With a vindication of anthems and cathedral services. London: Rivington, 1833.

4900. DIETZ, Philipp. Die Restauration des evangelischen Kirchenliedes. Hildesheim: G. Olms Verlag, n. d. (Reprt. - of Ausgabe Marburg 1903 ed. vol. 1.)

4901. FULLER-MAITLAND, J. A. The need for reform in church music. Church Music Society. Occasional Papers #1, 1912. (BM)

4902. KWASNIK, Walter. Emile Rupp als Orgelreformer, Kirchenmusiker and Mensch. Frankfurt a. M.: Verlag Das Musikinstrument, 1967.

4903. LITURGICAL Conference Incorporation. Crisis in church music? Washington: Proceedings of Conference, 1967.

4904. MEULEMEESTER, Arthur de. The reform of church music, a handbook for the use of the clergy, organists, choirmasters, choristers, and all who are concerned in the progress of ecclesiastical art. Dublin: Catholic truth society of Ireland, 1936.

4905. MOLITOR, Raphael. Die nachtridentinische Choralreform zu Rom. Hildesheim: G. Olms Verlag, 1967. (Reprt. - of Ausgabe Leipzig 1901-02 ed.)

4906. MORTIMER, Peter. Der Choralgesang zur Zeit der Reformation. Hildesheim: G. Olms Verlag, 1967. (Reprt. - Ausgabe Berlin 1821 ed.)

4907. MUSCOVIUS, Johann. Gestraffter Missbrauch der Kirchen-Musik/und Kirchhofe/aus Gottes Wort zur Warnung und Besserung vorgestellet durch. Lauban: N. G., 1694. (LC-29-2817)

4908. MUSICA Sacra und Liturgiereform nach dem 2. Vatikanischen Konzil. Internationaler Kongress für Kirchenmusik. Regensburg: F. Pustet, 1968.

4909. RILEY, William. Parochial music corrected. Containing remarks on the performance of psalmody in country churches, and on the ridiculous and profane manner of singing practiced by the Methodist. London: William Riley, 1762.

4910. SHEPHERD, Massey Hamilton. The reform of liturgical worship. The Bohlen lectures 1959. New York: Oxford Univ. Press, 1961.

4911. TERRY, Sir Richard. Voodooism in music and other essays. London: Burns, Oates, & Washbourne, ltd., 1934.

4912. TRADITION und Reformen in der Kirchenmusik: Festschrift für Konrad Ameln, zum 75. Geburtstag am 6. Juli, 1974 Hrsg. von G. Schumacher. Basel: Bärenreiter, 1974.

4913. UNION Féderale Française de Musique Sacrée. La musique sacrée après la reform liturgique, décisions, directives, orientations. Paris: Editions du Centurion, 1967.

4914. VAUGHAN, E. C. The romantic revolt. N.G.: N.G., 1907.

4915. VOIGT, C. Gespräch von der Musik, zwischen einem Organisten und Adjuvanten, darinnen nicht nur von verschiedenen Missbraüchen, so bey der Musik eingerissen, gehandelt, sondern auch eines und des anderen heim Klavier-und Orgel-spielen angemerket wird ... an das Licht gestellet von einem, der von Jugend auf christlich unterrichtet und oeffentlich die Wahrheit an den Tag gegeben. Erpurth: J. D. Jungnicol, 1742.

4916. WEINMANN, Karl. Geschichte der Kirchenmusik, mit besonderer Berücksichtigung der kirchenmusikalischen Restauration im 19. Jahrhundert. Kempten: J. Kösel, 1913.

4917. ______. Geschichte der Kirchenmusik. München: J. Kösel und F. Pustet, 1925, rev. ed.

4918. WILLIAMS, Schafer. Gregorian epoch, reformation, revolution, reaction? Boston: Heath, 1964.

See also: 61, 232, 721, 919, 932, 1031, 1032, 1095, 1105, 1137, 1141, 1149, 1165, 1176, 1217, 1301, 1310, 1315, 1354, 1439, 1574, 1751, 1803, 1854, 2003, 2065, 2124, 2128, 2268, 2638, 2934, 3088, 3162, 3171, 3359, 3377, 3477, 3507, 3583, 3910, 4545, 4656, 4730, 4764, 4775, 4776, 4780, 4781, 4787, 4793, 4794, 4813, 5384.

RELIGION and SECULAR MUSIC

4919. HERRMANN, William A., Jr. Religion in the operas of Giuseppe Verdi. Ann Arbor: Univ. Microfilms, Univ. of California, Berkeley diss., 1963.

4920. MILLER, William Robert. The Christian encounters the world of pop music and jazz. St. Louis, Mo.: Concordia, n.d.

4921. RÜSCH, Walter. Gottheit und Natur im Werke Ludwig van Beethovens. Gedanken zur Pastoral Symphonie. Wien: Bergland Verl., 1973.

RESEARCH

4922. A BIBLIOGRAPHY of master's theses and doctoral dissertations in music completed at Texas Colleges and Universities. Houston: Texas Music Educators Association, 1964.

4923. BOYER, Horace Clarence. An analysis of Black church music. Ann Arbor: Univ. Microfilms, diss. 1973.

4924. CANADIAN Music Library Association. A union list of music periodicals in Canadian libraries. McNeill, Ogreta, Comp. Edmonton, Alberta: Edmonton Public Library, 1966.

4925. DAMP, George Edward. The apparatus musico-organisticus of Gerge Muffat. (1623-1704). Ann Arbor: Univ. Microfilms Eastman School of Music diss., 1973.

4926. DELACOUR de BRISAY, A. C. "A la recherche des Orgues." The Organ. July, 1928.

4927. DE MARCO, Angelus A. The church of Rome and the problem of the vernacular versus the liturgical language. An abstract of a dissertation, etc. Catholic Univ. of America, Studies in Sacred Theology. ser. 2. no. 123-A. Washington: Catholic Univ. of America Press, 1960.

4928. DODGE, Mary Lee. A bibliography of doctoral dissertations in Europe. In progress and unpublished at this writing.

4929. DUCKLES, Vincent Harris. Music reference and research materials; an annotated bibliography. (3rd ed.) New York: Free Press, 1974.

4930. DUNLOP. Processions: A dissertation together with practical suggestions. Alcuin Club Tracts. no. 20. Oxford, England: Univ. Press, 1932.

4931. HARTLEY, Kenneth D. A bibliography of theses and dissertations in sacred music and related areas. Detroit: Information Service Inc. (Detroit studies in Music Bibliography), 1966.

4932. HEWITT, Helen. Doctoral dissertations in musicology. Philadelphia: American Musicological Society, 1965.

4933. HOFFMAN, William Charles. The origin and development of the Roman chants of the mass. Nashville, Tenn.: George Peabody College for Teachers, M.Ed., 1953.

4934. HONEMEYER, Karl. Thomas Müntzer und Martin Luther: ihr Ringen um d. Musik d. Gottesdienstes. (Untersuchung z. "Deutzsch Kirchenampt." 1523.) Berlin: Verlag-Merseburger, 1974.

4935. KEHL, Nikolaus. Der Christushymnus im Kolosserbrief. Stuttgart: Verlag Katholisches Bibelwerk, 1967.

4936. LABHARDT, Frank Joachim. Das Sequentiar Cod. 546 der Stiftsbibliothek von St. Gallen und seine Quellen. Inaugural-dissertation, etc. with plates. Bern, Switzerland: Haupt, 1959, 1963.

4937. MEAD, Rita. Doctoral dissertations in American music: a classified bibliography. Brooklyn: Institute for Studies in American Music, 1974.

4938. MIXTER, Keith Eugene. General bibliography for music research (2nd edition). Detroit: Information Coordinators, 1975.

4939. MORGAN, John Garlin. "A celebration of love": an innovative worship service demonstrating new music for choir and congregation. Ann Arbor: Univ. Microfilms, Univ. of Southern California diss., 1973.

4940. OVERATH, Johannes. Untersuchungen über die Melodien des Liedpsalters von Kaspar Ulenberg, Köln 1582. Ein Beitrag zur Geschichte des Kirchenliedes im 16. Jahrhundert. Beiträge zur rheinischen Musikgeschichte. Hft. 33. With musical examples. Köln: N. G., 1960.

4941. PATTENGALE, Robert Richard. The cantatas of Niccolò Jommelli. Ann Arbor: Univ. Microfilms, Univ. of Mich. diss., 1973.

4942. PIERSIG, Johannes. Beiträge zu einer Rechtssozialogie der Kirchenmusik. Regensburg: G. Bosse, 1972.

4943. RECHERCHES sur la musique française. v. 18. Paris: A. et J. Picard, 1973.

4944. ROSS, Sylvia Lucy. A comparison of six Misere settings from the eighteenth century conservatories. Ann Arbor: Univ. Microfilm, Univ. of Ill. diss., 1972.

4945. SOMERVILLE, Thomas Charles. A study of the performance of sacred music by contemporary Scottish composers 1950-1970. Ann Arbor: Univ. Microfilms, Univ. of Southern California diss., 1972.

See also: 88, 89, 99, 96, 98, 187, 190, 194, 205, 214, 215, 221, 228, 229, 247, 248, 249, 254, 259, 260, 261,

265, 271, 279, 287, 289, 312, 314, 318, 319, 481, 494, 516, 523, 617, 648, 677, 689, 787, 825, 827, 835, 841, 858, 879, 881, 888, 931, 943, 946, 948, 953, 969, 985, 1001, 1002, 1041, 1043, 1044, 1046, 1047, 1049, 1053, 1059, 1060, 1061, 1067, 1068, 1070, 1071, 1072, 1073, 1076, 1077, 1200, 1228, 1230, 1231, 1232, 1233, 1234, 1235, 1236, 1238, 1240, 1244, 1312, 1316, 1320, 1324, 1329, 1343, 1345, 1350, 1353, 1359, 1362, 1365, 1366, 1378, 1382, 1390, 1391, 1399, 1406, 1410, 1413, 1424, 1427, 1438, 1442, 1443, 1444, 1451, 1453, 1454, 1457, 1469, 1592, 1607, 1610, 1614, 1616, 1623, 1626, 1627, 1636, 1644, 1658, 1664, 1671, 1850, 1869, 1962, 2097, 2128, 2240, 2246, 2249, 2251, 2257, 2288, 2374, 2385, 2390, 2391, 2401, 2403, 2404, 2407, 2464, 2503, 2508, 2517, 2525, 2533, 2586, 2589, 2591, 2627, 2643, 2670, 2674, 2678, 2690, 2704, 2714, 2717, 2718, 2719, 2726, 2728, 2729, 2731, 2736, 2743, 2750, 2758, 2766, 2770, 2780, 2782, 2793, 2795, 2797, 2807, 2841, 2845, 2846, 2866, 2890, 2973, 2974, 3013, 3031, 3036, 3043, 3049, 3050, 3053, 3062, 3064, 3067, 3070, 3071, 3073, 3076, 3077, 3078, 3079, 3080, 3081, 3086, 3089, 3093, 3100, 3101, 3105, 3113, 3115, 3116, 3118, 3122, 3123, 3141, 3142, 3151, 3154, 3160, 3161, 3163, 3164, 3165, 3166, 3171, 3190, 3193, 3200, 3202, 3204, 3205, 3206, 3207, 3208, 3210, 3211, 3212, 3213, 3214, 3215, 3216, 3217, 3219, 3222, 3223, 3226, 3229, 3232, 3233, 3235, 3236, 3240, 3241, 3242, 3279, 3367, 3449, 3463, 3486, 3498, 3515, 3527, 3543, 3544, 3600, 3617, 3632, 3645, 3647, 3650, 3652, 3653, 3661, 3664, 3674, 3675, 3693, 3712, 3716, 3721, 3749, 3770, 3780, 3802, 3913, 3951, 3957, 3958, 3975, 4030, 4035, 4045, 4110, 4111, 4113, 4114, 4123, 4124, 4129, 4147, 4157, 4159, 4204, 4210, 4225, 4230, 4232, 4239, 4244, 4253, 4283, 4321, 4325, 4327, 4336, 4339, 4341, 4345, 4349, 4351, 4352, 4353, 4354, 4360, 4381, 4382, 4394, 4395, 4397, 4442, 4454, 4457, 4464, 4466, 4481, 4489, 4491, 4505, 4512, 4516, 4526, 4540, 4542, 4543, 4548, 4556, 4558, 4573, 4591, 4592, 4601, 4608, 4630, 4647, 4670, 4712, 4722, 4728, 4760, 4772, 4785, 4790, 4792, 4805, 4816, 4818, 4822, 4828, 4842, 4852, 4856, 4880, 4888, 4893, 4950, 4951, 4952, 4964, 4965, 4969, 4971, 4976, 4997, 4998, 5003, 5004, 5006, 5008, 5012, 5013, 5017, 5019, 5021, 5024, 5027, 5033, 5041, 5042, 5043, 5062, 5063, 5108, 5109, 5125, 5141, 5142, 5149, 5160, 5161, 5162, 5165, 5167, 5169, 5170, 5172, 5179, 5187, 5188, 5202, 5203, 5209, 5212, 5239, 5250, 5256, 5257, 5284, 5285, 5331, 5336, 5352, 5354, 5358, 5420, 5430.

RHYTHM and METER

4946. AUBRY, Pierre. Le rythme tonique dans la poesie liturgique et dans le chant des églises chrétiennes au moyen âge. Paris: H. Welter, 1903.

4947. COWAN, William. The music of the church hymnary and the psalter in metre, its sources and composers. New York: H. Frowde, 1901.

4948. DARAS, Dom. Le vrai rythme grégorien; étude basée sur les sources. Louvain: Abbaye du Mont César, 1965.

4949. DAVIES, H. W. Rhythm in church. N.G.: S. Riorden, 1914. (BM)

4950. GARDNER, Elwyn Fredrick. A consideration of certain historical and philosophical trends in the rhythmic structure of music. Dallas, Tex.: Southern Methodist Univ., M.M., 1965.

4951. HURDLE, James. A determination of rhythmic relationship with prose and music as an emotional stimulus in certain religious worship practices. Houston: Texas Southern Univ., M.M.E., 1961.

4952. LUCAS, John Samuel. Rhythms of Negro music and Negro poetry. Minneapolis, Minn.: Minnesota, M.A., 1945.

4953. MURRAY, Anthony Gregory. Accentual cadences in Gregorian chant. P. 12. Bath: Downside Abbey, 1958.

4954. _______. The authentic rhythm of Gregorian Chant. P. 15. Bath: Downside Abbey, 1959.

4955. _______. Gregorian rhythm in the Gregorian centuries. The literary evidence. Bath: Downside Abbey, 1957.

4956. _______. Plainsong rhythm. The editorial methods of Solesmes. Bath: Downside Abbey, 1956.

4957. ROTHSCHILD, Fritz. The lost tradition in music: Rhythm and tempo in J. S. Bach's time. New York: Oxford Univ. Press, 1953.

4958. No entry.

4959. SACHS, Curt. Rhythm and tempo: a study in music history. New York: W. W. Norton, 1953.

4960. WINICK, Steven D. Rhythm: an annotated bibliography. Metuchen, N.J.: Scarecrow Press, 1974.

4961. WOLF, Johannes. "Geschichte der Mensural-Notation von 1250-1460." Wiesbaden: Breitkopf und Härtel, 1965.

4962. YESTON, Maury. The stratification of musical rhythm. New Haven: Yale Univ. Press, 1976.

See also: 289, 559, 588, 623, 643, 702, 3175, 3429, 3566, 4732.

SCHOOLS--CHURCH and SUNDAY SCHOOLS--MUSIC FOR

4963. BUTTLE, I. M. Musical moments in the Sunday school. London: H. V. Capsey, 1939.

4964. HILTON, Hope. The use of music in the religious education of primary and junior children. Los Angeles: Univ. of Southern California, 1961.

4965. HOLLIS, Jo D. An evaluation of hymn-tunes and singing practices in Protestant church schools. Nashville, Tenn.: George Peabody College for Teachers, 1952.

4966. HYMNS and songs for church schools. Augsburg: N. G., 1962.

4967. MORCH, Vivian Sharp. The use of music in Christian Education. Philadelphia: Westminster Press, 1956.

4968. NEUBACHER, Klaus. Lieder des evangelischen Religionsunterricht. Frankfurt a. M.: Diesterweg, 1968.

4969. PATTERSON, Floyd H., Jr. The Southern Baptist Sunday School Board's program of church music. Publishing No. 24,482. Nashville: George Peabody College for Teachers, 1957.

4970. PSALMS and hymns for school and home. London: N. G., 1892.

4971. RYBERG, Lucile Hayman. The correlation of music in the church school with improved church music. Chicago: Chicago Musical College, 1947.

4972. SMITH, Henry Augustine. Worship in the church school through music, pageantry, and pictures. Elgin: David C. Cook Publishing Co., 1928.

4973. SMITH, Jean Louise. Great art and children's worship. Nashville, Tenn.: Abingdon Press, 1948.

4974. THOMAS, Edith Lovell. Music in Christian education. New York & Nashville: Abingdon-Cokesbury Press, 1953.

4975. The VOICE of praise for Sunday school and home ... four hundred and thirty-seven thousand. London: Sunday School Union, 1887.

4976. WITT, David Hughes. Music in the religious education program of the Protestant Sunday school. Dallas, Tex.: Southern Methodist Univ., M. M., 1957.

See also: 754, 755, 765, 1569, 1753, 2750, 2797.

SEMIOTICS and SEMIOLOGY

4977. INTERNATIONAL Congress on Semiotics of Music, 1st, Belgrad 1973. Actes du 1. Congrès international de semiotique musicale, Belgrad, 17-21 Oct. 1973. Proceedings of the First International Congress on Semiotics of Music. (In English, French or German). Pesaro: Centro di initiativa culturale, 1975.

4978. NATTIEZ, Jean Jacques. Fondements d'une semiology de la musique. Paris: Union générale, d'éditions, 1976.

See also: 571.

SEQUENCES

4979. BARTSCH, K. Die Lateinischen Sequenzen des Mittelalters. Hildesheim, Germany: Georg Olms-Reprint, 1966. (orig. Rostock, 1868.)

4980. HAYDE, Mary Loyola, Sister. The source of the Latin trope. Urbana: Illinois Univ. Lib. n. p., 1949.

4981. KEHREIN, Joseph. Lateinische Sequenzen des Mittelalters. Hildesheim, Germany: Georg Olms-Reprint, 1967. (orig. Mainz, 1873.)

4982. LABHARDT, Frank. Das sequentiar Cod. 546 der Stiftsbibliothek von St. Gallen und seine Quellen. Compiled by Joachim Cuontz. Bern: Publikationen der Schweizerischen Musikforschenden Gesellschaft, 1959.

4983. MESSENGER, Ruth Ellis. The medieval Latin hymn. Washington: Capital Press, 1953.

4982. MOBERG, Carl Allan. Über die schwedischen Sequenzen, eine musikgeschichtliche Studie. Mit 5 Tafeln und 69 Sequenzenweisen nebst melodischen Varianten aus schwedischen und anderen Quellen. Uppsala: Almqvist & Wiksells boktrycke, 1927.

4985. VOGT, Hubert. Die Sequenzen der Graduale Abinghof aus Paderborn. Münster (Westf.): N. G., 1972.

4986. ZWICK, Gabriel. Les proses en usage à l'usage de Saint Nicolas à Fribourg jusqu'au dix-huitième siècle. N. G.: n. p. (LC-ML 3080. z9)

See also: 2221, 2491, 2624, 2632, 2660, 3004, 3013, 4936.

SERVICE MUSIC

4987. ARCHER and Reed (ed.). The choral service book. Philadelphia: General Council Publication Board, 1901.

4988. ARLT, Wulf. Ein Festoffizium des Mittelalters aus Beauvais in seiner liturgischen und musikalischen Bedeutung. Köln: Volk, 1970. (Reprint, Bonn 1819 ed.)

4989. ARNOLD, John Henry. The music of Holy Communion. London: S. P. C. K., 1933.

4990. BATTEN. Magnificat and Nunc Dimittis. London: Oxford Univ. Press, n. d.

4991. BECKER, Hansjakob. Das Tonale Guidos I: ein Beitrag zur Geschichte des liturgischen Gesanges und der Ars musica im Mittelalter. München: Arbeo-Gesellschaft, 1975.

4992. BENEVOLI, Orazio. Magnificat secundi toni (Monumenta liturgiae Polychoralis Sanctae Ecclesiae Romanae, Psalmodia cum tribus choris concertata, No. 1). Rome: Societas Universalis Sanctae Ceciliae, 1955.

4993. BEVIN. Morning and evening service. London: Bayley & Ferguson, n. d.

4994. BRITT, Matthew. The hymns of the Breviary and Missal. New York: Beneger Brothers, 1952.

4995. CRIGHTON, Arthur B. Te Deum Laudamus in 20th century coronations. Ann Arbor: Univ. Microfilms, 1967.

4996. DANIELS, Louis E. A service book and short Psalter. New York: Oxford Univ. Press, 1940.

4997. DAVIS, Oma Grier. A selected, annotated bibliography of Te Deums in the Library of Congress, and a history of this hymn since 1600. Ann Arbor: Univ. Microfilms, 1967.

4998. DEMPSTER, Fred E. The magnificat settings of Orlando di Lasso. Iowa City: State Univ. of Iowa, 1961.

4999. DETTELBACH, Hans von. Breviarium musicae; Werke, Probleme, Gestalten. Graz: Stiasny, 1967.

5000. DOUGLAS, Charles Winfred (ed.). The canticles at Evensong. New York: H. W. Gray Co., Inc., 1915.

5001. ________. Compline. New York: H. W. Gray Co., n. d.

5002. EPISCOPAL Church--Compiled by the Liturgical Commission. The Book of Offices. Services for certain occasions not provided for in the Book of Common Prayer. 2nd. Ed. New York: The Church Pension Fund, 1949.

5003. FRANDELL, Gordon Harold. Development of Magnificat organ settings by representative German composers between 1450-1750. Vol. I & II. Ann Arbor: Univ. Microfilms, 1966.

5004. ______. The organ Magnificat in the 17th century. Ann Arbor: Univ. of Michigan, 1961.

5005. FRERE, Walter Howard. Antiphonale Sarisburiense. Ridgewood, N. J.: Gregg Press-Reprint, 1967. (orig. London, 1923.)

5006. GIULIANA, Paul. History and development of Magnificat settings in the 15th and 16th centuries. New York: School of Sacred Music, Union Theological Seminary, 1949.

5007. GOODRICH, Wallace and Winfred Douglas. The choral service. New York: H. W. Gray Co., 1927.

5008. GREEN, Francis Marion. Magnificats of Orlandus Lassus. Ann Arbor: Univ. Microfilms, 1968.

5009. HUSMANN, Heinrich (ed.). Die Melodien des chaldäischen Breviers Commune nach den Traditionen Vorderasiens und der Malabarkuste. Roma: Pont. Institutum Orientalium Studiorum, 1967.

5010. HUTCHINS, Gordon (ed.). The new service book. Containing the choral service for Morning and Evening Prayer; Chants for the Canticles; Music for the Communion Service; Chants for the Burial office, etc. Boston, Mass.: The Parish Choir, 1944.

5011. JENKINS, Graham. Praying the Breviary. Liturgical Library. London: Challoner Publications, 1960.

5012. JOHNSON, Axie Allen. Choral settings of the Magnificat. Ann Arbor: Univ. Microfilms, 1968.

5013. KIRSCH, Winfried. Die Quellen der mehrstimmigen Magnificat-und Te Deum-Vertonungen bis zur Mitte des 16. Jahrhunderts. Tutzing: Hans Schneider, 1966.

5014. KNOWLES, Atherton. Text-book of Anglican service-music. Tracing its development from Thomas Tallis to Samuel Sebastian Wesley. London: E. Stock, 1895.

5015. MAAS, Christianus Joannes. Geschiedenis van het meerstemmig Magnificat tot omstreeks 1525. Groningen: V. R. B., 1967.

5016. McCRAY, James Elwin. The British Magnificat in the 20th century. Ann Arbor: Univ. Microfilms, 1968.

5017. McGOWAN, John Bailey. Sixteenth-century polyphonic settings of the Latin hymn Te Deum laudamus. Ann Arbor: Univ. Microfilms, 1967.

5018. MATTFELD, Victor H. George Rhaw's publication for Vespers. Brooklyn: Institute of Medieval Music, 1966.

5019. MEINHOLZ, Josef. Untersuchungen zur Magnificat-Komposition des 15. Jahrhunderts. Köln: N. G., 1956. (LC58-27767)

5020. MOBERG, Carl Allan. Die liturgischen Hymnen in Schweden; Beitrage zur Liturgie-und-Musikgeschichte des Mittelalters und der Reformationszeit. Kopenhagen: E. Munksgaard, 1947.

5021. NORMANN, H. C. The music of the Lutheran service. New York: Columbia Univ. Ed. D., 1956.

5022. OFFICE hymns of the church. N. G.: Pfallucher, Carl and Fitts, Dudley, n. d.

5023. OFFICE of Compline. New York: Morehouse-Gorham Co., 1958.

5024. OSSING, Hans. Untersuchungen zum Antiphonale Monasteriense. Regensburg: Bosse, 1966.

5025. OUSELEY, Frederick A. G. Bart. Cathedral music, services and anthems. London: J. Alfred Novello, 1850 (?)

5026. PEABODY, Herbert C. The church service and its music. Fitchburg, Mass.: Sentinel Printing Co., 1919.

5027. PRIESTLY, William Paul. A performance edition and critical commentary of Festival Te Deum by Giovanni Paisiello 1740-1816. Ann Arbor: Univ. Microfilms, 1969.

5028. PROTESTANT Episcopal Church in the USA-Joint Commission on Church Music. Service music and anthems; for the nonprofessional choir. New York: The H. W. Gray Co., Inc., 1963; from Greenwich: Seabury Press, 1955, also, 1963.

5029. QUICK, M. Sing to the Lord. A course of lessons on canticles, National Society-Church Education Publications, 1943. (BM)

5030. REANEY, Gilbert (ed.). Breviarium regulare musicae. Ms. Brit. Mus. ed. n. p.: American Institute of Musicology, 1966.

5031. RENKER, Gustav. Die Musik des Mönches. 1. Heft der Novellen "Das Rätsel." Zürich: N. G., 1940. (BM)

5032. RICHARDS, G. D. The voluntaries and their place in the church service. New York: Schirmer, 1911.

5033. SCHEMPF, William. Magnificats from Hieronymus Praetorius to Heinrich Schütz. Rochester, N. Y.: Univ. of Rochester, Eastman School of Music, 1959.

5034. SCHILDBACH, Martin. Das einstimmige Agnus Dei und seine handschriftliche Überlieferung vom 10. bis zum 16. Jahrhundert. Erlangen: Offsetdruck-Fotodruck J. Hogl, 1967.

5035. SHEPPARD, Lancelot Capel. How to use the New Breviary. London: Dartman, Longman, & Todd, 1961.

5036. SIDLER, H. Studien zu den alten Offertorien mit ihren Versen. Freiburg: Veröffentlichungen der Gregorianischen Akademie zu Freiburg, Schweiz, Hft. 20, 1939.

5037. SOWA, H. Quellen zur Transformation der Antiphonen. Tonarund Rhythmus-studien. Kassel: Bärenreiter-verlag, 1935.

5038. SPIESS, Lincoln B. A mercedarian antiphonary. Sante Fe, N. M.: Museum of New Mexico Press, 1965.

5039. STUBBS, G. E. How to sing the Choral Service: a manual of intoning. London, New York: Novello, Ewer & Co., 1899.

5040. VALADEZ SANTOS, José. Los cabildos y el servicio coral. Morelia, Mexico: Escuela Superior de Musica Sagrado, 1945.

5041. WALTERS, William R. A study of the nature and scope of Christian Judgment service music. Western Reserve Union Library. Cleveland, Ohio: Western Reserve Univ., 1963.

5042. WARD, Tom Robert. The polyphonic office hymn from the late fourteenth century until the early sixteenth century. Ann Arbor: Univ. Microfilm, 1969.

5043. ZINGALE, J. L. Liturgical music arranged to meet the needs of grades VII, VIII, and IX singing groups in Catholic parochial schools of Florida (Parts I & II). Tallahassee: Florida State Univ., 1958.

See also: 2, 16, 19, 20, 36, 49, 285, 356, 376, 377, 380, 387, 443, 459, 486, 510, 554, 677, 678, 726, 971, 1005,

1160, 1163, 1206, 1207, 1219, 1220, 1227, 1285, 1305, 1392, 1815, 1867, 1872, 1873, 1874, 1875, 2048, 2070, 2186, 2221, 2269, 2448, 2523, 2578, 2628, 2673, 2819, 2844, 2873, 2874, 2890, 2896, 2927, 2958, 2959, 2997, 3003, 3027, 3103, 3107, 3117, 3135, 3630, 3836, 4489, 4572, 4716, 4855, 4885, 4908, 4944, 5119.

SERVICE PLAYING

5044. WALTER, Samuel. Basic principles of service playing. New York: Abingdon Press, 1963, 1964.

See also: 2068.

SHAPED NOTES

See: 2226, 5158.

SINGING, CONGREGATIONAL

5045. BROWN, F. Eugene, Jon A. Hosch and Dave Skrobak. The singing church. Nashville, Tenn.: I. L. Batey, 1968.

5046. CHURCHILL, John. Congregational singing: the congregation's part in public worship. Croydon: Royal School of Church Music, 1966.

5047. CURWEN, John Spencer. Studies in worship music, chiefly as regards congregational singing. London: J. Curwen & Sons, 1880.

5048. ________. Studies in worship music (second series). London: J. Curwen & Sons, 1885.

5049. ________. Studies in worship music, chiefly as regards congregational singing. London: Curwen & Sons, Ltd., 1901.

5050. DOWNEY, James Cecil. The music of American revivalism. Ann Arbor: Univ. Microfilms, 1968.

5051. FLEMING, George T. The music of the congregation. London: The Faith Press, 1923.

5052. KETTERING, Donald D. Steps toward a singing church. Philadelphia: Westminster Press, 1958.

5053. LIEMOHN, Edwin. The singing church. Columbus, Ohio: Wartburg Press, 1959.

5054. McCUTCHAN, Robert G. The congregation's part in the office of music worship. Evanston, Ill.: Northwestern Univ., 1934.

5055. MANUAL for Congregational singing. Mangalore: N.G., 1914.

5056. MANUAL of Congregational singing during the liturgical functions for the ecclesiastical year. Transliterated in Canarese. Mangalore: N.G., 1932.

5057. MASON, Lowell. Song in worship. Address with introduction. Boston: Marvin & Son, 1878.

5058. The ORGANIST and the congregation. Lectures and a sermon delivered at the 1st Conference of Congregational Organists, held at Mansfield College, Oxford, June 22-24, 1951. London: Independent Press, 1952.

5059. PHILLIPS, C. H. The singing church. An outline history of the music sung by choir and people. London: Faber & Faber, Ltd., 1945, 1947.

5060. REYNOLDS, William J. Singing churchmen # 2. Nashville: Broadman Press, n.d.

5061. SHORE, S. R. The congregational song, choir v. congregation: reconciliation or rivalry. Church Music Review, 1931.

5062. WATKINS, Cole. A study of some American developments in congregational church song. Greencastle: De Pauw Univ., Master's thesis., 1936.

5063. WATSON, D. C. Singing in the church program. New York: Columbia Univ., 1957.

5064. WESTENDORF, Omer. Music lessons for the man in the pew. Cincinnati: World Library of Sacred Music, 1965.

See also: 31, 55, 72, 836, 1011, 1015, 1147, 1222, 1455, 1709, 1834, 1976, 2186, 2512, 2529, 2631, 2683, 2699, 3504, 3533, 3639, 3678, 4075, 4480, 5119.

SOCIETIES--SINGING

5065. AARAU, Arbeiter-Sängerbund. Fünf und siebzig Jahre, 1885-1960, Arbeiter-Sängerbund Aarau. Aarau, Switzerland: The Sängerbund, 1960.

5066. ALLGEMEINER Cäcilien Verein zur Förderung der katholischen Kirchenmusik auf Grund des päpstlichen Briefes vom 16 Dezember, 1870. New York: J. Pustet, 1876.

5067. ALLGEMEINER Cäcilienverein für Deutschland, Österreich und die Schweiz. Cäcilienvereins-katalog. Selbständige Beilage zum Cäcilienvereins-organe. New York: F. Pustet, 1876-19--.

5068. BASLE, Basler Bach-Choir. Funfzig Jahre Basler Bach-Choir. With plates. Basle: N. G., 1961.

5069. BISCHOFSZELL, Männerchor. Achtzehn Hundert ein und sechzig bis zum neunzehn Hundert ein und sechzig, 100 Jahre Männerchor Bischofszell. Bischofszell: N. G., 1961.

5070. BLOMMEN, Heinz. Anfänge und Entwicklung des Männerchorwesens am Niederrhein. Beiträge zur rheinischen Musikgeschichte. Hft. 42. Köln: A. Volk, 1960.

5071. BRADFORD, Yorkshire, Bradford Festival Choral Society. A history of the Bradford Festival Choral Society. From its formation in 1856. By G. F. Sewell. Bradford: G. F. Sewell, 1907.

5072. BRUXNER, M. A hundred years of music making.... A history of the Windsor and Eton Choral Society, 1841-1941. Windsor: Oxley and Son, 1949.

5073. EDINBURGH institution for the encouragement of sacred music. Edinburgh: Oliver and Boyd, 1817-.

5074. EDUCATIONAL Commission of the Society of St. Gregory of America. White list, with a selection of papal documents and other information pertaining to Catholic church music. Glen Rock, N. J.: Society of St. Gregory of America, 1928, also augmentative edition, 1932, 1939, 1947.

5075. HABERL, F. (ed.). Caecilien kalendar. 5 vols. Regensburg: Society of Skt. Cäcilia, 1876-1885.

5076. HOFMANN, Erna Hedwig. The Dresden Kreuz Chor. Translated by Lena Jaeck. With illustrations. Leipzig: VEB edition, 1962.

5077. HUNDERT Jahre Kirchengesangverein in Walferdingen, 31. Mai 1962. Luxemburg: Sankt-Paulus-Druckerei, 1962.

5078. JOHNSON, Arthur of Nottingham. The Nottingham Sacred Harmonic Society. Nottingham: Caxton Press, 1905.

5079. JOHNSON, H. Earle. Hallelujah, Amen! The Story of the Handel and Haydn Society of Boston. Boston: Bruce Humphries, 1965.

5080. KILBURN, N. How to manage a choral society. London: W. Reeves, 1932.

5081. LEIPERT, Karl. Hundert Jahre Tiroler Sängerbund, 1860-1960. Bearbeitet und zusammengestellt von K. Leipert. Schlern-Schriften. n. 211. Innsbruck: Wagner, 1960.

5082. LIEDERKRANZ "Cäcilia," Griesinger. Festschrift zum 100 Jähringen Jubiläum des Liederkranzes "Cäcilia," Griesinger. Griesingen: Liederkranz "Cäcilia," 1961.

5083. PERKINS and Dwight. History of the Handel and Haydn Society. Boston: Mudge, 1883-93.

5084. SOLOTHURN, Canton of. Solothurnischer Kanionalgesangverein. Hundert Jahre Solothurnischer Kantonalgesangverein, 1863 bis 1963. Jubiläumsschrift ... von Alfred Disch. with plates. Olten: N. G., 1963. (BM-7887. b. 11)

5085. STIEDA, W. F. C. Der Pommersche Chor in Rostock. Schwerin: Verein für mecklenburgische und Altertumskunde. Jahrbucher. Jahrg., 1919.

5086. USTER, Sängerbund Uster. Hundert Jahre Sängerbund Uster. With illustrations. Uster: N. G., 1962.

5087. WESTBROOK, Francis. The Methodist church music society; what it stands for. London: Epworth Press, 1946.

See also: 64, 137, 386, 504, 821, 893, 1033, 1132, 1425, 2657, 3354, 3452, 3464, 3476, 3620, 4174, 4567, 5158.

SOCIOLOGY

5088. ADORNO, Theodor W. Introduction to the sociology of music. Trans. from the German by E. B. Ashton. Orig. title--"Einleitung in die Musiksoziologie." New York: Seabury Press, 1976.

5089. FELLERER, Karl Gustav. Soziologie der Kirchenmusik; Materialen zur Musik-und Religionssoziologie. Köln, Opladen: Westdeutscher Verlag, 1963.

5090. KARBUSICKY, Vladimir. Empirische Musiksoziologie: Erscheinungsformen, Theorie u. Philosophie d. Bezugs "Musik-Gesellschaft." Wiesbaden: Breitkopf und Härtel, 1975.

See also: 2366, 3364, 3906, 4942.

SONATAS

5091. KREMER, Rudolph J. The organ sonata since 1845. Ann Arbor: Univ. Microfilms, Washington Univ. diss., 1963.

See also: 148, 4629.

SONGS, SACRED

5092. ARNDT, Ernst Moritz. Von dem Wort und dem Kirchenliede nebst geistlichen Liedern. Hildesheim and New York: G. Olms Verlag, 1970. (Reprt. --of Ausbage Bonn, 1819 ed.)

5093. BÄUMKER, Wilhelm. Das katholische deutsche Kirchenlied in seinen Singweisen von den frühesten Zeiten. Auf Grund handschriftlicher und gedruckter Quellen bearb. St. Louis, Mo.: Herder, 1883-1911.

5094. _______. Das katholische deutsche Kirchenlied in seinen Singweisen; von den frühesten Zeiten bis gegen Ende des 17. Jahrhunderts. Auf Grund handschriftlicher und gedruckter Quellen bearbeitet (4 Bände) Band 1: (Unveränderter reprografischer Nachdruck der Ausgabe Freiburg 1886). Band 2: Begonnen von K. S. Meister. (Unveränderter reprografischer Nachdruck der Ausgabe Freiburg 1883). Hildesheim: Olms, 1962.

5095. CANTILENAE Piae. Ein und dreissig geistliche Lieder d. Hs. Paris, Bibl. Nat., nouv. fr. 1050. Hersg. von Friedrich Genrich. Frankfurt: (Selbstverlag), 1966.

5096. COBB, John Logan. Sacred solo music in the French Baroque. Ann Arbor: Univ. Microfilms, 1969.

5097. DEARMER, Percy. Songs of praise discussed. London, and Fair Lawn, N.J.: Oxford Univ. Press, 1933.

5098. DEUTSCHE Lied, Das. Geistlich und weltlich bis zum 18. Jahrhundert. Hildesheim: G. Olms Verlag, 1966. (Reprt. Berlin: Ausgabe, 1908.)

5099. ERB, Jörg. Dichter und Sänger des Kirchenliedes. Lahr-Dinglingen (Baden): Verl. der Sankt-Johannis-Druckerei Schweickhardt, 1970.

5100. ESPINA, Noni. Vocal solos for protestant services. New York: Noni Espina, 1966.

5101. FISCHER, Albert Friedrich. Das deutsche evangelische Kirchenlied des 17. Jahrhunderts. Hildesheim: G. Olms Verlag, 1964. (Reprt. Ausgabe Gotha, 1878-79.)

5102. FRANTZ, C. L. Geschichte der geistlichen Liedertexte vor der Reformation mit besonderer Beziehung auf Deutschland. Niederwalluf bei Eiesbaden: M. Sandig, 1970.

5103. FÜRST-WULLE, Margherita. Il canto della chiesa cristiana nella evoluzione della musica occidentale. (Pref. di V. Subilia.) Torino: Claudiana, 1974.

5104. GARDNER, Johann von. Das Problem des Altrussischen Demestischen Kirchengesanges und seiner linienlosen Notation. München: Sagner, 1967.

5105. HEERWAGEN, Friedrich Ferdinand. Literatur-Geschichte der geistlichen Lieder und Gedichte neuer Zeit. Hildesheim: George Olms, n. d. (Reprt. --of Schweinfurt 1797, ed. Vol. 2.)

5106. HOFFMAN von FALLERSLEBEN, August Heinrich. Geschichte des deutschen Kirchenliedes bis auf Luthers Zeit. Hildesheim: G. Olms, 1965. (Reprt. --of Hannover 1861 ed.)

5107. HORINE, John W. Sacred song. Philadelphia: The United Lutheran Publication House, 1934.

5108. JANOTA, Johannes. Studien zu Funktion und Typus des deutschen geistlichen Liedes im Mittelalter. München: Beck, 1968.

5109. KEHREIN, Joseph. Kirchen--und religiöse Lieder aus dem zwölfen bis fünfzehnten Jahrhundert. New York: G. Olms, 1969. (Reprografischer Nachdruck der Ausg. Paderborn 1853.)

5110. LUTHER, Martin. Deutsche geistliche Lieder. Hildesheim: G. Olms, 1966. (Reprt. --of Leipzig: 1840 ed.)

5111. ________. Die deutschen geistlichen Lieder. Neudrucke deutscher Literaturwerke. Tübingen: Niemeyer, 1967.

5112. ________. Geistliche Lieder. Hildesheim: G. Olms, 1971. (Reprt. --of Stuttgart, 1848.)

5113. MILLER, Josiah. Singers and songs of the church. New York: Longman, Green & Co., 1868, 1875.

5114. PATRICK, Millar. The story of the church's song. Revised. Richmond: John Knox Press, 1962.

5115. POLING, David. Songs of faith-signs of hope. Waco, Tex.: Word Books, 1976.

5116. POLSKIE Towarzystwo Spiewacze im. Fryderyka Szopena--Buenos Ayres. W sluzbie pieśni. Al servicio de la canción, etc. Buenos Aires: N. G., 1954. (BM07903. e. 18)

5117. RIST, Johann. Johann Schop, himmlische Lieder. Hildesheim: G. Olms, n. d. (Reprt. --of Luneburg: Johann und Heinrich die Stern, 1652.)

5118. SANKEY, Ira David. My life and the story of the gospel hymns and of sacred songs and solos. (With an introduction by T. L. Cuyler.) Philadelphia: Sunday School Times Co., also New York: A. M. S. Press (reprt.), 1974.

5119. SCHÖBERLEIN, Ludwig-Friedrich Riegel. Schatz des liturgischen Chor-und Gemeindegesangs. Hildesheim: G. Olms, n. d. (Reprt. --of Göttingen 1865, vol. 3.)

5120. SIEBEL, Katherine. Sacred songs. New York: H. W. Gray, 1966.

5121. SOPHIE, Elisabeth. Himmlische Lieder und Christfürstliches Davids-Harfen-Speil von Anton Ulrich. New York: Johnson Reprint, 1969.

5122. STAINER, John. Early Bodleian Music. Sacred and secular songs, ranging from about 1185 to 1505. Refer to Bodleian library founded by Sir Thomas Bodley, English diplomat and founder of the library (1545-1613). New York: Broude Brothers, 1966-67. (Reprt., London: 1901 and 1913 eds.)

5123. SUTTER, Ignace de. De dienst van het lied: muziek-historische en didaktische studies over het kerklied in de oecumene. Brugge: Emmaüs, 1974.

5124. TUCHER, G. F. von (ed.). Schatz des evangelischen Kirchengesangs im ersten Jahrhundert der Reformation. Hildesheim: G. Olms, n. d. (Reprt. --of Leipzig: Breitkopf und Härtel, 1848 ed.)

5125. ULRICH, Winfried. Semantische Untersuchungen zum Wortschatz des Kirchenliedes im 16. Jahrhundert. Lübeck, Hamburg: Matthiesen, 1969.

5126. VETTER, Daniel. Musicalische Kirch-und Haus-Ergötzlichkeit. Hildesheim: G. Olms, n. d. (Reprt. --of Leipzig 1709.)

5127. WACKERNAGEL, Philipp. Das deutsche Kirchenlied von der ältesten Zeit bis zum Anfang des 17. Jahrhundert. Hildesheim: G. Olms, 1964. (Reprt. Leipzig 1864-1877 ed. 5 vols.)

5128. WETZSTEIN, O. Das deutsche Kirchenlied im 16., 17. und 18. Jahrhunderts. Neustrelitz: N. G., 1888.

5129. WILHELMI, Herbert. Der ostdeutsche Beitrag zum evangelischen Kirchenlied. Leer (Ostfriesland): Rautenbera, 1968.

5130. WINTERFELD, Carl Georg August Vivigens. Der evangelische Kirchengesang und sein Verhältnis zur Kunst des

Tonsätzes. Hildesheim: G. Olms, 1966. (Reprt. --of Leipzig 1843-47 ed.)

5131. WIRTH, C. V. Der evangelische Liederschatz. Nurnberg: N. G., 1893.

5132. ZAHN, Johannes. Die Melodien der deutschen evangelischen Kirchenlieder aus den Quellen geschöpft und mitgeteilt. Hildesheim: G. Olms, 1963. (Reprt. --of Gutersloh 1889-93. Vol. 6.)

See also: 299, 565, 1314, 2695, 2721, 3273, 3381, 3449, 3467, 3473, 3586, 4219, 4373, 4374, 4467, 4483, 4821, 5133, 5365, 5411, 5437.

SPIRITUALS, WHITE and BLACK, and OTHER BLACK SACRED MUSIC

5133. ADES, Hawley. Three to make music. Delaware Water Gap: Shawnee Press, n. d.

5134. ANDERSON, Marian. My Lord, what a morning: an autobiography. New York: Viking Press and Macmillan Co. of Canada, 1956.

5135. ASBURY, Samuel and Henry E. Meyer. Old-time white camp-meetings spirituals. N. G.: Texas Folk-Lore Society, 1932.

5136. BAKER, David N., Lida M. Belt and Herman Hudson. The Black composer speaks. Metuchen, N. J.: Scarecrow Press, 1978.

5137. BUFFINGTON, Albert F. Dutchified German spirituals. Lancaster, Pa.: Franklin & Marshall College, Fackenthal Library, 1965.

5138. CHAMBERS, H. A. (ed.). The treasury of negro spirituals. New York: Emerson Books, 1968.

5139. CONE, James H. The spirituals and the Blues: an interpretation. New York: Seabury Press, 1972.

5140. COURLANDER, Harold. Negro folk music, U. S. A. New York and London: Columbia Univ. Press, 1963.

5141. CRUTCHFIELD, Mary Elizabeth. The white spiritual. New York: Union Theological Seminary, M. A., 1946.

5142. CULLINS, Ella Webb. Origin of American negro folkways. Boston, Mass.: Boston Univ., M. A., 1942.

5143. DALTON, Lilian Howard. Singing slaves. A biography of John Newton, 1725-1807. Eagle Books, no. 65. London: Edinburgh House Press, 1952.

5144. DE LERMA, Dominique-René. Black music in our culture. Kent, Ohio: Kent State Univ. Press, 1970.

5145. ________. Reflections on black music. Kent, Ohio: Kent State Univ. Press, 1973.

5146. DIXON, Christa. Negro spirituals: from Bible to folk song. Philadelphia: Fortress Press, 1976.

5147. ________. Wesen und Wandel geistlicher Volkslieder, negro spirituals. Wuppertal: Jugenddienst-Verlag, 1967.

5148. FISHER, Miles Mark. Negro slavesongs in the United States. Ithica, N. Y.: Publ. for the American Historical Society by Cornell Univ. Press, 1953.

5149. GLAZER, Irving William. Negro music in early America, from 1619 to the Civil War. New York: New York Univ. M. A., 1945.

5150. GRISSOM, Mary Allen. The negro sings a new Heaven. New York: Dover Publ., Inc., 1969. (Repr. of--Chapel Hill, N. C.: Univ. of North Carolina Press, 1930 ed.)

5151. HANDY, William Christopher. Negro authors and composers of the United States. New York: AMS Press, 1976. (Reprint, New York: Handy Bros. Music Co., 1938.)

5152. HANSEN, Kurt Heinrich. Go down, Moses; 100 spirituals and gospel songs. Hamburg: Furche-Verlag, 1963.

5153. HELLSTROM, Jan Arvid. Enny sang. Stockholm: Verbum; Studiebok-forlaget, 1969.

5154. JACKSON, George Pullen. Another sheaf of white spirituals. Gainesville: Univ. of Florida Press, 1952.

5155. ________. Down-East spirituals and others. Second edition. Locust Valley, N. Y.: J. J. Augustin Publ., 1953.

5156. ________. Spiritual folk songs of early America. Locust Valley, N. Y.: J. J. Augustin Publisher, 1953.

5157. ________. Spiritual folk-songs of early America. New York: Dover Publ., Inc., 1964. (Repr. of New York: J. J. Augustin, Publ., 1937.)

5158. ________. White spirituals in the Southern Uplands: The story of Fasola folk, their songs, singing, and "Buckwheat Notes." New York: Dover Publications, Inc., 1965. (Also Hatboro, Pa.: Folklore, Univ. of N.C. Press, Chapel Hill, 1933, 1965.)

5159. JOHNSON, James Weldon and J. Rosamond Johnson. The books of American negro spirituals, including--The Book of American Negro Spirituals and The Second Book of Negro Spirituals. New York: Viking Press, 1947.

5160. JOHNSON, Lillian. The significance of negro music to America. Houston: Texas Southern Univ., M.M.E., 1944.

5161. JONES, Geraldine Wells. The negro spiritual and its use as an integral part of music education. Hartford, Conn.: Hartt College of Music, 1953.

5162. KERR, Thomas Henderson. A critical survey of printed vocal arrangements of Afro-American religious folk songs. Rochester, N.Y.: Eastman, M.M., 1939.

5163. KREHBIEL, Henry Edward. Afro-American songs. (Repr. of 1913 ed.) New York: Frederick Ungar Publ. Co., 1962 and 1971.

5164. LEHMANN, Theo. Nobody knows; Negro-Spirituals mit Einführung und Nachwort. 2. Auflage. Leipzig: Koehler & Auflage, 1963.

5165. LEY, Margaret. Spirituals. Ein Beitrag zur Analyse der religiösen Liedschöpfung bei der nordamerikanischen Negern in der Zeit der Sklaverei. Munich, Germany: Munich Univ. Library, 1954.

5166. LOCKE, Alain. The negro and his music. Port Washington, N.Y.: Kennikat Press, 1968. (orig. 1936, Repr. of Associates in Negro Folk Education.)

5167. LONG, Norman G. The theology and psychology of the negroes' religion prior to 1860 as shown particularly in the spirituals. Oberlin, Ohio: Oberlin College, M.A., 1936.

5168. LOVELL, John. Black song: the forge and the flame; the story of how the Afro-American spiritual was hammered out. New York: MacMillan, 1972.

5169. MERRITT, Nancy G. Negro spirituals in American collections; a handbook for students studying negro spirituals. Washington, D.C.: Howard Univ., M.A., 1940.

5170. MEYER, Henry E. Southern spirituals from white singers. Georgetown, Tex.: Southwestern Univ., M.A., 1942.

5171. ODUM, Howard and Guy B. Johnson. The negro and his songs. Hatboro, Penn.: Folklore Associates, Inc., 1964.

5172. RICKS, G. R. Some aspects of the religious music of the United States negro: an ethnomusicological study with special emphasis on the Gospel tradition. Evanston, Ill.: Northwestern Univ., 1960.

5173. RIEDEL, Johannes. Soul music, black and white: the influence of black music on the churches. Minneapolis: Augsburg Publ. House, 1975.

5174. ROACH, Hildred. Black American music, past and present. Rev. ed. Boston: Crescendo Publ. Co., 1976.

5175. SCARBOROUGH, Dorothy. On the trail of negro folk-songs. Assisted by Ola Lee Gulledge. Hatboro, Pa.: Folklore Associates, 1963.

5176. SOUTHERN, Eileen. The music of the black Americans: a history. New York: W. W. Norton & Co., 1971.

5177. ______. Readings in black American music. New York: W. W. Norton & Co., 1971.

5178. SPIRITUALS triumphant. Nashville: Sunday School Publishing Board, n. d.

5179. THROWER, Sarah Selina. The spiritual of the Gullah negro in South Carolina. Cincinnati, Ohio: Coll-Conservatory of Music Cincinnati, 1954.

5180. THURMAN, Howard. Deep River and the negro spiritual speaks of life and death. Richmond, Ind.: Friends United Press, 1975.

5181. ______. The negro spiritual speaks of life and death. New York: Harper & Row, 1969.

5182. WHITE, Evelyn Davidson. Selected bibliography of published music by black composers. n. p., White, 1975.

5183. WORK, John Wesley. Folk song of the American negro. New York: Negro Univ. Press, 1969.

5184. WYLEI, Eugene. The white spiritual. Minneapolis: N. G., 1950.

5185. ZENETTI, Lothar. Peitsche und Psalm. Geschichte und Glaube, Spirituals und Gospel-songs der Neger Nordamerikas. München: Pfeiffer, 1967.

See also: 314, 820, 883, 1072, 1616, 2291, 2486, 2580, 2658, 2694a, 4638, 4760, 4821, 4923, 4952.

STYLE

5186. BERRYMAN, Rudolph B. Two methods of musical stylistic analysis: an experimental evaluation. Ann Arbor: Univ. Microfilms, 1965.

5187. BEVILL, Ruby L. Analysis of Verdi's choral style as found in the Manzioni Requiem. Denton, Tex.: North Texas State Univ. M. M., 1946.

5188. CLEMONS, Ouida. Typical elements of Brahms' choral style as found in the German Requiem. Denton, Tex.: North Texas State Univ., M. A., 1942.

5189. CROCKER, Richard L. A history of musical style. Berkley: Univ. California at Berkley: McGraw-Hill, 1966.

5190. DART, Thurston. The interpretation of music. N. G.: Hutchinson, 1954.

5191. DICKINSON, George S. A handbook of musical style. Poughkeepsie, N. Y.: Vassar College Cooperative Bookshop, 1965.

5192. DILLENBERGER, Jane. Style and content in Christian art. An orientation in the history of Christian art stressing an understanding of the style of art, plus the biblical and apocryphal sources of the subject matter. Nashville, Tenn.: Abingdon Press, 1965.

5193. DONINGTON, Robert. The interpretation of early music. London: Faber and Faber, 1963; also Boston Music Co., 1964.

5194. FELLERER, Karl Gustav. Der Stilwandel in der Abendlandischen Musik um 1600. Opladen: Westdeutscher Verlag, 1972.

5195. FROTSCHER, Gotthold. Auffuehrungspraxis alter Musik. New York: C. F. Peters Corporation, 1967.

5196. GRIESBACHER, Peter. Kirchenmusikalische Stilistik und Formenlehre. Regensburg: A. Coppenrath, 1912.

5197. HANDSCHIN, Jacques. Eine wenig beachtete Stilrichtung innerhalb der mittelalterlichen Mehrstimmigkeit. N. G.: N. G., 1924. (LC-ML5. S338)

5198. JEPPESEN, Knud. Palestrinastil med saerlight henblik paa dissonans-behandlingen. København: Levin & Munksgaard, 1923.

5199. ________. The style of Palestrina and the dissonance. London: Oxford Univ. Press, H. Milford, 1927.

5200. ________. The style of Palestrina and the dissonance. Introduced by Edward J. Dent. Copenhagen: Ejnar Munksgaard Publisher, 1946.

5201. KATHODRAAL Van St. Bavo-Muziek-Instituut. Stijl en vorm en het Gregariaansch. Een studie de aesthetica van de Gregoriaansche muziek door Dr. A. I. M. Kat. Haarlem: Hilversum, 1946.

5202. LEDDY, Margaret. A stylistic analysis of the masses and motets of Antonio Lotti. Washington, D. C.: Catholic Univ. of America, 1961.

5203. LOVELL, John Harrison. A stylistic study of the masses of Josquin des Pres. Ann Arbor: Univ. of Michigan, 1960.

5204. SCHOLL, Sharon Lynn. Religious connotation of musical style. Ann Arbor: Univ. Microfilms, 1966.

5205. STAPLIN, Carl Bayard. Stylistic changes in the chorale-preludes of J. S. Bach. Ann Arbor: Univ. Microfilms, 1966.

5206. TUSLER, Robert. The style of J. S. Bach's Chorale Preludes. New York: Da Capo Press-Reprint, 1966. (orig. Berkeley & Los Angeles, 1956.)

5207. WOLFF, Christoph. Der Stile antico in der Musik Johann Sebastian Bachs: Studien zu Bachs Spätwerk. Wiesbaden: Franz Steiner Verlag, 1968.

See also: 289, 617, 669, 670, 1061, 1307, 1336, 2007, 2144, 2385, 2412, 2935, 2972, 3116, 3208, 3225, 3290, 3366, 4054, 4077, 4104, 4131, 4153, 4457, 4516, 4528, 4531, 4592, 4612, 4725, 4728.

SYLLABUS

5208. HANNUM, Harold. Church music syllabus. Arlington-La Sierra College: Hannum, 1956.

SYMBOLISM

5209. ADAIR, Agnes Beard. Symbolism in Bach's St. John and St. Matthew Passions. Dallas, Tex.: Southern Methodist Univ., M. M., 1962.

5210. CIRLOT, J. E. Dictionary of symbols. New York: Philosophical Library, 1962; 2nd ed., 1971.

5211. McGEE, Ratha D. Symbols, signposts of devotion. Nashville: Upper Room, 1956.

5212. MOESER, James Charles. Symbolism in J. S. Bach's "Orgelbuechlein." Austin, Tex.: Univ. of Texas, M.M., 1964.

5213. RICE, T. T. Russian Icons. England: Spring, 1963.

5214. STAFFORD, Thomas. Christian symbolism in the Evangelical churches. New York and Nashville: Abingdon-Cokesbury, 1942.

5215. SYMBOLS of the church. Boston: Whittemore Associates, Inc., 1963.

5216. WILSON, Frank E. An outline of Christian symbolism. New York: Morehouse Gorham Co., 1938.

See also: 635, 967, 1052, 5412.

TALENT

5217. HAECKER, V. and T. Ziehen. Zur Vererbung und Entwicklung der musikalischen Begabung. On the hereditary transmission and development of the musical talent. Leipzig: J. A. Barth, 1922.

5218. SCHAUL, Johann Baptist. Über Tonkunst, die berühmtesten Tonkünstler und ihre Werke. Karlsruhe: G. Braun, 1818.

5219. TURNBULL, Robert. Musical genius and religion. London: S. Wellwood, 1907.

See also: 4220, 4316.

TEMPO

5220. GULLO, Salvatore. Das Tempo in der Musik des XIII. and XIV. Jahrhunderts. Bern, Switzerland: Verlag Paul Haupt, 1964.

See also: 4957, 4959.

TERMINOLOGY

5221. CARROLL, Joseph R. Compendium of liturgical music terms. Toledo, Ohio: Gregorian Institute of America, 1964.

5222. FARJEON, H. Musical words explained. London: Oxford Univ. Press, 1933.

5223. FIELDS, Victor Alexander. The singers glossary. Boston, Mass.: Boston Music Co., 1952.

5224. GREENISH, A. J. Students dictionary of musical terms. [New ed.] London: J. Williams; New York: Mills Music, 1953. (Rev. of Dictionary of Musical Terms. Joseph Williams Series of Practical Handbooks, 1917.)

5225. HOBOKEN, Anthony van. "Probleme der musikbibliographischen Terminologie." In Fontes artist musicae, 1958.

5226. LEE, F. G. Glossary of liturgical and ecclesiastical terms. London: Bernard Quaritch, 1877.

5227. PADELFORD, Frederick Morgan. Old English musical terms. Boston: Milford House, 1973.

5228. PARRY, J. Manual of musical terms. London: J. Curwen, 1920.

5229. SCHLÖTTERER, Reinhold. Die kirchenmusikalischen Terminologie der griechischen Kirchenväter. München: Inaug. Diss., n.d. (LC-ML 3060.S35)

5230. SLOYAN, Gerard. Vocabulary for the Roman Catholic faith. Flushing, N.Y.: Data-Guide, Inc., 1963.

5231. YOUNG, M. C. Musical terms. London: Novello, 1911.

See also: 630, 686, 1481, 1489, 1490, 1491, 1499, 1504, 1505, 1507, 1511, 1514, 1523, 1525, 1540, 1545, 3903.

THEATER, USE OF CHURCH MUSIC IN

See: 1091.

THEOLOGY

5232. ARNOLD, Matthew. God and the Bible. (Repr.) New York: Macmillan & Co., 1901.

5233. RIDER, Daniel E. The musical thought and activities of the New England transcendentalists. Ann Arbor: Univ. Microfilms, 1964.

5234. ROUTLEY, Erik. Church music and theology. Philadelphia: Fortress Press, 1960.

5235. SCHMIDT, Johann Michael. Musico-theologica of Stigtelyke toepassing van muzikaale waarheden. Amsterdam: A. Olofsen, 1756.

5236. SÖHNGEN, Oskar. Theologie der Musik. Kassel: Johannes Stauda Verlag, 1967.

5237. WALSH, Walter. History of the Romeward movement. N. G. : N. G. , 1900.

See also: 1763, 2003, 2147, 5167.

THEORY--MUSIC

5238. BAKER, J. P. Choir boy's hand book of musical theory and vocal exercises. London: N. G. , 1898.

5239. BRITTON, Allen Perdue. Theoretical introductions in American tune-books to 1800. East Lansing, Mich. : Michigan, Ph. D. , 1950.

5240. COUSSEMAKER, Edmond de. L'art harmonique aux XIIe et XIIIe siècles. Collected Editions-Historical Sets. New York: Broude Brothers, 1965-1966.

5241. ________. Histoire de l'harmonie au Moyen Age. Paris: Didron, 1852, also New York: Broude Brothers.

5242. PRUVAST, P. La musique rénovée selon la synthése acoustique. N. G. : N. G. , 1931. (BM)

5243. RAYMOND, Georges Marie. Lettre à M. Villoteau, touchant ses veus sur la possibilité et l'utilité d'une theorie exacte des principes naturels de la musique; suivie d'un memoire et de quelques opuscules sur l'usage de la musique dans les églises et l'utilité de rétablissement des maîtrises de chapelle dans les cathédrales de France, et de la refutation d'un systême particulier sur les causes de l'expression musicale. Paris: Chez Courcier, 1811.

5244. SHIR-CLIFF, Jay and Rauscher. Chromatic harmony. Riverside: The Free Press, 1964.

5245. TATHAM, J. Rudiments of music explained for choirs. London: N. G. , 1890.

5246. TELL, Werner. Die Kirchentonarten und ihre Harmonik. Mit Notenbeispielen. Auszug aus einer Harmonielehre mit Improvisations und Tonsatzübungen. Berlin: Evangelische Verlagsanstalt, 1949.

5247. WILSON, Harry Robert. Choral arranging for schools, glee clubs, and publication. A complete guide. New York: Robbins Music Corp. , 1949.

5248. WOOLDRIDGE, H. E. Early English harmony, Vol. 1. B. Quaritch, 1913.

See also: 32, 1004, 1005, 1145, 1998, 2743, 3008, 3491, 4490, 4726.

THERAPY--MUSICAL

5249. ALVIN, Juliette. Music therapy. New York: Basic Books, also London: Hutchinson, 1975.

5250. BOEHM, Beat. Heilende Musik im griechischen Altertum. Basel Univ. Library. Basel, Switzerland: Zeitschr. für Psychotherapie u. med. Psychologie 8, 1958.

5251. BRIGHT, Ruth. Music in geriatric care. New York: St. Martin's Press, 1972.

5252. BRITISH Society for Music Therapy. Different aspects of music therapy: Papers read at the conference held at St. Michael's School, Graham Terrace, London, S.W. 3, 8th July 1967. London: The Society, 1967.

5253. ________. The nature and scope of music therapy with handicapped children. London: The Society, 1975.

5254. EAGLE, Charles (ed.). Music therapy index. (International) Vol. I. Lawrence, Kan.: National Assn. for Music Therapy (P. O. Box 610), 1976.

5255. GINGLEND, David R. and Winifred E. Stiles. Music activities for retarded children. Nashville: Abingdon, n. d.

5256. HARBERT, Wilhelmina Keniston. Some principles, practices and techniques in musical therapy. Stockton, Cal.: Pacific, M.A. (psych.), 1947.

5257. JOPLIN, Mary Tucker. Music therapy: a study as related to the emotionally disturbed child. Lubbock, Tex.: Texas Technological College, M.M.Ed., 1966.

5258. MUSIKTHERAPIE: Theorie und Methodik. Überarb. Beiträge einer wissenschaftlichen Konferenz. Jena: G. Fischer, 1971.

5259. NORDHOFF, Paul and Clive Robbins. Creative music therapy: individualized treatment for the handicapped child. New York: John Day Co., 1975.

5260. ________. Music therapy for handicapped children. New York: Rudolf Steiner Publications, Inc., n. d.

5261. PAHLEN, Kurt. Musik-Therapie: Behandlung v. Heilung geistiger u. seel. Störung durch Musik. München: Heyne, 1973.

5262. PRIESTLEY, Mary. Music therapy in action. New York: St. Martin's Press, also London: Constable, 1975.

5263. REVERS, Wilhelm J., G. Harrer, and C. M. Simmons (eds.). Neue Wege der Musiktherapie: Grundzüge einer alten und neuen Heilmethode. 1. Aufl. Düsseldorf: Econ Verlag, 1974.

5264. THOMAS, Claus. Bibliographie zur Musiktherapie. Amriswil, Switzerland: Amriswiler-Bücherei, 1973.

See also: 3906.

THOROUGH BASS (THROUGH BASS)
General Bass and Basso Continuo

5265. ABRAHAM, Lars Ulrich. Der Generalbass im Schaffen des Michael Praetorius and seine harmonischen Voraussetzungen. Berlin: Verlag Merseburger, 1961.

5266. BUELOW, George J. Through-Bass accompaniment according to Johann D. Heinichen. Berkeley: Univ. of California Press, 1966.

5267. HAAKE, Helmut. Anfänge der Generalbass-Sätzes: die "Cento concerti ecclesiastici (1620) von Lodovico Viadana." Tutzing: Schneider, 1974.

5268. HEINICHEN, Johann David. Der Generalbass in der Komposition. Hildesheim, Germany: Georg Olms-Reprint, 1967. (orig. Dresden, 1728.)

5269. HEINMANN, Walter. Der Generalbassatz und sein Rolle in Bachs Choralsatz. München: Musikverlag Katzbitzler, 1973.

5270. KELLER, Hermann. Schule des Generalbass--Spiels (5. Aufl.) Kassel and New York: Bärenreiter, 196-.

5271. _______. Thoroughbass method. Edited by Carl Parrish. New York: Norton, 1965 also London: Barrie & Rockliff, 1966.

5272. LAMPE, John Frederick. A plain and compendious method of teaching thorough-bass. Monuments of Music & Music Literature. New York: Broude Brothers (Facsimile), 1969. (orig. London: J. Wilcox, 1737.)

5273. LOCKE, Matthew. Melothesia. Monuments of Music & Music Literature. New York: Broude Brothers

(Facsimile), n. d. (orig. London: Printed for J. Carr, 1673.)

5274. MARPURG, Friedrich Wilhelm. Handbuch bey dem Generalbasse und der Composition. Hildesheim, Germany: Georg Olms-Reprint, 1967, also 1974. (orig. 1757-62.)

5275. MOSER, H. J. Das ist: Geschichte des mehrstimmigen Generalbassliedes und des Quodlibets im deutschen Barock. Braunschweig: N. G., 1933.

5276. MOZART, Wolfgang Amadeus. Practical elements of thorough-bass. With introd. by Baird Hastings. (orig. 1817.) New York: Joseph Patelson Music House, n. d.

5277. PASQUALI, Nicolo. Thorough-bass made easy. Ed. with an introduction by J. Churchill. Facs. ed. London; New York: Oxford Univ. Press, 1974.

See also: 9, 21.

TRANSLATIONS

5278. AMOS, Flora R. Early theories of translations. New York: Columbia Univ. Press, 1920.

5279. HODGSON, Julian. Music titles in translation: a checklist of musical compositions. London: Clive Bingley; also Hamden, Conn.: Linnett Books, 1976.

5280. PHILLIMORE, J. S. Some remarks on translations and translators. London: Oxford, 1919.

5281. SCHUERK, Ingrid. Deutsche Übertragungen mittellateinischer Hymnen im 18. und 19. Jahrhundert. Tübingen: Hermaea. Neue Folge, 1963.

See also: 1241, 2506, 2513, 2527, 2673, 3344, 4150, 4654, 5313.

TRANSPOSITION

5282. CLARK, J. Bunker. Transposition in seventeenth century English organ accompaniments and the transposing organ. Detroit: Information Coordinators, 1974.

TRINITY

See: 2284.

TROPES

5283. PLANCHART, Alejandro Enrique. The repertory of tropes at Winchester. Princeton, N. J.: Princeton Univ. Press, 1977.

5284. STUDIA Latina Stockholmiesia, 21. Corpus Troporum I. Tropes du propre de la messe. 1. Cycle de Noël; par l'équipe de recherches sur les tropes placées sous la direction de Ritva Jonsson. Stockholm: Almqvist and Wiksell International, 1975.

5285. ______, 22. Ed. by Olaf Marcusson. Corpus Troporum II. Prosules de la messe. 1. Tropes de l'alleluia. Stockholm: Almqvist and Wiksell International, 1976.

See also: 1254, 2959, 3194, 4980.

TWENTIETH CENTURY CHURCH MUSIC

5286. ALBET, Montserrat. La musica del siglo XX. Personalidad entrevistada: Karlheinz Stockhausen. Barcelona: Salvat, 1974.

5287. BACHARACH, A. L. (ed.). British music of our time. London: Pelican Books, 1946.

5288. BAUER, Marion. Twentieth-Century music. New York: G. P. Putnam's Sons, 1933.

5289. BORETZ, Benjamin. Perspectives of new music. Princeton, N. J.: Princeton Univ. Press, 1962-1965.

5290. BULL, Storm. Index to biographies of contemporary composers (Vol. I). Metuchen, N. J.: Scarecrow Press, 1964.

5291. ______. Index to biographies of contemporary composers, (Vol. II). Metuchen, N. J.: Scarecrow Press, 1974.

5292. CASTLE, L. Church music of to-day. N. G.: Church Music Review, 1933.

5293. COHN, Arthur. Twentieth century music in Western Europe. New York: Da Capo Press, 1972. (Repr. of Philadelphia and New York: J. B. Lippincott Co., 1965.)

5294. COMPOSIUM Directory of New Music; an Annual. Index of contemporary compositions--published for a number of years. Los Angeles: Chrystal Record Co., 1976.

5295. DEMUTH, Norman. Musical trends in the 20th century. London: Rockliff Publishing Corp., 1952.

5296. ELSON, L. C. Modern music and musicians. New York: N. G., 1913.

5297. EWEN, David. Complete book of twentieth century music. New York: Prentice-Hall, Inc., 1952.

5298. GRAF, Max. Modern music. New York: Philosophical Library, 1946.

5299. HANSON, Peter S. (ed.). Introduction to Twentieth century music. Rockleigh, N.J.: Allyn & Bacon, Inc., 1961.

5300. KARKOSCHKA, E. Das Schriftbild der neuen Musik. Celle: A. Broude Brothers, 1966.

5301. MANFREDINI, Vincenzo. Difesa della musica moderna e de suoi celebri esecutori. Bologna: Forna, 1972.

5302. MAY, James D. Avant-garde choral music, an annotated selected bibliography. Metuchen, N.J.: Scarecrow Press, 1977.

5303. MELLERS, Wilfred. Man and his music (Vol. IV of Romanticism and the 20th Century). Fair Lawn, N.J.: Essential Books, Inc., 1957.

5304. MERSMANN, Hans. Die Kirchenmusik im XX Jahrhundert. Nürnberg: Glock und Lutz, 1958.

5305. RISATTI, Howard. New music vocabulary: a guide to notational signs for contemporary music. Urbana, Ill.: Univ. of Ill. Press, 1975.

5306. RÖHRING, Klaus. Neue Musik in der Welt des Christentums. München: C. Kaiser, 1975.

5307. SALZMAN, Eric. Twentieth-century music: an introduction. Englewood Cliffs: Prentice-Hall, 1967.

5308. SATEREN, Leland B. The new song. A guide to modern music for use in the church choir. Minneapolis: Augsburg Publ. House, 1958.

5309. SLONIMSKY, Nicolas. Music since 1900. New York: W. W. Norton & Co., 1938.

5310. ________. Music since 1900. (Third ed.) (1st ed--1937; 2nd ed. 1938.) (With papal Motu Proprio and Mediator Dei.) New York: Coleman Ross Co., Inc., 1949.

5311. THOMPSON, Kenneth. A dictionary of twentieth century composers (1911-1971). New York: St. Martin's Press, 1973.

See also: 277, 622, 993, 1020, 1342, 1512, 1697, 1710, 1715, 1773, 1777, 1813, 1832, 2802, 3049, 3148, 3161, 3319, 3355, 3565, 3595, 3647, 3702, 3759, 3771, 3800, 3987, 4023, 4995, 5016.

VERNACULAR

5312. NICHOLSON, David. Vernacular and music in the missions. Cincinnati: World Library of Sacred Music, 1962.

5313. SCHMIDT, Herman A. P. Liturgie et langue vulgaire. Le problème de la langue liturgique chez les premiers réformateurs et au Concile de Trente.... Traduction du néerlandais par Dom Suitbert Caron. Vol. 53. p. 212. Romae: Analecta Gregoriana, 1950.

See also: 4927.

VESTMENTS

5314. LESAGE, Robert. Vestments and church furniture. Objets et habits liturgiques. Translation by Fergus Murphy. pp. 152. Faith and Fact Books, No. 113. London: Burns & Oates, 1960.

5315. LINCOLN-USHER Art Gallery. Festival exhibition of church plate and vestments, 27th June to end of August 1951. A catalogue. With plates. Lincoln: N. G., 1951. (BM 7960. de 54)

See also: 2950, 2952.

VISUAL AIDS

See: 1696.

VOCAL MUSIC

5316. BUCK, P. C. and others (ed. comm.). Tudor church music. New York: Oxford Univ. Press, 1922, 1923.

5317. CECILIE; casopis pro katolickou hudbu hudbu pasvatnou v Cechách, na moravě a ve Slezsku. V. Praze: Knehtiskarna Mikulase a Knappa, 1874.

5318. COLLES, H. C. Voice and verse. New York: Carl Fischer (Oxford Univ. Press), 1928.

5319. FISCHER, A. F. W. Kirchenlieder-Lexicon. Hildesheim, Germany: Georg Olms-Reprint, 1966. (orig. Gotha 1878-79; Suppl. 1886.)

5320. GABRIEL, Paul. Das deutsche evangelische Kirchenlied von Martin Luther bis zur Gegenwart. Berlin: Evangelische Verlagsanstalt, 1951.

5321. GRIESBACHER, Peter. Choral und Kirchenlied, historische Entwickelung und systematische Bewertung ihrer musikalischen Formen nach praktischen Gesichtspunkten dargestellt. Regensburg: A. Coppenrath, 1912.

5322. INGRAM, Madeline D. and William C. Rice. Vocal technique for children and youth. Nashville, N.Y.: Abingdon Press, 1962.

5323. LUTHER, Martin. Christliche Gesänge Lateinisch und Deutsch. Wittenberg: N.G., 1542.

5324. NATORP, Bernhard Christoph Ludwig. Über den Gesang in den Kirchen der Protestanten. Ein Beytrag zu den Vorarbeiten der Synoden für die Verrdlung der Liturgie. Essen und Duisburg: G. D. Bädeker, 1817.

5325. RADIO Revival Specials. Dayton, Tenn.: R. E. Winsett Company, n.d.

5326. SAUTER, Benediktus. Der liturgische Choral. Freiburg: Herder, 1903.

5327. The STORY of the church's song. Edinburgh, Scotland: The Church of Scotland Committee, 1927.

5328. STRAVINSKY, I. Abraham and Isaac. A sacred ballad for baritone and chamber orchestra. Hebrew text. New York: A. Broude, Inc., 1965.

5329. WYETH, John. Wyeth's repository of sacred music. Part I and part II. New York: Da Capo Press, 1964, 1966.

See also: 160, 204, 250, 280, 343, 362, 374, 386, 490, 516, 763, 1015, 1089, 1100, 1237, 1307, 1354, 1357, 1358, 1637, 1707, 1930, 1943, 2098, 2143, 2892, 3288, 3293, 3294, 3313, 3487, 3516, 3537, 3625, 3627, 3628, 4131, 4340, 4482, 4484, 4604, 4773, 4992, 5339, 5345, 5350, 5369.

VOCAL TECHNIQUES

5330. BATES, J. Young singers: their voice cultivation and preservation. London: Stainer and Bell, 1926.

5331. BECKETT, Harold Irwin. Group voice for the church choir. Columbus, Ohio: Ohio State Univ., M.A., 1950.

5332. BRODNITZ, Friedrich S. Keep your voice healthy. New York: Harper Bros., 1953.

5333. BROWN, William Earl. Vocal wisdom. Editor, Lillian Strongin, through printer, Hudson Offset Co., 22 Stoddard Pl., Maxims of Giovanni Battista Lamperti. Brooklyn, N. Y., 1931-57.

5334. CLEALL, Charles. Voice production, in choral technique. London: Novello and Co., 1969.

5335. COLEMAN, H. Five minutes weekly--a sight-singing course. London: Oxford Univ. Press, 1960.

5336. DAVIS, William Woodrow. A proposed plan for guiding adolescent boys in singing. Dallas, Tex.: Southern Methodist Univ., M. M., 1952.

5337. FIELD-HYDE, F. C. The art and science of voice training. London: Oxford Univ. Press, 1950.

5338. GARCIA, Manuel. Hints on singing. Translated from the French by Beata Garcia. London: Aschenberg, Hopwood and Crew, Ltd. (New York: Schuberth, and Co.), 1894.

5339. HENDERSON, William J. The art of the singer. New York: Charles Scribner's Sons, 1906.

5340. ________. Early history of singing. New York: Longmans, Green and Co., 1921.

5341. HOLLOWAY, H. Singing voice of boys. Birmingham: The Midland Educational Company, ltd., 1899.

5342. HULLAH, John Pyke. The duty and advantage of learning to sing. London: J. W. Parker, 1846.

5343. LAMPERTI, G. B. Vocal wisdom. Edited by William Earl Brown. New York: Hudson Offset Company, 1953.

5344. REGIDOR ARRIBAS, Ramón. Temas de canto, el aparato de fonación (cómo es y cómo funciona), el "pasaje" de la voz. Madrid: Real Musical, 1975.

5345. RICE, William C. Basic principles of singing. New York and Hashville: Abingdon Press, 1961, 1964.

5346. ROMA, Lisa. The science and art of singing. New York: G. Schirmer, Inc., 1956.

5347. SHAKESPEARE, William. The art of singing. Bryn Mawr: The Oliver Ditson Co., 1898, revised 1921.

5348. VENNARD, William. Singing, the mechanism and technique. Illus. by the author. Los Angeles: N. G., 1949. (Second ed. Los Angeles, 1950.)

5349. WHITE, R. T. Hints for singers. Designed especially for the use of choirs. London: imp. by Boston Music Co., 1898.

5350. WITHERSPOON, Herbert. Singing. New York: G. Schirmer, Inc., 1925.

5351. ________. Thirty-six lessons in singing. Chicago: Miessner Institute, 1930.

See also: 498, 499, 500. 513, 798, 807, 809, 842, 860, 882, 891, 1891, 1923, 2139, 2606, 2745, 3575, 4773, 4785, 4796, 4820, 4909, 5039, 5162, 5238, 5322.

WEDDING MUSIC

5352. COHEN, Ethel S. The wedding songs of the Babylonian Jews. New York: New York Univ., M. A. (music), 1940.

5353. FRYXELL, Regina. Wedding music. Rock Island: Augustana Book Concern, 1956.

5354. KRADER, Barbara Lattimer. Serbian peasant wedding songs; a formal semantic and functional analysis. Cambridge, Mass.: Radcliffe College Library, 1955.

5355. LANTZ, Russell A. Music for weddings. Newton, Kan.: Faith and Life Press, 1965.

5356. MUSIC for church weddings. Greenwich: The Seabury Press, 1952.

5357. PROTESTANT Episcopal Church in the USA, The. Music for Church weddings. Issued by the joint commission on church music of the Protestant Episcopal church in the USA. New York: H. W. Gray Co., Inc., 1963.

5358. RICHARDS, Betty Dove. Wedding festival music of the Renaissance and Baroque Periods. Waco, Tex.: Baylor Univ., M. M., 1965.

See also: 3000.

WOMEN IN MUSIC

5359. CLEMENT, Clara Erskine. Women in the fine arts; from the seventh century B. C. to the twentieth century A. D.

(orig. publ. --1904.) Williamstown, Mass.: Corner House, avail. through Nicholas Books--(Reprt.), 1976.

5360. DRINKER, Sophie Lewis Hutchinson. Music and women: the story of women in their relation to music. (Reprint, New York: Coward-McCann.) Washington: Zenger Pub. Co., 1975.

5361. ELSON, Arthur and Everett E. Truette. Woman's work in music, being an account of her influence on the art in ancient as well as modern times, a summary of her musical compositions in the different countries of the civilized world, and an estimate of their rank in comparison with those of men. (New rev. ed.) (Reprint-Boston: L. C. Page.) Washington: Zenger Pub. Co., 1975.

5362. HIXON, Don L. and Don Hennessee. Women in music, a biobibliography. Metuchen, N.J.: The Scarecrow Press, 1975.

5363. PIERRE-CHARLES, Livie. Femmes et chansons. Pref. de L. Chaleau. Paris: L. Soulanges, 1975.

5364. PITTMAN, E. R. Lady hymn writers. London: N.G., 1892. (BM)

5365. SMITH, E. M. Woman in sacred song. Library of hymns by women. Boston: N.G., 1885. (BM)

WORKBOOKS

5366. NORDEN, D. W. The choirmaster's workbook. Rock Island, Ill.: Augustance Book Concern, n.d.

WORSHIP, MUSIC IN

5367. ABBA, Raymond. Principles of Christian worship. New York: Oxford Univ. Press, 1957.

5368. ASHTON, Joseph Nickerson. Music in worship. Boston: Pilgrim Press, 1947 (4th ed.). Orig., 1943.

5369. BATEY, Irma Lee. Singing in worship. Filmstrip series, Illustrated by Billy Leavell. Nashville, Tenn.: Marshall Gunselman (Producer, 1962).

5370. BAYS, Alice A. Worship programs in the fine arts. Nashville: Abingdon-Cokesbury, 1940.

5371. BLACKWOOD, A. W. The fine art of public worship. Nashville: Abingdon Press & Cokesbury Press, 1939, 1946.

5372. COFFIN, H. S. The public worship of God. Philadelphia: The Westminster Press, 1946.

5373. CONCERNING worship. New York: Oxford Univ. Press, 1948.

5374. CURRY, Louise H. and Chester M. Wetzel. Worship services using the arts. Philadelphia: Westminster, 1961.

5375. DAVIES, Henry Walford. Music and Christian worship; a short survey and analysis. London: H. Milford, 1913.

5376. ________ and Harvey Grace (eds.). Music and worship. London: Eyre & Spottiswoode, 1935.

5377. DEARMER, Percy. The art of public worship. Milwaukee: Morehouse Publishing Co., 1919.

5378. ________. The church at prayer and the world outside. New York: George H. Doran Co., 1923.

5379. DEVAN, Samuel Arthur. Ascent to Zion. Illustrations by George F. Ketcham, Jr. New York: The Macmillan Co., 1942.

5380. DUCHESNE, L. Christian worship: its origin and evolution. London: S. P. C. K., 1903.

5381. EASTON, Burton Scott and Howard C. Robbins. The eternal word in the modern world. New York: Charles Scribner's Sons, 1937.

5382. ELLARD, Gerald. Christian life and worship (Roman Catholic). Milwaukee: The Bruce Publishing Co., 1943.

5383. ________. Men at work at worship (Roman Catholic). New York: Longmans, Green & Co., 1940.

5384. FISKE, George W. The recovery of worship. New York: The Macmillan Co., 1931.

5385. FITCH, Florence Mary. One God, the ways we worship him. New York: Lothrop, Lee & Shepard Co., 1944.

5386. ________. Their search for God. New York: Lothrop, Lee & Shepard Co., 1944.

5387. GARRET, Thomas Samuel. Christian worship. An introductory outline. London: Oxford Univ. Press, 1961.

5388. GIBSON, George M. The story of the Christian Year. New York-Nashville: Abingdon-Cokesbury Press, 1945.

5389. GOLDSWORTHY, E. A. Plain thoughts on worship. Chicago-New York: Willett Clark & Co., 1936.

5390. HARDIN, H. Grady, Joseph D. Quillian, Jr. and James F. White. The celebration of the Gospel. A study in Christian worship. New York-Nashville: Abingdon Press, 1964.

5391. HARDMAN, Oscar. The history of Christian worship. London: Hodder & Stoughton, 1937.

5392. HAVERGAL, William Henry. Holy praise offered by means of holy music, and the union of sacrifice and song. Stratford-on-Avon: R. Lapworth, 1843.

5393. HEDLEY, George. Christian worship. New York: Macmillan, 1953.

5394. HISLOP, D. H. Our heritage in public worship. New York: Charles Scribner's Sons, 1935.

5395. HUNTER, Stanley Armstrong. Music and religion. New York: AMS Press, 1973.

5396. IRWIN, K. and R. Ortmayer. Worship and the arts. Nashville: Board of Education of the Methodist Church, 1953.

5397. JENKINS, Graham. The study of worship. Tenbury Wells: Challoner Publications, 1963.

5398. JUNGMANN, Joseph A. Liturgical worship (Roman Catholic). New York: Frederick Pustet Co., 1941.

5399. LOTZ, Philip. The quest for God through worship; a book of worship services for churches, church schools, departmental assemblies, college chapel services, young people's meetings, youth conferences, and similar gatherings. St. Louis: The Bethany Press, 1934.

5400. LOVELACE, Austin Cole and William C. Rice. Music and worship in the church. Nashville: Abingdon Press, 1960.

5401. McDORMAND, Thomas B. The art of building worship service. Nashville: Broadman, 1942.

5402. McILWAIN, Orene. Worship God. Richmond: John Knox Press, 1954.

5403. MAXWELL, W. D. Concerning worship. London: G. Cumberledge, 1948.

5404. ______. An outline of Christian worship. New York: Oxford Univ. Press, 1936.

5405. MICKLEM, N. Christians worship: studies in its history and meaning. Oxford: Clarendon Press, 1936.

5406. MUSIC in the church. New York: Archbishops of Canterbury and New York, Committee on the Place of Music in the Worship of the Church, 1951.

5407. MUSIC in worship. Report of the Archbishop's Committee. London: S. P. C. K., 1932, also New York: Macmillan.

5408. PALMER, A. O come let us worship. New York: The Macmillan Co., 1939.

5409. QUICK, Oliver Chase. The Christian sacraments. New York: Harper & Brothers, 1927.

5410. REED, Luther D. Worship: A study of corporate devotion. Philadelphia, Pa.: Muhlenberg Press, 1959.

5411. SCHAFF, Philip. Christ in song. New York: Anson D. F. Randolph & Co., 1868.

5412. SEEDENSPENNER, C. Form and freedom in worship. Chicago-New York: Willett, Clark, & Co., 1941.

5413. SHEPHARD, Massey H., Jr. (ed.). Worship in Scripture and tradition. New York: Oxford Univ. Press, 1963.

5414. SHEPPARD, Lanclot Capel. True worship. Edited by L. Sheppard. London: Darton, Longman & Todd, also Baltimore: Helicon Press, 1963.

5415. SPERRY, W. H. Reality in worship. New York: The Macmillan Co., 1926.

5416. STONE, James Samuel. Music in worship and the spirit of chivalry. Chicago: Doughaday & Co., 1921.

5417. THOM, J. H. Hymns for Christian worship. London: N. G., 1898.

5418. UNDERHILL, Evelyn. Worship. New York: Harper & Brothers, 1936, 1957.

5419. VOGT, Von Ogden. Art and religion. New Haven: Yale Univ. Press, 1921.

5420. WRIGHT, Leroy Evert. The place of music in worship. The physical and psychological justification of music in the worship experience in the Protestant Churches of America. Evanston, Ill.: Northwestern Univ., 1949.

5421. ZIEGLER, E. K. A book of worship for village churches. New York: Agriculture Mission Foundation, 1939.

See also: 114, 618, 1035, 1048, 1164, 1229, 1284, 1302, 1303, 1430, 1686, 1687, 1708, 1738, 1750, 1761, 1764, 1770, 1835, 1836, 1837, 1841, 1858, 1876, 1886, 1891, 1917, 2162, 2215, 2550, 2583, 2592, 2616, 2619, 2777, 2843, 2853, 2861, 2892, 2893, 2905, 2917, 2923, 2925, 2930, 2931, 2942, 2966, 2982, 2987, 3047, 3098, 3310, 3504, 3583, 3937, 4013, 4139, 4146, 4340, 4575, 4642, 4735, 4738, 4741, 4744, 4830, 4834, 4843, 4939, 4973, 5046, 5047, 5048, 5049, 5053, 5057, 5204, 5211, 5214, 5216.

WRITERS (SACRED MUSIC TEXTS)

5422. BACH, Carl Philipp E. Herrn Professor Gellerts geistliche Oden und Lieder. Hildesheim: G. Olms, n. d. (Reprt. - of Berlin 1758-64 ed.)

5423. BENNETT, J. Lionel. Famous hymns: their writers and tunes. London: Skeffington & Son, 1932.

5424. BURRAGE, Henry S. Baptist hymn writers. Portland: Brown, Thurston & Co., 1888.

5425. CHRISTOPHERS, S. W. Hymns-writers and their hymns. London: S. W. Partridge & Co., 1866.

5426. DUFFIELD, Samuel. Latin hymn writers and their hymns. New York: Funk & Wagnalls, 1889.

5427. FRIESE, Hans. Gib mir die Gnadenhände; Thüringer Liederdichter aus der Barockzeit. Hrsg. von der Evangelisch-lutheranischen Kirche in Thüringen. Berlin: Evangelische Verlagsanstalt, 1962.

5428. ________. Gloria sei dir gesungen! Liederdichter aus der Zeit Martin Luthers. Hrsg. von der Pressestelle der Evangelisch-lutherischen Kirche in Thüringen. Berlin: Evangelische Verlagsanstalt, 1963.

5429. GRASSBERGER, Franz. The author catalogue of published music, Vol. 1. New York: C. F. Peters Corporation, 1967.

5430. HÜBNER, Götz Eberhard. Kirchenliedrezeption und Rezeptionswegforschung. Tübingen: M. Niemeyer, 1969.

5431. JOHNSON, Samuel. Lives of the English poets. Oxford: Clarendon Press, 1905.

5432. LEASK, H. A. Hymn-writers of the 19th century. London: The Author, 1902.

5433. MARTIN, Hugh. They wrote our hymns. London: SCM Press, 1961. (also Alec R. Allenson, Inc., Naperville, Ill.)

5434. MARTIN, J. Currie. The church and the hymn writers. London: James Clarke & Co., 1928.

5435. NEWMAN, John. Verses on various occasions. London, New York: Longmans, Green and Co., 1903.

5436. NUTTER, Charles S. and Wilbur T. Tillet. The hymns and hymn writers of the church. New York: The Methodist Book Concern, 1911.

5437. PFEIFFER, Johannes. Dichtkunst und Kirchenlied. Über das geistliche Lied im Zeitalter der Säkularisation. Hamburg: N. G., 1961. (BM3111, d. 43)

5438. PRESTON, Novella D. Makers of hymns. Illustrated by Sandor Bodo. Nashville, Tenn.: Convention Press, 1962.

5439. SYMONS, Arthur. Romantic movement in English poetry. New York: E. P. Dutton & Co., 1909.

5440. TILLETT, Wilbur T. Our hymns and their authors. Nashville: Barbee & Smith, 1900.

5441. WHITTEMORE, Mildred C. Hymn writers of the Christian Church. Boston: Whittemore Assoc., Inc., 1963.

See also: 1425, 1426, 1618, 2069, 2111, 2114, 2428, 2443, 2461, 2469, 2495, 2505, 2508, 2648, 2652, 2656, 2658, 2667, 2697, 2703, 2836, 3662, 4366, 4367, 4399, 4456, 4460, 4471, 4521, 4641, 4642, 4643, 4644, 5099, 5102.

YEARBOOKS

5442. The CATHOLIC choirmaster's diary, with rubrical and historical notes. Boston: McLaughlin & Reilly Co., 1953, 1954.

5443. JAHRBUCH für Liturgik und Hymnologie. Kassel: J. Stauda, 1955.

5444. KIRCHENMUSIKALISCHES Jahrbuch. Regensburg: Harberl, 1876-190-.

5445. ROYAL College of Organists. Yearbook, 1973-74. London, Kensington Gore, SW7-2Qs: Royal College of Organists, 1973.

See also: 1617, 2901, 2930, 2969, 3323, 3478, 3480, 3481, 4764.

AUTHOR, EDITOR AND COMPILER INDEX